Tax Lists
of
Somerset County Maryland
1730–1740

J. Elliott Russo

HERITAGE BOOKS
2011

HERITAGE BOOKS
AN IMPRINT OF HERITAGE BOOKS, INC.

Books, CDs, and more—Worldwide

For our listing of thousands of titles see our website at
www.HeritageBooks.com

Published 2011 by
HERITAGE BOOKS, INC.
Publishing Division
100 Railroad Ave. #104
Westminster, Maryland 21157

Copyright © 1992 Lois Green Carr

All rights reserved. No part of this book may be reproduced or transmitted in any form or by any means, electronic or mechanical, including photocopying, recording or by any information storage and retrieval system without written permission from the author, except for the inclusion of brief quotations in a review.

International Standard Book Numbers
Paperbound: 978-1-58549-198-8
Clothbound: 978-0-7884-8849-8

CONTENTS

Introduction v

Technical Notes vii

1730 Tax List (Accession number: MdHR 20,397-5) ... 1

1731 Tax List (Accession number: MdHR 20,397-6) ... 21

1733 Tax List (Accession number: MdHR 20,397-7) ... 43

1734 Tax List (Accession number: MdHR 20,397-8) ... 64

1735 Tax List (Accession number: MdHR 20,397-9) ... 85

1736 Tax List (Accession number: MdHR 20,397-10) .. 107

1737 Tax List (Accession number: MdHR 20,397-11) .. 128

1738 Tax List (Accession number: MdHR 20,397-12) .. 143

1739 Tax List (Accession number: MdHR 20,397-13) .. 166

1740 Tax List (Accession number: MdHR 20,397-14) .. 190

Index 215

INTRODUCTION

Lists of taxables are valuable tools for social historians and genealogists who wish to study households and families in the period before the census. Somerset County, Maryland, has an extraordinary run of such lists from 1722 through 1759. Lists remain for 30 of the 38 years, although not all are in good condition. We offer here the lists for the years 1730 through 1740.

Except for a brief period during the Seven Years War, only heads were taxed in colonial Maryland. The definition of a taxable varied in the early years of the colony, but had stabilized by 1674. From that time taxables were males and black females aged 16 or above. Those disabled by illness or injury or old age could be exempt at the discretion of the county justices. Ministers--and priests until 1692--were also excused.

The constable of each hundred--an administrative division of the county--compiled the list of taxables by going from door to door. Invariably he organized his list by household. He put the head of the household first and next listed the whites and then the blacks, who were usually, but not always, slaves. Not every household head was taxable, some were women or exempted for other reasons, but even those who were not taxed were listed in order to identify the house. The lists were then nailed to the court house door for all to see. Neighbors were expected to notice and report on who had concealed any taxables. The county justices investigated complaints of concealment and fined those found guilty. Once the lists were complete, the justices divided the county "charge" by the number of taxables to determine the tax due from each. The lists were also used to determine provincial and church taxes owed.

Undoubtedly some taxable people were missed in this procedure. Single men moved often in response to the demand for labor. Early in the eighteenth century, Maryland law began to require that all such men find a "housekeeper" to guarantee payment of the tax, but some probably fell through the cracks. In addition, when such men became disabled, they ceased to appear. Nevertheless, the tax lists offer the best information we can get of the numbers of white adult males and their distribution in households.

These lists have many other uses, although the researcher often must consult other available documents, such as wills and other probate records, to ensure accuracy in linking names.[1] Here is a goldmine for genealogists and social historians. Genealogists can find help in tracing families. Students of family history can use the lists to follow changes in household structure and household formation over time. One can see the appearance of sons as they reached age 16 and follow them as they worked for their parents and then established households of their own. A run of tax lists as long as that available for Somerset can give general information about the ages at which men first formed their households, which, by the eighteenth century, was usually when they married. It may be feasible to relate household formation to economic change in the area. Where men more likely to make such a move when times were good? Migration studies are also possible, although complicated by the difficulties of tracing movers and identifying men who died but whose estates did not go through probate.[2]

Much remains to be done with the Somerset tax lists. All need to be transcribed and published. In addition, the names need to be linked from list to list, a formidable task, given the duplication of names. The ten lists offered here, although not yet linked, at least make a substantial portion of all the surviving lists widely available.

Researchers owe much to the Maryland State Archives, which has preserved these lists and made them accessible. Archivists have rescued them from obscurity in boxes of court papers, sorted them, and repaired them enough to make consulting them possible. We are all also indebted to J. Elliot Russo (Jean E.) for putting the lists printed here into publishable form. With her hard work, they are now legible to anyone who cares to consult them. May the good work continue.

Lois Green Carr
Historian, Historic
St. Mary's City

[1] Jean E. Russo describes the difficulties encountered in linking names from list to list in "The Constables' Lists: An Invaluable Resource," Maryland Historical Magazine 85 (1990), 164-170.

[2] On the difficulties of migration studies, see Russo, "Constables' Lists."

TECHNICAL NOTES

This volume contains transcriptions of the constables' lists of Somerset County taxables. For every year, there is an individual list for each of the county's nine hundreds. The transcripts are arranged alphabetically by hundred within each year. The constables organized the tax lists by household. In this transcription households have been assigned sequential numbers; these numbers do not appear on the original lists. The numbering, beginning with the household in the upper left hand corner, follows the column format used by the constable.

The present volume includes the extant tax lists for the period 1730 through 1740. The list for 1732 does not survive. The quality of the early lists (through 1735) is consistently good, with all of the hundreds appearing to be complete. The 1736 and 1737 lists, however, are in poor condition. For many of the hundreds, only fragments of the lists remain. By comparing these two lists with preceding and subsequent lists, I have reconstructed many of the incomplete names. These reconstructions appear in the lists in brackets; I have only inserted material of which I am quite confident. The lists for 1738 and 1739 are in excellent condition. The 1740 list, also in good condition, is included in this volume because it is the last surviving list from the period prior to the establishment of Worcester County out of territory formerly part of Somerset County. Where individual lines or small sections of a list are difficult to read, I reconstructed the entries in the same manner as used for the fragmentary lists, a process again indicated by the use of brackets.

Every effort has been made to provide a verbatim transcription of the tax lists. However, technical considerations necessitated limiting the size of the name field to 25 characters. As a result, some of the descriptive notations have been abbreviated or truncated. In the index I used standardized names to group phonetically similar entries. These standardized names are intended to facilitate locating individuals in the lists; they are not offered as "correct" spellings. I tried to retain the spelling used most commonly by the constables across the county and across the time period. In some cases, however, I used contemporary spellings (such as Montgomery rather than Mungumry) when the eighteenth-century spellings were so unusual that researchers might not locate relevant entries. Abbreviations of given names are those used by the constables. In the index I expanded the names. In some cases, constables used the same abbreviation for different but related given names; for example: "Jos" was used for Joseph, Joshua, and possibly Josiah and "Matt" was used for Matthew and Mathias. I consistently expanded such abbreviations to the most commonly used name, such as Joseph for "Jos" and Matthew for "Matt."

J. Elliott Russo
3215 37th Ave. S.
Minneapolis, MN 55406

ABBREVIATIONS AND MEANINGS

Those abbreviations in brackets have been introduced by the compilers to conserve space. Others are found verbatim in the records.

[aq] =
[hp] = half planter
[hs] = half share
jour, junr., jur., jun., ju., j. = junior
[na] =
quarter = collection of cabins on a plantation
s. = son or senior
sinior, sener, senr., ser. = senior
[ws] = whole share
widd., wid., widw. = widow

The following entry may cause confusion:
"1319 DAVIS, JNO., SENR. for son
"1319 DAVIS, THOS."

It indicates that John Davis, senr. is being taxed for his son Thomas Davis [and not for himself].

These tax lists may be examined at the Maryland State Archives. In requesting examination of these documents or copies of them (in person or by mail), refer to the following Accession Numbers.

```
1730 Tax List - MdHR 20,397-5
1731 Tax List - MdHR 20,397-6
1733 Tax List - MdHR 20,397-7
1734 Tax List - MdHR 20,397-8
1735 Tax List - MdHR 20,397-9
1736 Tax List - MdHR 20,397-10
1737 Tax List - MdHR 20,397-11
1738 Tax List - MdHR 20,397-12
1739 Tax List - MdHR 20,397-13
1740 Tax List - MdHR 20,397-14
```

How to use the Index

The surname (last name) is underlined. In brackets are some of the variations which have been equated to the underlined surname. Following the surname are given names with the year of the tax and the household number. Turn to the section with the appropriate year (shown on the top of the right hand pages and locate the entries with the given household number.

For example, Christopher Glass is listed in the index with an entry of 30-1185. This means that there is an entry in the 1730 tax list, household number 1185. Once you find the entry (on page 16), you will note that there are several persons living in the household with Christopher Glass: John Glass, and slaves, Frank, Pompy and Diana. All persons listed are aged 16 or older.

1730 TAX LIST [Household number/Name/Remarks]

ANNEMESSEX HUNDRED

1 Sailer, Jno
2 Hall, Charles
2 Davies, Richd [hs]
2 slave Dominick
3 Hall, Richd.
3 Hall, Jno. [na]
3 Walstone, Joy
4 Benson, Jno.
4 Benson, Wm. [na]
4 Benson, Sollom. [na]
5 Waters, Wm. senr.
5 slave Davie
6 Waters, Eliz. att
6 Waters, Littleton [na]
6 Hall, Wm. [na]
6 Londin, Henry
6 slave Sepio
6 slave Alex [na]
6 slave Hanniball [na]
6 slave Hagar
6 slave Major
6 slave Pegg [hs]
7 Cotmons, Mary att
7 Cotmon, Jos. [hs]
7 Cotmon, Laz. [hs]
7 slave Mingo
7 slave Gennie [hs]
8 Waters, Jno.
8 Spruance, Jno. [na]
8 Owens, Moses [na]
8 slave Jack
8 slave Harry
8 slave Tom
8 slave Will
8 slave Sesana
8 slave Maser
9 Waters, Wm. senr.
9 slave Goliah
9 slave Sambo
9 slave Dinah
9 slave Bristoll [hs]
9 slave Pompey [hs]
10 Tull, Thos.
10 Cottinhome, Thos.
10 Tull, Wm. [hs]
10 slave Quamino
11 Barnes, Robt.
12 Trehern, Jno.
12 Herry, Geo.
12 Roach, Nath. [hs]
12 Trehern, Jams. [hs]
12 Roach, Danl. [hs]
12 slave Gennie
13 Handy, Samll.
13 Handy, Thos.
13 slave Kate
13 slave Dido
13 slave Nann [hs]
14 Curtice, Cha.

14 Jnoson, Wm.
14 slave Tabith
14 slave Dick
15 Cullen, Edmd.
16 Betsworth, Jams.
17 Long, Jeffrey
17 Long, Samll.
17 Long, Jeffrey
17 Long, Sowell [hs]
17 slave Kate
18 Stocdill, Edwd.
18 Turk, Magnes
19 Lister, Wm.
19 Ligg, Benjn.
19 Lister, Wm. [hs]
19 Lister, Thos. [hs]
19 slave Ceaser
20 Hull, Danll.
21 Beauchamp, Wm.
22 Marshall, Geo.
23 Boston, Wm.
24 King, Jams.
25 Williams, Thos. sr.
25 Williams, Thos.
25 Beauchamp, Isaac
25 Lackey, Pattrick [na]
25 slave Dick
25 slave Andrew
25 slave Ceaser
25 slave Patience
25 slave Sarah [hs]
26 Planner, Wm.
26 Adams, Jno. [na]
26 slave Hector
26 slave Sambo
26 slave Watt
26 slave George
26 slave Tom
26 slave Adam
26 slave Titus
26 slave Quesh
26 slave Divaum
26 slave Jean
26 slave Hannah
26 slave Robbin [hs]
26 slave Glascow [hs]
27 Puesey, Wm.
28 Dikes, Jno.
29 Smith, Henry
29 Grigin, Paull
30 Wards, Mary att
30 Bormon, Jno.
31 Dixon, Thos.
31 slave Harry
31 slave Tobeth
31 slave Dinah
31 slave Livey
31 slave Dick [hs]
32 Horsey, Samll.

32 Horsey, Smith
32 Horsey, Stephen
33 Horsey, Nathl.
33 Jervice, Wm.
33 Barrat, Henry
33 slave Nid
33 slave Cake
33 slave Patience
33 slave Kate
33 slave Quamino [hs]
33 slave Prince [hs]
33 slave Jennie [hs]
34 Horsey, Isaac
34 Kelley, Jno.
34 slave Jon[a]than [hs]
35 Dixon, Wm.
35 Cogsberry, Henry
35 slave Bettey [na]
36 Hallond, Michl. sr.
36 slave Jack
37 Hallond, Michl. jnr.
37 slave Dick
37 slave Moull
38 Tayler, Wm.
38 Williams, Henry
39 Coulburn, Wm.
39 Coulburn, Wm.
39 Coulburn, Saml. [na]
39 Coulburn, Sollom.
39 Christey, Jno. [na]
39 Coulburn, Michal [hs]
39 slave Quaco
39 slave Lucie
40 Coulburn, Anne att
40 slave Abram
41 Coulburn, Sollomon
41 McCennie, Patt.
41 Coulburn, Sollom. [hs]
41 slave Guy
42 Frayzer, Petter
42 More, Jno.
43 Coward, Mary att
43 slave Mariea
44 Davies, Jams.
45 Miles, Henry
45 Stanthin, Edwd.
45 slave Fillice
45 slave Dinah
46 Dohotey, Jno.
47 More, Fran.
47 More, Jno.
47 More, Thos.
47 More, Jacob [hs]
48 Johnson, Jno.
48 Smith, Jams. [na]
48 Jnoson, Jno.
48 Dies, Phill. [hs]
49 Lord, Fran.
49 Lord, Thos. [hs]

TAX LISTS OF SOMERSET COUNTY: 1730-1740

ANNEMESSEX HUNDRED

49 Lord, Alexandr. [hs]
50 Ward, Stephn. senr.
50 slave Fillice
50 slave Sarah
50 slave Pompey
51 Ward, Stepn. junr.
52 Ward, Cournelious
53 Riggins, Jno.
53 Riggins, Jonathn.
53 Riggins, Jno.
53 Riggins, Stepten [hs]
53 Dukes, Rob. [hs]
54 Allen, Joseph
55 Sumers, Thos.
55 Sumers, Jonathn.
55 Sumers, Geo.
55 Sumers, Thos. [hs]
56 Ward, Samll.
56 Lord, Henry
56 Ward, Jno. [hs]
57 Sumers, Jno.
57 Sumers, David
57 slave Locus
58 Vessell, Jams.
59 Bird, David
60 Booth, Rogr.
61 Wheler, Jno.
62 Ward, Thos.
62 Ward, Jams.
62 Ward, Jacob
63 Sterlin, Jno. senr.
63 Sterlin, Jno. junr.
63 Sterlin, Henry
63 More, Wm.
63 Sterlin, Aron
63 More, Samll. [hs]
64 Bird, Jos.
64 Wilson, Jno.
64 Cullin, Jacob
65 Roach, Jno.
65 Obeer, Isaac
66 Cullen, Henry
67 Robarts, Robr. [na]
68 Gardener, Thos.
68 Long, Randoll
68 slave Silby
68 slave Pegg
69 Davies, Jno.
69 Carrie, Fran. [na]
69 slave Sambo
69 slave Harry
69 slave Sue
69 slave Bes
69 slave Jack
69 slave Wott
70 Horsey, Stephn.

70 Bailey, Thos.
70 Kelly, Jams. [hs]
70 slave Bess
70 slave Jack [hs]
71 Bell, Antoney
71 Bell, Thos.
71 Arnald, Wm.
71 Bell, Antoney
71 Bell, Josephus [hs]
71 slave Robbin
71 slave Kate
71 slave Nannie
72 Gunby, Jno.
72 Spiby, Jonathn.
72 slave Jack
72 slave Kate
73 Kellem, Jno.
73 Dikes, Edwd.
73 Kellem, Jno.
73 Kellem, Joshua [hs]
74 Ware, Robt.
74 Swaine, Jno.
74 Mathis, Wm.
74 Mathis, Robr.
75 Hern, Edwd.
76 White, Jno.
76 McGomrame, Thos.
77 Adkins, Joshua
77 Oneall, Henry
77 slave Bess [hs]
78 Long, Rendall
78 slave Shilo
79 Scott, Robt. senr.
79 Scott, Robt. junr.
79 Scott, Jno.
79 slave Bettey
80 Gunby, Kirk
80 Dikes, Jno.
80 Riddin, Cha.
81 Peusey, Ayles att
81 Puesey, Jno.
82 Cahoone, Jno.
83 Cottinhame, Cha.
83 Cottinhame, Cha.
83 Cottinhame, Thos.
83 Cullen, Nichelos
83 Cottinhame, Jno. [hs]
84 Dies, Robt.
85 Potter, Anne att
85 Potter, Henry
85 Potter, Josephus
86 Adams, David
86 Adams, Thos.
86 Adams, Jacob
87 Roaches, Sarah att
87 Wheatly, Sampson
87 Riddin, Petter
87 Wheatly, Wm. [hs]
88 Conner, Jno.

88 Conner, Jno. [hs]
89 Conner, Wm.
90 Oughton, Jno.
90 Outten, Jno. [hs]
90 slave Dick
91 Maddux, Thos.
91 Maddux, Alexandr.
91 Maddux, Bell
92 Mitchall, Rondall
92 Lord, Jno.
93 Prier, Thos.
93 Tayler, Elies
94 Wilson, Wm.
94 Wilson, Geo.
94 Wilson, Jno.
94 Wilson, Jos. [hs]
95 Trehern, Jams.
95 Long, Coulburn [hs]
96 Long, Samll.
96 Long, Wm.
96 Long, David
97 White, Jno.
97 White, Jno. [hs]
97 slave Essex
98 More, Thos.
99 Porter, Jos.
100 Beachamp, Edmd.
100 Beauchamp, Edmd.
100 Beachamp, Jno. [hs]
100 Beachamp, Robt. [hs]
100 Beachamp, Smith [hs]
101 Kings, Robt. [aq]
101 slave Mingo
101 slave Tamer
102 Brimiagin, Walter
103 Rennold, Jno. [na]
104 Williams, Jno.
104 Fenton, Martin [na]
104 slave Sambo
104 slave Sarah [hs]
105 Catlin, Wm.
105 Catlin, Robt. [hs]
105 slave Harry
106 Williams, Isaac
106 Eairs, Jacob
106 Dockeday, Jams.
107 Lanford, Jos.
107 Lanford, Benj.
107 Lanford, Jos.
108 Parks, Arthr.
108 Parks, Jno. [hs]
109 Tailer, Thos.
110 Tailer, Jno. senr. att Jno. Tailer (only Isaac Parks taxable)
110 Parks, Isaac
111 Tailer, Jno. junr.
112 Parks, Jno. senr.
112 Parks, Arthr. [hs]
113 Mister, Wm.

1730 TAX LIST [Household number/Name/Remarks]

ANNEMESSEX/BALTIMORE HUNDREDS

113 Pritchett, Wm.
113 Mister, Wm. [hs]
114 Evans, Jno.
114 Husk, Jno.
115 Wheler, Samll.
116 Hopkins, Geo.
116 Hopkins, Jno.
116 Hopkins, Geo. [hs]
117 Allensworth, Richd.
117 Allensworth, Richd.
117 Allensworth, Nehemiah [hs]
118 Horsman, Henry
119 Long, Danll.
119 Long, Dall. [na]
119 Long, David
119 slave Friendship [hs]
120 Stockwell, Thos.
121 Vessells, Ephrm.
121 Vessells, Ephm. [hs]

BALTIMORE HUNDRED
122 Onarton, John
122 slave Jack
122 slave Filles
123 Wharton, Daniel
123 Wharton, Henmon
123 Derikson, Joseph
124 Rickardson, Jones
124 slave Bees
125 Whalley, Willm. son of John
126 Hazzard, David senior
126 Hazzard, David junr.
126 slave Dinih
127 Hazzard, Conard
127 slave Robbin
128 Marsey, Jno.
129 Mersiey, Edkins
130 Eviens, Willm.
130 Eviens, John
131 Evines, John son of Waltor
132 Dasiey, Thom.
133 Godwen, Ceaser senr.
133 Godwen, Ceaser junr.
134 Rickards, John junr.
135 Robbinson, Thom.
135 Hazzard, Willm.
135 slave Jeffery
135 slave Janey

136 Godwen, Michel
137 Johnson, Lenard
138 Dikeson, Sturges
138 Johnson, John
139 West, George
139 Roberts, Alxr.
140 Roberts, Thomas senr.
140 Roberts, Thom. junr.
141 Morrs, Sarah
141 Moriss, Dennies
141 Morriss, Willm.
142 West, Willm.
143 West, Thomas
144 Idlit, John senr.
144 Idlit, John junr.
144 slave Jack
145 Idlit, Benjamen
146 Samons, Willm.
147 Hickmon, Rich. junr.
148 Dirixson, Benjman
149 illegible
150 Dikieson, Hannah
150 slave Boos
151 Collings, Willm.
152 Hickmen, Richard senr.
152 slave Sarah
153 Freeman, Willm.
154 Moriss, Bibbins
155 Tindle, Samuel
155 Coupper, Charles
156 Camble, John
157 Dineho, Willm.
157 Williams, John
158 Wayiaples, Paul
158 Karrey, Richard
158 slave Charles
159 Howard, George
159 Howard, Nehemiah
159 slave Kent
159 slave Bees
160 Smith, John senr.
160 Smith, Jon. junr.
160 Smith, Robert
161 Bernet, Mary
161 Bernet, John
161 Bernet, James
162 Grooms, Willm.
162 Gudrick, Willm.
163 Beassey, Willm.
164 Burton, Willm.
164 Burton, John
164 slave Tittous
164 slave Rechal
165 Lowes, Joseph
166 Joseph, [Fr]edrieck
167 Indlos, Abraham

168 Morriss, John
169 Kenney, Joseph
170 Kenney, Stephn.
170 Kenney, Willm.
171 Indloes, Thom.
172 West, Allexr.
173 Ronalds, Richard
174 Kerrieys, Thomas
175 Johns, Ebenezr.
175 Fletwood, Thom.
176 Haighway, Abraham
177 Smith, John senr. capt.
177 Smith, John junr.
177 Smith, Thomas
177 Hamlton, John
177 slave Herrey
177 slave Mary
178 Rickards, John
178 slave Simon
178 slave Bossn
178 slave Mall
178 slave Bridget
179 Linch, John
180 Robbinson, Michel
181 Robinson, Mary
181 Robinson, Josiah
181 slave Bees
182 Perrey, James
183 Tingle, Hough sinior
184 Tingle, John
185 Tingle, Hugh jour.
186 Woodcraft, John
187 Woodcraft, Richard
188 Robinson, John
188 Robinson, George
189 Botten, Thomas
190 Botten, John
191 Cabb, John
192 Coffing, Thomas
192 Coffing, Joseph
193 Smith, Jones
194 Townson, Boweman
195 Hutson, George
196 Whorton, Francis
197 Miller, John
197 Godwen, Moses
197 slave Primes
197 slave Pigg
198 Linch, Allexr.
198 Cabb, Natthll.
199 Weight, Joseph
199 Weight, Willm.
199 Weight, Joseph junr.
200 Cabb, Willm.
201 Linch, John
201 Linch, Abraham
202 Holland, John
202 Eviens, Elias

TAX LISTS OF SOMERSET COUNTY: 1730-1740

BALTIMORE HUNDRED

203 Stevenson, John
203 Stevenson, Joseph
204 Smith, Willm.
205 Tull, John
205 Wabb, Willm.
206 Clark, R[ace]
207 Hutson, Richard junr.
208 Hall, John
209 Hall, Joseph
210 Hutson, John
211 Hutson, Samuel
212 Lithbery, Abgail
212 Lethbery, Arther
213 Fassitt, Willm.
214 Fassitt, Francling
214 Tyrie, Robert
214 slave Nanie
215 Mumford, Willm.
216 Hallaway, John
216 Hallay, Joseph
217 Bredwell, Isiah
217 Bridwel, Stephn.
217 Forsight, Thomas
217 slave Simon
217 slave Coffie
217 slave Adam
218 Brittingham, Joseph snr
219 Gray, Joseph
219 Gray, Thomas
219 slave Simon
219 slave Quaco
220 Harison, Willm.
220 Chanchle, George
221 Murrey, James
222 Dalle, Archibald
222 Dall, John
222 slave Ross
223 Gray, Willm.
224 Powell, Thomas son of John
225 Dalle, John sinor
226 Timions, Willm.
227 Hamlon, John
228 Russiel, Andw.
229 Mumford, James
229 Mumford, Thom.
229 slave Jenne
230 Woodcraft, Mary
230 Woodcraft, Willm.
230 Woodcraft, Thomas
231 Allison, John
232 Williams, Argliues
232 Murrey, Robert
233 Truet, George
234 Drikens, Dibrex
235 Johnson, David
236 Hampton, Mary mrs.

236 Woods, Adam
236 slave Nerow
236 slave Jack
236 slave Pigg
236 slave Hannah
237 Davidson, Willm.
238 Fervell, Thomas
239 Menklyn, Richard
240 Collings, John
240 Ratlife, Elias
241 Collings, Thomas
242 Robertson, Andrew
242 Fall, Abraham
243 Tall, John
244 Kennet, Martain
245 Turvile, Willm. sinior
245 Turvile, Willm. jour.
246 Gault, Robert
246 Gault, Willm.
246 Gault, John
247 Kennet, Willm.
248 Hill, Robert
248 Hill, Johnson
249 Hutson, Richard
249 Gray, John
249 Gray, Willm.
249 Gabb, John
249 Street, Mensfeet
249 slave Coffe
249 slave Dick
250 Loogwood, Richard
250 Loggwood, Armale
250 Eviens, Willm.
251 Neweble, John
252 Camble, John
253 Wallace, Thomas
253 slave Hector
254 Pattey, John
254 Mersiey, Willm.
254 Johnson, Benjam.
255 Fassat, Willm. capt.
255 Johns, John
255 slave Frank
255 slave Sue
255 slave Doll
255 slave Merisey
255 slave Tittors
255 slave Lue
256 Fassit, Willm. son of Capt. Wm. Fassit
256 Deeds, Larance
257 Mersey, Allexr.
257 slave Jack
258 Hamlon, Francies
259 Coller, Petter
259 slave Pompey
260 Mersiey, Willm.

261 Kinnisey, John
262 Walton, Willm. sinior
262 Walton, Willm. jour.
262 slave Casear
262 slave Judah
262 slave Maglaster
263 Wheller, John sinr.
263 Wheller, John jour.
264 Crapper, Edmand
264 Camble, Solloman
264 slave Petter
264 slave Pompey
264 slave Dick
264 slave Febbe
265 Hopkins, Samuel
265 Bredfoott, Adam
265 one shoemaker
266 Crapper, Netth. senior
266 Crapper, Sollm.
266 Crapper, Edmond
266 Hamilton, William
266 Crapper, Netth. jour.
267 Holland, Richard
268 Ratlife, Charels
268 Ratlife, Edward
268 slave Tom
268 slave Robin
268 slave Mall
268 slave Charles
268 slave Ceatt
268 slave Sutie
269 Olford, David
270 Fassitt, John
271 Marchel, Isaac
271 Marchel, Jaccob
271 slave Jon. Morris
271 slave Ben
271 slave Bees
271 slave Diniah
272 Purnel, John
272 Ratlife, Charals s. Ellise Ratlife
272 Ratlife, Charales
272 Abbet, Willm.
272 slave Will
272 slave Sambo
272 slave Mall
272 slave Dall
272 slave Marry
272 slave Dinah
273 Herpweel, Robert
273 Latcham, Thoma.
274 Whalley, Willm.
274 Whalley, Edward
275 Liptroatt, John
276 Pridox, Thomas

1730 TAX LIST [Household number/Name/Remarks]

BALTIMORE/BOGERTERNORTON HUNDREDS

277 Gilland, John
277 Mekie, Thom.
277 slave Sambo
278 Boien, Rodah
278 Dueit, Nath.
278 slave Qamoney
279 Duett, Willm.
279 Warrent, Robert
280 Quilling, Joseph
281 Simson, Richard
282 Tayller, Walter
283 Purkins, Thomas
284 Powell, Susanah
284 Powel, Charles
285 Whilling, --rey, mr. plantation - 2 slaves
286 Richardson, Thomas
287 Morgyine, Evirey
288 Conror, Daniel
289 Henrey, John marchnt.
290 Willson, John
290 Willson, Israll
291 Ingram, Jaccob
291 Mersey, Thomas
292 Blizsurd, Bnjm.
293 Hallaway, John sr.
294 Showel, Samuel
295 Harvey, Thos.
295 Bishop, Thos.

BOGERTENORTON HUNDRED
296 Leay, John
296 Ball, Samuell
296 slave
297 Murray, John
297 Gillinin, Hugh
297 Rathbon, Richd.
297 slave
298 Slinger, Thomas
299 Brown, John
300 English, Thomas
301 Stevenson, James
302 Penewell, Charles
303 Truitt, Benjamain
303 Weeb, Samuell
304 Purnall, Mathew
304 slave
305 Tompson, James
306 Penewell, John
307 Davis, Robert
307 Davis, Wm.
307 Davis, Ishmaell
308 Davis, Thomas
309 Heather, Ephiraim
309 Heather, Epheraim
309 2 slaves
310 Blizard, Richard

311 Garman, John
312 Truitt, Wm.
313 Cavenough, John
314 Clark, Daniel
315 Truitt, Ellenir widow
315 4 slaves
316 Truitt, George son of George
317 Mumford, James
318 Turner, Henery
318 Henderson, Charles
319 Dennis, Wm.
320 Steele, James
320 Steele, Daniell
321 Scott, Mark
322 Hall, Wm.
322 2 slaves
323 Hall, Robert
324 Shockley, Wm.
325 Gillitt, John
326 Tayler, John Lee
327 Wilcocks, George
328 Crapper, Ebeynezar
328 Crapper, Ebynezar
329 Gangun, Edward
330 Porter, Wm.
331 Davis, Edward
332 Tull, Benjamain
333 Tull, Richard
334 Timmons, Francis
335 Timmons, Aron
336 Timmons, Thomas
337 Timmons, Joseph
338 Timmons, James
339 Timmons, Sameull
340 Timmons, Wm.
341 Timmons, John
342 Warrin, Robert
342 Townsand, Wm.
343 Warrin, Nicholos
343 Gray, Nicholos
344 Dasey, John
345 Baker, John
346 Richardson, Charles
346 slave
347 Bishop, John senr.
347 Bishop, Benjamain
347 Bishop, Joseph
347 Bishop, David
348 Bishop, John son of Henry
349 Donelson, John
349 Tustin, Wm.
349 Weeb, John
349 Kelly, Nicholas
349 Lewis, Wm.
349 Barrick, Wm.
349 2 slaves
350 Tayler, Joseph

350 Tayler, John
351 Alixander, Paul
352 Stevens, Samuell
352 Daisy, Thomas
353 Braton, Quanton
354 Truitt, George
354 slave
355 Brittingham, Isaac
355 Brittingham, Wm.
355 slave
356 Ennis, Nathaniell
356 Townsand, Jeremiah
357 Ennis, Wm.
358 Bishop, Charles
359 Frankling, Edward
360 Smock, Henery
361 Pointer, Edward
362 Williams, Prisgrane
363 Realy, Thomas
363 slave
364 Evans, Edward
364 Evans, Ebeynezar
365 Bradford, John
365 Bradford, Wm.
366 Collings, Thomas
366 slave
367 Midsley, Thomas
368 Walton, Richard
368 Walton, John
369 Robinson, Wm.
369 Robinson, Wm. junr.
369 slave
370 Sharly, James
370 Cusadey, Owin
371 Patrick, Mathew
372 Holstone, John
373 Edwards, Benony
374 Pepper, John
375 Truitt, Joseph
376 Hook, Wm.
377 Truitt, George son of Philip
378 Hutson, Wm.
379 Braton, James
379 Bell, Adam
380 Hutson, Margrett widow
380 Holland, Wm.
380 Bishop, Bowin
380 slave
381 Ponton, Robert
382 Holstone, Wm.
383 Claywell, Thomas
383 slave
384 Godfrey, Charles
384 slave
385 Low, George
386 Jones, George
386 Hammond, Charles
387 Hammond, John

TAX LISTS OF SOMERSET COUNTY: 1730-1740

BOGERTERNORTON HUNDRED

388 Hammond, Isaac
389 Hammond, Edward
389 Hammond, Jacob
390 Hammond, John son of Jno.
391 Penewell, Thomas
392 Burbage, Edward
393 Truitt, John
394 Bowin, Littleon
395 Bowin, John
396 Bowin, Luke
396 Bowin, George
396 slave
397 Evans, John
397 slave
398 Williams, John
398 Bisick, Absolom
399 Hadder, Warrin
400 Beaderd, Richard
401 Parker, John
401 Parker, George
401 Parker, John
401 Parker, Charles
401 Parker, Philip
401 Parker, Samuell
401 4 slaves
402 Atkins, Stanton
403 Jarman, Job
404 Truitt, James
405 Truitt, Thomas
406 Raine, Mathew
407 Truitt, Samuell
408 Porter, John
409 Handcock, Wm.
410 Pointer, Elias
410 Pointer, Wm.
411 Selbey, Parker
412 Handcock, Daniell
413 Porter, Joseph
413 slave
414 Jones, Joseph
414 Swaine, Wm.
415 Smith, Wm.
416 Nock, John
416 Burton, John
416 Noles, Samuell
416 slave
417 Townsand, Jeremiah
417 Townsand, Brickhouse
417 slave
417 slave
418 Purnall, Thomas
418 slave
418 slave
418 slave
418 slave
419 Pointer, Thomas
420 Truitt, Mary widow

420 Truitt, George
420 Truitt, Nehemiah
421 Fletcher, Thomas
421 Sockwell, George
421 slave
422 Atkins, John
423 Hampton, Mary widdow
423 3 slaves
424 Collings, Charles
425 Peckett, Peter
425 Church, Samuell
426 Hodge, Robt.
427 Williams, Thomas Nath.
427 Williams, Samuell
428 Richards, Wm.
429 Ironshire, Isaac
430 Smith, John
431 Simson, Wm.
431 2 slave
432 Whittington, Wm.
432 5 slaves
433 Powell, Samuell
434 Tingle, Samuell
435 Powell, Rachell widdow
435 Powell, Thomas
436 Williams, Joab
437 Bassitt, Ailice widd.
437 Bassitt, John
438 Brittingham, Wm.
438 Brittingham, Wm. junr.
438 Brittingham, Solomon
439 Jarman, Robt.
440 Jarman, Wm.
441 Ennis, Mary widow
441 Ennis, Cornelious
442 Parnall, Elisha
442 Lindall, Peter
442 2 slaves
443 Davis, Wm.
444 Bradford, Nathaniell
445 Purnall, Catharine
445 4 slaves
446 Beaderd, Wm.
447 Johnson, Afreya Doze
447 Johnson, George
447 Johnson, John
447 Johnson, Thomas
447 Johnson, Samuell
447 slave
448 Jarman, Henery
449 Hader, Anthoney
450 Crapper, Nehemiah

451 Crapper, Wrixam
452 Dreadon, Hanah wid.
452 Dreadon, John
453 Dreadon, Robtert
454 Denis, Donuk
455 Stevenson, Lesey wid.
455 Richardson, James
456 Collings, Mary widd.
456 Collings, Andrew
457 Collings, Wm.
458 Crapper, John
458 Molonie, Patrick
459 Porter, Wm.
459 Mackmanus, James
460 Selbey, Wm.
460 6 slaves
461 Arabia, Jacobus
461 Collings, Solomon
462 Richardson, Robt.
462 Richardson, Wm.
463 Gore, James
464 Martin, James
464 Rewark, Bryan
464 5 slaves
465 Spence, Adam senr.
465 2 slaves
466 Davis, Robert junr.
467 Penewell, Anne wid.
467 Penewell, Wm.
467 Penewell, Richard
468 Bridgewaters, Emaneuell
469 Sheehanus, Wm.
470 MacCales, John
470 Lindall, Robt.
471 Murray, Donkin
471 Greer, Adam
471 McKinsey, Patrick
472 Braton, Samuell
472 Braton, James
472 Braton, Wm.
473 Spence, Adam
473 2 slaves
474 Low, George
475 Rownd, James
475 3 slaves
476 Rownd, Edward
476 Charles, John
476 2 slaves
477 Smith, Abraham
477 Smith, John
478 Williams, Jonathan
478 Williams, John
479 Morris, Wm.
479 Morris, Joseph
480 Weeb, Grace widd.
480 Weeb, Elisha
481 Hailes, Jeremiah

1730 TAX LIST [Household number/Name/Remarks]

BOGERTERNORTON/MANOKIN HUNDREDS

482 Clark, Charles
483 Hutson, Donis
483 Mcherson, Peter
483 slave
484 Pointer, Wm.
484 Pointer, Nathaniell
485 Brittingham, Jeremiah
486 Stevenson, Hugh
486 Mullin, Christopher
487 Smith, Andrew
488 Jarman, George
489 Bishop, Wm.

MANOKIN HUNDRED

490 Wilson, Ephrum
490 Wotson, James
490 Clark, Alexander
490 Cames, John
490 Hath, Abraham
490 slave Monday
490 slave Hanah
490 slave Moll
490 slave Coffe
490 slave Jenne
490 slave Tom
490 slave Nane
490 slave Benne
490 slave Peter
490 slave Harre
490 slave Cezer
491 Wilson, David
491 Swift, Richard
491 slave Jacob
491 slave Monday
491 slave Phillip
491 slave Cudgo
491 slave Nany
491 slave Holoday
492 Tegue, John senr.
492 Tegue, John junr.
493 Sharp, Benjamin
493 Walston, William
493 Walston, Thomas
493 Jones, Matthew
493 Ginkins, John
494 Davis, Arther
495 To Tull, Esther
495 Tull, Joshua
495 slave Moll
496 Miles, Samell
496 slave Dick
496 slave Benn
497 Maddox, Lazarus
497 slave Coffe
497 slave Jo
497 slave Dick
498 Furnis, William

498 slave Abbo
499 Phillips, John
500 Sandus, Richard
501 Westt, Antony
502 Turpin, William sen.
502 Tull, John
502 slave Moll
502 slave Tom
502 slave Hary
502 slave Jack
502 slave Fillis
502 slave Bess
503 Thomson, Andrew
503 Thomson, William
503 Thomson, John
503 Phillips, James
503 Banister, Charles
503 slave Tony
503 slave Cezer
503 slave Ros
504 West, William
505 Banister, Thomas
505 Rigins, William
506 Smith, John
506 slave Charles
507 To Fountain, Mary junr.
507 Brown, Turvill
507 Hopkens, Beniamon
508 Chamburs, Richard
508 Chapell, William
508 slave Coko
509 [Turp]in, William jun.
509 slave Will
509 slave Besor
509 slave Frost
509 slave Conibe
509 slave Gorge
509 slave Peg
509 slave Moll
510 Bausman, William sener.
510 Bulger, Richard
510 slave Doso
510 slave Bess
511 Fountain, Nicoless
511 Wilson, John
511 Tull, Thomas
512 Butler, Nathanill
513 McDormon, William
514 Ford, Absolom
515 Miles, William
516 Polk, William
516 Polk, David
516 slave Owen
516 slave Abner
516 slave Hanne
517 Strobridg, James

517 Camill, John
517 Magraugh, James
517 slave David
517 slave Coffe
517 slave Hager
518 Stuard, Willam revd.
518 slave Jemme
518 slave Abbo
519 Stutt, Arsbill
520 Nox, Willam
521 Jones, Willam hed [head of] monokin
521 slave Gy
521 slave Moodo
521 slave Eve
522 Gray, John juner.
522 slave Hano
523 Gray, John sener.
523 Bryon, Richard
524 Smith, Robert
525 Flemon, Willam
526 Magraugh, Jhon
527 Fo[ll]er, John
528 Newman, Henry
528 Layfild, Robert
529 Magraugh, Willam
530 Lockwood, Willam
531 Laws, James
532 Mornie, John
533 Mat[li]tt, James
534 Gold Smith, John
535 Polk, James
536 Pope, James
537 Hath, Willam
538 Magraugh, Jean to
538 Layfield, Thomas
539 Benston, George
540 King, Beniamon
541 Owens, John
542 Dormon, Matthew junr.
543 Dorman, Michell
544 Grinless, John
544 Gullitt, Abraham
545 Mellrow, Danill
545 Mulrow, Alexander
546 Smith, Edward
546 Smith, Thomas
547 Gray, Willam
548 Wilson, Robert
548 slave Sambo
549 Brown, David
549 Benston, Robart
549 slave Cogo
550 Defap, Charles
551 Spiser, Phillup
552 Woolcocks, John
553 Horsy, Revill
553 Hammon, Daniell

TAX LISTS OF SOMERSET COUNTY: 1730-1740

MANOKIN HUNDRED

553 Cunelo, Darbe
553 slave Nick
554 Horsy, Willam
555 Hall, Alexander senr.
555 Hall, Alexander junr.
556 Steward, Alexander
556 Dischall, James
556 Montery, Danill
557 Hales, John
557 Layfield, Willam
558 Fitchjarril, Peter
558 slave Tom
559 Carny, Robart
559 Gilegin, Bryon
560 Fisher, Bartly
560 slave Jack
560 slave Beck
561 Hardin, Joseph
562 Shaw, Jonathan
563 Shipard, Matthew
564 Horsy, John
564 Killy, John
564 Hill, John
564 slave Peter
564 slave Moll
565 Tunstall, John
565 slave Somersett
565 slave Mill
565 slave Lohill
565 slave Lewrpole
565 slave Tony
565 slave Fremon
565 slave Truman
565 slave Norris
565 slave Bess
565 slave Nabelah
565 slave Dinah
566 Not, Issack
567 Maddox, Thomas
567 slave Soo
567 slave Will
568 Maddox, Daniell
568 slave Jack
568 slave Sary
569 Turpin, John
569 Turpin, Willam
569 slave Coffe
569 slave Tobe
569 slave Cork
570 To King, Eliner
570 slave Jubeter
570 slave Roos
571 Wey, Willam
571 slave Sipeo
572 Flawed, Katron to
572 Fawed, John
573 Hath, Jacob
574 [To]ckles, Willam

575 Dorman, Matthew sener.
575 slave Doll
576 Hath, Abraham sener.
576 Hath, Abraham
576 A[nd]er[son], Roger
577 Ascridg, Willam
577 slave Peter
577 slave Moll
578 Rusell, Richard
579 Fosky, Thomas
580 [Wi]lliss, Barnebe
581 To Woolford, Roger
581 slave Samson
581 slave Will
581 slave Tamer
581 slave Rose
582 Jones, Willam goos crk
582 slave Benn
582 slave Tom
583 Bawsmon, Willam i Cove
583 Bawsmon, Willam
584 Bawsmon, George jun.
584 slave Sambo
585 Tull, Samewill
586 Lawed, Tucker
587 Mitchell, Thomas
587 Mitchell, Isac
587 slave Mingo
587 slave Sary
588 Chamberlin, Willam
589 Revell, Randull
589 slave Harry
589 slave Tobe
589 slave Marth
590 Roach, William
590 Roach, Isac
590 Roach, Charls
590 slave Kitt
590 slave Patince
591 Right, Abill
592 MacDaniell, David
593 Revell, Charles
593 Davis, John
593 slave Venus
594 To Lindow, James
594 Robards, Joseph
594 Ruke, Willam
594 Haley, Timothy
594 slave Moses
594 slave Hazard
594 slave Bess
594 slave Jenny
595 King, Whitenton
595 Fisher, Henery
595 slave Tony

595 slave Harry
595 slave Tom
595 slave Pace
595 slave Bess Pampefoot
596 Haymon, Arther
596 Haymon, Willam
596 Haymon, Beniamon
597 To Woolford, Marth
597 Labruce, Beniamon
597 slave Moll
597 slave Sary
598 Smith, Willam
598 slave Pace
599 Tillmon, Aron
600 Tillman, Joseph
600 slave Lonon
601 Tullmon, John
602 West, Randull
602 Wilson, James
602 slave Mingo
603 Wolston, Boz
603 Right, Randull
604 Young, John
605 Bawsmon, George sener.
606 Bawsmon, John
607 Jarves, William
608 Ballard, Jarves
608 Ballard, William
608 slave Roos
608 slave Ame
609 Brown, Thomas
609 Brown, David junr.
609 slave Cudgo
609 slave Judy
610 Moo, John
611 Pukum, Abraham
612 Staples, James
613 Horner, George
613 Horner, Tull
613 Horner, George
613 Horner, James
614 Febus, George sener.
614 Febus, Samewill
614 slave Into
615 Febus, George juner.
615 Ho[rn]er, Willam
616 Rigsbe, Lewis
616 Cinegum, Thomas
616 slave Atte
617 Cro[u]der, Francis
617 La[ry], Timothy
618 Birgin, Danill
619 Elsey, John sener.
619 Elsey, John juner.
619 Forgerson, John
619 slave Cezer
619 slave Judy

8

1730 TAX LIST [Household number/Name/Remarks]

MANOKIN/MATTAPANY HUNDREDS

619 slave Betty
619 slave Sibb
619 slave Nun
619 slave Sambo
620 Colins, Willam
620 Colens, Thomas
621 Odear, Steven
   sener.
621 Odear, Steven
   jun.
621 Odear, Farness
622 Givans, John
   sener.
622 Givans, Thomas
622 Shery, Job
623 [Giv]ens, John
   junr.
624 Long, Sollomon
625 Mathas, Partrick
625 Tindull, James
626 Furnes, James
627 Boler, Willam
628 Ballard, Henery
628 Wilks, John
628 Magraugh, David
628 Huitt, Thommis
628 slave Seser
628 slave Venter
628 slave Syrus
628 slave Jeny
628 slave Bendah
629 To Ballard, Elener
629 Jacobs, Will
629 slave Mory
629 slave Betty
630 Elsey, Arnold
630 Chambers, Edward
630 Coldwill, William
630 Jacobs, Edward
   moluto
630 slave Cussau
630 slave Jack
630 slave Urow
630 slave Nan
630 slave Hanne
630 slave Blinah
631 Fo[unt]ain, Mary
   sen.
631 Fountin, Samwill
631 Fountin, Thomas
631 Semour, Digby
631 slave Harry
631 slave More
632 To Robarson, James
632 Roberson, John
632 slave Jack
632 slave Tobe
632 slave Naro
632 slave Prew
633 Gilless, Joseph

633 Surmon, John
633 Pallis, John
633 Lesherbury, Thomas
633 slave Boson
634 Mclamey, Willam
634 Abitt, John
634 slave Naro
635 King, [Robert]
635 King, Nehemiah
635 Nisbett, William
635 Butt, John
635 slave Fortin
635 slave Jose
635 slave Sezer
635 slave Tobe
635 slave Momare
635 slave Muke
635 slave Nibett
635 slave Bess
635 slave Moll
635 slave Judy
635 slave Judy
635 slave Didah
635 slave Didah
636 Husk, John
636 slave Attee
637 King, Capell
637 slave Pompe
637 slave Tite
637 slave Grace
638 [Alexander], Moses
638 Cane, James
639 Plunkit, Oner
639 Cane, William
640 Gones, Wm.
641 Hath, Dorman
642 Blu[itt], Thomas

   MATTAPANY HUNDRED
643 Claywell, Petter
643 Claywell, Ezecell
643 slave Jude
644 Pope, John
644 Wise, Ezekell
644 slave Cook
644 slave Tom
644 slave Rose
644 slave Jane
645 Sturges, Richard
645 Taylor, Josiah
646 Tarr, Micall
647 Tarr, John
648 Willitt, Ambrous
648 Willitt, Tom
649 Claywell, Petter
   junr.
650 Peper, Tobias
651 Peper, Wm.
652 Brownbill, Nathll.
653 Vesey, Charl.

654 Chapman, Humphre
655 Henderson, Bishop
656 Wattson, Robart
656 Wattson, Charl.
656 Fisher, Balley
656 slave Amereler
657 Hill, Abraham
658 Allin, Joseph
659 Allen, John
660 Hosiear, Samuell
660 Hosiear, Sam. junr.
661 Croford, Andrew
661 Croford, John
662 [Dred]en, J[ohn]
663 Guttry, Patrick
664 Porter, McClantuck
665 Answorth, Wm.
666 Beachbord, Wm.
667 Parremore, Tho.
667 slave Will
667 slave Pegg
668 Tarr, Samll.
668 Hudson, Johnathan
668 slave Dick
669 Ginkins, John
670 Nutton, Tho.
670 Nuton, Starling
671 Turner, Wm.
671 Rigen, Ambrous
672 Sturgis, John
673 Johnson, Petter
674 Johnson, John
675 Harman, Immanuell
676 Wise, Tho.
676 Wiant, John
676 slave Rachell
677 Hopkins, Nathanill
677 Hopkins, Hamton
677 Murrow, David
677 Walker, John
677 slave Abner
678 Hopkins, Nathll.
   junr.
678 Ares, Henry
679 Richardson, John
680 Wise, Mathew
681 Aires, John
682 Hopkins, Samuell
682 Hopkins, Sam. junr.
682 Hopkins, John
682 Hopkins, Josiah
683 Pope, Samuell
683 slave Will
684 Pope, George
684 slave Bess
685 Milbourn, Tho.
685 Gurley, George
686 Taylor, Phillip
687 Hill, Johnson
687 Nuton, Johnathan

TAX LISTS OF SOMERSET COUNTY: 1730-1740

MATTAPANY/MONIE HUNDREDS

687 Hill, Lishea
688 Hill, Hutton
689 Hill, Robart
690 Sturgis, John senr.
690 Sturgis, Danill
690 Rode, John
691 Hopkins, Wm.
691 slave Rose
692 Walton, Fisher
692 Mackiell, John
692 slave Petter
692 slave Moll
693 Walton, Stephen
693 [Walton], Stephen junr.
693 Davis, C[harl.]
694 illegible, Tho.
695 illegible, Ja-----
695 illegible
696 illegible, Jno.
696 illegible, William
696 slave Dick
696 slave Nan
697 Hopkins, Mathew
697 Nickals, Matthias
698 Selby, Phillip
698 Selby, Mathew
698 Selby, Danil
698 [Selby], Phillip junr.
698 Selby, William
698 slave Sezer
698 slave Pine
698 slave Betty
699 Selby, Parker
699 La---, John
699 slave Jack
699 slave Tamow
699 slave Gloster
700 Masen, Abraham
701 Cord, William
701 slave Doll
701 slave Jane
702 Wagaman, Jacob
702 Wagaman, Wm.
702 Wagaman, Henry
702 slave George
702 slave Jack
702 slave Moll
703 Walker, John
703 slave Jack
704 Wattson, John
705 Wattson, Robart
706 Scott, Robart
706 S[cott], Robart
706 illegible, William
706 illegible
707 illegible

708 [A]rnall, [illegible]
709 illegible at quarter
709 slave Robin
709 slave Pegg
709 slave Abigall
710 Hodson, Rowland
710 Hodson, John
711 Cade, Charl.
712 Duberly, Tho.
713 Wattson, Luke
714 Pane, J[ohn]
714 Pane, Joseph
715 Prise, David
716 Bratten, William
716 Bratten, John
716 Westry, ---iall
716 slave Guy
717 Vannetson, Wm.
718 Robins, Tho.
718 slave Nedd
718 slave Jack
718 slave Hannah
718 slave Sarah
719 Booth, Wm.
719 Cary, Sollomon
719 Adkins, illegible
720 Nilson, Wm.
721 Jones, John
722 Tow, Jonas
722 Wattson, Petter
723 Holland, Nehemiah
723 Burke, John
724 Aydolett, Wm.
724 slave illegible
725 [Holla]nd, Benjamin
725 slave Janne
726 Chapman, Edward
726 slave Joe
727 Slingo, Tho.
728 Answorth, widow
728 Taylor, John
728 Answorth, Petter
729 Johnson, Wm.
729 Johnson, Hezekiah
730 Clarke, John
731 Purnell, John
731 slave Tobe
731 slave Sesar
731 slave Tom
731 slave Marrera
731 slave Sarah
731 slave Phillis
731 slave Nimrod
732 Brownbill, Henry
732 slave Pompe
733 Waite, Nathanill
734 Wattson, widow
734 Wattson, James

MONIE HUNDRED

735 White, Francis
736 White, John
737 Walker, James
738 Wallace, Mathew
738 slave Sibilla
739 Wallace, Richard
739 Wallace, Thomas
739 Wallace, James
739 Wallace, David
739 slave Ceaser
739 slave Bess
740 Roberts, Edward
740 slave Jeffery
740 slave Sarah
741 Harris, Jeremiah
742 More, Rowland
743 Morgan, Wallter
744 Grundey, John
744 Grundey, Rensher
745 Martin, George
746 Jones, Lewis
746 Jones, Samuell
746 slave Hannah
746 slave Moll
746 slave Ceasor
746 slave Jack
747 Hobbs, Noble
747 Wallter, Thomas
748 Laws, John
748 Wallace, William
748 slave Prince
748 slave Ceaser
748 slave Dunah
749 Miller, John
749 Miller, Thomas
749 Williams, John
750 Laws, Thomas
750 Wallace, John
750 King, Duncan
750 slave Joro
750 slave Marreah
751 Roe, Thomas
751 Jones, Charles
752 Roe, Joseph
753 Bassell, Thomas
754 Jones, Richard
755 Ferding, Randall
756 Winsor, Lazarus
756 Winsor, John
757 Pollock, Joseph
757 Neal, John
758 Pollock, David
758 slave Rodger
758 slave Sambo
759 Wright, Thomas
759 Wright, Henry
759 Austin, William
760 Shores, John
760 Shores, William

1730 TAX LIST [Household number/Name/Remarks]

MONIE/NANTICOKE HUNDREDS

761 Stringer, George
762 Stoughton, William
762 Skene, Robert
762 Ennis, Robert
762 Fosque, Benjo.
762 slave Busser
762 slave Jupeter
762 slave Cato
762 slave Simon
762 slave Fender
762 slave Dinah
763 Waller, John
763 Waller, Nelson
763 slave Jane
764 Waller, Major
765 Waller, William
766 Irving, George
766 Culberson, William
766 slave Toby
766 slave Jeffery
766 slave Judath
767 Laws, Robert
767 Laws, Panter
767 Laws, William
767 slave Boony
767 slave Jack
767 slave Samson
768 Cary, Thomas
768 slave Lonnon
768 slave Hannah
769 Ruark, John
770 Macomb, Robert
771 Jones, John
771 Jones, Robert
771 Jones, George
771 Cunungham, Arthur
771 slave London
771 slave Gallaway
771 slave Amock
771 slave Jeny
771 slave Rachell
772 Downs, George
772 Downes, Robert
772 Covington, Benjamin
772 Jones, Thomas
772 slave Toby
772 slave Frank
772 slave Bender
773 Jones, William
773 slave Will
773 slave Sepio
773 slave Sue
774 Gale, Mathias
774 slave Joo
774 slave Jacob
774 slave James
774 slave Dublin
774 slave Steven
774 slave Ceasor

774 slave Will
774 slave Peter
774 slave Rose
774 slave Pollinah
774 slave Jenney
774 slave Bess
774 slave Phebey
774 slave Rose junr.
774 slave Violett
774 slave Grace
775 Gale, George
775 slave Limehouse
775 slave Sepio
775 slave James
775 slave Jock
775 slave Nanney
775 slave Pitter
775 slave Sarah
776 Jones, James
776 Jones, John
776 slave Sambo
776 slave Moll
776 slave Sibb
777 Hobbs, Mersillas
778 Dashiell, Thomas
778 Dashiell, Levin
778 Harrison, John
778 slave Will
778 slave Jack
778 slave Harculis
778 slave Harey
778 slave Jack jur.
778 slave Merando
778 slave Bess
778 slave Jane
778 slave Thamar
779 Covinton, Philip
779 Covinton, John
779 Billins, James
779 slave Sambo
779 slave Cucko
779 slave Joo
779 slave Betty
780 Hobbs, Joy junr.
780 Mungar, John
781 Hobbs, Thomas
782 Leatherbury, John
782 slave Pompy
782 slave Samboo
782 slave Samson
782 slave Africa
782 slave Benn
782 slave Toney
782 slave Bridgett
782 slave Rose
783 Jones, Daniell
783 Covinton, Abraham
783 slave Whitehaven
783 slave Doll
784 Covinton, Thomas

784 Jones, Mathias
785 Waller, George
786 Dorman, Henry
787 Dorman, John
788 Durham, Thomas
789 Fisgarrard, Edmond
790 Stanton, Jonathan
790 Murrah, John

NANTICOKE HUNDRED

791 McClester, Jno. capt.
791 McClester, Wm.
791 McClester, Samll.
791 slave Coffie
791 slave Sambo
791 slave Tom
791 slave Adam
791 slave Siss
791 slave Abba
791 slave Phillis
792 Hopkins, Stephen
792 Chambers, Samll.
793 Samuells, Richard senr.
793 slave Cocorah
794 Samuells, Peter junr.
794 Hurst, Wm.
795 Martin, John
796 Bartley, John senr.
797 Bartley, John junr.
798 Hi[ck]man, Joshua
799 Walter, John
800 Dunn, Elizabeth
800 Walter, Daniell
801 Phipps, John
802 Hopkins, John junr.
803 Nutwell, Brunt
804 Hurst, Joseph
805 Hickman, Wm. senr.
805 slave Jack
805 slave Sambo
805 slave Mareah
805 slave Rose
806 Hickman, Wm. junr.
806 slave Orrey
807 Macomb, Timothy
807 Mezeck, Benja.
808 Mezek, Isaac
809 Dunn, Richard
810 Anderson, Sarah
810 Anderson, Jno.
811 Swilivin, Michall
812 Venadson, Lias
812 More, Wm.
813 Usears, John
813 Cooper, Jno.
814 Laramore, Thos. senr.

TAX LISTS OF SOMERSET COUNTY: 1730-1740

NANTICOKE HUNDRED

814 Laramore, Thos. junr.
814 Daughety, James
815 Macabe, Henry
816 Beard, Lewis senr.
816 Beard, John
816 Beard, Lewis
817 Henderson, Robt.
818 Collier, Robt.
818 Collier, Doughty
818 Parkerson, Jno.
819 Game, Sambo
819 Game, Robt.
819 slave Grace
820 Fluellin, Samll.
820 slave Sirus
821 Larramore, John senr.
821 Larramore, John
821 Larramore, Thos.
821 slave Coffie
821 slave Sibb
821 slave Moll
822 Dashiell, Henry
822 slave Gift
822 slave Sibb
823 Winright, Cannan
823 Winright, Stephen
823 Winright, John
824 Hopkins, Robt. senr.
824 Hopkins, Robt.
824 slave Toby
824 slave Pegg
824 slave Jenney
825 Hopkins, John senr.
825 Hopkins, John
825 Gurling, John
825 slave Jack
826 Dashiell, James
826 slave Robt.
826 slave Will
826 slave Will
826 slave Grace
826 slave Frank
827 Macants, Alexandr.
828 Williams, Richard
829 Shurman, Thos. senr.
830 Vahan, Wm.
831 Deen, John
832 Collins, John
832 Shurman, Thos.
833 Dashiell, Wm.
834 Bound, Joseph
835 Harris, Phillip
835 Speare, Henry
835 Gillisphie, Henry
835 Neasom, Jno.
836 Butler, Nicholas

837 Richardson, John
838 Culver, John
839 Nicholson, Roger
840 Dashiell, Joseph
840 slave David
840 slave Rendell
841 Dashiell, George senr.
841 Dashiell, Benja.
841 Dashiell, Robt.
841 slave Harry
841 slave Tamer
841 slave Didoe
842 Parsons, Francis
843 Ciningam, Daniell
844 Benston, Thos.
844 Shurridon, John
844 slave Will
845 Collier, Betts
846 McClester, Joseph
846 McClester, Neal
846 slave Samson
847 Russell, James senr.
848 Russell, James junr.
849 Relph, Thomas
850 Goslin, James
851 Jackson, Jonathan
851 Jackson, Thos.
852 Richardson, Wm.
853 Rider, Richd.
853 Rider, Hathley
853 Rider, Wilson
853 slave Taler
854 Collins, Richd.
855 Giles, Wm. senr.
855 Giles, Thos.
855 Giles, Wm.
855 slave Florah
856 Bordley, Wm.
856 Billings, Benja.
856 Murphey, James
857 Weatherlee, James
857 slave Tom
857 slave Pegg
858 Johnson, David
858 Cordrey, Jacob
859 Jacobs, Walter
859 Shiels, Partrick
859 slave Jack
859 slave Sibb
859 slave Bess
860 Given, Robt. senr.
860 Makeey, Michall
860 slave Sezer
860 slave Charles
860 slave Hanah
860 slave Nan
860 slave Bess
861 Burne, James
862 Carter, John senr.

862 Carter, Samll.
862 Carter, Thos.
863 Carter, John junr.
864 Carter, Philip
865 Farrington, Wm.
865 slave Alce
866 Train, James senr.
866 Train, James
866 Train, Roger
866 slave Coffie
866 slave Rose
867 Hardy, James
867 Hardy, Joseph
868 Piper, Wm.
868 Ackworth, Henry
868 slave Ben
868 slave Sambo
868 slave Sarah
868 slave Nell
868 slave Rose
869 Oliver, Wm.
870 Nutter, Huet
870 Nutter, Mathew
870 slave Punch
870 slave Tites
870 slave Dinah
871 Dunken, James
872 Nutter, Margaret
872 slave Philip
872 slave Sippeo
872 slave Moll
872 slave Rose
873 Nutter, Christophr.
873 Jones, John
873 slave Seaser
873 slave Tom
873 slave Barbary
873 slave Rose
873 slave Minadab
874 Nutter, Wm.
874 slave Ben
874 slave Cattoe
874 slave Jean
874 slave Catherine
875 Austen, Wm.
876 More, Jno. senr.
876 More, Wm.
877 Cordery, Isaac
878 More, Jno. junr.
879 More, Wm.
880 Tulley, Stephen senr.
881 Tulley, Benja.
882 Rodes, Timothy
883 McDowell, John
884 Green, Richd.
885 West, James
885 [B]urcam, James
886 Lanford, Thos.
887 Caldwell, James
887 slave Sambo
887 slave Robin

1730 TAX LIST [Household number/Name/Remarks]

NANTICOKE HUNDRED

887 slave Rose	920 Hovington, John senr.	953 Baker, James
888 Dashiell, Mitchell	920 Hovington, Jonathan	954 Middleton, Daniell senr
888 Currey, Philip	920 Tully, Joseph	954 Middleton, Daniell
889 Right, Wm.	920 slave Adam	955 Johnson, Thos.
890 Tayler, Abram	920 slave Iago	956 ONeal, John
890 slave Quasha	920 slave Domonick	957 Ingram, Abraham
891 Rodes, Daniell	920 slave Jenney	957 Ingram, Isaac
891 Rodes, Timothy	921 Cordry, Edward	957 Fleetwood, John
892 Beek, Isabell	922 Young, Charles	957 Highway, Abraham
892 Langston, Wm.	923 Melson, Samll. senr.	958 Short, Edward senr.
893 Baker, Thos.	923 Melson, Joseph	958 Short, Edwd.
893 Langston, Spear	923 Melson, Samll.	958 Short, Jno.
894 Weatherlee, Wm.	924 Wright, Soloman	958 Martin, Thos.
894 slave Sevinah	924 Wright, Edward	959 Ingram, Isaac
895 Twilly, Elizabeth	925 Green, Ezekiell	960 Ingram, Jacob
895 Nicholson, James	925 Hull, John	961 Wingate, Philip
895 Twilly, Robt.	926 English, Wm.	962 Dunken, Thos.
895 Twilly, George	926 Ell[ens]worth, Robt.	963 Samuells, Petter senr.
896 Nicholson, Richd.	927 Marvil, Thos.	963 Samuells, Richard
897 Heatch, Solloman	928 Rotten, Josiah	964 Dolby, Peter
897 slave Cook	929 Hovington, Richd.	965 Walter, Thos.
898 Parramore, James	930 Hovington, Thos.	966 Draper, Alexandr.
898 Shehe, Potter	931 Roberson, John	966 Draper, Wm.
899 Cheaseman, John	932 Nuten, Christopher	966 ONeal, James
899 slave Seaser	932 Harper, Wm.	966 slave Toney
899 slave Nansy	933 Russell, Wm.	967 Gray, Wm.
900 Ackworth, Samll.	934 Deen, Charles	967 Marcy, Thos.
900 slave Sue	934 Wheatley, Wm.	967 slave Margret
901 Ackworth, Charles	934 slave Tom	968 Shockley, David
901 Ackworth, Richd.	935 Walter, Henry	969 Boyce, Daniel
901 Wailes, John	936 Nouls, Edmond	970 Darby, Daniell
902 Ackworth, Thos.	937 Rowell, Thomas	970 Fulton, Wm.
902 slave Will	938 Tully, James	971 Tindall, Charles
903 Olphey, John	938 Tully, Benja.	972 Smith, John
904 Brown, Wm.	939 Nuton, Patience	973 Bound, Jacob
905 Gilliss, John	939 Nuton, John	974 Harvey, John
906 Scott, George	940 Huggins, Charles	975 Williams, Charles
907 Scott, Windom	941 Roberson, Wm.	976 Manlose, Emanuell
908 Young, William	942 Suman, Peter junr.	976 slave Quaco
909 Jackson, Samll.	943 Thornes, Edwd.	976 slave Nell
910 Wilson, John	944 Stilley, Mary	977 Polk, Charles
911 Cooper, Gabrill senr.	944 Floyd, Major	978 Owens, Robt.
911 Cooper, Thos.	945 Edge, Joshua	978 slave Cate
912 Gravener, Thos.	946 Roberson, David	979 Polk, John
913 Cooper, Gabrill junr.	947 Maglolin, Jno.	980 Hyminons, Thomas
914 Cooper, Samll.	948 Lynn, Aron	981 Newbald, Francis
915 Cooper, Isaac	948 White, John	982 Sharp, John
916 Tayler, Wm.	948 Gynkins, Thos.	983 Ingram, Robart
917 Wood, Thos.	948 slave Will	984 Winzer, Henry
917 Wood, John	948 slave Harry	985 Noble, Isaac senr.
918 Killam, Edwd.	948 slave Abram	986 Noble, Isaac junr.
918 Darby, John	949 Marcy, Elizabeth	987 Callaway, Peter junr.
918 slave Dick	949 Marcy, Wm.	988 Winzer, John
918 slave Marian	950 George, Wm.	988 Hayward, Wm.
919 Hovington, John junr.	951 Baker, Wm.	988 Friggs, Robt.
919 Churine, John	952 Mezek, Jno.	989 Givens, Robert junr.
	952 Mezek, George	989 Maclalin, Joseph

TAX LISTS OF SOMERSET COUNTY: 1730-1740

NANTICOKE/POCOMOKE HUNDREDS

990 Owten, John
991 Hosey, Mathew
992 Cooper, James
993 Owten, Edwd.
993 Tatman, Wm.
994 Stephens, John
995 Parramore, Joseph
996 Surman, Thos.
   junr.
997 Hugg, Joanah
997 Polk, John
998 Benston, Henry
999 Benston, Wm.
1000 Caldwell,
   Partrick
1001 Parramore, Mathew
1002 Goddart, Jno.
1002 Hickson, Joseph
1003 Cliften, George
   senr.
1003 Cliften, George
1004 Cliften, Philip
1005 More, Jno.
   forrest
1005 Kinney, Wm.
1006 Callaway, Jno.
   senr.
1006 Callaway, Edward
1006 Callaway, Jno.
1007 Haynes, Francis
1008 Caldwell, John
   junr.
1008 Jones, Wm.
1008 slave Sambo
1009 Waller, Nathaniel
1010 Callaway, Wm.
1010 Callaway, Jno.
1011 Waller, Thos.
   senr.
1011 Waller, Nathll.
1011 Waller, Thos.
1012 Harvey, Wm.
1013 Parramore, Thos.
1014 King, Wm.
1015 Downes, Robert
1016 Hardy, John
1017 Jones, John
1018 Oliver, George
1019 Maclure, Robert
1020 Jones, James
   junr.
1021 King, Philip
1022 Relph, Wm.
1023 Records, John
1024 Callaway, Peter
   senr.
1024 Williams, John
1025 Spear, Henry
1026 More, Catrin
1026 More, Wm.

1027 Henry, John
1028 Wallis, Richd.
1029 Anderson, John
1030 Cotman, Ebenezer
1031 Danilson, Jane
1031 slave Tom
1031 slave Belindo
1032 Low, Rase
1033 Langford, John
1034 Collins, Edmond
1035 Jones, James
   senr.
1035 Jones, Daniell
1036 Wright, Soloman
1036 Brown, Jno.
1037 Twiford, Jno.
1037 Brown, Jno.
1038 Tully, Stephen
   junr.
1039 Bennet, Edwd.
   senr.
1039 Bennet, Edwd.
1039 Bennet, George
1039 Bennet, John
1040 Shurman, Wm.
1041 Mezek, Jacob
1042 Read, John senr.
1042 Read, John
1042 slave Pegg
1043 Abdon, Wm.
1044 Quaturmus, James
1045 Gales, John [aq]
1045 slave Barsheba
1045 slave Simon
1045 slave Harculas
1045 slave Messenger
1045 slave Judah
1045 slave Moll
1046 Darby, Walter
1047 Relph, Ann
1047 Buckworth, Charles
1048 Langston, John
1048 Smith, David
1049 Game, Fortune
1049 Game, Betty
1050 Mezek, Nehemiah
1050 Mezek, Jacob
1050 Paul, Jacob
1051 Paul, George
1052 Nicholson, John
1053 Donohoe, Nathall.

POCOMOKE HUNDRED
 1054 Benton's, Comfort
1054 slave Messorai
1054 slave Holborn
1054 slave Sambo
1054 slave Coffee
1054 slave Bess
1054 slave Pegg

1054 slave Hannah
1054 slave Joan
1055 Coston, Isaac
1056 Harper, Richard
1057 Coston, Stephen
1058 Jordine, Aaron
1059 Tull, John
1059 Pilcher, John
1060 Knight, Richard
1060 Knight, James
1060 Knight, Joshua
1061 McCollegin, Hugh
1062 Harper, Edwd.
1063 Harris, Caleb
1064 Riggin, Teague
1064 Cantwell, Thomas
1064 slave Ceaser
1064 slave Nan
1065 Harris, Robt.
1065 Logey, Alexr.
1065 slave Moll
1065 slave Harry
1066 Riggin, Ambross
1066 Riggin, Teague
1066 Bonum, Willm.
1067 Riggin, Joseph
1067 Condon, Edwd.
1068 Daily, Patrick
1069 Porter, William
1070 Denston, John
1071 Scott, Thomas
1072 Donohoe, Teague
1073 Ottell, Francis
   sen.
1073 Ottwell, Solm.
1074 Riggin, Darby
1075 To Townsend,
   Elizth.
1075 slave Tom
1075 slave Tawney
1076 Colbourn, Jno.
1076 Colebourn, William
   [hs]
1077 Mayo, Saml.
1078 Dickerson, Edmd.
   senr.
1078 slave George
1079 Dickerson, Edmd.
   junr.
1080 Dickerson, Charles
1081 Dickerson,
   Cornelius
1081 slave Dinah
1082 Townsend, John
   junr.
1082 Townsend, Jno. his
   son
1082 Ottell, Charles
1083 Bennett, Jno.
1084 Fleming, Jno.

1730 TAX LIST [Household number/Name/Remarks]

POCOMOKE HUNDRED

1084 Fleming, Isaac
1084 Steevens, Edwd.
1084 Fleming, Willm.
1084 slave Robin
1084 slave Dina
1084 slave Pompy [hs]
1085 Donoho, Dorman
1085 Cooper, Saml.
1086 Smulling, Randall
1087 Ward, Joseph
1087 Ward, Cornelius
1087 slave Bess
1088 Warrick, Arthur
1088 Oatwell, Francis junr.
1089 Harper, Francis
1089 Harper, James [hs]
1089 Harper, Mosses [hs]
1090 Tull, William
1091 Harper, John
1091 Wilson, Francis
1091 Huggins, Roger
1092 Tull, George
1092 Tull, Noble
1092 slave Abner
1092 slave Dinah
1093 Mills, William
1093 Mills, Samuel
1093 Mills, Jonathn. [hs]
1094 Hampton, Mary madm.
1094 Dreeden, David taylor
1094 Gudgeon, Benjn.
1094 Miller, Jno.
1094 slave Ceaser
1094 slave Tarrill
1094 slave Chick
1094 slave Adam
1094 slave Joan
1094 slave Pompy
1094 slave Joan
1094 slave Lucey
1094 slave Old Genney
1094 slave Old Genney
1094 slave Young Genn
1094 slave Patience
1095 Adams, Thomas senr.
1095 Adams, Thomas junr.
1095 Adams, David
1095 slave Jenny
1096 Dickerson, Peter
1096 Dickerson, John
1096 Dickerson, Edwd.
1096 Dickerson, Isaac
1096 Dickerson, Charles
1096 slave Squashoby
1097 Cox, William
1097 slave Jonas
1097 slave Doll
1098 Dies, Robt.
1098 Dies, Daniel
1099 Ellis, John
1100 Evans, Thomas
1100 slave Jeney
1101 Boyer, Robt.
1102 White, Jno. at Point
1102 Collins, Samuell
1102 Conner, Wm.
1103 Handy, Wm.
1103 Handy, Saml. [hs]
1103 slave Nedd
1103 slave Harry
1104 Porter, Hugh
1104 Goar, Richd.
1104 Porter, Jonathn. [hs]
1105 Dennis, John junr.
1105 Dennis, Theophilus
1105 slave Kingston
1105 slave Patience
1106 Mitchell, Robt.
1106 Boyce, Wm.
1106 slave Townsydes
1107 Dorman, Saml.
1107 Stevens, Wm. [hs]
1108 Adams, Abraham
1109 Marshall, Samuel
1109 Marshall, Thomas
1110 Wood, William
1110 Long, Jno.
1111 Taylor, Robt.
1112 Boston, Isaac
1112 slave Sambo
1112 slave Venus
1112 mulatto Darkus
1113 Boston, Esow
1114 Adams, Jacob
1114 Adams, Saml.
1114 Adams, Colons
1114 Adams, Thomas [hs]
1114 slave Sambo
1114 slave Nann
1115 White, Willm.
1115 slave Great Harry
1115 slave Little Harry
1115 slave James
1115 slave Jeney
1115 slave Sew
1115 slave Sarah
1116 Whittingham, Heber
1116 Hapcraft, Thos.
1117 Calvert, William
1118 Fenton's, Margett
1118 Blair, Robt.
1118 slave Bess
1119 Brown, Thomas
1120 Benston, Thos.
1120 Johnson, Joshua
1121 Peacock, Edwd.
1122 Noble, James senr.
1123 Tomlinson, Saml.
1123 Tomlins, Soll.
1123 Tomlinson, Edwd.
1123 slave Abner
1124 Perkins, Jno.
1125 To Perkins, Sarah
1125 Perkins, Wm.
1125 Perkins, Michall
1126 Buywaters, Richd.
1127 Mattux, Lazrus
1127 Jenkins, Christopher
1128 Broughton, Jno.
1129 Broughton, Bruff
1129 Parker, Philip
1130 Cluff, Edwd.
1130 Dukes, Wm.
1131 Clogg, Saml.
1132 Townsend, Danl.
1132 slave Pegg
1132 slave Kate
1133 Townsend, James
1133 slave Guy
1134 Scholfield, Henry
1134 Davis, Elizth. [hs]
1135 Adams, Wm.
1135 Adams, Dennis
1135 Adams, Wm.
1135 slave Jack
1136 Adams, George
1136 Adams, Jacob [hs]
1137 Powell, John
1137 slave Sarah [hs]
1138 Benston, Willm.
1139 To Harris, Ann
1139 Pilcher, Wm.
1140 Holland, Willm.
1140 slave Tony
1140 slave Tom
1140 slave Darkus
1141 Billing, Thomas
1141 slave Robert
1142 Milbourn, Caleb
1142 slave Mingo
1142 slave Annah
1143 Milbourn, Jno.
1144 Ellis, Thomas
1145 Nearon, Robt. senr.
1145 slave Will
1145 slave Harry
1146 Nearon, Robt. junr.
1146 slave Sarah

TAX LISTS OF SOMERSET COUNTY: 1730-1740

POCOMOKE HUNDRED

1147 Nearon, James
1147 Cambridge, William
1147 slave Moll
1148 White, Jno. pocomoke
1148 slave George
1148 slave Patience
1149 McDaniel, Allen
1149 McDaniel, Mosses [hs]
1150 McCready, Alex
1151 White, Archibld.
1151 West, Thos.
1152 Dreaden, David senr.
1152 Dreaden, Wm.
1152 Dreaden, David junr.
1153 Carsey, Peter
1153 Carsey, Wm.
1153 Carsey, Saml.
1154 Hull, Edwd.
1154 Hull, Beacham
1155 Beachamp, Edwd.
1155 Beachamp, Marcy
1155 Beachamp, Thos.
1155 slave Morie
1156 Matthews, Teague
1157 Adams, Philip
1157 Adams, Hope
1157 Davis, Jno.
1158 Matthews, Saml.
1159 Matthews, Jno.
1160 Riggin, Jno. senr.
1160 Riggin, Stephen
1160 Riggin, John junr.
1160 slave Jeny
1161 Riggin, Saml.
1161 slave Bess
1162 Riggin, Jno. secudes
1163 To Riggen, Eliz.
1163 Riggin, Charles
1163 slave Mark
1163 slave Nan
1163 slave Peter
1164 Clifton, Jno.
1165 Allen, Francis
1165 Allen, John
1165 Hindman, Jacob
1165 slave Sibbery
1165 slave Ceasar
1165 slave Sampson
1165 slave Will
1165 slave Judea
1165 slave Nell
1165 slave Margery

1166 Scott, John
1166 Ray, James
1166 Goldsmith, Thomas
1166 slave Toany
1166 slave Peter
1166 slave Jack
1166 slave Sawney
1166 slave Pheaby
1166 slave Rose
1167 Sheldon, Jno.
1167 slave Isaac
1168 Grey, Thomas
1168 slave Abraham
1169 Adkinsons, Patience
1169 Atkinson, Saml.
1170 Atkinson, Isaac
1170 slave Guy
1171 Atkinson, Angelo
1171 Barrett, Henry
1171 Jones, Abraham
1172 Gibbs's, Robt. capt.
1172 Gibbs, Abraham
1173 Stewart, Jno.
1173 Warters, Patrick
1173 Cockling, Francis
1173 Christophers, Aristobulus
1173 Vahon, Wm.
1173 Davis, Evan
1173 slave Fisher
1173 slave Sandy
1173 slave Jack
1173 slave Bockwo
1173 slave Fungo
1173 slave Brawney
1174 Magan, John
1175 Porter, Francis
1175 Porter, Meckimney
1176 Townsend, Charles senr.
1176 Townsend, Charles junr.
1176 Townsend, Sollomon
1176 Townsend, Elias
1177 Townsend, Jno. senr.
1177 Townsend, Saul
1177 slave Murreah
1178 Peal, Thomas
1178 Peal, Thurrogood
1178 Gades, Robt.
1178 slave Sampson
1179 Andrews, Jno.
1180 Cottingham, Jonathn.
1180 Cottingham, Charles
1180 Cottingham, Wm.

1181 Beavans, Thos.
1181 Townsend, Jno. son of Chas.
1182 Beavins, Roland
1182 Beavans, Cornelius
1182 Beavans, Wm.
1182 Beavans, Elias
1183 Worder, Sesannah
1183 Cornon, Cornelius
1183 slave Mass
1183 slave Tom
1183 slave Bellah
1183 slave Phabia
1184 Sturges, Joshua
1184 Laws, Wm.
1184 slave Tom
1184 slave Moll
1185 Glass, Christopher
1185 Glass, John
1185 slave Frank
1185 slave Pompy
1185 slave Diana
1186 Duffen, George
1187 Noble, James
1187 Steevens, Jno.
1188 ODear, Jno.
1189 Tillman, Gideon
1189 slave Pompy
1189 slave Grace
1190 Niblett, Burnell
1190 slave Pompy
1191 Johnson, Elizth.
1191 slave Bess
1192 Houston, Joseph
1192 slave Bell
1193 Beavans, Jno. senr.
1193 Beavans, Caleb
1193 Beavans, Jno. junr.
1193 slave Sambo
1194 Nelson, Hugh
1194 Grey, Allen
1194 Dieton, Isaac
1194 slave Jos
1195 Houlston, Benja.
1195 Worrington, Thos.
1195 slave Dick
1196 Taylor, Saml. senr.
1196 Taylor, Saml. junr.
1197 Godfrey, Jos.
1198 Turner, Saml.
1199 Turner, Jno.
1200 Buttler, Thos.
1201 Morris, Isaac
1201 Morris, Luke
1201 Davis, Jos.
1201 slave Ayo
1201 slave Ben
1201 slave Surrey

1730 TAX LIST [Household number/Name/Remarks]

POCOMOKE/WICOMICO HUNDREDS

1201 slave Abner
1202 Hutton, Abram
1202 slave Will [hs]
1203 Sturgis, Jonathn.
1204 Dennis, John senr.
1204 Dennis, Solm.
1204 Dennis, Danl.
1204 slave Joa
1204 slave Kate
1205 Houston, Robt.
1206 White, Jno.
1206 White, Majr.
1207 Davis, Nat.
1208 Selby, Thos.
1208 slave Dinah
1208 slave Tom
1209 Fitzwaters, Henry
1210 Whittington, Southy
1210 Beavans, Joshua
1210 Landman, Jno.
1210 slave Ceaser
1210 slave Hannah
1211 Hough, Edmd.
1211 slave Will
1211 slave Sambo
1211 slave George
1211 slave Titus
1211 slave Nanny
1212 Townsend, Solm.
1213 Taylor, James
1213 Brown, Willm.
1214 Whittington, Wm.
1214 slave Franck
1214 slave Babb
1215 Nicholson, James
1216 Nicholson, Jno.
1216 Nicholson, Jos.
1217 Lane, George
1218 Henderson, John senr.
1218 slave Guy
1218 slave George
1218 slave Joan
1218 slave Bess
1219 Ellis, William
1220 Henderson, Benja.
1221 Henderson, James
1221 slave Adam
1222 Lamberson, Abraham
1223 Melvin, Robt.
1223 Melvin, Willm. [hs]
1224 Gillett, Jno.
1224 Gillett, Wm.
1224 slave Harry
1225 Henderson, Jno. junr.
1226 Holston, James
1226 slave Kate
1227 Holston, Jno. senr.
1227 slave Rose
1228 Holston, Jno. junr.
1229 Gillett, Saml.
1229 slave Darkus
1230 Dickerson, James
1230 Dickerson, Robt.
1231 Burnett, James
1231 McDaniel, James
1232 Benston, Edwd.
1233 McHendry, Charles
1234 Brittingham, Jno.
1234 slave Mecubo
1235 Jones, Edwd.
1236 Lindow, James
1236 Luke, Wm.
1236 slave Mosses
1237 Banes, George
1238 Quinton, Philip
1238 slave Jack
1239 Scholfield, Joseph
1239 slave Primus
1239 slave Will
1240 Henderson, Charles
1240 Young, Paul
1241 Lane, Willm.
1241 slave Harry
1241 slave Kate
1242 Mills, Jno.
1242 Mills, Wm.
1242 Mills, Robt.
1242 Mills, Nat.
1242 Mills, Alex
1242 slave Ayu
1243 Mills, Saml.
1243 Mills, Nathl.
1243 Speeden, James
1243 Speeden, Robt.
1244 Cary, John
1245 Merrill, Jno.
1245 Merrill, Joshua
1245 Chambers, Jeremiah
1245 slave Nann
1246 Marchment, Wm.
1246 Marchment, Charles
1247 Benston, Alexr.
1248 Braizer, Wm.
1248 Corbine, Thos.
1249 Taylor, Hope
1250 Lamberson, Jno.
1251 Pitts, Jno.
1252 Layfield, Thos.
1252 Layfield, Geo.
1252 Penngally, Thos.
1252 slave Tollomy
1253 Mills, Mary widw.
1253 slave Hector
1254 Hayward, Thos. mr.
1254 Davis, Tudar
1254 slave Sambo
1254 slave Jasper
1254 slave Sinaser
1254 slave Tom
1254 slave Priss
1254 slave Jenney
1255 Wonell, James taylors
1255 Bennett, Wm. taylors
1256 Smith, Wm. doctor
1257 Townsend, Littleton
1257 Carry, Jeremiah
1258 Couserly, Patrick

WICOMICO HUNDRED

1259 Handy, John
1259 Williams, John
1259 Houston, George
1259 Handy, Samuel
1259 Seahorn, Thos.
1259 Desheild, Matt.
1259 slave Merrah
1259 slave Dick
1259 slave Prince
1259 slave Benj
1259 slave Jean
1260 Humphris, Thos.
1260 Maglachlan, Dom.
1260 Roads, Jno.
1260 slave Quamino
1260 slave Cuffy
1260 slave Bess
1260 slave Sibby
1261 Pipper, Christopher
1261 slave Dick
1261 slave Sambo
1261 slave Toby
1261 slave Sue
1261 slave Dido
1262 Crutch, Jacob
1262 Crutch, Robt.
1263 Child, Thos.
1264 Lankcake, Francis
1264 slave Jack
1264 slave Toby
1264 slave Bess
1265 Vincent, Thos. junr.
1265 Vincent, James
1266 Nicholson, Richd.
1266 Nicholson, Joseph
1266 Samuels, Abel
1267 Nicholson, James
1268 James, John
1269 Bready, John
1270 Price, Eve

TAX LISTS OF SOMERSET COUNTY: 1730-1740

WICOMICO HUNDRED

1270 slave Will
1270 slave Bridgett
1271 Heatch, Samuel
1271 Riggen, Ambrose
1272 Bird, Thos. senr.
1272 Bird, Thos.
1273 Jones, Finch
1274 Lankcake, Gorge
1274 Cartor, Charles
1275 Records, John
1275 Records, Benj.
1275 Records, Alex.
1275 Records, Joseph
1275 Thomson, Geo.
1276 Codry, John
1277 Heatch, Adam
1277 Heatch, Elgate
1277 slave Toby
1277 slave Frank
1277 slave Hanna
1277 slave Mow
1277 slave Cannador
1278 Price, Jno.
1279 Linch, Cornelius
1280 Heatch, John
1281 Atkinson, Timothy
1281 Evans, Wm.
1282 Collins, James
1282 Collins, Richd.
1283 Handy, Isaac
1283 slave Sherp
1283 slave Prue
1284 Taylour, Joseph
1285 Vincent, Thos. senr.
1285 Vincent, Geo.
1286 Lecate, Jno.
1286 Lecate, Bartho.
1287 Hall, Thos.
1288 Elgate, Wm.
1289 Timmons, Thos.
1290 Covintone, Thos.
1290 slave Thos.
1291 Mattix, Alex.
1292 Mattix, Wm.
1293 Carr, Jno.
1294 Caldwell, Jno.
1294 Caldwell, Joshua
1294 Crawford, Jno.
1294 Lenard, Joseph
1294 Rathbon, Andrew
1294 slave Cofy
1294 slave Tom
1294 slave Ishmall
1294 slave Wm.
1294 slave Jone
1294 slave Squash
1294 slave Wm
1294 slave Doll

1295 Holtone, John
1296 Lindow, Thos.
1297 Hearon, Thos.
1297 slave Hanna
1298 Hearon, Wm.
1298 slave Mall
1299 Reddy, Nicholas
1299 Reddy, Jno.
1299 Reddy, Thos.
1300 Freny, Petter
1301 King, James
1302 Taylour, Thos.
1303 Gordy, Moses
1304 Parmore, Richd.
1305 Christopher, Jno. junr.
1306 Handy, Ebenezer
1306 slave Thom
1306 slave Sambo
1306 slave Mumford
1306 slave Hanna
1306 slave Bonaber
1306 slave Eme
1307 Longer, James
1308 Phillips, Jacob
1309 Smith, James senr.
1309 Smith, James
1309 Smith, David
1309 Smith, Moses
1310 Lingo, Daniel
1311 Maglimmery, Geo.
1312 Maglimmery, Edward
1312 Olifant, John
1313 Disharoon, Jno. junr.
1314 Tetum, Jno.
1315 Cocks, Thos.
1316 Hall, Fenix
1317 Lingo, Jno.
1318 Davis, Daniel
1319 Davis, Jno. senr. for son
1319 Davis, Thos.
1320 Kezey, Patt.
1320 Kezey, Jno.
1321 Lingo, Jacob
1322 Purdue, Jno.
1323 Davis, Jno. junr.
1323 Magee, Petter
1324 Magee, Geo.
1325 Magee, Jno.
1326 Chathell, James
1327 Disharoon, Lewis
1327 Disharoon, Leven
1328 Right, Jeramiah senr.
1328 Right, Jeramiah
1329 Hill, Thos.
1330 Smith, Geo.

1331 Turnor, Samuel
1331 Turnor, Nicholas
1332 Hayman, Wm.
1332 Hayman, Charles
1333 Shokley, Jno.
1333 Shokley, Jonat.
1334 Duskie, Moses
1334 Griffen, Oliver
1335 Lingo, Roberson
1336 Davis, Sam.
1337 Maybillie, Patt.
1338 Duskie, Richd.
1339 Attkins, Robt.
1339 Attkins, Jacob
1340 Duskie, Denis
1340 Diall, James
1341 Fuckes, Benj.
1341 Highway, Isaac
1341 slave Toby
1341 slave Patience
1342 Todvine, Mary
1342 Todvine, Isaac
1343 Croutch, Isaac
1344 Bowen, Wm.
1345 Todvine, Henry
1345 Todvine, Thos.
1345 Vance, Alex.
1345 slave Gulya
1345 slave Fran
1345 slave James
1346 Todvine, Nicholas
1347 Carry, Wm.
1347 Carry, Jonathan
1348 Rotch, Else
1348 Rotch, Steven
1348 Goldsmith, Antoney
1348 slave Thom
1348 slave Pegg
1349 Disharoon, John senr.
1349 Disharoon, Jno.
1349 Disharoon, Wm.
1349 Stephens, Wm.
1349 slave Cuffy
1349 slave Aboe
1350 Disharoon, Michall
1350 Green, James
1351 Croutch, Jno.
1352 Radish, Jno.
1353 Bushaw, Ann
1353 Hougine, Wm.
1353 Makanells, Jno.
1353 slave Suntor
1354 Collier, Thos.
1354 slave Grace
1355 Vinibles, Jno.
1356 Bordman, Sarah
1356 Bordman, Graves
1357 Corbett, Daniel
1358 Goslin, Thos.

1730 TAX LIST [Household number/Name/Remarks]

WICOMICO HUNDRED

1359 Phillips, Richd. junr.
1359 Phillips, Thos.
1359 Phillips, Jno.
1360 Venibles, Wm.
1361 Phillips, Richd. senr.
1361 slave Grace
1362 Gordy, Petter
1363 Christopher, Jno. senr.
1363 Christopher, Clem.
1364 Dowdle, Christopher
1365 Hunt, Jno.
1366 Anderson, Thos.
1366 Pope, Richd.
1367 Gathert, Thos.
1368 Such, Oliver
1369 Hasteen, Robt.
1370 Caldwell, Hugh
1371 Sharp, Geo.
1371 slave Rose
1371 slave Frank
1372 Gillise, Thos.
1372 Denwood, Geo.
1372 Vance, Thos.
1372 slave Nedd
1372 slave Aby
1372 slave Stepney
1372 slave Dom
1372 slave Nema
1372 slave Pegg
1372 slave Jean
1373 Alexander, Wm.
1373 Alexander, James
1374 Alexander, Sam.
1375 Alexander, Moses
1376 Griffin, Jno.
1377 Murphie, Joseph
1377 Collens, Jno.
1378 Sherman, Petter
1378 Sherman, Petter
1378 slave Thom
1379 Gathert, Geo.
1379 Mitchell, Jno.
1379 Mitchell, Benj.
1379 Lokie, Thos.
1380 Mitchell, Richd.
1381 Swillivan, Wm.
1381 Noble, Isaac
1382 Cottman, Joseph
1382 Gastinew, Mathew
1382 Lokie, Jno.
1382 Roberson, Jno.
1382 slave Bubo
1382 slave Sarrah
1383 Cottman, Wm.
1384 Wallace, Richd.

1385 Robertson, Wm.
1386 Mode, Petter
1387 Walker, Thos.
1387 Chambers, Robert
1387 slave Sam
1387 slave Jonathan
1387 slave Dinoe
1388 Ellis, Merick
1388 Stewart, doctor
1388 Gibson, Geo.
1388 slave Into
1388 slave Buboo
1388 slave Thom
1388 slave Mary
1388 slave Hanna
1389 Holbrook, Thos.
1389 Rennolds, Jno.
1390 Howard, Thos.
1391 Brookshaw, An[n]
1391 Wilkinson, James
1392 Fowler, Edward
1392 Austeen, Robert
1392 slave Mary
1393 Harris, Wm. junr.
1394 Harris, Jean
1394 Harris, Geo.
1394 Right, Wm.
1395 Harris, Wm. senr.
1395 Harris, Richd.
1396 Deshield, Thos.
1396 Forbus, Petter
1396 slave Tobe
1397 Hodg, Richd.
1398 Gale, Leven
1398 Stewart, Jno.
1398 Noble, Mark
1398 Warton, Wm.
1398 slave Hope
1398 slave Pleasent
1398 slave Vuber
1398 slave Titiue
1398 slave Joyce
1398 slave Pullert
1398 slave Bridgist
1399 Mclean, Daniel
1399 Morris, Jerimiah
1400 Howard, John
1401 Cope, Jno.
1401 Cope, Wm.
1402 Sherman, Edward junr.
1402 Croutch, Jacob
1403 Hobbs, Joy
1403 Hobbs, Absolim
1403 slave Polly
1404 Mungare, Mary
1404 Mungare, Mathew
1405 Adda, Owen
1406 Mellone, Robt.
1407 Mcgee, Petter

1408 Balife, Geo.
1409 Bailife, Jonathan
1410 Bailife, Sarrah
1410 Carry, Leven
1411 Christopher, Ephram
1412 Vance, David
1413 Edly, Wm.
1414 Vance, Alex.
1415 Thompson, John
1416 Seahan, John
1417 Lowes, Henry
1417 slave Jeptha
1417 slave Rose
1418 North, Edward
1418 North, Wm.
1418 Stephens, Thos.
1418 slave James
1418 slave Beck
1419 Stephins, Richd.
1419 slave Pumboo
1419 slave Cesar
1419 slave Sew
1420 Cable, Wm.
1421 Bounds, Jonathan
1421 slave Bess
1422 Stephins, Jno.
1422 Terry, Jno. Geo.
1422 slave Bess
1423 Stevens, Ann
1423 slave Jack
1424 Dishield, Geo.
1424 Pointer, Wm.
1424 slave Polly
1424 slave Samboo
1424 slave Samboo
1424 slave Dublin
1424 slave Rose
1424 slave Nan
1424 slave Jean
1424 slave Katt
1425 Meers, John
1425 Meers, Robt.
1426 Persons, Jno.
1427 Persons, Geo.
1428 Jenkins, Jervice
1429 Benns, Jno.
1430 Miller, Petter
1430 Hodge, Jno.
1431 Hill, Charles
1431 Ellis, Francis
1432 Hillman, Edward
1433 Chadwecks, James
1433 Chadwecks, James
1434 Stangford, Joseph
1434 Christopher, Rixon
1435 Disharoon, Ann
1435 Disharoon, Michall
1436 Dixson, Wm.
1437 Knox, Robt.
1438 Hayman, James

TAX LISTS OF SOMERSET COUNTY: 1730-1740

WICOMICO HUNDRED

1438 Hayman, John
1438 Hayman, Charles
1438 Hayman, Isaac
1439 Pullett, Thos.
1440 Waller, Jno.
1440 Cushiney, Jno.
1441 Brewertone, Wm.
1441 slave Patience
1442 Adams, Alex.
1442 Garnill, Thos.
1442 Harwood, Richd.
1442 Puckan, Richd.
1442 Sylivan, Timothy
1442 slave Jack
1442 slave Squash
1442 slave Flora
1442 slave Beck
1443 Rancher, Thos.
1443 slave Petter
1443 slave Pomp
1444 Rancher, Honorwood
1444 slave Jack
1444 slave Bess
1445 Ballard, Charles
1445 slave Ceater
1446 Ballard, Elenar
1446 slave Hope
1446 slave Mall
1446 slave Jack
1446 slave Mariah
1447 Evans, John
1447 Kemp, John
1447 slave Tobee
1447 slave Tom
1447 slave Messer
1447 slave Robt
1447 slave Eboe
1447 slave Sibb
1448 Deleney, Wm.
1449 Childs, John
1450 Crockett, Richd.
1450 Spicier, James
1450 slave Crope
1450 slave Grace
1451 Crockett, John
1451 Heren, Jno.
1451 slave Wappin
1452 Crockett, Robt.
1452 slave Mannto
1453 Evans, John senr.
1453 Fowler, Thos.
1453 slave illegible
1454 Everton, Jno.
1455 Higgman, Benj.
1456 Neilson, Wm.
1457 Neilson, John
1458 Wooten, Thos.
1458 slave Sarrah

1459 Leckie, Alex.
1459 slave Darby
1459 slave Sam
1459 slave Nimi
1460 Disheild, Geo.
1460 slave Thom
1461 Codry, Daniel
1461 slave Robt.
1461 slave Sampson
1461 slave Sibb
1462 Scott, Geo.
1462 Scott, Day
1462 slave Sam
1462 slave Hector
1462 slave Wm
1462 slave Tom
1462 slave Sanders
1462 slave Sipio
1462 slave Tom
1463 Walles, Joseph
1464 Codry, Abraham
1464 Codry, Morgan
1465 King, Kepweil
1465 slave Major
1465 slave Jack
1465 slave Parkett
1465 slave Bess
1465 slave Kett
1465 slave Ross
1466 Makmorie, James
1466 slave Batt
1466 slave Pomp
1466 slave Rose
1466 slave Timmer
1467 Venibles, Benj.
1467 slave Cuffy
1468 Venibles, Joseph
1468 Venibles, Wm.
1468 Winder, Thos.
1468 Givens, James
1468 slave Jeffry
1468 slave Mingo
1468 slave Frank
1468 slave Wm
1468 slave Hagor
1468 slave Nedd
1468 slave Bess
1469 Goslin, John
1469 Goslin, Richd.
1470 Hardie, Robt.
1471 Bartlett, Thos.
1471 Bartlett, Wm.
1471 Bartlett, Pasky
1472 Porter, Joshua
1473 Morris, Juda
1473 Morris, Jacob
1473 Morris, Joseph
1474 Hougin, Sarah
1474 Fulertone, Alex.
1474 Fulertone, James

1474 Guild, John
1475 Davis, Wm.
1476 Raglin, Mikel
1477 Sormon, Edard ser.
1477 Sormon, Jobe
1478 Hatch, Richard

1731 TAX LIST [Household number/Name/Remarks]

ANNEMESSEX HUNDRED

1 Planner, Wm. capt.	17 slave Sambo	41 McClatt, Jonathn.
1 Adams, Jno.	17 slave Dina	42 Dixon, Wm.
1 slave Hector	18 Waters, Elisa. mrs.	42 Cosere, Hugh
1 slave Sambo	18 Waters, Littleton	42 slave Betty
1 slave Watt	18 Landen, Henry	43 Horsey, Nathl.
1 slave George	18 slave Scipio	43 Nichols, Wm.
1 slave Tom	18 slave Alexr. Allen	43 Barritt, Henry
1 slave Titus	18 slave Hanniball	43 slave Ned
1 slave Adam	18 slave Major	43 slave Cook
1 slave Quam	18 slave Hagar	43 slave Prince
1 slave Quash	19 Waters, Wm. senr.	43 slave Quamino
1 slave Joan	19 slave Davy	43 slave Kate
1 slave Hannah	20 Hall, Charles	43 slave Patience
2 Williams, Isaac	20 slave Dominick	44 Horsey, Saml.
2 Ayres, Jacob	21 Hall, Richd.	45 Horsey, Smith
2 slave Sampson	21 Wallstone, Joy	45 Allen, Henry
3 Williams, Jno.	22 Benson, Jno.	46 Horsey, Stepn. junr.
3 Fenton, Martin	22 Benson, Wm.	47 Holland, Mich. senr.
3 slave Sambo	22 Benson, Sol.	47 slave Jack
4 Cattlin, Wm.	23 Beauchamp, Edmd.	48 Holland, Michl. junr.
4 slave Harry	23 Beauchamp, Edmd.	
5 Lister, Wm.	23 Beauchamp, Robt.	48 slave Dick
5 Molleston, Jno.	24 Beauchamp, Wm.	48 slave Moll
5 Legg, Benja.	24 Marshall, Tho.	49 Frazer, Peter
5 slave Casar	25 Hull, Danl.	49 Mooe, Jno.
6 Stockdell, Edwd.	26 King, Jams.	50 Davis, Jams.
7 Handy, Saml.	27 Boston, Wm.	51 Coulbourne, Wm. senr.
7 Handy, Thos.	28 Marshall, Geo.	51 Coulbourne, Wm.
7 slave Nan	29 Porter, Jos.	51 Coulbourne, Saml.
7 molattoe Cate	30 Moor, Thos.	51 Coulbourne, Sol.
8 Curtis, Charles	31 To King, Robt. majr.	51 slave Quaque
8 Johnson, Wm.	31 slave Mingoe	51 slave Lucie
8 slave Dick	31 slave Tamar	52 Coulbourne, Solomn.
8 slave Tony	32 Williams, Tho.	52 Seamour, Digby
19 Long, Jeoffrey	32 Williams, Tho.	52 McKenny, Patrick
9 Long, Saml.	32 Beauchamp, Isaac	52 slave Guy
9 Long, Jeoffrey	32 indian Andrew	52 slave Dido
9 slave Kate	32 slave Dick	53 Miles, Henry
10 Cullen, Edmond	32 slave Cesar	53 Scandlin, Edwd.
11 Tull, Tho.	32 slave Patience	53 slave Phillis
11 slave Quam	33 Puissey, Wm.	53 slave Dinah
12 Brimengen, Walter	33 Boarman, Jno.	54 Johnson, Jno.
12 Hopkins, Benja.	34 Langford, Benja.	54 Smith, Jams.
13 Bettsworth, Jams.	35 Smith, Henry	54 Johnson, Jno.
14 Trahern, Jno.	35 Treagin, Paul	54 Dyes, Philby
14 Trahern, Jams.	36 Taylor, Wm.	55 Moor, Francis
14 molatto Harry	37 To Coulbourn, Anne	55 Redding, Peter
14 slave Jinny	37 slave Abram	55 Moor, Jno.
15 Waters, Jno.	38 Allen, Jos.	55 Moor, Thos.
15 Tomlinson, Harry	39 Doughety, Jno.	55 Moor, Isaac
15 Spruance, Jno.	40 Dixon, Thos.	56 Laud, Francis
15 slave Jack	40 Cristee, Jno.	56 Laud, Henry
15 slave Will	40 slave Harry	56 Laud, Jno.
15 slave Sue	40 slave Toby	56 Laud, Thos.
15 slave Maria	40 slave Dick	57 Ward, Stepn. senr.
16 To Cottman, Mary	40 slave Lilly	57 slave Phillis
16 slave Mingo	40 slave Dinah	57 slave Sarah
17 Waters, Wm. junr.	41 Horsey, Isaac	57 slave Pompy
17 Parriss, Jno.	41 Kelley, Jno.	58 Ward, Saml.
17 slave Goliah		

TAX LISTS OF SOMERSET COUNTY: 1730-1740

ANNEMESSEX/BALTIMORE HUNDREDS

59 Riggin, Jno. senr.
59 Riggin, Jona.
60 Ward, Stepn. junr.
61 Sumners, Tho.
61 Sumners, Geo.
61 Sumners, Jona.
61 Dukes, Jno.
62 Sumners, Jno.
62 Sumners, David
62 slave Lopus
63 Wassells, James
64 Ward, Tho.
64 Ward, Jams.
64 Ward, Jacob
65 Bird, David
66 Claywell, Selby
67 Roach, Jno.
67 Obear, Isaac
68 Roach, Saml.
69 Booth, Roger
70 Wheeler, Jno.
71 Dyes, Robt.
71 Dyes, Danl.
72 Stockwell, Thos.
73 Cullen, Henry
74 Starling, Jno.
74 Starling, Jno.
74 Starling, Henry
74 Starling, Aaron
74 Moor, Wm.
75 Roberts, Robt.
76 Bird, Joseph
76 Willson, Jno.
76 Cullen, Jacob
76 Booth, Jams.
77 Daviss, Jno.
77 slave Sambo
77 slave Harry
77 slave Watt
77 slave Sue
77 slave Bess
77 slave Jinny
78 Horsey, Stepn.
78 Bayly, Tho.
78 slave Bess
79 Bell, Antho. sen.
79 Arnell, Wm.
79 slave Robin
79 slave Kate
80 Bell, Thos.
80 slave Nan
81 Bell, Antho. junr.
82 Bell, Jno.
83 Cahoon, Jno.
84 Gunby, Jno.
84 Spybie, Jona.
84 slave Jack
84 slave Kate
85 Kellam, Jno.
85 Kellam, Jno.

85 Kellam, Joshua
85 Dakes, Edwd.
86 Gunby, Kirk
86 Redding, Charles
87 White, Jno. junr.
87 Magoo, Tho.
88 Herne, Edwd.
88 Laud, Randall
89 Atkinson, Joshua
89 Oneal, Henry
89 Matthews, Wm.
90 Scott, Robt.
90 Scott, Jno.
90 slave Betty
91 Cottingham, Charles
91 Cottingham, Charles
91 Cottingham, Tho.
91 Cullen, Nicho.
92 To Cottingham, Mary
92 Cottingham, Jno.
93 To Potter, Anne
93 Potter, Henry
93 Potter, Josephus
94 Adams, David
94 Adams, Tho.
94 Adams, Jacob
95 At Roachs, Sarah
95 Wheatley, Sampson
96 Conner, Jno.
97 Conner, Wm.
98 Outen, Jno.
98 slave Dick
99 White, Thos.
100 Maddux, Tho.
100 Maddux, Alexr.
100 Maddux, Bell
101 Willson, Wm.
101 Willson, Geo.
101 Willson, Jno.
102 Prior, Tho.
103 Langford, Jos.
103 Langford, Jos.
104 To Puissey, Alice
104 Puissey, Jno.
105 Trahern, James
106 Long, Saml.
106 Long, Wm.
106 Long, David
107 Long, Danl.
107 Long, Danl.
107 Long, David
108 White, Jno. senr.
108 slave Essex
109 Ward, Cornelius
109 Riggin, Jno.
110 Owen, Elisa
110 Willson, Jno.
110 Owen, Phillip
111 Waters, Edwd.
112 Williams, Henry

113 Long, Randall
113 Taylors, Elias
113 slave Sibb
114 Horsman, Henry
115 Williams, Wm.
116 Evans, Jno.
117 Wheeler, Saml.
118 Mister, Wm.
119 Tyler, Jno. junr.
120 Tyler, Thos.
121 To Tyler, Jno. senr.
121 Parker, Isaac
122 Parks, Arthur
122 Parks, Arthur
122 Parks, Jno.
123 Parks, Jno.
123 Parks, Mark
124 Hopkins, Geo.
124 Hopkins, Jno.
125 Ellingsworth, Richd.
126 White, Wm.
127 White, Isaac
128 Kersey, Wm.
129 Outerbridge, Jno.
130 Hall, Wm.

BALTIMORE HUNDRED

131 Fassit, Willm. capt. sr
131 Fassit, Rouse
131 Jones, Jon.
131 slave Frank
131 slave Sambo
131 slave Sue
131 slave Dalle
131 slave Tites
131 slave Cusey [hs]
132 Walton, Willm. senr.
132 Walton, Willm. junr.
132 Walton, Benjeman
132 slave Gloster
132 slave Ceaser
132 slave Judah
133 Crapper, Edmond
133 Camble, Solomon
133 slave Petter
133 slave Pompey
133 slave Dick
133 slave Febbey
134 Hopkins, Samuel junr.
134 Brawfoot, Adam
134 Conner, Michel
135 Crapper, Nethanel senr.
135 Crapper, Edmond
135 Hamlton, Willm.

1731 TAX LIST [Household number/Name/Remarks]

BALTIMORE HUNDRED

135 Crapper, Solomon
136 Marchel, Isacc
136 Peal, Thorowgood
136 slave John Morris
136 slave Ben
136 slave Dinah
136 slave Bess
137 Holland, Richard
138 Alford, David
139 Whalie, Willm.
139 Ratlife, Charles
140 Ratlife, Charles senr.
140 Ratlife, Purnel [hs]
140 slave Tom
140 slave Sarah
140 slave Robin
140 slave Charles
140 slave Cate
140 slave Mall
140 slave Will [hs]
140 slave Matt [hs]
141 Purnel, John
141 Dueit, Nethaniel
141 Ratlife, Charles
141 Abbet, Willm.
141 Ratlife, Wrixam [hs]
141 slave Will
141 slave Mary
141 slave Dinah
141 slave Dall
141 slave Zone [hs]
141 slave Quameney [hs]
142 Whaliey, Mary
142 Whaliey, Edward
142 Whalie, Charles [hs]
143 Produx, Thomas
143 slave Filles [hs]
144 Gilland, John
144 Megumrey, Robert [hs]
144 slave Sambo
145 Boien, Rodah
145 Boien, John
145 Boien, Willm.
145 slave Quamnah
146 Dueit, Willm.
147 Quellin, Mary
147 Quellin, Joseph
147 Quellin, Benjaman
147 Quelling, John [hs]
148 Crapper, Nathaniel junr
148 Crapper, Vincet [hs]

149 Fasit, Jon.
149 slave Luey
149 slave Money
150 Tull, John senr.
150 Tull, John junr.
150 Webb, Mark [hs]
151 Smith, Willm.
152 Stevenson, John
152 Stevenson, William [hs]
153 Holland, John
153 Walton, Willm.
154 Purkins, Thomas
155 Linch, John senr.
155 Linch, Abram
155 Chambers, Alexr.
156 Cabb, Willm.
156 Cabb, Nathaniel
156 Tingle, Littleton [hs]
157 Weight, Joseph senr.
157 Weight, Willm.
157 Weight, Joseph junr.
157 Weight, Nathaniell
158 Linch, Alexr.
159 Bouton, John
160 Miller, John
160 Gooding, Moses
160 slave Primus
160 slave Pady
161 Allison, Jon.
162 Tingle, Hugh
163 Robinson, John
163 Robinson, George
164 Woodcraft, John
165 Woodcraft, Richard
166 Tingle, Hugh senr.
167 Tingle, John
167 slave Harrey [hs]
168 Cabb, John senr.
168 Cabb, John junr.
169 Tounsend, Bowman
170 Bouton, Thomas
170 Bouton, Able
171 Smith, Jones
172 Woodcraft, Mary
172 Woodcraft, William
172 Woodcraft, Thomas
173 Hudson, David
174 Smith, John capt. senr.
174 Smith, John junr.
174 Smith, Thomas
174 slave Harrey
174 slave Mareiah
174 slave Bess
175 Rickards, John
175 slave Simon

175 slave Boson
175 slave Mall
175 slave Bridget
176 Evins, John
177 Whaliey, William
178 Hall, John
179 Hall, Joseph
180 Evins, Willm.
180 Evins, John
181 Mersey, John
181 Banks, Nibbling
182 Mersiey, Attkens
183 Hazzard, David senr.
183 Hazzard, Willm.
183 slave Dinah
184 Wharton, Daniel
185 Wharton, Henman
186 Onarton, John
186 slave Jack
186 slave Filles
187 Rickards, Jonnas
187 slave Sarah
188 Rickards, John junr.
189 Morris, Sarah
189 Morris, Willm.
190 Godwen, Ceasar senr.
190 Godwen, Ceasar junr.
191 Godwen, Michel
191 slave Bess
192 Robinson, Thomas
192 Gray, John
192 slave Jeffrey
192 slave Jane
193 Johnson, Linoard
194 Dickson, Sturges
194 Johnson, John
195 Baldrey, Francies
196 Dickson, John
197 West, William
198 Dasiey, Thomas
199 Idlot, Benjaman
199 Gilstrap, Petter
200 West, George
200 Metherd, Jonathen
201 Idlot, John senr.
201 Idlot, John junr.
201 slave Jack
202 West, Thomas
203 Harniey, Thomas
204 Hall, Samuel
205 Linch, John junr.
206 Dirkson, Joseph
207 Parrey, James
208 Hill, Ann
208 Hill, Benone
209 Robinson, Mary

TAX LISTS OF SOMERSET COUNTY: 1730-1740

BALTIMORE HUNDRED

209 Robinson, Joshuah
209 slave Bess
210 Robinson, Michal
211 Mariner, Henrey
212 Roberts, Thomas senr.
212 Roberts, Thomas junr.
212 Roberts, Samuel son [hs]
213 Howard, George senr.
213 Howard, Nehmiah
213 Howard, George junr.
213 slave Kent
213 slave Bess
214 Hickman, Richard senr.
214 Roberts, Allexr.
214 slave Lady
215 Freeman, Willm.
215 Freeman, William son [hs]
216 Collings, Willm.
217 Dirickson, Benjaman
218 Salmon, Willm.
218 Bernet, John
219 Wharton, Francies
220 Dickeson, Hannah
220 Dickson, Charles
220 slave Patiance
221 Smith, John senr.
221 Smith, John junr.
221 Smith, Robert
221 Bernet, James
222 Wayaples, Paul
222 slave Charles
223 Besiey, Willm.
224 Napman, John
225 Morris, Bibbins
226 Burton, Willm.
226 Burton, John
226 Pepper, Willm.
226 Burton, Joshua son [hs]
226 slave Touse
226 slave Rachel
227 Camble, John
228 Joseph, Fedrick
229 Lewes, Joseph
230 Lewes, Arter
231 Lewes, Willm.
232 Ingrim, Jacob
233 Coffin, Thomas
233 Coffin, John
233 Coffin, Joseph
234 Short, Edward
235 Jones, Ebenzr.
235 Fletwood, Thomas
236 Carriey, Thomas
237 Carriey, Willm.
238 Inloss, Thom.
239 Kenney, Stephn.
239 Kenney, Lazares son [hs]
240 Kenney, Joseph
241 Morris, John
241 Morris, Dinnis
242 Runnels, Richard
242 West, Thom.
243 Drigus, Dibrex
244 Johnson, David
244 slave Jack [hs]
245 Wilson, John
245 Wilson, Isreal
245 Wilson, John son[hs]
246 Davidson, William
246 Davidson, Rowes son [hs]
247 Woods, Adam
248 Hampton, mydam
248 slave Jack
248 slave Nero
248 slave Pigg
248 slave Hannah
248 slave Hannable [hs]
249 Miller, Joseph
250 Bradwel, Isaiah
250 Bradwel, James Stephn
250 Forthsight, Thomas
250 slave Simon
250 slave Adam
250 slave Pender
251 Halaway, John senr.
252 Halaway, John junr.
253 Harison, Willm.
254 Gray, Joseph
254 Gray, Thomas
254 slave Simon
254 slave Quaco
255 Gray, Willm.
256 Dal, John senr.
257 Dal, John junr.
258 Brettenham, Joseph
258 Brittingham, Robert son
259 Murrey, James
259 Murrey, Robert
260 Dal, Archable
261 Hamlon, John
262 Powell, Thomas senr.
263 Williams, Arglus
264 Mumford, James
264 slave Jene
265 Showel, Samuel
266 Russel, Andw.
267 Mumford, Willm.
268 Fassit, Franklyn
268 Tyrie, Robt.
268 slave Nane
269 Hickman, Richard junr.
270 Powel, Susanah
270 Powel, Charles
271 Lethbery, Abgile
271 Lethbery, Arter
272 Hudson, John
273 Hudson, Richard junr.
274 Hudson, Samuel
274 Evins, Elias
275 Clark, Race
275 Clark, John
276 Bradfoot, Willm.
277 Trueit, George
278 Gault, Robert
278 Gault, Willm.
278 Gault, John
279 Tylor, Walter
279 Conner, Daniel
280 Newbold, John
281 Simpson, Richard
282 Camble, John
282 Wattrs, Patrick
282 slave Mall
283 Walace, Thomas
283 slave Hector
284 Goddard, Thomas
285 Kennet, Willm.
285 Ratlife, John
286 Hudson, Richard senr.
286 Gabb, John
286 Gray, John
286 Gray, Willm.
286 slave Coffe
286 slave Dick
286 slave Beack [hs]
287 Logwood, Richard
287 Evens, William
288 Hudson, William
289 Hill, Robert
289 Hill, Johnson
289 Tyler, Samuel [hs]
289 Hill, William Stephen [hs]
289 slave Will
290 Hamlon, Francies
291 Pattey, John
291 Mathas, Willm.
291 Pattey, Powel [hs]
291 slave Lonon
292 Mersiey, Willm.

1731 TAX LIST [Household number/Name/Remarks]

BALTIMORE/BOGERTERNORTON HUNDREDS

293 Mumford, Charles
294 Collings, Thomas junr.
295 Fall, John
296 Fervewl, Thomas
297 Manklyn, Richard
298 Robertson, Andrew
298 Fall, Abram
299 Delanie, John Patrick
300 Coller, Petter
300 Latchim, Thomas
300 slave Pompey
301 Fassit, Willm. junr.
301 Edde, Larance
302 Whittinghim, Sury
302 slave Robbin
302 slave Chebing
303 Mersiey, Allexr.
303 slave Jack
304 Wheller, John senr.
304 Wheller, John junr.
305 Walton, John
306 Turvile, Willm. senr.
306 Turvile, Willm. junr.
306 Webb, Willm.
306 Whalie, John [hs]
307 Kennet, Martain
307 Bishop, Bowen
307 Turvile, John [hs]
308 Collings, John
308 Ratlife, Elias
308 Collings, Able [hs]

BOGERTERNORTON HUNDRED
309 Evans, John
309 slave
310 Evans, Edward
310 Evans, Ebenezar
310 Evans, Laurence
311 Walton, Richard
312 Collins, Thomas
313 Truett, John
313 Turvill, Presgrave
314 Collins, Charles
315 Franklin, Edward
315 Franklin, William
315 slave
316 Nock, John
316 Burton, John
316 slave
317 Reily, Thomas
318 Donelson, capt.
318 Justin, William

318 Davis, Lazarus
318 Kelley, Nickoles
318 Lues, William
318 2 slaves
319 Purnell, Cathrine
319 4 slaves
320 Bedard, William
320 Besek, Absolam
321 Backitt, Peter
322 Church, Samuell
323 Timmons, William
324 Timmons, John
325 Timmons, Francis
326 Timmons, Thomas
327 Timmons, Samuell
328 Timmons, Aron
329 Timmons, Joseph
330 Timmons, James
331 Jones, Joseph
331 Swain, William
332 Brown, John
332 Hammond, Charles
332 Kerey, Richard
333 Martin, James
333 Downes, Robert
333 Jones, Thomas
333 Covington, Benjamin
333 Roark, Bryan
333 Richeson, William
333 5 slaves
334 Bratten, Samuell senr.
334 Bratten, William
334 Bratten, Samuell junr.
335 Bratten, Samuell junr.
336 Willcox, George
337 Bowen, John
338 Morris, William
338 Morris, Joseph
339 Townsend, Jeremiah
339 Townsend, Brickus
339 2 slaves
340 Crapper, Ebenezar senr.
340 Crapper, Ebenezar junr.
341 Bushop, John junr.
341 Pennewell, Richard
342 Johnson, Afradozia
342 Johnson, Georg
342 Johnson, John
342 Johnson, Thomas
342 Johnson, Samuell
342 slave
343 Brittingham, Isaac
343 Brittingham, Isaac
343 slave
344 Ennis, William

345 Ennis, Nathaniell
346 Davis, William seaside
347 Richardson, Charles
347 Richardson, Jams.
347 slave
348 Pointer, Thomas
348 Pointer, Ratcliff
349 Dennis, William
350 Pointer, Edward
351 Williams, Prisgrave
352 Shirley, Jams.
352 Davis, Theophilus
353 Hudson, Margrett
353 slave
354 Loe, George
354 Glindell, Robert
355 Houlston, William
356 McCauly, John
357 Stevens, Samuell
357 Dicks, Thomas
358 Robieson, William senr.
358 Robieson, William
358 slave
359 Bushop, John senr.
359 Bushop, Joseph
359 Bushop, David
360 Bushop, William
360 Bushop, Benja.
360 Outen, John
361 Scoolfield, Joseph
361 slaves
362 Teague, John senr.
362 Teague, William
362 Teague, John junr.
362 Woods, William
363 Powell, Rachell
363 Powell, Thoms.
364 Powell, Samuell
364 Chancler, George
365 Tingle, Daniell
366 Evins, Mary
366 Evins, Gammage
366 Evins, Powell
367 Beddart, Richard
368 Ironshire, Isaac
368 slave
369 Richardson, Robert
369 Lang, John
370 Parker, Tabitha
370 Parker, Samuell
370 Parker, Charles
370 4 slave
371 Truett, George son of Joa
371 Truett, Nemiah
372 Brittingham, William senr.

TAX LISTS OF SOMERSET COUNTY: 1730-1740

BOGERTERNORTON HUNDRED

372 Brittingham, William ju
372 Brittingham, Sollomon
373 Brittingham, Jeremiah
374 Mumford, James
375 Mumford, George
376 Truett, William
377 Truett, George son of Philip
378 Truett, Elenor
378 4 slaves
379 Turner, Henry
380 Henderson, Charles
381 Steel, James
381 Steel, William
381 Steel, Daniell
382 Dennis, Donnock
383 Reyden, Robert
384 Scott, Mark
385 Burbridge, John
386 Cavenock, John
387 Thomson, James
388 Mitchell, Thomas
388 slave
389 Hammond, John senr.
390 Hammond, John junr.
391 Hammond, Edward
392 Hanncock, William
393 Townsend, William
394 Richards, William
395 Simson, William
395 slave
396 Smith, Andrew
397 Smith, William
398 Smith, John
399 Midsley, Thomas
400 Haddor, Anthony
401 Rownd, James
401 Mitchell, James
401 3 slaves
402 Selby, John
402 2 slaves
403 Murray, John
403 Gillman, Hugh
403 Brown, William
403 slave
404 Hall, William
404 Hall, Adam
404 2 slaves
405 Murray, Duncan
405 Grier, Adam
405 McCartnick, Patrick
405 Holloway, John
405 slave
406 Tull, Richard

407 Williams, John
408 Crapper, Nemiah
409 Tull, Benjamin
410 Davis, Edward
411 Smith, William Porter
412 Porter, Joseph
412 slave
413 Lay, John
413 slave
414 Crapper, John
415 Crapper, Wrixam
416 Bassett, Alice
416 Bassett, John
417 Devrox, John
417 Pryer, Webb
417 slave
418 Gogen, Edward
419 Heather, Ephrim senr.
419 Heather, Ephrim junr.
419 2 slaves
420 Penniwell, John
421 Blizard, Richard
422 Selby, Parker
423 Smock, Henry
424 Smith, Abraham
424 Pointer, Nathaniell
424 Pointer, John
425 Hudson, Dennis
425 slave
426 Selby, William
426 6 slave
427 Arabin, Jacobus
427 Colins, Solomon
428 Dreyden, Hannah
428 Dreyden, John
429 Stevenson, James
430 English, Thomas
431 Clark, Charles
432 Godfrey, Charles
432 slave
433 Dasie, John
434 Alexander, Paul
435 Whittington, William
435 6 slaves
436 Clawell, Thomas
436 slave
437 Porter, William
438 Houlston, John
439 Edwards, Benony
440 Pepper, John
441 Fletcher, Thomas mr.
441 Stockwell, George
441 Johnson, Thomas
441 3 slaves
442 Rownd, Edward

442 Charles, John
442 2 slaves
443 Tayler, Joseph
443 Tayler, William
444 Hales, Jeremiah
445 Truett, George son of George
445 Truett, John
446 German, Henry
446 Webb, Samuell
447 Hook, William
448 Spence, Adam senr.
448 2 slaves
449 Spence, Adam junr.
449 3 slaves
450 Slingo, Thomas
451 Lane, George
452 Dennis, Solomon
452 Dennis, Daniell
453 Shockley, William
454 Purnell, Thomas
454 6 slaves
455 Purnell, Elisha
455 2 slaves
456 Stevens, William
457 Bratten, James
457 Bell, doctor
458 Ennis, Mary
458 Ennis, Cornelius
458 Ennis, Samuell
459 Bushop, Charles
460 Hall, Robert
461 Handcock, Daniell
462 Adkins, Elizabeth
462 Bowen, William
463 Shohannas, William
463 Keneday, Simmons
464 Bridgewater, Emanuell
465 Davis, Robert junr.
466 Davis, Robert senr.
466 Davis, Willm.
466 Davis, Eshmail
466 Davis, Thomas
467 Davis, Thomas
468 Collins, Mary
468 Collins, Andrew
468 Collins, John
469 Penniewell, Charles
470 Peniewell, Ann
470 Peniewell, William
471 Williams, Johnathan
471 Williams, John
471 Williams, Littleton
472 Adkins, Stenton
473 German, Job
474 Truett, Thomas
475 Truett, James
476 Raine, Mathw.
477 Truett, Samuell

1731 TAX LIST [Household number/Name/Remarks]

BOGERTERNORTON/MANOKIN HUNDREDS

478 Porter, John
479 Davis, William
479 Davis, William
479 Davis, Phillip
479 Davis, Samuell
480 Parker, George
481 Parker, Phillip
482 Murray, David
483 Bradford, John
484 German, Robert
485 Hodge, Robert
486 Hadder, Warrin
487 Williams, Thoms. Nathl.
487 Williams, Samll.
488 Hampton, maddam
488 3 slaves
489 Warren, Nickolas
489 Gray, Nickolas
490 Warren, Robert
491 Baker, John
492 Clark, Daniell
493 German, William
494 German, George
495 Burbridge, Edward
495 Pointer, William
496 Purnell, Mathew
496 Hammond, Jacob
496 slave
497 German, John
498 Jones, George
499 Truett, Benjamin
500 Truett, Joseph
501 Bowen, Luke
501 Bowen, George
501 slave
502 Truett, Henry
503 Bowen, Littleton
504 Webb, Grace
504 Webb, Elisha
505 Pointer, Elias
505 Lendell, Peter
506 Penniewell, Thomas
507 Gelitt, John

MANOKIN HUNDRED

508 Wilson, Ephrum
508 Wots, James
508 Clark, Alexander
508 Camis, John
508 Hath, Abraham
508 slave Mondy
508 slave Coffe
508 slave Peter
508 slave Hary
508 slave Seser
508 slave Moll
508 slave Hano
508 slave Nan
508 slave Jeny
508 slave Bona
509 Tunstall, John
509 Christopher, Arrostoblus
509 Banister, Charles
509 Haly, Timothy
509 Jannan, Paris
509 Magraw, James
509 slave Somersett
509 slave Soloy
509 slave Wille
509 slave Lohill
509 slave Leuerpole
509 slave Truman
509 slave Fremon
509 slave Tom
509 slave Noriss
509 slave Dick
509 slave Pompy
509 slave Tom Law
509 slave Bess
509 slave Isabelah
509 slave Dinah
510 Dugless, Volin tine
511 Denison, Robart
512 Ballard, Henery
512 Magraw, David
512 slave Venter
512 slave Seser
512 slave Sines
512 slave Jenny
512 slave Bendaw
513 Struard, Wm. revrnd
513 slave Jemy
513 slave Abbo
514 King, Robart
514 King, Nehemiah
514 Nisbett, Willam
514 Oglisbus, John
514 Butt, John
514 slave Fortin
514 slave Jose
514 slave Seser
514 slave Seser
514 slave Tobe
514 slave Manary
514 slave Vilitt
514 slave Bess
514 slave Moll
514 slave Dido
514 slave Dido
514 slave Judy
514 slave Judy
515 Wilson, David
515 Swift, Richard
515 Thomson, Joseph
515 slave Cudo
515 slave Mondy
515 slave Philup
515 slave Jacob
515 slave Holada
515 slave illegible
516 Benston, Gorge
517 Gray, Willam
517 Grinless, Willam
518 Gray, John sener
519 Smith, Robart
519 Smith, Thomas
520 Chambus, Richard
520 Chapell, Willam
520 slave Yoco
521 Fisher, Barkly
521 slave John
521 slave Beck
522 Haymon, Beniamon
522 Haymon, Willam
523 Hay mon, Arther
524 Turpin, Willam juner
524 slave Will
524 slave Boso
524 slave George
524 slave Frost
524 slave Punelepy
524 slave Peg
524 slave Moll
525 Owens, John
526 Dorman, Michell
527 Morn, John
528 Matlen, James
529 Law, James
530 Hath, Abrum sener
530 Hath, Dorman
530 Hath, Abraham
531 Fintch, John
531 Ring Rose, Danill
531 slave Murear
532 Dorman, Matthew j.
533 Lindow, James
533 Birk, Patrick
533 Robards, Jos.
533 slave Moin
533 slave Jeny
533 slave Bess
534 Brown, Thomas
534 Brown, David
534 Inas, Robart
534 Chain, Alexandr
534 slave Cugo
534 slave Judy
534 slave Bess
535 Brown, David senr.
535 slave Cugo
536 Smith, Edward
536 Smith, Thomas
537 Hales, John
537 Lafild, Robart
537 Lafild, Willam
538 To Carny, Ann

TAX LISTS OF SOMERSET COUNTY: 1730-1740

MANOKIN HUNDRED

538 Lafild, Thomas
539 Lockwood, Willam
539 Hicks, Willam
540 Foler, John
541 Denwood, Thomas
541 Cinegum, Arther
541 slave Cugo
541 slave Grace
542 Dorman, Matthew senr.
542 slave Jack
542 slave Doll
543 Boler, Willam
544 To Mullrow, Danill
544 Mulrow, Elexander
545 Magraw, William
546 New man, Henry
547 Magraw, John
548 To Magraw, Jean
548 Magraw, Robart
549 To Ballard, Eliner
549 slave Will
549 slave Hogo
549 slave Bess
549 slave Mary
550 Long, Solomon
551 Carny, Robart
551 Gillegin, Bryon
552 Flemon, Willam
553 Furness, James
554 Colens, Willam
555 Wilcoks, John
556 Hath, Willam
557 Pope, James
558 Stutt, Archebild
559 Strobridg, James
559 slave David
559 slave Coffe
559 slave Hager
560 Dorman, Henery junr.
561 Wilson, Robart
561 slave Sambo
562 Polk, James
563 Nott, Isac
564 Thomson, Andrew
564 Thomson, Willam
564 Thomson, John
564 slave Tony
564 slave Sesor
564 slave Bess
565 Sandus, Richard
566 Mitchell, Thomas
566 Mitchell, Isac
566 slave Mingo
566 slave Sary
567 Jones, Willam
567 Brooks, Partrick
567 slave Momado
567 slave Gy
567 slave Eve
568 Huntt, John
569 Goold smith, John
569 Grinless, John
569 Cain, Willam
570 Davis, Auther
571 McDonill, David
572 Lewis, Willam
572 slave Benn
572 slave Tom
573 Ford, Absolom
574 McDorman, Willam
575 Sharp, BenJamon
575 Jones, Matthew
575 Ginkens, John
575 Wolston, Willam
575 Wolston, Thomas
576 Tull, Joshew
576 slave Moll
577 Barns, Robart
577 Elexandr, James
578 Miles, Samell
578 slave Dick
578 slave Benn
579 Butler, Nathanill
580 Madox, Lazarus
580 slave Coffe
580 slave Dick
580 slave Joo
581 Madox, Thomas
581 slave Will
581 slave Suu
582 Tull, Samewill
583 Madox, Danill
583 slave Jacob
583 slave Sary
584 Tull, Solomon
584 Tull, Richard
585 Miles, Willam
586 Willis, Barnobe
587 Tockell, Willam
588 Hardin, Joseph
589 Turpin, Willam sen.
589 Owens, Mosis
589 Fordred, Willam
589 slave Tom
589 slave Jack
589 slave Tobe
589 slave Fillis
590 Fountin, Nicholess ju.
590 Whorton, Willam
590 Brown, Tarill
591 Fountin, Nicholes se.
591 Smith, John
591 slave Cha
591 slave London
591 slave Tom
592 Blewit, Thomas
593 King, BenJamon
594 Turpin, John
594 Turpin, Willam
594 slave Cofe
594 slave Tobe
594 slave Cork
595 Fountin, Mary se.
595 Fountin, Samewill
595 Fountin, Thomas
595 MakDanil, James
595 slave Hartles
595 slave Moll
596 Flawed, John
596 Fisher, Henery
597 Shaw, Jonathan
598 Shipard, Matthew
599 King, Whitenton
599 Gullet, Abraham
599 King, John
599 slave Harry
599 slave Tony
599 slave Tom
599 slave Pase
600 King, Eliner
600 slave Jubiter
600 slave Rose
601 To King, Elibeh
601 slave Pase
602 Hall, Alexander sener
603 Hall, Alexander j.
604 West, Antony
605 West, Willam
606 Horsy, Revill
606 Horsy, Willam
606 Hanon, Danill
606 slave Nick
607 Ascridg, Willam
607 slave Ned
607 slave Moll
608 Hath, Jacob
609 Banister, Thomas
609 Rusill, Willam
609 Bryon, Richard
610 Mathis, Partrick
611 Labruce, Beniamon
612 Right, Abill
613 Horsy, John
613 Hill, John
613 Kille, John
613 slave Peter
613 slave Moll
614 Wolston, Boos
614 Right, Randell
615 Revill, Charles
615 Davis, John
615 slave Nenes
616 Delop, Charles
617 Roach, Willam

1731 TAX LIST [Household number/Name/Remarks]

MANOKIN/MATTAPANY HUNDRED

617 Roach, Isac
617 slave Kitt
617 slave Pacince
618 Revill, Randell
618 slave Harry
618 slave Tobe
618 slave Matha
619 Smith, Willam
620 To Wye, Mary
620 slave Sipeo
620 slave Moll
621 Wolford, John
621 slave Samson
621 slave Rose
622 Febus, George sen.
622 Febus, Samell
622 Febus, Willam
622 slave Into
623 Horner, George
623 Horner, Till
623 Horner, James
624 Fosky, Thomas
625 Lales, John
626 Rusill, Richard
627 Spiser, Phillup
628 Young, John
629 Ballard, Jarvis
629 Ballard, Willam
629 Ballard, Jarvis
629 slave Ame
629 slave Rose
630 Rigsbe, Lewis
630 Cunegum, Thomas
630 MacDanill, Randall
630 slave Atte
631 Febus, George juner
631 Horner, Willam
632 Elsey, John sener
632 Elsey, John
632 slave Sambo
632 slave Seser
632 slave Bety
632 slave Nan
632 slave Judy
632 slave Sib
633 Elsy, Arnold
633 Chambus, Edward
633 Coldwill, William
633 Elsey, Arnold
633 Horner, George
633 slave Ned
633 slave Cusaw
633 slave Jack
633 slave Nan
633 slave Hanno
633 slave Billindo
634 Wolker, James
635 Birgin, Danill
636 McClemy, Willam
636 Tull, John
636 Abit, John
636 slave Naro
637 Bozman, Willam sen.
637 slave Doso
637 slave Bess
638 Bozman, Willam
638 Bozman, Willam
639 Bozman, George sener
640 Brown, Sidney
641 Jones, Willam goos cre.
641 slave Benn
641 slave Benn
642 Staples, James
643 Bozman, George juner
643 Edwards, John
643 Camill, John
643 slave Sambo
644 Gilless, Joseph
644 Surman, John
644 Letherbery, Thomas
644 slave Boson
644 slave Jack
645 To Robertson, James
645 Roberson, John
645 Hall, John
645 slave Jack
645 slave Tobe
645 slave Naro
645 slave Prew
646 Bozman, John s.
646 Bozman, John
647 Jarvis, William
648 To Woolford, Martha
648 Moo, John
648 slave Moll
648 slave Sary
649 To King, Capill
649 slave Dick
649 slave Pompe
649 slave Tite
649 slave Judy
650 Crow Der, Francis
650 Lare, Timothy
651 Tillmon, Joseph
651 slave Lonon
652 Gray, John juner
652 slave Hanno
653 Furnss, William
653 slave Appo
654 Tillmon, John
655 Tillmon, Aron
656 Gebins, John juner
657 Gibins, John sener
657 Shery, Job
657 Gibins, Thomas
658 Odear, Steven
658 Dear, Furnes
659 Odear, Steven jun.
660 Polk, William
660 Polk, David
660 slave Oreen
660 slave Adner
660 slave Harer
661 Fitch Jarrill, Peter
661 slave Tom
662 To Elexander, Moses
662 Cain, James
663 Wye, Willam revrend
663 slave Jemy
663 slave Elex
663 slave Jubetor
664 Macolin, Hugh
665 Odear, John

MATTAPANY HUNDRED

666 Purnell, John
666 6 slaves
667 Walton, Stephen
667 unnamed
668 Odwe, Thomas
669 Masson, Abraham
670 Tow, Jonas
670 unnamed
671 Walton, Fisher
671 unnamed
671 2 slaves
672 Davis, Charles
672 unnamed/slave
673 Cord, Wm.
673 unnamed/slave
674 Hopkins, Nathaniell
674 unnamed
674 unnamed
674 slave
675 Ayres, John
676 Brownbill, Henry
677 Gutrey, Patrick
678 Booth, Wm.
678 unnamed
678 unnamed
679 Hopkins, Samuell
679 unnamed
679 unnamed
679 unnamed
680 Answorth, Sarah
680 unnamed
681 Answorth, Wm.
682 Milbroune, Tho.
683 Scarbrough, Jno.
683 unnamed
683 2 slaves
684 Phunelson, Williams
685 Hill, Robert
686 Johnson, Wm.

TAX LISTS OF SOMERSET COUNTY: 1730-1740

MATTAPANY/MONIE HUNDRED

686 unnamed
687 Wise, Tho.
687 unnamed/slave
688 Tar, Mikell
689 Tayler, Phillip
690 Wise, Matthew
690 unnamed/slave
691 Selby, Phillip
691 unnamed
691 unnamed
691 unnamed
691 unnamed
691 3 slaves
692 Selby, Parker
692 3 unnamed/slaves
693 Sturgis, John senr.
693 unnamed
693 unnamed
694 Hopkins, Matthew
694 unnamed
694 unnamed
695 Pope, John
695 unnamed
695 4 slave
696 Pope, George
696 2 slave
697 Pope, Samll.
698 Hill, Johnson
698 unnamed
698 unnamed
698 unnamed
699 Parremore, Thomas
699 unnamed/slave
699 3 slaves
700 Sturgis, John junr.
701 Turner, Wm.
702 Nutten, Thos.
702 unnamed
702 unnamed
703 Cherix, James
703 unnamed/slave
704 Johnson, John
705 Tar, Sam.
705 unnamed
705 slave
706 Clark, John
707 Shawr, Abraham
708 Johnson, Petter
708 unnamed/slave
709 Lane, George
710 Hermon, Manuell
711 Richardson, John
711 slave
712 Nelson, Wm.
712 unnamed
713 Bratten, Wm.
713 unnamed
713 slave

714 Sturgis, Richard
714 unnamed
715 Dredin, John
716 Beachbord, Wm.
717 Scott, Robert pot
717 unnamed
718 Sheha, Potter
719 Hall, John
720 Mexfild, Joseph
720 2 slaves
721 Arnold, Wm.
721 unnamed
722 Robins, Eliza
722 4 slaves
722 slave
723 Jones, John
723 unnamed/slave
724 Waggamon, Jacob
724 unnamed
724 unnamed
724 2 slaves
725 Walker, John
725 slave
726 Hodgson, Rowland
726 unnamed
727 Conner, Richd.
728 Allen, Jos.
729 Watson, Luke
730 Bensbow, Joshua
731 Watson, Petter
731 unnamed/slave
732 Hill, Abra.
733 Duberley, Thos.
734 Watson, John
735 Watson, Robert
735 unnamed
735 unnamed
735 slave
736 Chapmon, Humphrey
737 Veze, Charles
738 Watson, Robert junr.
739 Watson, Moses
740 Willet, Ambros
740 unnamed
741 Pepper, Tobias
742 Wyat, Nathall.
743 Dur, Wm.
744 Pepper, Wm.
745 Porter, Clintuck
746 Steen, James
747 Brownbill, Nathall.
748 Clavell, Peter senr.
748 unnamed
748 slave
749 Allen, John
750 Aydelott, Wm.
750 slave
751 Hosiear, Samll.

751 unnamed/slave
752 Holland, Benja.
752 unnamed/slave
753 Chapmon, Margrett
753 slave
754 Crafford, Andrew
754 unnamed
755 Sammons, Benja.
756 Holland, Nehemiah
756 unnamed
756 unnamed
757 Claywell, Petter junr.
758 Henderson, Bishop
759 Russell, Cuthburt

MONIE HUNDRED

760 Gale, George mr.
760 Maughon, Christopher
760 slave Limos
760 slave Scipio
760 slave Sarah
760 slave Naney
760 slave Jammey
760 slave Jack
760 slave Parthena
761 Gales, madam taxables
761 slave Joe
761 slave Jammey
761 slave Ceesar
761 slave Stephen
761 slave Will
761 slave Peter
761 slave Dublen
761 slave Jacob
761 slave Rose
761 slave Rose
761 slave Pollena
761 slave Jeany
761 slave Bess
761 slave Violet
761 slave Phebe
761 slave Bendor
762 Rouock, John
763 Jones, William
763 Miles, John
763 slave Jack
763 slave Scipio
763 slave Sue
764 Dalsheill, Thos.
764 Dalsheill, Lewin
764 Coventoun, Nehemiah
764 Firguson, John
764 slave Jack
764 slave Will
764 slave Hercules
764 slave Harrey
764 slave Jack
764 slave Jean

1731 TAX LIST [Household number/Name/Remarks]

MONIE/NANTICOKE HUNDREDS

764 slave Bess	783 Roberts, Jno.	809 Hobbs, Joy
764 slave Miranda	783 Roberts, Rencher	809 Montgair, Matthew
764 slave Thamar	784 Martin, George	810 Hobbs, Thos.
765 Downs, George	785 Harris, Jeremiah	811 Mode, Peter
765 slave Toby	786 Waller, Wm.	812 Jones, James
765 slave Frank	786 Jones, Samll.	812 Jones, Jno.
765 slave Bendor	786 slave Cesar	812 Dughing, Walter
766 Jones, Elizabeth	787 White, Francis	812 slave Sambo
766 slave London	787 White, John	812 slave Moll
766 slave Amuck	788 White, John	812 slave Sibb
766 slave Jean	789 Wallace, Matthew	813 Storrie, widdow
766 slave Rachell	789 slave Sibb	813 Coventoun, Abraham
767 Jones, Robert	790 Wallace, Richard	813 Jones, Daniel
767 Jones, George	790 Wallace, Thos.	813 slave Whitehaven
767 Martin, Thos.	790 Wallace, James	813 slave Doll
767 slave Galloway	790 Wallace, David	814 Coventoun, Thos.
768 Lawes, Robert	790 slave Ceesar	814 Jones, Mathais
768 Lawes, Panther	790 slave Bess	815 Fitzgerald, Edmond
768 Skeen, Robert	791 Roberts, Edward	816 Malingo, Jacob
768 Lawes, Wm.	791 slave Jeffrey	817 Durham, Thomas
768 slave Bubo	791 slave Sarah	818 Leatherberry, Jno.
768 slave Jack	792 Jones, Lewis	818 slave Sambo
768 slave Samson	792 slave Jack	818 slave Toney
769 Malcom, Robert	792 slave Hannah	818 slave Bridget
769 Malcom, George	792 slave Mall	818 slave Africa
770 Wilson, John	793 Hobbs, Noble	818 slave Rose
771 Irwing, George	794 Miller, John	818 slave Ben
771 Kellason, Will.	794 Miller, Thos.	818 slave Pompey
771 slave Toby	795 Lawes, Jno.	819 Dorman, John
771 slave Jeffrey	795 Williams, Jno.	820 Dorman, Henrey
771 slave Judah	795 Wallace, Will.	
772 Waller, John	795 slave Prince	NANTICOKE HUNDRED
772 Waller, Neilson	795 slave Duew	821 McClister, John
772 slave Jenny	795 slave Secar	821 McClister, William
773 Waller, Major	796 Lawes, Thos.	821 McClister, Samuell
774 Staughton, Wm. mr.	796 Wallace, Jno.	821 slave Coffie
774 Loe, Charles	796 slave Jack	821 slave Sambo
774 Husk, John	796 slave Marrea	821 slave Addam
774 slave Sibbyna	797 Bazill, Thos.	821 slave Tom
774 slave Allai	798 Williams, Jeremiah	821 slave Siss
774 slave Busser	799 Roe, Joseph	821 slave Philliss
774 slave Simon	800 Jones, Richard	821 slave Abbo
774 slave Fendor	801 Roe, Thos.	822 Hopkins, Stephan
774 slave Cato	801 Jones, Charles	822 Hopkins, Robert
775 Wright, Thos.	802 Foedden, Randell	823 Barkley, John ser.
775 Wright, Henrey	803 Roe, widdow	824 Barkley, John jur.
776 Shores, John	803 Spens, Jno.	825 Samuells, Peter
776 Shores, Wm.	804 Windsor, Lazarus	825 Hust, William
777 Stringer, George	804 Windsor, Jno.	826 Timons, John
778 Pollock, widdow	805 Shanks, Benjamin	827 Samuells, Richard
778 slave Sambo	806 Carrey, Thos.	827 Walter, Daniell
778 slave Rodger	806 slave Lemmon	827 slave Coffe
779 Waller, George	807 Coventoun, capt.	828 Phips, John
779 King, Duncan	807 Coventoun, Jno.	829 Makum, Timothy
780 Pollock, Joseph	807 Rose, Samuell	829 Messix, Benjamin
780 Howell, John	807 slave Sambo	830 Messex, Isaac
781 Morgan, Walter	807 slave Cuckow	831 Dunn, Richard
782 Muir, Rolland	807 slave Bess	832 Anderson, Sarah
783 Roberts, widdow	808 Hobbs, Marthillias	832 Anderson, John
	808 Montgair, Jno.	833 Caldwill, John jur.

TAX LISTS OF SOMERSET COUNTY: 1730-1740

NANTICOKE HUNDRED

833 Jones, William
833 slave Sambo
834 Calaway, John ser.
834 Callaway, Edward
834 Callaway, John
835 Parmore, Matthew
836 Caldwell, Patrick
837 Callaway, William
837 Callaway, John
837 Callaway, William jur.
838 Harvey, William
839 Waller, Thomas ser.
839 Waller, Nathaniell
839 Waller, Thomas
840 Spear, Henery
841 Govan, Robart jur.
842 Jones, James ser.
842 Jones, Danill
843 Phillips, Richard
843 Phillips, John
844 Jackson, Samuell
845 Collins, James
845 Garins, Samuell
846 Nutter, Christipher
846 Jones, John
846 slave Leaser
846 slave Tom
846 slave Rose
846 slave Barbrey
846 slave Minidab
847 Vatnatson, Elias
848 Useears, John
849 Larmore, Thomas jur.
849 Larmore, Thomas sr.
849 More, William
850 Makab, Henery
851 Henderson, Robart
852 Beard, Leuis ser.
852 Beard, John
852 Beard, Lewis
853 Coyllar, Robart ser.
853 Coyllar, Dotey
853 Coyllar, Robart
854 Gam, Sambo
854 Gam, Robart
854 slave Grace
855 Right, William ser.
855 Right, William
855 Brown, John
856 Collins, George
857 Dashiels, James

857 slave Robin
857 slave Will
857 slave Will
857 slave Grace
858 Cupper, John
859 Dashiells, Henery
859 slave Gift
859 slave Sibb
860 Relph, Thomas
861 Oneall, John
862 Collins, John
862 Surman, Thomas
863 Melson, Samuell ser.
863 Melson, Joseph
863 Melson, Samuell
863 Melson, Benjamin
864 Austin, William
864 Bordely, William
865 Cheasman, John
865 slave Seaser
865 slave Nancey
866 McClister, Joseph
866 McClister, Neall
866 slave Sampson
867 Right, Solomon
868 Cotman, Ebenezar
869 Rodes, Timothy ser.
869 Rodes, Timothy
870 Wallace, Richard
871 Kellum, Edward
871 Wale, John
871 Goslae, Ezekill
871 slave Dick
871 slave Marow
872 Ackworth, Charles
872 Ackworth, Richard
872 Gloster, Thomas
873 Flualen, Samuell
873 slave Silas
874 Hickman, Jashua
875 More, William
876 Richardson, William
877 Gosle, James
878 Gam, Fortin
878 Gam, Betty
879 Surman, Thomas
880 Dean, John
881 Vawn, William
881 Ball, John
882 Williams, Richard
883 Hopkins, John ser.
883 Hopkins, John
883 slave Jack
884 McCants, Alexander
885 Hopkins, John jur.
886 Hopkins, Robart
886 Windright, John
886 Owars, Ephram

886 slave Tobey
886 slave Page
887 Windright, Cannon
887 Windright, Stephan
887 Parsons, Robart
888 Larmore, John ser.
888 Larmore, John
888 Larmore, Thomas
888 slave Coffe
888 slave Sibb
889 Ackworth, Thomas
889 slave Will
890 More, John
890 More, William
891 Green, Richard
892 Mackdowll, John
893 Nickolson, Richard
894 Taylor, William
895 Scot, George
896 Twiford, John
896 Askiley, Daniell
896 Mufey, James
897 Tuley, Stephen jr.
898 Tuley, Bejm.
899 Tuley, Stephen ser.
900 Tweley, Robertt
901 Giles, William snr.
901 Giles, Thomas
901 Giles, William jur.
901 slave Floro
902 Rider, Richard
902 Rider, Hathley
902 Rider, Wilson
902 slave Tulle
903 Talyr, Abraham
903 slave Squash
904 Anderson, John
905 Darby, John
906 Young, Charles
906 Tuley, Joseph
906 Gibb, Alxr.
906 Boyce, John
907 Benett, Elesebeth wido.
907 Benett, Edward
907 Benett, Gorge
907 Benett, John
908 Sherman, William
909 Mcginey, Jenn wido.
909 Deputy, James
910 Robertson, John
910 slave Sue
911 Rusell, Wm.
911 Whilley, William
912 Daine, Charles
912 Rightt, Edward
912 Harper, William
912 slave Tom
913 Hardy, John
914 Nickelson, John

32

1731 TAX LIST [Household number/Name/Remarks]

NANTICOKE HUNDRED

914 slave Cock
914 slave Vinus
915 Nickelson, Roger
916 Coluer, John
917 Richardson, John
918 Windrightt, William
919 Haresh, Philip
919 Spear, Henery
920 Bounds, Joseph
921 Dashiels, William
922 Olefentt, William
923 Carter, John ser.
923 Carter, Samuell
923 Carter, Thomas
924 Hufington, John
924 Polson, William
924 slave Jeck
924 slave Jeney
924 slave Plesentt
925 Hufinton, Johathen
926 Hufington, John jur.
926 Churn, John
927 Cooper, Gabrell
927 Cooper, Thomas
928 Cooper, Gabrell jur.
929 Witherley, William
929 slave Findo
930 Parkerson, John
931 Hikman, William
931 slave Jeck
931 slave Murah
931 slave Sambo
931 slave Sistt
932 Hickman, William jur.
932 slave Ora
933 Hustt, Joseph
934 Jeckson, Johanathen
935 Nickellson, James
936 Nuter, William
936 slave Benn
936 slave Catto
936 slave Cating
936 slave Rose
937 Train, James ser.
937 Train, James jur.
937 Train, Rodger
937 Shales, Patrick
937 slave Rose
938 Givan, Robertt ser.
938 Mcckeey, Mikeall
938 slave Seser
938 slave Charles
938 slave Hanah
938 slave Nane

938 slave Bes
939 Darbey, Walter
939 Macoy, John
940 Ackworth, Samuell
940 slave Sue
941 Neubeld, Francis
941 slave Amey
942 Ryden, James
942 Ryden, James jur.
943 Coler, Gorge Betts
944 Benston, Thomas
944 Camp, John
944 slave Will
945 Dashiels, Joseph
945 Shireden, Daniell
945 slave Perey
945 slave Randell
945 slave Buss
946 Nuter, Margrett
946 slave Philip
946 slave Sipio
946 slave Jenne
946 slave Mole
947 Johnson, David
948 Cooper, Samuell
949 Willson, John
950 Tuley, James
950 Price, Francis
951 Westt, James
951 Burken, James
952 Hick, Solomon
952 Billins, Bejm.
952 slave Frank
952 slave Cock
953 Backer, Thomas
954 Langsdell, William
954 Fulton, William
955 Ferington, William
955 Brown, John
956 Cooper, Isaac
956 Tuley, Bejm.
957 Langford, Thomas
958 Paromor, James
959 Cartter, Philip
960 Records, John jur.
960 Inglesh, Robertt
961 McCluer, Robertt
962 Olefentt, Gorge
963 More, Catron wido.
963 More, William
964 Roberson, William
965 Dashiles, Gorge
965 Dashiles, Bejm.
965 Dashiels, Robertt
965 slave Hery
965 slave Turner
965 slave Dido
966 Codrey, Isaac
967 Persons, Francis
968 Read, John

968 Read, John jur.
968 Read, Zacharies
968 slave Pege
969 Quteromus, James
970 Mesick, Natheniall
970 Mesick, Jacob
970 Rickey, Archbuld
971 Polk, Gorge
972 Meseck, Jacob ser.
973 Abdon, William
974 Kinigam, Dainell
975 Galle, John
975 Horeshson, John
975 slave Mesnger
975 slave Bosely
975 slave Simond
975 slave Largeg
975 slave Juda
975 slave Matt
975 slave Ross
976 Stilley, Mary wido.
976 Floyed, Magir
977 Ege, Joshua
978 Qutormus, Isaha
978 Gibens, John
978 Hall, Thomas
979 Roberttson, David
980 Mcglaclen, John
981 Nettwell, Briantt
982 Winser, Henery
982 Friggs, Robertt
983 Winser, John
984 Bounds, Jacob
985 Nobell, Isaac jnr.
986 Nobell, Isaac snr.
987 Bouger, Frances wido.
987 Bouger, James
988 Johnson, Thomas
989 Oneall, John
990 Boyce, Danell
991 Darby, Daniell
992 Wootten, John
993 Wootten, Edward
994 Hosey, Matthew
995 Stevens, John
996 Sherman, Thomas jur.
997 Clefton, Gorge ser.
997 Clefton, Gorge jur.
998 Piper, William
998 Ackworth, Henery
998 slave Sambo
998 slave Boney
998 slave Nell
998 slave Sarah
998 slave Ross
999 Tweley, Elzebett wido.
999 Tweley, Gorge

TAX LISTS OF SOMERSET COUNTY: 1730-1740

NANTICOKE/POCOMOKE HUNDREDS

1000 Browne, William
1001 Henery, John
1001 Henery, Robertt
1002 Dashiell, Michell
1002 Correy, Philip
1003 Colens, Edmond
1004 Donas, Robertt
1005 Calaway, Petter
1006 Parromor, Thomas
1007 King, Philip
1008 Carrter, John
1009 King, William
1010 Jones, James jur.
1011 Relph, William
1012 Jones, John
1013 Clifton, Philip
1014 Records, Bejm.
1014 Thomson, Gorge
1015 Benston, William
1016 Cooper, James
1017 Hugge, Johanah wido.
1017 Polke, John
1018 Calaw[ay], Petter jur.
1019 Benston, Henery
1019 Benston, Gorge
1020 Godard, John
1020 Hickson, Joseph
1021 More, John forestt
1022 Keney, William
1023 Nuton, Chripther
1024 Walter, Henery
1024 Walter, Daniell
1025 Ingram, Isaac
1025 Massey, Thomas
1026 Ingram, Robertt
1027 Wingett, Philip
1028 Doanesh, Juvns
1029 Dolby, Petter
1030 Wilems, Charles
1031 Samuels, Richard
1032 Gray, William
1032 War[ne]r, Isaac
1032 slave Margrett
1033 Polke, John
1034 Manlef, Manuelwe
1034 slave Ned
1035 Fowler, Arthur
1036 Lansdell, John
1036 Lan[sd]ell, Sper
1037 S[ho]rtt, Edward snr.
1038 [Sh]ortt, Edward jnr.
1039 [Ba]ker, William
1040 [Ma]rsey, William
1041 [Th]orns, Edward

1042 T[hor]ns, Alxr.
1043 Sherman, Petter
1044 Codr[e]y, John snr.
1045 Dr[ap]er, Alex.
1045 Dreper, William
1045 Oneall, James
1046 Low, Reafe
1047 Wetherly, Elesebeth wid
1047 Wetherly, James
1047 slave Tom
1047 slave Pieg
1048 Lynn, Aaron
1048 Anderson, John
1048 slave Will
1048 slave Abraham
1049 Shokley, David
1049 Shokley, James
1050 Messix, John
1050 Messix, George
1050 Messix, Obediah
1051 Ingrom, Abraham
1051 Ingrom, Jacob
1051 Fleatwood, John
1051 Kelly, John
1052 Harvey, John
1053 Sharp, John
1054 Owins, Robart
1054 slave Tom
1055 Polk, Charles
1056 Clifton, Daniell
1057 Bushop, Henery
1058 Samuells, Petter
1059 More, John jnr.
1060 Huggans, Charles
1061 English, William
1062 Green, Ezekell
1063 Marvell, Thomas
1064 Hardey, James
1064 Hardey, Joseph
1065 Jacobs, Walter
1065 slave Sibb
1066 Russell, James ser.
1066 Russell, Thomas
1067 Russell, James
1068 Wood, Thomas
1068 Wood, John
1069 Young, William
1070 Roads, Daniell
1071 Right, Solomon
1072 Langford, John
1072 Collins, Richard
1073 Hufington, Thomas
1074 Danilson, Jean
1074 slave Tom
1074 slave Blando
1075 Rotten, Josiah
1076 Hufington, Richard

1077 Nowils, Edmund
1077 Nowils, Richard
1078 Caudrey, Edward
1078 Caudrey, Daniell
1079 Nutter, Matthew
1079 slave Dominick
1080 Scott, Windom
1081 Dunken, James
1082 Buckley, Nickliss
1083 Sulevan, Michaell
1084 Martain, John
1085 Nutter, John Huitt
1085 slave Punch
1085 slave Diana
1085 slave Tite
1086 Walter, John
1087 Govan, James
1087 slave Frank
1088 Waller, Nathanill
1088 Williams, John
1089 Caldwell, James
1089 slave Cobb
1089 slave Sambo
1089 slave Rose

POCOMOKE HUNDRED
1090 Riggin, John senr.
1090 Riggin, John
1090 Riggin, Steven
1090 slave Jenney
1091 Riggin, Samll.
1091 slave Ciss
1092 Riggin, Jno. junr.
1092 Riggin, Charles
1092 slave Peter
1092 slave Nan
1092 slave Mark
1093 Dickeson, Peter senr.
1093 Dickeson, John
1093 Dickeson, Edw.
1093 Dickeson, Isaac
1093 Dickeson, Chas.
1093 slave Coshab
1094 Cocks, Wm.
1094 slave Jonas
1094 slave Dol
1094 slave Sesar
1095 Ellis, John
1096 Cliften, John
1097 White, John
1097 Coner, Wm.
1097 slave Tom
1098 Evens, Tho.
1098 slave Viy
1099 Hollon, Wm.
1099 slave Tom
1099 slave Darkes
1100 Collens, Samll.
1101 Billins, Tho.

1731 TAX LIST [Household number/Name/Remarks]

POCOMOKE HUNDRED

1101 slave Robin
1102 Britt, John
1102 slave Quash
1102 slave Oxfortt
1103 Melborn, Ralph
1103 slave Dago
1104 Milbourn, widdow
1104 Millbourn, Caleb
1104 slave Mingo
1104 slave Ana
1105 Melbourn, John
1106 Nearn, Robtt. senr.
1106 slave Harry
1106 slave Will
1107 Nearn, Robtt. junr.
1107 slave Jenney
1108 Nearn, James
1108 slave Will
1108 slave Mall
1109 White, John
1109 Beachamp, John
1109 slave George
1109 slave Pase
1110 McRedde, Alexr.
1111 Cary, Francis
1112 White, Archabel
1113 Broughton, Bruf
1113 Linsey, Tho.
1113 Parker, Phillip
1114 Benston, Tho.
1114 slave Pleasant
1115 Brown, Tho.
1116 Powell, John
1117 Buywater, Richart
1118 Newbold, Tho.
1118 slave Mol
1118 slave Patience
1119 Maddux, Lazarus
1119 Jenkins, Christopher
1120 Buyard, Robtt.
1120 Cliften, George [hp]
1120 Buyer, Jonathan [hp]
1121 McDaniel, Allen
1121 Mackdaniel, Moses [hs]
1122 Tomlin, Samll.
1122 Tomlin, Solomun
1122 Tomlin, Seward
1122 Tomlin, Naboth [hp]
1122 slave Abner
1122 slave London [hp]
1123 Broughton, John
1123 Broughton, Wm. [hp]

1124 Scholfield, Henry
1124 Roland, Elisabeth [hs]
1125 Whittingham, mr.
1125 Happeraft, Tho.
1126 Cluff, Edw.
1126 Dukes, Wm.
1127 Clegg, Samll.
1127 Banks, Kit
1128 Dorman, Samll.
1128 Stevens, Edw.
1129 Dennis, John junr.
1129 Otwell, Francis
1129 slave Kingstown
1129 slave Jo
1129 slave Caleme
1130 Townsend, Littleton
1131 Gibs, capt.
1131 Gibs, Abraham his son
1132 Dickeson, Cornelius
1133 Townsend, John senr.
1133 Townsend, Jno. junr.
1133 Otwell, Cha.
1134 Mayo, Samll.
1135 Cottengem, Jonathan
1135 Cottengem, Cha.
1135 Cotengem, Wm.
1135 Cottengem, Jonathan [hs]
1136 Sturges, Joshua
1136 Loe, Wm.
1136 slave Tom
1136 slave Mol
1137 Turner, Samll. junr.
1138 Turner, Jno.
1139 Butler, Tho.
1140 Taylor, Samuel
1140 Taylor, Samll.
1141 Townsend, Cha.
1141 Townsend, Elias
1141 Townsend, Solomon
1142 Jones, Wm.
1143 Rennels, John
1144 Tillman, Gideon
1144 slave Pompe
1144 slave Grace
1145 Noble, James
1145 Stevens, John
1146 Whittington, Southey
1146 Bevens, Joshua
1146 slave Sesar

1146 slave John
1146 slave Lawneullana
1147 Bevens, John
1147 Bevens, Caleb
1147 slave Sambo
1148 Nicols, James
1149 Nicols, John
1149 Nicols, Joseph
1150 Nicols, Elizabeth
1150 Hammon, Edw.
1150 slave Fillis
1151 Johnson, Elisabeth
1151 slave Betty
1152 Lyptrot, John
1153 Houston, Joseph
1153 Cillim, John
1153 slave Esbell
1154 Townsend, Solomon
1155 Huff, Edmon
1155 slave Will
1155 slave Sambo
1155 slave Gorge
1155 slave Titus
1155 slave Nan
1155 slave Floro
1156 Whittington, Wm.
1156 slave Frank
1156 slave Bab
1157 Duffins, George
1158 Nelson, Hugh
1158 Diton, Isaac
1158 slave Jo
1159 Gray, Allen
1160 Morris, Isaac
1160 Morris, Luke
1160 slave Surry
1160 slave Ben
1160 slave Abner
1160 slave Ayo
1161 Dennis, Jno. senr.
1161 Dennis, Whetly
1161 slave Jo
1161 slave Cate
1162 Outen, Abraham
1162 slave Will
1163 Sturges, Jonathan
1163 slave Jane
1164 Melven, Robtt.
1164 Melvin, Wm.
1165 Henderson, Beniamin
1166 Wheeler, Isaac
1167 Burnet, James
1167 Burnet, James
1168 Henderson, Francis
1169 Lamdon, Tho.
1169 Burk, John
1170 Glass, Christofer
1170 Glass, John
1170 Glass, Christofer
1170 slave Frank

TAX LISTS OF SOMERSET COUNTY: 1730-1740

POCOMOKE HUNDRED

1170 slave Pompey
1170 slave Dina
1171 Godfre, Joseph
1172 Davis, Joseph
1173 Davis, Elisabeth
1173 slave Will
1173 slave Simon
1173 slave Mary
1174 Selby, Tho.
1174 slave Dina
1175 Davis, Nathaniel
1175 Davis, Jno.
1176 White, Hannah
1176 White, Henry
1177 Houston, Benjamin
1177 Townsend, John
1177 slave Dick
1178 Wordy, Susanna
1178 slave Tom
1178 slave Mass
1178 slave Febe
1178 slave Belo
1179 Fishwater, Henry
1180 Andres, John
1181 Bevins, Rolon
1181 Bevins, Wm.
1181 Bevins, Elias
1182 Peall, Tho.
1182 slave Samson
1183 Stuard, John
1183 Cocklin, Francis
1183 slave Fisher
1183 slave Tom
1183 slave Jack
1183 slave Bromon
1183 slave Funur
1183 slave Nane
1183 slave Rose
1184 Gullips, James
1185 Conly, Patrick
1186 Brittingham, Jno. junr.
1187 Merill, Joseph
1188 Lamberson, Jno.
1188 Lamberson, Robtt.
1189 Cary, Jno.
1190 Braser, Wm.
1190 Braser, James
1190 Curvine, Tho.
1191 Gudgen, Benj.
1192 Benston, Alexr.
1193 Lamberson, Abraham
1194 Lamberson, Johannus
1195 Hudson, Wm.
1196 McHenry, Charles
1197 Henderson, Jno. junr.
1198 Scott, capt.

1198 Ray, James
1198 Goldsmith, Tho.
1198 slave Tom
1198 slave Peter
1198 slave Soney
1198 slave Phebe
1198 slave Rose
1199 Haward, Tho. mr.
1199 Davis, Tuder
1199 slave Sambo
1199 slave Sevea
1199 slave Tom
1199 slave Jesper
1199 slave Priss
1199 slave Jenny
1199 slave Rose
1200 Allen, Francis
1200 Hinman, Jacob
1200 Allen, Jno.
1200 Chaille, Moses junr.
1200 Gaddass, Robert
1200 slave Judith
1200 slave Saborah
1200 slave Nell
1200 slave Mangeree
1200 slave Sampson
1201 Handy, Wm. mr.
1201 Handy, Samll.
1201 slave Ned
1201 slave Harry
1201 slave Heger
1202 Riggin, Ambrose
1202 Riggin, Teague
1203 Harris, John
1203 Harris, Benton
1204 Magan, Jno.
1205 Harper, Edw.
1206 Tull, John
1207 Costen, Isaac
1208 Benton, Comfort
1208 slave Masorrath
1208 slave Houborn
1208 slave Sambo
1208 slave Cofee
1208 slave Pegg
1208 slave Bess
1208 slave John
1208 slave Hannah
1209 Costen, Stephen
1209 Pilcher, John
1210 Mitchell, Robtt.
1210 Boyse, Wm.
1210 slave Townsides
1210 slave Silbey
1211 Townsend, Daniel
1211 slave Pegg
1211 slave Jenne
1212 Jorden, Aron
1213 Tindell, James

1214 Harris, Caleb
1215 Ward, Joseph
1215 Ward, Cornelius
1215 slave Bobo
1216 Worwick, Arther
1217 Riggen, Teague
1217 Cantwell, Thomas
1217 slave Cesar
1217 slave Nan
1218 Harris, Robtt.
1218 Logen, Alexr.
1218 slave Harry
1218 slave Mol
1219 Riggin, Joseph
1219 Condum, Edward
1220 Smullen, Randuplh
1221 Denston, John
1222 Daily, Patrick
1223 Porter, Wm.
1224 Townsend, Elisabeth
1224 Townsend, Danford
1224 slave Tom
1224 slave Toney
1225 Scott, Tho.
1226 Layn, Jno.
1227 Wonnel, James
1227 Bennet, Wm.
1228 Otwell, Francis
1228 Otwell, Solomon
1229 Riggin, Darby
1229 Riggin, Pierce
1230 Dennaho, Teague
1230 Dennaho, Daniel [hp]
1230 Dennaho, Teague [hp]
1231 Flemen, John
1231 Flemmen, Wm.
1231 slave Robin
1231 slave Dina
1232 Colbourn, John
1232 Reden, Michail
1233 Dickeson, Edw.
1233 Dickeson, Cha.
1233 slave Gonge
1234 Dennaho, Dorman
1234 Cuper, Samll.
1235 Townsend, James
1235 slave Guy
1236 Shilden, John
1236 Bonum, Wm.
1236 slave Isaac
1237 Porter, Hugh
1237 Gore, Richart
1237 Porter, Jonathan
1238 Gray, Tho.
1238 slave Abraham
1239 Porter, Francis
1239 Porter, Mackemey
1239 Townsend, Cha.

1731 TAX LIST [Household number/Name/Remarks]

POCOMOKE HUNDRED

1240 Akeson, Angelo
1240 Jones, Abraham
1240 Redden, Cha.
1241 Townsend, J[no.] senr.
1241 Townsend, Saul
1241 slave Mirerah
1242 Bevens, Tho.
1243 Adkitson, Patience
1243 Adkeson, Samll.
1244 Adkeson, Isaac
1244 slave Guie
1245 Mills, Wm.
1245 Mills, Samll.
1246 Tull, George
1246 Tull, Noble
1246 slave Abner
1246 slave Dinah
1247 Knite, Richart
1247 Knite, James
1247 Knight, Joshua
1248 Harper, Francis
1248 Pilchard, James
1249 Pirkins, widow
1249 Pirkins, Wm.
1249 Pirkins, Michail
1250 Pirkins, Jno.
1251 Benstone, Wm.
1252 Dreden, David
1252 Dreden, Wm.
1252 Dreden, David
1253 Colvart, Wm.
1254 Fenton, widdow
1254 Blair, Robtt.
1255 Pecock, Edw.
1256 Beachamp, Edw.
1256 Beachamp, Tho.
1256 slave More
1257 Hull, Edw.
1257 Davis, Beachamp
1258 Addams, Phillip
1258 Davis, Jno.
1259 Adams, Wm.
1259 Adams, Dennis
1259 Adams, Wm.
1259 slave Jack
1260 Adams, George
1261 Adams, Hope
1262 Marshell, Samll.
1263 Adams, Tho.
1263 Adams, David
1263 Adams, Isaac
1263 slave Vine
1264 Adams, Abraham
1265 Wood, Wm.
1265 Long, Jno.
1266 Carsey, Peter
1266 Carsey, Samll.
1267 Boston, Neser

1268 Tayler, Robtt.
1269 Boston, Isaac
1269 slave Sambo
1269 slave Venus
1269 slave Dark
1270 Tayler, Hope
1271 Adams, Jacob
1271 Adams, Samll.
1271 Adams, Collens
1271 Adams, Phillip
1271 Matthues, Robtt.
1271 slave Samson
1271 slave Nan
1272 Matthues, Teague
1273 Matthues, Wm.
1274 Matthues, John
1275 Matthues, Samull.
1276 Houston, John junr.
1276 Fittgarald, Jno.
1277 Henderson, James
1277 slave Adam
1278 Henderson, Jno. senr.
1278 slave Guy
1278 slave George
1278 slave Bess
1278 slave Eve
1278 slave Jone
1279 Quinten, Phillip
1279 Quinten, Dixon
1279 slave John
1280 Merrill, John
1280 Merrill, Joshua
1280 Chambers, Jeremiah
1281 Gogin, David
1282 Jones, Edw.
1282 Melton, Jno.
1283 Small, John
1283 Young, Daniel
1284 Layfield, Tho.
1284 Layfield, George
1284 Pilgalley, Tho.
1284 slave Tolomy
1285 Blaids, Robtt.
1285 Wright, Comfort
1286 Henderson, Cha.
1286 Johnson, Joshua
1287 Baker, James
1287 Baker, Henderson
1287 Benstone, Benjamin
1287 slave York
1288 Houston, James
1288 Powell, Levin
1288 slave Cate
1289 Houstone, John senr.
1289 slave Bettey
1290 Houstone, Joseph
1291 Ramsey, Cha.

1291 Ramsey, Barret
1292 Houston, Robtt.
1293 Dickeson, Peter
1293 Matthes, Kindal
1294 Webb, John
1294 Webb, Solomon
1294 Webb, Jno.
1295 Mills, widdow
1295 Mills, Moses
1295 slave Heckter
1296 Jones, Tho.
1297 Blaids, John
1297 Blaids, Benjamin
1298 Mills, John
1298 Mills, Wm.
1298 Mills, Robtt.
1298 Mills, Nathaniel
1298 Mills, Alexr.
1298 slave Nanne
1299 Greer, Archabel
1299 Greer, Henry
1299 Greer, John
1300 Piper, Isaac
1301 Benston, Edw.
1302 Gillett, Samll.
1302 slave Dorcus
1303 Gillit, John
1303 Stevenson, Joseph
1303 slave Harry
1303 slave Nanne
1304 Mills, Samll.
1304 Mills, Nathaniel
1304 Stevenson, Robtt.
1304 Paden, John
1305 Ellis, Wm.
1305 Adkins, John
1306 Dickeson, James
1306 Dickeson, Robtt.
1307 Layn, Wm. mr.
1307 slave Harry
1307 slave Cate
1308 Warrinton, Tho.
1309 White, Wm.
1309 slave James
1309 slave Old Harry
1309 slave Young Harry
1309 slave Robin
1309 slave Sarah
1309 slave Jenny
1309 slave Pris
1309 slave Sue
1310 Hampton, madam
1310 Henry, John
1310 slave Jone
1310 slave Genny
1310 slave Lucy
1310 slave Patience
1310 slave Pompy
1310 slave Chick
1310 slave Tarrill

TAX LISTS OF SOMERSET COUNTY: 1730-1740

POCOMOKE/WICOMICO HUNDREDS

1310 slave Addam
1310 slave Clear
1310 slave Tom
1310 slave Joho
1310 slave Aginney
1311 Harper, John
1311 Rigging, John
1311 Hugin, Roger

WICOMICO HUNDRED
1312 Steward, Allexander
1312 Folster, John
1312 Mcintire, Daniell
1312 slave Jeane [ws]
1313 Evans, John junr.
1313 Chambers, Samuel
1313 slave Toby
1313 slave Merser
1313 slave Tom [ws]
1313 slave Robin [ws]
1313 slave Sibb [ws]
1313 slave Abo [ws]
1314 Dulany, William
1315 Holebrook, Thomas [ws]
1315 Rennalds, John [ws]
1315 Shirrodon, John [ws]
1316 Shiles, John [ws]
1316 slave Tom [ws]
1317 Crockett, John [ws]
1317 slave Wooping [ws]
1318 Crockett, Richard [ws]
1318 slave Grace [ws]
1319 Phillips, Richard [ws]
1319 slave Grace
1320 Shiles, Thomas [ws]
1321 Nelson, John [ws]
1322 Crockett, Robt. [ws]
1322 slave Cropp [ws]
1322 slave Mank [ws]
1323 Nelson, William
1324 Everton, John
1325 Evans, John senr. [ws]
1325 Fowler, Thomas
1326 Pow, John [ws]
1326 slave Abo [ws]
1327 Lecatt, John [ws]
1328 Vinsent, Thomas junr. [ws]

1328 Vinsent, James junr. [ws]
1329 Cox, Thomas [ws]
1330 Cox, Hill [ws]
1331 Tatom, John
1332 Disharoon, Lewis [ws]
1332 Disharoon, Levin [ws]
1333 Disharoon, John junr.
1334 Handy, Abennezer [ws]
1334 slave Sambo [ws]
1334 slave Tom [ws]
1334 slave Mumfurd [ws]
1334 slave Hannah [ws]
1334 slave Bonny [ws]
1334 slave Ame
1334 slave Will boy [hs]
1335 Taylor, Thomas [ws]
1336 Gorde, Peter [ws]
1337 Gorde, Moses [ws]
1338 Phillips, Jacob [ws]
1339 King, James [ws]
1340 Phidsimons, Thomas [ws]
1341 Shockley, John [ws]
1342 Lindo, Thomas [ws]
1343 Redy, Nicholas [ws]
1343 Redy, Thomas [ws]
1343 Redy, John
1344 Carr, John
1345 Todevine, Nicholas, miller
1346 Turk, Magne, miller
1347 Nicholson, Richard [ws]
1347 Nicholson, Joseph [ws]
1347 Samuells, Abell [ws]
1348 Lancake, George
1348 Cartor, Charles
1348 Evans, William
1349 Lackey, Allexander [ws]
1349 slave Darby [ws]
1349 slave Sam [ws]
1349 slave Ame [ws]
1349 slave Surry [hs]
1350 Caudry, Daniell
1350 slave Robin [ws]
1350 slave Samson [ws]

1350 slave Sibb [ws]
1351 King, Capell
1351 Boutell, Benjamin
1351 slave Parakeet [ws]
1351 slave Major [ws]
1351 slave Mingo [ws]
1351 slave Bess [ws]
1351 slave Rose [ws]
1351 slave Cate [ws]
1352 Caudry, Abraham [ws]
1352 Caudry, Morgan [ws]
1353 Wailes, Joseph [ws]
1353 Kidchin, William
1353 slave Leander boy [hs]
1353 slave Odry girl [hs]
1354 Mcmorie, James
1354 slave Batt [ws]
1354 slave Pompie
1354 slave Rose [ws]
1354 slave Tamer [ws]
1354 slave Abner boy [hs]
1355 Hardy, Robt. [ws]
1355 Hardy, Georg [hs]
1356 Nicholson, James [ws]
1357 James, John [ws]
1358 Goslin, John [ws]
1358 Goslin, Richard [ws]
1359 Piper, Christopher
1359 slave Dick
1359 slave Sambo
1359 slave Toby
1359 slave Sue
1359 slave Dinah
1360 Venables, Joseph senr.
1360 Venables, Benjamin [ws]
1360 Venables, William [ws]
1360 slave Toby
1360 slave Coffe [ws]
1360 slave Jeffery [ws]
1360 slave Tom [ws]
1360 slave Will [ws]
1360 slave Betty [ws]
1360 slave Hager [ws]
1361 Winder, Thomas [ws]
1361 slave Mingo [ws]
1362 Wafers, Ignatious
1363 Bartlett, Thomas [ws]
1363 Bartlett, Paskue [ws]
1364 Handy, John

1731 TAX LIST [Household number/Name/Remarks]

WICOMICO HUNDRED

1364 slave Marriah
1364 slave Dick
1364 slave Prince
1364 slave Jeane
1364 slave Moll
1365 Bartlett, William [ws]
1366 Handy, Isaac
1366 Crouch, Jacob [ws]
1366 slave Sharper [ws]
1366 slave Prew
1366 slave Oxford boy[hs]
1366 slave Quammino boy [hs]
1367 Smith, Jame. [ws]
1367 Price, Allexander [hs]
1368 Breedy, John [ws]
1369 Bird, Thomas [ws]
1369 Bird, Tho. junr. [ws]
1370 Jones, Finch [ws]
1370 Price, Allexander
1371 Humphris, Thomas
1371 Roads, John
1371 Humphris, Thomas junr.
1371 slave Quamino [ws]
1371 slave Coffe [ws]
1371 slave Abo [ws]
1371 slave Bess [ws]
1372 Lancake, Francis
1372 slave Jack [ws]
1372 slave Toby [ws]
1372 slave Bess [ws]
1373 Records, John [ws]
1373 Records, Allexander [ws]
1373 Records, Joseph [ws]
1374 Caudry, John [ws]
1375 Ackinson, Timothy
1376 Maddox, William [ws]
1377 Maddox, Allexander [ws]
1378 Linch, Curnelus [ws]
1379 Hitch, John [ws]
1379 slave Mow [ws]
1380 Hitch, Samuell [ws]
1381 Price, John [ws]
1381 slave Hannah [ws]
1382 Hitch, Elgate [ws]
1382 slave Cunnoondah [ws]
1382 slave Toby [ws]
1383 Johnson, Purnell [ws]
1384 Hall, Thomas [ws]
1385 Evans, William [ws]
1386 Elgate, William [ws]
1387 Taylor, Joseph
1388 Davis, John junr. [ws]
1389 Carzey, Patrick [ws]
1389 Carzey, William
1390 Murfee, Joseph [ws]
1391 Maglamry, Edward][ws]
1392 Lingo, John [ws]
1393 Vinson, Thomas
1393 Vinson, George [ws]
1393 Vinson, Benjamin [ws]
1394 Covinton, Thomas [ws]
1394 slave Tom [ws]
1395 Hastin, Robert [ws]
1395 Hastin, William [ws]
1396 Hairn, Thomas
1396 Hairn, Nehemiah [ws]
1396 slave Hannah [ws]
1397 Hairn, William [ws]
1397 Hairn, Thomas boy [hs]
1397 slave Moll [ws]
1398 Harris, William senr. [ws]
1398 Harris, Richd. [ws]
1398 Harris, John [ws]
1399 Dashiell, Thomas junr.
1399 Furbush, Peter [ws]
1399 slave Toby [ws]
1400 Renshaw, Thomas [ws]
1400 slave Peter [ws]
1400 slave Pompe [ws]
1401 Renshaw, Underwood [ws]
1401 slave Jack [ws]
1401 slave Bess [ws]
1402 Ballard, Charles [ws]
1402 Grant, John [hs]
1402 slave Secer [ws]
1403 Walker, Thomas
1403 Chambers, Robt [ws]
1403 slave Tom [ws]
1403 slave Jonathan [ws]
1403 slave Dino [ws]
1404 Robyson, John [ws]
1404 Goslin, Mathew
1405 Gale, Levin coll.
1405 Steward, John
1405 Noble, Mark
1405 Savage, William
1405 Dilcher, John Parsons
1405 slave Hope
1405 slave Pleasant
1405 slave Ventor
1405 slave Jehue
1405 slave Joyce
1405 slave Pollord
1405 slave Betty
1406 Robyson, William
1406 Crauford, John
1407 Cottman, Joseph
1407 Locke, John
1407 slave Boobo [ws]
1407 slave Jack [ws]
1407 slave Sarah [ws]
1408 Cottman, William
1409 Pointter, William
1410 Ballard, mrs.
1410 slave Hago
1410 slave Moll
1410 slave Jack [ws]
1410 slave Murreah [ws]
1411 Swillavan, William [ws]
1411 Noble, Isaac [ws]
1412 Goddard, George
1412 Mitchell, John
1412 Mitchell, Benjamin
1412 slave man [ws]
1413 Milhard, Richard
1413 Locee, Thomas
1414 Shirman, Peter
1414 Shirman, Peter junr. [ws]
1414 slave Tom [ws]
1415 Dashiell, George junr.
1415 slave Tom
1416 Willin, Thomas [ws]
1416 slave Sarah [ws]
1417 Willin, Edward [ws]
1418 Ellis, Merick

TAX LISTS OF SOMERSET COUNTY: 1730-1740

WICOMICO HUNDRED

1418 Steward, Patrick
1418 Gibson, George
1418 Simson, Archebald
1418 Wilkins, James
1418 slave Boobo
1418 slave Tom [ws]
1418 slave Mary [ws]
1418 slave Hannah
1418 slave Whurra
1419 William, John
1419 Seahorn, Thoma.
1419 Handy, Samuell
1419 Dashiell, Matthias
1420 Fowler, Edward [ws]
1420 Austen, Robt.
1420 Austen, George [hs]
1420 Fowler, John [hs]
1420 slave Mary
1421 Harris, William junr. w
1422 Durrum, James senr. [ws]
1422 Harris, George [ws]
1422 Durrum, James junr.
1423 Addams, Allexander
1423 Syllavan, Timothy
1423 Farnall, Thomas
1423 Short, John
1423 Harewood, Richard
1423 slave Quash
1423 slave Jack
1423 slave Beck
1424 Pollett, Thomas [ws]
1424 Ruark, William [hs]
1424 Pollett, Thomas junr. [hs]
1425 Allexander, William [ws]
1425 Allexander, James [ws]
1425 Allexander, Lestin [ws]
1426 Griffin, John
1427 Adley, William
1428 Allexander, Samuell
1429 Allexander, Moses
1430 Wallace, Richard
1430 Stevens, Isaac
1431 Bound, Jonathan
1431 slave Bess [ws]
1432 North, Edward
1432 North, William
1432 slave Buck
1432 slave Beck
1433 Hurt, Daniell
1434 Stephens, Richard
1434 slave Ceaser [ws]
1434 slave Pumbo [ws]
1434 slave Alse [ws]
1434 slave Sue [ws]
1435 Chadawicks James sr. [ws]
1435 Chadawicks, James jr. [ws]
1436 Carry, William [ws]
1436 Carry, Levin [ws]
1436 Cary, Jonathan
1436 Cary, Tho.
1437 Att Hamans, Sarah
1437 Haman, James
1437 Haman, John [ws]
1437 Haman, Charles [ws]
1437 Haman, Isaac [ws]
1438 Duskell, Moses
1438 Griffen, Olliver [ws]
1439 Mallaly, Patrick [ws]
1440 Akins, Robt.
1441 Shockley, John [ws]
1441 Shockley, Jonathan
1441 Shockley, John
1441 Shockley, Richard [hs]
1441 Shockley, William [hs]
1442 Haymond, William
1442 Haymond, William
1442 Haymond, Nicholas [hs]
1443 Crouch, John [ws]
1444 Att Crouches, Anne
1444 Crouch, Nicholas [ws]
1445 Att Disharoons, Anne
1445 Disharoon, Mickell [ws]
1446 Mcglamery, George
1447 Boins, William [ws]
1448 Caldwell, John senr.
1448 Caldwell, Joshua
1448 Lamard, Joseph
1448 Caldwell, Robt.
1448 slave Tom
1448 slave Will
1448 slave Coffe
1448 slave Tom
1448 slave Will
1448 slave Ishmaell
1448 slave Doll
1448 slave Sqush
1449 Caldwell, Hugh
1450 Wright, Jeremiah senr.
1450 Wright, Jeremiah junr.
1451 Turner, Samuell [ws]
1451 Turner, Nicholas [ws]
1452 Smith, David
1453 Smith, James [ws]
1453 Smith, Moses
1454 Smith, George
1455 Longgo, James
1455 Ollifan, John [ws]
1456 Purdue, John
1457 Davis, John
1457 Davis, Thomas [ws]
1458 Magge, George [ws]
1459 Davis, Daniell [ws]
1459 Corzey, John
1460 Shehorn, John [ws]
1461 Shuch, Oliver [ws]
1462 Christopher, John jr. [ws]
1463 Disharoon, John senr. [ws]
1463 Disharoon, John junr. [ws]
1463 Disharoon, William [ws]
1463 slave Coffee [ws]
1463 slave Eve [ws]
1464 Todevine, Henry
1464 Todevine, Thomas
1464 Vance, Allexander junr.
1464 slave Golliah [ws]
1464 slave Sarah [ws]
1464 slave Jeane [ws]
1465 Scott, George [ws]
1465 slave Sam
1465 slave Pompe [ws]
1465 slave Sanders
1465 slave Will
1466 Scott, Day [ws]
1466 slave Hecttor [ws]
1466 slave Tom

1731 TAX LIST [Household number/Name/Remarks]

WICOMICO HUNDRED

1466 slave Sippeo [ws]
1467 Parrimore, Richard [ws]
1468 Cathell, Jame. [ws]
1469 Davis, Samuell [ws]
1470 Duskell, Dennis [ws]
1471 Ragley, Mikell [ws]
1472 Knox, Robt. [ws]
1473 Foox, Benjamin [ws]
1473 Hyway, Isaac
1473 slave Patience [ws]
1474 Vance, David
1475 Vance, Allexander sr. [ws]
1476 Banes, John [ws]
1477 Christopher, Richard [ws]
1478 Christopher, John [ws]
1478 Christopher, Clement [ws]
1479 Balye, Jonathan [ws]
1480 Balye, George [ws]
1480 Balye, Benjamin [hs]
1481 Brueton, William [ws]
1481 Brueton, William [hs]
1481 slave Patience [ws]
1482 Moors, John [ws]
1482 Moors, Robt. [ws]
1482 Pope, Richard
1483 Garrard, Wm.
1483 slave Uxor
1484 Maggee, Peter [ws]
1484 Maggee, John
1485 Molone, Robt. [ws]
1485 Megee, Peter
1486 ODay, Owen [ws]
1486 Oday, John [hs]
1486 Oday, Owen [hs]
1486 Oday, Henry [hs]
1487 Hobs, Joy [ws]
1487 Hobs, Aboslon [ws]
1487 slave Pollebus [ws]
1488 Shirman, Jeane
1488 Haymond, Charle [ws]
1489 Shirman, Edwar [ws]
1489 Shirman, Job [ws]
1490 Cope, John [ws]
1490 Cope, William [ws]
1491 McClanan, Daniel
1491 Morris, Jeremiah [ws]
1492 Parsons, John [ws]
1493 Parsons, George
1494 Miller, Peter [ws]
1495 Hall, Phenix [ws]
1495 Cusshene, John
1495 slave Jack [ws]
1496 Stephens, John [ws]
1496 slave Bess [ws]
1496 slave Jack [ws]
1497 Dowdell, Christopher
1498 Tomsom, John
1499 Disharoon, Mikell
1499 Canaday, John [hs]
1500 Hill, Charles
1500 Ellis, Joseph [ws]
1500 Ellis, Frances [ws]
1501 Att Houghgens, Sarah
1501 Follerton, Allexander [ws]
1501 Follerton, James [ws]
1501 Golden, John
1502 Reddish, John [ws]
1503 Corbitt, Daniell [ws]
1504 Goddard, Thomas
1505 Lows, Henry
1505 slave Jeptto [ws]
1505 slave Rose [ws]
1506 Collier, Thoma [ws]
1506 Phillips, George [hs]
1506 slave Buck [ws]
1507 Dashiell, George capt.
1507 slave Polly
1507 slave Samboe
1507 slave Dublin
1507 slave Samboe
1507 slave Harry
1507 slave Ame
1507 slave Rose
1507 slave Kate
1507 slave Jane
1508 Cawdrie, Jacob [ws]
1508 Heron, William [ws]
1508 Mackinally, John [ws]
1508 slave Sultan [ws]
1509 Davis, William [ws]
1509 Hodge, John [ws]
1510 Goslin, Thomas
1511 Venables, John [ws]
1511 Crouch, Robt. [hs]
1512 Venables, William [ws]
1513 Phillips, Thos. [ws]
1514 Bushaw, Gerrard [ws]
1515 Keble, William senr. [ws]
1515 Keble, William junr. [ws]
1516 Gillis, Thomas
1516 Dennard, George
1516 Vaunce, Thomas
1516 McLaughlin, Domonick
1516 slave Nedd
1516 slave Aby
1516 slave Stepney
1516 slave Namore
1516 slave Pegg
1516 slave Jenny
1516 slave Domonick
1517 Standford, Joseph [ws]
1517 Christopher, Rixson [ws]
1518 Lingoe, Robeson [ws]
1519 Lingoe, Daniell [ws]
1520 Toadvine, Mary
1520 Toadvine, John [ws]
1521 Crouch, Jacob
1521 Crouch, Robert
1522 Crouch, Isaack
1523 Puckam, Richard [ws]
1524 Roach, Ealse
1524 Roach, Charles
1524 Roach, Stephen [ws]
1524 Goldsmith, Anthony [ws]
1524 slave Tom [ws]
1524 slave Pegg [ws]
1524 slave Harry [hs]
1525 Sharp, George
1525 slave Mary

TAX LISTS OF SOMERSET COUNTY: 1730-1740

WICOMICO HUNDRED

1525 slave Fanny
1526 Porter, Joshua
1527 Morris, Judy
1527 Morris, Jacob
   [ws]
1527 Morris, Joseph
   [ws]
1528 Howard, John
1528 Owen, Peter
1529 Hillman, Edward
1530 Jenkins, Jarvis
1531 Christopher,
   Ephraim
1532 Hodge, Richard
1533 Howard, Thomas

1733 TAX LIST [Household number/Name/Remarks]

ANNEMESSEX HUNDRED

1 Hall, Charles
1 slave Dominick
2 Hall, Richd.
2 Wallston, Joy
3 Waters, Abigail
3 Ashton, Thomas
3 slave Davie
4 Benson, Jno.
4 Benson, Solomn.
4 Benson, Geo.
5 Waters, Elisa.
5 Waters, Richd.
5 slave Alexa.
5 slave Hanniball
5 slave Hagar
5 slave Scipio
5 slave Pegg
6 Landen, Henry
7 Cottman, Mary
7 Cottman, Jos.
7 slave Jenny
8 Waters, Jno.
8 Williams, Jno.
8 slave Jack
8 slave Harry
8 slave Will
8 slave Maria
9 Waters, William
9 slave Goliah
9 slave Sambo
9 slave Dinah
10 Tull, Thos.
10 Tull, Wm.
10 slave Quamino
11 Cullen, Edmd.
12 Wharton, Wm.
13 Bettsworth, Jams.
14 Trahern, Jno.
14 Trahern, Jams.
14 Roach, Nathl.
14 slave Jenny
15 Handy, Thos.
16 Handy, Saml.
16 Handy, Samuel, junr.
16 slave Nan
16 slave Cate
17 Curtis, Charles
17 slave Dick
17 slave Tony
18 Long, Saml., junr.
18 slave Cate
19 Stockdell, Edwd.
19 Tayler, Jno.
19 Tomlinson, Henry
20 Lister, Jane
20 Holland, Isaac
20 slave Casar
21 Cattlin, Wm.
21 Cattlin, Robt.
21 slave Harry
22 Williams, Jno.
22 Fenton, Martin
22 Spartman, Geo.
22 slave Sambo
22 slave Mall
23 Beauchamp, Isaac
23 slave Patience
24 Sanders, Richd.
24 Sanders, Thos.
25 Beauchamp, Wm.
26 Beauchamp, Edmd., junr.
27 Boston, Wm.
28 King, Jams.
29 Brimegham, Waltr.
30 Hull, Danl.
31 Marshall, Geo.
31 Marshall, Thos.
32 Porter, Jos.
33 Moor, Thos.
34 King, Robt., majr.
34 slave Mingoe
34 slave Tamar
35 Williams, Thos., senr.mr
35 Williams, Thos., junr.
35 Addams, Jno.
35 indian Andrew
35 slave Dick
35 slave Casar
35 slave Frank
35 slave Sarah
35 slave Geluda
36 Williams, Isaac
36 slave Sampson
37 Planner, Wm., majr.
37 slave Hector
37 slave Watt
37 slave George
37 slave Titus
37 slave Adam
37 slave Tom
37 slave Robin
37 slave Dwam
37 slave Quash
37 slave Hanah
37 slave Glasgow
37 slave Sarah
38 Parker, Saml.
38 Ayres, Jacob
38 Turpin, Wm.
39 Langfort, Benj.
39 Langfort, Jos.
39 Cragin, Paul
40 Dixon, Thos.
40 slave Hary
40 slave Toby
40 slave Dick
40 slave Dinah
40 slave Lilly
41 Smith, Henry
41 Smith, Archa.
42 Dixon, Wm.
42 slave Bess
43 Horsey, Isaac
43 mulatto Jona.
43 slave Dick
43 slave Dorindo
44 Horsey, Nathl.
44 Moses, Edwd.
44 slave Cook
44 slave Quamino
44 slave Prince
44 slave Cate
44 slave Patience
45 Horsey, Saml.
45 Horsey, Smith
46 Horsey, Stephn., junr.
47 Holland, Micha., senr.
47 Holland, Wm.
47 slave Jack
48 Holland, Micha., junr.
48 slave Mall
49 Taylor, Wm.
50 Coulbourn, Wm.
50 Coulbourn, Wm., junr.
50 Coulbourn, Solomn.
50 Coulbourn, Micha.
50 Nicholls, Wm.
50 Colebourn, Saml.
50 slave Quaco
50 slave Lucy
51 Coulbourn, Anne
51 McCane, Patrick
51 slave Abram
52 Coulbourn, Solomn., senr
52 Coulbourn, Solom., junr.
52 slave Guy
52 slave Dido
53 Frazer, Peter
53 slave Maria
54 Miles, Henry
54 slave Phillis
54 slave Dinah
55 Johnston, Jno., senr.
55 Johnston, Jno., junr.
55 Smith, James
55 Dies, Filby
56 Daviss, Jams.
56 Bayly, Thos.
57 Moor, Fran.
57 Moor, Jno.
57 Moor, Isaac

TAX LISTS OF SOMERSET COUNTY: 1730-1740

ANNEMESSEX/BALTIMORE HUNDREDS

58 Doughety, Jno.
59 Lord, Francis
59 Lord, Henry
59 Lord, Randall
59 Lord, Thos.
59 Lord, Alexa.
60 Ward, Stepn., senr.
60 slave Pompey
60 slave Phillis
60 slave Sarah
61 Ward, Saml.
61 Ward, Jno.
61 Moor, Thos.
62 Ward, Stepn., junr.
62 Redding, Peter
63 Ward, Cornelius
64 Riggin, Jno., senr.
64 Riggin, Jno., junr.
64 Riggin, Stepn.
64 Riggin, Jona.
64 Dukes, Robt.
65 Sumers, Jno.
65 Sumers, David
66 Sumers, Thos.
66 Sumers, Jonath.
66 Sumers, Geo.
66 Redding, Jno.
67 Wassells, Jams.
67 Wassells, Ephra.
67 Smith, Robt.
68 Ward, Thos.
68 Ward, Jams.
68 Ward, Jacob
69 Claywell, Selby
70 Bird, David
71 Booth, Roger
72 Grimes, James
73 Dies, Robt.
73 Dies, Danl.
74 Starling, Jno., senr.
74 Starling, Jno. jnr.
74 Starling, Henry
74 Starling, Aaron
74 Obear, Isaac
75 Yankswaw, Jno.
76 Dickinson, Jams.
77 Allen, Jos.
78 Bird, Jos.
78 Cullen, Jacob
78 Booth, Jams.
79 Price, Edwd.
79 Price, Fran.
79 Price, Thos.
79 slave Jenny
80 Roach, Charles
80 slave Jone
81 Roach, Jno.
81 Moor, Wm.
82 Daviss, Sarah
82 Daviss, Jno.
82 slave Harry
82 slave Watt
82 slave Sue
82 slave Jenny
83 Cullen, Henry
84 Bennitt, Henry
84 Ward, Richd.
84 Mackowen, Thos.
85 Willson, Jno.
86 Horsey, Stepn., senr
86 Kelley, Jams.
86 slave Bess
86 slave Jack
87 Bell, Antho., senr.
87 Bell, Antho., junr.
87 Lord, Jno.
88 Bell, Thos.
89 Gunby, Jno.
89 Spybe, Jona.
89 slave Jack
89 slave Cate
90 Townsend, Littleton
90 Johnston, Wm.
91 Kellam, Jno.
91 Kellam, Isaac
91 Kellam, Jno.
91 Dykes, Edwd.
92 Gunby, Kirk
92 Redding, Charles
93 Hern, Edwd.
93 Kendall, Wm.
93 Dukes, Jno.
94 Atkinson, Joshua
94 slave Bess
95 White, Jno., junr.
96 Long, Randl.
96 slave Sibb
96 slave Nan
97 Scott, Robt.
97 Scott, Jno.
97 slave Betty
98 Allen, Henry
99 Cottingham, Charles
99 Cottingham, Jno.
99 Cottingham, Charles
99 Cottingham, Thos.
100 Pewsey, Jno.
101 Langfort, Jos.
101 Langfort, Solm.
102 Scandalon, Edwd.
103 Pewsey, Wm.
104 Adams, David
104 Adams, Thos.
104 Adams, Jacob
105 Willson, Jno.
106 Cahoon, Jno.
106 Cottinghm, Thos.
107 Roach, Saml.
108 Potter, Henry
108 Matthews, Wm.
109 Beauchamp, Edmd.
109 Beauchamp, Robt.
110 Willson, Jno.
111 Conner, Jno.
112 Conner, Wm.
113 Willson, Geo.
114 White, Thos.
114 Wilson, Jos.
115 Wheatley, Sampson
116 Prior, Thos.
116 Taylor, Elias
117 Maddux, Thos.
117 Maddux, Bell
117 slave Kate
118 Outen, Jno., senr.
118 Outen, Jno., junr.
118 slave Bess
119 Trahern, Jams.
120 Long, Danl., senr.
120 Long, David
120 slave Friendship
120 slave Nan
121 Long, Saml., senr.
121 Long, Wm.
121 Long, David
121 Long, Coulbourn
122 Long, Jeoffrey
123 Long, Danl., junr.
124 White, Jno., senr.
124 slave Essex
125 Cary, Francis
126 Bell, Isaac
127 Owen, Elisa.
127 Owen, Phillip
128 Killby, Wm.
129 Hopkins, Geo.
129 Hopkins, Jno.
129 Hopkins, Wm.
130 Horsman, Henry
131 Parker, Isaac
132 Woolf, Henry
133 Mister, Wm.
134 Evans, Jno.
135 Parks, Jno.
135 Parks, Mark
136 Parks, Arthur
136 Parks, Jno.
136 Parks, Arthur
137 Tyler, Thos.
137 Salisbury, Wm.
138 Tyler, Jno., junr.
139 Wheeler, Saml.
140 Redding, Peter

BALTIMORE HUNDRED

141 Fassit, Willm., capt.
141 Fassit, Rous
141 Fassit, Lambord

1733 TAX LIST [Household number/Name/Remarks]

BALTIMORE HUNDRED

141 Silivain, Timothy
141 slave Frank
141 slave Sambo
141 slave Sue
141 slave Dall
142 Tull, John, senr.
142 Tull, John, junr.
142 Weeb, Mark
143 Crapper, Nath.
143 Crapper, Sollomon
144 Hudson, Richard, junr.
144 Lathberey, Arter
145 Hudson, Samuel
146 Laugh House, William
147 Forsight, Thom.
148 Bowen, Rodah
148 Dueit, Nath.
148 Bowen, John
148 Bowen, Willm.
148 slave Quomoney
149 Crapper, Nath., junr.
150 Jenkins, Benjamen
151 Godard, Thom.
152 Quiling, Mary
152 Quiling, Joseph
152 Quiling, Jon.
152 Quiling, Benjmen
153 Whaley, Mary
153 Whalley, Charles
154 Harrison, Willm.
154 Walton, Willm.
155 Evins, Willm.
155 Evins, John
155 Evins, Willm., junr.
156 Hopkins, Josiah
157 Hopkins, John
158 Robinson, Joshua
158 Tingle, Littleton
159 Linch, John, junr.
160 Morgine, Avere
160 Crapper, Edmond
161 Fassitt, John
161 slave Amineydal
161 slave Lues
162 Fassit, Willm.
162 Gay, James
162 Edge, Larince
162 slave Tittes
162 slave Rechal
162 slave Harrey
163 Hudson, John
163 Cupper, Ch.
164 Bernet, James
165 Smith, John, senr.
165 Smith, Robt.
166 Gillstrap, Peter
167 Wayaples, Paul
167 slave Charles
167 slave Dublon
168 Bessey, Willm.
168 Goodrick, Willm.
169 Carrey, Richard
170 Burton, Willm.
170 Burton, John
170 Burton, Josuah
170 Peper, Willm.
170 slave Rachel
170 slave Touss
170 slave Adam
171 Camble, John
172 Runels, Richard
173 Carrey, Willm.
174 Kenney, Joseph
175 Kenney, Stephen
175 Kenney, Laseres
176 Warner, Isaac
177 Short, Edward
178 Lweis, Joseph
179 Lewes, Arter
180 Pittrikine, David
181 Moris, Dinis
182 Ingrom, Jacob
183 Carrey, Tho.
183 Fleatwood, Thomas
184 Warrenton, Tho.
185 Morris, John
186 Jones, Ebenezer
186 slave Jack
187 Weeb, Willm.
188 Day, Willm.
189 Rickards, Jones
189 slave Sarah
190 Rickards, John, junr.
191 Depray, John
192 Onarton, John
192 slave Filles
192 slave Jack
193 Wharton, Hemmon
194 Wharton, Daniel
195 Hazzard, David, senr.
195 Hazzard, David
195 Hazzard, Willm.
195 slave Dinah
196 Clark, Mary
196 Clark, Edward
197 Morris, Sarah
197 Morris, Willm.
198 Godwing, Ceaser, senr.
198 Godwing, Ceaser
198 Godwing, Daniel
199 Dasiey, Tho.
200 Mersey, John
200 Banks, Niblet
201 Mersey, Adkins
202 Evins, John
203 Hall, John
204 Miller, Joseph
204 slave Tom
204 slave Nane
204 slave Chas.
204 slave Jack
205 Parrey, James
206 Hill, Ann
206 Hill, Benjamen
207 Godweing, Michel
207 slave Bess
208 Johnson, Linerard
208 Monk, Willm.
209 Robinson, Tho.
209 Roberts, Alexr.
209 slave Bess
210 Dickson, Sturges
210 Johnson, Jon.
211 Dickson, John
212 Baldrey, Francies
213 Idlot, Benjamon
214 West, Willm.
215 West, George
215 Bernet, John
216 West, Thomas
217 Kerney, Tho.
218 Idlot, John, senr.
218 Gray, John
218 Boweman, Henrey
218 slave Jack
219 Idlot, John, jur.
220 Howard, George, senr.
220 Howard, Nemiah
220 Howard, George
220 Carter, Joseph
220 Macken, Hugh
220 slave Kent
220 slave Bess
221 Hall, Samuel
222 Smith, John, capt.
222 Smith, John
222 Smith, Tho.
222 slave Harrey
222 slave Bess
222 slave Mereah
223 Rickards, John
223 slave Simon
223 slave Boson
223 slave Mall
223 slave Bridget
224 Roberts, Thom.
224 Roberts, Samuel
225 Dirickson, Joseph
226 Hickman, Richard
226 Roberts, Tho.
227 Wise, Mathew
228 Collings, Willm.

TAX LISTS OF SOMERSET COUNTY: 1730-1740

BALTIMORE HUNDRED

229 Mairner, Hennery
230 Robinson, Michel
231 Dickason, Hannah
231 Dickason, Ch.
231 slave Patiance
232 Dirickson, Benjamen
233 Salmon, Willm.
234 Wharton, Frincies
235 Morris, Bibbins
236 Robinson, John
236 Robinson, George
237 Tingle, Hugh, senr.
237 Tingle, Hugh, jur.
238 Woodcraft, Richard
239 Tingle, John
240 Sauls, John
241 Rodgers, Solomon
241 slave Cain
242 Coffing, Tho.
242 Coffing, Joseph
242 Coffing, Jon.
242 Coffing, Thomas
243 Tounsend, Bowman
244 Smith, Jones
245 Linch, Abraham
246 Hudson, David
246 Hudson, George
246 Hudson, Absolom
247 Woodcraft, Mary
247 Woodcraft, Willm.
247 Woodcraft, Tho.
247 Wildgoose, Rich.
248 Miller, Jon.
248 Gooden, Moses
248 slave Prines
248 slave Pigg
249 Alison, John
250 Boden, John
251 Boden, Tho.
252 Boden, Able
253 Weight, Joseph, senr.
253 Weight, Joseph
253 Latchim, Tho.
254 Cabb, Willm.
255 Linch, John, senr.
255 Cabb, Natt.
255 Chambers, Alexr.
256 Purkins, Tho.
257 Holland, John
258 Stevenson, John
258 Stevenson, Willm.
259 Smith, Willm.
260 Clark, Rase
260 Clark, John
260 Clark, Benjmen
261 Wieght, Willm.
262 Powel, Susannah
262 Powel, Charles
263 Hickman, Richard, junr.
264 Fassit, Franklyn
264 Tyre, Robt.
264 slave Nane
265 Mumford, Willm.
266 Rusel, Andw.
267 Showel, Samuel
268 Murrey, James
269 Hallaway, John, senr.
270 Hallay, John, junr.
271 Hallaway, Joseph
272 Mumford, Charles
272 Mumford, Tho.
273 Bradwel, Isaiah
273 Bradwel, Stephen
273 slave Simon
273 slave Adam
273 slave Pender
273 slave Minieo
274 Brittingham, Elesabth
274 Brittingham, Willm.
274 Brittingham, Rob.
275 Gray, Joseph
275 Murrey, Robt.
275 slave Simon
275 slave Quaco
276 Gray, William
277 Powel, Tho.
278 Dalle, Archabald
279 Gray, Tho.
280 Dale, John, senr.
281 Dalle, John, junr.
282 Mumford, James
283 Johnson, David
283 Camble, Sollomon
283 Wilson, John
284 Wilson, Mary
284 Wilson, Isral
285 Linch, Alexr.
286 Hampton, Mary, mrs.
286 slave Jack
286 slave Pigge
286 slave Hannah
287 Manklyn, Richard
288 Fearwell, Tho.
289 Turvile, William, senr.
289 Whalley, John
289 Turvile, Prisgrave
290 Turvile, Willm., junr.
290 slave Joney
291 Kennitt, Martaine
291 Bishop, Bowen
291 Turvile, John
292 Robertson, Andrew
293 Fall, Abraham
294 Fall, John
295 Collings, Tho.
296 Collings, John
296 Racklife, Elias
297 Gault, Robert
297 Gault, Willm.
297 Gault, John
298 Hudson, Willm.
298 Gray, Willm.
299 Hudson, Richard, senr.
299 Gray, John
299 slave Coffey
299 slave Dick
300 Loggwood, Richard
301 Kennett, Willm.
301 Racklife, John
302 Hill, Comfort
302 slave Will
303 Hamlon, Francies
304 Pattey, John
304 Mathews, Willm.
304 slave London
305 Wheler, John, senr.
305 Wheler, John
306 Jons, John
307 Driges, Dibrex
308 Mersey, Willm.
309 Walton, Benjamin
309 slave Nane
310 Mersey, Alexr.
310 slave Jack
310 slave Judah
311 Coller, Petter
311 slave Pompey
311 slave Mall
312 Delaniey, John Patrick
313 Walton, Willm., senr.
313 Walton, Willm.
313 slave Ceaser
313 slave Gloster
313 slave Judah
314 Walton, John, jr.
315 Crapper, Edmond
315 Steel, Augustes
315 slave Dick
315 slave Petter
315 slave Pompey
315 slave Febey
316 Purnel, John
316 Abbett, Willm.
316 Racklife, Charles
316 Racklife, Wrixom
316 Killey, John
316 Watters, Richard
316 Mackcunick, Pattrick
316 slave Will

1733 TAX LIST [Household number/Name/Remarks]

BALTIMORE/BOGERTERNORTON HUNDREDS

316 slave Toney
316 slave Dall
316 slave Mall
317 Marshel, Isaac
317 Morris, John
317 slave Ben
317 slave Dinah
317 slave Bass
318 Whalley, Willm.
319 Hollond, Richard
320 Prodox, Tho.
321 Bradfoot, Natt.
321 slave Toney
322 Gilland, John
322 slave Sambo
322 slave Febey
322 slave Floro
323 Woods, Robert
324 Conner, Daniel
325 Liptroott, John
326 Racklife, Char.
326 Peel, Thorogood
326 slave Robbin
326 slave Sarrah
326 slave Katte
327 Alford, David
328 Newbold, John
328 slave Cato
329 Wallice, Tho.
329 slave Hector
330 Camble, John
331 Simpson, Richard
332 Taylor, Walter
333 Hall, Joseph
334 Joseph, Fredrik
335 West, Thomas
336 Jefferson, Richard
337 Juitt, Wm.
337 slave Ned
338 Hopkins, Samuel, junr.
338 Bradford, Adam
338 Conner, Michall

BOGERTERNORTON HUNDRED
339 Whittington, Wm., snr.
339 Whittington, Wm., jnr.
339 Whittington, Suthey
339 8 slaves
340 Sebry, William
340 5 slaves
341 Spence, Adam, snr.
341 2 slaves
342 Claywell, Tho.
343 Porter, Wm.
343 Patrick, Rodger
344 Atkins, John

345 Bishop, John, snr.
345 Bishop, Joseph
345 Bishop, David
346 Bishop, Wm.
346 Bishop, Benjamain
346 Houten, John
346 Houten, Tho.
347 Selbey, John
347 Cusadey, Owen
347 2 slaves
348 Edwards, Benoney
349 Pepper, John
350 Victer, Magladen
350 Victer, James
351 Purnall, Thomas
351 Purnall, Benjamain
351 4 slaves
352 Lowe, George
353 Richardson, Charles
353 Parker, Philip
353 slave
354 Richardson, Robt.
354 Lindall, Robt.
355 Braton, Samuell
355 Braton, Wm.
356 Richardson, James
357 Braten, Samuell, jnr.
358 Scholfield, Joseph
358 Scholfield, John
358 Gabe, Joseph
358 2 slaves
359 Purnall, Elisha
359 2 slaves
360 Holestone, John
361 Holestone, Wm.
361 Holestone, Charles
362 McCaley, John
363 Brittingham, Jeremiah
364 Brittingham, Wm.
364 Brittingham, Soloman
365 Brittingham, Isaac
365 Brittingham, Nathan
365 slave
366 Davis, Wm., sea side
366 slave
367 Stevens, Samuel
368 Shockley, John
369 Ennes, Wm.
369 Ducks, Tho.
370 Ennis, Nath.
371 Ennis, Mary
371 Ennis, Cornelius
371 Ennis, Saml.
372 Porter, Joseph
372 slave
373 Williams, John

373 Townsand, Wm.
374 Tull, Richard
375 Purnall, Katharine
375 Purnall, Walter
375 2 slaves
376 Williams, Prasgrave
376 Bisick, Absollam
377 Beaderd, Wm.
378 Beckeets, Peter
379 Hader, Anthoney
380 Murray, Duncan
380 4 slaves
381 Donelson, John
381 Tuftin, Wm.
381 Davis, Lazarus
381 Hambelton, Wm.
381 Kelley, Nicholas
381 3 slaves
382 Railey, Tho.
382 Hill, Johnson
383 Whaley, Wm., snr.
384 Lindall, Peter
385 Nock, John
385 Burton, John
385 Nock, Nehemiah
385 2 slaves
386 Frankling, Edward
386 Frankling, Charles
386 slave
387 Lay, John
387 slave
388 Evans, Elias
389 White, John, point
389 2 slaves
390 Gillitt, John
391 Hutson, Denis
392 Smith, John
393 Bowin, Wm.
394 Handcock, Daniell
395 Bishop John, son Henry
395 Chansler, George
396 Sherley, James
397 Pointer, Wm.
398 Hall, Robert
399 Denis, Wm.
400 Pointer, Tho.
400 Pointer, Ratcklife
400 Borman, John
400 Pointer, Wm.
401 Smock, Henery
401 Smock, John
402 Blizard, Richard
403 Selbey, Parker
403 Griffin, Oliver
404 Penewell, John
405 Heather, Epheraim, snr.
405 Heather, Epheraim, jnr.

TAX LISTS OF SOMERSET COUNTY: 1730-1740

BOGERTERNORTON HUNDRED

405 2 slaves
406 Gahagun, Edward
407 Handcock, Wm.
408 Crapper, Ebenezar, snr.
409 Crapper, Ebenezar, jnr.
410 Crapper, Wrixam
411 Jarman, Robt.
412 Jones, Joseph
413 Swaine, Wm.
414 Jarman, Wm.
415 Hammond, Edward
416 Hammond, John
416 Baswell, John
417 Jarman, George
418 Clark, Daniell
419 Duncan, Tho.
420 Purnall, Mathew
420 Hammond, Jacob
421 Hammond, Isaac
422 Jarman, John, snr.
422 Jarman, John, jnr.
423 Brown, John
424 Jones, George
425 Ratcklife, Charles
425 2 slaves
426 Webb, Elisha
427 Weeb, Samuell
428 Bowin, Littleton
428 slave
429 Tompson, James
430 Bowin, John
431 Truitt, George, accomak
431 Truitt, George
431 slave
432 Truitt, Henry
433 Morris, Wm.
434 Truitt, George, son James
435 Morris, Joseph
436 Burbage, John
437 Mitchell, Thomas
437 slave
438 Fletcher, Tho., mr.
438 Johnson, Tho.
438 3 slaves
439 Truitt, George, son George
439 Truitt, John
439 2 slaves
440 Stephinsin, Hugh, mr.
440 Travis, Richard
441 Mumford, James
442 Truitt, Wm.
443 Truitt, Philip
443 Davis, Wm.

444 Truitt, George, son Ph.
445 Mumford, George
446 Dreaden, John
447 Stevenson, James
448 English, Tho.
449 Braten, James
450 Godfrey, Charles
450 slave
451 Denis, Donick
452 Deverix, John
452 Prier, Weeb
452 slave
453 Hall, Wm.
453 Hall, Adam
453 2 slaves
454 Johnson, Afriadoze
454 Johnson, George
454 Johnson, John
454 Johnson, Tho.
454 Johnson, Samuell
454 slave
455 Hodge, Robt.
455 slave
456 Richards, Wm.
457 Townsand, Jeremiah
457 Townsand, Brickhouse
457 2 slaves
458 Gornwell, John
458 Lewes, Wm.
458 slave
459 Smith, Wm.
459 Harman, Zachariah
460 Grear, Ursula
460 Harman, Wm.
461 Midsley, Tho.
461 Baynom, Bartholemew
462 Simpson, Wm.
462 Simpson, Tho.
462 Hill, Richard
462 2 slaves
463 Williams, Argulus
464 Crapper, Nehemiah
465 Davis, Edward
466 Tull, Benjamain
466 Townsand, Jeremiah
467 Templin, John
468 Timmons, Francies
469 Timmons, John
470 Timmons, Tho.
471 Timmons, Wm.
472 Timmons, Samuell
473 Timmons, Aron
474 Timmons, Joseph
475 Timmons, James
476 Lee, John, snr.
476 Lee, John, jnr.
477 Smith, John Truitt
477 Evans, Powell

478 Stephens, Wm.
479 Collings, Thomas
480 Tayler, Joseph
480 Tayler, Wm.
481 Jones, John
482 Walton, Richard
483 Evans, John
483 Evans, Ebenezer
483 Evans, Larance
483 slave
484 Warrin, Nicholas
484 Gray, Nicholas
485 Warrin, Robert
485 Denis, Wm.
486 Dasey, John
487 Ironshire, Isaac
487 slave
488 Beaderd, Richard
489 Powell, Samuell
490 Tingle, Daniell
490 Evans, Wm.
491 Evans, Gamage
492 Williams, Tho. Nat.
492 Williams, Sam.
493 Bradford, John
494 Bradford, Wm.
495 Hader, Warrin
496 Truitt, George, son Job
496 Truitt, Nehemiah
497 Spence, Adam, jnr.
497 Woods, John
497 3 slaves
498 Woods, Wm.
499 Hook, Wm.
500 Truitt, Joseph
501 Wilcox, George
502 Smith, Abraham
502 Pointer, John
503 Robison, Hanah
503 Robison, Wm.
504 Murray, John
504 Brown, Wm.
505 Slinger, Tho., snr.
505 Slinger, Tho., jnr.
506 Denis, Solomon
507 Clark, Charles
508 Rathbone, Robert
509 Scott, Mark
510 Rownd, James
510 Stanton, Wm.
510 4 slaves
511 Waters, Patrick
512 Pointer, Nathaniell
513 Pointer, Elias
514 Rownd, Edward
514 2 slaves
515 Murray, David
516 Parker, Samuell
516 5 slaves

1733 TAX LIST [Household number/Name/Remarks]

BOGERTERNORTON/MANOKIN HUNDREDS

517 Parker, Charles
518 Parker, Philip
519 Shohanis, Wm.
519 Canady, Simon
520 Bridgints, Emanull
521 Davis, Robt., jnr.
522 Davis, Tho.
523 Davis, Robt., snr.
523 Davis, Wm.
523 Davis, Ishmaell
523 Davis, Benjamain
524 Parker, George
525 Davis, Wm., snr.
525 Davis, Philip
525 Davis, Samuell
525 Davis, George
526 Porter, John
527 Porter, James
528 Truitt, Saml.
528 slave
529 Collins, Mary
529 Collins, John
530 Collins, Wm.
531 Penewell, Wm.
531 Penewell, George
532 Penewell, Charles
533 Penewell, Tho.
534 Penewell, Richard
535 Williams, Jonathan
535 Williams, John
535 Williams, Lettilton
536 Atkins, Stanton
537 Jarman, Job
538 Truitt, James
539 Raine, Mathew
540 Tayler, William Rigin
541 Jarman, Henery
541 Angeloe, James
542 Burbage, Edward

MANOKIN HUNDRED
543 Wilson, David
543 Davis, Jno.
543 Heath, Abraham
543 slave Jacob
543 slave Cudgo
543 slave Harry
543 slave Josey
543 slave Kent
543 slave Pompey
543 slave Nanny
543 slave Holladay
544 Wilson, Samuel
544 Swift, Richard
544 Thompson, Joseph
544 slave Peter
544 slave Murmudo
544 slave Will
544 slave Naney
544 slave Hannah
544 slave Moll
544 slave Moll
544 slave Bess
544 slave Sarah
545 Fountain, Nicholes
545 Hall, Wm.
545 B[row]n, Alex.
545 slave Charles
545 slave London
545 slave Sam
546 Turpin, John
546 Turpin, Willm.
546 Fordred, Willm.
546 slave Coffy
546 slave Toby
546 slave Nanny
547 Hall, Alex., junr.
548 Benson, George
548 Benson, Mathias
548 Jones, George
549 Elzey, John, senr.
549 Elzey, John, junr.
549 Tate, Francis
549 slave Casar
549 slave Sambo
549 slave Bess
549 slave Nanny
549 slave Judith
549 slave Sibb
550 Phebus, George, senr.
550 Phebus, Samuell
550 slave Juno
551 Elzey, Sarah, mrs.
551 Chambers, Edwd.
551 Caldwell, William
551 Elzey, Arnold
551 slave Edward
551 slave Jacob
551 slave Jack
551 slave Ann
551 slave Belinda
551 slave Hannah
552 Phebus, George, junr.
553 Turpin, Wm., junr.
553 Floyd, John
553 slave Will
553 slave Frost
553 slave George
553 slave Buson
553 slave Penelope
553 slave Moll
554 Denwood, Thos.
554 Manwering, Abraham
554 slave Cugo
554 slave Munday
554 slave Will
554 slave Grace
554 slave Thamar
555 Ballard, Henry
555 Campbell, Jno.
555 Smith, Thos., sailor
555 slave Casar
555 slave Venture
555 slave Jenny
555 slave Belinda
556 Ballard, Ellenor, mrs.
556 slave Betty
556 slave Mary
557 Dorman, Wm.
558 Fountain, Thos.
558 Tull, John
558 slave Morey
558 slave Hercules
559 Carns, John
560 Roberts, Joseph
561 Mitchel, Ann
561 Mitchel, Thomas
561 Mitchel, Isaac
561 slave Mungo
561 slave Sarah
562 Leebruse, Benj.
563 Revell, Randall
563 slave Toby
563 slave Harry
563 slave Martha
564 Roach, Wm.
564 slave Kitt
564 slave Passy
565 Walston, Bows
565 Hill, John
565 Davis, Arthur, junr.
566 Tillman, Joseph
566 slave London
567 Niblett, Burnett
568 Dear, Robert
569 ODear, Stephen, junr.
570 Furnace, Ann
570 slave Lappo
571 Bowler, Wm.
572 Collins, Wm.
573 Furnace, James
573 slave Tom
574 Layfield, [Robert]
574 Layfield, Wm.
575 Pope, James
576 Strawbridge, James
576 slave Davy
576 slave Coffy
576 slave Hago
576 slave Asbell
577 Stitt, Archibald
578 Stuart,, revd. mr.
578 slave Tom
579 Heman, Wm.

TAX LISTS OF SOMERSET COUNTY: 1730-1740

MANOKIN HUNDRED

579 Heman, Benj.
580 Goldsmith, John
581 Smith, Magdalain
581 slave Pearson
582 Smith, Robert
582 Smith, Thomas
583 Dorman, Matthew, senr.
583 Dorman, Wm.
583 Wetherby, John
583 slave Jack
583 slave Doll
584 Dorman, Michal
585 Owens, John
586 King, Duncan
587 Hardy, Joseph
588 Bozman, Wm., senr.
588 Jarvise, Willm.
588 slave Dozy
588 slave Bess
589 Bosman, William, secundus
589 Bosman, William, jr.
590 Davis, Arthur
591 McDaniel, David
592 Tull, Samuel
593 Ford, Absalom
594 Sharp, Benj.
594 Jenkins, Jno.
594 Walston, Henry
594 Brian, Thos.
595 Maddox, Lazzarus
595 slave Coffy
595 slave Jo
595 slave Dick
596 Maddox, Thos.
596 slave Will
596 slave Sue
597 Willis, Barnaby
598 Turpin, Wm., senr.
598 Abbit, John
598 slave Tom
598 slave Jack
598 slave Feby
598 slave Phillis
599 Laws, James
600 Brown, David
600 Smith, John
600 slave Cudgo
601 Smith, Thos.
602 Walston, Wm.
602 Walston, Joseph
603 Shaw, Jonathan
604 Lindow, James
604 slave Bess
604 slave Moses
605 Moe, John
605 Ringrow, Daniel
605 Wilks, John

606 Bosman, John, senr.
606 Bosman, John, junr.
607 Bosman, George, junr.
607 slave Sambo
608 Jones, Wm.
608 slave Benj.
609 Horner, George, junr.
610 Robertson, James
610 Robertson, John
610 slave Jack
610 slave Tobee
610 slave Nero
610 slave Ceasar
610 slave Prew
610 slave Diana
610 slave Phillis
611 McClamy, Wm.
611 Hamon, Charles
611 Henderson, Wm.
611 slave Nero
611 slave Frank
612 Burgin, Daniel
613 Denniston, Rober
614 Rigsbee, Lewis
614 McDannish, Randall
614 slave Ally
615 Shank, Benj.
615 Spence, John
616 Morgan, Walter
617 Crowder, Francis
617 Cunningham, Thos.
617 Larren, Teague
618 Horner, George, senr.
618 Horner, James
618 Horner, Martilda
619 Malcolm, Robert
619 Malcolm, George
620 Heath, Wm.
621 Polk, Wm.
621 Polk, David
621 Gray, Alen
621 slave Totan
621 slave Abner
621 slave Hannah
622 Polk, James
623 Fountain, Michal, junr.
624 Long, Sollomon
624 Spruens, John
624 Mathews, Thomas
625 Matthews, Patrick
626 McGraa, James
627 Munro, Alex.
628 Chain, Alex.
629 Calverson, Wm.
630 Wilson, Robert
630 slave Sambo

631 Wilcocks, John
632 Brooks, Patrick
633 Gray, Thomas
633 McClamy, Woney
633 slave Ishmael
634 ODear, Stephen, senr.
634 ODear, Furnace
635 Haley, Timothy
636 Bosman, George, senr.
636 Tanner, John
636 slave Frank
637 Heath, Jacob
638 Fisher, Bartholemew
638 slave John
638 slave Will
638 slave Beck
639 Jones, Wm., monokin
639 Tate, Thos.
639 slave Guy
639 slave Eve
639 slave Mumudo
639 slave Anthony
640 Gillis, Joseph
640 Jones, Mitchell
640 Erving, John
640 slave --neman
640 slave Bassen
640 slave Jack
640 slave Rose
641 Denwood, George
641 Hues, Wm.
641 slave Ned
642 Brown, Thos.
642 Brown, David
642 Staples, James
642 slave Codgo
642 slave Ben
643 Ballard, Jarvis, senr.
643 Ballard, Wm.
643 Ballard, Jarvis, junr.
643 slave Nanny
643 slave Rose
644 Woolford, John
644 Muidman, Thomas
644 slave Sampson
644 slave Rose
644 slave Malbrow
644 slave Tamar
645 Knott, Isaac
646 Diamond, Richard
647 Tunstall, John
647 Parris, Jarman
647 slave Somersett
647 slave Tom
647 slave Will
647 slave Leverpool

1733 TAX LIST [Household number/Name/Remarks]

MANOKIN/MATTAPANY HUNDREDS

647 slave Freeman
647 slave Dick
647 slave Isable
647 slave Diana
647 slave Lowhill
647 slave Pompey
647 slave Norris
647 slave Tomboy
647 slave Rose
647 slave Siby
647 slave Dick
647 slave Hollons
648 King, Robert, col.
648 King, Nehemiah
648 Butt, John
648 Luwes, Wm.
648 McCallian, Hugh
648 Kindall, Patrick
648 slave Fortune
648 slave Toby
648 slave Cesar
648 slave Cesar, junr.
648 slave Josey
648 slave Mannary
648 slave Joe
648 slave Betty
648 slave Moll
648 slave Judah
648 slave Nan
648 slave Dido
648 slave Dido, junr.
649 Tull, Joshua
649 Tull, Richard
649 slave Moll
650 Barns, Robert
651 Butler, Nathaniel
652 Miles, Samel
652 slave Dick
652 slave Ben
653 Madux, Daniel
653 slave Harrey
653 slave Harry, junr.
654 Tull, Solomon
654 Tull, Thomas
655 Miles, Wm.
656 Young, John
657 Shepherd, Martin
658 Hicks, Wm.
659 King, Whittington
659 King, John
659 slave Toney
659 slave Harry
659 slave Tom
659 slave Parsey
660 Chambers, Richard
660 Collins, Price
660 Fisher, Henry
660 slave Betty
661 Horsey, Revell
661 slave Nick

662 Horsey, Wm.
662 slave Cudgo
663 Eskridge, Wm.
663 slave Ned
664 Wilson, [James]
665 Bannaster, Thomas
665 OBryan, Richard
666 Right, Abell
666 Right, John
667 Revell, Charles
667 Hall, John
667 Davis, John
667 Right, Randal
667 slave Naney
668 Horsey, John
668 Killey, John
668 Whealey, Wm.
668 slave Peter
668 slave Moll
669 Smith,, widow, back cree
669 Hopkins, Benj.
670 West, Anthony
670 Cantwell, Thos.
671 Gibbins, John, senr.
671 Gibbins, Thomas
671 Surrey, Job
672 Gibbins, John, junr.
673 Tillman, Aaron
674 Thompson, Andrew
674 Thompson, Wm.
674 Sanders, Richard
674 Thompson, Jno.
674 slave Cesar
674 slave Rose
675 Gray, Wm.
675 Grinless, Wm.
675 Morrah, Richard
676 Gray, John
676 Gray, Thos.
676 slave Hannah
677 Finch, John
677 slave Jamey
677 slave Marriah
678 Heath, Dorman
679 Heath, Abraham
679 Heath, Abraham, junr.
680 King, Capwell
680 Mackinteer, Daniel
680 slave Major
680 slave Tite
680 slave Paragate
680 slave Pompy
680 slave Jack
680 slave Grace
680 slave Kate
680 slave Rose

681 Brown, Sidney
682 West, Wm.
683 Fitzgerrald, Peter
683 slave Tom
684 McGra, Rob.
685 Lockwood, Wm.
686 McGra, Wm.
687 Brown, Terill
688 Spicer, Phillip
689 Wallston, Thomas

MATTAPANY HUNDRED

690 Pope, John
690 Pluder, Joseph
690 slave Tom
690 slave Book
690 slave Jiney
690 slave Rose
691 Sturgis, John, jun.
692 Sturgis, Dainell
692 Reid, John
693 Selby, Philip
693 Selby, Matthw.
693 Selby, Daniell
693 Selby, Philip
693 Selby, Wm.
693 slave Sangro
693 slave Pimey
693 3 slaves
694 Craford, Andrew
694 Craford, John
695 Selby, Parker
695 Reid, Walter
695 Marchment, Charles
695 indian Jack
695 slave Glorstor
695 slave Tamer
696 Dreaden, John
697 Pope, Samll.
698 Evens, John
699 Shihea, Petter
700 Richardson, John
700 slave Rachall
701 Hosiear, Samll., jnr.
701 slave Peague
702 Hopkins, Samll., senr.
702 Hopkins, Samll., jur.
703 Hopkins, Wm.
704 Johnson, Wm.
704 Johnson, Hixakiah
704 Taylor, Thos.
705 Johnson, Peter
706 Johnson, John
707 Hopkins, Nathall.
707 Ayars, Henry
707 Walker, John
707 slave Abnor

TAX LISTS OF SOMERSET COUNTY: 1730-1740

MATTAPANY/MONIE HUNDREDS

708 Steain, James
709 Hopkins, Matthew
709 Ayars, Richd.
709 Nickorles, Marthias
709 Ayars, Harson
710 Scarbrough, John
710 Desen, Gorge
710 Houlston, Benja.
710 Wise, Ezkiell
710 slave Dick
710 slave Naney
711 Milburne, Thomas
712 Slingor, Thos., senr.
712 Slingor, Thos.
713 Nealson, Wm.
713 Nealson, James
714 Braton, Wm.
714 Westrons, Mickel
714 slave
715 Scott, Robert
715 Scott, Wm.
715 Scott, Robert, jur.
716 Tarr, Samll.
716 Hudson, Jonathun
717 Turner, Wm.
718 Nuten, Thos., senr.
718 Nuten, Thos., jur.
719 Nuten, Jonathun
720 Watson, Peter
720 Hanlen, Pattrick
721 Hill, Abraham
722 Duberley, Thomas
722 Pain, Jos.
723 Coner, Richd.
724 Hodgson, Roling
724 Hodge, Robert
724 slave Jo
725 Hall, Gorge
726 Davis, Charles
726 Wimbror, Paul
727 Benston, Joshua
728 Wattson, Luke
729 Allen, Joseph
730 Chapman, Humphry
731 Henderson, Bishup
731 Tomson, Andrew
732 Walker, John
732 slave Jack
733 Wagaman, Jacob
733 Wagaman, Ephram
733 2 slaves
734 Claywell, Peter, ser.
734 Claywell, Ezekiell
734 slave Sambo
734 slave Gorge

734 slave Judey
735 Claywell, Peter, jur.
736 Willett, Ambrus
736 Willett, Wm.
737 Pepper, Wm.
738 Brownbill, Natha.
739 Pepper, Tobias
740 Wattson, Moses
741 Wattson, Robert, jur.
742 Porter, Clintuck
743 Tarr, Michell
744 Allen, John
745 Wattson, Robert, senr.
745 Wattson, Charles
745 slave
746 Rusell, Cuthbud
746 Wattson, James
746 Wattson, Uriah
747 Walton, Fisher
747 McRa[ll], John
747 slave Peter
747 slave Moll
748 Jones, John
749 Robins, Eliz., widow
749 slave Nead
749 slave Jack
749 slave Hanah
749 slave Sarah
750 Purnell, John
750 Young, Gorge
750 slave Tobey
750 slave Tom
750 slave Nimrod
750 slave Sarah
751 Guttridge, Pattrick
751 Guttridge, James
752 Sturgis, Richd.
753 Taylor, Rodger
753 Taylor, John
754 Beachbord, Wm.
755 Mallon, Christopher
756 Taylor, Philip
757 Wise, Thomas
758 Hill, Johnson
758 Hill, Eilsha
758 Gurley, Gorge
758 Richardson, John
759 Hill, Hutten
759 slave Dick
760 Holland, Nehemiah
760 Taylor, Elias
760 Ardis, Hazard
761 Walton, Steven, senr.
761 Walton, Stephen
762 Harman, Emanewell

762 Roberts, John
763 Benitt, Mary, widow
763 Lenzey, James
764 Ducare, Wm.
765 Vezey, Charles
766 McHendery, Charles
766 McHendry, Walter
767 Arnold, Wm.
768 Answorth, Wm.
768 Answorth, Jobe
769 Brownbill, Hendry
770 Hall, John
771 Gill, John
772 Meason, Abraham
773 Holland, Benja.
773 Williams, Thos.
773 slave Jeney
774 Wattson, John
774 Fisher, Balley
775 Davis, Charles
776 Samons, Benoney
777 Pope, George
777 slave Will
777 slave Bes
778 Booth, Wm.
778 Vohan, Wm.
779 Veneatson, Willums
780 Ceary, Solomon
781 Cord, Wm., senr.
781 Cord, Wm., junr.
781 Cord, Arthur
781 slave Jeney
782 Maxfeild, Joseph
782 3 slaves
783 ODewey, Thomas
784 Hill, Robt.

MONIE HUNDRED

785 Fiddey, Randall
786 Jones, Richard
787 Winsor, Lazarus
787 Winsor, John
788 Adams, Edward
789 Row, Thos.
789 Jones, Charles
789 Hopkins, George
790 Row, Joseph
791 Lawes, Thos.
791 slave Jack
791 slave Marea
792 Dugless, John
793 Miller, John
793 Miller, James
794 Miller, Thos.
795 Lawes, John
795 Rose, Saml.
795 slave Prince
795 slave Lunea
795 slave Ceasar
796 Jones, Lewis

1733 TAX LIST [Household number/Name/Remarks]

MONIE HUNDRED

796 Jones, Saml.
796 slave Jack
796 slave Ceasar
796 slave Hanah
796 slave Moll
797 Martin, George
798 Fargarrell, Edmd.
799 White, John
800 Harriss, Jeremiah
801 Williams, Jeremiah
802 Waller, George
803 Bassell, Thos.
804 Husk, John
805 Shores, Edw.
806 White, Frans.
806 White, Jno.
806 White, Thos.
807 Winsor, John
808 Walliss, Mathew
808 slave Sibb
809 Walliss, Richard
809 Walliss, Thos.
809 Walliss, James
809 Walliss, David
809 slave Ceasar
809 slave Bess
810 Roberts, Edw.
810 slave Jeffery
811 Roberts, Ranshaw
811 Roberts, John
812 Pollock, Joseph
812 Oneal, John
812 Macdaniel, Owen
813 Wright, Thos.
813 Wright, Hen.
814 Shores, Jno.
814 Shores, Wm.
815 Stoughton, Wm., esq.
815 Low, Chas.
815 slave Bursy
815 slave Cato
815 slave Symon
815 slave Fender
815 slave Sabrica
816 Wye, Wm., junr.
816 slave Jemy
816 slave Alix
816 slave Scipio
816 slave Moll
816 slave Donleer
817 Waller, John
817 slave Jane
818 Irving, George
818 slave Tobey
818 slave Coffee
818 slave Jeney
818 slave Jane
819 Willson, John
820 Martin, Thos.

821 Waller, Mager
821 Waller, Wm.
821 Waller, Nelson
822 Lawes, Robert
822 Skeen, Robert
822 Lawes, Panter
822 Lawes, Wm.
822 slave Bogo
822 slave Jack
822 slave Samson
823 Jones, Robert
823 Jones, Geo.
823 Jones, Thos.
823 slave London
823 slave Amok
823 slave Dick
823 slave Jean
823 slave Rachell
824 Fosque, Benjamin
825 Downes, Geo.
825 slave Tobey
825 slave Frank
826 Dashiell, Thos.
826 Dashiell, Levin
826 Harison, John
826 Chambers, Saml.
826 slave Jack
826 slave Will
826 slave Hary
826 slave Jack
826 slave Jane
826 slave Bess
826 slave Marando
826 slave Tamer
827 Jones, Wm.
827 Miles, John
827 slave Will
827 slave Jane
827 slave Sue
828 Rork, John
829 Gale, Betty, mrs. for
829 Kenny, John
829 slave Joe
829 slave Ceaser
829 slave Stephen
829 slave Jacob
829 slave Will
829 slave Dublin
829 slave Peater
829 slave Oved
829 slave Janey
829 slave Rose
829 slave Palina
829 slave Bess
829 slave Pheby
829 slave Palina
829 slave Vilet
829 slave Jamey
830 Gale, George

830 Maughone, Christopher
830 Tolinson, John
830 slave Limas
830 slave Sipeo
830 slave Jamey
830 slave Jack
830 slave Parthena
830 slave Nany
830 slave Sarah
831 Hobbs, Mathelli
832 Hobbs, Joy
833 Hobbs, Thos.
834 Magrach, John
834 Campbell, James
835 Follows, John
835 Gellasibey, Tarrance
836 Newman, Henry
836 Luke, Williamson
837 Dorman, Henry
838 Metlain, James
839 Mungar, John
840 Mode, Peter
841 Jones, James
841 Jones, John
841 Duhigg, Walter
841 Brooksher, Manaring
841 slave Sambo
841 slave Sib
841 slave Moll
842 Durham, Thos.
843 Cary, Thos.
844 Covington, John
844 slave Sambo
844 slave Cookoo
844 slave Bess
844 slave Dinah
845 Jones, Daniell
845 slave Whitehaven
845 slave Doll
846 Hickson, Joseph
847 Gale, Mathias
847 slave Relph
847 slave Sarah
848 Letherbery, John
848 slave Sambo
848 slave Samson
848 slave Tone
848 slave Dampe
848 slave Bess
848 slave Bridgett
848 slave Rose
848 slave Nane
848 slave Nane
849 Marraugh, John
850 Dorman, Henry
850 unnamed/slave
851 Dorman, John
852 Covington, Thomas
852 unnamed/slave

TAX LISTS OF SOMERSET COUNTY: 1730-1740

NANTICOKE HUNDRED

853 Donoho, Nathanell
854 Bushop, Henry
855 Manlove, Mannuell
855 slave Quoco
856 Polke, John
856 slave Atty
857 Owens, Robt.
857 slave Cate
858 Polk, Charles
859 Wille, John
860 Newbold, Frances
860 slave Ame
861 Neall, John
862 Owens, Peter
863 Bacer, Wm.
864 Thorns, Elxdr.
865 Thorns, Edward
866 Daughters, William
866 Daughters, Wm.
867 Hickman, James
868 Phips, John
869 Smith, Stephen
870 O[z]burn, John
871 Benston, Wm.
872 Whinwrite, Willm.
872 Whinwrite, John
873 Cleften, Geo.
873 Cleften, Geo., jnr.
874 Sharp, John
874 Kille, John
875 Ingram, Abraham
875 Ingrom, Davd.
875 Ingram, Isaac
876 Samuells, Peter
877 Samuells, Richd.
878 Collings, Andrew
879 Lankdell, John
880 Kinigin, Arther
881 Ingram, Robt.
882 Smith, David
883 Rowell, Thos.
884 Dodriell, James
885 Shirman, Wm.
886 Beniett, Edward
887 Twyford, John
887 Kelley, Daniell
888 Tuley, Stephen
889 Tuley, Stephen, senr.
889 Tuley, Benj.
890 Roads, Timothy
891 Macdowell, John
892 Green, Richd.
893 West, James
893 Burkim, Roger
894 Piper, Wm.
894 Ackworth, Henry
894 slave Benn
894 slave Sambo
894 slave Nell
894 slave Sara
894 slave Rose
895 Harvey, John
896 Williams, Charles
897 Potter, Josefus
898 Short, Edward, senr.
898 Short, John
899 Tindell, Charles
900 Mezeck, John
900 Mezeck, Geo.
900 Mezeck, Obediah
901 Ginkins, Thos.
902 Johnson, Thos.
902 Murah, John
903 Neall, James
903 slave Dino
904 Mercy, Wm.
904 Mercy, Thos.
905 Parsons, Charles
905 Morris, Michell
906 Sherman, Peter
906 Christopher, Rickson
907 Wingate, Phillip
908 [M]elson, Joseph
909 King, Phillip
910 King, Willm.
911 Right, Edwd.
912 Dolbey, Peter
912 Isaac, John
913 Smith, John
914 Nould, Edmond
914 Nould, Richd.
915 Walter, Henry
915 Walter, Daniell
915 Walter, John
916 Hufington, Richd.
917 Roberson, John
917 slave Swo
918 Dean, Charles
919 Hufington, Thos.
920 Marvell, Thos.
921 Nuten, Christopher
922 Nuten, John
923 Rotten, Josiah
924 Noble, Isaac
925 Wooten, Edward
925 Tatman, James
926 Dashiell, Joseph
926 Sheradan, Daniell
926 slave David
926 slave Randell
926 slave Bess
926 slave Coffe
927 Dashiell, Geo.
927 Dashiell, Robt.
927 slave Harre
927 slave Tamo
927 slave Dido
927 slave Cago
927 slave Nerow
928 Benston, Thos.
928 Cooper, John
928 slave Will
929 Collier, Betts
930 Gale, John
930 slave Mese
930 slave Barshe
930 slave Rose
930 slave Moll
930 slave Jude
931 Dashiell, Wm.
932 Wooten, John
933 Callaway, Wm.
933 Callaway, John
934 Tomson, Geo.
935 Lingoe, Daniell
936 James, John
937 Hozeir, Mathew
938 Williams, John
939 Cooper, James
940 Polke, John
941 Stephens, John
942 Callaway, John
943 Callaway, Edward
944 Callaway, John
945 Waller, Nathanell
945 Waller, John
945 Gibens, Alexdr.
946 Waller, Thos.
946 Waller, Nathanell
946 Waller, Thos.
946 Waller, Robt.
946 Inglish, Robt.
947 Kinne, William
948 Paremore, Thos.
948 Paremore, Thos.
949 Benston, Henry
949 Benston, Geo.
949 Benston, Henry
950 Benston, William
951 Godard, John
951 Evans, William
952 Caldwell, John
952 OSarvand, William
952 slave Sambo
953 Caldwell, Patrick
954 Paremore, Mathew
955 More, John
956 Jones, Williams
957 Caldwell, Thos.
958 Callaway, Peter
959 Harvey, William
959 Hange, John
960 Rickords, John, jur.
961 Rusell, James
961 Rusell, Thos.
961 Rider, Hetley

1733 TAX LIST [Household number/Name/Remarks]

NANTICOKE HUNDRED

962 Relph, Thos.	998 Green, Ezecell	1027 Mercey, Henrey
962 Shirman, Peter	999 Inglish, Wm.	1028 Wales, John
963 Rusell, James, junr.	1000 Nicholson, Richd.	1029 Young, Charles
964 Goslin, James	1000 Twiley, Geo.	1029 Boyes, John
965 Rider, Richd.	1001 Elenworth, Robt.	1030 Cordrey, Edward
965 Rider, Wilson	1002 Ackworth, Samll.	1030 Cordry, David
965 slave Twoler	1002 slave woman	1031 Hufington, Jonathan
966 Richardson, Wm.	1003 Collings, Geo.	1032 Hufington, John
967 Voyhn, William	1004 Nicholson, Betty	1032 Polson, William
968 Deane, John	1004 slave Cook	1032 slave Iagoe
969 Shirman, Thos.	1005 Read, John	1032 slave Jeney
970 Williams, Richd.	1005 Read, John	1032 slave Plesent
971 Dashiell, James	1005 Read, Zacuriah	1033 Killiam, Edward
971 slave Roben	1005 slave Peg	1033 Killiam, John
971 slave Will	1006 Richardson, John	1033 Hicks, Wm.
971 slave Will	1006 Richardson, Wm.	1033 Goslin, Ezecell
971 slave Grace	1007 Quarturmus, James	1033 Churn, John
972 Harris, Phillip	1008 Elenworth, Richd.	1033 slave Meron
972 Spear, Henry	1008 Ellingworth, Richd.	1034 Hufington, John, junr.
973 Edge, Joshua	1008 Elenworth, Nehem.	1035 Faringtone, William
974 Quartermas, Issah	1009 Parsons, Frances	1035 Brown, John
974 Gibbins, John	1010 Macclester, Jos.	1036 Train, James
975 Roberson, David	1010 Macclester, Neall	1036 Train, James
976 Roberson, Wm.	1010 slave Samson	1036 Train, Roger
977 Macclure, Robart	1011 Givbens, Robt.	1036 slave Robin
978 Olefer, Geo.	1011 slave Sezer	1036 slave Rose
979 Jones, James, junr.	1011 slave Charles	1037 Hardy, James
980 Olefen, Wm.	1011 slave Samson	1037 Hardy, Benj.
981 Relph, Wm.	1011 slave Hanno	1038 Mezeck, Jacob
982 Downs, Robt.	1011 slave Nann	1038 Mezeck, Elihu
983 Hardy, John	1011 slave Bess	1039 Cuningham, Daniell
984 Calleway, Peter	1012 Givbens, Robt.	1040 Cordry, Isaac
984 Calleway, Thos.	1013 Nutter, Mathew	1041 Dashiell, Mitchell
985 Collings, Ebenr.	1013 slave Dominick	1041 Curey, Philip
986 Carter, Phillip	1014 Hitch, Solomon	1041 slave Vesa
987 Cooper, Gabriell	1014 Swilivin, Michell	1042 Dashiell, Henry
987 Cooper, Thos.	1014 Chapman, Richd.	1042 slave Gift
987 Cooper, Gabrell	1014 slave Frank	1042 slave Sib
988 Cooper, Samll.	1014 slave Cooke	1043 Hopkins, Jean, wido.
989 Cooper, Isaac	1015 Nicholson, James	1043 Hopkins, Robt.
990 Carter, John, junr.	1016 Felton, Will	1043 slave Tobe
991 Carter, John	1017 Owins, Edward	1044 Pall, Geo.
991 Carter, Samll.	1018 Lankston, Wm.	1044 Hust, Wm.
991 Carter, Charles	1019 Chesman, John	1045 Parkerson, John
991 Carter, Wm.	1019 slave Seser	1046 Young, William
991 Carter, Thos.	1019 slave Nancey	1046 Young, Jehu
991 Roads, John	1020 Paremore, James	1047 Smith, Thos.
992 Jones, John	1021 Ackworth, Charles	1048 Right, Solomon
993 Spear, Henry	1021 Ackworth, Richd.	1049 Darby, Walter
993 Speare, Robt.	1021 Glaster, Thos.	1049 Mercey, John
994 More,, widow	1022 Ackworth, Thos.	1050 Tuley, James
994 More, Wm.	1022 slave Sambow	1050 Tuley, Joseph
995 Backwor, Charles	1023 Brown, William	1050 Tuley, Benj.
996 M[elson], Samuel	1024 Gillis, John	1050 Price, Frances
996 Melson, Samll.	1024 Gillis, Thos.	1051 Tayler, Wm.
996 Melson, Benj.	1025 Scott, Geo.	1052 Darby, Daniell
997 Scott, Windom	1026 Wilson, John	1053 Twille, Robt.
	1026 Lankson, Speare	1054 Henry, John
	1027 Gravenor, Thos.	

TAX LISTS OF SOMERSET COUNTY: 1730-1740

NANTICOKE HUNDRED

1054 Henry, Roben
1055 Wollis, Richd.
1056 Lowe, Ralph
1056 Lowe, Robt.
1057 Danielson,, widow
1057 slave Belender
1058 Anderson, James
1058 Maclenen, Jos.
1059 Cottman, Ebenezer
1059 Cottman, Nathanell
1059 More, John, junr.
1060 Givbens, James
1060 slave Roger
1060 slave Frank
1061 Caldwell, James
1061 Gibens, John
1061 slave Tobe
1061 slave Bob
1061 slave Sambo
1061 slave Rose
1061 slave Siss
1062 Tayler, Abraham
1062 slave Quash
1063 Roads, Daniell
1063 Roads, Timothy
1064 Nutter, Christopher
1064 slave Sesor
1064 slave Tom
1064 slave Sipeho
1064 slave Rose
1064 slave Barbere
1065 Jones, John
1066 M[ezeck], Nehemiah
1066 Mezeck, Jacob
1066 Ouws, Ephram
1067 Whinwrite, Cannon
1068 Game, Sambow
1069 Hopkins, John
1069 Greer, James
1070 Collings, John
1070 Shirman, Thos.
1071 Bounds, Joseph
1071 Hust, Lazrus
1072 Buckle, Nicholas
1073 Collier, Robt.
1073 Collier, Doughty
1073 Collier, Robt.
1073 Collier, Geo.
1074 Beard, Lues
1074 Beard, John
1074 Beard, Lewis
1075 Laremore, Thos.
1075 More, Wm.
1076 Venedson, Elige
1076 Venedson, Elias
1077 Henderson, Robt.
1078 Richtie, Archeble

1079 Anderson, Sarah
1079 Anderson, John
1080 Weatherley, William
1080 Weatherley, Willm., jur.
1080 slave Sebiner
1081 Alexander, Moses
1081 Weatheley, James
1081 Billings, Benj.
1081 slave Tom
1081 slave Peg
1082 Nutter, William
1082 slave Philip
1082 slave Ben
1082 slave Cato
1082 slave Moll
1082 slave Rose
1082 slave Jean
1082 slave Catraner
1083 Phillips, Richd.
1083 Phillips, John
1083 Phillips, Wm.
1084 Jackson, Samll.
1085 Collings, James
1086 Maglin, John
1087 Lin, Aron
1087 Andraws, John
1087 slave Abraham
1087 slave Bess
1088 Collings, John
1089 Nutwell, Brunt
1090 Win[sor], Henry
1091 Winsor, John
1092 Bowger, James
1093 Gray, William
1093 Danton, Jonas
1093 slave Cofey
1093 slave Margrett
1094 Draper,, mr., att
1094 Draper, Wm.
1094 Fletwood, John
1094 slave Toney
1095 Noble,, widow
1095 Noble, John
1096 Walter, Tho.
1096 Johnson, Nathanell
1096 Notingame, Benj.
1097 Boyce, Daniell
1097 Donton, Wm.
1098 Davis, Neall
1099 Dunn, Richd.
1100 Mezeck, Isaac
1101 Macom, Timothy
1101 Mezeck, Benj.
1102 Mezeck, Jacob
1103 Hickman, Wm., junr.
1103 slave Oure
1104 Hickman, Wm.

1104 Hickman, Henry
1104 slave Jack
1104 slave Morrear
1104 slave Rose
1104 slave Sambo
1105 Hickman, Arther
1106 Hickman, Joshua
1107 Hust, Joseph
1108 Hopkins, John, junr.
1109 Walter, Daniell
1109 Stuard, Charles
1110 Samuells,, wido
1110 slave Cocero
1111 Hopkins, Stephen
1112 Walter, John
1112 Walter, Robt.
1113 Barkley, John
1114 Barkley, John, jur.
1115 Shockley, David
1115 Shockley, James
1115 Shockley, Samll.
1115 Outwell, Solm.
1116 Lingo, Richd.
1117 Riley, Geo.
1118 Right, Willm.
1118 Right, Wm.
1119 Lankford, Thos.
1120 Lankford, John
1120 Lankford, John
1121 Jones, James, snr.
1122 More, Willm., jur.
1123 More, John, senr.
1124 Right, Solm.
1125 Jackson, Jonathan
1125 Roach, John
1125 Jackson, Joshua
1126 Giles, Wm.
1126 Giles, Wm.
1126 slave Floro
1127 Meginne, Jean
1127 Daughty, James
1128 Giles, Tho.
1129 Johnson, David
1130 Austen, Wm.
1130 Bodly, William
1131 Jones, John
1132 Jacobs, Walter
1132 slave Sibb
1132 slave Jane
1132 slave Sambo
1132 slave James Murfey
1133 Muridon, John
1134 Mereday, John
1135 Dunkin, James
1136 Nutter, Huett
1136 slave Titt
1136 slave Finch
1136 slave Dino
1137 More, Wm., senr.

1733 TAX LIST [Household number/Name/Remarks]

NANTICOKE/POCOMOKE HUNDREDS

1137 Benett, Geo.
1138 Macclester, John
1138 Macclester, Samll.
1138 Macclester, Geo.
1138 slave Cofe
1138 slave Sambo
1138 slave illegible
1138 slave illegible
1138 slave Fillis
1138 slave Priss
1138 slave Abbe
1139 Fluellen, Samll.
1139 slave Sib
1140 Laremore, John
1140 Laremore, Tho.
1140 slave Cofey
1140 slave Sibb
1141 Game, Robt.
1141 Game, Elender
1142 Game, Forten
1142 Game, Betty
1142 Game, Rose

POCOMOKE HUNDRED
1143 Long, William, mr.
1143 Boyce, William
1143 slave Harry
1144 Gillet, Samuel
1144 slave Dorcas
1145 Gillet, John, jur.
1145 Stephenson, Joseph
1145 slave Harry
1145 slave Nancy
1146 Grear, Archable
1146 Grear, Henery
1146 Grear, John
1147 Chapman, Joshua
1148 Jones, Edward
1149 Ellis, William
1150 Mills, John
1150 Franklin, William
1150 Mills, Nathan
1150 Mills, Alexr.
1150 Mills, William
1151 Houston, John, senr.
1152 Houston, James
1152 slave Cate
1152 slave Bess
1153 Houston, Joseph
1154 Britingham, William
1155 Baker, James
1155 Baker, Henderson
1155 Benstone, Benja.

1155 slave Comfort Rite
1155 slave York
1156 Layfield, Catherun, widw
1156 Layfield, George
1156 slave Talaman
1157 Benstone, Alexr.
1158 Gooding, Benja.
1159 Quinton, Philip
1159 Quinton, Dickson
1159 slave Jack
1160 Small, John
1161 Dickeson, James
1161 Dickeson, Robert
1161 Dickeson, Frans.
1162 Dickeson, Peter, jur.
1162 Dickeson, Teague
1162 Dickeson, John
1162 Mathews, Willm. Kindel
1163 Melton, John
1164 Henderson, Benja.
1165 Young, Daniel
1166 Merrill, John
1166 Chambers, Jeremiah
1167 Burnitt, [Jean], widw.
1167 Burnitt, [James]
1168 Henderson, [John], jur.
1169 Henderson, [James]
1169 Henderson, [John]
1169 slave [Adam]
1170 Lamberson, [John]
1170 Lamberson, [Rob]ert
1171 Brasher, [A]nn, widw.
1171 Brasher, James
1171 Carvine, Thomas
1172 Henderson, John, senr.
1172 slave George
1172 slave Gie
1172 slave Jone
1172 slave Eve
1172 slave Bess
1173 Blades, Robert
1173 Blades, Joseph
1174 Blades, John
1175 Britingham, John, jur.
1175 slave Cesar
1175 slave Naney
1176 Mills, Samuel
1176 Mills, Nathanael
1176 Mills, Hugh
1176 Paden, John
1176 Noble, James

1177 Mills, Mary, widw.
1177 Mills, Moses
1177 Mills, Smith
1177 Taylor, Roger
1178 Melvin, Robert
1178 Melvin, William
1179 Lambden, Thomas
1179 Breman, James
1179 Burk, John
1179 slave Cesar
1180 Henderson, Charles
1181 Henderson, Frans.
1182 Davis, Evins
1183 Cane, Thomas
1184 Merrill, Joseph
1185 Ramsey, Charles
1185 Ramsey, John
1186 Lamberson, Johanas
1187 Lamberson, Abraham
1187 Lamberson, Abraham
1187 Lamberson, Samuel
1188 Wheeler, Isaac
1188 Wheeler, Edward
1189 Jones, Thomas
1190 Piper, Isaac
1191 Goging, David
1191 Brooks, Henery
1192 Brooks, Francis
1193 Cary, Ama, widw.
1193 Pilcherd, Moses
1194 Cary, Jeremiah
1195 Webb, John
1195 Webb, John
1195 Pilchard, James
1196 Dormond, Samuel
1197 Stephens, William
1198 Drading, David, jur.
1199 Cluff, Edward
1199 Duckes, William
1200 Brothon, Brough
1201 Clogg, Samuel
1202 Brothon, John
1203 Madix, Lazarus
1204 Purkins, Sarah, widw.
1204 Purkins, William
1204 Purkins, Michael
1205 Purkins, John
1206 Tilman, Gideon
1206 slave Pompy
1207 Newbold, Thomas
1207 Butler, Manuel
1207 slave Moll
1207 slave Patience
1208 Powell, John
1208 slave Sarah
1209 Brooks, Richard
1209 slave Lett
1210 Benstone, Thomas

TAX LISTS OF SOMERSET COUNTY: 1730-1740

POCOMOKE HUNDRED

1210 Johnson, Joshua
1211 White, William
1211 Christopher, Aristo.
1211 Banester, Charles
1211 slave James
1211 slave Harry
1211 slave Robin
1211 slave Nimrod
1211 slave Jene
1211 slave Sue
1212 Tomerlin, Sayward
1212 slave Pleasant
1213 Whitingham, Heber
1214 Benstone, William
1215 Scofield, Henery
1216 Tomerlin, Samuel
1216 Tomerlin, Solomon
1216 slave London
1217 Henery, Robert
1217 Henery, John
1217 Eve, George
1217 slave John
1217 slave Cesar
1217 slave Chick
1217 slave Tarrill
1217 slave Pompy
1217 slave Adam
1217 slave Tom
1217 slave Jone
1217 slave Jamie
1217 slave Jame
1217 slave Luca
1217 slave Patience
1217 slave Phillip
1217 slave Jeney
1218 White, Archable
1218 White, William
1219 Mathews, Teague
1220 Riggin, Samuel
1220 slave Bess
1221 Riggin, John, senr.
1221 Riggin, John
1221 Riggin, Stephen
1221 Riggin, Teague
1221 slave Jame
1222 Mathews, William
1223 Mathews, Samuel
1224 Mathews, John
1225 Clifton, John
1226 Riggin, Charles
1226 Riggin, John
1226 Riggin, Solmon
1226 slave Peter
1226 slave Nan
1227 Dickeson, Peter, senr.
1227 Dickeson, Isaac
1227 Dickseon, Charles
1227 slave Squashaho
1228 Cocks, William
1228 slave Jonas
1228 slave Cesar
1228 slave Doll
1229 Ellis, John
1230 Boyer, Robert
1230 Clifton, George
1230 Boyer, Jonathan
1231 Evins, Thomas
1231 slave Janne
1232 White, John
1232 Conner, William
1232 Murray, Daniel
1232 slave Tom
1232 slave Jack
1232 slave Adam
1233 Holland, William
1233 slave Tom
1233 slave Dorcas
1234 Billings, Thomas
1235 Britt, John
1236 Milbourn, Ralph
1236 slave Dago
1237 Milbourn, Caleb
1237 slave Mingo
1237 slave Hannah
1238 Milbourn, John
1239 Collins, Samuel
1240 Nairn, James
1240 slave Will
1240 slave Harry
1240 slave Moll
1241 Nairn, Robert
1241 slave Sarah
1241 slave Mage
1242 Evins, John
1243 Riggin, William
1244 White, John
1244 slave Patience
1244 slave Nan
1245 Renalls, Henery
1245 Cudogin, Dennis
1246 McDaniel, Allen
1246 McDaniel, Moses
1247 Slocumb, Thomas
1248 McCredy, Alexr.
1248 McCredy, Alexr.
1249 Taylor, Hope
1250 Taylor, Robert
1251 Wood, William
1251 Arnold, William
1252 Cearsey, Peter
1252 Cearsey, Samuel
1252 Cearsey, Robert
1253 Adams, Jacob
1253 Adams, Samuel
1253 Adams, Philip
1253 Mathews, Robert
1253 slave Sampson
1253 slave Nan
1254 Boston, Isaac
1254 slave Venas
1254 slave Gloster
1255 Boston, Aesuc
1256 Adams, Thomas, senr.
1256 Adams, Isaac
1256 slave Harry
1256 slave James
1257 Adams, Thomas, jur.
1258 Marshell, Samuel
1259 Adams, Hope
1260 Adams, Cathorun, widw.
1260 Cearsey, William
1261 Adams, George
1262 Adams, Philip
1263 Hull, Edward
1263 Davis, Beachamp
1263 Beachamp, John
1263 slave George
1264 Townsend, Littleton
1264 Townsend, John
1265 Beachamp, Edward
1265 Beachamp, Thomas
1265 Beachamp, John
1265 slave Mora
1266 Bywaters, Richard
1267 Adams, William
1267 Adams, Dennis
1267 Adams, William
1267 slave Jack
1268 Peacock, Edward
1269 Fenton, Margarett, widw.
1269 Blear, Robert
1270 Calvert, William
1271 Drading, David, senr.
1271 Drading, William
1272 Hayward, Thomas
1272 slave Sambo
1272 slave Seneca
1272 slave Tom
1272 slave Jesper
1272 slave Cuggoe
1272 slave Pris
1272 slave Jame
1272 slave Rose
1273 Dennis, John, jur.
1273 Davis, Tudar
1273 slave Kinston
1273 slave Oxford
1273 slave Patience
1273 slave Abo
1274 Allen, Francis
1274 Allen, John
1274 Allen, Francis
1274 Geddes, Robert

1733 TAX LIST [Household number/Name/Remarks]

POCOMOKE HUNDRED

1274 Obrian, Christopher
1274 Duffy, James
1274 Simpson, Archibald
1274 Johnson, Abraham
1274 slave Sibbery
1274 slave Nell
1274 slave Judith
1274 slave Margery
1274 slave Alice
1275 Connelly, Patrick
1276 Mitchell, Robert
1276 slave Townsides
1276 slave Silbey
1277 Handy, William
1277 Handy, Samuel
1277 Handy, Thomas
1277 Bennitt, Wm.
1277 slave Nedd
1277 slave Harry
1277 slave Hager
1277 slave Judith
1278 Gores, Richard
1279 Jones, Ann, widw.
1279 Jones, William
1280 Mills, William
1280 Mills, Samuel
1280 Mills, Jonathan
1281 Tull, George
1281 Tull, Noble
1281 slave Abner
1281 slave Dinah
1282 Harper, John
1283 Harper, Francis
1284 Costin, Stephen
1284 Pilchard, John
1285 Benton, Comford
1285 slave Mesarows
1285 slave Hoborn
1285 slave Coffee
1285 slave Sambo
1285 slave Bess
1285 slave Pegg
1285 slave Jane
1285 slave Hannah
1286 Costin, Isaac
1286 slave Andrew
1287 Tull, John
1288 Harris, John
1288 Harris, Benton
1289 Knight, Richard
1289 Knight, James
1290 Jordine, Aaron
1291 Tindall, James
1292 Harper, Edward
1293 Smith, John
1294 Riggin, Tegue
1294 slave Cesar
1294 slave Nan
1295 Warwick, Ater
1295 Hopcraft, Thomas
1296 Harris, Robert
1296 Login, Alexr.
1296 slave Harry
1296 slave Cesar
1296 slave Moll
1296 slave Moll
1297 Riggin, Joseph
1297 Condun, Edward
1298 Smulling, Randall
1298 Smulling, Randall
1299 Ward, Joseph
1299 Ward, Cornelius
1300 Riggin, Ambros, senr.
1300 Riggin, Teague
1301 Phillips, John
1301 Gullet, George
1302 Daley, Patrick
1303 Denstone, John
1304 Porter, William
1305 Scott, Thomas
1306 Wonell, James
1307 Lane, John
1308 Townsend, Eliz., widw.
1308 Townsend, Danford
1308 slave Towney
1309 Riggin, Ambros, jur.
1309 Riggin, John
1310 Coulbourn, John
1310 Coulbourn, William
1311 McCuddy, John
1311 Porter, Jonathan
1312 Riggin, Darby
1312 Riggin, Peirce
1312 Riggin, Teague
1313 Autwill, Francis, senr.
1314 Autwill, Charles
1315 Fleming, John
1315 Fleming, William
1315 Stephens, Edward
1315 slave Robin
1315 slave Pompey
1315 slave Dinah
1316 Mayo, Samuel
1316 Kelnik, Thomas
1317 Dickeson, Edward, jur.
1318 Dickeson, Edward, senr.
1318 slave George
1319 Donohow, Teague
1319 Donohow, Daniel
1319 Dohow, Teague
1319 Duckes, Robert
1319 Harwood, Richard
1320 Donohow, Dormond
1320 Cooper, Samuel
1321 Townsend, Daniel
1321 slave Pegg
1321 slave Sawney
1322 Dickeson, Cornelius
1322 slave Dinah
1323 Dickeson, Charles
1324 Townsend, John, jur.
1324 Townsend, John
1324 Autwill, Francis
1325 Townsend, John, senr.
1325 Townsend, Paul
1325 slave Murrear
1326 Porter, Francis
1326 Porter, Mecemy
1327 Scott, John, capt.
1327 Ray, James
1327 Goldsmith, Tom
1327 slave Peter
1327 slave Jamey
1327 slave Rose
1327 slave Pheby
1328 Gibbs, Abraham
1329 Atkinson, Samuel
1330 Atkinson, Isaac
1331 Atkinson, John
1332 Atkinson, Angellow
1332 Blades, Benja.
1332 Warington, Benja.
1332 Jones, Abraham
1333 Gray, Mary, widw.
1333 Anderson, Isaac
1333 slave Abraham
1334 Bennitt, John
1335 Townsend, James
1335 slave Gie
1336 Stewart, Sarah, widw.
1336 slave Fisher
1336 slave Tom
1336 slave Jack
1336 slave Cork
1336 slave Funso
1336 slave Rose
1337 Peal, Thomas
1337 slave Sampson
1338 Bivans, Rowland
1338 Bivans, William
1338 Bivans, Elias
1339 Andrews, John
1339 Andrews, Peal
1340 Wordy, Susanah, widw.
1340 slave Mass
1340 slave Tom
1341 Sheldon, John
1341 Dickeson, Edward

TAX LISTS OF SOMERSET COUNTY: 1730-1740

POCOMOKE/WICOMICO HUNDREDS

1341 slave Isaac
1342 Townsend, Charles
1342 Townsend, Solomon
1342 Townsend, Elias
1343 Bivans, Thomas
1344 Cotingham, Jonathan
1344 Cotingham, Charles
1344 Cotingham, William
1344 Cotingham, Jonathan
1345 Whitington, Southy
1345 Lanman, John
1345 slave Robin
1345 slave Cesar
1345 slave Hannah
1346 Houston, Benja.
1346 slave Dick
1347 Davis, Nathanail
1348 Selby, Thomas
1349 Turner, Samuel, jur.
1350 Turner, John
1351 Worington, Thomas
1352 Taylor, Samuel, senr.
1352 Taylor, George
1353 Butler, Thomas
1354 Bivans, John
1354 Bivans, John
1354 Bivans, Thomas
1354 slave Sambo
1355 Johnson, Eliz., widw.
1355 slave Betty
1356 Nichols, James
1356 slave Hannah
1357 Nichols, John
1358 Nichols, Joseph
1359 Townsend, Solomon
1360 Bivans, Caleb
1360 Taylor, William
1361 White, Henery
1362 Houston, Robert, jur.
1363 Houston, John, jur.
1364 Houston, Joseph
1364 Kilam, John
1364 Kilam, William
1364 slave Bell
1365 Gray, Allen
1366 Hough, Edmond
1366 Collins, William
1366 slave George
1366 slave Sambo
1366 slave Titus

1366 slave Naney
1367 Outton, Abraham
1367 slave Will
1368 Sturgis, Jonathan
1369 Nelson, Hugh
1369 slave Joe
1370 Dennis, John, senr.
1370 Dennis, Wheetly
1370 Dennis, Volantine
1370 Teney, John
1370 slave Joy
1370 slave Cate
1371 Glass, Christopher
1371 Glass, Christopher
1371 Glass, Elis
1371 slave Franck
1371 slave Dinah
1372 Davis,, , maden
1372 Farmer, William
1372 slave Simon
1372 slave Will
1373 Godfrey, Joseph
1374 Morris, Isaac
1374 Morris, Luke
1374 slave Ayo
1374 slave Urry
1374 slave Ben
1374 slave Abner
1375 Davis, Joseph
1376 Sturgis, Joshua
1376 Laws, William
1376 Laws, John
1376 slave Tom
1376 slave Moll
1377 Runells, John
1378 Jones, William
1379 Odear, John
1380 McDaniel, James
1381 Noble, James
1382 Stephens, John
1383 Dier, John
1384 Martin, James
1384 Downs, Robert
1384 Bennett, John
1384 Wollace, Robert
1384 Long, John
1384 slave Pompy
1384 slave Cato
1384 slave Cesar
1384 slave Nan
1385 Webb, Solomon
1386 Paine, John

WICOMICO HUNDRED

1387 Everton, Jno.
1388 Edwarts, Jno.
1389 Nellson, Willm.
1390 Willen, Thos.
1390 Willen, Robt.

1390 slave
1391 Nellson, Jno.
1392 Willen, Edwd.
1393 Shiles, Thos.
1393 Shiles, Jno.
1393 Macoy, Jno.
1394 Crocked, Jno.
1394 slave
1395 Crocked, Robt.
1395 2 slaves
1396 Evans, Jno., senr.
1396 Evans, Jno., junr.
1396 Pow, Jno.
1396 Fouler, Thos.
1396 slave Sambow
1396 slave Abow
1397 Crocked, Richard
1397 Laramore, Jno.
1398 Winder, Thos.
1398 slave Mingo
1399 Evans, Ann, widow
1399 slave Toby
1399 slave Mesow
1399 slave Robin
1399 slave Abow
1399 slave Sibb
1400 Dashiell, Geo., junr.
1400 slave Tom
1401 Stuard, Alexr.
1401 Dashiell, Willm.
1401 slave Bess
1401 slave Jane
1401 slave Sibb
1402 Lackie, Alexr.
1402 slave Darby
1402 slave Sam
1402 slave Surrey
1402 slave Amey
1403 Scott, Geo.
1403 slave Sam
1403 slave Pompey
1403 slave Sanders
1404 Scott, Day
1404 Hariss, Jno.
1404 slave Hecter
1404 slave Tom
1404 slave Sipeo
1405 Cordrey, Daniel
1405 slave Sampson
1405 slave Sibb
1406 Dashiell, James
1406 slave Frank
1407 Gillis, Thos.
1407 Vance, Thos.
1407 slave Steponey
1407 slave Domineck
1407 slave Namock
1407 slave Pegg

1733 TAX LIST [Household number/Name/Remarks]

WICOMICO HUNDRED

1408 Humphriss, Thos., sr.
1408 Humphriss, Thos., jur.
1408 slave Cofey
1408 slave Bess
1409 Cordrey, Abr.
1409 Jackson, Jno.
1410 Wailes, Joseph
1410 Burn, James
1410 slave
1411 Mackmorey, James
1411 slave Batt
1411 slave Pompy
1411 slave Rose
1411 slave Tamer
1412 Hardy, Robt.
1412 Hardy, Geo.
1412 Hardy, Jos.
1413 Piper, Christopher
1413 slave Dick
1413 slave Sambow
1413 slave Toby
1413 slave Sue
1413 slave Dido
1414 Howard, Thos.
1414 Chaimbers, Saml.
1415 Venables, Benj.
1415 Venables, Willm.
1415 slave Jefferey
1415 slave Tom
1415 slave Cofey
1415 slave Will
1415 slave Bess
1416 Bartlett, Thos.
1416 Bartlett, Paskey
1416 Bartlett, Willm.
1417 Byrd, Thos., senr.
1417 Byrd, Thos., junr.
1417 Byrd, Wm.
1418 Handy, Jno., mr.
1418 slave Charles Sprutt
1418 slave Joseph Lenard
1418 slave Dick
1418 slave Moll
1418 slave Jane
1419 Nicholson, Richd.
1420 Nicholson, James
1421 Nicholson, Joseph
1422 Records, Jno.
1422 Records, Alexr.
1422 Records, Joseph
1422 Records, Jas.
1423 Garrott, Will
1423 Garot, Comfort
1424 Cordrey, Jno.
1424 Cordrey, Morgin
1425 Vinson, Geo.
1425 Linch, Mikell
1426 Price, Jno.
1427 Culver, Jno.
1428 Hitch, Saml.
1429 Hitch, Jno.
1429 slave
1430 Hitch, Elgett
1430 slave Conowndow
1430 slave Hannow
1431 Hitch, Mary, widow
1431 Rigin, Ambros
1431 slave Toby
1432 Lancake, Franses
1432 slave Jack
1432 slave Toby
1432 slave Bess
1433 Lancake, Geo.
1433 Phillips, Geo.
1434 Macance, Alexr.
1435 Maglamary, Willm.
1436 Hall, Thos.
1437 Johnson, Purnall
1437 Johnson, Saml.
1438 Handy, Isaac
1438 slave Sharper
1438 slave Oxford
1438 slave Prew
1439 Vinson, Thos., junr.
1440 Vinson, Thos., senr.
1440 Vinson, Benj.
1441 Vinson, James
1442 Carr, Jno.
1443 Tatum, John
1443 Tomeson, Thos.
1444 Handy, Ebinz.
1444 slave Tom
1444 slave Mumford
1444 slave Sambow
1444 slave Will
1444 slave Boney
1444 slave Hanow
1444 slave Amey
1445 Disherune, Lewis
1446 Disherune, Jno., junr.
1447 Cocks, Thos.
1448 Disherune, Leven
1449 Turner, Saml.
1450 Smith, Geo.
1450 Smith, Archd.
1451 Tayler, Thos.
1452 Gordie, Moses
1453 Gordie, Peter
1454 Smith, David
1455 Smith, James, senr.
1455 Smith, Moses
1456 Hill,, widow
1456 Hill, James
1457 Carsey, Patrick, senr.
1457 Carsey, Patrick, junr.
1457 Carsey, Willm.
1458 Carsey, John
1458 Henerey, Marten
1459 Lingow, Jno.
1460 Lingow, Jacob
1461 Lingow, Robt.
1462 Longow, James
1463 Purdew, Jno.
1463 Evans, Willm.
1464 Maglamerey, Edwd.
1464 Oleyfent, Mathew
1465 Macorpint, Robt.
1466 Ready, Bryan
1466 Ready, James
1467 Freaney, Peter
1468 Lindow, Thos.
1469 Cardwell, Hugh
1469 Calaway, Willm.
1470 Hearn, Willm.
1470 Hearn, Thos.
1470 slave Moll
1471 Hearn, Thos.
1471 Hearn, Nehm.
1471 slave Hannow
1472 Phillips, Jacob
1472 Cocks, Hill
1473 Hastin, Robt.
1473 Haistin, Willm.
1474 Caldwell, Jno.
1474 Caldwell, Jso.
1474 Cornwell, Robt.
1474 slave Will
1474 slave Cofey
1474 slave Ishmell
1474 slave Squash
1474 slave Doll
1475 Hall, Saml.
1476 Sneed, Bryn.
1476 Ready, Jno.
1477 Clifpton, Phillip
1478 Waless, Richd.
1479 Murfey, Joseph
1480 Daviss, Danl.
1481 Bowlin, Thos.
1482 Right, Jeremiah
1483 Maglamery, Geo.
1483 Turk, Mgness
1484 Parsons, Geo.
1484 Magey, Peter
1485 Shokley, Jno.
1485 Shokley, Jont.
1485 Shokley, Jno.

TAX LISTS OF SOMERSET COUNTY: 1730-1740

WICOMICO HUNDRED

1485 Shokely, Richd.
1486 Haymon, Willm., sr.
1486 Haymon, Willm.
1487 Duskell, Moses
1487 Caine, James
1488 Daviss, Saml.
1489 Caththill, James
1490 Mallile, Patrick
1491 Christopher, Jno., senr.
1491 Christopher, Jno., junr.
1492 Paramore, Richd.
1493 Hailes, Jno.
1494 Atkins, Robt.
1495 Adley, Wm.
1496 Ragley, Mikell
1497 Nox, Robt.
1497 Nox, Willm.
1498 Haymon,, widow
1498 Haymon, Jas.
1498 Haymon, Jno.
1498 Haymon, Charles
1498 Haymon, Isaac
1499 Seahon, Jno.
1500 Fooks, Benja.
1500 slave Patience
1501 Todevine, Henr.
1501 Todevine, Thos.
1501 Vance, Alexr.
1501 slave Goliah
1501 slave Sarah
1501 slave Janey
1502 Carey, Willm.
1502 Carey, Levin
1502 Carey, Thos.
1503 Rouch,, widow
1503 Rouch, Isaac
1503 Roch, Stephen
1503 slave Tom
1503 slave Hary
1503 slave Peg
1504 Disherune, Jno., senr.
1504 Disherune, Willm.
1504 slave Cofey
1504 slave Grace
1505 Disherune, Jno., junr.
1506 Disherune, Mikell
1507 Colett, James
1507 Crouch, Jacob, junr.
1507 Todevine, Jno.
1507 Perrey, Jas.
1508 Crouch, Jacob
1508 Crouch, Robt.
1509 Crouch, Isaac
1510 Covington, Thos.
1510 Covington, Benj.
1510 slave Tom
1511 Stephins, Willm.
1512 Sharpe, Geo.
1512 slave Mary
1512 slave Faney
1512 slave Ruth
1513 Crouch, Jno.
1513 Crouch, Nicol.
1514 Such, Olifer
1515 Hill, Charles
1515 Ellis, Jno.
1516 Howard, Jno.
1517 Hillmon, Edwd.
1518 Disherune,, widow
1518 Disherune, Mikell
1519 Chadiwax, James, senr.
1519 Chadiwax, Jas., jur.
1520 Miller, Peter
1521 Christopher, Ephm.
1522 Magey, Geo.
1523 Doudell, Christoper
1524 Tompson, Jno.
1525 Puckham, Richd.
1526 Pullet, Thos.
1527 Ginkins, Garviss
1528 Cary, Johnta.
1529 Baley, Geo.
1529 Baley, Benja.
1530 Baley, Johna.
1531 Christopher, Jno.
1531 Christopher, Clemont
1531 Christopher, Jos.
1532 Mears, John
1532 Mears, Robt.
1533 Magey, Peter
1534 Malone, Robt.
1535 Mungarr,, widow
1535 Mungarr, Mathew
1536 Leatherbury, Thos.
1537 Hobbs, Joye
1537 Hobbs, Absolum
1537 slave Polepus
1538 Lokey, Thos.
1539 Sirmon, Edwd.
1540 Maclaine, Danl.
1540 Moress, Jeremiah
1541 Parsons, Jno.
1542 Dashiell, Geo., major
1542 Cemp, Jno.
1542 Boushaw, Graves
1542 Pinter, Willm.
1542 slave Poledore
1542 slave Sambow
1542 slave Frank
1542 slave Mingow
1542 slave Dubline
1542 slave Harey
1542 slave Nann
1542 slave Rose
1542 slave Cate
1542 slave Jane
1543 Cotmon, Benja.
1543 Sockwell, Geo.
1543 Loley, Jas.
1543 slave Jno.
1543 slave Sarah
1544 Cotmon, Joseph
1545 Venables, Willm.
1546 Venables, Jno.
1547 Hall, Fenex
1547 Hodgin, Jno.
1548 Frasher, Hugh
1549 Stephins, Jno.
1549 slave Jack
1549 slave Bess
1550 Kibbell, Willm.
1550 Kibbell, Willm., jun.
1550 Kibbell, Jno.
1550 Owins, Moses
1551 Stephins, Richd.
1551 slave Pumbow
1551 slave Sue
1551 slave Alce
1552 Bounds, Johna.
1552 slave Bess
1553 North,, widow
1553 North, Jno.
1553 slave Buck
1553 slave Peter
1554 Phillips, Richd.
1555 Daviss, Willm.
1556 Elliss, Franses
1557 Craford, Jno.
1557 Rider, Jas.
1558 Colier, Thos.
1558 slave Grace
1559 Bormon,, widow
1559 Bormon, Saml.
1560 Goslen, Thos.
1560 Goslen, Richd.
1561 Cordrey, Jacob
1561 Hearn, Willm.
1562 Boushaw, Garrott
1563 Bruerton, Willm.
1563 slave Patience
1564 Adams, Alexr.
1564 Pawl, Willm.
1564 Haymon, Charles
1564 slave Jack
1564 slave Quash
1564 slave Beck
1565 Alexander, Willm.
1565 Alexander, James

1733 TAX LIST [Household number/Name/Remarks]

WICOMICO HUNDRED

1565 Alexander, Lisan
1566 Griffen, John
1567 Dulaney, Willm.
1568 Sirmon, Peter
1568 Sirmon, Jno.
1568 Sirmon, Peter
1568 slave Tom
1568 slave Lemon
1569 Mitchell, Richd.
1569 Daye, Jno.
1570 Mitchell, Benja.
1571 Mitchell, Jno.
1572 Swillavin, Willm.
1572 Noble, Isaac
1573 Goslen, Mathew
1574 Cotmon, Willm.
1575 Robertson, Willm.
1576 Redish, John
1577 Hougin,, widdow
1577 Fullerton, Alexr.
1577 Fullerton, Jas.
1578 Moress,, widdow
1578 Moress, Jacob
1579 Lows,, mrs.
1579 Maconeley, Jno.
1579 slave Jeptha
1579 slave Rose
1580 Porter, Joshua
1580 Barrart, Saml.
1581 Godert, Thos.
1582 Godert, Geo.
1582 Mitchell, Alexr.
1582 Stephins, Isaac
1583 Todevine,, widow
1583 Todevine, Isaac
1584 Mattox, Allexr.
1584 slave Moreaw
1585 Matox, Willm.
1585 slave Abr.
1586 Jones, Finch
1586 Cushney, Jno.
1587 Scott, Andrew
1588 Upton, Thos.
1589 Gale, Levin, corl.
1589 Custis, Levin
1589 Sprogle, Godfrey
1589 Seahawne, Thos.
1589 Noble, Marke
1589 Savige, Willm.
1589 Devorix, Jno.
1589 Welch, Jas.
1589 Dashiell, Mathias
1589 Chambers, Richd.
1589 slave Hope
1589 slave Tahew
1589 slave Pleasent
1589 slave Venter
1589 slave Robin
1589 slave Joycet

1589 slave Pulort
1589 slave Bridgett
1589 slave Ziprow
1590 Walker, Thos.
1590 slave Tom
1590 slave Johat.
1590 slave Dinew
1591 Elliss,, mrs.
1591 Wilkins, James
1591 slave Bubo
1591 slave Hanno
1591 slave Tom
1591 slave Moll
1591 slave Mary
1591 slave Nann
1592 Atkinson, Timo.
1592 Pope, Richd.
1593 Stuard, Patr., docter
1593 Stuard, Jno.
1593 Parriss, Jno.
1593 Austin, Will
1593 slave Whirraw
1594 Cope, John
1594 Cope, Willm.
1595 Ballerd,, mrs.
1595 slave
1596 Ballerd, Charles
1596 slave Pompy
1597 Reancher, Underwood
1597 slave Jack
1597 slave Bess
1598 Reancher, Thos.
1598 slave Peter
1598 slave Seser
1599 Dashiell, Thos.
1600 Hariss, Willm.
1600 Hariss, Richd.
1600 Hariss, Jno.
1601 Durram, James
1601 Hariss, Geo.
1602 Austin, Robt.
1603 Fouler, Edwd.
1603 slave Moll
1604 Houlbrouk, Thos.
1604 Renalls, Jno.
1605 Hariss, Willm., jur.
1606 Backerr, Thos.
1607 Lecatt, Jno.
1608 Smith, James
1609 Goslen, John
1610 Daviss, Jno., junr.
1610 Magey, Saml.
1611 Duskell, Denness
1612 Furbush, Peter
1613 Shiles, John
1613 slave Tom

1614 Stanford, Joseph
1615 Magee, John
1616 Vance, David
1616 unnamed/slave
1617 Stephens, Thoms.

TAX LISTS OF SOMERSET COUNTY: 1730-1740

ANNEMESSEX HUNDRED

1 Cottman, Mary	18 slave Jonathan	39 Outten, Jno., senr.
1 Cottman, Joseph	18 slave Dick	39 Outten, Jno., junr.
1 slave Jenny	18 slave Dorendo	39 slave Bess
2 Waters, Eliz.	19 Horsey, Nath.	40 Maddux, Thos.
2 Waters, Rich.	19 slave Cook	40 Maddux, Bell
2 slave Alex	19 slave Quamener	40 slave Kate
2 slave Hannable	19 slave Kate	41 Addams, David
2 slave Sippy	19 slave Patience	41 Addams, Thos.
2 slave Hagar	19 slave Prince	41 Addams, Jacob
2 slave Peg	19 slave Tarroh	41 Addams, Wm.
3 Barns, Robt.	19 slave Ned	42 Cottingham, Charles
4 Katan, George	20 Horsey, Samuel	42 Cottingham, Thos.
5 Hall, Rich.	20 Horsey, Smith	42 Cottingham, Jno.
5 Wolston, Joy	21 Horsey, Stephen	43 Cottingham, Charles
6 Hall, Charles	22 Scot, Robt., senr.	44 Potter, Anne
6 slave Dominick	22 Scot, Robt., junr.	44 Lord, Henry
7 Hall, Jno.	22 Scot, Jno.	44 Potter, Henry
7 Treharn, James, jr.	22 slave Betty	45 Allen, Henry
8 Waters, Abigail	23 Long, Randall	46 Scandelon, Edwd.
8 Hall, Wm.	23 Powell, Thos.	47 Booth, Rogger
8 slave Dave	23 slave Sibb	48 Redden, Jno.
9 Watters, Jno.	24 White, Jno., junr.	48 Redden, Peter
9 slave Jack	24 Powell, Gabriel	49 Prier, Thos.
9 slave Harry	25 Atkinson, Joshua	49 Tailor, Elias
9 slave Will	25 Onail, Hennery	50 White, Thos.
9 slave Dick	25 slave Bess	50 Willson, Joseph
9 slave Jenny	25 slave Frank	51 Wilson, George
9 slave Morreah	26 Hearn, Edwd.	51 Megummerah, Thos.
10 Watters, Wm.	27 Gunby, Kirk	52 Trehearn, James
10 slave Goliah	27 Moore, Samuel	52 Long, Jno.
10 slave Sambo	28 Kellam, Jno., senr.	53 Roach, Charles
10 slave Dinah	28 Kellam, Isaac	53 slave Jo
10 slave Bristah	28 Kendall, Wm.	54 Roach, Jno.
11 Tull, Thos.	29 Kellam, Jno., junr.	54 Tomlinson, Henry
11 slave Quamerer	30 Gunby, Jno.	55 Riggen, Samuel
12 Planner, Wm., maj.	30 Spibe, Jonathan	55 slave Bess
12 slave Watt	30 Buckle, Cornelious	56 Johnson, Wm.
12 slave George	30 slave Jack	57 Pewsey, Wm.
12 slave Tom	30 slave Kate	58 Williams, Thos.
12 slave Titas	31 Gillemore, Wm.	58 Williams, Thos.
12 slave Addam	32 Bell, Anthony, j.	58 Addams, Jno.
12 slave Cush	33 Bell, Anthony, senr.	58 indian, Andrew
12 slave Robin	33 Lord, Jno.	58 slave Dick
12 slave Hannah	33 Bell, Josephas	58 slave Sesar
12 slave Glaseo	33 Jones, Mathew	58 slave Addam
12 slave Sarah	34 Bell, Thos.	58 slave Jonas
13 Williams, Isaac	34 slave Nan	58 slave Gelico
13 Dohety, James	35 Davis, Sarah	58 slave Sarah
13 slave Samson	35 Davis, Jno.	59 Trehearn, Jno.
14 Lankford, Benja.	35 slave Sue	59 Roach, Nathaniel
15 Pewsey, Jno.	35 slave Harry	59 Roach, Daniel
16 Dixon, Thos.	35 slave Watt	60 Long, Samuel, junr.
16 slave Harry	35 slave Jenny	60 slave Samson
16 slave Dick	35 slave Dick	60 slave Kate
16 slave Lilly	36 Wheatly, Sampson	61 Cullen, Edmd.
16 slave Dinah	36 Cregin, Paul	61 Cullen, Isaac
16 slave Toby	37 Connor, Wm.	62 Whorton, Wm.
17 Dixon, Wm.	37 Cottingham, Thos.	63 Roach, Samuel
17 slave Bess	38 Connor, Jno., senr.	64 Owens, Eliz.
18 Horsey, Isaac, col.	38 Connor, Jno., junr.	64 Owen, Phillip

1734 TAX LIST [Household number/Name/Remarks]

ANNEMESSEX HUNDRED

- 65 Kilby, Wm.
- 66 Tailor, Wm.
- 67 Allen, Joseph
- 68 Sumners, Thos.
- 68 Sumners, George
- 68 Sumners, Thos., junr.
- 69 Lord, Frances
- 69 Lord, Randall
- 69 Lord, Thos.
- 69 Lord, Alexd.
- 70 Ward, Cornelious
- 71 Sumners, Jonathan
- 72 Johnson, Jno., junr.
- 73 Sumners, Jno.
- 73 Sumners, David
- 74 Dixon, James
- 75 Moore, Frances
- 75 Moore, Thos.
- 75 Moore, Isaac
- 75 Moore, Jacob
- 76 Moore, Jno., senr.
- 77 Ward, Stephen, junr.
- 78 Ward, Stephen, senr.
- 78 slave Pompy
- 78 slave Phillis
- 78 slave Sarah
- 79 Ward, Samuel
- 79 Ward, Jno.
- 80 Dies, Robert
- 80 Booth, James
- 81 Bird, Joseph
- 81 Cullen, Jacob
- 81 Dies, Daniel
- 82 Ward, Thos.
- 82 Ward, James
- 82 Ward, Jacob
- 83 Grimes, James
- 84 Coulbroun, Sollo.
- 84 Coulbroun, Soll., junr.
- 85 Starling, Jno.
- 85 Starling, Jno., junr.
- 85 Starling, Henry
- 85 Starling, Aaron
- 86 Lankford, Joseph
- 86 Lankford, Joseph, junr.
- 86 Lankford, Soll.
- 87 Wilson, Jno., senr.
- 88 Wilson, Jno., junr.
- 89 Cohoon, Jno.
- 89 Kellam, Joshua
- 90 King,, col., quarter
- 90 slave Tamor
- 90 slave Mingo
- 91 Sanders, Richd.
- 91 Sanders, Thos.
- 92 Beacham, Sarah
- 92 Beachum, Robt.
- 93 Beacham, Wm.
- 94 Beacham, Edmd.
- 95 King, James
- 96 Boston, Wm.
- 97 Beacham, Isaac
- 97 Obear, Isaac
- 97 slave Patience
- 98 Brimegon, Walter
- 99 Hull, Daniel
- 99 Brown, Terrell
- 100 Catling, Wm.
- 100 Catling, Robt.
- 100 slave Harry
- 101 Marshall, George
- 101 Marshall, Thos.
- 102 Porter, Joseph
- 102 Porter, Wm.
- 103 Stogdell, Edwd.
- 104 Lister, Jean
- 104 Holland, Isaac
- 104 slave Sezar
- 105 Curtis, Charles
- 105 slave Dick
- 105 slave Toney
- 106 Handy, Thos.
- 107 Frazer, Peter
- 107 Moore, Jno.
- 107 slave Morreah
- 108 Miles, Henry
- 108 Loyd, Wm.
- 108 Beach, Thos.
- 108 slave Phillis
- 108 slave Dinah
- 109 Davis, James
- 109 Baily, Thos.
- 110 Moore, Thos.
- 111 White, Jno., senr.
- 111 White, Jno., junr.
- 111 slave Essex
- 112 Ceary, Frances
- 113 Long, Daniel, junr.
- 114 Long, Daniel, senr.
- 114 slave Friendship
- 114 slave Nan
- 115 Long, David
- 116 Johnson, Jno., senr.
- 116 Smith, James
- 116 Dies, Philby
- 117 Wepells, James
- 117 Wepells, Ephraim
- 118 Claywell, Selby
- 119 Bird, David
- 120 Wheler, Jno.
- 121 Cullen, Henry
- 122 Bennit, Henry
- 122 Ward, Rich.
- 123 Horsey, Stephen
- 123 Killy, James
- 123 slave Bess
- 123 slave Jack
- 124 Holland, Mich., junr.
- 124 slave Moll
- 125 Dougherty, Jno.
- 126 Price, Edwd.
- 126 Price, Thos.
- 126 Price, Frances
- 126 slave Jenny
- 127 Long, Samuel
- 127 Long, Wm.
- 127 Long, David
- 127 Long, Coulbroun
- 128 Long, Jeffery
- 128 slave Nish
- 129 Riggen, Jno., senr.
- 129 Riggen, Jno., junr.
- 129 Dukes, Robt.
- 129 Riggen, Stephen
- 130 Riggen, Jonathan
- 131 Handy, Samuel
- 131 Handy, Samuel, junr.
- 131 slave Kate
- 131 slave Nan
- 132 Williams, Jno.
- 132 Fenton, Martin
- 132 Dolkin, Wm.
- 132 slave Sambo
- 132 slave Moll
- 133 Coulbroun, Wm.
- 133 Coulbroun, Wm.
- 133 Coulbroun, Samuell
- 133 Coulbroun, Soll.
- 133 Coulbroun, Mich.
- 133 Mecanny, Patrick
- 133 slave Quake
- 133 slave Abram
- 133 slave Lucy
- 134 Smith, Herny
- 134 Smith, Archable
- 134 Smith, Wm.
- 135 Tiler, Thos.
- 135 Solsbury, Wm.
- 135 Goff, Joseph
- 136 Parks, Arthur
- 136 Parks, Arthur
- 136 Parks, Jno.
- 137 Tiler, Jno.
- 138 Parks, Jno.
- 138 Parks, Mark
- 139 Hopkins, George
- 139 Hopkins, Jno.
- 139 Hopkins, Wm.
- 140 Horsman, Henry
- 141 Moore, Isaac

TAX LISTS OF SOMERSET COUNTY: 1730-1740

ANNEMESSEX/BALTIMORE HUNDREDS

142 Williams, Wm.
143 Woolf, Henry
144 Evins, Jno.
145 Parker, Isaac
146 Mister, Wm.

BALTIMORE HUNDRED
147 Smith, John, capt. sr.
147 Smith, John, jr.
147 Smith, Thomas
147 slave Harre
147 slave Bess
147 slave Merah
148 Simpson, Richard
148 Anglo, James
149 Bredel, Isaiah
149 Bredel, James Stephen
149 4 slaves,
150 Hampton, Mary, mrs.
150 5 slaves
151 Rickards, Jones
151 slave Sarah
152 Depray, John
153 Rickards, John
153 Roberts, Alexander
154 Clark, Mary
154 Clark, Edward
155 Moriss, William
156 Godwing, Ceasar, sr.
156 Godwing, Ceasar
156 Godwing, Daniel
157 Dasiey, Thomas
158 Wharton, Henman
159 Wharton, Daniel
160 Onarton, John
160 slave Fills
160 slave Jack
161 Hazzard, David, sr.
161 Hazzard, David
161 Hazzard, Arter
161 slave Dinah
161 slave Jacob
162 Mersey, John
163 Mersey, Adkins
164 Evins, John
165 Fassit, William, capt.
165 Fassit, Rous
165 Fassit, Lambard
165 slave Sambo
165 slave Coffe
165 slave Dall
165 slave Bettey
165 slave Sue
165 slave Fillas
165 slave Frank
165 slave Nanney
166 Crapper, Nathaniel, sr.
166 slave Kenner
167 Wallace, Thomas
167 slave Norton
168 Newbold, John
168 slave Kate
169 Purnel, John
169 Racklife, Charles
169 Racklife, Wrixom
169 Lowe, Charles
169 slave Coney
169 slave Mall
169 slave Dall
169 slave Gr
170 Tyler, Josiah
170 All, John
171 Bradfoot, Nathaniel
171 slave White
172 Whaley, Charles
173 Whaley, William
173 McCormick, Patrick
174 Crapper, Edmond, jr.
175 Fassit, William, jr.
175 Fassit, Benles
175 slave Philos
175 slave Rachel
175 slave Nerey
176 Nook, William
176 slave Will
177 Godard, Thomas
178 Powel, Thomas
179 Hallayway, Joseph
180 Pattey, John
180 slave London
181 Hamlon, Francies
182 Hallaway, John, sr.
183 Hallaway, John, jr.
184 Collier, Peter
184 slave Pompey
184 slave Mall
185 Mersey, Alexander
185 slave Jack
185 slave Juday
186 Delany, Patrick
186 Mathes, William
187 Walton, William, sr.
187 Walton, William, jr.
187 slave Cesar
187 slave Gloster
187 slave Juday
188 Crapper, Edmond, sr.
188 Camill, Solomon
188 slave Petter
188 slave Sampson
188 slave Dick
188 slave Feley
189 Fassit, John
189 Quilling, Joseph
189 slave Menidah
189 slave Lucas
190 Camble, John
190 slave Feb
191 Marchel, Isaac
191 Dueit, Nathaniel
191 Morris, John
191 slave Ben
191 slave Dinah
191 slave Bess
192 Gray, Joseph
192 slave Simon
192 slave Quaco
193 Dall, John, sr.
194 Gray, William
195 Gray, Thomas
196 Dall, John, jr.
197 Dueitt, William
197 slave Ned
198 Lathinghouse, William
198 slave Mall
199 Gaiey, James
200 Murray, James
201 Forsight, Thomas
202 Smith, Jonas
203 Idlot, John
203 Bernot, John
203 Jackson, Jonathan
203 Bowman, Henry
203 slave Jack
204 Hudson, David
204 Hudson, Absolom
205 Tounsend, Bowman
206 Linch, Abraham
207 Liptrott, John
208 Rogers, Solomon
208 slave Cain
209 Holland, John
210 Weight, Joseph, sr.
210 Weight, Joseph, jr.
211 Cabb, William
212 Linch, John, sr.
212 Lathbery, Arter
212 Chambers, Alexander
213 Purkins, Thomas
214 Bonton, Able
215 Bouton, John
216 Smith, William
217 Betriken, David
218 Stevenson, John
218 Stevenson, William
219 Weight, William
220 Webb, William

1734 TAX LIST [Household number/Name/Remarks]

BALTIMORE HUNDRED

221 Tull, John, sr.
221 Tull, John, jr.
221 Webb, Mark
222 Clark, Race
222 Clark, John
222 Clark, Benjamin
223 Miller, John
223 Tingle, Littleting
223 slave Primus
223 slave Pigge
224 Bouton, Thomas
224 Bouton, Benjamin
225 Woodcraft, William
226 Tingle, John
227 Tingle, Hugh, sr.
227 Tingle, Hugh
228 Robinson, John
228 Robinson, George
229 Wildgoose, Thomas
229 Woodcraft, Thomas
229 Woodcraft, Mary
230 Coffing, Thomas
230 Coffine, Joseph
230 Coffine, John
230 Coffine, Thomas, jr.
231 Miller, Joseph
231 slave Tom
231 slave Mall
231 slave Charles
231 slave Jack
232 Walton, Benjamin
232 slave Martha
233 Matlason, John
234 Bowen, Rodah
234 Bowen, John
234 Bowen, William
234 slave,
235 Crapper, Nathaniel, jr.
236 Wheler, John, sr.
236 Wheler, John
237 Mersey, William
238 Turvile, William, sr.
238 Turvile, John
238 Turvile, Prisgrave
238 Whaley, John
239 Johnson, David
239 Wilson, Isaac
239 Wilson, John
239 slave Jack
240 Linch, Alexander
241 Bradfoot, William
242 Kennitt, Martain
243 Hudson, Richard, jr.
244 Hudson, Samuel
245 Hudson, John
246 Mumford, William
247 Mumford, Charles
248 Brittingham, Elizabeth
248 Brittingham, Robert
249 Ratlife, Charles, capt.
249 Lues, William
249 slave Robbin
249 slave Sarah
249 slave Cate
250 Morign, Aviery
250 Cor-, Daniel
251 Grimes, Henry
252 Gault, Robert
252 Gault, William
252 Gault, John
253 Showel, Samuel
254 Hickman, Richard
255 Howard, George, sr.
255 Howard, Nehemiah
255 Howard, George
255 Carter, Joseph
255 slave Kent
255 slave Bess
256 Bessen, Absolom
257 Murrey, Robert
258 Morner, Henry
259 Robinson, Michael
260 Rickard, John
260 Rickard, William
260 slave Bosson
260 slave Briget
260 slave Simon
260 slave Mall
261 Morris, Dennis
262 Burton, William
262 Burton, John
262 Burton, Joshua
262 Pepper, William
262 slave Josh
262 slave Rachell
263 Morris, John
263 slave Kate
264 Renolds, Richard
265 Jefferson, Richard
266 Briteyman, Thomas
267 Jones, Ebenezer
267 slave Bosson
268 Carey, Thomas
269 West, Thomas, jr.
270 Ingrum, Jacob
271 Short, Edward
272 Carey, William
272 Fleatwood, Thomas
273 Philips, William
274 Hunins, Philip
275 Lewes, Arther
276 Lewes, Joseph
277 Camble, John
278 Wilson, John
279 Carey, Richard
280 Kennet, William
280 Ratlife, John
281 Robertson, Andrew
282 Fall, Abraham
283 Fall, John
283 Bishop, Brien
284 Collings, John
284 Ratlife, Elias
285 Turvile, William, jr.
285 slave Toney
286 Smith, John
286 Smith, Robert
287 Gilstrap, Peter
288 Wayaples, Paul
288 Throgood, Paul
288 slave Charles
288 slave Sibb
289 Bewsiey, William
289 Goodrix, William
290 Tylor, Walter
291 Lockwood, Richard
291 Evins, William
292 Hudson, Richard
292 Makentosh, Hugh
292 slave Dick
292 slave Coffey
292 slave Beck
293 Alford, David
294 Peal, Thorogood
295 Collings, Thomas
296 Holland, Richard
296 Carweel, Agnatius Stephe
297 Evins, William
297 Evins, John
297 Evins, William, jr.
298 Mumford, James
299 Russel, Andrew
300 Fassit, Franklyn
300 slave Nane
301 Manklyn, Richard
302 Jones, John
303 Latchim, Thomas
304 Parrey, James
305 Hudson, William
305 Gray, William
306 Godwing, Michael
306 slave Bess
307 Robinson, Thomas
307 slave Bess
308 Hill, Ann
308 Hazzard, Benoney
309 Johnson, Linard
310 Dickson, Sturges
311 West, William
312 West, George
313 West, Thomas
314 Harney, Thomas

TAX LISTS OF SOMERSET COUNTY: 1730-1740

BALTIMORE/BOGERTERNORTON HUNDREDS

315 Bell, Isaac
316 Whalley, William
317 Dalle, Archabal
317 Doward, Adam
318 Roberts, Thomas
318 Roberts, Samuel
319 Hall, Samuel
320 Linch, John
321 Idlot, Benjamin
322 Wise, Mathew
323 Hopkins, John
324 Robinson, Joshua
325 Hopkins, Josiah
325 Walker, John
326 Idlot, John, jr.
327 Direxson, Joseph
327 Roberts, Thomas
328 Collings, William
329 Hickman, Richard
330 Morris, Bibens
331 Dirixson, Benjamin
332 Salmon, William
333 Wharton, Francis
333 Wharton, William
334 Bernet, James
335 Woodcraft, Richard
336 Killey, John
337 Carweel, Thomas
338 Harrison, William
339 Quilling, Mary
339 Quilling, John
339 Quilling, Benjamin
340 Walton, John
341 Conner, Daniel
342 Johnson, John
343 Mulesto, John
344 Hall, Joseph
344 Munks, William
345 Hopkins, Samuel
346 Prodox, Thomas
347 Fisher, Thomas
348 Crapper, Solomon
349 Jinkins, John

BOGERTERNORTON HUNDRED
350 Whittington, Wm., senr.
350 Whittington, Wm., junr.
350 7 slaves
351 Claywell, Thos.
352 Porter, Wm.
352 Patrick, Roger
353 Holston, John
354 Bishop, John, senr.
354 Bishop, Joseph
354 Bishop, David
355 Atkins, John
356 Selbie, John
356 2 slaves
357 Bishop, Wm.
357 Outon, John
357 Outon, Thos.
358 Selbie, Wm.
358 5 slaves
359 Purnell, Thos.
359 Purnell, Benj.
359 5 slaves
360 Low, George
361 Bishop, Benj.
362 Victor, Magdalen
362 Victor, James
363 Richardson, Charles
363 slave,
364 Richardson, Robt.
364 Holston, Charls
365 Richardson, Jams.
366 Gilleland, John
366 Taylor, Anthony
366 3 slaves,
367 Atkins, Elizabeth
367 Bowen, Wm.
367 Bowen, George
368 Handcock, Daniell
369 Pointer, Wm., senr.
370 Truitt, Samuell
370 slave,
371 Dennis, Wm.
372 Smock, Henry
372 Smock, John
373 Blizard, Richard
374 Pointer, Natl.
375 Handcock, William
376 Heather, Ephraim, senr.
376 Heather, Ephraim, junr.
376 2 slaves
377 Penewell, John
378 Selbie, Parker
379 Griffin, Oliver
380 Rownd, James
380 4 slaves
381 Crapper, Ebenezer, senr.
381 Penewell, Wm.
382 Crapper, Ebenezer, junr.
383 Crapper, Wrixam
383 Mason, Edmund
384 Crapper, John
385 Scofield, Joseph
385 Scofield, John
385 Hudson, George
385 2 slaves,
386 Purnell, Elisha
386 slave,
387 Brittingham, Isaac
387 slave,
388 Holston, Wm.
389 McCawley, John
389 Long, John
390 Riggin, Wm.
391 Teague, John, senr.
391 Teague, John, junr.
392 Brittingham, Jeremiah
393 Brittingham, Wm., senr.
393 Brittingham, Wm., junr.
393 Brittingham, Solomon
394 Mumford, George
395 Truitt, George, of Phil.
396 Truitt, William
397 Truitt, George, of Geo.
397 Truitt, John
397 Hammond, Edward
397 slave,
398 Mumford, James
399 Turner, Henry
400 Dreadon, John
401 Steele, James
401 Steele, Daniell
402 Stevenson, James
403 English, Thos.
404 Bratton, James
405 Tadlock, Agnes
405 Tadlock, Edward
406 Porter, Joseph
406 slave,
407 Williams, John
407 Hill, Richard
408 Tull, Richard
409 Purnell, Catherine, mrs.
409 Purnell, Walter
409 2 slaves,
410 Williams, Prisgrave
411 Buket, Peter
412 Smith, Abraham
412 Steele, William
413 Hadder, Anthony
414 Waters, Patrick
415 Murray, Duncan
415 Townsend, Wm.
415 5 slaves,
416 Donelson, Jno., capt.
416 Hamilton, Wm.
416 2 slaves,
417 Ryley, Thomas
417 Hill, Johnson
418 Greer, Adam
419 Nock, John
419 Burton, John
419 Nock, Nehemiah

1734 TAX LIST [Household number/Name/Remarks]

BOGERTERNORTON HUNDRED

419 4 slaves
420 Franklyn, Edwd.
420 Franklyn, Wm.
421 Lay, John
421 slave,
422 Collins, Thos.
423 Smith, John Truitt
424 Walton, Richard
425 Evans, John
425 Evans, Ebenezer
425 Evans, Lazarus
425 slave,
426 Bratton, Samuell, senr.
426 Bratton, James, junr.
426 Bratton, Hugh
427 Bratton, Samuell, junr.
427 Bratton, Wm.
427 Bratton, John
428 Cashedie, Owen
429 Turner, Nicholas
430 Dennis, Solomon
431 Dennis, Daniell
432 Godfrey, Charls
433 Scot, Mark
434 Deverix, John
434 Deverix, Cornelius
434 Prior, Webb
434 slave,
435 Johnston, Affradoza.
435 Johnston, John
435 slave,
436 Johnston, George
437 Johnston, Thos.
438 Robertson, Wm.
439 Hall, Wm.
439 Hall, Adam
439 2 slaves,
440 Bell, Adam
440 Richardson, Wm.
441 Drigus, John
442 Shellie, Moses
442 Shellie, Peter
443 McNeale, Archebald
444 Atkinson, John
445 Murray, John
445 Perkins, Hugh
446 Haller, Wm. Dubbin
447 Evans, Elias
447 Taylor, William
448 Tingle, Daniell
449 Powell, Samuell
450 Powell, Thomas, red
451 Powell, Rachell
451 Mumford, Thomas
452 Evans, Gamadge
453 Evans, Powell
454 Bedard, Richd.
455 Ironshire, Mary
455 Hammond, Jacob
455 slave,
456 Warren, Nicholas
456 Gray, Nicholus
457 Warren, Robert
457 Gray, John
457 Bedard, Wm.
458 Dasie, John
458 Whitehead, John
459 Taylor, Joseph
460 Jarman, Robert
461 Swaine, William
462 Jones, Joseph
463 Hammond, Edward
464 Burbadge, Edward
465 Duncan, Thomas
466 Jarman, George
467 Hammond, John
467 Bassitt, John
468 Webb, Grace
468 Webb, John
469 Hammond, Isaac
470 Jones, George
471 Murray, David
472 Jarman, Wm.
473 Parker, Samuell
473 4 slaves
474 Parker, Phillip
475 Parker, Charles
476 Oshonus, Wm.
476 Cannady, Nehemiah
477 Kersie, John
478 Bridgwaters, Emanuell
479 Parker, George
480 Davis, Robert
481 Springle, Charles
482 Davis, Robert, senr.
482 Davis, Wm.
482 Davis, Ismaell
482 Davis, Benj.
483 Davis, Wm., senr.
483 Davis, Samuell
483 Davis, George
484 Davis, Phillip
485 Porter, John
486 Dennis, Donnack, junr.
486 Davis, Wm.
487 Ryan, Mathew
487 Ryan, John
488 Truitt, James
489 Truitt, George, of James
490 Jarman, Job
491 Atkins, Stanton
492 Williams, Jonathn
492 Williams, John
492 Williams, Littleton
493 Jarman, John, senr.
493 Jarman, John, junr.
493 slave,
494 Brown, John
494 Wells, Daniell
494 Farmer, William
495 Ratcliff, Charles
495 2 slaves,
496 Bowen, John
497 Thompson, James
498 Bowen, Littleton
498 slave,
499 Truitt, George, accamack
499 Truitt, George, junr.
499 Truitt, Michaell
499 slave,
500 Morris, William
501 Morris, Joseph
502 Mitchell, Thomas
502 2 slaves
503 Bishop, John, junr.
504 Pointer, Elias
504 Pointer, John
504 Toadvine, Isaac
505 Fletcher, Thos., revd.
505 Mannaring, Abraham
505 Johnson
505 3 slaves,
506 Timmons, Francis
507 Timmons, Thomas
508 Timmons, Samuell
509 Timmons, James
510 Timmons, Joseph
510 Timmons, Wm.
511 Timmons, John
512 Timmons, Aaron
513 Pointer, Thomas
513 Pointer, Ratcliff
514 Richards, William
515 Penewell, Charles
516 Penewell, Thos.
516 Penewell, George
517 Collins, Mary
517 Collins, John
518 Collins, Wm.
519 Davis, Thos.
520 Spence, Adam, junr.
520 Spence, Adam, senr.
520 Wood, John
520 5 slaves
521 Truitt, Joseph
522 Teague, Wm.
523 Jarman, Henry
523 Webb, Elisha

TAX LISTS OF SOMERSET COUNTY: 1730-1740

BOGERTERNORTON/MANOKIN HUNDREDS

523 Tinnis, Wm.
524 Purnell, Matthew
525 Rathbone, Robert
525 Bromly, Thomas
526 Davis, Wm.
526 slave,
527 Stevens, Samuell
528 Ennis, Nathaniell
529 Ennis, William
529 Dukes, Thos.
530 Ennis, Mary
530 Ennis, Samuell
530 Collins, Solomon
531 Ennis, Cornelius
532 Gillet, John
533 Hall, Robert
534 Hudson, Dennis
534 slave,
535 Smith, John
535 Pointer, Wm.
536 Gornwell, John
536 3 slaves
537 Townsend, Jeremiah
537 slave,
538 Townsend, Brickhouce
539 Truitt, George, of Job
539 Truitt, Nehemiah
540 Hodge, Robert
540 3 slaves
541 Clark, Daniell
542 Webb, Samuell
543 Smith, Andrew
544 Midgley, Thomas
544 Bainum, Bartholomew
545 Greer, Ursley
545 Harman, Zachariah
545 Harman, William
546 Smith, William
547 Henderson, Charles
548 Simson, William
548 Simson, Thomas
548 [Hill], Nicholas
548 3 slaves
549 Tull, Benjamen
550 Davis, Edward
551 Crapper, Nehemiah
552 Porter, James
553 Stevenson, Hugh, revd.
553 Traverse, Richard
554 Jones, John
555 Templing, John
556 Bradford, John
557 Edwards, Bennoni
558 Rownd, Edward, capt.
558 Bradford, Adam

558 Tuftin, William
558 2 slaves
559 Eydes, Laram
560 Stevens, William
561 Baker, John
562 Williams, Thos. Nathanie
562 Williams, Samuell
563 Lindow, Peter
564 Hollond, William
565 Burbadge, John
566 Williams, Argulis
567 Charles, John, free black
568 Buncle, Alexander
569 Hader, Warrin
570 Clark, Charles

MANOKIN HUNDRED

571 King,, coll.
571 King, Nehemiah
571 King, Robert
571 Mccallagan, Hugh
571 Butt, John
571 Kendall, Patrick
571 slave Fortin
571 slave Jessee
571 slave Tobee
571 slave Long Cesar
571 slave Short Cesar
571 slave Maning
571 slave Joe
571 slave Betty
571 slave Moll
571 slave Judah
571 slave Nany
571 slave Dido, senr.
571 slave Dido, junr.
572 Elzey, Sarah, acct.
572 Chambres,, esgr.
572 Elzey, Arnold
572 Randals, Wm.
572 slave Ned
572 slave Jack
572 slave Nany
572 slave Hannah
572 slave Balindo
573 McClemmey, Wm.
573 McClemmey, Woney
573 Henderson, Wm.
573 Abbit, Wm.
573 slave Frank
573 slave Nearo
574 Turpin, John, senr.
574 Turpin, Wm.
574 slave Coffee
574 slave Tobee
574 slave Nany
575 Kitchin, Wm.
576 Fodred, Wm.

577 Maddux, Thos.
577 slave Will
577 slave Sew
578 Bazman, Geo., junr.
578 slave Sambo
579 Revell, Charles
579 Davis, John
579 slave Vanices
580 Landon, Henry
581 Walstone, Booz
581 Davis, Arthur, untaxed
582 Milles, Wm.
583 Mcdaniel, Davd.
584 Tull, Solomon
584 Tull, Thos.
585 Davis, Arthur, senr.
586 Ford, Absolam
587 Tull, Joshua
587 Cousins, Thos.
588 Tull, Esther
588 Tull, Richard
588 Tull, Steven
588 slave Moll
589 Tilman, Joseph
589 Sherry, Job
589 slave London
590 Niblet, Burn
590 slave Coffey
591 Tilman, Rouse
591 Swift, Richd.
591 Tilman, Benj.
592 Tilman, Moses
592 slave Sampson
593 Tilman, Aaran
594 Gibens, John, senr.
594 Gibens, Thos.
594 Leather, Steven
594 slave Pleasent
595 Gebins,, widow
595 Cain, James
596 Stitt, Archibald
597 Knott, Isaac
598 Maddux, Lazarus
598 slave Coffee
598 slave Joe
598 slave Dick
599 Murroh, Alxd.
600 Sharp, Benj.
600 Walstone, Henry
600 Obrian, Thos.
601 Maddux, Danl.
601 slave Sarah
602 Hall, Alxd., junr.
602 Jenkins, John
603 Daimond, Richd.
604 Fountain, Nicholas
604 Hopkens, Benja.
604 Brown, Alxd.
604 slave Tom

1734 TAX LIST [Household number/Name/Remarks]

MANOKIN HUNDRED

604 slave London	623 Grandless, Wm.	648 Clerk, Alexd.
604 slave Charls	623 Morrow, Richd.	649 Long, Solomon
604 slave Merum	624 Carney, Robert	649 Spruance, John
605 Saillor, John	624 Culberson, Wm.	649 slave man
606 Fountain, Mary	625 Bowler, Wm., senr.	650 Fountain, Nicholas
606 Fountain, Thos.	625 Bowler, Wm., junr.	651 Collins, Wm.
606 Tull, John	626 Chain, Alexd.	652 Furnace, James
606 slave Moor	627 Brown, Thos.	653 Shaw, Jonathan
606 slave Harkless	627 Brown, David	654 Milles, Samuel
607 Gray, Thos.	627 slave Cudga	654 slave Ben
607 Hill, John	628 Brown, David	654 slave Dick
607 slave Ishmell	628 Smith, John	655 Ballard, Jarvis
608 Robertson, James	628 slave Cudga	655 Ballard, Wm.
608 Robertson, John	629 Lockwood, Wm.	655 Ballard, Jarvis, junr.
608 slave Toby	630 McGraw, Wm.	
608 slave Cesar	630 Murfey, John	655 Ballard, Arnold
608 slave Nero	631 Smith, Thos.	655 slave Emee
608 slave Pru	631 Heath, Abraham	655 slave Rose
608 slave Jack	631 slave Heger	656 Walston, Thos.
608 slave Dinah	632 Smith, Robt.	657 Owens, John
608 slave Phills	632 Smith, Thos.	658 McDurmock, Wm.
608 slave Sciss	633 Tindel, James	659 Butler, Nathaniel
609 Banaster, Thos.	634 Poak, Wm.	660 Jones, Wm., goose creek
609 Matthews, Wm.	634 Gray, Allan	
609 Matthews, Robert	634 slave Outten	660 Macam, George
609 Brian, Richd.	634 slave Obur	660 slave Ben
609 Fidday, Thos.	634 slave Hannah	661 Bazman, Geo., senr.
610 Diers, Robert	635 Steward,, widow monocan	661 Bazman, Geo., junr.
610 Hughs, Wm.		661 Tanna, John
611 Eskridge, Wm.	635 slave Tom	661 slave Frank
612 Horsee, Sarah	636 Heath, Wm.	662 Young, John
612 slave Nick	637 Gray, John	663 Bazman, Wm., senr.
613 Denwood, Geo.	637 Gray, Thos.	663 slave Ducer
613 Haly, Timothy	637 slave Hannah	663 slave Bess
613 slave Polina	638 Wilson, Robert	664 Wilson, David
613 slave Ned	638 Carns, John	664 King, Planner
614 Heath, Dormand	638 slave Sibb	664 slave Henry
615 Laws, James	639 Lesull, Robt.	664 slave Josey
616 McGraw, Jane	639 Lesull, Wm.	664 slave Bessow
616 McGraw, Robt.	639 Lesull, Thos.	664 slave Kent
617 Heath, Abram.	639 Lesull, David	664 slave Pompey
617 Heath, John	640 Strawbridge, Jams.	664 slave Cudjow
618 Benston, Geo.	640 slave Coffee	664 slave Jacob
618 Benston, Matthais	640 slave Davey	664 slave Haliday
618 Jones, Geo.	640 indian Heger	664 slave Nany
619 Pope, James	641 Chambers, Richd.	665 Wilson, Samuel
620 Lindow, Jams.	641 Fisher, Henry	665 Thompson, Joseph
620 slave Mosee	641 Colins, Price	665 Roberts, John
620 slave Bess	642 Bruce, Benjamin	665 Cantwell, Thos.
621 Turpin, Wm.	643 Shephard, Martin	665 Sprogal, Godfery
621 slave Frost	644 ODear, Stephen	665 Coleburn, Wm.
621 slave Will	645 ODeare, Furnace	665 slave Peter
621 slave George	646 ODear,, widow	665 slave Mada
621 slave Jacob	646 slave Apo	665 slave Black Nany
621 slave Moll	647 Turpin, Wm., senr.	665 slave Hannah
622 Dormant, Mattw.	647 Turpin, John	665 slave Moll
622 Dormant, Wm.	647 slave Jack	665 slave Sarah
622 slave Jack	647 slave Tom	665 slave Bess
622 slave Doll	647 slave Phills	666 King, Whittington
623 Gray, Wm.	647 slave Tobe	666 King, John

TAX LISTS OF SOMERSET COUNTY: 1730-1740

MANOKIN/MATTAPANY HUNDREDS

666 slave Tony
666 slave Harry
666 slave Tom
666 slave Paie
666 slave Medera
667 Elzey,, capt.
667 Elzey, John, junr.
667 Tate, Francis
667 Cadwell, Wm.
667 slave Cesar
667 slave Sambo
667 slave Bess
667 slave Judga
667 slave Nany
667 slave Sibb
668 Faskey, Benj.
669 Gille, Joseph
669 Jones, Mitchel
669 Irvin, John
669 slave Truman
669 slave Boatswain
669 slave Jack
669 slave Rose
670 Horner, George
670 Horner, Jas.
670 Horner, John
670 slave Till
671 Revel, Randal
671 Revell, Wm.
671 Boyd, John
671 Breman, James
671 slave Tom
671 slave Tobee
671 slave Herrey
671 slave Martha
672 Horsey, John
672 slave Cudga
673 Wright, Abel
673 Wright, John
674 Roch, Wm.
674 slave Kitt
674 slave Patiance
675 Morgan, Walter
676 Rigsby, Lewis
676 Mcdaniel, Randal
676 slave Tondo
677 Crouder, Francis
677 Larry, Timothy
677 Horney, Wm.
678 Bazman, John, senr.
678 Bazman, John
678 Walsh, Wm.
679 Willis, Barnabe
680 Hammond, Charles
681 Horsey, Hannah
681 Killee, John
681 slave Moll
681 slave Peter
682 West, Wm.

683 Burgan, Daniel
684 Wilson, James
685 Phebus, Geo., senr.
685 Phebus, Samuel
685 Phebus, John
685 slave Into
686 Phebus, George
687 Moor, John
688 Abbit, John
689 Cuningam, Thos.
690 Betsford, Jas.
691 Bazman, Wm., junr.
691 Bazman, Wm.
691 Jarvis, Wm.
692 Denstone, Robt.
693 Brown, Signey
694 Mitchell, Thos.
694 slave Ann
694 slave Mingo
695 King, Capbell
695 Mackintyre, Danl.
695 Heath, Abrahm.
695 slave Major
695 slave Titus
695 slave Paricate
695 slave Jack
695 slave Pompey
695 slave Rose
695 slave Cato
696 Jones, Wm.
696 Tate, Thos.
696 slave Goy
696 slave Antony
696 slave Muda
696 slave Eve
697 Heman, Wm.
697 Heman, Benjm.
698 Finch, John
698 Wetherby, Jno.
698 slave Mary
699 Brooks, Patrick
700 Thompson, Andrew
700 Thompson, John
700 Thompson, And., junr.
700 Jones, Richd.
700 slave Ceasar
700 slave Rose
701 Thompson, Wm.
702 West, Anton.
703 Woolford, John
703 Marderman, Thos.
703 slave Sampson
703 slave Moll
703 slave Tamar
703 slave Rose
704 Staples, Jas.
704 slave Ben
705 Fichgarll, Peter
705 slave, Tom

706 Tull, Saml.
707 Tunstall, Jon.
707 Rochester, Ralph
707 Lord, Thos.
707 slave Somersett
707 slave Will
707 slave Freeman
707 slave Tom
707 slave Dick
707 slave Leverpoole
707 slave Dinah
707 slave Elzabell
707 slave Low Hill
707 slave Pompy
707 slave Sibey
707 slave Norris
707 slave Tomboy
707 slave Bess
707 slave Sibb
708 Ballard, Henry
708 Wilks, Jno.
708 Smith, Thoms.
708 Campbell, Jno.
708 slave Henter
708 slave Cesar
708 slave Janney
708 slave Bendo
709 Ballard, Elliner
709 slave Mary
710 Spicer, Philip
711 Denwood, Thos.
711 Crowly, Timothy
711 slave Cogo
711 slave Munday
711 slave Will
711 slave Tamer
711 slave Grass
712 Wallston, Wm.
712 Wallston, Joseph
713 Dorman, Michall
714 Fisher, Bartw.
714 slave Jno.
714 slave Beck
714 slave Will
715 Floyd, Jon.
716 Hardy, Joseph
717 Wilcoks, John
718 Goldsmith, Jno.
719 Poak, James
720 Shanks, Benjamin

MATTAPANY HUNDRED

721 Richardson, John
721 slave,
722 Lane, George
723 Wise, Thos.
723 Mills, Jams.
724 Johnson, William
724 Johnson, Hezekiah
725 Tarr, Saml.

1734 TAX LIST [Household number/Name/Remarks]

MATTAPANY HUNDRED

725 Answorth, Petter
726 Hosiear, Saml.
726 slave,
727 Johnson, Petter
727 Taylor, Thos.
728 Turner, William
729 Sturgis, John
729 Sturgis, Littleton
730 Sturgis, Daniell
731 Nutton, Thos.
731 Nutton, Jobe
731 Nutton, Thos.
732 Hill, Johnson
732 Hill, Elisha
732 Gurley, George
732 Richardson, John
733 Hill, Hutten
733 Scott, William
733 Robards, John
734 Pope, John
734 Pudderrer, Joseph
734 Taylor, John
734 4 slaves
735 Tarr, Micall
736 Dicer, William
737 Nutton, Johnathan
738 Selby, Phillip
738 Selby, Matthew
738 Selby, Daniell
738 Selby, Phillip
738 Selby, Wm.
738 5 slaves
739 Crofford, Andrew
739 Crofford, John
740 Hill, Robart
741 Selby, Parker
741 4 slaves
742 Purnell, John
742 Young, George
742 6 slaves
743 Taylor, Phillip
743 Taylor, Elias
744 Answorth, William
745 ODue, Thos.
746 Walton, Fisher
746 2 slave
747 Walton, Stephen
747 Walton, Stephen
747 Williams, Thos.
748 Cord, William
748 Cord, Arter
748 slave,
749 Arnall, William
750 Mason, Abraham
751 Shehe, Petter
752 Eavans, John
753 Brownbill, Henry
753 Brownbill, John
754 Answorth, Sarah
755 Aydelott, Wm.

755 slave,
756 Davis, Charles
756 Davis, Lazarus
756 Walton, Wm.
756 Tompson, Andrew
757 Hosiear, Saml.
758 Holland, Benjamin
758 Nandlon, Patrick
758 slave,
759 Holland, Nehemiah
759 Nutton, Johnathan
760 Guttry, Patrick
760 Guttry, Jams.
761 Slingo, Thos.
761 Slingo, Thos.
762 Johnson, John
762 Dicks, Edward
763 Pope, George
763 slave,
764 Wattson, Moses
765 Willet, Ambrus
765 Willet, Wm.
766 Nelson, Wm.
766 Nelson, Jams.
767 Wattson, Robart
767 Wattson, Charles
767 slave,
768 Chapman, Humphre
769 Henderson, Bishop
770 Booth, Wm.
770 Vaun, Wm.
771 Cary, Sollomon
772 Pane, John
772 Pane, Joseph
773 Hopkins, Wm.
774 Wattson, John
774 Trador, Wm.
775 Duberly, Thos.
776 Wattson, Petter
777 Wattson, Luke
778 Hill, Abraham
779 Allen, Joseph
780 Davis, Charles
781 Vannetson, Willm.
781 Vannetson, Nathl.
782 Scott, Robart
782 Scott, Robt.
783 Wattson, Robart
784 Brownbill, Nathl.
785 Pepper, Wm.
786 Pepper, Tobias
787 Bennit, Mary
788 Beachbord, Wm.
789 Porter, McClantuck
790 Claywell, Petter
791 Claywell, Petter
791 Claywell, Ezekell
791 3 slaves
792 Sammons, Benjamen
793 Gill, John

794 Mallin, Christopher
795 Bratton, William
795 Vestry, Micaell
795 slave,
796 Hopkins, Saml., senr.
796 Hopkins, Saml.
796 Piperbanes, Isaac
797 Hall, John
797 Hall, Henry
798 Walker, John
798 slave,
799 Wagaman, Jacob
799 Wagaman, Ephraem
799 Arnall, Jams.
799 2 slaves
800 Robins, Elizabeth
800 Robins, Bowdin
800 4 slaves
801 Mcfeilds, Joseph, quarter
801 3 slaves
802 Russell, Cuthburd
802 Wattson, Jams.
802 Wattson, Uriah
803 Scarbourgh, John
803 Wise, Ezekell
803 Murray, John, mercht.
803 Houston, Benjamen
803 2 slaves
804 Hopkins, Nathaniell
804 Ares, Henry
804 slave,
805 Hopkins, Mathew
805 Nickols, Mathias
805 Ayers, Richard
805 Ayers, Harison
806 Jones, John
807 Allen, John
808 Pope, Saml.
808 slave,
809 Dreaden, John
810 Milbourn, Thos.
811 Taylor, Roger
811 Taylor, John
812 Duffin, George
813 Hodson, Rowlon
813 slave,
814 Vesey, Charles
815 Cade, Charles
816 Harman, Manuell
817 Conner, Richard
818 Backer, Thos.
818 Hodson, Robt.
819 Sturgis, Richard

TAX LISTS OF SOMERSET COUNTY: 1730-1740

MONIE HUNDRED

820 Leatherbury, John
820 Leatherbury, Perry
820 Dorman, Hezekiah
820 slave Pompey
820 slave Samson
820 slave Sambo
820 slave Toney
820 slave Ben
820 slave Nany
820 slave Bridgett
820 slave Rose
820 slave Nany
821 Dorman, John
822 Makin, Robert
823 Covington, Thos.
824 Durham, Thos.
825 Macklin, James
826 Hobs, Thomas
827 Hobs, Joy
828 Hobs, Marsilias
828 Stephens, Isaac
828 Mungarr, Matthew
829 Haly, Nicholas
830 Follows, John
831 Covington, John
831 Hays, James
831 slave Sambo
831 slave Coko
831 slave Betty
831 slave Dianah
832 Jones, James
832 Jones, John
832 Jones, Matthias
832 Duhig, Walter
832 Brucksher, Manerring
832 slave Sambo
832 slave David
832 slave Sib
832 slave Moll
833 Jones, Daniel
833 Roberts, Renshaw
833 slave Whitehaven
833 slave Doll
834 Magrah, John
834 Hill, William
835 Dorman, Henry
836 Neuman, Henry
836 Lahee, Andrew
837 Mongarr, John
838 Gale, Betty, madam
838 Kenney, John
838 slave Joe
838 slave Jacob
838 slave Jemmey
838 slave Dublin
838 slave Stephen
838 slave Ovid
838 slave Will
838 slave Ceasar

838 slave Rose
838 slave Pliner
838 slave Vilat
838 slave Bess
838 slave Pheba
838 slave Beandar
838 slave Janny
839 Gale, Matthias
839 slave Sarah
840 Gale, George
840 slave Sipio
840 slave Limas
840 slave Jemmy
840 slave Jack
840 slave Nany
840 slave Sarah
840 slave Parthena
841 Dashiell, Thomas, senr.
841 Dashiell, Levin
841 Chambers, Samuell
841 slave Will
841 slave Jack
841 slave Harry
841 slave Jack
841 slave Robin
841 slave Bess
841 slave Tamer
842 Laws, Robert
842 Laws, Panter
842 Laws, William
842 slave Boobo
842 slave Jack
842 slave Samson
843 Downes, George
843 slave Tobey
843 slave Frank
844 Stoughton, William
844 Lawles, James
844 Reighan, James
844 slave Buss
844 slave Catto
844 slave Simon
844 slave Tindo
844 slave Sibbino
845 Jones, Robert
845 Jones, George
845 Jones, Thos.
845 slave London
845 slave Dick
845 slave Amock
845 slave Jean
845 slave Rachell
846 Fitzgarell, Edmund
847 Waller, George
848 Shores, Edward
849 Laws, John
849 slave Prince
849 slave Ceasar
849 slave Dooniar

850 Millar, Thos.
851 Laws, Thos.
851 slave Jack
851 slave Mirear
852 Roe, Joseph
853 Roe, Thos.
853 Jones, Charles
853 Hopkins, George
853 Grig, Henry
854 Jones, Ritchard
855 Winsor, Lazarus
855 Winsor, John
855 Winsor, Lazarus
856 Millar, John
856 Millar, James
857 Williams, John
858 Jones, Lewis
858 Jones, Samuell
858 slave Jack
858 slave Ceasar
858 slave Moll
859 Bazwell, Thomas
860 Martin, George
861 Roberts, John
861 Roberts, Thomas
862 Husk, John
863 White, Francis
863 White, John
863 White, Thomas
864 Winsor, Mary
864 Winsor, John
865 White, John
865 Rose, Samuell
866 Wallis, Matthew
866 slave Tom
866 slave Sibb
867 Wallis, Ritchard
867 Wallis, Thomas
867 Wallis, James
867 slave Ceasar
867 slave Bess
868 Roberts, Edward
868 slave Jeffrey
869 Polk, Joseph
869 Neall, John
869 Makdaniel, John
870 Horner, George, junr.
871 Right, Thos.
871 Right, Henry
871 Welch, John
871 Skean, Robert
872 Shores, John
872 Shores, William
873 Irving, George
873 slave Tobey
873 slave Cuffy
873 slave Jean
873 slave Jenney
874 Waller, Major

1734 TAX LIST [Household number/Name/Remarks]

MONIE/NANTICOKE HUNDREDS

875 Waller, John	903 Anderson, John	934 slave Cooke
875 slave Jean	904 Mezeck, Isaac	935 Mezeck, Jacob
876 Waller, Nelson	905 Venetson, Elias	935 Mezeck, Elihu
877 Magrah, James	905 Venetson, Elshe	936 Mezeck, Neh.
878 Jones, William	906 Hickson, Joseph	936 Owens, Ephrem
878 Miles, John	907 Leremor, Thos.	937 Pall, Geo.
878 slave Will	908 Beard, Lewis	937 Hust, Wm.
878 slave Jemmey	908 Beard, John	938 Roberson, Wm.
878 slave Sue	908 Beard, Lewis	939 Read, John
879 Martin, Thos.	909 Henderson, Robt.	939 Read, John
880 Luke, Williamson	910 Collier, Robt.	939 Read, Zachr.
881 Waller, William	910 Collier, Dowty	939 slave Pegg
882 Carry, Thos.	910 Collier, Robt.	940 Quarturmas, James
883 Cary, Rachel	910 Collier, Geo.	941 Parson, Frances
883 Crouch, Thomas	911 Game, Robt.	942 McClester, Jos.
884 Wye, William	912 Fuellen, Samll.	942 McClester, Neall
884 Wye, William	912 slave Silas	942 Gouldberek, Wm.
884 slave Jemmy	913 Laremore, John	942 Beckingham, Wm.
884 slave Donleer	913 Laremore, Thos.	942 slave Samson
885 Rowe, Eliz.	913 slave Cofey	943 Dashiell, Joseph
886 Spence, John	913 slave Sibb	943 Sheraden, Daniell
	914 Dashiell, Henry	943 slave Randell
NANTICOKE HUNDRED	914 Steward, Ch.	943 slave Bettey
887 McClester, John	914 slave Gift	944 Dashiell, Robt.
887 McClester, Samll.	914 slave Sibb	944 slave Harey
887 McClester, Geo.	915 Whinwrite, Canan	944 slave Tom
887 slave Cofey	916 Hopkins, Robt.	944 slave Cago
887 slave Sambo	916 slave Tobe	944 slave Mara
887 slave Tom	917 Mezeck, Benj.	945 Benston, Thos.
887 slave Adam	918 Hopkins, John	945 Cooper, John
887 slave Siss	918 Hopkins, John	945 slave Will
887 slave Abbo	918 slave Sue	946 Gale, John
888 Hopkins, Stephen	918 slave Nan Game	946 Sehorn, Thos.
889 At the wido. Samuells	919 Game, Forten	946 Leatherbery, John
889 slave Cocoro	920 Dashiell, James	946 Kempe, John
890 Walter, Daniell	920 slave Roben	946 Houlder, Samll.
891 Wallis, David	920 slave Will	946 slave Barsha
892 Hopkins, John	920 slave Will	946 slave Messey
893 Hickman, Joshua	920 slave Jack	946 slave Townsitt
893 Hickman, Henry	921 Rickey, Archeble	946 slave Rose
894 Barkley, John	922 Williams, Richd.	946 slave Moll
895 Barkley, John, junr.	922 More, Wm.	946 slave Jude
896 Hickman, Wm.	923 Shirman, Thos.	947 Rusell, James
896 slave Jack	924 Dean, John	947 Rusell, Thos.
896 slave Sambo	925 Vohan, Wm.	947 Rusell, Wm.
896 slave Moreer	925 Bacon, Dudson	948 Rusell, James, junr.
896 slave Rose	926 Collins, Geo.	949 Goslin, James
897 Hickman, Wm., jur.	927 Collins, John	950 Relph, Thos.
897 slave Orre	927 Sherman, Thos.	950 Shirman, Peter
898 Hust, Jos.	928 Green, James	951 Ryder, Willson
899 Walter, John	929 Bounds, Joseph	952 Richardson, Wm.
899 Walter, Robt.	929 Hust, Lazrs.	953 Jackson, Jonathan
900 Hickman, Arther	930 Dashiell, Wm.	953 Jackson, Joshua
901 Macom, Thimoty	931 Harris, Phill.	953 Jackson, Zecll.
901 Mezeck, Juell	931 Speare, Henry	954 Giles, Wm.
902 Dun, Richd.	932 Buckley, Nichos.	954 Giles, Wm.
903 At the widow. Andersons	933 Richardson, John	954 slave Floro
	933 Richardson, Wm.	955 Giles, Thos.
	934 At ye wido. Nicholsons	956 Shirman, Wm.
		957 Benett, Edwd.

TAX LISTS OF SOMERSET COUNTY: 1730-1740

NANTICOKE HUNDRED

957 Benett, Geo.
958 Tulley, Stephen
958 Tulley, Benj.
959 Roads, Timothy
960 More, Wm., Q.
961 Tulley, Stephen, jr.
962 Twyford, John
963 Green, Richd.
963 Green, Richd.
964 More, John, Q.
964 More, Isaac
965 Phillips, John
966 At ye wido. Megenes
966 Doxtey, James
967 Bodley, Wm.
968 Austen, Wm.
968 Murfey, James
969 Johnson, David
970 Jones, John
971 At ye wido. Jacobs
971 slave Sambo
971 slave Sibb
972 Nutter, Huett
972 slave Tite
972 slave Dino
972 slave Mingoe
973 Nutter, Wm.
973 slave Phill
973 slave Ben
973 slave Catoe
973 slave Rose
973 slave Cateraner
973 slave Moll
974 Nutter, Ch.
974 slave Seser
974 slave Tom
974 slave Sipo
974 slave Rose
974 slave Berbory
975 Dunkin, James
976 Mereday, John
977 Hardy, James
978 Train, James
978 Train, James
978 Train, Roger
978 slave Roben
978 slave Bess
979 Farentine, Wm.
980 Goven, Robt., senr.
980 slave Sambo
980 slave Hannor
980 slave Bess
981 Goven, James
981 slave Frank
982 Fulton, Willm.
983 Roads, Daniell
983 Roads, Timothy

984 Tayler, Abraham
984 slave Quake
985 Dashiell, Mitchell
985 slave Venas
986 Caldwell, James
986 Given, John
986 slave Roben
986 slave Sambo
986 slave Tobe
986 slave Rose
986 slave Siss
987 West, James
987 Burkam, Roger
988 Nutter, Mathew
988 slave Domonick
989 Right, Solom.
990 Wetheley, James
990 slave Peg
991 Wetherley, Wm.
991 Wetherley, Wm.
991 slave Subiner
992 Hitch, Solom.
992 slave Frank
992 slave Cook
993 Nicholson, Richd.
993 Twiley, Geo.
994 Nicholson, James
995 Ackworth, Samll.
995 Ackworth, Henry
995 slave Sue
996 Paramor, James
997 Chesman, John
997 slave Seser
997 slave Naniey
998 Ackworth, Ch.
998 Glaster, Thos.
999 Ackworth, Thos.
999 slave Will
1000 More, Wm.
1001 At ye wido. Hitches
1001 Rigen, Ambrus
1001 slave Tobe
1002 Brown, Wm.
1003 Gillis, John
1003 Gillis, Thos.
1004 Young, Wm.
1004 Young, John
1005 Polson, Wm.
1006 Hufington, Jonathan
1007 Killiam, Edwd.
1007 Killiam, John
1007 Hicks, Wm.
1007 slave Roben
1007 slave Meron
1008 Hufington, John
1008 Churn, John
1008 Glaster, Solom.
1008 slave Jegoe

1008 slave Jeney
1008 slave Plesant
1009 Hufington, John, jur.
1010 At ye wido. Young
1010 Boyce, John
1011 Cordry, Edwd.
1012 Cordry, David
1013 Smith, Thos.
1014 Darby, Walter
1014 Mercey, John
1015 Tulley, Joseph
1016 Twilley, Robt.
1017 Tayler, Wm.
1018 At ye wido. Ellingworth
1018 Ellingworth, Richd.
1018 Ellingworth, Neh.
1019 Mackdowell, John
1020 Ellingworth, Robt.
1021 Mervell, Thos.
1022 Scott, Windom
1023 Rotten, Josias
1024 Melson, Samll.
1024 Melson, Benj.
1024 Melson, Samll.
1025 Green, Ezecll.
1026 English, Wm.
1027 Deane, Ch.
1028 Hufington, Thos.
1029 Hufington, Richd.
1030 Daudrell, James
1031 Wallis, Richd., senr.
1031 slave Mineo
1032 Scott, Geo., b.c.
1033 Roberson, John
1033 slave Sue
1034 Walter, Henry
1034 Walter, Daniell
1034 Walter, John
1034 Walter, Wm.
1035 Nowles, Edmd.
1035 Nowles, Richd.
1036 Nuten, John
1037 Keley, Geo.
1038 Edge, Joshua
1039 Roberson, David
1040 Maglolin, John
1041 Collings, John
1041 Collings, Thos.
1042 Linn, Aaron
1042 Anders, John
1042 slave Abrem
1042 slave Bess
1043 Keney, Wm.
1044 Carter, Phill.
1045 Caldwell, John
1045 Carnell, Thos.
1045 slave Sambo

1734 TAX LIST [Household number/Name/Remarks]

NANTICOKE HUNDRED

1046 Paremor, Joseph
1047 Godard, Geo.
1048 Godard, John
1049 Paremore, Mathew
1050 Hardey, John
1050 Carter, Ch.
1051 More, John, jur.
1052 Calaway, Wm.
1053 Waller, Thos., junr.
1054 Ange, Frances
1055 Pa[rker], John
1056 Tompson, George
1057 Lingoe, Daniell
1058 James, John
1059 Williams, John
1060 Cooper, James
1060 Polke, John
1061 Calaway, John, junr.
1062 Calaway, Edwd.
1063 Calaway, John, senr.
1064 Waller, Nathn., senr.
1064 Waller, John
1065 Waller, Nathn.
1065 Gibins, John
1066 Waller, Thos.
1066 Waller, Richd.
1067 English, Robt.
1068 Paremore, Thos.
1068 Paremore, Thos.
1069 Benston, Henry
1069 Benston, Geo.
1069 Benston, Henry
1070 Caldwell, Patrick
1071 Spear, Henry
1071 Spear, Robt.
1072 More, Wm., junr.
1073 Phillips, Richd.
1074 Phillips, Thos.
1074 Phillips, Wm.
1075 Collings, James
1076 Shirman, Thos.
1077 Bowlin, Thos.
1078 Jones, James
1079 Lankford, John, senr.
1079 Lankford, John
1079 Lankford, Edwd.
1080 At ye wido. Stileys
1080 Floyd, Majr.
1081 Gravener, Thos.
1081 Mercy, Henry
1082 McCluer, Robt.
1083 Olefer, Geo.
1084 Jones, James, junr.
1085 Relph, Wm.
1086 Jones, John
1087 Lowe, Ralph
1087 Lowe, Robt.
1087 Lowe, John
1088 Cottman, Ebenr.
1089 More, John, junr.
1090 Lankford, Thos.
1091 Right, Wm.
1091 Right, Wm.
1091 Right, Ezecll.
1092 Wooden, Edwd.
1092 Tatman, James
1093 Wooden, John
1094 Calaway, John
1095 Benston, Wm.
1096 Henry, John
1096 Henry, Robt.
1097 Landell, Wm.
1098 Cooper, Isaac
1099 Cooper, Gabrell
1099 Cooper, Gabrell
1099 Cooper, Thos.
1100 Ricords, John
1101 Ricords, Alexdr.
1102 Cooper, Samll.
1103 Willson, Jno.
1104 Keley, Daniell
1105 Downs, Robt.
1106 Collings, Edmd.
1107 Tulley, James
1107 Tulley, Benj.
1108 Gerett, Wm.
1108 Gerett, Comfort
1109 Jackson, Samll.
1109 slave Grace
1110 Anderson, James
1110 Maclanin, Jos.
1110 slave Belander
1111 Olefent, Wm.
1112 Caldwell, Thos.
1112 Arthbone, Andrew
1113 Carter, John, senr.
1113 Carter, Samll.
1113 Carter, Wm.
1114 Carter, John
1114 Carter, Thos.
1114 Bass, John
1115 Ryder, Hatly
1116 Kinigam, Daniell
1117 Darbey, Daniell
1118 Hosey, Mathew
1119 Stephens, John
1120 Ange, John
1121 Calaway, Peter
1122 Govans, Robt., jr.
1122 slave Seser
1122 slave Charles
1123 Kirkman, Roger
1124 Right, Edwd.
1125 Winser, John
1126 Bibbins, Joshua
1127 Betholemy, Samll.
1128 Shockley, David
1128 Shockley, James
1128 Shockley, Solom.
1128 Isaacks, John
1129 Davis, Neall
1130 Hall, John
1131 Boyce, Daniell
1131 Denton, Jonas
1132 Walter, Thos.
1132 Notingham, Benj.
1133 Genkins, Thos.
1134 Draper, , mr.
1134 Fletwood, John
1134 slave Toney
1135 Gray, Wm.
1135 Denton, Wm.
1135 slave Cofey
1136 Noble, Isaac
1137 Bouger, James
1138 Winser, Henry
1139 At ye wido. Nobles
1139 Noble, John
1140 Smith, John
1141 Blizard, Richd.
1142 Dolbey, Peter
1143 King, Wm.
1144 King, Phill.
1145 Mores, Micell
1146 Parsons, Ch.
1147 Mercey, Wm.
1148 Oneall, James
1148 slave Dino
1149 Mercey, John
1150 Johnson, Thos.
1151 Tindell, Ch.
1152 Ubank, Molton
1153 Short, John
1154 Short, Edwd., senr.
1155 Potter, Josefas
1156 Williams, Ch.
1157 Harvey, John
1158 Smith, David
1159 Ingram, Robt.
1160 Kiningam, Arther
1161 Landall, John
1161 Smith, James
1162 West, Alexdr.
1163 Collings, Andrew
1164 Samuells, Richd.
1165 Samuells, Peter
1166 Ingram, Abraham
1166 Ingram, Isaac
1166 Ingram, Abraham
1166 slave Prisiller
1167 Kemey, Henry
1168 Shirman, Jobe

TAX LISTS OF SOMERSET COUNTY: 1730-1740
NANTICOKE/POCOMOKE HUNDREDS

1169 Kelley, John
1170 Bounds, Jacob
1171 Sharpe, John
1172 Clifen, Geo., senr.
1172 Clifen, Geo.
1172 Clifen, Thos.
1173 Whinwrite, Wm.
1174 Benston, Wm., senr.
1174 Whinwrite, John
1175 Smith, Stephen
1176 Phips, John
1177 Hickman, James
1178 Daughters, Wm.
1179 Thornes, Edwd.
1180 Thornes, Alexdr.
1181 Bacor, Wm.
1181 Gibens, John
1182 Owen, Peter
1183 Oneall, John
1184 Nubold, Frances
1184 slave Amey
1185 Mezeck, John
1185 Mezeck, Geo.
1185 Mezeck, Obediah
1186 Welley, John
1187 Polke, Ch.
1188 Owens, Robt.
1188 Nocks, John
1188 slave Cate
1189 P[olke], John
1189 slave Attey
1190 Maniste, Amanll.
1190 slave Will
1190 slave Quaco
1191 Donoho, Nathn.
1192 Melson, Job
1193 Wingate, Phil.
1194 Caldwell, Hew
1195 Wallis, Richd.

POCOMOKE HUNDRED
1196 Hayward, Thos., mr.
1196 slave Sambow
1196 slave Sincho
1196 slave Jesper
1196 slave Cuggo
1196 slave Pris
1196 slave Jenney
1196 slave Rose
1197 Whitington, Suthey
1197 Lanman, Jno.
1197 slave Robin
1197 slave Ceasar
1197 slave Hannah
1198 Scott, Jno., capt.

1198 Scott, John, junr.
1198 Goldsmith, Thos.
1198 slave Tony
1198 slave Petter
1198 slave Rose
1198 slave Pheabe
1199 Stewart, Sarah
1199 slave Fisher
1199 slave Tom
1199 slave Jack
1199 slave Cosek
1199 slave Fungo
1199 slave Men----
1200 Anderson, Mary
1200 slave Abraham
1201 Porter, Francis
1201 Porter, McCemy
1201 slave Jack
1202 Atkinson, Isaac
1203 Atkins, Samuell
1204 Atkinson, Aingelow
1204 Warington, Benj.
1205 Tull, George
1205 Tull, Nobell
1205 slave Abner
1205 slave Dinah
1206 Mills, Wm.
1206 Mills, Samuell
1206 Mills, Jona.
1207 Harper, Anne
1207 Pilcher, Wm.
1208 Harper, Francis
1209 Riggin, Joseph
1209 Condum, Edw.
1210 Warrick, Arthur
1210 Hoopcraft, Thos.
1211 Riggin, Ambros, senr.
1211 Riggin, Teague
1211 Taylor, Jacob
1212 Riggin, Teague
1212 slave Nan
1213 Smuling, Randall
1213 Smuling, Randall
1213 Smuling, Natn.
1214 Ward, Joseph
1214 Ward, Cornelis
1215 Costen, Mathies
1215 slave James
1216 Daley, Patrick
1217 Harriss, John
1217 Harris, Benton
1218 Luis, Willim
1218 Pilcher, John
1219 Carey, Neomy
1219 Pilcher, Moses
1220 Jourdine, Aaron
1221 Tull, John
1222 McCuddey, John
1222 Porter, Jona.

1223 Toundson, Charles
1223 Toundson, Solomon
1223 Toundson, Elius
1223 Toundson, Wm.
1224 Toundson, John, senr.
1224 Toundson, Saull
1224 slave Merah
1225 Peall, Thos.
1225 slave Sampson
1226 Bibbins, Rolond
1226 Bibbins, Wm.
1226 Bibbins, Elias
1227 Conerley, Patrick
1228 Andrews, John
1228 Andrews, Peall
1229 Toundson, John
1229 Toundson, John
1230 Mahow, Samuell
1230 Jones, Abraham
1231 Riggin, Ambros, junr.
1232 Dickerson, Edw., senr.
1232 slave George
1233 Dickerson, Edw.
1234 Dickerson, Charles
1235 Donehow, Dorman
1235 Cupper, Samuell
1235 Otwell, Francis
1236 Dukes, William
1237 Toundson, Daniell
1237 Toundson, Dickerson
1237 slave Tauney
1237 slave Peg
1238 Dickerson, Cornelis
1238 slave Dinah
1239 Toundson, James
1239 slave Goie
1240 Bennitt, John
1241 Blades, John
1242 Henderson, Benj.
1243 Henderson, James
1243 Henderson, John
1243 slave Adam
1244 Henderson, Chars.
1245 Henderson, John
1245 slave George
1245 slave Guy
1245 slave Bess
1245 slave Eave
1245 slave Jane
1246 Johnson, Joshua
1247 Small, John
1248 Dickerson, James
1248 Dickerson, Francis
1248 Dickerson, Robert
1249 Henderson, Francis
1250 Henderson, John
1251 Lane, Wm.

1734 TAX LIST [Household number/Name/Remarks]

POCOMOKE HUNDRED

1251 Boyce, Wm.
1251 slave Dick
1251 slave Harrey
1252 Layfield, Cathrine
1252 Layfield, George
1252 Coner, Wm.
1252 slave Tollomey
1253 Brittingham, John
1253 slave Ceasar
1253 slave Nan
1254 Baker, James
1254 Baker, Henderson
1254 Benston, Benj.
1254 Willoms, John
1254 Right, Cumfort
1254 slave Yorke
1255 Gaddis, Robt.
1255 slave Tom
1256 Cane, Thos.
1257 Quinton, Phillip
1257 Quinton, Dixon
1257 slave Jack
1258 Coston, Stephen
1258 Fogg, Moses
1258 slave Sambo
1259 Dickerson, Petter
1259 Mathis, Kindell
1259 Dickerson, John
1260 Britingham, Thos.
1261 Dickerson, Isaac
1261 slave Quashaby
1262 Brittingham, Wm.
1262 slave Rose
1263 Davis, Evin
1264 Merrill, John
1265 Mills, Wm., junr.
1266 Shankling, Wm.
1266 Mills, Nathan
1266 Mills, Alex.
1266 Bull, Patrick
1267 Lamberson, Abraham
1267 Lamberson, Saml.
1267 Lamberson, Abrh.
1268 Ramsey, Char.
1269 Jones, Thos.
1270 Mills, Samuell
1270 Mills, Nathl.
1270 Mills, Hugh
1270 Pading, John
1270 Nobell, James
1271 Mills, Mary
1271 Mills, Smith
1271 Taylor, Roger
1271 slave Simon
1272 Mills, Moses
1273 Jones, Edw.
1273 Jones, Elisha
1274 Goging, David

1274 Brooks, Henery
1275 Melton, John
1276 Brooks, Francis
1277 Fisher, Baley
1278 Harper, Edw.
1279 Hadder, Ignatious
1280 Harris, Jeremiah
1281 Knight, Richd.
1281 Knight, James
1282 Sturgis, Jos.
1282 Laws, Wm.
1282 Laws, John
1282 slave Tom
1282 slave Moll
1283 Bibbins, John
1283 Bibbins, John
1283 Bibbins, Thos.
1283 slave Sambo
1284 Diere, John
1285 Taylor, Saml.
1285 Taylor, Saml.
1285 Taylor, George
1286 Warrington, Thos.
1287 Nobell, James
1288 Stevens, John
1289 McDaniell, Jas.
1290 Webb, John
1290 Webb, Solomon
1290 Webb, John
1291 Wheler, Isaac
1291 Wheler, Edw.
1292 Melvin, Robt.
1292 Melvin, Wm.
1293 Elless, Wm.
1294 Gillett, John
1294 slave Henery
1294 slave Nan
1295 Gillett, Samuell
1295 Gillett, Wm.
1295 slave Bess
1296 Porter, Wm.
1296 Riggin, Pease
1297 Denston, John
1297 Denston, John
1298 Phillips, John
1298 Gillett, George
1299 Lane, John
1300 Otwell, Francis
1301 Buttler, Thos.
1302 Bibbins, Thos.
1303 Toundson, Comfort
1303 Toundson, Wm.
1304 Otwell, Charles
1305 Cordugon, Dennis
1306 Handy, Eliz.
1306 Handy, Saml.
1306 Handy, Thos.
1306 Handy, Wm.
1306 Bennett, Wm.
1306 slave Harry

1306 slave Nedd
1306 slave Hagar
1306 slave Inde
1307 Allen, Francis
1307 Allen, Francis
1307 Duffey, James
1307 Johnson, Abrah.
1307 slave Ceborah
1307 slave Hill
1307 slave Inde
1307 slave Margory
1308 Renolds, Henery
1308 Dingally, Thos.
1308 Hubbord, Richd.
1309 Lamberson, John
1309 Lamberson, Robt.
1310 Merrell, Joseph
1311 Lindall, Robt.
1312 Newbold, Thos.
1312 Butler, Manuell
1312 slave Patience
1313 Dredon, David
1313 Dredon, Wm.
1314 Perkins, John
1315 Perkins, Sarah
1315 Perkins, Wm.
1315 Perkins, Michaell
1316 Clogg, Samuel
1317 Tilman, Gidding
1317 slave Pompy
1318 Brauton, John
1319 Brauton, Bruff
1319 Parker, Phillip
1320 Cluff, Edw.
1321 Dredon, Daniel
1322 Dorman, Samuell
1323 Stevens, Wm.
1323 Stevens, Edw.
1324 Obrion, Christopher
1325 Piper, Isaac
1326 Mitchell, Robt.
1326 slave Townsides
1326 slave Selby
1327 Toundson, Littleton
1328 Denniss, John, senr.
1328 Deniss, Whetley
1328 Dones, Wollintine
1328 Denniss, Lazr.
1328 Twoman, Jno.
1328 slave Joseph
1328 slave Cate
1329 Cotingham, Jonathan
1329 Cotingham, Charles
1329 Cotingham, Jona.
1329 Cotingham, Wm.
1330 Muttex, Lazzros
1331 Flemming, John
1331 Flemming, Wm.
1331 slave Pompy

TAX LISTS OF SOMERSET COUNTY: 1730-1740

POCOMOKE HUNDRED

1331 slave Robin
1331 slave Dinah
1332 Colborn, John
1332 Colborn, Wm.
1333 Morriss, Isaac
1333 Morriss, Luke
1333 slave Ayllo
1333 slave Ben
1333 slave Suthy
1333 slave Abner
1334 Harriss, Robt.
1334 Loge, Alexr.
1334 slave Harrey
1334 slave Ceasar
1334 slave Moll
1334 slave Moll jr.
1335 Benston, John
1335 Benston, Saull
1335 Benston, George
1336 Benton, Cumfort
1336 Costen, Mathies
1336 slave Massorow
1336 slave Hobough
1336 slave Coffey
1336 slave Ben
1336 slave Pegg
1336 slave Jane
1336 slave Manuell
1337 Costen, Isaac
1337 slave Andrew
1338 Owten, Abrah.
1338 Marshall, Jacob
1338 slave Will
1339 Nicholds, Jas.
1339 slave Hannah
1340 Nicholds, Jno.
1341 Nicholds, Joseph
1342 Holstone, Jno., junr.
1343 Houstone, Robt.
1344 Houstone, Joseph, senr.
1344 Killam, Wm.
1344 slave Dick
1344 slave Bell
1345 Purnell, Elisha
1345 Gabey, Joseph
1345 slave Pippin
1346 Huff, Edw.
1346 slave Will
1346 slave Titus
1346 slave Sambo
1346 slave George
1346 slave Naney
1347 Martain, James
1347 Downs, Robt.
1347 Wallace, Robt.
1347 Bennett, John
1347 slave Pompy
1347 slave Ceasar
1347 slave Cato
1347 slave Nann
1348 Jones, Wm.
1349 Right, Randall
1350 Odeare, John
1351 Sturgis, Jona.
1351 Sandwith, Wm.
1352 Nelson, Hugh
1352 slave Jack
1353 Glass, Christopher
1353 Glass, Elius
1353 Glass, Chris.
1353 Steall, James
1353 slave Frank
1354 Godfery, Joseph
1355 Davis, Joseph
1356 Bibbins, Calib
1356 Taylor, Wm.
1357 Killum, John
1358 Toundson, Solomon
1359 Turner, Samuell
1360 Turner, John
1361 Baull, Samuell
1361 Toundson, Jeremiah
1362 Davis, Nathanill
1363 Selbey, Thos.
1363 slave, Sam
1364 Johnson, Elizabeth
1364 slave Bess
1365 Davis,, madom
1365 slave Simon
1365 slave Will
1365 slave Sam
1366 Bounds, George
1367 Grear, Archabald
1368 Houston, John, senr.
1369 Houston, James
1369 slave Cate
1370 Houston, Joseph, junr.
1370 slave Bess
1371 Gore, Richard
1372 Jones, Ann
1372 Jones, Wm.
1373 Wonnell, James
1373 Reading, Charles
1373 Harwood, Richard
1374 Caldwell, Joshua
1374 slave Mass
1375 Dennis, John, junr.
1375 Merrell, Joshua
1375 Whinright, Stephen
1375 Matthis, Thos.
1375 slave Kingston
1375 slave Oxford
1375 slave Jack
1375 slave Patience
1375 slave Abbow
1376 Pecock, Edward
1377 Tomilson, Sayward
1377 slave Plesant
1378 Colbord, William
1379 Fenton, Margrett
1379 Blare, Robert
1379 Grage, Hugh
1380 Davis, Becham
1381 Beywatters, Richard
1381 Hull, Edward
1382 Beuchem, John
1382 slave George
1383 Glass, John
1384 Adams, Hope
1385 Marshall, Samuell
1386 Adams, Thomas, senr.
1386 Adams, David
1386 Adams, Isaac
1386 slave Harrey
1386 slave Jenney
1387 Adams, Thos., junr.
1388 Carsey, Petter
1388 Carsey, Samuell
1388 Carsey, Robertt
1388 Cottingham, John
1389 Carsey, Wm.
1390 Adams, Jacob
1390 Adams, Samuell
1390 Adams, Philip
1390 slave Nan
1390 slave Sampson
1391 Matthies, Teague
1392 Matthues, John
1393 Matthues, William
1394 Matthues, Samuell
1395 Clifton, John
1396 Riggin, John, junr.
1397 Riggin, Elizabeth
1397 Riggin, Solomon
1397 slave Petter
1398 Riggin, Charles
1398 slave Nan
1399 Dickerson, Teague
1400 Milborn, Ralph
1400 slave Dajar
1400 slave Betty
1401 Holland, William, capt.
1401 slave Tom
1401 slave Dinah
1402 Boyer, Robertt
1402 Boyer, Jonathan
1402 Clifton, George
1403 Evins, Thomas
1403 slave Jenney
1404 Evins, Joshua
1405 Elliss, John
1406 Naron, Robert
1406 slave Margey

1734 TAX LIST [Household number/Name/Remarks]

POCOMOKE/WICOMICO HUNDREDS

1406 slave Sarah
1407 White, Archabald
1407 White, Wm.
1408 McDanniell, Allin
1408 McDanniell, Moses
1409 McCredy, Alexr.
1409 McCredy, Alexr.
1410 Tomilinson, Abbigell
1410 Tomblinson, Solomon
1410 Marchment, Charles
1410 slave Lunon
1411 Brayser, Ann
1411 Brayser, James
1411 Corobine, Thomas
1412 White, William
1412 Christophus, Aristobilus
1412 Long, Sowell
1412 slave Jamey
1412 slave Harrey
1412 slave Robin
1412 slave Nimrod
1412 slave Pheuin
1412 slave Sue
1412 slave Jenny
1413 Schofield, Henery
1414 Benston, Wm.
1415 Benston, Thomas
1416 Brown, Thomas
1417 Powell, John
1417 slave Sarah
1418 Brooks, Richard
1418 slave Lott
1419 Blades, Robertt
1419 Blades, Benjamin
1419 Blades, Joseph
1420 Lamdon, Thomas
1421 White, John, pocomoke
1421 Slocom, Benton
1421 2 slaves
1422 Billings, Thomas
1423 Milborn, Calob
1423 2 slaves
1424 Milborn, John
1425 Collings, Samuell
1426 Slocom, Thomas
1427 Naron, James
1427 3 slaves
1428 Cox, William
1428 3 slaves
1429 Hampton, Mary, madom
1429 Henerey, Robt. Jenkins
1429 Henerey, John
1429 13 slaves

1430 White, John, point
1430 2 slaves
1431 Dickerson, Charles
1431 Dickerson, Edward
1432 Taylor, Robert
1433 Adams, Phillip
1434 Adams, Wm.
1434 Adams, Dennis
1434 Adams, Phillip
1434 slave,
1435 Boston, Isaac
1435 2 slaves
1436 Riggin, John, senr.
1436 Riggin, Stephen
1436 Riggin, John
1436 Riggin, Teague
1436 slave,
1437 Becham, Edward
1437 Becham, Thomas
1437 Becham, John
1437 slave,
1438 Boston, Easaw
1439 Woods, Wm.
1439 Arnold, William
1440 Sheldon, John
1440 slave Isaac
1441 Toundson, Eliz.
1441 Toundson, Danford
1441 slave Bess
1442 Gibs, Abraham
1443 Burnett, Jeane
1443 Burnett, James
1444 Dunehow, Teague
1444 Donehow, Daniell
1444 Dukes, Robertt
1444 Donehow, Teague
1445 Riggin, Darby
1445 Riggin, Teage
1446 Young, Daniell
1447 Carey, Jeremiah
1448 Gray, Allin
1449 Adams, George
1450 Britt, John
1450 slave Jack

WICOMICO HUNDRED

1451 Coldwell, John, mr.
1451 Coldwell, Robert
1451 Highway, Abraham
1451 slave Coffey
1451 slave Will
1451 slave Ishmaell
1451 slave Doll
1451 slave Squash
1451 slave Gardiner
1452 Hearn, Tho.
1452 [Hearn], Nehemyah, son

1452 [Hearn], George, son
1452 slave Hannah
1453 Sloane, James
1454 Lindan, Tho.
1455 Phillips, Jacob
1456 Hastins, Robert
1456 [Hastins], Will., son
1457 Coldwell, Heugh
1458 Freny, Petter
1459 White, Henry
1460 Gordy, Petter
1461 Gordy, Moses
1462 Taylor, Thomas
1463 Hearn, Will.
1463 [Hearn], Tho., son
1463 slave Niall
1464 Mattax, Will.
1464 slave Abram
1465 Mattax, Alix.
1465 slave Mariah
1466 Covington, Tho.
1466 [Covington], Bingimin, son
1466 slave Tom
1467 Cox, Thomas
1468 Hall, Sam.
1468 Ready, Bryant
1469 Vincent, Tho., senr.
1469 [Vincent], Bengimin, son
1470 Tatum, John
1470 [Tatum], Thomas, son
1471 McGlachlin, Robert
1472 Vincent, Thomas, junr.
1473 Lecatt, John
1474 Wale, John
1475 Creagh, Will.
1475 Cox, Hill
1475 Hennry, Martain
1475 [Creagh], Cornelius, son
1476 Turner, Sam.
1476 [Turner], Edward, son
1476 Smith, Archibald
1477 Smith, George
1478 Smith, David
1479 Smith, James, senr.
1479 [Smith], Moses, son
1480 Hill,, widow
1480 [Hill], James, her son
1481 Davis, John
1481 Roark, Jams.
1482 Davis, Daniell

TAX LISTS OF SOMERSET COUNTY: 1730-1740

POCOMOKE HUNDRED

1483 Davis, John, junr.
1483 McGee, John
1484 Parsons, George
1485 Croutch, Isack
1485 Croutch, Robert
1486 Perry, James
1487 Shockly, John
1487 [Shockley], Jonathan, son
1487 [Shockley], John, son
1487 [Shockley], Richard, son
1488 McGlamry, George
1489 Boyen, William
1490 Duskey, Moses
1491 Davis, Samuell
1492 Dixon, Will.
1493 Atkins, Robert
1494 Hales, John
1495 Roark, John
1496 Parrimore, Richard
1497 Cathill, James
1498 Cristopher, John, junr.
1498 Taylor, John
1499 Duskey, Dunis
1499 Tolbat, John
1500 Fooks, Bengimin
1500 slave Patience
1501 Vance, Alix., junr.
1502 Toadvins,, widow
1502 [Toadvine], William, son
1503 Hayman, Will.
1503 [Hayman], Will., son
1504 Adly, William
1505 Ragly, Micaell
1506 Knox, Robert
1506 [Knox], Will., son
1507 Pollet, Thomas
1508 Stanford, Joseph
1509 Chadwick, James
1509 [Chadwick], James, son
1510 Disherone, John, junr.
1511 Disherone, John, forrest
1512 Disherone, Lewis
1513 Disherone, Levin
1514 Dishrone, Micaell
1514 Canid[or], John
1515 Miller, Petter
1516 Puckham, Richard

1517 Cristopher, Ephraim
1518 Jankins, Jarvis
1518 [Jenkins], John, son
1519 Thomson, John
1520 McGee, George
1521 Doudle, Christopher
1522 Shahane, John
1523 Vance, David
1524 Croutch, John
1524 [Croutch], Nicolas
1525 Sutch, Oliver
1526 Dishrone,, widow
1526 [Disharoon], Mickaell, son
1527 Hillman, Edward
1528 Howard, John
1529 Roatches,, mrs.
1529 [Roach], Isack, son
1529 [Roach], Stephen, son
1529 slave Tom
1529 slave Harry
1529 slave Peg
1530 Dishrone, John, mr.
1530 [Disharoon], Will., son
1530 slave Coffy
1530 slavve Grase
1530 slave Fanny
1531 Sharp,, capt.
1531 slave Pompy
1531 slave Mary
1532 Goldsmith, Anthony
1533 Todevine, Hennry
1533 [Todvine], Thomas, son
1533 Hiway, Isack
1533 slave Golyah
1533 slave Oxford
1533 slave Jane
1533 slave Sarah
1534 Careys,, widow
1534 [Carey], Thos., son
1535 Carey, Levin
1536 Carey, Jonathan
1537 Tounsand, Ben., mr.
1537 slave Bess
1538 Hayman, James
1538 [Hayman], Charles, brother
1538 [Hayman], Isaac, brother
1539 Hayman, John

1540 Goddard, Thomas
1541 Fullerton, Alix.
1541 [Fullerton], James, brother
1542 Radish, John
1543 Lows,, capt.
1543 slave Jeptha
1543 slave Roase
1544 Cadry, Jacob
1544 Cadry, Morgan
1545 Colier, Tho.
1545 slave Grace
1546 Addams, Alix., reverant
1546 Hayman, Charles
1546 Hill, John
1546 Christopher, Rixan
1546 slave Jack
1546 slave Squak
1546 slave Bess
1547 G[i]lles, Thomas, mr.
1547 Turk, Magnus
1547 slave Dannuk
1547 slave Stepny
1547 slave Namor
1547 slave Pegg
1548 Goslin, Thomas
1549 Goslin, Mathew
1550 Cadry, Isack
1551 Elliot, Francis
1552 Balley, Jonathan
1553 Davis, William
1554 Goslin, Richard
1555 Vennabls, William
1556 Mitchell, Isack
1557 Phillips, Richard
1558 Crauford, John
1558 Rider, James
1559 Bounds, Jonathan
1559 Ward, James
1559 slave Bess
1560 Stephens, Richard
1560 slave Pompy
1560 slave Alis
1561 Kible,, widow
1561 [Kibble], Will., son
1562 Fosque, Thomas
1563 Stephens, John
1563 Roatch, John
1563 slave Isack
1563 slave Bess
1564 Hall, Thomas
1565 Hall, Phenix
1566 Dashiell, Magor
1566 North, John
1566 slave Polidore
1566 slave Sambo
1566 slave Frank

1734 TAX LIST [Household number/Name/Remarks]

WICOMICO HUNDRED

1566 slave Harry
1566 slave Dublin
1566 slave Jane
1566 slave Nan
1566 slave Cate
1566 slave Roase
1566 5 slaves
1567 Parsons, John
1568 McGee, Petter, junr.
1569 McGle[n]e, Daniell
1570 Cope, John
1570 Cope, Will.
1571 Surman, Edward
1571 Morris, Jerimiah
1572 Hobs, Joy
1572 [Hobs], Absolum, son
1572 slave Polipus
1573 Bashaw, Graves
1574 McCone, Robert
1575 McGee, Petter, senr.
1576 Kible, John
1577 Mears, John
1577 [Mears], Robert, son
1578 Cristopher, John
1578 [Christopher], Clement
1578 [Christopher], Joseph, son
1579 Ellis, Joseph
1580 Hill, Charles
1580 Ellis, John
1581 Baley, George
1581 [Baily], Ben., son
1581 Pope, Richard
1582 Alixander, Will.
1582 [Alexander], Liston, son
1583 Alixander, James
1583 Hodg, John
1584 Alixander, Moses
1584 slave Tom
1585 Grifen, John
1586 Surman, Petter
1586 [Surman], Petter
1586 [Surman], John
1586 slave Tom
1586 slave Lemon
1587 Mitchell, Richard
1588 [Mitchell], Alex.
1588 Mitchell, Benjimin
1589 Mitchell, John
1589 Aday, John
1590 Swillifant, Will.

1590 Noble, Isack
1591 Sockwell, George
1592 Miflin, Thomas
1593 Brearton, Will.
1593 slave Patiens
1594 Cottman, Will.
1595 Cottman, Benjimin
1595 slave John
1595 slave Sarah
1596 Cottman, Joseph
1596 Aday, Owen
1597 Robison, Will.
1598 Robison, John
1599 Lokey, Thomas
1600 Walker, Thos.
1600 slave Tom
1600 slave Jonathan
1600 slave Dyna
1600 slave Cate
1601 Handy, Ebinezer
1601 slave Sambo
1601 slave Mumford
1601 slave Tom
1601 slave Will
1601 slave Amy
1601 slave Hannah
1601 slave Bonny
1602 Holdbrooke, Thomas
1603 Ellis,, mrs.
1603 Fouler, Tho.
1603 slave Boubo
1603 slave Hannah
1603 slave Nanny
1603 slave Moll
1604 Gale,, hon. collonell
1604 Debvix, John
1604 Rinsrose, Daniell
1604 Specks, Robert
1604 Welch, James
1604 slave Hope
1604 slave Plesant
1604 slave Jehew
1604 slave Venter
1604 slave Robin
1604 slave Petter
1604 slave Joyce
1604 slave Pullett
1604 slave Bridget
1604 slave Zephora
1604 slave Jack
1604 slave Kingston
1604 slave Robin
1605 Stiuart, Patrick
1605 Stuart, John
1605 slave Wfra
1606 Harris, Will., senr.
1606 [Harris], Richard, son

1606 [Harris], John, son
1606 [Harris], Charls, son
1607 Harris, Will., junr.
1608 Durham, James
1609 Harris, George
1610 Astin, Robert
1610 slave Mall
1611 Ballards,, mrs.
1611 slave Mariah
1612 Dashiell, Tho.
1613 Ballard, Charles
1613 slave Cesar
1614 Rencher, Underwood
1614 slave Jack
1614 slave Bess
1615 Renchar, Tho.
1615 slave Pompy
1615 slave Petter
1616 Leggs, Bengimin
1617 Shiles, John
1617 slave Tom
1618 Croket, Richard
1618 Larimore, John
1619 Croket, John
1619 slave Wapin
1620 Croket, Robert
1620 slave Crop
1620 slave Munk
1621 Cadry, Daniell
1621 slave Samson
1621 slave Sib
1622 Evans,, mrs.
1622 slave Toby
1622 slave Mesar
1622 slave Robin
1622 slave Sibb
1622 slave Abo
1623 Dashiell, George
1623 Foster, John
1623 slave Coffey
1624 Lackey, Alix.
1624 slave Darby
1624 slave Sam
1624 slave Surrey
1624 slave Amey
1625 Evans, John, senr.
1625 [Evans], John, son
1625 slave Sambo
1625 slave Abo
1626 Dashiell, Charles
1626 Tipet, Tho.
1627 Shiles, Tho.
1627 McCoy, John
1628 Willin, Edward
1629 Nelson, John
1630 Nelson, Will.
1631 Willin, Tho.
1631 [Willin], Robert

TAX LISTS OF SOMERSET COUNTY: 1730-1740

WICOMICO HUNDRED

1631 slave Sarah
1632 Everton, John
1632 [Everton], Will
1633 Howard, Tho.
1633 Jarvice, Sam.
1634 Upton, Thos.
1634 Poe, John
1635 Scott, Day, mr.
1635 slave Hector
1635 slave Sipeo
1635 slave Tom
1635 slave Leucy
1636 Scott, George, mr.
1636 slave Sam
1636 slave Sanders
1636 slave Pompy
1636 slave Mingo
1637 Cadry, Abraham
1638 Wales, John
1638 slave Galaway
1639 Stuart, Alix
1639 Dashiell, Will.
1639 slave Jane
1639 slave Bess
1639 slave Sibb
1640 Dashiell, James, junr.
1640 slave Frank
1641 McMorry, James
1641 slave Batt
1641 slave Pompy
1641 slave Abner
1641 slave Roase
1642 Hardy, Robert
1642 Hardy, George
1642 Boreman, Sam.
1643 Piper, Cristopher
1643 slave Dick
1643 slave Sambo
1643 slave Toby
1643 slave Senr
1644 Goslin, John
1645 Vennabls, Bengimin
1645 slave Tom
1645 slave Coffey
1645 slave Will
1645 slave Bess
1646 Venabls, Will.
1646 slave Jafrey
1647 Recirds, John
1647 [Records], Ben., son
1647 [Records], James, son
1647 [Records], Tho., son
1647 slave Caine
1648 Humfris,, capt.
1648 [Humphris], Thomas, son
1648 slave Cofey
1648 slave Bess
1649 Bird, Tho.
1649 [Bird], Tho., son
1649 [Bird], Will., son
1650 Smith, James, junr.
1651 Baker, Thomas
1652 Nicoldson, Joseph
1653 Nicoldson, James
1654 Nicoldson, Richard
1655 Bartlit, Tho.
1655 [Bartlett], Pasky, son
1656 Bartlit, William
1657 Culver, John
1658 Cadry, John
1659 Dalany, Will.
1660 Owen, Edward
1661 Handy, John, capt.
1661 slave Dick
1661 slave Moll
1661 slave Jane
1662 Morris, Jacob
1663 Crouth, Jacob
1663 [Crouth], Jacob, son
1664 Porter, Joshua
1665 Collet, James
1665 Salt, Balmforth
1665 Todevine, John
1665 Berry, James
1666 Lancake, Francis
1666 [Lancake], Stephen, son
1666 slave Jack
1666 slave Toby
1666 slave Bess
1667 Lancake, George
1667 Phillips, George
1668 Price, John
1669 McGlamry, Will.
1669 [Brady,, widow]
1670 Brady, William, to his mother
1671 Heatch, Elgate
1671 Price, Elix.
1671 slave Canuna
1671 slave Hannah
1672 Johnson, Purnall
1673 Handy, Isack, mr.
1673 slave Sharper
1673 slave Prew
1674 Hitch, Sam.
1674 Price, Frank
1675 Heatch, John
1675 slave Mow
1676 Vincent, George
1676 Hith, Will.
1677 Clifton, Phillip
1678 Murfey, John
1679 Lingo, Robison
1680 Lingo, Jacob
1681 Dorman, Hennry
1681 [Dorman], Maior, son
1682 Lingo, Richard
1683 Willis, Nathaniell
1684 Longo, James
1685 McGlamry, Edward
1685 Olifant, Mathew
1686 Carsey, Patrick
1686 [Carsey], Will., son
1686 [Carsey], Patrick, son
1687 Lingo, John
1688 Perdue, John
1689 Ready, Thomas
1690 Bashaw, Garrat
1691 Man, Thomas
1692 Jones, Finch
1693 Linch, Micaell
1694 Burn, James
1694 Heath, John
1695 Atkinson, Tim.
1695 Evans, William
1696 [Croutch, Ann]
1696 Croutch, Jacob, son
1697 Cornwell, Robert
1698 Leonard, Joseph
1699 Winder, Thos.
1699 unnamed/slave
1700 Polk, David
1701 Stevens, Thos.
1702 Stevens, William

1735 TAX LIST [Household number/Name/Remarks]

ANNEMESSEX HUNDRED

1 Coulbroun, William, senr
1 Coulbroun, Wm., jur.
1 Coulbroun, Samuel
1 Coulbroun, Sollomon
1 Coulbroun, Michael
1 slave Quako
1 slave Abram
1 slave Lucy
2 Coulbroun, Sollomon
2 Coulbroun, Soll.
2 Mecanny, Patrick
3 Katan, George
4 Tailor, Willm.
5 Holland, Michael, jur.
5 Obrian, Clark
5 slave Moll
6 Bennett, Henry
6 Ward, Richd.
7 Roach, Charles
7 slave Jo
8 Bird, Joseph
8 Cullen, Jacob
8 Dies, Daniel
9 Starling, Jno., senr.
9 Starling, Jno., junr.
9 Starling, Henry
9 Starling, Aaron
10 Dixon, James
11 Bird, David
12 Grimes, James
13 Moore, William
14 Ward, Thos.
14 Ward, James
14 Ward, Jacob
15 Juett, William
15 slave Ned
16 Sumners, Thos.
16 Sumners, Geo.
16 Sumners, Thos.
17 Sumners, Jonathan
18 Sumners, Jno.
18 Sumners, David
19 Claywell, Selby
20 Tyler, Thos.
21 Tyler, Jno.
21 Tyler, Jno.
22 Parks, Arthur
22 Parks, Jno.
22 Parks, Arthur
22 Parks, Job
22 Solsberry, William
23 Williams, William
24 Parks, Jno.
24 Parks, Mark
25 Evens, Jno.
25 Hurst, Jno.
26 Mister, Wm.
26 Mister, Abraham
26 Mister, Benjamin
27 Hopkins, George
27 Hopkins, Jno.
27 Hopkins, Willm.
27 Hopkins, Charles
28 Woolf, Henry
29 Spibey, Jonathan
30 Fogg, Daniel
31 Parker, Isaac
32 Moore, Isaac
33 Allen, Joseph
34 Redden, Jno.
35 Riggen, Jonathan
36 Riggen, Jno., senr.
36 Riggen, Jno., jur.
36 Riggen, Willm.
37 Ward, Cornelious
37 Riggen, Stephen
38 Ward, Stephen, junr.
39 Ward, Samuell
39 Ward, Jno.
40 Lord, Frances
40 Lord, Randall
40 Lord, Jno.
40 Lord, Thos.
40 Lord, Alexdr.
41 Ward, Stephen, senr.
41 slave Pompy
41 slave Phillis
41 slave Sarah
42 Dougherty, Jno.
42 Dougherty, Nathll.
43 Moore, Frances
43 Moore, Thos.
43 Moore, Jacob
44 Frazer, Peter
44 slave Moreah
45 Johnson, Jno., senr.
45 Smith, James
46 Johnson, Jno., jur.
47 Davis, James
48 Miles, Henry
48 slave Dinah
48 slave Fillis
48 slave Robbin
49 Bell, Anthony, ser.
49 Arnall, Willm.
49 Bell, Josephas
49 Jones, Matthew
50 Bell, Anthony, jur.
51 Davis, Jno.
51 Megummery, Thos.
51 slave Harry
51 slave Watt
51 slave Sue
51 slave Dick
51 slave Jenny
52 Roach, Jno.
52 Roach, Isaac
53 Price, Edward
53 Price, Jno.
53 Price, Frances
53 Price, Johnson
54 Cullen, Henry
54 Dukes, Jno.
55 Allen, Henry
56 Scandelin, Edward
57 Lankford, Joseph, senr.
57 Lankford, Sollomon
57 Owen, Moses
58 Lankford, Joseph, jur.
59 Horsey, Stephen, jur.
60 Horsey, Samll.
60 Horsey, Smith
61 Horsey, Isaac
61 slave Jonathan
62 Horsey, Natl.
62 slave Quomene
62 slave Cook
62 slave Prince
62 slave Kate
62 slave Patience
62 slave Parroah
63 Dixon, Willm.
63 slave Bess
63 slave Ben
64 Smith, Henry
64 Smith, Archble.
64 Smith, Willm.
65 Dixon, Thos., senr.
65 Dixon, Thos., junr.
65 slave Harry
65 slave Tobey
65 slave Dick
65 slave Gidden
65 slave Dinah
65 slave Hannah
66 Lankford, Benjamin
67 Long, Jno.
67 slave Robin
67 slave Sarah
68 Pewsey, Willm.
69 Owen, Elizabeth
69 Owen, Phillip
70 Williams, Isaac
70 Dohety, James
71 Williams, Thos., junr.
71 Addams, Jno.
71 slave Dick
71 slave Sesar
71 slave Quash
71 slave Lilly
72 Fanton, Marten
72 Dolkin, Willm.

TAX LISTS OF SOMERSET COUNTY: 1730-1740

ANNEMESSEX HUNDRED

73 Williams, Thos., senr.
73 Cottingham, Thos.
73 Green, Thos.
73 Johnson, Willm.
73 slave Titas
73 slave Adam
73 slave George
73 slave Tom
73 slave Jonas
73 slave Addam
73 slave Glaseo
73 slave Sarah
73 slave Gelico
74 Williams, Jno.
74 Williams, Jacob
74 slave Sambo
74 slave Moll
75 Catlin, Wllm.
75 slave Harry
76 Curtis, Charles
76 slave Dick
76 slave Toney
76 slave Kate
77 Handy, Thos.
77 slave Nan
78 Long, Samuel, anamessex
78 slave Samson
78 slave Kate
79 Tull, Sollomon
80 Tull, Thos.
80 slave Quamenor
81 Trehearn, Jno.
82 mollatto Watt
83 Watters, Willm.
83 slave Goliah
83 slave Sambo
83 slave Bristah
83 slave Dinah
84 Watters, John
84 slave Harry
84 slave Jane
84 slave Moreah
84 slave Will
84 slave Dick
85 Watters, Edward
86 Cotman, Mary
86 Cottman, Joseph
86 slave Jenny
87 Watters, Abigail
87 slave David
88 Barns, Robart
89 Whorton, Willm.
89 Slocum, Riley
90 Hall, Charles
90 Davis, Richd.
90 slave Domminick
91 Hall, Richd.
91 Wolston, Joy

92 Landon, Henry
93 Watters, Eliz., mrs.
93 Watters, Richd.
93 Loyd, Willm.
93 Beach, Thos.
93 slave Allex
93 slave Hannable
93 slave Sippeo
93 slave Hagar
93 slave Peg
94 Stockdell, Edward
95 Lister, Jane
95 Lister, Thos.
95 Lister, Willm.
95 slave Sesar
96 Outten, Jno., senr.
96 Outten, Jno., junr.
96 slave Bess
97 Maddux, Thos.
97 Maddux, Bell
98 Connor, Jno., senr.
98 Connor, Jno., junr.
98 mollatto Kate
99 Connor, Willm.
100 Wheatly, Sampson
101 Addams, David
101 Addams, Thos.
101 Addams, Jacob
101 Addams, Willm.
102 Potter, Henry
102 Dukes, Robert
103 Lord, Henry
104 Linzy, Thos.
105 Cottingham, Charles
105 Cottingham, Thos.
105 Cottingham, Jno.
106 Cottingham, Charles
107 Scott, Robt., senr.
107 Scot, John
107 slave Bess
108 Long, Randall
108 Powell, Gabriel
108 slave Sibb
109 White, Jno., junr.
109 Powell, Thos.
110 Hearn, Edward
110 Riggen, Jonathan
111 slave Frank
111 slave Bess
111 Atkinson, Joshua
112 Gunby, Jno.
112 Buckler, Cornelious
112 slave Jack
112 slave Kate
113 Gunby, Kirk
113 Kendall, Willm.
114 Kellam, Jno., senr.
114 Kellam, Jno., jur.
114 Kellam, Isaac

115 Horsey, Stephen, senr.
115 Foddred, Willm.
115 Killy, James
116 Bell, Thos.
116 slave Nan
117 Bywaters, Richd.
118 Sanders, Rchd.
118 Sanders, Thos.
119 King, Robert, col. quarter
119 slave Mingo
119 slave Tamore
120 Beachamp, Isaac
120 slave Patience
121 King, James
122 Beachamp, Edmond
122 Dakes, Edward
122 Beachamp, Robert
123 Beachamp, Willm.
124 Beachamp, Sarah
124 Beachamp, Jno.
125 Boston, William
125 Catlin, Robt.
126 Brimmegom, Walter
127 Marshall, George
128 Porter, Joseph
128 Porter, William
129 Moore, Thos., merunseo
130 White, Jno., senr.
130 White, Jno.
130 slave Essex
131 Ceary, Frances
132 Cohoone, Jno.
133 Riggen, Samuel
133 slave Bess
134 Long, Daniell, junr.
135 Long, Jeffery
135 slave Nish
136 Long, Samuell merunseo
136 Long, Wm.
136 Long, David
137 Wilson, Jno.
138 Long, Daniell, senr.
138 Long, David
138 slave Friendship
138 slave Nan
139 Trehearn, James
140 Wilson, George
141 Prier, Thos.
141 Tayler, Elias
142 White, Thos.
142 Wilson, Joseph
143 Roach, Nathaniel
144 Pewsey, Jno.
145 Roach, Samll.
146 Scott, Robt., junr.
147 Lindone, Jno.

1735 TAX LIST [Household number/Name/Remarks]

ANNEMESSEX/BALTIMORE HUNDREDS

148 Moore, Frances
148 Moore, Jno., senr.
148 Moore, Isaac
149 Moore, William
149 Moore, Samll.

BALTIMORE HUNDRED
150 Carey, Thomas
151 Morris, John
151 slave Cate
152 Morriss, Dennis
153 Waker, William
154 Runnels, Richard
155 Jones, Ebenezer
155 slave Bess
156 Radney, William
157 Prittyman, Thomas
158 Murray, James
158 slave Bess
159 Burton, William
159 Burton, John
159 Burton, Joshua
159 Pepper, Wm.
159 slave Tows
159 slave Rachell
159 slave Adam
160 Wilson, John
161 Carey, Richard
162 Bearnett, John
163 Beasey, William
163 Goodrich, William
164 Waples, Paul
164 Thoroughgood, Paul
164 slave Charles
164 slave Dublen
165 Gilstrap, Peter
166 Bowden, John
167 Cobb, William
167 Tingle, Samuell
168 Wait, Joseph
168 Cobb, Joseph
169 Weight, William
170 Lathberry, George
171 Purkins, Thomas
171 Colfing, Joseph
172 Stevenson, John
173 Smith, William
174 Townsend, Bowman
175 Hudson, David
175 Hudson, Absalom
175 Hudson, William
176 Coffing, Thomas
176 Coffing, Thomas
177 Tingle, Hugh
177 Tingle, Hugh
178 Hudson, Samuel
179 Adams, Thomas
179 Blizard, Thomas
180 Gray, Joseph
180 Killey, Nicholas
180 slave Simon
180 slave Quaco
181 Smith, John
181 Smith, Robert
182 Grayham, George
183 Barnett, James
184 Wharton, Francis
184 Wharton, William
185 Morris, Bibbins
186 Blizard, Richard
187 Derixon, Joseph
188 Linch, John, junr.
188 Roberts, Saml.
189 Hall, Samuel
190 Roberts, Thomas
190 Roberts, Alexander
191 Hazzard, David, sr.
191 Hazzard, Wm.
191 Hazzard, Arther
191 slave Jacob
191 slave Dinah
192 Wharton, Daniel
193 Wharton, Henmon
193 slave Amerello
194 Clark, Mary
194 Clark, Edward
195 Bredell, Isaiah
195 Bredell, Stephen
195 slave Simon
195 slave Adam
195 slave Pender
195 slave Menah
196 Brittingham, Elizabeth
196 Brittingham, Robert
196 Gatt, John
197 Crapper, Edmond, junr.
198 Collins, John
199 Fall, John
199 Lucker, Wm.
200 Smallwood, Samuel
201 Mumford, James
201 slave Oram
202 Linch, Alexander
203 Hollaway, John, senr.
204 Hampton, Mary, mrs.
204 slave Jack
204 slave Hannah
204 slave Hanable
205 Hollaway, Joseph
206 Hollaway, John, junr.
207 Mumford, Charles
208 Mumford, Thomas
209 Russell, Andrew
210 Bessix, Absolam
211 Mumford, Wm.
212 Shewell, Samuel
213 Fassitt, Franklin
213 Wilson, John
213 slave Nan
214 Talburt, John
215 Richards, John, junr.
216 Richards, Jones
216 slave Sarah
217 Depray, John
218 ONorton, John
219 Godwin, Ceaser
219 Godwin, Ceaser
219 Godwin, Daniel
220 Hazzard, David, junr.
221 Daizey, Thomas
222 Hopkins, Josiah
223 Wise, Mathew
224 Aydelott, John, senr.
224 Bowman, Henry
224 slave Jack
225 Howard, George, senr.
225 Howard, George, junr.
225 slave Kent
225 slave Bess
226 Robinson, Joshua
226 slave Bess
227 Howard, Nehemiah
228 West, Thomas
229 West, Wm.
230 Hickman, Richard, junr.
231 Hudson, Richard, junr.
231 Lathberry, Arthur
232 Nottman, John
233 Hudson, John
234 Tull, John, senr.
234 Tull, John, junr.
235 Clark, Rase
235 Clark, John
235 Clark, Benjamin
235 Clark, Joseph
236 Evans, Wm., senr.
236 Evans, John
236 Evans, William
236 Evans, Walter
237 Liptrott, John
238 Rodger, Solomon
238 slave Cain
239 Tingle, John
239 slave Harry
240 Woodcraft, Richard
241 Woodcraft, Mary
241 Wildgoose, Richard
241 Wildgoose, Thomas
242 Woodcraft, William

TAX LISTS OF SOMERSET COUNTY: 1730-1740

BALTIMORE HUNDRED

243 Deall, Archibald
244 West, George
245 Aydelott, Benjamin
246 Dixon, Sturgis
246 Johnson, Levin
247 Johnson, Leonard
248 Godwin, Michael
248 slave Bess
249 Hill, Ann
249 Hazzard, Benjamin, son
250 Robinson, Thomas
251 Marsey, John
251 Banks, Niblett
252 Mersey, Atkins
253 Evans, John, senr.
254 Records, John, sr.
254 Records, Wm.
254 slave Boston
254 slave Simon
254 slave Bridgett
254 slave Moll
255 Robinson, Michael
255 Robinson, William
256 Webb, William
257 Linch, Abram
258 Miller, John
258 Tingle, Littleton
258 slave Primrose
258 slave Pegg
259 Bowden, Abell
260 Robinson, John
260 Robinson, George
261 Perry, James, junr.
262 Hardin, Thomas
263 Hopkins, John
264 Joseph, Frederick
265 Lewis, Joseph
265 Lewis, Wm.
266 Lewis, Arthur
267 Anderson, Wm.
268 Collins, George
269 Ingram, Jacob
270 Short, Edward
271 Cary, William
272 Johnson, Bartholomew
273 West, Thomas, junr.
274 Philips, Wm.
274 Hudson, Charles
275 Campbell, John
276 Hickman, Richard, senr.
277 Collins, Wm.
278 Derrixon, Benjamin
279 Murray, James
280 Murray, Robert
281 Deall, John, junr.
281 Tatlock, Edward
282 Deall, John, senr.
283 Gray, Thomas
284 Powell, Thomas, junr.
285 Harrison, Wm.
286 Kennitt, Martin
287 Johnson, David
288 Wilson, Isaac
289 Laughinghours, Wm.
289 slave Moll
290 Jones, John
291 Latchim, Thos.
292 Campbell, John
292 slave Pheaby
293 Walliss, Thomas
294 Simpson, Richard
295 Newbold, John
295 slave Cato
296 Taylor, Walter
297 Loggwood, Richard
298 Collins, Thomas
299 Wale, Charles
300 Crapper, Nathaniel, jr.
301 Morgan, Avere
301 slave Apo
302 Fisher, Benton
303 Gay, James
304 Forsight, Thomas
305 Tier, Robert
306 Bell, Isaac
307 Johnson, John
308 Miller, Joseph
308 Monks, Wm.
308 slave Charles
308 slave Jack
308 slave Moll
308 slave Tom
309 Aydelott, John, junr.
310 Peterkin, David
311 Hall, Joseph
312 Smith, John, capt.
312 Smith, John, junr.
312 Smith, Thomas
312 slave Harry
312 slave Bess
312 slave Mereah
313 Marshall, Isaac
313 slave Benjamin
313 slave Thom
313 slave Bess
313 slave Dinah
314 Bradford, Nathaniel
315 Predox, Thomas
316 Fasitt, Lambert
316 slave Coffey
317 Fasitt, John
317 slave Mingo
317 slave Lucy
318 Marey, Alexander
318 slave Jack
318 slave Jaude
319 Delamati, John Patrick
320 Walton, Comfort
320 slave Nan
321 Cambill, Solomon
322 Wheler, John, senr.
322 Wheler, John
323 Crapper, Nathanl., senr.
323 Crapper, Vencint
323 slave Kener
324 Judett, Nathaniel
325 Walton, Willm. senr.
325 Walton, William, jr.
325 slave Ceaser
325 slave Jude
325 slave Gloster
326 Laurance, Henry
327 Wolton, John
328 Crapper, Solomon
329 Pattey, Jno.
329 slave London
330 Waker, John
331 Hook, William
331 Taylor, Samuell
332 Wale, William, senr.
333 Forwell, Thomas
334 Hudson, Richard, senr.
334 Hudson, John
334 slave Dick
334 slave Beck
334 slave Charles
334 slave Coffey
335 Collier, Peter
335 slave Pompey
335 slave Moll
336 Crapper, Edmond
336 slave Nick
336 slave Peter
336 slave Pompy
336 slave Phebe
336 slave Margrat
337 Holland, Richard
337 Caldwell, Agustin
337 slave Hannah
338 Wale, William, junr.
338 McConnock, Patrick
339 Kennett, Wm.
339 Ractcliff, John
340 Godard, Thomas
341 Gault, Wm.
341 Turvill, John
342 Robinson, Andrew
343 Fall, Abram
344 Manklyn, Richard

1735 TAX LIST [Household number/Name/Remarks]

BALTIMORE/BOGERTERNORTON HUNDREDS

345 Bradford, William
346 Turvill, Wm., sr.
346 Turvill, Prisgrave
346 Rackliffe, Elias
346 Wale, John
347 Turvill, Wm., jr.
348 Bowin, Rodiah
348 [Bowin], William
348 Bowin, Jno.
348 Cowe, Danl.
348 slave Quamne
349 Fassit, Rouce
350 Racklife, Charles, capt.
350 Rackliffe, Purnall
350 Flowith, George
350 slave Robin
350 slave Cate
350 slave Fosque
350 slave Matt
350 slave Sarah
350 slave Will
351 Alford, David
352 Fassit, Willm.
352 slave Sambo
352 slave Will
352 slave Harry
352 slave Titus
352 slave Rachel
352 slave Nancy
352 slave Frank
352 slave Sew
352 slave Doll
352 slave Berry
352 slave Phillis
353 Peal, Thoroughgood
354 Quillin, Joseph
354 Quillin, John
354 Quillin, Benja.
355 Hudson, William
355 Gray, William
356 Purnell, John
356 Lowe, Charles
356 Rackliffe, Charles
356 Rackliffe, Rixam
356 slave Toney, sr.
356 slave Toney
356 slave Doll
356 slave Mary
357 Hopkins, Samuel, capt.
358 Gault, Robt.
359 Morris, Wm.
360 Jefferson, Richd.
361 Cuningam, Arthur

BOGERTERNORTON HUNDRED
362 Murray, John
363 Dobbin, William
364 Mcneal, Archbald

365 Challie, Moses
365 Challie, Peter
366 Buncle, Alexander
367 Stewart, Peter
368 Wildman, John
369 Ellison, Richd.
370 Clawell, Thos.
370 slave
371 Whittington, William
371 6 slaves
372 Porter, William
372 Patrick, Roger
372 Patrick, Daniell
373 Houlston, John
374 Bushop, John, senr.
374 Bushop, Joseph
375 Adkins, John
376 Pepper, John
377 Selby, John
377 3 slaves
378 Bushop, William
378 Outten, John
378 Outten, Thos.
379 Purnell, Thos.
379 4 slaves
380 Selby, William
380 4 slaves
381 Loe, George
382 Bushop, Benja.
383 Victor, James
384 Richardson, Charles
384 slave
385 Richardson, Robt.
385 slave
386 Richardson, James
387 Richardson, William
388 Scofield, Joseph
388 Scofield, John
388 2 slaves
389 Purnell, Elisha
389 slave
390 Brittingham, Isaac
390 Brittingham, Nathan
390 slave
391 Rattcliffe, Charles
392 Edwards, Benony
393 Purnell, Benja.
393 slave
394 Houlston, William
394 Purkins, Hugh
395 Mcaley, John
396 Greer, Archbald
397 Teague, John, senr.
397 Teague, John, junr.
398 Brittingham, Jeremiah
399 Brittingham, William, sr

399 Brittingham, William, jr
399 Brittingham, Solomon
399 Brittingham, Absolom
400 Davis, William, seaside
400 Ducks, Thos.
400 slave
401 Stevens, Samuell
402 Shockley, John
403 Holland, William
404 Ennis, Nathl.
405 Ennis, William
406 Ennis, Mary
406 Ennis, Saml.
407 Ennis, Cornelius
408 Mumford, George
409 Truit, George, son of Philip
410 Truit, William
411 Truit, Geo., son of George
411 Truit, John
411 Davis, William
411 slave
412 Mumford, James
412 [Mumford], James
413 Turner, Henry
414 Dreyden, John, junr.
415 Dreyden, Robert
416 Steel, James
416 Steel, Daniell
417 Sturgis, John
418 Turner, Nickolas
419 Stevenson, James
420 English, Thos.
421 Bratten, James
422 Bratten, Saml., senr.
422 Bratten, Hugh
423 Bratten, Saml., junr.
423 Bratten, William
423 Bratten, John
424 Dennis, Solomon
425 Dennis, Wh[eatl]y
426 Godfrey, Charles
427 Scott, Mark
428 Devrox, John
428 Prior, Webb
428 Devrox, Cornelius
428 slave
429 Johnson, George
430 Johnson, Thomas
431 Johnson, Affradozi
431 Johnson, John
431 slave
432 Robieson, William
432 Wells, Daniell
433 Hall, William

TAX LISTS OF SOMERSET COUNTY: 1730-1740

BOGERTERNORTON HUNDRED

433 Hall, Adam
433 Hall, Phenix
433 2 slaves
434 Bell, Adam
434 slave
435 Drigroes, John
436 Spence, Adam
436 4 slaves
437 Murray, David
438 Jarmin, William
439 Parker, Saml.
439 4 slaves
440 Oshohannas, William
441 Carsey, John
442 Bridgewaters, Immanuel
442 Bridgwaters, Isaac
443 Parker, George
444 Davis, Robert, junr.
445 Davis, Robert, senr.
445 Davis, William
445 Davis, Ishmaell
445 Davis, Benja.
446 Davis, William, senr., ind. town
446 Davis, Saml.
446 Davis, Phill.
446 Davis, George
447 Porter, John
448 Dennis, Donnock
448 Dennis, William
449 Raine, Mathew
449 Raine, John
450 Truitt, James
451 Truitt, Geo., son of James
452 Jarmin, Job
453 Adkins, Stenten
453 Adkins, Stephen
454 Williams, Jonathan
454 Williams, John
454 Williams, Littleton
455 Penniewell, Charles
456 Penniewell, Thos.
457 Penniewell, John
457 Penniewell, Geo.
458 Collins, Mary
458 Collins, John
459 Collins, William
460 Davis, Thos.
461 Mollison, John
462 Gillet, John
463 Hudson, Major
464 Hall, Robert
464 slave

465 Hudson, Dennis
465 slave
466 Smith, John
467 Gilleland, John
467 2 slaves
468 Bowen, William
469 Handcock, Daniell
470 Pointer, William
470 Pointer, Nehemiah
471 Smachie, William
472 Truit, Saml.
472 slave
473 Dennis, William
474 Pointer, Thos.
474 Pointer, Ratcliffe
474 Pointer, Turvil
474 Steel, Wm.
475 Smock, Henry
475 Smock, John
476 Pointer, Elias
477 Mannering, Abraham
478 Pointer, Nathl.
479 Blizard, Richard
480 Heather, Ephraim, senr.
480 Heather, Ephraim, junr.
480 slave
480 slave
481 Rownd, James
481 4 slaves
482 Crapper, Ebenezer, senr.
483 Crapper, Ebenezer, junr.
484 Crapper, John
485 Crapper, Rixam
486 Tadlock, Agnes
486 Tadlock, Edward
487 Porter, Joseph
488 Purnell, Cathrine
488 Purnell, Walter
488 2 slaves
489 Williams, John
490 Hill, Richard
491 Tull, Richard
492 Williams, Presgrave
492 Harmon, Zackariah
493 Beckett, Peter
494 Smith, Abraham
494 Pointer, John
495 Hadder, Anthony
496 Waters, Patrick
497 Selby, Parker
498 Griffen, Oliver
499 Murray, Dunkin
499 5 slaves
500 Donelson, John
500 Justian, William
500 slave

500 slave
501 Reyley, Thos.
501 Coffen, William
502 Hill, Johnson
502 Hill, William
503 Evans, Charles
503 Morris, John
504 Greer, Adam
505 Charles, John
506 Nock, John
506 2 slaves
507 Burton, John
508 Franklin, Edward
508 Franklin, William
509 Lay, John
509 slave
510 Collins, Thomas
511 Truit, John
512 Evans, John
512 slave
513 Evans, Ebenezer
514 Tingle, Daniell
515 Powell, Saml.
516 Evans, Gammage
517 Evans, Powell
518 Beddard, Richard
519 Brevard, Adam
519 slave
520 Warren, Nickolas
521 Warren, Robert
521 Gray, John
522 Dazey, John
522 Gray, Nicholas
523 Tayler, William
524 Jarmin, Robert
525 Swaine, William
526 Jones, Joseph
527 Hammond, Edward, junr.
528 Burbridge, Edward
528 Pointer, William
529 Duncan, Thos.
530 Jarmin, George
530 Hammond, William
531 Hammond, John
531 Bassit, John
532 Hammond, Isaac
533 Purnell, Mattw.
533 slave
534 Hammond, Edward, senr.
535 Jones, George
536 Clark, Daniell
537 Jarmin, John, senr.
537 Jarmin, John, junr.
537 slave
538 Jenkins, John
538 2 slaves
539 Bowen, John
540 Thompson, James

1735 TAX LIST [Household number/Name/Remarks]

BOGERTERNORTON/MANOKIN HUNDREDS

541 Bowen, Littleton
541 slave
542 Bushop, John
542 Henderson, Wm.
543 Bowen, George
544 Truit, George, accomack
544 [Truit], George
544 slave
545 Morris, William
546 Morris, Joseph
547 Marchment, Charles
548 Brazier, James
549 Mitchell, Thos.
549 2 slaves
550 Cavenough, John
551 Steen, James
552 Lues, William
553 Burbridge, John
554 Fletcher, Thos.
554 Stockwell, Geo.
554 3 slaves
555 Timmons, John
555 Timmons, Saml.
556 Timmons, Joseph
557 Timmons, Thos.
558 Timmons, Aron
559 Timmons, James
560 Timmons, William
561 Timmons, Saml.
562 Gornwell, John
562 2 slaves
563 Townsend, Jeremiah
563 2 slaves
564 Townsend, Brickhouse
565 Townsend, William
566 Truit, Geo., son of Job
566 Truit, Nehemiah
567 Hodge, Robert
567 slave
568 Richards, William
569 Webb, Saml.
570 Smith, Andrew
571 Midsley, Thomas
572 Smith, William
573 Harmon, William
574 Banum, Bartholemew
575 Hadder, Warren
576 Bradford, John
577 Williams, Thomas Nathl.
577 Williams, Saml.
578 Simson, William
578 Simpson, Thos.
578 4 slaves
579 Crapper, Nehemiah
580 Davis, Edward
581 Templin, John

582 Tull, Benja.
583 Porter, James
583 Porter, John
584 Teague, William
584 Penniewell, Wm.
585 Rownd, Edward, capt.
585 Hughes, William
585 Burk, Patrick
585 slave
585 slave
586 Braford, Adam
587 Stevenson, Hugh, mr.
587 Traverse, Richard
588 Eddes, Lawrence
589 Baker, John
589 Tillman, Solomon
590 Clark, Charles
591 Jarmin, Henry
591 Webb, Elisha
592 Parker, Charles
593 Parker, Phillip
594 Truitt, Joseph
595 Collins, Solomon
596 Henderson, Charles
597 Mason, Edmund
598 Powell, Thos.
599 Jackson, Henry

MANOKIN HUNDRED
600 King, White
600 King, John
600 slave Tony
600 slave Pacy
600 slave Tome
600 slave Harry
601 Turpin, Wm., junr.
601 slave Will
601 slave Froast
601 slave George
601 slave Moll
602 Floyd, John
603 Tilman, Moses
603 Cane, James
604 Eskridge, Wm.
605 Given, Katherine
605 Cane, Wm.
606 Givens, Ann
606 Givens, Thos.
606 slave Pleasant
607 Tilmon, Aaron
608 Tilmon, Joseph
608 slave Lonnon
609 Nirblit, Burnit
609 slave Coffee
610 Dorman, Wm.
611 Tull, Easther
611 Tull, Richd.
611 Tull, Steven

611 slave Moll
612 Wilson, Saml.
612 Cantwell, Thos.
612 slave Pettor
612 slave Mammuda
612 slave Will
612 slave Nanne
612 slave Hanner
612 slave Moll
612 slave Sarah
612 slave Bess
613 Coston, Mathias
614 Macdaniel, David
615 Davis, Arthur
616 Forge, Absolom
617 Walston, Thos.
618 Wolston, Wm.
618 Wolston, Joseph
619 Miles, Saml.
619 slave Dick
619 slave Benn
620 Butler, Nat
620 slave Sarah
621 Abbit, John
622 Sharp, Benjamin
622 Bryan, Thos.
622 Wolston, Henry
623 Tull, Saml.
624 Tull, Joshua
624 Cussens, Thos.
625 Bedsworth, James
626 Wilson, David
626 King, Planner
626 Davis, Jno.
626 slave Harrey
626 slave Kent
626 slave Pompey
626 slave Cudjo
626 slave Josey
626 slave Bristoe
626 slave Holloday
626 slave Nanne
626 slave Robbin
627 Wetherbey, Jno.
628 Fountain, Mary
628 Fountain, Thos.
628 Tull, Jno.
628 slave Harcles
628 slave Mary
629 Willis, Barnaby
630 Turpin, Wm. senr.
630 Turpin, Jno.
630 slave Tom
630 slave Jack
630 slave Toby
630 slave Fillis
631 Hammon, Charles
632 Cullin, Edmon
632 Cullin, Isaac
633 Miles, Wm.

91

TAX LISTS OF SOMERSET COUNTY: 1730-1740

MANOKIN HUNDRED

634 Maddox, Daniel	657 slave Mary	675 Riggby, Lewis
634 Tull, Thos.	658 Wallston, Booz	675 Conner, Cornelius
634 slave Sarah	658 Hill, Jno.	675 slave
635 Gray, Wm.	659 Reavell, Charles	676 Denwood, Thos.
635 Morrow, Richd.	659 slave Venus	676 Vance, Thos.
636 Tilman, Rose	660 Davis, Jno.	676 Tomlinson, Henry
636 Holland, Isaac	661 Reavell, Randl.	676 5 slaves
636 Tilman, Benjamin	661 slave Tobe	677 Heath, Abraham
637 Furnes, Ann	661 slave Martha	678 Heath, Abraham
637 slave Apow	662 Reavell, Wm.	678 Heath, Jno.
638 Denston, Robart	662 slave Tom	679 Finch, Jno.
639 West, Anthony	663 Chambers, Rchd.	679 slave
640 Morow, Alexander	663 Fisher, Henry	680 Polk, James
641 Tindal, James	664 Dorman, Mathew	681 Polk, Wm.
642 Collins, William	664 Dorman, Wm.	681 Gray, Allen
642 Pullit, Abra.	664 Dorman, Nemiah	681 3 slaves
643 Booler, Elinor	664 slave Jno.	682 Wilson, Robt.
643 Booler, Wm.	664 slave Doll	682 slave Sambo
644 Fountain, Nicholas	665 Hall, Alexr.	683 Thompson, Andrew
645 Furnis, James	665 molato Nan	683 Thompson, Andrew
646 Shiphard, Martin	666 Owens, Jno.	683 Thompson, Jno.
647 Long, Solomon	667 Laws, James	683 2 slaves
647 Roch, Daniel	668 Phebus, George, senr.	684 Thompson, Wm., junr.
647 slave Sarah	668 Phebus, Samuel	685 Pope, James
648 Benston, George	668 Phebus, Jno.	686 Stewart,, widow
648 Benston, Mathias	668 slave Into	686 slave Tom
648 Jones, George	669 Ballard, Jarvis, senr.	687 Lesull, Robt.
649 Strawbridge, James	669 Ballard, Wm.	687 Lesull, Wm.
649 slave Davey	669 Ballard, Jarvis	687 Lesull, Thos.
649 slave Cuffee	669 Ballard, Arnold	688 Gray, Jno.
649 slave Dick	669 slave Ame	688 slave Hannah
649 slave Hagger	669 slave Rose	689 King, Capell
650 Jones, Wm., junr.	670 Swift, Richd.	689 5 slaves
650 Mocum, George	671 Fountain, Nicho., senr.	690 King, Robt., senr.
650 slave Ben	671 Hopkins, Benja.	690 King, Robt., junr.
651 McClammey, Woney	671 Brown, Alexander	690 King, Nehemiah
651 Odear, [James]	671 4 slaves	690 McCallagan, Hugh
651 slave Frank	672 Elzey, Jno., senr.	690 Kendall, Patrick
652 Bozman, George, junr.	672 Elzey, Jno., junr.	690 slave Fortin
652 slave Sambo	672 slave Caesar	690 slave Jessee
653 Bozman, Wm., junr.	672 slave Sambo	690 slave Joe
653 Bozman, Wm., junr.	672 slave Betty	690 slave Long Ceasar
654 McClemmy, Wm.	672 slave Sibb	690 slave Short Ceasar
654 Camell, Nehemiah	672 slave Nancey	690 slave Manary
654 slave Nero	673 Robertson,, mr.	690 slave Betty
655 Brown, Thos.	673 Campell, Jno.	690 slave Judah
655 Brown, David	673 Robertson, Jno.	690 slave Dido, senr.
655 Wilcocks, Wm.	673 slave Jack	690 slave Dido, junr.
655 slave Coger	673 slave Caesar	690 slave Nan
655 slave Jack	673 slave Toby	691 Smith, Robt.
655 slave Bess	673 slave Nero	691 Smith, Thos.
656 Ballard, Henry	673 slave Pru	692 Mitchel, Ann
656 Cammell, Jno.	673 slave Dinah	692 slave Sarah
656 Wilks, Jno.	673 slave Philis	693 Mitchel, Thos.
656 slave Jemmy	673 slave Sciss	694 Haman, Wm.
656 slave Ceesar	674 Jones, Wm., senr.	694 Haman, Ben.
656 slave Venter	674 8 slaves	695 Smith, Magdillon
656 slave Bendo		695 slave Race
657 Ballard, Elinor		696 Harris, Philip
		696 Spere, Henry

1735 TAX LIST [Household number/Name/Remarks]

MANOKIN/MATTAPANY HUNDREDS

697 Brown, Sidnie	721 Elsey, Sarah	745 slave
698 Row, Isaac	721 Elsey, Arnold	746 Foscue, Benja.
699 Heath, Dorman	721 slave Need	747 Kearns, Jno.
700 Dorman, Michael	721 slave Jack	748 Crowder, Francis
701 Fisher, Barkely	721 slave Nany	748 Lairy, Timothy
701 2 slaves	721 slave Belendo	749 Gray, Thos.
702 Lindow, James	721 slave Hannah	749 Kelly, Jno.
702 slave Bess	722 Burgin, Daniel	749 Abet, Wm.
703 Follor, Jno.	722 Galaspie, Terrance	750 Hall, William
704 Matle, James	723 Madix, Thos., senr.	751 Outerbridge, John
705 Horner, George, junr.	723 Madix, Thos., junr.	751 slave Tom
706 Horner, George, senr.	723 slave Will	752 Bozman, John, senr.
706 Horner, Till	723 slave Sue	752 Bozman, John, junr.
706 Horner, James	724 Kitchin, Wm.	753 Dorman, Margarett
706 Horner, Jno.	725 Bozman, George, senr.	753 slave Medera
707 Lockwood, Wm.	725 Bozman, George	753 Smith, John
708 Staples, James	725 Tanner, Jno.	754 Brown, Rebecca
708 slave Ben	725 slave Frank	754 slave Cudgo
709 Banister, Thos.	726 Bozman, Wm., senr.	755 Stutt, Archibald
709 Banister, Charles	726 slave Doose	
709 Feddy, Thos.	726 slave Bess	MATTAPANY HUNDRED
710 Dias, Robt.	727 Young, Jno.	756 Purnell, John
711 Whittingham, Wm.	728 Gillis, Joseph	756 5 slaves
712 Mathas, Wm.	728 Jones, Mitchel	757 Richardson, John
713 West, Wm.	728 Arvin, Jno.	757 slave
714 Macgrah, Jean	728 Welsh, Wm.	758 Harman, Manewell
714 Macgrah, Robt.	728 slave Truman	759 Lane, George
715 Tate, Thos.	728 slave Boatswain	760 Wise, Thos.
715 Tate, Francis	728 slave Rose	760 Mells, James
716 Hally, Timothy	729 Phebus, George, junr.	760 Richardson, Saml.
717 Denwood, George	729 Horner, Wm.	761 Johnson, Wm.
717 Bryon, Richd.	730 Spicer, Philip	762 Tarr, Samuel
717 Welsh, James	731 Cuningham, Thos.	762 Garley, Gorge
717 slave Ned	732 Clark, Alexr.	763 Hosiear, Saml., junr.
717 slave Plinar	733 Roch, Wm.	764 Johnson, Peter
718 Fitzgarald, Peter	733 slave Kill	765 Turner, Wm.
718 slave Tom	733 slave Patience	766 Sturgis, Rich.
719 Tunstall, Jno.	734 Morgan, Walter	767 Sturgis, Daniel
719 Lord, Thos.	735 Horsey, Jno.	767 Reed, John
719 slave Low Hill	735 slave Cudgo	768 Nutten, Thos.
719 slave Tomboy	736 Horsey, Stephen	768 Nutten, Jobe
719 slave Sibie	736 slave Peter	768 Nutten, Thomas
719 slave Norris	737 Mathas, Patrick	768 Nutten, Starling
719 slave Beck	738 Shanks, Benja.	769 Hill, Johnson
719 slave Pompey	739 Roberts, Joseph	769 Hill, Elisha
719 slave Bess	740 Debruce, Benja.	769 Richardson, John
719 slave Somerset	741 Jarvis, Wm.	769 slave
719 slave Will	742 Madix, Lazarus	770 Hill, Hutten
719 slave Tom	742 slave Coffee	770 Robarts, John
719 slave Freeman	742 slave Joe	771 Pope, John
719 slave Dinah	743 Woolford, Jno.	771 Taylor, Thos.
719 slave Isabella	743 Woolford, Thos.	771 Taylor, John
720 Turpin, Jno.	743 slave Sampson	771 4 slaves
720 Turpin, Wm.	743 slave Rose	772 Tarr, Michel
720 slave Cuffee	743 slave Tamer	773 Ducar, William
720 slave Tobe	743 slave Moll	774 Nutten, Jonathan
720 slave Nan	744 Martin, Thos.	775 Selby, Philip
720 slave Tom	745 Horsey, Sarah	775 Selby, Matt.
		775 Selby, Daniel

TAX LISTS OF SOMERSET COUNTY: 1730-1740

MATTAPANY/MONIE HUNDREDS

775 Selby, Philip
775 Selby, Wm.
775 5 slaves
776 Craford, Andrew
776 Craford, John
777 Hill, Robt.
778 Selby, Parker
778 Tollman, James
778 4 slaves
779 Taylor, Philip
779 Taylor, Elias
780 Answorth, Wm.
781 ODewey, Thos.
782 Walton, Fisher
782 2 slaves
783 Walton, Stephen
783 Walton, Stephen, junr.
783 Walton, Wm.
783 Hardis, Hazard
784 Cord, Wm.
784 Cord, Arthur
784 slave
785 Arnell, Wm.
785 Arnell, Laurenc
786 Mason, Abra.
787 Evens, John
788 Brownbill, Henry
788 Brownbill, Jno.
789 Answorth, Sarah, widow
789 Taylor, John
790 Answorth, Peter
790 Answorth, Jobe
791 Aydlott, William
791 slave
792 Davis, Charles
792 Williams, Thos.
792 Davis, Lazarus
793 Hosiear, Saml., senr.
794 Holland, Benja.
794 slave
795 Hudson, Jonathan
796 Holland, Nehemiah
796 Wattson, James
797 Guttry, Pattrick
797 Guttry, James
798 Slingor, Thos., senr.
798 Slingor, Thos.
799 Johnson, John
800 Pope, Gorg
800 2 slaves
801 Wattson, Moses
802 Willett, Ambrus
802 Willett, Wm.
803 Wattson, Robt., senr.
803 Wattson, Charles

803 Harkis, Thos.
803 slave
804 Chapman, Umphrey
805 Henderson, Bishop
806 Ceary, Solomon
807 Pain, John
808 Wattson, John
809 Duberley, Thos.
810 Wattson, Peter
810 Wattson, Uriah
811 Wattson, Luke
812 Hill, Abraham
813 Davis, Charles
814 Allen, Joseph
815 Venatson, Wm.
815 Venatson, Nathan
816 Scott, Robt., senr.
816 Scott, Wm.
816 Scott, Robt.
817 Wattson, Robt., junr.
818 Brownbill, Nathal.
819 Peper, Wm.
820 Peper, Tobias
821 Benett, Mary, widow
821 Lenzey, James
822 Bechbord, Wm.
823 Porter, Clintuck
824 Claywell, Peter, junr.
825 Claywell, Peter, senr.
825 3 slaves
826 Bratton, Wm.
826 slave
827 Hopkins, Saml.
828 Hall, Jno.
828 Hall, Henry
829 Hopkins, Wm.
830 Walker, Jno.
830 slave
831 Wagaman, Jacob
831 Wagaman, Ephraim
831 Thomson, Andrew
831 Harman, John
831 slave
832 Robins, Elizth., widow
832 4 slaves
833 Samons, Benoney
834 Maxfield, Jos.
834 3 slaves
835 Rusell, Cuthbud
836 Scarbrough, John
836 Murray, John
836 Wise, Ezekiel
836 2 slaves
837 Hopkins, Nathal.
837 Ayars, Henry
837 slave

838 Hopkins, Mattw.
838 Ayars, Harson
838 Ayars, Richd.
839 Jones, John
840 Allen, Jno.
841 Pope, Saml.
842 Dreadin, John
843 Milburne, Thos.
844 Taylor, Rodger
845 Dufin, Gorge
846 Hodgson, Rolling
846 slave
847 Vezey, Charles
848 Coner, Richd.
849 Mallen, Christo.
850 Wimbrough, Paul
851 Jackson, Wm.
852 Ceary, Jeremiah
853 Long, John
854 Porter, Wm.
855 Puddrah, Jos.
856 Benston, Joshua
857 Nelson, Wm.
858 Booth, Wm.

MONIE HUNDRED

859 Roe, Joseph
860 Laws, Thomas
860 slave Jack
860 slave Morreour
861 Wallace, John
862 Laws, John
862 slave Prince
862 slave Juner
862 slave Ceasar
863 MccDormon, Darbey
864 Jones, Luas
864 Jones, Samueall
864 slave Ceasar
864 slave Jack
864 slave Moll
865 Wye, William
865 slave Jamey
865 slave Dunleour
866 Carey, Thomas
867 Carey, Rachel
867 Crouch, Thomas
868 Luak, Williamson
869 Mongar, John
870 Dorman, Henry
871 Newman, Henry
871 Layhill, Andrew
872 Mograw, John
872 Hill, William
873 Hobbs, Thomas
874 Hobbs, Joy
874 Mongar, Mathew
875 Hobbs, Marthelus
875 Stepeans, Isack
876 Covington, John

1735 TAX LIST [Household number/Name/Remarks]

MONIE/NANTICOKE HUNDREDS

876 slave Sambo
876 slave Cookie
876 slave Betty
876 slave Dinour
877 Wallear, William
878 Jones, James
878 Dughig, Walter
878 Brusher, Manring
878 slave Davad
878 slave Sibb
878 slave Moll
879 Jones, Daniell
880 Storey, Susanah
880 slave Whighthaven
880 slave Doll
881 Harding, Joseph
882 Milles, Edward
883 Dorham, Thomas
884 Covington, Thomas
884 Handay, Samuel
885 Letherburey, John, mr.
885 Letherburey, Perey
885 Dorman, Ezekiah
885 slave Janey
885 slave Sambo
885 slave Pompey
885 slave Benn
885 slave Bridgett
885 slave Rose
885 slave Nanny
885 slave Nany
885 slave Bess
886 Dorman, John
887 Malkem, Robert
888 Blueat, Thomas
889 Downs, Robert
889 Wallace, Robert
890 Haley, Nicolis
891 Hamfort, John
892 Gale, Betty, madam
892 Kenny, John
892 slave Joe
892 slave Sephean
892 slave Jacob
892 slave Jamey
892 slave Dubling
892 slave Ovid
892 slave Ceazar
892 slave Will
892 slave Pheba
892 slave Rose
892 slave Bess
892 slave Bendah
892 slave Jamey
892 slave Vilate
892 slave Palinah
893 Gale, George, capt.

893 Maughone, Christopher
893 slave Sipio
893 slave Limas
893 slave Jamey
893 slave Jack
893 slave Nanny
893 slave Sarah
893 slave Parthena
894 Gale, Mathieas
894 slave Sarah
895 Jones, William
895 Milles, John
895 slave Will
895 slave Jamey
895 slave Suwe
896 Dashiell, Thomas
896 Dashiell, Levin
896 Brodhead, Joseph
896 slave Will
896 slave Jack
896 slave Harrey
896 slave Robin
896 slave Jack
896 slave Joe
896 slave Bess
896 slave Tamer
896 slave Sarah
896 slave Hanah
897 Downs, George
897 slave Tobey
897 slave Frank
898 Jones, Robert
898 Jones, Thomas
898 Chambers, Samuall
898 slave London
898 slave Ammok
898 slave Dick
898 slave Jane
898 slave Rachel
899 Jones, George
900 Lows, Robert
900 Lows, Painter
900 Lows, Willm.
900 slave Bubbo
900 slave Jack
900 slave Sampson
901 Irving, Geo.
901 slave Tobey
901 slave Coffey
901 slave Jane
901 slave Jane
902 Mograw, James
903 Waller, John
903 Wallace, Thomas
903 slave Jane
904 Walear, Maior
905 Stoughton, William, sgur
905 Coldweld, William

905 Lawlis, James
905 Obear, Isack
905 slave Busie
905 slave Siman
905 slave Sabbina
906 Wright, Thomas
906 [Wright], Henrey
906 Skein, Robert
906 Welcks, John
907 Showrs, John
907 Showrs, William
907 slave Pompey
908 Showrs, Ewd.
909 Waller, George
909 Saucer, William
910 Polk, Joseph
910 Neial, John
910 McDonald, Owen
911 Roberts, Ewd.
911 slave Jeffrey
912 Wallace, Rikeard
912 Walace, Thomas
912 Walace, James
912 slave Cesear
912 slave Bess
913 Husk, John
914 Whight, John
915 Wallace, Mathew
915 Rose, Samueall
915 slave Tome
915 slave Sibb
916 Windser, Mary, widow
916 Windser, John
917 Duglis, John
918 Whight, Francis
918 Whight, Thomas
918 Whight, John
919 Roberts, John
919 Roberts, Thomas
920 Martin, Geo.
921 Williams, John
922 Bozsuell, Thomas
923 Roe, Thomas
923 Gamueall, George
923 Hopkins, Geo.
923 Feding, Randol
924 Jones, Richeard
925 Chaine, Alexander
926 Windser, Lazrus
926 Windser, John
926 Windser, Lazrus
927 Miller, Thomas

NANTICOKE HUNDRED

928 McClester, John, capt.
928 McClester, Samuel
928 McClester, George
928 slave Sambo
928 slave Coffee

TAX LISTS OF SOMERSET COUNTY: 1730-1740

NANTICOKE HUNDRED

928 slave Tom
928 slave Adam
928 slave Ciss
928 slave Abbo
928 slave Dinah
929 Hopkins, Steven
930 Walter, Daniel
931 Samuels, Ann, widow
931 slave Cocoro
932 Phipps, John
933 Wallis, David
934 Hopkins, John, junr.
935 Hickman, Joshua
936 Berklee, John, junr.
937 Berklee, John
937 Berklee, Abraham
938 Hickson, Joseph
939 Hust, Joseph
940 Macom, Timothy
941 Mezick, Isaac
942 Dunn, Richard
943 Anderson, Sarah
943 Anderson, John
944 Walter, John
944 Walter, Robert
944 Hickman, Henry
945 slave Jack
945 slave Sambo
945 slave Mercer
945 slave Rose
945 Hickman, Wm.
946 slave Orre
946 Hickman, Wm., junr.
947 Venatson, Elias
948 Larimore, Thomas
948 Larimore, James
949 Collier, Dowty
950 Rickee, Archabald
951 Beard, Lewis
951 Beard, John
951 Beard, Lewis, junr.
951 Hust, Lazarus
952 Henderson, Robert
953 Collier, Robert
953 Collier, Robert
953 Collier, George
953 Mezick, Julian
954 Fluellin, Samuel
954 slave Silas
955 Larimore, John
955 slave Coffee
955 slave Sibb
956 Dean, John
957 Game, Robert
958 Dashiell, Henry
958 Stewart, Cha.
958 slave Gift
958 slave Sibb
959 Winwright, Canaan
959 Winwright, John
959 slave Quacco
960 Hopkins, Robert
960 slave Tobe
961 Mezick, Benjamin
962 Hopkins, John
962 Hopkins, John
962 slave Nan
962 slave Sue
963 Game, Fortin
964 Dashiell, James
964 Dashiell, James
964 slave Robin
964 slave Will
964 slave Will
964 slave Jack
964 slave Didow
965 Williams, Richard
965 Williams, John
966 Shurman, Thos.
966 Shurman, Thos.
967 Thorns, Alexr.
968 Vaughan, Wm.
968 Baccon, Dudson
969 Collins, John
970 Dashiell, Wm.
971 Bounds, Joseph
972 Bucklee, Nicholus
973 Richardson, John
973 Richardson, Wm.
974 Roberson, Wm.
975 Mezick, Jacob
976 Mezick, Jacob, junr.
977 Mezick, Nehemiah
977 Owens, Epharim
978 Paul, Geo.
979 Read, John
979 Read, John, junr.
979 Read, Zachariah
979 Read, Obediah
979 slave Pegg
980 Quatermus, James
980 Quatermus, James
981 Green, James
982 Persons, Francis
982 slave Bess
983 Dashiell, Joseph
983 Cromwell, Thos.
983 Shiradon, Daniel
983 slave Randol
984 Dashiell, Robert
984 slave Harry
984 slave Cago
984 slave Nero
984 slave Tamer
985 Taylor, Anthony
986 Benson, Thos.
986 Cooper, Jno.
986 slave Will
987 Giles, Thos.
988 Giles, Wm.
988 Giles, Wm., junr.
988 slave Floro
989 Jackson, Jonathan
989 Jackson, Joshua
989 Jackson, Ezekiel
990 Richardson, Wm.
991 Rider, Hathley
992 Rider, Wilson
993 Rusel, James, junr.
994 Goslee, James
994 Meclane, Archabald
995 Relph, Thos.
995 slave Pompee
996 Rusel, James
996 Rusel, Thos.
996 Rusel, Wm.
997 Gale, John
997 Kemp, John
997 slave Beashee
997 slave Messe
997 slave Galaway
997 slave Townsides
997 slave Judith
997 slave Moll
997 slave Rose
998 Shurman, Wm.
998 Shurman, Isaac
999 Bennit, Edward
999 Bennit, John
1000 Twiford, John
1001 Tulley, Steven, junr.
1001 Tulley, Richd.
1002 Records, Alexander
1003 More, Wm., junr.
1004 More, John, quantico
1004 More, Isaac
1005 Wright, Solomon
1006 Crouch,, widow
1006 Phillips, Wm.
1007 Godart, Thos.
1008 Waller, Nelson
1009 More, John, junr.
1010 Green, Richard
1010 Green, Richd.
1011 West, James
1011 Baslee, Thos.
1012 Langford, Thos.
1013 Right, Judith, widow

1735 TAX LIST [Household number/Name/Remarks]

NANTICOKE HUNDRED

1013 Right, Wm.
1014 Cottman, Ebenezer
1014 Cottman, Natha.
1015 Lowe, Ralph
1015 Lowe, Robt.
1015 Lowe, John
1016 Langford, John
1016 Langford, John
1016 Langford, Edwd.
1017 Phillips, Thos.
1018 Wallis, Richard, carp.
1018 Oday, Henry
1019 Anderson, James
1019 Meclannin, Joseph
1020 Henry, John
1020 Henry, Robt.
1020 Henry, Hugh
1021 Dashiell, Mitchel
1021 slave Venus
1022 Gravenor, Thos.
1022 Mercey, Henry
1023 Wilson, John
1024 Cooper, Gabriel
1024 Cooper, Gabriel, junr.
1024 Cooper, Thos.
1025 Cooper, Samuel
1026 Cooper, Isaac
1027 Langsdell, Wm.
1028 Sheridine, Wm.
1029 Tulley, James
1029 Price, Frank
1029 Tulley, Benja.
1029 Churn, John
1030 Phillips, Richd.
1031 Olifer, George
1032 Hardy, John
1033 Meclure, Robert
1034 Carter, John, junr.
1035 Jones, John
1036 Jones, James
1036 Carter, Thos.
1037 Inglish, Robert
1037 Olifer, Thos.
1038 Olifent, Wm.
1038 Ready, Cornelius
1039 McClester, Joseph
1039 McClester, Neal
1039 Hicks, Levin
1039 Billings, James
1039 Goldsborough, Wm.
1039 Beckingham, Wm.
1039 slave Sampson
1040 Relph, Wm.
1041 Parimore,, widow
1041 Parimore, Thos.
1042 Collins, Edmund
1043 Downs, Robert
1044 Fulton, Wm.
1045 Calaway, Peter
1045 Calaway, Thos.
1045 Calaway, John
1046 Carter, John
1046 Carter, Samuel
1047 Speer, Henry
1047 Spear, Robert
1048 Wallis, Richd.
1048 slave Mical
1049 Waller, Thomas, junr.
1050 Waller, Thos.
1050 Waller, Richd.
1050 Roads, John
1051 Waller, Nathaniel, junr.
1052 Waller, Nathl.
1052 Waller, John
1053 Greire,, widow
1053 Greire, Wm.
1054 Moore,, widow
1054 More, Wm.
1055 Caldwell, Thomas
1056 Calaway, Wm.
1057 Calaway, Wm., junr.
1058 Calaway, John
1059 Calaway, John, senr.
1060 Calaway, Edward
1061 Calaway, John, junr.
1062 Caldwell, John, junr.
1062 Caldwell, Robert
1062 Carvel, Thomas
1062 slave Sambo
1063 Jones, Wm.
1064 Kenney, Wm.
1065 Caldwell, Patrick
1066 More, John, forest
1067 Williams, John
1068 Godard, John
1069 Mitchell, John
1070 Benson, Henry
1070 Benson, Henry
1071 Cooper, James
1071 Polk, John
1072 Benson, Wm.
1073 Benson, Wm.
1073 Carter, Charles
1074 Shurman, Thos.
1075 Godard, George
1075 Mitchel, Alexr.
1075 Mitchel, Thos.
1076 James, John
1077 Bollen, Thos.
1078 Wooten, Edward
1078 Tatman, James
1079 Wooten, John
1079 Howel, John
1080 Hosey, Mathew
1081 Stevens, John
1082 Stevens, Thos.
1083 Lynn, Aaron
1083 Jenckins, Thos.
1083 Moris, Michal
1083 slave Abraham
1083 slave Bess
1084 Killey, George
1085 Meglohlin, John
1086 Gibins, John
1086 Freaks, Wm.
1087 Mackdowel, John
1088 Collings, Thos.
1089 Venson, James
1090 Collins, John
1091 Newton, John
1092 Keninghan, Daniel
1093 Nowles, Edmund
1093 Nowles, Richard
1094 Dodrill, James
1095 Boadley, John
1096 Walter, Henry
1096 Walter, Daniel
1096 Walter, John
1096 Walter, Wm.
1097 Dean, Charles
1098 Roberson, John
1099 Hovington, Thos.
1100 Hovington, Richard
1101 Rotten, Josiah
1102 Rowel, Thomas
1103 Scott, George, baron crk
1104 Scott, Windom
1105 Marvel, Thos.
1105 Marvel, Richard
1106 Green, Ezekiel
1106 Hall, Joseph
1107 Wright, Solomon, baron c.
1108 Elingsworth, Robert
1109 Nicholson, Richard
1110 Elingsworth,, widow
1110 Elingsworth, Richard
1110 Elingsworth, Nehemiah
1111 English, Wm.
1112 Caldwell, James
1112 Caldwell, Wm.
1112 slave Bobb
1112 slave Sambo
1112 slave Tobee
1112 slave Rose
1112 slave Ciss
1113 Ready, Thos.
1114 Cordrey, David

TAX LISTS OF SOMERSET COUNTY: 1730-1740

NANTICOKE HUNDRED

1115 Cordrey, Edward
1116 Melson, Samuel
1116 Melson, Saml., junr.
1117 Jones, Finch
1118 Young,, widow
1118 Boyce, John
1119 Hovington, Jonathan
1119 Glaster, Thos.
1120 Hovington, John
1120 Gastinau, Mathuw
1120 Glaster, Solomon
1120 slave Iago
1120 slave Isaac
1120 slave Pleasant
1121 Hovington, John, junr.
1122 Darby, Walter
1123 Tayler, Wm.
1124 Polson, Wm.
1125 Kelam, Edward
1125 slave Robin
1125 slave Merian
1126 Young, Wm.
1126 Young, John
1127 Venables, Benja.
1127 Mersey, John
1127 slave Tom
1128 Brown, Wm.
1128 Carmical, John
1129 Gillis, John
1129 Gillis, Thos.
1130 Hitch,, widow
1130 Riggin, Ambros
1130 slave Tobee
1131 Ackworth, Thos.
1131 slave Will
1132 Ackworth, Charles
1133 Tulley, Joseph
1134 Wafer, Ignatius
1135 Cheesman, John
1135 slave Cesor
1135 slave Naney
1136 Parimore, James
1137 Ackworth, Samuel
1137 slave Sue
1138 Ackworth, Henry
1139 Hitch, Solomon
1139 slave Cook
1139 slave Frank
1140 Weatherley,, widow
1140 slave Sebinah
1141 Twilley, Robert
1141 Twilley, George
1141 Wright, Zebulon
1142 Weatherley, James
1142 slave Pegg
1143 Carter, Phillip
1143 Carter, Wm.
1144 Rhoades, Daniel
1144 Givens, John
1145 Taylor, Abraham
1145 slave Quash
1146 Givans, James
1146 slave Frank
1147 Smith, Thomas, junr.
1147 slave Hager
1148 Givans, Robert
1148 slave Cesar
1148 slave Charles
1148 slave Hanah
1148 slave Rose
1149 Train, James
1149 Train, James
1149 Train, Roger
1149 slave Robin
1149 slave Rose
1150 Farintine, Wm.
1151 Hardy, James
1151 Hardy, Joseph
1152 Nutter, Christopher
1152 slave Cesar
1152 slave Sipio
1152 slave Tom
1152 slave Barbry
1152 slave Rose
1153 Nutter, Wm.
1153 slave Phillip
1153 slave Cato
1153 slave Ben
1153 slave Moll
1153 slave Rose
1153 slave Citran
1154 Nutter, Mathew
1155 Dunkin, James
1156 Nutter, Huet
1156 slave Tite
1156 slave Mingo
1157 Jacobs, Eliz.
1157 Murphey, James
1157 slave Sambo
1157 slave Sibb
1158 Bennit, George
1159 Martin, John
1160 Jones, John, quantico
1161 Austin, Wm.
1161 Austin, Wm.
1161 Holder, Saml.
1162 Bodley, Wm.
1163 Phillips, John
1164 Rhodes, Timothy
1164 Rhodes, Timothy, junr.
1165 Tulley, Steven
1165 Tulley, Benja.
1166 More, Wm., quantico
1167 Maginey,, widow
1167 Dauhity, James
1168 Burn, James
1169 Nicholson, James
1170 Rickords, John
1170 Turk, Magnus
1171 Backworth, Charles
1172 Noble, Isaac
1173 Chipman, Parris
1173 Robinnut, Samuel
1173 Robinut, Samuel
1173 Hunter, John
1173 Fleetwood, John
1173 slave Betty
1174 Noble,, widow
1174 Noble, John
1175 Bougar, James
1175 Bass, John
1176 Winsor, John
1177 Winsor, Henry
1178 Bounds, Jacob
1179 Givans, Robert, junr.
1179 slave
1180 Calaway, Peter, junr.
1181 Thompson, George
1182 Parimore, Mathew
1182 Parimore, Ezekiel
1183 Kirkman, Roger
1184 Wright, Edward
1185 King, Phillip
1186 Parimore, Joseph
1187 King, Wm.
1188 Paramore, James, junr.
1188 Parsons, Charles
1189 Melson, Joseph
1189 Melson, Benja.
1190 Hall, John
1191 Wingate, Philip
1192 Potter, Josephas
1193 Smith, John
1194 Tindell, Charles
1194 Joseph, Jeremiah
1195 Ingram, Robert
1196 Short, Edward
1196 Short, Abraham
1196 Fleetwood, Thomas
1197 Williams, Charles
1198 Dolby, Peter
1199 Kemeny, Walter
1200 Taylor, John
1200 Taylor, Wm.
1200 Powel, Joseph
1201 Short, John
1202 Hurvey, John
1203 Smith, David
1204 Langsdell, John

1735 TAX LIST [Household number/Name/Remarks]
NANTICOKE/POCOMOKE HUNDREDS

1204 Smith, James
1205 Kennigham, Arthur
1206 Johnson, Simon
1207 Ubank, Molton
1208 Samuells, Peter
1209 Samuells, Richard
1210 Collings, Andrew
1211 Ingram, Abraham
1211 Ingram, David
1211 Ingram, Abraham
1211 slave Priscilla
1212 Ingram, Isaac
1213 Donohoe, Nathaniel
1214 Manliff, Emanuel
1214 slave Quaco
1215 Bartholemew, Samuel
1216 Polk, John
1216 Polk, James
1216 slave Atto
1217 Owens, Robert
1217 slave Cate
1218 Polk, Charles
1218 Polk, Epharim
1219 Willey, John
1219 Cope, Wm.
1219 slave Coffee
1220 Newbold, Francis
1220 slave Amee
1221 Fisher, George
1222 Kelley, John
1223 Sharp, John
1224 Smith, Steven
1224 Friggs, Robert
1225 Draper, Wm.
1225 slave George
1225 slave Tony
1226 McClester, Randoll
1227 Oneal, James
1227 slave Dinah
1228 Oneal, John
1229 Johnson, Thomas
1230 Mersey, Wm.
1231 Collings, Richard
1232 Shockley, David
1232 Shockley, Solomon
1232 Shockley, James
1233 Winwright, William
1234 Gray, Wm.
1234 Isaacks, John
1234 slave Coffee
1235 Walter, Thos.
1235 Nottingham, Benja.
1236 Boyce, Daniel
1236 Dunton, Jonas
1236 Donton, Wm.

1237 George, Wm.
1238 Hickman, James
1239 Owens, Peter
1240 Clifton, George
1240 Clifton, George
1240 Clifton, Thomas
1240 Clifton, Nehemiah
1241 Mezick, John
1241 Mezick, Obediah
1241 Mezick, James
1241 Ingram, Isaac
1242 Mezick, George
1243 Askeley, Daniel
1244 Shurman, Peter
1245 Shurman, Joab
1246 Baker, Wm.
1247 Edge, Joshua
1247 Floyd, Major
1248 Hall, Tho.

POCOMOKE HUNDRED
1249 Hayward, Thomas, mr.
1249 Handlin, Patrick
1249 slave Cuggo
1249 slave Sambo
1249 slave Sineco
1249 slave Tom
1249 slave Jasper
1249 slave Pris
1249 slave Rose
1249 slave Jeney
1250 Tillmon, Giddion
1250 slave Popey
1251 Dormon, Saml.
1252 Cluff, Edwd.
1253 Maddox, Lazr.
1254 Clogg, Saml.
1255 Pirkins, John
1256 Pirkins, Sarah
1256 Pirkins, Wm.
1256 Pirkins, Mitchell
1257 Paden, John
1257 slave Oxford
1258 Dredon, David, junr.
1259 Pingalley, Thos.
1259 Buttler, Manuell
1260 Johnson, Joshua
1261 Dickerson, Edwd., son of Pet.
1262 Browne, Thoms.
1263 Benston, Thoms.
1264 Powell, John
1264 Powell, Levin
1264 slave Sarah
1265 White, Esther, mrs.
1265 slave Jemmey
1265 slave Robin

1265 slave Harrey
1265 slave Nimrod
1265 slave Phenie
1265 slave Jenney
1265 slave Pris
1265 slave Sue
1266 Colbert, Wm.
1267 Scolfield, Henry
1268 Harrey, George
1269 Slocomb, Thomas
1269 Long, Colbourn
1270 Tull, George
1270 Tull, Noble
1270 Tull, Jonathan
1270 slave Abner
1270 slave Dinah
1271 Mills, Wm.
1271 Mills, Saml.
1271 Mills, Jonathan
1272 Pilcher, Wm.
1272 Jones, Abraham
1273 Pilcher, John
1274 Gillet, Saml.
1274 Gillet, Wm.
1274 slave Darkis
1275 Webb, John
1275 Webb, Solomon
1275 Webb, John, junr.
1276 Melven, Robt.
1276 Melven, Wm.
1276 Melven, Robt., junr.
1277 Mills, Mary
1277 Mills, Moses
1277 Mills, Smith
1277 Taylor, Roger
1277 slave Simon
1278 Houston, James
1278 slave Betty
1278 slave Cate
1279 Brittingham, Wm.
1279 slave Rose
1280 Quinton, Philip
1280 Quinton, Dixon
1280 slave Jack
1281 Henderson, Benja.
1282 Ellis, Wm.
1283 Henderson, Francis
1284 Connelly, Patrick
1285 Gillet, John
1285 slave Harrey
1285 slave Nanne
1286 Blades, John
1287 Brittingham, Thoms.
1288 Layfield, George
1289 Breeman, James
1289 slave Tolomey
1290 Melton, John
1291 Books, Francis
1292 Piper, Isaac

TAX LISTS OF SOMERSET COUNTY: 1730-1740

POCOMOKE HUNDRED

1293 Goggin, David
1293 Brooks, Henry
1294 Jones, Edward
1294 Jones, Elisha
1295 Goodin, Benj.
1296 Conner, Wm.
1297 Small, John
1298 Blades, Robt.
1298 Blades, Benj.
1299 Benston, Anne
1299 Wotikins, William
1300 Curvine, Thoms.
1301 Davis, Evan
1302 Ramsey, Charles
1302 Ramsey, John
1303 Mills, Saml.
1303 Mills, Nathl.
1303 Mills, Hugh
1304 Merrell, John
1305 Jones, Thoms.
1305 Taylor, James
1306 Henderson, John, junr.
1306 Henderson, Saml.
1307 Henderson, James
1307 Henderson, John
1307 slave Adam
1308 Henderson, Charles
1308 Right, Comfort
1309 Young, Daniel
1310 Dickerson, Peter
1310 Dickerson, John
1311 Lamberson, John
1311 Lamberson, Robt.
1312 Lindall, Robt.
1313 Merrell, Jos.
1313 Chambers, Jeremiah
1314 Broughton, Bruff
1314 Culenan, John
1314 Hattfield, Wm.
1315 Broughton, John
1315 Broughton, Wm.
1316 Houston, Joseph, junr.
1317 Houston, John, senr.
1318 Henderson, John, senr.
1318 slave Gye
1318 slave George
1318 slave Bess
1318 slave Jane
1318 slave Eve
1319 Dickerson, James
1319 Dickerson, Robt.
1319 Dickerson, Francis
1320 Stephens, Wm.
1320 Stephens, Edward
1321 Jones, Anne
1321 Jones, Wm.
1322 Gore, Richard
1323 Obrien, Chris.
1324 Shanklin, Wm.
1324 Mills, Nathan
1324 Mills, Alexr.
1325 Mills, Wm., junr.
1326 Brittingham, John
1326 slave Seser
1326 slave Nane
1327 Dickerson, Isaac
1327 slave
1328 Lamberson, Abra.
1328 Lamberson, Saml.
1328 Lamberson, Abra.
1329 Newbold, Thoms.
1329 Newbold, Purnell
1329 slave Patience
1330 Beachamp, Edward
1330 Beachamp, Marcey
1330 Beachamp, Thomas
1330 Beachamp, John
1330 slave
1331 Worwick, Arther
1332 Riggin, Ambrose, senr.
1332 Riggin, Teague
1332 Taylor, Jacob
1333 Smullen, Randell
1333 Smullen, Randell
1333 Smullen, Nathan
1334 Riggin, Joseph
1335 Hadock, Ignatious
1336 Colburson, Wm.
1337 Knight, Richard
1337 Knight, James
1338 Harris, John
1338 Harris, Benton
1339 Harris, Jeremiah
1340 Lewis, Wm.
1341 Harris, Robt.
1341 slave Harrey
1341 slave Moll
1341 slave Sesor
1342 Jourdine, Aron
1343 Harper, Edwd.
1344 Ward, Joseph
1344 Ward, Cornelius
1345 Phillips, John
1346 Odear, Stephen
1347 Riggin, Teague
1347 2 slaves
1348 Denston, John
1348 Denston, John
1349 Dukes, Wm.
1350 Harper, Francis
1350 Pilcher, Moses
1351 Lane, John
1352 Martin, James, capt.
1352 slave Pompey
1352 slave Moss
1352 slave Sesor
1352 slave Caton
1352 slave Will
1352 slave Nannie
1353 Sturgis, Joshua
1353 Laws, John
1353 slave Tom
1354 Laws, Wm.
1355 McDaniel, James
1356 Towensand, Littleton
1357 Beavens, John
1357 Beavens, John
1357 Beavens, Thoms.
1357 slave Sambo
1358 Hough, Edmond
1358 slave Will
1358 slave Titus
1358 slave Sambo
1358 slave Nanne
1359 Nelson, James
1360 Benson, John
1360 Benston, George
1360 Benston, Saul
1361 Dennis, John, senr.
1361 Dennis, Valentine
1361 Dennis, Lazarus
1361 Nueman, John
1361 slave Joe
1361 slave Cate
1362 Davis, Nathl.
1362 Davis, Nathl.
1363 Scarbrough,, madam
1363 slave Plesant
1363 slave Landell
1363 slave Betty
1364 Bodl, Saml.
1365 Glass, Jno.
1366 Caldwell, Jos.
1367 Davis, Jos.
1368 Goodfree, Joseph
1369 White, Hannah
1369 White, John
1370 Outen, Abraham
1370 slave Will
1371 Calem, John
1372 Beavens, Caleb
1372 Taylor, Wm.
1373 Johnson, Mary
1373 slave Betty
1374 Houston, John
1375 Houston, Robt.
1376 Whittington, Wm.
1376 slave Noney
1377 Morris, Isaac
1377 Morris, Luke

1735 TAX LIST [Household number/Name/Remarks]

POCOMOKE HUNDRED

1377 slave Ben
1377 slave Will Fariner
1377 slave Abner
1377 slave Will
1377 slave Sam
1377 slave Sulkey
1377 slave Abo
1378 Dennis, Daniel
1379 Beavens, Joshua
1380 Taylor, Saml., senr.
1380 Taylor, George
1381 Taylor, Saml.
1382 Glass, Chrisr.
1382 Glass, Elias
1382 Glass, Chris.
1382 slave Frank
1383 Purnell, Elisha
1383 slave Pipen
1384 Nickols, John
1385 Nickols, James
1385 slave Hanah
1386 Nickols, Mathias
1387 Paine, Joseph
1388 Nickols, Joseph
1389 Turner, John
1390 Warrinton, Thomas
1391 Jones, Wm., forest
1392 Right, Randell
1393 Noble, James
1394 Stevens, John
1395 [Smith], John
1396 White, John, pocomoke
1396 slave George
1396 slave Patience
1396 slave Nan
1397 Naron, James
1397 slave Will
1397 slave Harey
1397 slave Moll
1398 Naron, Robt.
1398 slave Sarah
1398 slave Margre
1399 Hall, John
1399 Treherne, James
1400 McCredey, Alexr.
1400 McCredey, Alexr.
1400 McCredey, Solomon
1401 McDaniel, Allen
1401 McDaniel, Moses
1402 Carsey, Wm.
1403 Riggin, John, junr.
1404 Tomerlinson, Soward
1404 slave Plesent
1405 Tomerlinson, Abagall
1405 Tomerlinson, Solomon
1405 slave Lemon
1406 Renalds, Henry
1406 Hubbard, Richd.
1406 Cocane, George
1407 Brooks, Richd.
1407 Brooks, Henry
1407 slave Lett
1408 Benston, Wm.
1409 Willson, John
1410 Collins, Saml.
1411 Backer, James
1411 Baker, Henderson
1411 Neloins, John
1411 slave Yourk
1412 Adams, Isaac
1413 Adams, Wm., senr.
1413 Adams, Dennis
1413 Adams, Phillip
1413 slave Jack
1414 Adams, Wm., junr.
1415 Adams, Hope
1416 Adams, Philip
1416 slave Nane
1417 Davis, Beachamp
1418 Dredon, David, senr.
1418 Dredon, Wm.
1419 Fenton, Margret
1419 Blaer, Robt.
1420 Peacock, Edwd.
1421 Adams, George
1422 Marchell, Saml.
1423 Adams, David
1423 slave Harrey
1423 slave Jeney
1424 Woods, Wm.
1425 Boston, Isaac
1425 slave Gloster
1425 slave, molato
1425 slave Venus
1426 Boston, Easah
1427 Taylor, Robt.
1428 Carsey, Peter
1428 Carsey, Saml.
1428 Carsey, Robt.
1428 Cottingham, John
1429 Adams, Jacob
1429 Adams, Saml.
1429 Adams, Philip
1429 slave Sampson
1429 slave Nan
1430 Mathews, Saml.
1431 Mathews, Wm.
1432 Mathews, Teague
1433 Mathews, John
1434 Clifton, John
1435 Riggin, John, senr.
1435 Riggin, John
1435 Riggin, Stephen
1435 Riggin, Teague
1435 slave Jenney
1436 Kellem, Joshua
1437 Riggin, Eliz.
1437 Riggin, Solomon
1437 slave Peter
1438 Riggin, Charles
1438 slave Nane
1439 Dickerson, Charles, junr
1440 Cox, Wm.
1440 slave Jonas
1440 slave Seser
1440 slave Doll
1441 Dickerson, Teague
1442 Ellis, John
1443 Boyer, Robt.
1443 Clifton, George
1443 Boyer, Jonathan
1443 slave Harey
1444 White, John, at point
1444 slave Jack
1444 slave Tom
1445 Holland, Wm., capt.
1445 slave Tom
1445 slave Dinah
1446 Milbourn, Ralph
1446 slave
1447 Evans, Thomas
1447 slave
1448 Evans, John
1449 Milbourn, Mary
1449 Milbourne, Caleb
1449 slave Mingoe
1449 slave Hanah
1450 Milbourne, John
1451 Adams, Collins
1452 Britt, John
1453 White, Archabald
1453 White, Wm.
1454 Bell, John
1455 Burnet, Jane
1455 Burnet, James
1456 Wheeler, Isaac
1457 Lambdon, Thomas
1458 Scott, Jno., capt.
1458 Scott, John
1458 Goldsmith, Thomas
1458 slave Peter
1458 slave Toney
1458 slave Rose
1458 slave Pheby
1459 Lane, Wm., capt.
1459 slave Harey
1459 slave Dick
1460 Mitchell, Robt.

TAX LISTS OF SOMERSET COUNTY: 1730-1740

POCOMOKE HUNDRED

1460 Mitchell, Joshua
1460 slave Townsides
1460 slave Selby
1461 Handy, Eliz.
1461 Handy, Saml.
1461 Handy, Stephen
1461 Bennet, Wm.
1461 slave Hager
1461 slave Harey
1461 slave Judey
1462 Dennis, John, junr.
1462 Mathews, Thos.
1462 slave Kinstone
1462 slave Oxford
1462 slave Jack
1462 slave Patience
1462 slave Abo
1463 Parsons, Robt.
1464 Anderson, Mary
1464 slave Abram
1465 Riggin, Ambros junr.
1466 Allen, Francis, mr.
1466 Dufey, James
1466 Johnson, Abraham
1466 slave Sibrey
1466 slave Judey
1466 slave Nell
1466 slave Margree
1467 Goslin, John, indian
1468 Bounds, George
1468 Winright, Stephen
1469 Beavens, Thomas
1470 Atkinson, Saml.
1471 Atkinson, Isaac
1472 Towensand, Charles
1472 Towensand, Solomon
1472 Towensand, Elias
1472 Towensand, Wm.
1473 Towensand, John, senr.
1473 Hambleton, Wm.
1473 Towensand, Saul
1473 slave Dick
1473 slave Merer
1474 Towensand, Comfort
1474 Towensand, Wm Barkley
1475 Towensand, Solomon
1476 Towensand, James
1476 slave Gye
1477 Shelden, John
1477 slave Isaac
1478 Benet, John
1479 Fogg, Moses
1480 Donohoe, Dormon
1480 Cupper, Saml.
1481 Beavens, Rowland
1481 Beavens, Wm.
1482 Beavens, Cornelius
1483 Coulbourn, John
1483 Coulbourne, Wm.
1484 Porter, Francis
1484 Porter, McCemey
1484 Porter, Jonathan
1484 slave Jack
1485 Butler, Thos.
1486 Townsand, John, junr.
1486 Townsand, John
1487 Mayo, Saml.
1488 Dickerson, Charles, senr.
1489 Dickerson, Edmd., senr.
1489 slave George
1490 Donoho, Teague
1490 Donoho, Teague
1490 Donoho, Daniel
1490 Dukes, Robt.
1491 Dickerson, Edmd., junr.
1491 Reding, Charles
1492 Dickerson, Cornelius
1492 slave Lenor
1493 Cottingham, Jonathan
1493 Cottingham, Wm.
1494 Benton, Comfort
1494 Costen, Mathias
1494 slave Sambo
1494 slave Hobon
1494 slave Coffe
1494 slave Pegg
1494 slave Jone
1494 slave Hannah
1495 Costen, Isaac
1495 slave Andrew
1496 Tull, John
1497 Costen, Stephen
1498 Gaddis, Robt.
1498 slave Tom
1498 slave Febo
1499 Houston, Joseph, senr.
1499 Celum, Wm.
1499 slave Bell
1499 slave Joe
1500 Sturgis, Jonathan
1501 McCuddey, John
1502 Marchant, Benj.
1502 slave Adam
1503 Atkinson, Angelow
1503 Warinton, Benj.
1503 Boyce, Wm.
1504 Stewart, Sarah, mrs.
1504 slave Jack
1504 slave Corck
1504 slave Fisher
1504 slave Tom
1504 slave Fungo
1505 Otwell, Francis
1506 Hampton,, madam
1506 Henry, Robt., capt.
1506 Henry, John, capt.
1506 slave Tarell
1506 slave Chick
1506 slave Adam
1506 slave Harrey
1506 slave Pompey
1506 slave Seser
1506 slave Lusey
1506 slave Old Jeney
1506 slave Little Jeney
1506 slave Patience
1506 slave Fillis
1507 Peal, Thomas
1507 slave Sampson
1508 Andrews, John
1508 Andrews, Peal
1508 Andrews, Shipard
1509 Otwell, Charles
1509 Otwell, Francis
1510 Riggin, Darby
1510 Riggin, Pearce
1510 Riggin, Teague
1510 Riggin, Jno.
1511 Fleming, John
1511 Fleming, Wm.
1511 slave Robin
1511 slave Dinah
1511 slave Pompey
1511 slave Joe
1512 Whittington, Southy
1512 Whittington, Wm.
1512 slave Robin
1512 slave Hannah
1512 slave Sarah
1513 Wonell, James
1514 Towensand, Daniel
1514 Towensand, Dickerson
1514 slave Elizabeth
1514 slave Andeny
1515 Lindow, James
1515 slave Moses
1516 Caldwell, John
1516 Elliot, Fra.
1517 Merrill, Joshua
1518 Selby, Thos.
1518 Selby, Thos., junr.

1735 TAX LIST [Household number/Name/Remarks]

POCOMOKE/WICOMICO HUNDREDS

1518 slave

WICOMICO HUNDRED
1519 Gale, Levin, col.
1519 Leatherbury, Jno.
1519 Noble, Mark
1519 Seahorn, Thomas
1519 slave Hope
1519 slave Pleasent
1519 slave Jahew
1519 slave Robin
1519 slave Peter
1519 slave Jack
1519 slave Joice
1519 slave Pollert
1519 slave Zeprah
1519 slave Hannah
1520 Dashiell, George, col.
1520 Dashiell,, Doctor
1520 Evans, John
1520 North, John
1520 Leatherbury, Thomas
1520 18 slaves
1521 Handy, John
1521 slave Dick
1521 slave Tom
1521 slave Moll
1521 slave Jane
1522 Gilliss, Thomas
1522 Bluitt, John
1522 slave Stepney
1522 slave Dominick
1522 slave Namah
1522 slave Pegg
1523 Adams, Alexander
1523 Adams, Alexr., junr.
1523 Hill, John
1523 slave Jack
1523 slave Squash
1523 slave Beck
1524 Hobbs, Joy
1524 Hobbs, Absolom
1524 slave Pollibus
1525 Cope, John
1526 Cope, William
1527 McGee, Peter
1528 Malloon, Robert
1529 McGee, Peter, senr.
1530 McClanney, Daniel
1530 Mitchell, John
1531 Goslin, Thomas
1532 Hearn, William
1533 Cordery, Isaac
1534 Goslin, Mathew
1535 Davis, William
1536 Collier, Thomas

1536 slave Grace
1537 Goslin, Richard
1538 Mitchell, Isaac
1539 Kibble, John
1540 McGee, George
1540 McGee, Saml.
1541 Jenckins, Jarvis
1541 Jenckins, John
1542 Ellis, Joseph
1543 Miller, Peter
1544 Brereton, William
1544 Brereton, Willm.
1544 slave Patience
1545 Bailey, George
1545 Bailey, Benjamin
1546 Disharoon, Michael
1546 Coniday, John
1547 Hill, Charles
1547 Ellis, William
1548 Hillman, Edward
1549 Chiles, Edmond
1550 Disharoon, Michael, jr.
1551 Porter, Joshua
1552 Such, Oliver
1553 Ellis, Francis
1554 Morris, Jacob
1554 Morris, Joseph
1555 Howard, John
1556 Collet, James
1556 Hayman, Charles
1556 Salt, Balmforth
1557 Sharp, George
1557 slave Pompey
1557 slave Mary
1558 Crouch, John
1558 Crouch, Nicholas
1559 Toadvine, Henry
1559 slave Goliah
1559 slave Oxford
1559 slave Jenney
1559 slave Sarah
1559 slave Hiway
1560 Shockley, John
1560 Shockley, John
1560 Shockley, Richard
1561 Shockley, Jonathan
1562 Toadvine, Thomas
1562 Ellis, John
1563 Duskey, Dennis
1563 Talbort, John
1564 Duskey, Moses
1565 McGraw, William
1566 Fooks, Benja.
1566 Toadvine, John
1566 slave Patience
1567 Bashaw, Graves
1568 Crouch, Jacob
1569 Perrey, James
1570 Crouch, Isaac

1571 Christopher, John
1571 Christopher, John
1572 Parsons, George
1573 McGlamary, George
1574 McGlamary, Willm.
1575 Cathell, James
1576 Davis, Samuell
1577 Hayman, William, sr.
1577 Hayman, Willm., junr.
1578 Davis, Daniel
1578 Davis, Thomas
1579 Davis, John, junr.
1579 McGee, John
1580 Lingoe, Richard
1581 Sheydy, Elizabeth
1581 Sheydy, Stephen
1581 Sheydy, John
1582 Lingoe, Jacob
1583 Dorman, Henry
1583 Dorman, Henry, junr.
1584 Williss, Nathaniell
1585 Lingoe, Robinson
1586 Vaunce, David
1587 Hayman, James
1587 Hayman, Charles
1587 Hayman, Isaac
1588 Hayman, John
1589 Griffen, John
1590 Alexander, Moses
1590 slave Tom
1591 Adley, William
1592 Vance, Alexander
1593 Knox, Robert
1593 Knox, William
1594 Ragley, Michael
1595 Adkins, Robert
1596 Hailes, John
1596 Layfield, David
1597 Shehorn, John
1598 Roach,, mrs.
1598 Goldsmith, Anthony
1598 Roach, Stephen
1598 slave Tom
1598 slave Harry
1598 slave Peg
1599 Carey, Levin
1600 Carey, Jonathan
1601 Carey, Thomas
1602 Tounsend, Benjamin
1602 slave Dick
1602 slave Bess
1603 Dashiell, George
1603 slave Coffey
1604 Evans, John, senr.
1604 Evans, John, junr.
1604 slave Sambo
1605 Crocket, John

TAX LISTS OF SOMERSET COUNTY: 1730-1740

WICOMICO HUNDRED

1605 slave Sib
1606 Dashiell, Charles
1606 slave Pelyner
1607 Tippet, Thomas
1608 Shiles, Thomas
1608 McCoye, John
1609 Willin, Thomas
1609 Willin, Robert
1609 slave Sarah
1610 Nelson, William
1610 Pritchet, William
1611 Everton, John
1611 Everton, William
1612 Crocket, Robert
1612 slave Crap
1612 slave Munk
1613 Crocket, Richard
1613 Larrimore, John
1614 Lackie, Alexander
1614 slave Tobie
1614 slave Messer
1614 slave Robin
1614 slave Sib
1614 slave Abba
1614 slave Sam
1614 slave Southey
1614 slave Darbey
1615 Harris, George
1616 Durram, James
1617 Shiles, John
1617 slave Tom
1617 slave Hanabel
1618 Harris, William, junr.
1619 Harris, William, senr.
1619 Harris, Richard
1619 Harris, John
1619 Harris, Charles
1620 Dashiell, Thomas
1620 Jones, John
1620 Wilson, Wm.
1621 Rencher, Thomas
1621 Leggs, Benja.
1621 slave Peter
1621 slave Pompey
1622 Ballard, Charles
1622 slave Ceasar
1623 Ballard, Elizabeth
1623 slave Mercer
1624 Austin, Robert
1624 Austin, William
1624 slave Moll
1625 Walker, Thomas
1625 slave Tom
1625 slave Jonathan
1625 slave Dinah
1625 slave Cate
1626 Stewart, Patrick

1626 slave Jane
1627 Elliss,, mrs.
1627 Fowler, Thomas
1627 slave Bubow
1627 slave Hannah
1627 slave Ann
1627 slave Mary
1628 Holbrooke, Thomas
1628 Allexr., Willm.
1629 Robinson, Willm.
1630 Lokey, Thomas
1631 Robinson, John
1632 Moad, Peter
1633 Howard, Thomas
1633 Jarvis, Saml.
1634 Cottman, Joseph
1634 Adaw, Owen
1635 Cottman, Benjamin
1635 Newman, John
1635 slave Sarah
1636 Cottman, William
1637 Swillaven, William
1638 Melven, Thomas
1639 Mitchell, Benjamin
1640 Mitchell, Richard
1640 Adaw, John
1641 Noble, John
1642 Sermon, Peter, senr.
1642 Sermon, Peter, junr.
1642 slave Tom
1642 slave Lemon
1643 Sermon, John
1643 Austin, Geo.
1644 Alexander, Liston
1644 Hodgen, John
1645 Chaddawacks, James, senr
1645 Chaddawacks, James, junr
1646 Standford, Joseph
1646 Christopher, Rixsom
1647 Dowdle, Christopher
1648 Hearn, Thomas
1648 Hearn, Nehemiah
1648 Hearn, George
1648 slave Hannah
1649 Caldwell, John
1649 Farlor, Jno.
1649 Caldwell, Robert
1649 Rider, James
1649 Rathbone, Andrew
1649 slave Coffey
1649 slave Will
1649 slave Coffey
1649 slave Quash
1649 slave Doll

1650 Covington, Thomas
1650 slave Tom
1651 Gray, Allin
1652 Maddox, William
1652 slave Abraham
1653 Maddox, Alexander
1653 slave Mercer
1654 Culver, John
1655 Vincent, George
1655 Hitch, William
1656 Vincent, Thomas, senr.
1656 Vincent, Benja.
1657 Hall, Samuell
1658 Wale, John
1659 Vincent, Thomas, junr.
1660 Hitch, John
1660 slave Mercer
1661 Hitch, Elgate
1661 Smith, Archibald
1661 Berrey, James
1661 slave Conounder
1661 slave Hannah
1662 Baker, Thomas
1663 Owens, Edward
1663 Lahydill, Speir
1664 Price, John
1664 Price, Thomas
1665 Smith, James, senr.
1666 Nicholson, Joseph
1667 Nicholson, James
1668 Nicholson, Richard
1668 Wetherly, William
1669 Bartlett, William
1670 Bartlett, Thomas
1670 Bartlett, Paskey
1671 Handy, Isaac
1671 slave Sharper
1671 slave Prue
1672 Johnson, Purnall
1673 Hall, Thomas
1674 Johnson, Samuell
1675 Bready, Rebecca
1675 Bready, William
1676 Bird, Thomas, senr.
1676 Bird, Thomas, junr.
1676 Bird, William
1677 Humphris, Mary
1677 Humphris, Thomas
1677 slave Bess
1678 Rickards, John
1678 Rickards, James
1678 Rickards, Thomas
1679 Rickards, Benjamin
1679 slave Cant
1680 Lank, Francis
1680 slave Tobee
1680 slave Bess
1680 slave Jack

1735 TAX LIST [Household number/Name/Remarks]

WICOMICO HUNDRED

1681 Lank, George
1681 Price, Alexander
1681 Phillips, George
1682 Farrell, William
1682 slave Comfort
1683 Vennables, William
1683 Price, David
1684 Vennables, Benja.
1684 slave Will
1684 slave Bess
1685 Bailey, Jonathan
1686 Bounds, Jonathan
1686 slave Bess
1687 Kibble, William
1688 Vennables, Willm.
1688 Vennables, Joseph
1689 Chamber, Edward, esq.
1689 slave Will
1690 Stevens, Richard
1690 slave Tobie
1690 slave Chilse
1691 Stevens, John
1691 slave Bess
1692 Fasque, Thomas
1693 Hall, Ann
1693 Taylor, James
1694 Sirman, Edward
1694 Morris, Jeremiah
1695 Smith, James, junr.
1696 Meers, John
1696 Meers, Robert
1697 Christopher, John, senr.
1697 Christopher, Clem
1697 Christopher, Joseph
1698 Christopher, Ephraim
1699 Thompson, John
1700 Goslin, John
1701 Piper, Christopher
1701 slave Dick
1701 slave Sambo
1701 slave Tobee
1701 slave Sew
1702 Hardey, Robert
1702 Hardey, George
1702 Bashaw, Joiles
1702 Boardman, Samuell
1703 Winder, Thomas
1703 slave Mingo
1704 Wales, Joseph
1704 slave Ordery
1705 McMurray, James
1705 slave Ball
1705 slave Pompey
1705 slave Abner
1705 slave Rose
1706 Stewart, Alexander
1706 slave Ball
1707 Dashiell, Mathias
1707 slave Mingo
1707 slave, woman
1708 Cordery, Abraham
1709 Scott, George
1709 slave Samuel
1709 slave Sanders
1709 slave Pomp
1710 Scott, Day
1710 Lewis, Christopher
1710 slave Hecter
1710 slave Sippio
1710 slave Tom
1710 slave Lucey
1711 Cordery, Daniel
1711 Faster, John
1711 slave Samson
1711 slave Sibb
1712 Upton, Thomas
1713 Codery, Jacob
1713 Cordery, Morgan
1714 Keirsey, Patrick, senr.
1714 Keirsey, Patrick, junr.
1715 Perdue, John
1716 Longoe, James
1717 McGlamarey, Edward
1717 Oliphant, Mathew
1718 Hill, James
1719 Murfey, Joseph
1720 Smith, Moses
1721 Smith, David
1722 Smith, George
1722 Smith, John
1723 Turner, Samuell
1723 Turner, Edward
1724 Disharoon, John, forrest
1724 Cornwell, Robert
1725 Disharoon, Lewis
1725 Cox, Hill
1726 Disharoon, Levin
1727 Handy, Ebenezer
1727 Cragen, Paul
1727 slave Tom
1727 slave Sambo
1727 slave Mumford
1727 slave Will
1727 slave Amey
1727 slave Hannah
1728 McCalpin, Robert
1729 Cray, William
1729 Ready, Brian
1729 Ready, Daniell
1730 Hearn, William
1730 Hearn, John
1730 slave Moll
1731 Freiny, Peter
1731 Freiny, John
1732 White, Henry
1733 Mellson, Daniell
1734 Taylor, Thomas
1735 Gordey, Peter
1736 Gordey, Moses
1737 Lindow, Thomas
1738 Phillips, Jacob
1739 Hastin, Robert
1739 Hastin, William
1739 Hastin, Benjamin
1740 Linch, Michael
1741 Atkinson, Timothy
1742 Disharoon, Willm.
1743 Stevens, Willm.
1744 Jackson, Samuell
1744 slave Grace
1745 Fullerton, Alex.
1745 Parremore, Richard
1746 Fullerton, James
1747 Lowes, Henry, capt.
1747 slave Jepta
1747 slave Dover
1747 slave Rose
1747 slave Betty
1748 Hitch, Samuell
1748 slave Jack
1749 Tatum, John
1750 Leanord, Joseph
1751 Williams, John
1751 Whittington, Southey
1751 Fenelson, Elisha
1751 slave Robin
1752 Cox, Thomas, senr.
1752 Cox, Thomas, junr.
1753 Pullett, Thomas
1754 Polk, David
1755 Dashiell, Willm.
1756 Lingoe, John
1757 Caldwell, Hugh
1758 Crouch, Jacob, senr.
1758 Crouch, Jacob, junr.
1758 Crouch, Robt.
1759 Reddish, John
1759 Crouch, Robert
1760 Right, Jeremiah, senr.
1760 Right, Jeremiah
1761 Lecatt, John
1762 Disharoon, John, senr.
1762 slave Coffey
1762 slave Fanney
1762 slave Grace

TAX LISTS OF SOMERSET COUNTY: 1730-1740

WICOMICO HUNDRED

1763 Rencher, Wood
1763 slave Jack
1763 slave Bess
1764 Collins, James
1765 Parsons, John
1766 Disharoon, John
1767 Cordery, John
1768 Willin, Edward
1769 Shiles, John
1770 Gale, Matt.
1770 slave Jack
1770 slave Palph
1771 Phillips, Richd.
1772 Toadvine, Mary
1772 slave Jack
1772 slave Ralph
1773 Covinton, Benja.
1774 Davis, John, senr.
1774 unnamed/slave
1775 Harris, Robt.
1775 slave woman

1736 TAX LIST [Household number/Name/Remarks]

ANNEMESSEX HUNDRED

1 Handy, Thomas
1 slave Nan
2 Tull, Thomas
3 Wharton, William
4 Hall, Richard
4 Wolston, Joy
5 Hall, Charles
5 Davis, Richard
6 L[anden, Henry]
7 Maelpin, Robert
8 Curtis, Charles
8 slave Dick
8 slave Toney
9 Trehearn, John
10 Roach, Nathaniell
11 Tull, Solomon
12 Catlin, William
12 slave Harrey
13 Stockdell, Edward
14 Long, Sameull, anna
14 slave Kate
14 slave Samson
15 Fenton, Martin
15 Dolkin, William
16 Waters, John
16 slave Harrey
16 slave Will
16 slave Dick
16 slave Sam
16 slave Berry
16 slave Jenny
16 slave Moreah
17 Waters, William
17 slave Goliah
17 slave Sambo
17 slave Bristah
17 slave Pompy
17 slave Dinah
18 Waters, Eliza.
18 slave Allex
18 slave Hannable
18 slave Sippeo
18 slave Hagar
18 slave Pegg
19 Katan, George
20 Waters, Abigll.
20 slave Davey
20 slave York
21 To Cottman, Mary
21 Cottman, Joseph
21 Cottman, Benja.
21 slave Jenny
22 Waters, Edward
23 Riggen, Jno., junr.
24 Ward, Cornelius
25 Ward, Stephen, junr.
26 Addams, David
26 Addams, Jacob
26 Addams, William
27 Addams, Thomas
28 Potter, Henry
29 Pewsey, John
30 Cottingham, Charles
30 Cottingham, Jno.
31 Cottingham, Charles, jr.
32 Langford, Joseph, senr.
32 Langford, Soll.
33 Scandelin, Edward
34 Langford, Joseph, junr.
35 Linsey, Thomas
36 Cohoone, Jno.
37 Scott, Robert, senr.
37 Scott, Jno.
37 slave Bess
38 Scott, Robert, junr.
39 Bannester, Charles
40 Long, Randall
40 slave Sibe
41 White, John, senr.
42 Hearn, Edward
42 Kindell, William
43 Atkinson, Joshua
43 Powell, Thomas
43 slave Frank
43 slave Bess
44 Gunby, Kirk
44 Moore, Samuell
45 Kellam, John, senr.
45 Kellam, Isaac
46 Kellam, John, junr.
47 Gunby, Jno.
47 Bucker, Cornelious
47 slave Jack
47 slave Kate
48 Whittingtons, Southey, - quarter
48 slave Robin
49 Bell, Thos.
49 slave Nann
50 Bell, Anthony
50 Bell, Josephas
50 Jones, Mathew
51 Horsey, Stephen, sr.
51 Killey, Jas.
51 slave Sarah
52 Davis, Jno.
52 Megumery, Thomas
52 slave Harry
52 slave Will
52 slave Dick
52 slave Sue
52 slave Jenny
53 Mott, Jno.
54 Cullen, Henry
55 Price, Edward
55 Price, Jno.
55 Price, Francis
55 Price, Johnson
56 Bennett, Henry
56 Ward, Richard
57 Lord, Francis
57 Lord, Randall
57 Lord, Thos.
57 Lord, Alexander
58 Lord, Henry
59 Roach, Charles
59 slave Joe
60 Roach, [Jno.]
60 Park, Arthur
61 Cullen, Jacob
62 Starling, Jno., sr.
62 Starling, Henry
62 Starling, Aaron
63 Starling, Jno., junr.
64 Grimes, James
65 Wheeler, John
66 Moore, Isaac
67 Bird, David
68 Dies, Daniel
69 Ward, Thomas
69 Ward, Jacob
69 Ward, Moses
70 Ward, James
71 Juett, William
71 slave Ned
72 Sumners, Jonathan
73 Reddin, John
74 Allen, Joseph
74 Allen, Henry
75 Sumners, John
75 Sumners, David
75 Sumners, Benja.
76 Sumners, Thomas
76 Sumners, George
76 Sumners, Thomas
77 Riggen, Jno., senr.
77 Riggen, William
78 [Ri]ggen, [Jonathan]
78 [Rigg]en], [Stephen]
79 Ward, Samuell
79 Ward, Jno.
79 Ward, William
80 Ward, Stephen, senr.
80 slave Pompy
80 slave Phillis
80 slave Sarah
81 Doughety, Jno.
81 Doughety, Nathn.
82 Davis, James
82 Beach, Thomas
83 Moore, Frances
83 Moore, Jno.
83 More, Thos.
83 More, Isaac
83 Moore, Jacob
84 Johnson, Jno., senr.

TAX LISTS OF SOMERSET COUNTY: 1730-1740

ANNEMESSEX HUNDRED

84 Johnson, Jno., jr.
84 Smith, Jams.
85 Miles, Henry
85 slave Robin
85 slave Dinah
85 slave Phillis
86 Frazer, Peter
86 slave Moreah
87 Coulbourn, Solomon
87 Coulbourn, Solomon, jr.
88 Coulbourn, Wm., senr.
88 Coulbourn, Samll.
88 Coulbourn, Soll.
88 Coulbourn, Michael
88 slave Quako
88 slave Abram
88 slave Lucy
89 Coulbourn, Willm., junr.
89 slave Kate
90 Tayler, William
91 Holland, Michaell, junr.
91 slave Moll
92 Horsey, Stephen, junr.
93 Horsey, Smith
94 Horsey, Isaac, coll.
94 Parks, Charles
94 mollatto Johnathan
95 Johnson, William
96 Williams, Thomas, jr.
96 slave Dick
96 slave Cesar
96 slave Quashy
96 slave Lilly
97 Horsey, Nathn.
97 Horsey, Outerbridge
97 slave Kook
97 slave Quamenah
97 slave Prince
97 slave Patience
97 slave Kate
97 slave Tarroah
98 Dixon, William
98 Dixon, Ambross
98 slave Bess
98 slave Benn
99 Dixon, Thomas, senr.
99 Dixon, Thomas, junr.
99 slave Harry
99 slave Toby
99 slave Dick
99 slave Gidden
99 slave Hanah
99 slave Dinah
100 Lankford, Benja.
101 Long, John
101 slave Robin
101 slave Sarah
102 Smith, Henry
102 Smith, Arcable
102 Smith, Wm.
103 Cottingham, Thos., senr.
103 Cottingham, Jno.
104 Williams, Thos., capt.
104 Addams, John
104 Owen, Thomas
104 slave Titus
104 slave Addam
104 slave George
104 slave Tom
104 slave Addam
104 slave Jonas
104 slave Glasco
104 slave Sarah
104 slave Gelico
105 Pewsey, William
106 Bywaters, Richard
107 free black Watt
108 Williams, Isaac
108 Dougherty, James
108 Wood, David
109 To Owen, Eliza.
109 Owen, Phillip
110 At col. King's quarter
110 slave Mingo
110 slave Tamor
111 Sanders, Richard
111 Sanders, Thomas
112 Beauchamp, Isaac
112 slave Patience
113 Williams, Jno.
113 Williams, Jacob
113 slave Sambo
113 slave Moll
114 To Lister, Jane
114 Lister, Thomas
114 Lister, William
114 slave Cesar
115 Beauchamp, Edmond
115 Trehearn, James
116 Beachamp, William
117 Brumegum, Walter
118 Boston, William
119 Marshall, George
120 Marshall, [Samuel]
121 Adams, [Dennis]
122 Porter, Joseph
122 Porter, William
123 White, Jno., junr.
124 Ceary, Francis
125 Moore, Thomas, merum.
126 Long, Daniel, junr.
127 Long, Jeffery
127 Long, Sawell
127 slave Nish
128 Long, Samll., merumsco
128 Long, William
128 Long, David
129 Long, Daniell, senr.
129 slave Friendship
130 Long, David, senr.
131 Trehearn, James
132 Willson, George
133 Prier, Thomas
134 White, Thomas
134 Willson, Joseph
134 slave Essex
135 Wheatly, Sampson
135 slave Jack
136 Readen, Peter
137 To Maddux, Mary
137 slave Kate
138 Maddux, Bell
139 Conner, John, senr.
139 Conner, John, junr.
140 Conner, William
141 Willson, Jno., junr.
142 To Parks, Arthur
142 Parks, Jno.
142 Parks, Job
142 Hurst, John
143 Parks, John, senr.
143 Parks, Marke
144 Williams, William
145 Tyler, Thomas
146 Tyler, Jno., senr.
146 Tyler, Jno., junr.
146 Tyler, Thomas
147 Dixon, James
148 Evins, Jno.
149 Mister, William
149 Mister, Abraham
149 M[ister], Benjamin
150 Hop[kins], George
150 Hopkins, Jno.
150 Hopkins, William
150 Hopkins, Charles
151 Woolf, Henry
152 Fogg, Daniell
153 Cottingham, Thomas, jr.

1736 TAX LIST [Household number/Name/Remarks]

BALTIMORE HUNDRED

154 Smith, John, senr. capt.
154 Smith, John, junr.
154 Smith, Thomas
154 slave Haery
154 slave Marah
154 slave Bess
155 Wharton, Henmon
155 slave Amarall
156 Rickards, John, sr.
156 Rickards, Wm.
156 slave Simon
156 slave --tson
156 slave Mary
156 slave Bridgett
157 Harney, Thomas
157 Harney, Thomas
158 Hazard, David, senr.
158 Hazard, Wm.
158 slave Jacob
158 slave Dinah
159 Hazard, David, junr.
160 Roberson, Thomas
161 Hopkins, John
162 Roberson, John
162 Roberson, George
163 Gilstrap, [Pe]ter
163 Goodrick, [William]
164 ---i-y, illegible
164 Townsend, William
165 Coffon, Thomas
165 Coffen, Thomas
165 Coffen, Joseph
166 Roberson, Michael
166 Roberson, William
167 Smith, William
168 Aydelott, John, junr.
169 Wise, Mathew
170 Hopkins, Josiah
171 Tull, John, senr.
171 Tull, John
172 Johnson, Lenneard
173 Wyatt, William
174 Gray, William
175 Linch, Abraham
175 Wharton, Thomas
176 Miller, William Gray
177 Willson, Israel
178 Miller, John, mr.
178 slave Primas
178 slave Peggey
179 Howard, Nehemiah
180 Waples, Paul
180 Thorowgood, Paul
180 slave Charles
180 slave Dublin
181 Boden, John
182 Aydelott, Benjamin
183 Derickson, Benjamin
184 Woodcraft, William
184 Wilegoose, Richard
184 Wilegoose, Thomas
184 Cobb, Joseph
185 Aydelott, John, senr.
185 slave Jacob
186 Tingle, Hugh, senr.
186 Tingle, Hugh, junr.
187 Tingle, John
187 slave Harry
188 Rickards, Jones
189 Rickards, John, junr.
190 Depray, John
191 Cobb, William
191 Tingle, Samuell
192 Evans, Wm.
192 Evans, Jno.
192 Evans, Wm.
192 Evans, Walter
193 Bredall, [Isaia]h
193 Bredall, Jams. Stephen
193 slave Pendo
193 slave Mino
193 slave Adam
193 slave Simon
194 Hall, Samuell
195 Smith, Ann
195 Tingle, Littleton
196 Deale, John, senr.
197 Holland, Richard
197 Caldwell, Augusten
197 slave Hanah
198 Linch, Alexander
199 Patty, John
199 Patty, Powell
199 slave man
200 Gray, Thomas
201 Collier, Petter
201 slave Pompey
201 slave Moll
202 Johnson, David
203 Loggwood, Richard
204 Besecks, Absolom
205 Russell, Andrew
206 Bradford, William
207 Colings, Thomas
208 Farrill, Thomas
209 Latcham, Thomas
210 Hudson, Richard, sr.
210 Jones, Thomas
210 Hudson, John
210 slave Coffee
210 slave Chick
210 slave Charles
210 slave Beck
211 Kennett, William
212 Evans, Ebenezer
213 Mumford, Charles
214 Besicks, Nathaniel
215 Peterkin, David
216 Robarts, Thomas
216 Robarts, Alexander
217 Smith, John, piney neck
217 Smith, Robart
218 Deale, John, junr.
218 Brotton, John
219 Deale, Archable
219 Blizard, Thomas
219 Deale, Quanton
220 Stevenson, John
221 Howard, George, sr.
221 Howard, George, jr.
221 slave [Ken]t
221 slave Bess
222 Fassitt, [LAMB]AR[D]
222 slave Fellice
223 Morrow, Robart
224 Morrow, James
224 Moore, Willm.
225 Fassitt, Rouse
225 slave Core
226 Whaley, Willim., senepux
226 Rackliffe, Nathaniell
227 Gault, William
228 Newbold, John
228 Whitehead, Jno.
228 slave Cato
228 slave Sille
229 Hook, William
229 Wheeler, John
229 Taylor, Samll.
230 Marsey, Alexander
230 slave Jack
230 slave Jude
231 Marshall, Isaac
231 Marshell, Jacob
231 slave Ben
231 slave Dinah
232 Walton, John
233 Bradford, Nathaniell
233 Quilling, Benjamin
234 Hampton, Mary, madm.
234 slave Jack
234 slave Hannable
234 slave Petter
234 slave Pegg
234 slave Hanah

TAX LISTS OF SOMERSET COUNTY: 1730-1740

BALTIMORE HUNDRED

235 Fassitt, William, mr.
235 slave Will
235 slave Harry
235 slave Rachell
235 slave Titus
235 slave Sambo
236 Miller, Joseph
236 slave Tom
236 slave Moll
236 slave Charles
236 slave Jack
237 Wyatt, Joseph
237 Wyatt, Nathaniell
238 Walker, John
239 Nickles, John
240 Liptrott, John
241 Well, William
242 Boden, Susanah
242 Clark, Joseph
243 Pirkins, William
244 Turvill, Presgrave
244 Hill, Johnson
244 Collings, Price
244 Collings, Able
244 Hill, Wm. Steven
245 Townsend, Bowman
245 Wharton, Rixam
246 Kelley, Nicklas
247 Momford, James
247 Cade, Thos.
247 slave Orom
248 Holloway, John
249 Holloway, Joseph
250 Hill, illegible, widow
250 Hazard, ------y
251 ------orth, illegible
252 Morris, Dennis
253 Tippitt, Thomas
254 Gray, Joseph
254 Jenkins, John
254 slave Simon
254 slave Quaco
255 Tyer, Robert
256 Brittingham, Eliza.
256 Brittingham, Robert
257 Hudson, David
257 Hudson, William
258 Blizard, Richard
258 Munks, William
259 Adams, Thomas
260 Woodcraft, Richard
261 Boden, Able
262 Wharton, Francis
262 Whorton, Wm.
263 Samans, Wm.
264 Laughinghouse, Wm.
264 slave Moll
265 Onorton, John
265 Brown, John
266 Dixson, Sturges
266 Banks, Niblett
267 Barnett, John
268 ---ag---, illegible
269 Cammile, John
269 slave Felace
270 Wallas, Thomas
270 Juitt, Nathanill
270 Bowls, Urias
271 Quilling, Joseph
272 Wheeler, John
273 Manklin, Richard
274 Mumford, William
275 Hopkins, Samuell
275 Evens, William
276 Robertson, Andrew
277 Fall, John
278 Fall, Abraham
279 Aulford, David
280 Turvell, William
280 Whealey, John
281 Delaley, Jno. Patrick
282 Crapper, Nathaniel, jr.
283 Beasey, William
284 Fisher, Bentill
285 Crapper, Edmund, jr.
286 Morgan, Avery
286 Coe, [Danie]ll
286 illegible
286 slave [Q]uaminy
287 Pridix, Thomas
288 Rackliffe, Charles, capt
288 Rackliffe, Purnall
288 Tayler, John Jones
288 slave Robin
288 slave Sarah
288 slave Will
288 slave Matt
288 slave Kate
289 Larrance, Henry
290 Hill, Richard
291 Perry, James, tax free
291 Perry, James, junr.
292 Purnell, Jno., mr.
292 Rackliffe, Charles
292 Heugitt, George
292 Lowant, Charles
292 slave Will
292 slave Toney
292 slave Quaminy
292 slave Toney
292 slave Marray
292 slave Dolley
293 Crapper, Nathanil, snr.
293 Crapper, Vinson
293 slave Kenner
294 Goddard, Thomas
295 Fasitt, Mary, mrs.
295 Bowen, John
295 slave Frank
295 slave Doll
295 slave Sue
295 slave Barney
296 Walton, [Wm.], jr.
297 Turvell, John
298 Kennett, Martin
298 Willson, John
299 Forsight, Sarah
299 Hogg, James
300 Roberson, Joshua
300 slave Bess
301 Dasey, Thomas
302 West, George
303 West, Thomas
304 West, William
305 Watson, John
305 Shelerneng, Timothy
306 Wharton, Daniel, sr.
306 Wharton, Daniel, jr.
307 Clark, Mary
307 Clark, Edward
307 Clark, Wm.
308 Morris, William
309 Godwin, Ceaser, jr.
310 Evens, John
311 Godwin, Ceaser, sr.
311 Godwin, Daniell
312 Hall, Joseph
313 Crapper, [Edmond]
313 Mecoy, James
313 Cammil, Solomon
313 slave Peter
313 slave Pompey
313 slave Dick
313 slave Febe
314 Walton, Willm., sr.
314 Walton, William
314 slave Ceasar
314 slave Gloster
314 slave Juday
315 Masey, William
316 Knock, Nehemiah
316 slave woman
317 Hudson, William
317 Gray, William
318 Gault, Robart
318 Gault, John

1736 TAX LIST [Household number/Name/Remarks]

BALTIMORE/BOGERTERNORTON HUNDREDS

319 Graham, George
320 Lewis, Joseph
320 Lewis, William
321 Barnett, James
322 Gibins, Thomas
323 Carry, Richard
324 Morris, Bibbins
325 Eades, James
326 Kelley, George
327 Cammile, John, indian river
328 Lewis, Arthur
329 Phillips, John
330 Morris, John
330 slave Kate
331 Carry, Thomas
332 Pritteyman, Thomas
333 Jeoferson, Richard
334 Jones, Ebenezer
334 slave Boson
335 Short, Edward
336 Ingrom, Jacob
337 Green, Ezekiel
337 Hall, Thomas
337 Hall, Joseph
338 Hickman, Richd., indn.ri
339 Willson, John
340 Drifen, George
341 Hudson, Richard
341 Lathberry, Arthur
342 Hudson, Samuell
343 Natman, John
344 Fassitt, [Fran]klin
344 slave Bess
345 Smythers, Sargant
346 Showell, Samuell
346 Dolby, William
347 Holloway, John, sr.
348 Collings, John
348 Rackliff, Elias
349 Purkins, Thomas
350 Clark, Race
350 Clark, Jno.
350 Clark, Benjaman
350 Clark, Race
351 Johnson, John
351 Johnson, Levin
352 Johnson, Bartholomew
353 Simpson, Richard
353 Quilling, John
353 Looker, William
354 Harrison, William
355 Smalwood, Samuell
356 Powell, Thomas
357 Burton, William
357 Burton, Jno.
357 Burton, Joseph
357 slave Touse
357 slave Bomand
357 slave Adam
357 slave Rachell
358 Collings, Wm.
359 Phillips, Wm.
360 Collings, George
361 Marsey, Adkins

BOGERTERNORTON HUNDRED
362 Smith, William
363 Hammond, Edward
364 Haddor, Warrin
364 Hammond, William
365 Harmon, William
365 Harmon, Zachariah
366 Hammond, John
366 Bassett, John
366 Bassett, James
367 Hodge, Robert
367 slave
368 Smith, Andrew
368 Smith, George
369 Porter, Joseph
369 Porter, John
370 Templin, John
370 Templin, Richard
371 Blizard, Richard
372 Smoshie, William
373 Collins, Thomas, senr.
374 Becketts, Peter
375 Truitt, John
376 Timmons, Thomas
377 Timmons, Aaron
378 Timmons, Joseph
379 Timmons, James
380 Timmons, John
381 Timmons, Samll.
381 Timmons, Aaron
382 Jones, Joseph
383 Townsend, William
384 Peal, Thorogood
384 slave
385 Green, Adam
386 Evans, Elias
386 Coffing, John
387 Donnelson, Catherine
387 2 slaves
388 Tadlock, Agnes
388 Tadlock, Edward
389 Crapper, Ebenezer, sr.
390 Crapper, Ebenezer, jr.
391 Crapper, John
392 Stain, James
393 Rownd, James
393 Cutless, John
393 5 slaves
394 Brittingham, Willm., sr.
394 Brittingham, Solomon
394 Brittingham, Absolom
394 Brittingham, Nathll.
395 Brittingham, Wm., junr.
396 Hall, Robert
396 Hall, Spence
396 slave
397 Dennis, William, senr.
398 Gillett, John
399 Hudson, John
400 Hudson, Major
401 Bowen, William
402 Handcock, Daniel
402 Handcock, Wm.
403 Pointer, Wm., senr.
404 Hudson, Dennis
404 2 slaves
405 Ennis, William, senr.
405 Ennis, William, junr.
406 Stone, James
407 Ennis, Natha.
408 Duncan, Thomas
409 Murray, Duncan
409 McCormuck, Patrick
409 Morris, John
409 Hambleton, Wm.
409 5 slaves
410 Purnell, Catherine
410 Purnell, Walter
410 2 slaves
411 Godfrey, Charles
412 Bishop, Joseph
412 Patrick, Daniel
413 Bishop, William
413 Owten, John
413 Owten, William
414 Schofield, Joseph
414 Schofield, John
414 2 slaves
415 Davis, Robert, senr.
415 Davis, William
415 Davis, Ishmael
415 Davis, Benja.
415 Davis, Robert
416 Dennis, Solomon
417 Dennis, Daniel
418 Davis, Wm.
418 Davis, Samuell
419 Davis, Philip
419 Davis, George
420 Adkins, Stanton
420 Adkins, Stephen
421 Dennis, Wm., junr.
422 Pennewell, Jno.

TAX LISTS OF SOMERSET COUNTY: 1730-1740

BOGERTERNORTON HUNDRED

423 Pennewell, Geo.
424 Gillaland, John
424 McGumery, Robert
424 2 slaves
425 Bishop, Benjamin
425 Patrick, Roger
426 Williams, Jonathan
426 Williams, Littleton
427 Pennewell, Thomas
428 Murrain, Mathew
428 Murrain, John
429 Trewitt, James
430 Trewitt, Geo., son James
431 Jarman, Job
432 Lowe, George
433 Porter, John
434 Collins, John
435 Collins, William
436 Collins, Mary
436 Collins, Thomas
437 Davis, Robert, junr.
438 Parker, Tabitha
438 Parker, Samuell
438 4 slaves
439 Keirsie, John
439 Keirsie, Patrick
439 Canady, [Nehemiah] Siman
440 Oshohanies, William
441 Parker, Charles
442 Parker, Philip
443 Selby, William
443 Selby, Wm., jr.
443 4 slaves
444 Porter, Wm., seaside
445 Richardson, Robert
446 Richardson, Charles
446 slave
447 Bratten, Samll., senr.
447 Bratten, Hugh
448 Bratten, Samll., junr.
449 Richardson, J[one]s
450 Selby, John
450 3 slaves
451 Lane, George
452 Deverix, John
452 Prier, Webb
452 Deverix, Cornelius
452 slave
453 Scott, Mark
454 Holston, John

455 Adkins, John
456 Victor, James
456 Victor, Thomas
457 Jackson, Henry
458 Jarman, Henry
458 Webb, Elisha
459 Johnson, Afradozie
459 slave
460 Johnson, John
461 Johnson, George
462 Johnson, Thomas
463 Jackson, Agnes
463 Jackson, John
464 Beddard, William
465 Waters, Richard
465 Taylor, Josiah
465 Bryan, James
466 Williams, Thos. Nathll.
466 Williams, Samuell
466 Gray, Nicholas
467 Lay, John
467 2 slaves
468 Sturgis, John
468 Sturgis, Littleton
469 Burton, John
470 Heather, Ephraim, sr.
470 Heather, Ephraim, jr.
470 slave
471 Selby, Parker
472 Stevens, Samuell
473 Holston, William
474 Davis, Wm., seaside
474 Dukes, Thomas
474 slave
475 Brittingham, Isaac
475 Brittingham, Nathan
475 slave
476 Greer, Archibald
476 Greer, Henry
477 Brittingham, Jeremiah
478 Purnell, Thomas
478 6 slaves
479 Taylor, William
480 Turner, Nicholas
481 Turner, Henry
482 Mason, Edmond
483 Dredon, John
484 Dredon, Robert
485 Purnell, Benjamin
485 slave
486 McCaley, John
487 Bratten, James
488 Stevenson, James
488 Stevenson, Adam
489 Ennis, Mary
489 Ennis, Samuel

489 Ennis, John
490 Edwards, Benjamin
491 Hammond, Jacob
492 Holland, William
493 Marchment, Charle
494 Swaine, William
495 Penewell, Charles
496 Tull, Benjamin
497 Richards, William
498 Smith, Abraham
499 Baynom, Bartholomew
500 Warren, Nicholas
501 Warren, Robert
502 Gray, John
503 Daizey, John
504 St[earns], William
505 Baker, John
505 Tillmon, William
506 Crapper, Nehemiah
507 Pointer, Thomas
507 Pointer, Ratcklife
507 Pointer, Turvill
507 Pointer, William
508 Mumford, George
509 Truitt, William
510 Bell, Adam
510 Holston, Benjamn.
510 Holston, Charles
510 slave
511 Bradford, Adam
512 Drigguss, John
513 Buncle, Alexander
514 Hall, Wm.
514 Hall, Adam
514 Hall, Pheenix
514 2 slaves
515 Bratten, James, junr.
516 Richardson, William
517 Pepper, John
517 Pepper, William
518 Rownd, Edward
518 Davis, Thomas
518 Bowen, Edward
518 2 slaves
519 Ellison, Richard
520 Purnell, Mathew
520 Williams, John
520 slave
521 Sandwith, William
522 Morriss, Joseph
523 Fletcher, Thomas
523 3 slaves
524 Mumford, James, sr.
524 Mumford, James, jr.
525 Jarman, John, sr.
525 Jarman, John, jr.
525 Jarman, William
525 slave
526 Crapper, Wrixham

1736 TAX LIST [Household number/Name/Remarks]

BOGERTERNORTON/MANOKIN HUNDRED

527 Knock, John
527 Mollison, John
527 3 slaves
528 Simpson, William
528 Simpson, Thomas
528 4 slaves
529 Riley, Thomas
529 Evans, Larraunce
530 Lues, William
531 Porter, Jonathan
532 Jenkins, John
533 Wildman, John
534 Chaille, Moses
535 Stewart, Peter
536 Murray, John
537 Bell, John
538 Gillmor, Hugh
539 Atkinson, John
540 Spence, [Ad]am
540 5 slaves
541 Higgins, Nathaniel
542 Robinson, William
542 Wells, Daniel
543 Morriss, William
543 Trewitt, Joseph
544 Townsend, Jeremiah
544 3 slaves
545 Townsend, Brickhouse
546 Tingle, Daniel
547 Powell, Thomas
548 Evans, Gamage
549 Jarman, William, sr.
550 Webb, Samuell
551 Stevenson, Hugh
551 Traverse, Richard
551 Stevenson, Samuell
552 Franklin, Edward
553 Dennis, Wheatly
554 Holt, John
555 Hammond, Edward, son Joh
556 Ingoe, James
557 Murray, David
558 Trewitt, George, son of George
558 Trewitt, John
558 slave
559 Truitt, George, son P.O. [or Pd.]
560 Tompson, James
561 Bowen, John
562 Bowen, Littleton
562 slave
563 Bishop, John
563 Henderson, William
564 Eddes, Larrance
565 Bowen, George
566 Hammond, Isaac

567 Brozer, Jams. Mumford
568 Jarman, Robert
569 Bradford, John
570 Brevard, Adam
570 slave
571 Jarman, George
572 Timmons, Samuell
573 Griffin, Oliver
574 Mannering, Abra.
575 Midsley, Thomas
575 Church, William
576 Pointer, Chas.
577 Handcock, Willm.
578 Waters, Patrick
579 Davis, Edward
579 Davis, Samuell
580 Henderson, Charles
581 Jones, Geo.
582 Davis, Thos.
583 Shockley, John
584 Greer, John
585 Gornwell, John
586 Purnall, Elisha
586 slave
587 Hampton, Mary, madam
587 3 slaves
588 Steale, James
588 Steale, Daniell
588 Steale, Wm.
589 Powell, Samll.
590 Tull, Richd.
591 Teague, John, senr.
591 Teague, John
592 Denis, Donuck
593 Clawell, Thos.
594 Lindall, Peter
595 Truitt, Geo., accomack
595 Truitt, Geo.
595 2 slaves
596 Smock, Henry
596 Smock, John
597 Beddard, Richard
598 Burbridge, Edward
599 Burbridge, John
600 Smith, John
601 Williams, Argalus
602 Williams, Presgrave
603 Bridgewaters, Emanuell
603 Bridgewaters,, son
604 Collins, Solomon
605 Ake, John
606 Truitt, Geo., son of Job
607 Truitt, Nehemiah
608 Evans, John
608 slave

MANOKIN HUNDRED

609 Willson, David, capt.
609 King, Planner
609 slave Ceasar
609 slave Harry
609 slave Josey
609 slave Robbin
609 slave Kent
609 slave Cudjo
609 slave Pompy
609 slave Bristol
609 slave Hollady
609 slave Nanny
610 Willson, Samll., capt.
610 slave Peter
610 slave Mammudo
610 slave Will
610 slave Sampson
610 slave Nanny
610 slave Hannah
610 slave Moll
610 slave Bess
610 slave Rose
610 slave Sarah
611 Revill, [Cha]rles
611 slave Venus
612 Walston, Boaz
612 Walston, Obed
613 Revell, Randall
613 slave Toby
613 slave Martha
614 West, William
615 Bailey, Thomas
615 Cason, Alexr.
615 slave Daniell
616 Roach, Wm.
616 slave Kitt
616 slave Patience
617 Hall, Wm.
618 Hammond, Charles
619 Miles, William, senr.
619 Miles, William, junr.
620 Tull, Thomas
621 Turpin, Wm., son of Wm.
621 slave Will
621 slave Frost
621 slave George
621 slave Moll
622 Butler, Nathaniell
622 slave Sarah
623 Willis, Barnaby
623 Walston, Joseph
623 Dorman, Wilson
624 Turpin, William, capt.

TAX LISTS OF SOMERSET COUNTY: 1730-1740

MANOKIN HUNDRED

624 Turpin, Jno.
624 Turpin, Whittey
624 slave Jack
624 slave Tom
624 slave Toby
624 slave Philliss
625 Fountain, [Nicholas]
625 Brown, Alexander
625 slave London
625 slave Tom
625 slave Charles
625 slave Mirriam
626 Fountain, Mary
626 Fountain, Thomas
626 Tull, John
626 slave Hercules
626 slave Moree
627 Wetherby, John
628 Bedsworth, James
629 Strawbridge, James
629 slave Cuffy
629 slave Davey
629 slave Dick
629 indian Hagar
630 McDaniell, David
631 Davis, Arthur
632 Costin, Mathias
633 Ford, Absolom
634 Maddox, Thomas
634 Maddox, John
634 slave Will
634 slave Sue
635 Abbott, John
636 Tull, Samuell
637 Davis, John
638 Tull, Joshua
638 Cousins, Thomas
639 Walston, Thomas
639 Walston, Henry
640 Sharp, Benjamin
640 Obryan, Thomas
641 Walston, William
642 Tull, Esther
642 Tull, Richard
642 Tull, Stephen
642 slave Moll
643 Maddox, Daniel
643 slave Adam
643 slave Sarah
644 McDorman, William
645 Maddox, Lazarus
645 illegible
645 slave Joe
645 slave Cuffee
646 Miles, Samuell
646 slave Dick
646 slave Ben
647 Jones, Wm., goose creek
648 Bozman, George, junr.
648 slave Sambo
649 McClemmey, William
649 Campbell, Nehemiah
649 Abbott, Wm.
649 slave Narrow
649 slave Judah
650 Young, John
651 Clark, Alexr.
652 Cantwell, Thomas
653 Culverson, Wm.
654 Cunningham, Thomas
655 Fitzgerald, Peter
655 Obryan, Richd.
655 slave Tom
656 Bozman, Jno., sr.
656 Bozman, Jno., jr.
656 Macom, Geo.
657 Robertson, Jams., revd.
657 Robertson, Jno.
657 slave Jack
657 slave Cesar
657 slave Toby
657 slave Narrow
657 slave Prew
657 slave Dinah
657 slave Phillis
657 slave Siss
658 Bozman, Geo., senr.
658 Bozman, Geo., junr.
658 Tanner, Jno.
658 slave Frank
659 Wye, William, junr.
659 slave Jamy
659 slave Aleck
659 slave Dunleer
660 Shank, Benjamin
661 McClemmey, Wonney
661 slave Frank
662 King, Robert, col.
662 King, Nehemiah
662 King, Robt., junr.
662 Andrew, John
662 McCalagan, Hugh
662 Creagh, William
662 slave Fortune
662 slave Josey
662 slave Long Cesar
662 slave Short Cesar
662 slave Joe
662 slave Menary
662 slave Tom
662 slave Bess
662 slave Judah
662 slave Dido
662 slave Back Creek Dido
662 slave Nan
663 Chambers, Richard
663 Collins, Samuel
663 Fisher, Henry
664 Finch, John
664 slave Mariah
665 Ballard, Henry, [col.]
665 Wilks, John
665 Campbell, Jno.
665 slave Venture
665 slave Cesar
665 slave Jenny
665 slave Biendo
666 Ballard, Eleanor, mrs.
666 mulatto Mary
667 Lindow, Margaret
667 slave Moses
667 slave Josey
667 slave Bess
668 Goldsmith, John
668 Goldsmith, Charles
669 King, Jno.
669 slave Harry
670 King, Whittington
670 slave Toney
670 slave Will
670 slave Andry
671 Knott, Isaac
672 Floid, John
673 Tillman, Aaron
674 Niblett, Burnall
674 slave Coffee
675 Odear, Rose
675 Cain, James
676 Marshall, Thomas
677 Layfield, William
677 Layfield, Thomas
678 Polk, William
678 Gray, Allen
678 slave Olan
678 slave Hannay
678 slave Abner
679 Heath, Ann
679 Brown, George
680 Polk, Jams.
680 slave Ogy
681 Gray, Jno.
681 slave Hannah
682 Gray, William
682 Murrah, Richd.
682 Goldsmith, Thomas
683 Pope, James
684 Smith, Magdalen
684 slave Patience
685 Laws, James
686 Lockwood, Wm.
687 Anderson, Jams.
687 Hailey, Timothy
687 slave Cudgo

1736 TAX LIST [Household number/Name/Remarks]

MANOKIN HUNDRED

688 Magraw, Jane
688 Magraw, Robert
689 Denwood, Geo.
689 slave Ned
689 slave Medara
690 Vaunce, Thomas
691 Staples, [James]
691 slave Benn
692 Benston, George
692 Benston, Mathias
692 Jones, George
693 Stitt, Archabald
694 Smith, Robert
694 Smith, Thos.
694 Smith, Jno.
695 Jones, Wm., monokin
695 slave Guy
695 slave Anthony
695 slave Eve
696 Swift, Richard
697 Mately, James
698 Harriss, Phillip
698 Spear, Henry
699 Whittingham, Heber
699 Tate, Francis
700 Sheperd, Martin
701 Horsey, Sarah
701 Fiddy, Randall
701 slave Nick
702 Mitchell, Thomas
703 Mitchell, Ann
703 slave Sarah
704 Tunstall, John, capt.
704 Oneal, Thomas
704 Lord, Thomas
704 slave Lowhill
704 slave Sibba
704 slave Dick
704 slave Pompey
704 slave Norris
704 slave Tomboy
704 slave Bess
704 slave Sibb
704 slave Somerset
704 slave Will
704 slave Tom
704 slave Freeman
704 slave Isabell
704 slave Dinah
704 slave Moll
705 Banister, Thomas
705 Jones, Charles
705 Fiddy, Thomas
705 slave Austin
706 Libruse, Benjamin
707 Mathews, William
708 Outerbridge, Jno., capt.

708 slave Dormido
708 slave Priss
709 West, Anthony
709 Thomson, Andrew
710 Holland, Isaac
710 slave Appo
711 Givens, Thomas
712 Givens, Ann
712 slave Pleasant
713 Hayman, William
713 Hayman, Benjamin
714 Fosque, Benjamin
715 Martin, Thomas
716 Burgan, Daniell
717 Woolford, John
717 slave Sampson
717 slave Rose
717 slave Tamor
717 slave Moll
718 Tindall, James
719 Cairns, John
720 Collins, William
721 Furnace, James
722 Gullett, Abraham
722 Gullett, George
723 Bolend, Eleanor
723 Bolend, Wm.
724 Long, [Solomon]
724 Tomslon, Doctor
724 Tillman, Benjamin
724 slave Nann
725 Murrow, Alexander
726 Mathews, Patrick
727 Follows, John
728 Owens, John
729 Bozman, Wm., senr.
729 Killy, Jno.
729 slave Duso
729 slave Bess
730 Dorman, Mathew
730 Dorman, William
730 Dorman, Nehemiah
730 slave Jack
730 slave Doll
731 Dorman, Michael
732 Heath, Dorman
733 Willson, Sarah
733 slave Sambo
734 Pookum, Richard
735 Heath, Abraham, jr.
736 Fisher, Sarah
736 slave Jack
736 slave Will
736 slave Beck
737 King, Capell, capt.
737 slave Parragate
737 slave Jack
737 slave Tite
737 slave Major
737 slave Kate

738 Denwood, Thomas
738 Kinny, John
738 slave Cudjo
738 slave Pompy
738 slave Will
738 slave Sarah
738 slave Grace
738 slave Tamar
739 Elzey, John
739 Caldwell, Wm.
739 slave Ceasar
739 slave Sambo
739 slave Betty
739 slave Sibby
739 slave Nancy
740 Elzey, Sarah, mrs.
740 Elzey, Arnold
740 slave Ned
740 slave Jack
740 slave Nan
740 slave Fendo
740 slave Polindo
740 slave Hannah
741 Rigbey, Lewis
741 Fashe, Cornelious
741 slave Fendo
742 Crowder, Francis
742 Lary, Timothy
743 Ballard, Jarvis, senr.
743 Ballard, Wm.
743 Ballard, Jarvis, junr.
743 Ballard, Arnold
743 slave Amey
743 slave Rose
744 Phebus, George, senr.
744 Phebus, Jno.
744 slave Into
745 Phebus, George, junr.
746 Turpin, Wm., son of Jno.
746 slave Mingo
747 Horner, George, sr.
747 Horner, Matilda
747 Horner, Jno.
748 Browne, Thomas
748 Browne, David
748 Willcox, Wm.
748 slave Jack
748 slave Cojo
748 slave Bess
749 Tillman, Joseph
749 Beauchamp, Robert
749 slave London
750 Turpin, Hannah
750 slave Cuffee
750 slave Toby

TAX LISTS OF SOMERSET COUNTY: 1730-1740

MANOKIN/MATTAPANY HUNDREDS

- 750 slave Nan
- 751 Bozman, William, jr.
- 751 Miles, Edward
- 752 Gilliss, Joseph
- 752 Jones, Mitchell
- 752 Ewing, John
- 752 slave Truman
- 752 slave Boatswain
- 752 slave Rose
- 753 Wheeler, Elizabeth
- 753 Jenckins, Samuell
- 754 Heath, Abraham, sr.
- 754 Heath, Jno., senr.
- 754 Heath, Jno., junr.
- 755 Thomson, Sarah
- 755 King, James, indian
- 756 Elzey, John, junr.
- 757 Davis, Jno., back creek
- 758 Denniston, Robert
- 759 Wilson, Geo.
- 760 Hall, Mary
- 760 slave Nan

MATTAPANY HUNDRED

- 761 Selby, Phillip
- 761 Selby, Mathew
- 761 Selby, Daniel
- 761 Selby, Phillip, junr.
- 761 Selby, William
- 761 5 slaves
- 762 Selby, Parker
- 762 4 slaves
- 763 Cord, William
- 763 Cord, Arthur
- 763 slave
- 764 Aydelott, William
- 764 Aydelott, Wm., junr.
- 764 slave
- 765 Walton, Stephen
- 765 Walton, Stephen, junr.
- 765 Hardis, Hazard
- 766 Watson, Peter
- 766 Wate, Joseph
- 767 Russell, Cuthburt
- 767 Watson, Urias
- 768 Jones, John
- 769 Ainsworth, William
- 770 Davis, Charles
- 770 Davis, Lazarus
- 770 Williams, Thomas
- 771 Allen, John
- 772 Pepper, Tobias
- 773 Pepper, William
- 774 Brumble, Nathaniel
- 775 Pilcher, James
- 776 Carey, Solomon
- 777 Watson, Robert, jr.
- 778 Carey, Jeremiah
- 779 Watson, Moses
- 780 Booth, William
- 780 Haynefield, Wm.
- 781 Willett, Ambross
- 781 Willett, William
- 781 Willett, Thomas
- 782 Pope, John
- 782 Taylor, John
- 782 slave
- 783 Taylor, Roger
- 783 Taylor, John
- 784 Mallin, Christopher
- 785 Pope, George
- 785 slave
- 786 Ainsworth, Sarah
- 786 Ainsworth, Job
- 787 Beachbord, Willm.
- 787 Read, Walter
- 788 Claywell, Peter, jr.
- 789 Porter, Clentuck
- 790 Puddihny, Joseph
- 791 To Bennitt, Mary
- 791 Linsey, James
- 792 Claywell, Peter, sr.
- 792 Taylor, Thomas
- 792 3 slaves
- 793 Tarr, Michell
- 794 Sturgis, Richard
- 795 Funnelson, William
- 795 Funnelson, Nathan
- 796 Braten, William
- 796 slave
- 797 Duer, William
- 798 Nelson, William
- 798 Nelson, James
- 799 Scott, Robert
- 800 Hall, John
- 801 Holland, Nehemiah
- 801 Watson, James
- 802 Holland, Benjamin
- 802 slave
- 803 Wimbroe, Paul
- 804 Veazey, Charles
- 804 Veazey, William
- 805 Chapman, Humphry
- 806 Watson, Robert, senr.
- 806 Watson, Charles
- 806 Hieway, Isaac
- 806 slave
- 807 Wattson, John
- 807 Rogers, Samuell
- 808 Douberly, Thomas
- 809 Pain, John
- 810 Hill, Abraha
- 811 Wattson, Luke
- 812 Hodgson, Rolan
- 812 slave
- 813 Davis, Charles
- 814 Allen, Joseph
- 815 Benston, Joshua
- 816 To Watson, John
- 816 2 slaves
- 817 Jackson, William
- 818 Henderson, Bishop
- 819 Waggaman, Jacob
- 819 Waggaman, Ephraim
- 819 Harmon, John
- 819 slave
- 820 Maxfield, Joseph
- 820 4 slaves
- 821 Arnold, William
- 821 Arnold, Larraunce
- 822 Walton, Fisher
- 822 Hargas, Thomas
- 822 2 slaves
- 823 Odiewey, Thomas
- 824 Purnall, John
- 824 6 slaves
- 825 Hosier, Samuel
- 826 Crafford, Andrew
- 826 Crafford, John
- 827 Sturgis, Daniel
- 827 Read, John
- 827 Read, James
- 827 Ralphfield, Spencer
- 828 Hill, Johnson
- 828 Hill, [Elisha]
- 828 Richison, John
- 828 slave
- 829 Hill, Hutton
- 830 Turner, William
- 831 Hosier, Samuel, jr.
- 832 Newton, Thomas
- 832 Newton, Job
- 832 Newton, Southy
- 832 Newton, Thomas, junr.
- 833 Newton, Jona.
- 834 Tarr, Samuell
- 834 Cornwell, John
- 835 Huttson, Jonathan
- 836 Johnson, Peter
- 836 Johnson, Peter, jr.
- 837 Johnson, John
- 837 Dikes, Edward
- 837 Dikes, Daniell
- 837 Vaun, William
- 838 Johnson, William
- 838 Johnson, Hezekiah
- 838 Robarts, John
- 839 Wise, Thomas
- 839 Mills, James
- 839 slave
- 840 Richardson, John
- 840 Richardson, Samuell

1736 TAX LIST [Household number/Name/Remarks]

MATTAPANY/MONIE HUNDREDS

840 slave
841 Gill, John
842 Hopkins, Mathew
842 Airs, Harrison
842 Airs, Richard
843 Hopkins, Nathaniell
843 Airs, Henry
843 slave
844 Scarborough, John
844 Hall, Henry
844 Wise, Ezekiel
844 Tallman, James
844 slave
844 slave
845 Evans, John
846 Porter, William
847 Slingoe, Thomas, junr.
847 Slingoe, Thomas
848 Lang, John
849 Hopkins, Samuell, jr.
850 Hopkins, William
851 Guttery, Patrick
852 Dreddin, John
853 Milbourn, Thomas
854 Taylor, Phillip
854 Taylor, Elias
855 Brownbill, Henry
855 Brownbill, John
856 Sammons, Benja.
856 Harman, Benja.
857 Robbins, Elizabeth
857 Robbins, Thomas
857 4 slaves
858 Hill, Robert
859 Pope, Samuell
859 2 slaves
860 Harman, Emanuell
860 slave Simon

MONIE HUNDRED

861 Jones, Lewis
861 Jones, Samuell
861 slave Jack
861 slave Ceasar
861 slave Moll
862 Laws, Robert
862 Laws, Panthur
862 Laws, Wm.
862 slave Boobo
862 slave Jack
862 slave Samson
863 Mangare, John
864 Dorman, Henry
864 Obeir, Isaac
865 Newman, Henry
865 Layhe, Andrew
866 Macgraw, John
866 Hill, William

867 Hobbs, Thomas
867 Mangar, Mathew
868 Hobbs, Joy
869 Hobbs, Marsallas
869 Stevens, Isaac
870 Covington, John
870 slave Sambo
870 slave Coco
870 slave Busey
870 slave Jean
870 slave Betty
870 slave Peg
871 Jones, James
871 Duhigg, W[alter]
871 slave Dave
871 slave Sibb
871 slave Moll
872 Covington, Thomas
872 Leatherbury, Parry
873 Jones, Daniel
874 Story, Susanah
874 slave Whitehaven
874 slave Moll
875 Durham, Thomas
876 Leatherbury, John
876 Dorman, Isaiah
876 slave Tone
876 slave Pompe
876 slave Benn
876 slave Robbin
876 slave Sambo
876 slave Rose
876 slave Bridgett
876 slave Nanne
876 slave Nanne
876 slave Bess
877 Gale, George, capt.
877 Maughon, Christopher
877 Lawless, James
877 slave Sippeo
877 slave Limos
877 slave Jeamy
877 slave Jack
877 slave Nanney
877 slave Sarah
877 slave Parthena
877 slave Joe
877 slave Jeamy
877 slave Ceasar
877 slave Dublin
877 slave Will
877 slave Ovid
877 slave Jacob
877 slave Dominick
877 slave Palinah
877 slave Bess
877 slave Jenny
877 slave Pheby
877 slave Vilett
877 slave Beanda

878 Dashiell, Thomas
878 Dashiell, Leven
878 Chambers, Samuell
878 slave Will
878 slave Jack
878 slave Old Jack
878 slave Harry
878 slave Joe
878 slave Bess
878 slave Tamer
878 slave Hannah
878 slave Sarah
879 Carey, Thomas
880 Carey, Rachell
880 Crouch, Thomas
880 Crouch, David
881 Luke, Williamson
882 Downs, George
882 slave Tobe
882 slave Frank
883 Downs, Robert
883 Wallace, Robert
884 Jones, Robert
884 Welsh, William
884 slave London
884 slave Dick
884 slave Amok
884 slave Jean
884 slave Rachell
885 Jones, George
886 Erving, George
886 slave Tobee
886 slave Cuffee
886 slave Jenny
886 slave Jean
887 Magraw, James
888 Waller, George
888 Saucer, William
889 Jones, Thomas
890 Jones, William
890 Miles, John
890 slave Will
890 slave Jenny
890 slave Sue
891 Waller, John
891 slave Jean
892 Robarts, Edward
892 slave Jeffry
892 slave Binah
893 Wright, Thomas
893 Wright, Henry
893 Welch, John
894 Shores, John
894 [Shores], Wm.
895 Pollock, Joseph
895 Macdaniel, Owen
896 Bluett, Thomas
896 slave Dinah
897 Waller, Major

TAX LISTS OF SOMERSET COUNTY: 1730-1740

MONIE/NANTICOKE HUNDREDS

898 Spicer, Phillip
899 Hurst, John
900 Wallace, Mathew
900 slave Tom
900 slave Sibb
901 Wallace, Richard
901 Wallace, Thomas
901 Wallace, James
901 slave Ceasar
901 slave Bess
902 White, John
902 Rose, Samuel
903 Duglas, [John]
904 Williams, [John]
905 White, [Fr]ancis
905 White, [John]
905 White, [Thom]as
906 [Martin, George]
907 [Miller, Thomas]
908 illegible
909 [Roberts, John]
909 [Roberts, Thomas]
910 [McDorman, Darby]
911 B[azwill, Thomas]
912 Laws, [Tho]mas
912 slave [Jack]
912 slave Murrear
913 Windsor, Lazarus
913 Windsor, James
913 Windsor, Lazarus
914 Roe, Elizabeth
914 Roe, John
915 Jones, Richard
916 Chain, Alexander
917 Roe, Thomas
917 Windsor, John
917 Hopkins, George
917 Gamewell, George
918 Roe, Joseph
919 Laws, John
919 slave Prince
919 slave Ceasar
920 Wallace, John
920 Wallace, Thomas
921 Waller, William
922 Stoughton, Wm.
922 slave Bussie
922 slave Simon
922 slave Binah
922 slave Sarah

NANTICOKE HUNDRED
923 McClester, John
923 McClester, Samll.
923 McClester, George
923 slave Coffe
923 slave Sambo
923 slave Tomner
923 slave Adam
923 slave Nar
923 slave Dinow
923 slave Sisaboo
924 Cooper, Gabrell
924 Cooper, Thomas
924 Cooper, Gaby
924 Hazard, Henry
925 Cooper, Samuell
926 Cooper, Isaac
927 Willson, John
928 Gravener, Thos.
929 Ackworth, Thomas
929 slave Will
930 Ackworth, Charles
930 Giles, John
931 Brown, Wm.
931 Curmicell, John
932 Hardy, John
933 Culver, John, esqs.
934 Collings, Ebin
935 Hitch, Mary
935 Gilis, Thomas
935 slave Toby
936 Tulle, Ben
937 Taler, Wm.
938 Tullee, James
938 Price, Frank
939 Rowell, Thomas
940 Scott, Windom, esqr.
941 Scott, George, nant
942 Marvell, Thomas
942 Marvell, Robart
943 Collings, John, tipkin
944 Bucklee, Nicholas
945 Vahan, Wm.
946 Bacond, Dutson
947 Townsin, Benja.
947 slave Dick
947 slave Bess
948 Twiford, John
949 Rickords, Alexander
950 Moore, Wm., junr.
951 More, John, senr.
951 More, Isaac
951 More, James
952 Right, Solomon
953 Godarte, Thomas
953 Godarte, John
954 More, John, junr.
955 Langford, John, sr.
955 Langford, Edward
955 Langford, Thos.
956 Langford, John
957 Cottman, Ebin
957 Cottman, Wm.
958 Cottman, Nathaniell
959 Low, Ralph
959 Low, Robin
959 Low, John
960 Williams, Richard
960 Williams, John
961 Shurman, Thos.
962 Dashiell, Henry
962 slave Gift
962 slave Sib
963 Larmore, John
963 Grigs, Henry
963 slave Cofy
963 slave Seib
964 Fluelling, Samll.
964 slave Sile
965 Game, Robart
966 Walter, Danell
967 Walter, John
968 Bartlett, John, junr.
969 Bartlett, John
969 Bartlett, Abraham
970 Tullee, Joseph
971 Wafers, Ignatious
972 Hofinton, Thos.
973 Roberson, John
974 Darby, Walter
975 Jones, John, capt.
976 Rite, Saulle, baron creek
977 Olifir, Wm.
977 Reedy, Cornelus
978 More, Wm., forest
979 Waller, Nathaniell
979 W[aller], [John]
980 Waller, Nathaniell
981 Langston, Speare
982 Woller, Thomas, junr.
983 Grear, Elizabet
983 Grear, Wm.
984 Waller, Thomas
984 Waller, Richard
985 Parmore, Thomas
986 Relpte, Wm.
987 Calaway, Peter
987 Callaway, [T]hos.
987 Callaway, Jno.
988 Callaway, Wm., snr.
989 Callaway, Wm., jnr.
990 Polke, John
991 Couper, James
992 Olifer, George
993 Jarwile, Samll.
993 Carter, Charles
994 Carter, John, sr.
994 Carter, Sam
994 Carter, T[h]os.
994 Carter, Wm.
995 Spear, Henry
996 Callaway, [Jo]hn, senr.
997 Ange, [Fr]ances
997 Ange, [Fr]ancis
998 Stuard, [C]atharine
998 Macane, George

1736 TAX LIST [Household number/Name/Remarks]

NANTICOKE HUNDRED

998 slave Tom
998 slave Belend.
999 Hopkins, Stephen
999 Hopkins, David
999 More, Wm.
1000 Wallace, David
1001 Samuells, Ann
1001 slave Quaker
1002 Hopkins, John
1003 Brown, Signee
1004 Hickman, Henry
1005 Hickman, illegible
1006 Winser, Henry
1006 Winser, James
1007 Hickman, James
1008 Ingrom, Isaac
1009 Meseck, John
1009 Meseck, James
1009 Meseck, Obediah
1009 Ingrom, Jacob
1010 Meseck, George
1011 Askely, Daniell
1012 Draper, Wm.
1012 slave George
1012 slave Tom
1012 slave Lusander
1013 Kennigin, Arthur
1014 Polk, Charles
1014 Polk, Ephraim
1015 Polk, John
1015 Polk, Jams.
1015 slave Atte
1015 slave Sib
1016 Hall, James
1017 Collier, Robert
1017 Collier, George
1017 slave Sarah
1018 Collier, Doubty
1018 Collier, Robart
1019 Winrite, Cannon
1019 slave Quash
1020 Hopkins, Robart
1020 slave Toby
1021 Wouten, Edward
1022 Wooten, John
1023 Hosay, Mathew
1024 Stephens, John
1025 Godart, George
1025 Mitchell, Alexander
1026 Benston, Henry
1026 Benston, Henry
1027 Williams, John
1028 More, John, forest
1029 Rhodes, John
1030 Calaway, John
1031 Calaway, John
1032 Macluer, Robart
1033 Goddart, John

1034 Kenney, Wm.
1035 Surman, Thomas
1036 Parmore, Mathew
1036 Parmore, Ezekiell
1037 James, John
1038 Maclalen, Joseph
1039 Ackworth, Samuell
1039 slave Sue
1040 Ackworth, Henry
1041 Cheesman, John
1041 slave Sesor
1041 slave Ches
1041 slave Nan
1042 Parmore, James
1043 Jones, James
1043 Powell, Joseph
1044 Carter, John, junr.
1045 Hardy, James
1046 Hitch, Solomon
1046 Hitch, Adam
1046 slave Frank
1046 slave Cook
1047 Palle, George
1048 Meseck, Benjamin
1049 Hopkins, John, senr.
1049 Hopkins, John
1049 Hopkins, Roger
1049 slave Sue
1049 slave Nan
1050 Game, Fortin
1050 Game, Bety
1051 Dashiell, Bridget
1051 Dashiell, James
1051 slave Robin
1051 slave Will
1051 slave Will
1051 slave Jack
1052 Dashiell, Wm.
1053 Dean, John
1054 Bounds, Joseph
1055 Read, John
1056 Read, Wm.
1057 illegible
1057 Nicholson, George
1057 slave Venus
1057 slave Beamors
1058 Hust, Joseph
1059 Reed, John
1060 Callaway, Edward
1061 Roten, Josiah
1062 Hofinton, Ritchd.
1063 Polson, William
1064 Dashiell, Joseph
1064 slave Randall
1065 Henry, John
1065 Henry, Hew
1066 Langston, Wm.
1067 Nicholson, James
1068 Twille, Robert

1069 Wetherly, James
1069 slave Pegg
1070 Wetherly, Charaty
1070 Wetherly, Richard
1070 slave Sebina
1071 Henry, Robert
1072 Wallis, Richard, senr.
1073 Fulton, Wm.
1074 Smith, Thos., baron cr.
1075 Young, Rachell
1075 Young, Jehew
1076 Mellson, Samuell
1076 Mellson, Samuell
1076 [Mellson], John
1077 Mellson, Benjamin
1078 Hofinton, John
1078 Piper, Benja.
1079 Jones, Finch
1080 Givans, Robert
1080 slave Samson
1080 slave Sesor
1080 slave Charles
1080 slave Nann
1080 slave Bess
1081 Caldwell, James
1081 slave Toby
1081 slave Bob
1081 slave Sambo
1081 slave Rose
1081 slave Hagow
1082 Taylor, Abraham
1082 slave Quash
1083 Rhodes, Daniell
1083 Ackworth, Thomas
1084 Hofinton, Jonathan
1084 Glaster, Thomas
1085 Boyce, John
1086 Cordry, David
1087 Beeck, Isabel
1087 Beek, Isaac
1088 Ralphe, Thomas
1088 slave Pompe
1089 Trane, James
1089 Trane, James
1089 Trane, Roger
1089 slave Robin
1089 slave Benor
1089 slave Rose
1090 Russell, James, senr.
1090 Russell, Thos.
1090 Russell, Wm.
1091 Russell, James
1091 Archeble ye Boy
1092 Goslin, James
1093 Rider, Willson
1094 Rider, Hetly
1095 Richerson, Wm.
1096 Jackson, Jonathan

TAX LISTS OF SOMERSET COUNTY: 1730-1740

NANTICOKE HUNDRED

1096 Jackson, Joshua
1096 Jackson, Ezekiell
1097 Jackson, Thomas
1098 Giles, William
1098 Giles, Wm.
1098 slave Florow
1099 Giles, Thomas
1100 Burn, James
1101 Benett, George
1102 Shiles, Thomas
1102 Macay, John
1103 Boardly, Wm.
1103 Murphy, James
1104 Oystin, Wm.
1104 Oystin, Wm.
1105 Jones, John, quantico
1106 Jacobs, Elizabeth
1106 slave Sambo
1106 slave Sib
1107 James, Dunkin
1108 Gastinue, Mathewice
1109 Nutter, Mathew
1110 Taylor, Anthony
1111 Langford, Thomas
1112 Carter, Phillip
1113 Kellamb, Edward
1113 Kellamb, John
1113 Piper, Joseph
1113 slave Robin
1113 slave Meren
1114 Hofington, Jno., senr.
1114 Glaster, Saull
1114 slave Yourk
1114 slave Jayaw
1114 slave Jeane
1114 slave Pleasant
1115 Dean, Charles
1116 Bradly, Wm.
1117 Dodrall, James
1118 Nuten, John
1119 Walter, Henry
1119 Walter, Daniell
1119 Walter, John
1119 Walter, William
1120 Noulds, Edman
1120 Noulds, Dick
1121 Elensworth, Robert
1122 Elensworth, Richard
1123 Shuraden, William
1124 West, James, esqr.
1124 Besle, Thomas
1125 Green, Richard
1125 Green, Dick
1126 Phillips, John
1126 Phillips, Wm.
1127 Tulle, Stephen
1127 Tulle, Richard
1128 Tulle, Stephen
1129 Tulle, Benjamin
1130 Rhodes, Timothy
1131 More, Wm., quanticoe jr.
1131 More, Thomas
1132 Bennett, Edward
1133 Bennett, Elizabeth
1133 [Bennett], John
1133 Bennett, Wm.
1134 Shurman, Wm.
1134 Shurman, Isaac
1134 Shurman, Wm.
1135 Nutter, Wm.
1135 slave Phillip
1135 slave Benn
1135 slave Catow
1135 slave Moll
1135 slave Catherine
1135 slave Rose
1136 Nutter, Christopher
1136 slave Sesor
1136 slave Tom
1136 slave Sipio
1136 slave Rose
1136 slave Barbary
1137 Nutter, Huett
1137 slave Till
1137 slave Mingo
1138 Maclester, Joseph
1138 Maclester, Neal
1138 Billins, James
1138 Hix, Levin
1138 Goldsborough, William
1138 Beckingham, William
1138 slave Samson
1138 slave Narow
1139 Farntine, Wm.
1139 slave Michell
1140 Smith, Thomas, roasticoe
1141 Gibans, James
1141 slave Frank
1142 Baker, William
1143 Marcy, William
1144 Lynn, Aaron
1144 Lynn, John
1144 slave Abraham
1144 slave Bess
1145 Harve, John
1145 Moires, Michell
1146 Friggs, Robart
1147 Ginkins, Thomas
1148 Colings, Andrew
1149 Bounds, Jacob
1150 Smith, John
1151 Shurman, Peter
1152 Shurman, Jobe
1153 Kirkman, Roger
1154 Right, Edward
1155 Keme, Abraham
1156 Keme, John
1157 Tomson, George
1158 Tomson, Charles, senr.
1159 Tomson, Charles
1160 Downes, Robert
1161 King, William
1162 King, Phillip
1163 Mitchell, John
1164 Calaway, Peter
1165 Benston, Wm.
1166 Wingitt, Philip
1167 Owens, Peter
1168 Benston, Wm., senr.
1169 Keme, Walter
1170 Winrite, Wm.
1171 Parmore, James
1172 Parsons, Charles
1173 Dunton, Jonas
1173 Dunt[on], Wm.
1174 Smith, David
1175 Shortt, John
1176 Shortt, Edward, senr.
1176 Shorte, Abraham
1177 Oneall, John
1178 Oneall, James
1178 slave Dino
1179 Dolby, Peter
1180 Williams, Charles
1181 Walter, Thos.
1182 Winser, John
1183 Ingrom, Robart
1184 Langston, John
1184 Smith, Wm.
1185 Manlove, Amanuell
1185 slave Quacoe
1186 Noble, Isaac
1187 Tindoll, Charles
1188 Venadson, Elias
1189 Potter, Josefus
1190 Jonson, Simon
1191 Taler, John
1191 Taler, Wm.
1192 Boyce, Daniell
1192 Isaacks, John
1192 slave Bess
1193 Gray, Wm.
1193 slave Cofe
1194 Holston, John
1195 Chipman, Parris
1195 Fleetwood, John
1195 Bass, John
1196 Bowger, James
1197 Melson, Joseph
1198 Hall, John

1736 TAX LIST [Household number/Name/Remarks]

NANTICOKE/POCOMOKE HUNDREDS

1199 Wille, John
1199 Persons, Jno.
1199 slave Cate
1200 Jonson, Thomas
1200 Fleetwood, [T]ho.
1201 Meseck, Isaac
1202 Hickman, William
1202 Hickman, Jonathan
1202 slave Kate
1202 slave Sambo
1202 slave Murreah
1202 slave Rose
1203 Hust, Joseph
1204 Thornes, Alexander
1205 Macom, Timothy
1206 Anderson, John
1207 Richee, Archibald
1208 Dun, Richard
1208 Dunn, Nicholas
1209 Henderson, Robert
1210 Beard, Lues
1210 Bearde, Lewis
1211 Larmore, Thomas
1211 Larimore, James
1212 Beard, John
1213 Nicholson, Richard
1214 Ingrom, Abraham
1214 Ingrom, Abraham
1214 Ingrom, David
1214 slave Phebe
1215 MacClester, Randoll
1216 Andrus, John
1217 Walker, John
1218 Edge, Robert
1219 Edge, Joshua
1220 Floyd, Mager
1221 Kinnegen, Daniell
1222 Roberson, Wm.
1223 Colings, Thomas
1224 Givands, John
1225 Collings, John
1226 C[ollings], Thos., c---
1227 Stiley, Mary
1227 Stilley, John
1228 Nicholson, Elizabeth
1228 Walter, Robart
1229 Mackdowell, John
1230 Phillips, Thomas
1231 Phillips, Richard
1232 Wollis, Richard
1233 Phips, John
1234 Winrite, John
1235 Clifton, George
1235 Clifton, George
1235 Clifton, Nehemiah
1235 Clifton, Thomas

1235 -usef-, Jeremiah
1236 Rickords, John
1237 Vinson, James
1238 Caldwell, Thos.
1239 Caldwell, Patrick
1240 Caldwell, John
1240 Caldwell, Robart
1240 Cornwell, Thomas
1240 slave Sambo
1241 Sharp, John
1242 Ubank, Molten
1243 Nubold, Francis
1243 slave Ame
1244 Donohoe, Nathaniell
1245 Owens, Robart
1245 slave Cate
1246 Shockly, David
1246 Shockly, James
1247 Robinett, Samuell
1248 Robinet, Samuel, sr.
1249 Bolin, Thomas
1250 [Read], [Thomas]
1250 Read, [Obediah]
1250 slave Peg
1251 Quartermus, James
1252 Parsons, Francis
1253 Meseck, Jacob, sr.
1254 Meseck, Nehemiah
1254 Ores, Ephraim
1255 Mezeck, Jacob, junr.
1256 Richerson, John
1257 Dashiell, Robert
1257 slave Cato
1257 slave Tamer
1258 Dashiell, Precela
1258 slave Hary
1259 Benston, Thomas
1259 Couper, John
1259 slave Will
1259 slave Bess
1260 Martin, John
1261 Gale, John
1261 Maclan, Archibald
1261 Kemp, John
1261 slave Mese
1261 slave Galaway
1261 slave Barshe
1261 slave Townside
1261 slave Moll
1261 slave Juda
1261 slave Rose

POCOMOKE HUNDRED
1262 Hampton, Mary, madm.
1262 Henry, Robert, capt.

1262 Henry, John, [capt.]
1262 slave [Chick]
1262 slave Tarel
1262 slave Pompey
1262 slave [Harrey]
1262 slave Adam
1262 slave Sesar
1262 slave [Jenney]
1262 slave [Lucy]
1262 slave [Patience]
1262 slave [Phillis]
1263 illegible
1263 ----son, ------e
1263 Whittington, Southy
1263 Venelson, Elisha
1263 slave Jamey
1263 slave Robin
1263 slave Harrey
1263 slave Minrod
1263 slave Pheenix
1263 slave Jamey
1263 slave Sarah
1263 slave Priss
1264 Scolfield, Henry
1265 Benston, Thomas
1266 Benston, William
1267 Brown, Thomas
1268 Powell, John
1268 slave Sarey
1269 Brooks, Richard, mr.
1269 Brooks, Hugh
1269 Wright, John
1269 slave Lett
1270 Colburd, William
1271 Fenton, Margret
1271 Blayer, Robert
1272 Peacock, Edward
1273 Slocumb, Thomas
1273 Long, Colbourn
1274 Pingalley, Thomas
1274 Buttler, Manewell
1275 Newbold, Thomas
1275 Newbold, Purnell
1275 slave Patience
1276 Maddux, Margret
1276 Duckes, John
1276 Duckes, Robert
1277 Pirkins, John
1278 Perkins, Sarah
1278 Perkins, Michell
1279 Dredon, David, sr.
1279 Dredon, William
1280 Dredon, David, junr.
1281 Cox, Wm.
1281 slave Doll
1281 slave Ceasar
1282 Riggen, John, junr.
1282 slave Nan

TAX LISTS OF SOMERSET COUNTY: 1730-1740

POCOMOKE HUNDRED

1283 Riggen, Eliza.
1283 Riggen, Solomon
1284 Riggin, Charles
1285 Caldwell, Joshua
1285 slave Mass
1285 slave Cuggo
1286 Dickerson, Charles
1287 Dickerson, Teague
1288 Riggen, John, senr.
1288 Riggen, Teague
1288 Riggin, John
1288 Riggin, Steven
1288 slave Jemey
1289 Carsey, Wm.
1289 Carsey, Robt.
1289 Carsey, S[aml.]
1290 Taylor, Robert
1290 Taylor, Robert
1291 Taylor, Elias
1292 Willson, John
1293 Addams, Samuell
1293 Adams, Phillip
1294 Harris, Calep
1294 Smith, John
1295 Boyer, Robert
1295 Clifton, George
1295 slave Harrey
1296 Elles, John
1297 Marchant, Benja.
1297 slave Adam
1298 White, John, point
1298 slave Jack
1298 slave Toney
1299 Clifton, John
1300 Billings, Thomas
1301 Holland, Wm.
1301 Singleton, John
1301 slave Tom
1301 slave Dinah
1302 Milbourne, Ralph
1303 Evans, John
1304 Evans, Thos.
1304 slave Jenney
1305 Milborne, Calep
1305 slave Mingo
1305 slave Hannah
1306 Milbourne, John
1307 Adams, Colons
1308 Collins, Samll.
1309 Naron, Robert
1309 slave Sarah
1309 slave Madge
1310 Naron, James
1310 slave Harrey
1310 slave Will
1310 slave Moll
1311 White, John, poco.
1311 slave George
1311 slave Patience
1311 slave Nan
1312 White, Archabald
1312 White, Wm.
1313 Hogskin, Sue
1313 Hoggskin, James
1314 Boston, Isaac
1314 slave
1314 slave
1314 slave
1315 Boston, Esah
1316 Adams, Isaac
1316 slave Jenney
1317 Wood, William
1318 Adams, Rachell
1318 slave Jack
1319 Adams, George
1320 Adams, Phillip
1320 slave Jenney
1321 Adams, Hope
1322 Ad[a]ms, Wm., senr.
1322 Adams, Phillip
1322 slave Iaco
1323 Adams, William, junr.
1324 Beachamp, Edward
1324 Beachamp, Levin
1324 slave
1325 Beachamp, Marcey
1325 Beachamp, John
1326 Beachamp, Thomas
1327 Davis, Beachamp
1328 Webb, John
1328 Webb, Solomon
1328 Webb, John
1329 Mills, Moses
1329 slave Simon
1330 Paine, Joseph
1330 Pilsher, Moses
1331 Connelly, Patrick
1332 Melvin, Robert
1332 Melvin, Wm.
1332 Melvin, Robt., junr.
1333 Melton, John
1334 Brooks, Francis
1334 Brooks, Henry
1335 Elles, William
1336 Jones, Wm.
1336 Burnett, James
1337 Gillett, Samll.
1337 Gillett, Wm.
1337 Gillett, Samll., jr.
1337 slave Darkis
1338 Gillett, John
1338 slave Henry
1338 slave Naney
1339 Mills, Samuell
1339 Mills, Hugh
1339 Mills, Nathl.
1339 Mills, John
1340 Lane, Wm., capt.
1340 slave Harrey
1340 slave Dick
1340 slave Doll
1341 Piper, Isaac
1342 Goodin, Benjamin
1343 Jones, Edward
1343 Jones, Elisha
1344 Brittingham, John
1344 slave Sesar
1344 slave Nann
1345 Backer, James
1345 Chambers, Jeremiah
1345 slave Yourke
1346 Breeman, James
1346 slave Tolemey
1347 Quinton, Dixon
1348 Quinton, Philip
1348 slave Jack
1348 slave Tamor
1349 Lamberson, John
1350 Lindall, Robert
1350 Lamberson, Robert
1351 Merrill, Joseph
1352 Brittingham, Wm.
1352 slave Rose
1353 Brittingham, Thomas
1354 Baker, Henderson
1355 Houston, Joseph, jr.
1355 slave Bess
1355 slave Harrey
1356 Houston, James
1356 Powell, Leving
1356 slave Cate
1357 Houston, John, senr.
1358 Henderson, John, senr.
1358 slave Gie
1358 slave George
1358 slave Bess
1358 slave Jone
1358 slave Eve
1359 Henderson, Charles
1360 Henderson, Francis
1360 Right, Comfort
1361 Henderson, Benja.
1362 Blades, John
1362 Blades, Benja.

1736 TAX LIST [Household number/Name/Remarks]

POCOMOKE HUNDRED

1363 Young, Daniel
1364 Layfield, George
1365 Small, John
1366 Conner, William
1367 Davis, Evans
1368 Curvine, Thomas
1369 Dickerson, James
1369 Dickerson, Robt.
1369 Dickerson, Francis
1370 Henderson, James
1370 Henderson, John
1370 slave Adam
1371 Henderson, Jno., junr.
1371 Henderson, Samuell
1372 Blades, Robert
1373 Lambden, Thomas
1374 Merrell, John
1375 Wheeler, Isaac
1375 Wheeler, Wm.
1375 slave Joe
1376 Dickerson, Peter
1377 Cade, Charles
1378 Ramsey, Charles
1378 Ramsey, John
1379 Lamberson, Abraham
1379 Lamberson, Samll.
1379 Lamberson, Abra., jr.
1380 Jones, Thomas
1381 Mills, Smith
1381 Taylor, Roger
1382 Mills, Wm., junr.
1382 Mills, Nathon
1382 Mills, Alexa.
1383 Shanklin, Wm.
1383 slave
1384 Stevens, William
1385 Stevens, Eleanor
1385 Stevens, Edward
1386 Paden, John
1386 slave Oxford
1387 Cluff, Edward
1388 Dorman, Samuell
1388 Dorman, Samuell
1389 Clogg, Samuel
1390 Tillman, Gedion
1390 slave Pompey
1391 Broughton, Bruff
1392 Broughton, John
1392 Hattfield, Wm.
1392 Broughton, William
1393 Dennis, John, junr. mr.
1393 Taylor, John
1393 slave Kingston
1393 slave Jack
1393 slave Patience
1393 slave Abbo
1393 slave Kate
1394 Mitchell, Robert
1394 Mitchell, Joshua
1394 slave Townsides
1394 slave Selby
1395 Gore, Richard
1396 Gaddis, Robert
1396 slave Tom
1396 slave Pheby
1397 Rycraft, Richd., cold.
1397 Burckett, Thomas
1397 slave Moshey
1397 slave Atta
1398 Gibbs, Abraham
1399 Hayward, Thomas, mr.
1399 Dius, Robt.
1399 slave Sambo
1399 slave Sineca
1399 slave Tom
1399 slave Jesper
1399 slave Cuggo
1399 slave Priss
1399 slave Jenney
1399 slave Rose
1400 Handy, Eliza.
1400 Handy, Samll.
1400 Handy, Stephen
1400 Bennett, Wm.
1400 slave Harrey
1400 slave Hagar
1400 slave Judy
1401 Mills, William, senr.
1401 Mills, Jonathan
1402 Mills, Samuell, junr.
1403 Tull, George, mr.
1403 Tull, Noble
1403 Tull, Jonathan
1403 slave Abner
1403 slave Dinah
1404 Pilsher, Wm.
1405 Pilsher, John
1406 Costen, Stephen
1407 Benton, Comfort
1407 Coston, Mathias
1407 slave Sambo
1407 slave Coffey
1407 slave Pegg
1407 slave Jone
1407 slave Hannah
1407 slave Moll
1408 Coston, Isaac
1408 slave Andrew
1409 Tull, John
1410 Harris, John
1410 Harris, [Be]n[to]n
1410 slave Tom
1411 Harris, Jeremiah
1412 Haddock, Ignatious
1413 Knight, Richard
1413 Knight, James
1414 Jordine, Aaron
1415 Odear, Stephen
1416 Smullin, Randell
1416 Smullen, Randell, jr.
1416 Smullen, Nathl.
1416 Smullen, William
1417 Dailey, Patrick
1418 Phillips, John
1419 Ward, Joseph
1419 Ward, Cornelius
1419 Ward, Joseph
1420 Riggen, Ambross, senr.
1420 Riggen, Teague
1420 Dickerson, John
1421 Benston, John
1421 Benston, George
1422 Warwick, Arthur
1423 Riggen, Teague
1423 Riggen, Teague
1423 slave Peter
1423 slave Nan
1424 Harris, Robert
1424 slave Harrey
1424 slave Toney
1424 slave Moll
1425 Riggin, Joseph
1425 Taylor, Jacob
1426 Harper, Edward
1427 Riggen, Darby
1427 Riggen, John
1427 Riggen, Teague
1428 Otwell, Charles
1429 Otwell, Francis
1429 Otwell, Solomon
1430 Scott, John, capt.
1430 Scott, John, junr.
1430 slave Peter
1430 slave Rose
1430 slave Pheby
1430 slave Toney
1431 Porter, Francis
1431 Porter, McCimey
1431 McGraine, John
1431 Redding, Michaell
1431 slave Jack
1431 slave Soney
1432 Anderson, Mary
1432 slave Abram
1433 Sheldon, John
1433 slave Isaac
1434 Bennett, John
1435 Allen, Francis, mr.
1435 Allen, Francis, junr.

TAX LISTS OF SOMERSET COUNTY: 1730-1740

POCOMOKE HUNDRED

1435 Johnson, Joshua
1435 Fortin, John
1435 slave Judie
1435 slave Margary
1436 Townsend, James
1436 slave Gie
1436 slave Jack
1437 Townsend, Charles
1437 Townsend, Solomon
1437 Townsend, Wm.
1438 Atkinson, Angelo
1438 Powell, Gabriel
1439 Atkinson, Isaac
1440 Beavins, Thomas
1441 Townsend, Daniel
1441 Townsend, Dickerson
1441 Townsend, James
1441 slave Pegg
1442 Cottingham, Jonathn.
1442 Cottingham, Wm.
1443 Donohoe, Teague
1443 Donohoe, Teague
1443 Donohoe, Daniel
1443 Duckes, Robert
1444 Glass, Christopher
1444 Glass, Elias
1444 slave Frank
1445 Pope, John
1445 Beavins, John
1445 slave
1445 slave
1446 Donohoe, Dorman
1446 Cupper, Samuell
1447 Fogg, Moses
1448 Dickerson, Cornelious
1448 slave Dinah
1449 Dickerson, Edmond, senr.
1449 slave George
1450 Dickerson, Edmond, jr.
1450 Oldwell, Francis
1451 Dickerson, Charles
1452 Mayo, Samuell
1453 Townsend, John, junr.
1453 Townsend, John
1454 Townsend, Saul
1454 slave Moreah
1455 Flemming, John
1455 Flemming, Wm.
1455 Elleson, Patrick
1455 slave Robin
1455 slave Pompy
1455 slave Joe
1455 slave Dinah

1456 McCuddy, John
1457 Townsend, Eliza.
1457 slave Jenney
1458 Parsons, Robert
1459 Townsend, Danford
1460 Riggen, Ambross, junr.
1460 Riggen, Pearce
1461 Lane, John
1462 Coulbourne, John
1462 Coulbourne, William
1463 Woonell, James
1463 Reding, Charles
1464 Harper, Francis
1465 Dukes, Wm.
1466 Glass, Christopher, junr
1467 Newton, Starling
1468 Dickerson, Isaac
1469 Bownds, George
1469 Winwright, Stephen
1469 Gurley, George
1470 Taylor, Peter
1470 slave Jack
1471 Peal, Thomas
1471 slave Sampson
1472 Andrews, John
1472 Andrews, Sheperd
1473 Beavins, Roland
1473 Beavins, Wm.
1474 [Ward, Joseph]
1474 [Ward], Corn[elius]
1474 [Ward], J[oseph], junr.
1475 Kitchin, Wm.
1475 Savage, George
1475 slave Londer
1475 slave Harrey
1475 slave Monday
1475 slave Pleasant
1475 slave Betty
1476 Whittington, Southy
1476 Johnson, John
1476 Landman, John
1476 slave Robin
1476 slave Sesar
1476 slave Hanah
1476 slave Sarah
1477 Buttler, Thomas
1478 Taylor, Samll., senr.
1478 Taylor, George
1479 Taylor, Samuell, junr.
1480 Purnell, Elisha
1480 slave Pipin
1481 Martin, James, capt.

1481 slave Pompy
1481 slave Joe
1481 slave Sesar
1481 slave Cate
1481 slave Nan
1482 Morris, Isaac, mr.
1482 slave Ago
1482 slave Benn
1482 slave Southy
1482 slave Abner
1482 slave Will Farmor
1482 slave Will
1482 slave Sam
1482 slave Dinah
1483 Nichols, James
1483 slave Hanah
1484 Nichols, Joseph
1485 Nichols, Mathias
1486 Hough, Edmond
1486 slave Will
1486 slave Titus
1486 slave Sambo
1486 slave Nanny
1487 Townsend, Littleton
1487 Townsend, Wm. Barkley
1488 Cellam, Joh
1489 Beavens, Caleb
1489 Taylor, Wm.
1490 Johnson, Whittington
1490 slave Jacob Fox
1490 slave Betty
1490 slave Pleasant
1491 Dennis, John, senr.
1491 Dennis, Valentine
1491 Dennis, Lazarus
1491 Till, John
1492 Beavins, John
1492 Beavins, Thomas
1492 Taylor, James
1492 slave Sambo
1493 Warrington, Thos.
1494 Rewark, John
1495 Crouch, Isaac
1496 McDaniel, James
1497 Sturgis, Joshua
1497 Laws, John
1497 Laws, Lazarus
1497 Warranton, Benja.
1497 Kellum, William
1497 slave Tom
1498 Dubin, Wm.
1499 Townsend, Solomon
1500 Jones, Wm., forest
1501 Di[us], John
1502 Right, Randall
1503 Noble, James
1504 Stephans, John
1505 Fountain, Nicholas
1506 Townsend, Jeremiah

1736 TAX LIST [Household number/Name/Remarks]
POCOMOKE/WICOMICO HUNDREDS

1507 Oulden, Abraham
1507 Anderson, Peale
1507 slave Will
1508 Sturges, Jonathan
1509 Davis, [Jose]ph
1510 Godfrey, [Josep]h
1511 Huton, John Booth
1512 Merrill, Joshua
1513 Stevenson, Joseph
1513 Stevenson, Wm.
1514 Mathis, Mary
1514 Mathis, Wm.
1515 Denston, John
1515 Denston, Jno., jnr.
1516 Hall, John

WICOMICO HUNDRED
1517 Gale, Levin, coll.
1517 Leatherbury, John
1517 Noble, Mark
1517 Fowler, Thomas
1517 Noble, John
1517 Deverix, John
1517 12 slaves
1518 Dashiell, George, coll.
1518 Evans, John
1518 Dobbity, James
1518 16 slaves
1519 Handy, John, capt.
1519 4 slaves
1520 Everton, John
1520 Everton, William
1521 Nelson, William
1521 Stewart, Charles
1522 Willen, Thomas, sr.
1522 Willen, Robert
1522 Willen, Thomas, junr.
1522 slave
1523 Willin, Edward
1524 Dashiell, Charles
1524 slave
1525 Evans, John, senr.
1525 Evans, John, junr.
1525 slave
1526 Crockett, Robert
1526 slave
1527 Crockett, John
1527 Larrimore, John
1528 Shiles, John
1528 2 slaves
1529 Crockett, Richard
1530 Cordery, Daniell
1530 2 slaves
1531 Dashiell, George
1531 slave
1532 Scott, Day
1532 Lewis, Christopher
1532 4 slaves
1533 Jackson, John
1534 Scott, George
1534 McLane, John
1534 3 slaves
1535 Wailes, Joseph
1535 2 slaves
1536 Dashiell, Mat.
1536 Russell, Thomas
1536 2 slaves
1537 Stewart, Alexa.
1537 2 slaves
1538 Dashiell, Wm.
1538 2 slaves
1539 Cordery, Abraham
1540 McMorie, James
1540 4 slaves
1541 Winder, Thomas
1541 Shiles, John
1541 2 slaves
1542 Hardy, Robt.
1542 Hardy, George
1542 Bordman, Samll.
1543 Piper, Christopher
1543 4 slaves
1544 Goslee, John
1545 Vennables, Benja.
1545 3 slaves
1546 Vennables, William
1547 Twilley, George
1548 White, Francis
1549 Barklett, Thomas
1549 Barklett, Paskey
1550 Barklett, Wm.
1551 Jackson, Samll.
1551 slave
1552 Fullerton, Alexander
1553 Reddish, Jno.
1553 Crouch, Robert
1553 Crouch, Jacob
1554 Lows, Henry
1554 5 slaves
1555 Cordery, Jacob
1555 Beshaw, Wm.
1556 Goslee, Thomas
1557 Goslee, [Matthew]
1558 Goslee, Richard
1559 Morris, Jeremiah
1560 Vennables, Willm., sr.
1560 Vennables, J[os.]
1561 Mitchell, Isaac
1562 Phillips, Richard
1563 Collier, Thomas
1563 slave
1564 Bounds, Jona.
1564 slave
1565 Stevens, Richard
1565 2 slaves
1566 Foskey, Thomas
1567 Kibble, Wm.
1567 Magee, John
1567 2 slaves
1568 Dashiell, Arthur
1568 Taylor, Jams.
1568 4 slaves
1569 Hall, Pheenix
1570 Cope, John
1570 Cope, Wm.
1571 Parsons, John
1572 Smith, James, senr.
1573 McClannon, Daniell
1573 Mitchell, John
1574 Sirman, Edward
1574 Mears, Robert
1575 Hobbs, Joy
1575 Hobbs, Absolom
1575 slave
1576 Mitchell, Benjamin
1577 Mitchell, Richard
1577 Oday, John
1578 Sirman, Jeane
1578 Magee, Peter
1579 Mears, [Joh]n
1580 Brereton, Wm., senr.
1580 Brereton, Wm., jr.
1580 slave
1581 Adams, Alexa., jr.
1581 McKenney, Patrick
1581 2 slaves
1582 Crouch, Jacob, senr.
1583 Serman, Peter, sr.
1583 Serman, Peter, jr.
1583 2 slaves
1584 Serman, John
1584 Astons, George
1585 Sillivan, Wm.
1585 Noble, Wm.
1586 Noble, Isaac
1587 Howard, Thomas
1588 Cottman, William
1589 Cottman, Benja.
1589 Newman, John
1589 slave
1590 Cottman, Joseph
1590 Oday, Owen
1591 Robinson, John
1592 Harriss, George
1593 Lokee, Thomas
1594 Mode, Peter
1595 Walker, Thos.
1595 4 slaves
1596 Ellis, Alice
1596 Chambers, Edward, esq.
1596 Horner, James
1596 3 slaves

TAX LISTS OF SOMERSET COUNTY: 1730-1740

WICOMICO HUNDRED

1597 Stewart, Patrick
1597 Foster, John
1597 slave
1598 Gale, Mathias, esq.
1598 5 slaves
1599 Holbrooke, Thomas
1599 Alexander, Wm.
1600 Austin, Robert
1600 slave
1601 Harriss, William, junr.
1602 Durham, James
1603 Harriss, Richard
1604 Dashiell, Thos.
1604 slave
1605 Rencher, Thos.
1605 2 slaves
1606 Rencher, Wood
1606 Lake, Benja.
1606 2 slaves
1607 Ballard, Charles
1607 slave
1608 Ballard, Elen.
1608 slave
1609 Johnes, John
1610 Harriss, William, senr.
1610 Harriss, Jno.
1610 Harriss, Charles
1611 Disharoone, Michael
1612 Disharoone, John, jr.
1613 Disharoone, William
1614 Alexander, Listian
1615 Gilliss, Thomas
1615 Bluett, John
1615 4 slaves
1616 Doudle, Christopher
1617 Magee, Geo.
1617 Magee, Samll.
1618 Tomson, John
1619 Christopher, Ephraim
1620 Christopher, Clemon
1621 Christopher, John
1621 Christopher, Joseph
1622 Bailey, George
1623 Elliss, Joseph
1624 Bailey, Jonathan
1625 Dulany, William
1625 Madden, Tim
1626 Nicholdson, Jos.
1627 Nicholdson, James
1628 Price, John
1628 Price, Thomas
1628 Price, David
1629 Bird, Thos., sr.
1629 Bird, Thos.
1630 Hall, Thomas
1631 Johnston, Purnall
1632 Bready, Rebecca
1632 Bready, William
1633 Linch, Michael
1634 Vinson, Geo.
1634 Heatch, Wm.
1635 Heatch, John
1635 Bashaw, Giles
1635 slave
1636 Vinson, Thomas, junr.
1637 Heatch, Samll.
1637 slave
1638 Roach, Alice
1638 Roach, Isaac
1638 Roach, Stephen
1638 3 slaves
1639 Revell, Wm.
1639 slave
1640 Toadvine, Henry
1640 4 slaves
1641 Hayman, Jams.
1641 Hayman, Charles
1641 Hayman, Isaac
1642 Hayman, John
1643 Griffen, John
1644 Hayman, [Char]les
1645 Vaunce, David
1646 Stanford, Joseph
1647 Chadwicks, Jams., senr.
1647 Chadwicks, Jams., junr.
1648 Jenkins, Jarvis
1648 Jenckins, John
1649 Howard, John
1650 Hill, Chas.
1650 Ellis, John
1650 Ellis, William
1651 Ellis, Frank
1652 Hillman, Edward
1653 Porter, Joshua
1654 Disharoone, Michael, jr.
1655 Disharoon, John, sr.
1655 3 slaves
1656 Sehorn, John
1657 Chiles, Edmond
1658 Perrey, James
1658 Talbott, John
1659 Beshaw, Graves
1660 Carey, Thomas
1661 Meglamery, George
1662 Toadvine, Mary
1662 Toadvine, George
1663 Toadvine, Isaac
1663 Toadvine, William
1664 Raglin, Michael
1665 Hayman, Willm., sr.
1665 Hayman, Wm., junr.
1666 Shockley, Jno.
1666 Shockley, Jno., junr.
1666 Shockley, Richd.
1666 Shockley, Wm.
1667 Shockley, Jonathan
1668 Driskill, Moses
1668 Driskill, Wm.
1669 Magraw, William
1670 Daviss, Samuell
1671 Cathell, James
1672 Christopher, John
1672 Taylor, John
1673 Hailes, John
1674 Atkins, Robert
1675 Fooks, Benja.
1675 Fooks, Wm.
1675 slave
1676 Driskill, Dennis
1677 illegible
1678 Sharp, George
1678 3 slaves
1679 Crouch, Jno.
1679 Crouch, Nich.
1680 Morris, Jacob
1680 Morris, John
1681 Carey, Jona.
1682 Pollock, David
1683 Pullet, Thomas, senr.
1683 Pullet, Thomas, junr.
1684 At Harriss, Robert, quarter
1684 slave
1685 Covington, Thos.
1685 slave
1686 Gray, Allen
1687 Mattex, Wm.
1687 slave
1688 Mattex, Alex.
1688 slave
1689 Caudry, John
1689 Caudry, Morgan
1690 Waller, Neilson
1691 Jaritt, William
1691 Jarritt, Comfort
1692 Lecat, John
1693 Wale, John
1694 Collett, Jams.
1694 Perry, James
1694 Toadvine, Jno.
1694 Murphy, Daniell
1695 Records, Jno.
1695 Records, Thomas
1695 Riggin, Ambrose

1736 TAX LIST [Household number/Name/Remarks]

WICOMICO HUNDRED

1696 Humphris, Thos.
1697 King, William
1698 Lancake, Francis
1698 Lancake, Stepn.
1698 3 slaves
1699 Lank, Geo.
1699 Phillips, Geo.
1700 Alexander, Moses
1700 Hodge, Jno.
1700 slave
1701 Handy, Isaac
1701 5 slaves
1702 Stevens, William
1703 Knox, Robt.
1703 Knox, Wm.
1704 Adley, William, senr.
1704 Adley, William, junr.
1705 Salt, Balmforth
1706 Williss, Nathaniell
1707 Lingoe, Robertson
1708 Dorman, Henry
1708 Dorman, Major
1709 Scadey, Stephen
1709 Scadey, John
1710 Lingoe, James
1710 Ruoke, J[ames]
1711 Perdue, John
1712 McGlamary, Edwd.
1712 Ollifen, Mathew
1713 Persons, George
1713 Brereton, Alexa.
1714 Cox, Thos.
1714 Cox, Thos., junr.
1715 Taylor, Thomas
1716 Gordee, Peter
1717 White, Henry
1718 Mellson, Daniell
1719 Disharoone, John
1720 Disharoone, Levin
1721 Disharoone, Lewis
1722 Turner, Samuell
1722 Smith, Archibald
1722 Turner, Edward
1722 Turner, Joshua
1723 Smith, George
1724 Melvin, Thomas
1725 Kiersey, Patrick
1726 Lingo, John
1727 Hill, James
1728 Ready, Brian
1729 Tatum, John
1730 Leonard, Joseph
1731 Davis, Daniell
1732 Davis, John
1733 Smith, James
1733 Kennady, John
1734 Smith, David
1735 Murfey, Joseph
1736 Smith, Moses
1737 Hearn, Thomas
1737 Hearn, Geo.
1737 Hearn, Nehemiah
1737 slave
1738 Hearn, William
1738 Hearn, John
1738 slave
1739 Ready, Thomas
1740 Lindow, Thomas
1741 Phillips, Jacob
1742 Caldwell, Hugh
1743 Hastin, Robt.
1743 Hastin, Willm.
1743 Hastin, Benja.
1744 Freney, Peter
1744 Freney, John
1745 Collings, Jams.
1746 Heatch, Elgate
1746 Bird, Wm.
1746 -ent-ace, Samll.
1746 3 slaves
1747 Evans, William
1748 Bailey, Benjamin
1749 Magee, Peter, senr.
1749 Magee, Peter, junr.
1750 Maylone, Robert
1751 Fullerton, Jams.
1752 Davis, William
1753 Thomson, Thomas
1754 Caldwell, Jno., mr.
1754 Caldwell, Robt.
1754 Farlow, Jno.
1754 Cornwell, Robert
1754 Rathbone, Andrew
1754 4 slaves
1755 illegible
1756 Roberson, Wm.
1757 Lackie, Alexa.
1757 Mackintoie, Danll.
1757 7 slaves
1758 Lingoe, Richard
1759 Davis, Thos.
1760 Cox, Hill
1761 Vincon, Thos., senr.
1761 unnamed/slave
1762 Cragen, Paul
1763 Wright, Jerma., junr.
1764 Gordey, Moses

TAX LISTS OF SOMERSET COUNTY: 1730-1740

ANNEMESSEX HUNDRED

1 Cotting[ham], Charles
1 Cottingham, Jno.
2 Cottingham, Charles
3 Cottingham, Thos., jur.
4 Pewsey, Jno.
5 Cottingham, Thos., ser.
5 Cottingham, Jno.
6 Smith, Henry
6 Smith, Wm.
7 Lankford, Joseph, ser.
7 Lankford, Soll.
8 Lankford, Joseph, jur.
9 [Adams], D[avid]
9 [Adams], Wm.
9 Addams, D.
10 Addams, Thos.
11 Pott[er], Henry
12 Wilson, George
13 Wilson, Jno., [jur.]
14 Cohoone, Jno.
15 Prier, Thos.
15 Prier, Samll.
16 White, Thos.
16 Wilson, Jos.
17 To Maddux, Mary
17 mollatto Kate
18 Maddux, Bell
19 Kellam, Jno., ser.
19 Kellam, Isaac
20 Kellam, John, jur.
21 Lord, Franics
21 Lord, Thos.
22 Lord, Henry
22 Lord, Alexr.
23 Connor, Jno.
23 Connor, Jno., jur.
23 Connor, Levin
24 Connor, Wm.
25 To Ward, Mary
25 Rigg[in], Jonathan
26 W[h]ea[tly], Sampson
26 slave Jack
27 Davis, Jno.
27 slave Harry
27 slave Wat
27 slave Dick
27 slave Sue
28 Roach, Jno.
29 To Bird, Joseph
29 Cullen, Jacob
29 Dunnock, Wm.
30 Starling, Jno., senr.
30 Starling, Henry
30 Starling, Aaron
31 Tyler, Thos.
31 Hurst, Jno.
32 Hopkins, George
32 Hopkins, Jno.
32 [Hop]kin[s], Wm.
32 Hopkins, Charles
33 Horsman, Henry
34 Fogg, Danll.
35 Woolf, Henry
36 Dixon, James
37 Mister, Willm.
37 Mister, Abraham
37 Mister, Benjn.
38 Williams, Wm.
39 To Parks, A[rthu]r
39 Parks, Jobe
40 Parks, Jno.
40 Parks, Mark
41 [Parks], Isaac
42 Tyler, Jno., senr.
42 Tyler, Jno., junr.
42 Tyler, Haes
43 Evens, Jno.
44 Bell, Anthony
44 Bell, Josephas
44 Jones, Mathew
45 Gunby, Jno.
45 Buckl[e], Cornelious
45 slave Jack
45 slave Kate
46 Gunby, Kirk
47 Whittenton, Southy
47 slave Robin
47 slave Sesar
47 slave Hannah
47 slave Sary
48 Long, Randall
48 slave Sib
49 Hearn, Edwd.
49 Ward, Stephen, jur.
50 White, Jno.
50 Powell, Thos.
51 Linzey, Thos.
52 Readen, Peter
53 Scandelin, Edwd.
54 Scott, Robt., senr.
54 Scott, Jno.
55 Davis, James
56 Miles, Henry
56 slave Files
56 slave Dinah
56 slave Robin
57 Fraz[er], Peter
58 Ca[ton], George
59 [Coulbro]un, Sollomon
59 Coulbroun, Soll., [jur.]
59 M[eceny], Patrick
59 slave M[er]ah
60 Ore, Mic[hael]
60 Ore, Michael, jur.
61 Mott, Jno.
62 Horsey, Stephen, capt.
62 Horsey, Jno.
62 Killey, James
62 slave Sary
63 Bell, Thos.
63 [slave] [N]an
64 Starling, [Jn]o., jur.
65 Grimes, [James]
66 Wheler, Jno.
67 Bird, David
68 Moore, Isaac
68 Parks, John
69 Ward, James
70 Ward, Thos.
70 Ward, Jacob
70 Ward, Moses
70 slave Pompey
70 slave Fillis
71 Sumners, [Jona]than
72 [Ri]g[gen], Jno., jur.
73 Juett, Willm.
73 slave Ned
73 slave London
74 Sumners, Jno.
74 Sumners, David
74 Sumners, Benjn.
74 Parks, Arther
75 Sumners, Thos.
75 Sumners, Geo.
75 Sumners, Thos., jur.
75 Benson, Sollomon
76 Allen, Joseph
76 Allen, Henry
77 Readen, Jno.
77 Dies, Filby
78 Riggen, Jno., senr.
78 Riggen, Wm.
79 Riggen, Jonathan
80 Johnson, John, jur.
81 Ward, Cornelious
81 Riggen, Stephen
81 Dukes, Robt.
82 Ward, Stephen
83 Ward, Samll.
83 Ward, Jno.
83 Ward, Wm.
84 Doughety, Jno.
84 Doughety, Nall.

1737 TAX LIST [Household number/Name/Remarks]

ANNEMESSEX HUNDRED

85 Moore, Frances
85 Moore, Jacob
85 Key, Wm.
86 Johnson, Jno., senr.
86 Smith, James
86 Flin, Jno.
87 Coulbroun, Willm., senr.
87 [Coulbr]oun, S[am]ll.
87 slave Quake
87 slave Lucey
88 Coulbroun, Wm., jur.
88 mollatto Kate
89 Tayler, Wm.
90 Price, Edwd.
91 To Holland, Michael, ser.
91 slave Sary
92 Holland, Michael, jur.
92 slave Moll
93 Cullen, Henry
93 Ward, Richd.
94 Porter, Joseph
94 Porter, Wm.
95 Moore, Thos., merum.
96 White, Jno., jur.
97 Long, Danll., jur.
98 Long, Jeffery
98 slave Ishmell
99 Long, Samll., merumsco
99 Long, Wm.
99 Long, [Da]vid, jur.
100 Lo[ng], [Dan]ll., [se]nr
100 [slave] [Friendsh]ip
101 illegible, senr.
102 Tr---, illegible
103 Williams, Thos. [ca]pt.
103 [Ow]en, Th[os.]
103 slave Titus
103 slave Addam
103 slave George
103 slave Tom
103 slave Jonas
103 slave Addam
103 slave Sarah
103 slave Glaseo
103 slave Gelico
104 Johnson, Wm.
105 Maddux, Thos.
106 Roach, Charles
106 Bannester, Charles

106 slave Joe
106 slave Rose
106 slave Neomy
107 Scott, Robt., jur.
108 Addams, Dennis
109 Williams, Jno.
109 Williams, Jacob
109 slave Sambo
109 slave Moll
110 Catlin, Wm.
110 slave Harry
111 Long, Samll., anna
111 slave Kate
111 slave Sam[son]
112 Sto[ck]dell, Edwd.
113 Who[rto]n, [W]m.
113 [C]ulle[n], Isaac
114 Tull, Solomon
115 Trehearn, Jno.
116 Roach, Nathall.
116 slave Samson
117 Watters, Jno.
117 slave Will
117 slave Sam
117 slave Dick
117 slave Berry
117 slave Joane
118 To Cottman, Mary
118 Cottman, Joseph
118 Cottman, Benjn.
118 slave Jenny
119 Waters, William
119 Wilson, Jno.
119 slave Geliah
119 slave Sambo
119 slave Pompey
119 slave Bristoll
119 slave Dinah
120 Waters, Edwd.
121 Waters, Elizabeth
121 Beach, Thos.
121 slave Hagar
121 slave Sipeo
121 slave Margrett
121 slave Hannable
121 slave Allex
122 To Wa[ters], Abiga[il]
122 slave Dav[id]
122 slave York
123 Ha[ll], Richd.
123 Wa[lston], [J]oy
124 Hall, Wm.
125 --ll, Thos.
126 Landen, Henry
127 Hall, Charles
127 Davis, Richd.
128 To Handy, Jeane
128 slave Nan
129 Long, Saywell

130 To Lister, Jeane
130 Lister, Thos.
130 Lister, Wm.
130 slave Sesar
131 Beauchamp, Edmd.
132 Beauchamp, Wm.
132 Beauchamp, Robt.
133 Brimegom, Walter
134 Marshall, George
135 Marshall, Samll.
136 Marshall, Thos.
137 Horsey, Smith
138 Horsey, Stephen, jur.
139 H[orsey], Nathaniell
139 O[uter]br[idge], Thos.
139 Horsey, Outerbridge
139 slave Cook
139 slave Prince
139 slave Quamenor
139 slave Kate
139 slave Patience
139 slave --rroah
140 Horsey, Isaac, coll.
140 P[ar]ks, Charles
140 slave Jonathan
140 slave Beck
141 Dixo[n], Wm.
141 Dixon, Ambros
141 slave Betty
141 slave Ben
141 slave Cuffey
142 Long, Jno.
142 slave [Robin]
142 slave [Sary]
143 Dixon, Thos.
143 Dixon, Thos., jur.
143 slave Harry
143 slave Tobey
143 slave Dick
143 slave Gidden
143 slave Hannah
143 slave Dinah
144 Lan[k]ford, Benjamin
144 Kindell, Wm.
145 Williams, Thos., junr.
145 slave Dick
145 slave Sesar
145 slave Quash
145 slave Lilly
146 illegible, Wm.
147 By[water]s, Richd.
148 free black W[at]
149 W[illiams], Isaac
149 Doug[hety], James
149 [Wo]od, David
149 slave illeg
150 Beauchamp, Isaac

TAX LISTS OF SOMERSET COUNTY: 1730-1740

ANNAMESSEX/BALTIMORE HUNDREDS

150 slave Patience
151 Sanders, Richd.
151 Sanders, Thos.
152 At Kings, Robt., quarter
152 slave Mingo
152 slave Tamore
153 Curtis, Charles
153 slave Toney
153 slave Dick
154 To Owen, Elizabeth
154 Owen, Moses
154 Owen, Phillip
154 Owen, Wm.
155 Boston, Wm.

BALTIMORE HUNDRED
156 Tull, [John]
156 Tull, [John], junr.
157 Weeb, [Wm.]
158 Smith, Wm.
159 Hiue--, John
160 Wy[att], [Jos]eph
160 W[ya]tt, [Nat]haniel
161 [B]oden, John
162 [B]oden, Able
163 Nickelson, John
164 Purkins, Thomas
165 Wilson, Israll
166 Smith, Ann
166 Coffen, John
167 Cobb, Wm.
168 Linch, Abraham
169 Tingle, Littleton
170 Watson, John
170 Syliven, Timothy
170 Goodrick, Richard
171 Rogers, Solomon
171 slave Cane
172 Hudson, George
173 illegible, Wi[lliam]
174 -----lott, --n----
174 illegible, Tho[mas]
174 illegible, Ro----
175 illegible, G[eorge]
176 West, T[h]omas
177 illegible
178 illegible
179 illegible, [Tho]mas
179 -arrney, [Th]omas
180 Wise, [M]atthew
180 Wise, Zekeill
181 Howard, Nehemiah
182 Perry, James, sr.

182 Perry, James, jr.
183 Howard, George, sr.
183 Howard, George, jr.
183 slave Kent
183 slave Bess
184 Woods, Robert
184 Woods, John
185 Aydlott, John, jr.
186 Hall, Joseph
187 Derixson, Joseph
188 Dolbey, William
188 Jenkins, John
189 Hazzard, David, sr.
189 Hazzard, Wm.
189 slave Jacob
189 slave Jeney
189 slave Dinnah
190 Hazzard, David, jr.
191 W[har]t[on], Henman
191 slave Arma[rall]
192 Clark, Mary
192 Clark, Wm.
193 illegible
194 Dasey, Tho[ma]s
195 Godwin, [Ceaser], sr.
195 Godwin, [Dan]iel
196 Godwin, Ceaser, jr.
197 Morris, Wm.
197 [Morris], Ale[xander]
198 Rickcor[ds], Jones
199 Depray, [Jo]hn
200 Hall, Sam[ue]ll
201 Miller, Joseph
201 slave Tom
201 slave Moll
201 slave Charls
201 slave Jack
202 Rickcords, John, sr.
202 Rickcords, Wm.
202 slave Simon
202 slave Boson
202 slave Briggitt
202 slave Moll
203 Woodcraft, William
203 Wilegoose, Richard
203 Wilegoose, Thomas
204 Gray, Wm.
205 Tingle, John
205 slave Harry
206 Woodcraft, Richard
207 Walker, John
208 -----an, Jo----
209 illegible, Jo---
209 illegible, William
210 [Rob]erson, Michaell
210 Rob[erson], W[m.]

211 [Colling]s, W[m.]
211 Collings, Able
212 Larthinghouse, William
212 slave Moll
213 illegible, Roba[rt]
214 Mo-------, James
214 slave ORam
215 Foresith, Sarah
215 Hogg, James
216 Fas[si]tt, Mary, mrs.
216 slave Frank
216 slave Bess
216 slave Doll
216 slave Sew
217 Pridicks, Thomas
218 Rackliff, Charles, capt.
218 Rackliff, Purnell
218 Looker, Wm.
218 slave Robin
218 slave Cate
218 slave Will
218 slave Moll
219 Fassitt, Rouse
219 slave James
219 slave Fillis
220 Patey, John
220 Patey, Powell
220 slave London
221 Rob[erts], Thomas
221 slave Quash
221 slave Bess
222 Pe[al], Thorou[g]ood
223 illegible, Ebeneas[er]
223 Turvell, John
224 Powell, T[h]omas
225 Collings, John
226 [De]la[ney], John Patric
227 [Larra[nce, Hennery
228 Crapper, Edmund, jr.
229 Cr[app]er, Nathaniel, jr
230 Alford, David
231 [Tur]vell, William
231 Evines, Larrance
231 Wheatley, John
231 Merritt, Luke
231 Clocker, Daniel
232 Waters, Richard
233 Evens, William
233 Evens, John
233 Evens, Wm.
233 Evens, Walter
234 Tingle, Hugh, sr.
234 Tingle, Hugh, jr.
235 Rickcords, John

1737 TAX LIST [Household number/Name/Remarks]

BALTIMORE HUNDRED

235 Towsend, Wm.
236 Whorton, Daniel, sr.
236 Whorton, Daniel, jr.
236 Whorton, George
237 Dufen, George
238 Joseph, Fedrick
239 Lewis, Wm.
240 Cammile, John
241 Bur[ton], Will[iam]
241 [Burto]n, Joh[n]
241 Burton, Joshu[a]
241 slave Adam
241 slave Touse
241 slave Comod[e]
241 slave Rach[el]
242 Wilson, John
243 L[ewi]s, Arthur
244 [Co]llings, George
245 illegible, Phillip
246 Short, Edward
247 J[oh]nson, Batholomwma
248 Gibbin[s], Thomas
249 Tipitt, Thomas
250 Beasey, William
251 Morris, Bibins
252 Nock, Solomon
253 Carrey, Thomas
254 Green, Zeckett
254 Hall, Joseph, jr.
255 West, Thomas, jr.
256 Jones, Ebenezer
256 slave Boston
257 Rodeney, William
258 Simples, Paul
259 Hall, Thomas
260 Pridteyman, Thomas
261 Strabritt, Thomas
262 Lewis, Joseph
262 Lewis, William, jr.
263 Simp[son], Richard
264 Morris, John
264 slave Cate
265 Smythers, Sirgant
266 Whorton, Thomas
267 Whor[to]n, Francis
267 Whorton, Wm.
268 Smith, John, piney neck
268 Smith, Robart
269 Hickman, Richard
270 illegible, George
271 Whealler, John, sr.
271 Whealer, John, jr.

272 Freeman, William, sr.
272 Freeman, Wm., jr.
273 Smith, John, capt. sr.
273 Smith, John, jr.
273 Smith, Charles
273 Smith, Thomas
273 Munks, William
273 slave Harry
273 slave Marah
273 slave Bess
274 Waples, Paul
274 Paul, Thorowgood
274 slave Charles
274 slave Dublin
275 Miller, John
275 slave Primas
275 slave Peggey
276 Coffin, Thomas, sr.
277 Coffin, Joseph
278 Cofien, Thos., jr.
279 Morris, Dennis
280 Gil[lstr]ap, Peter
281 [Rob]erson, Thomas
282 Johnson, Lenard
283 Roberson, Joshua
283 slave Bess
284 Dixson, Stirges
284 Johnson, Leaven
284 Banks, Neblitt
285 Godwin, Mich[ae]ll
285 slave Bess
286 Derickson, Benjam[in]
287 Salm[o]ns, William
288 Purkins, William
288 Tingle, Samuel
289 Colling[s], Thomas
290 Farrall, Thomas
291 Latcham, Thomas
292 Mankl[yn], Richard
292 Rackliff, Elias
293 Fault, John
294 Fault, Abraham
295 Kennitt, William
295 Roberson, Androw
296 Hudson, David
296 Hudson, William
297 Bradford, William
298 Linch, Alexander
299 Harrison, William
300 Hutson, Wm.
301 Hampton, Mary, madam
301 slave Jack
301 slave Hanable
301 slave Pegg
301 slave Peter
302 Gray, Thomas

302 Johnson, John
303 Holloway, John
303 Holloway, Moses
303 Holloway, Aron
304 Masey, John
304 Robarts, Thomas
305 [Town]send, Boman
305 Wh[ar]ton, Ricksam
305 Baker, William
306 Masey, Adkins
307 Newbold, John
307 Ingo, James
307 ------ad, illegible
307 slave Cato
307 slave Sillo
308 Evens, John
309 Cammille, John
309 slave Fellis
310 Wal[l]er, Thomas
311 Fassitt, Lamburd
311 Bowls, Zeachariah
311 slave Coe
312 Holland, Richard
312 Caldwell, Agustain
312 slave Hannah
313 Wyatt, William
313 Larthbery, Arthar
314 Hudson, Samuel
315 Waton, William, sr.
315 Walton, Wm., jr.
315 slave Ceaser
315 slave George
315 slave Jude
316 Loggwood, Richard
317 Hopkins, Samuel
318 Quilling, Joseph
318 Quilling, Benjaman
319 Fassitt, Frankline
319 Wilson, John
319 slave Nan
320 Sho[w]ell, Samuel
320 Larthberry, George
320 Cammile, Solomon
321 Hudson, Richeard, sr.
322 Clark, Race
322 Clark, John
322 Clark, Benjaman
322 Clark, Race, jr.
323 Bridell, Isaiah
323 slave Simon
323 slave Adam
323 slave Pendo
323 slave Mino
324 Robarts, Thomas
325 Holloway, John, jr.
326 Mumford, Charles
327 Hardis, Hazzard
328 Deale, John, sr.
329 Deale, John, jr.

TAX LISTS OF SOMERSET COUNTY: 1730-1740

BALTIMORE/BOGERTERNORTON HUNDREDS

330 Tyer, Robart
331 Hickman, Richard
332 Brittingham, Elezebeth
332 Blizard, Thomas
333 Blizard, Richard
334 Chace, Isaac
335 Bunton, Jonathan
336 Mumford, William
337 Clark, Joseph
338 Kinnitt, Martain
339 Gautt, Robert
339 Gautt, John
339 Brittingham, Robart
340 Gautt, William
341 Bridell, James Steven
342 ----ok, illegible
342 Tayler, Samuel
343 Liptrott, John
343 Brumbely, John
344 Brumbely, Hennery
345 Hudson, John
346 Bradford, Nathan[ie]l
346 Quilling, John
347 Whealey, Mary
347 Whealley, Charles
347 Whealley, Nathanile
348 Whealley, William
348 Mackcioy, James
348 Mackcioy, Jno.
349 Purnell, John, mr.
349 Lowe, Charls
349 slave Will
349 slave Toney
349 slave Toney
349 slave Doll
349 slave Moll
349 slave Dinah
350 Gray, Joseph
350 slave Simon
350 slave Quaco
351 Deale, Archable
351 Brotton, John
351 Deale, Quanton
352 Turvell, Prisgrave
352 Taylor, Josiah
353 Bessicks, Absalam
354 Russell, Androw
355 Holloway, Joseph
356 Morrah, James
357 Bessicks, Nathanil
358 Hudson, Richeard, sr.
358 Hudson, John
358 Gray, Wm.
358 slave Cuffe

358 slave Dick
358 slave Charles
358 slave Beck
359 Godard, Thomas
360 Crapper, Nathaniel, sr.
360 Crapper, Vinson
360 slave Kinner
361 Fassitt, William
361 Jones, John
361 slave Will
361 slave Titus
361 slave Harry
361 slave Sambo
361 slave Racheall
362 Coller, Peter
362 slave Pompy
362 slave Moll
362 slave Sarah
363 Masey, Alexander
363 slave Jack
363 slave Jude
364 Nock, Nehemiah
364 slave Nan
365 Masey, William
366 illegible
367 Crapper, Edmund
367 slave Dick
367 slave Peter
367 slave Pompy
367 slave Fele
367 slave Mary
368 Fassitt, John
368 slave Minney
368 slave Lewsy
369 Morgan, Avery
369 Coe, Daniel
369 slave Hannah
370 Bowen, Rodey
370 Bowen, John
370 Bowen, Wm.
370 slave Quaminy
371 Johnson, David
372 Jeaferson, Richeard
372 Jeaferson, Richard
373 Johnson, John
374 Roberson, John
374 Roberson, Joshua
374 Roberson, Joseph
375 Aydlott, John, sr.
375 More, Wm.
376 Smallwood, Samuel

BOGERTERNORTON HUNDRED
377 Holt, John
377 illegible, Josh[ua]
378 Wildman, John
378 ----ay, [Sa]mll.
379 Challie, Moses
380 Stewart, Peter

381 Bell, John
381 French, John
382 Jarmin, Henry
383 Murray, John
384 Buncle, Alexander
385 Atkinson, John
386 Rownd, James
386 5 slaves
387 Guy, James
388 Porter, James
389 Porter, Joseph
389 slave
390 Tull, Benjamin
391 Crapper, John
392 Stevens, William
393 Murray, Dunken
393 7 slaves
394 Greer, Adam
395 Ryley, Thomas
396 Evans, Elias
397 Charles, John
398 Lay, John
398 2 slaves
399 Lay, William
400 Burton, John
400 Duett, Nathll.
401 Franklen, Edward
401 Harmon, John
401 Harmon, Zackariah
402 Frankli[n], William
403 Alexander, Paul
403 Harmon, [Benj.]
404 Wale, William
405 Beddard, William
406 White, John
406 2 slaves
407 Gornwell, John
407 3 slaves
408 Midsley, Thomas
409 Evans, John
409 Evans, William
409 slave
410 Tingle, Daniel
411 Evans, Gammage
412 E[v]ans, Powell
413 Po[w]ell, Thomas
414 Po[we]ll, Samll.
415 Wa[rren], [Nic]ho[li]s
416 [W]arren, [Robert]
417 Harmon, William
418 Dazey, John
418 Gray, Nickolas
419 Beddard, Richard
420 Townsend, Jeremiah
420 3 slaves
421 Townsend, Brickhouse
422 Timmons, William
423 Timmons, Aaron
424 Timmons, Joseph

1737 TAX LIST [Household number/Name/Remarks]

BOGERTERNORTON HUNDRED

425 Timmons, Thomas
426 Timmons, Samll.
427 Timmons, James
428 Timmons, John
428 Timmons, Samll.
428 Timmons, Aron
429 Smith, William
430 Greer, Ursula
430 Greer, John
431 Smith, Andrew
431 Smith, George
432 Loe, George
433 Jarmin, Robert
434 Hodge, Robert
434 slave
435 Richarts, William
436 Jones, Joseph
437 Swain, William
438 Jackson, Agnes
438 Jackson, John
439 Truett, John
440 Collins, Thomas, sr.
441 Hadder, Warren
442 Truit, George, son of Job
443 Truit, Nehemiah
444 Bradford, John
445 Gray, John
446 Davis, Edward
446 Davis, Samll.
447 Crapper, Nehemiah
448 Crapper, Rixam
449 Smith, John
450 Simson, William
450 Simson, Thos.
450 4 slaves
451 Templin, John
452 Tull, Richard
453 Tadlock, Agnes
453 Tadlock, Edward
454 Purnell, Catherine
454 Purnell, Walton
454 2 slaves
455 Becket, Peter
455 B[eck]et, William
456 [P]enniwell, Charles
457 [Mar]sh[al]l, [Isaac]
457 Marshall, Jacob
457 Webb, illegible
457 3 slave
458 Hudson, [Dennis]
458 Lowrie, William
458 2 slaves
459 Gilleland, John
459 Montgomery, John
459 2 slaves
460 Gillet, John

461 Hudson, Majer
462 Mannering, Abraham
463 Webb, Samll.
464 Davis, Tuder
465 Smith, Abraham
466 Handcock, Daniell
466 Handcock, Wm., jr.
467 Hall, Robert
467 slave
468 Dennis, William, senr.
469 Bratten, Samll., senr.
469 Bratten, Hugh
470 Bratten, Samll., junr.
471 Hall, Adam
472 Heather, Ephraim, senr.
472 slave
473 Heather, Ephraim, junr.
473 Templin, Richd.
474 Griffen, Oliver
475 Crapper, Ebenezar, senr.
476 Crapper, Ebenezar, junr.
477 Poynter, Thomas
477 Poynter, Ratcliffe
477 Poynter, Turvil
477 2 slaves
478 Poynter, John
479 Ake, John
480 Blizard, Richd.
481 Brittingham, William, sr
481 Brittingham, Absolam
481 Brittingham, Nathaniel
482 Brittingham, William, ju
483 Brittingham, Solomon
484 Ennis, William
484 Ennis, William, junr.
484 Dukes, Thomas
485 Ennis, Nathaniel
486 Ennis, Cornelius
487 Holland, William
488 Selby, Parker
489 Ennis, Mary
489 Ennis, Samll.
490 Davis, William, seaside
490 slave
491 Stevens, Samll.
492 Teague, John

492 Teague, John, junr.
493 Shockley, John
494 McCaly, [John]
495 [H]olston, [William]
495 [Holston], Charles
496 Collins, Samuel
497 Greer, Arc[hib]ald
497 Greer, John
498 Purnell, Elisha
498 2 slaves
499 Banum, Bartholemew
500 Nock, J[oh]n
500 2 slaves
501 Williams, [Sam]ll.
501 Williams, Nathaniel
502 Bell, Ad[a]m
502 slave
503 Vestrey, [Mich]ael
504 Spence, [Ada]m
504 Scott, William
504 5 slaves
505 [Ro]binson, illegible
506 ----lls, illegible
507 ---ford, illegible
508 Hall, [William]
508 Hall, Phenix
508 [2 slaves]
509 ---goes, J---
510 Johnson, A[fradozi]
510 slave
511 [Joh]nson, Jo[hn]
512 Johnson, George
513 Johnson, Th[om]as
514 [Devro]x, Jo[hn]
514 Devrox, Cornelius
514 slave
515 S[cot]t, Mark
516 [Stur]giss, Joh[n]
516 Sturgiss, Littleton
517 Steel, James
517 Steel, Daniell
517 [S]teel, Willi[am]
518 [T]urner, Nic[holas]
519 Godfrey, C[harle]s
520 Stevenson, James
520 Stevenson, Adam
520 Stevenson, Samll.
521 MacNeal, Ar[chibald]
522 [Tu]rner, H[enry]
523 [Dre[den, John
524 Dennis, So[lomon]
525 Dennis, D[anie]l
526 Dennis, D[o]n[o]ck
527 [S]tevenson, illegible
528 Prior, John Webb
529 Mumford, illegible
530 Truit, George, son of George

TAX LISTS OF SOMERSET COUNTY: 1730-1740

BOGERTERNORTON HUNDRED

530 Truit, John
530 slave
531 Mumford, [Jam]es
531 Mumford, James, junr.
532 Truit, [Willi]am
533 Truit, George, son of Philip
534 Mason, Edmund
535 [Willi]ams, illegible
535 [W]illiams, illegible
536 Adkins, Stenton
536 Adkins, Steven
537 Jarmin, Job
538 Truit, [Ja]mes
539 Porter, John
540 Collins, John
541 Collins, Mary
541 Collins, Thomas
542 Collins, William
543 Penniewell, John
544 Parker, George
545 Penniewell, George
546 Davis, William, senr.
546 [Davi]s, S[amll.]
547 Davis, Robert, junr.
548 Oshohannas, William
548 ---sey, illegible
549 Truit, Thomas
550 Taylor, Phillip
550 [Taylor], Elias
551 Davis, Thomas
552 Davis, Phillip
552 D[av]i[s], George
553 Parker, Charles
554 Parker, Phillip
555 Jarmin, William
556 Murray, David
557 Davis, Robert, senr.
557 Davis, William
557 Davis, Ishmael
557 [Davis], Benj.
557 Davis, Robert
558 Rain, Mathew
558 Ra[in], John
559 Parker, Tabitha
559 Parker, Samll.
559 5 slaves
560 Bridgewa[ters], Emmanuel
560 Bridgwaters, Isaac
560 Williams, illegible
561 Purnell, Mathew
561 Cambell, N[ehem]iah
561 slave
562 Burbridge, Edward
563 Rathbone, Robert
564 Hammond, Isaac
564 [Hamm]ond, Will[iam]
565 Burbridge, John
566 Dunken, Thomas
567 Smachie, William
568 Jones, George
569 Bowen, John
570 Mitchell, Thomas
570 2 slave
571 Bowen, Littleton
571 slave
572 Bowen, George
573 Thomson, James
574 illegible, John
574 illegible
575 Bow[in], William
576 Jarmin, John, senr.
576 [Jarmin], William
576 slave
577 Jarmin, John, junr.
578 Marchment, Charles
579 Jarmin, George
580 Truit, George, accomack
580 Truit, George, junr.
580 2 slaves
581 Truit, George, son James
582 Hammond, Edward, son Edward
583 Ratcliffe, John
584 Hill, Johnson, junr.
584 Hill, Robert
585 Lindell, Peter
586 Edwards, Benjn.
586 Edwards, James
587 Hammond, John
587 Bassit, James
588 Bassit, John
589 Sandwith, William
590 Fletcher,, mr.
590 3 slaves
591 Morris, William
592 Morris, Joseph
593 Truit, Joseph
594 Selby, John
594 3 slaves
595 Selby, William
595 Selby, William, jr.
595 Houlston, Benj.
595 3 slaves
596 Pepper, John
596 Pepper, William
597 Purnell, Thomas
597 6 slaves
598 Victor, James
598 Victor, Thomas
599 Richardson, James
600 Richardson, Charles
600 slave
601 Richardson, Robert
602 Richardson, William
603 Bratten, William, junr.
604 Bratten, James, junr.
605 Bratten, James, senr.
606 Scoefield, Joseph
606 Scofield, John
606 2 slaves
607 Bushop, William
608 Outten, John
609 Outten, Thomas
610 Bushop, Benja.
610 Patrick, Roger
611 Bushop, Joseph
612 Lane, George
613 Clawell, Thomas
614 H[ou]lston, John
615 Porter, William
616 Patrick, Daniel
617 Atkins, John
618 Bravard, Adam
618 slave
619 Tayler, William
620 Brittingham, Isaac
620 Brittingham, Nathan
620 slave
621 Ennis, John
622 Sturgiss, Joshua
622 Laws, John
622 Laws, Bolitha
622 slave
623 Jenkens, John
624 Brittingham, Jeremiah
625 Williams, Pressgrave
626 Rownd, Edward, capt.
626 Davis, Thos.
626 2 slaves
627 Givan, John
628 Dennis, Wheatly
629 Tuster, Bentall
630 Denis, Wm., [j]nr.
631 Townsand, Wm.
632 Penewell, Thomas
633 Smith, Wm.
634 Pointer, Elias
635 Penewell, Wm.
636 Rowin, Edward
637 Smock, Henery
637 Smock, John

1737 TAX LIST [Household number/Name/Remarks]

BOGERTERNORTON/MATTAPANY HUNDRED

638 Handcock, Wm.
639 Henderson, Charles
640 Hill, Johnson
640 Hill, Elisha

MATTAPANY HUNDRED
640 Richardson, John
641 Hill, Hutton
641 Voan, Wm.
642 Bratton, William
642 Willson, Wm.
642 slave
643 Sturgis, Richard
644 Clayuell, Peter, junr.
645 Guttry, Pattrick
645 Guttry, Jams.
646 Hall, John
646 Hall, Henry
647 Pain, John
647 Pilshiar, Mosses
647 Pain, Mosses
648 Aydlott, William
648 Williams, Thomas
648 slave
649 Wattson, Robt., junr.
650 Wattson, Mosses
651 Clayuell, Peter, senr.
651 Clayuell, Shadrich
651 3 slaves
652 Reed, Waltor
653 Slocum, Thos.
653 Long, Colburne
654 Porter, Clintuck
655 Pluder, Joseph
656 Benitt, Mary, widow
656 Linzey, Jams.
657 Venettson, Williams
657 Venettson, Nathan
658 Peper, Tobias
659 Peper, William
660 Brumbley, Nathall.
661 Answorth, William
661 Taylor, John
662 Henderson, Bishup
663 Samons, Benja.
663 Harman, Gorge
664 Walton, Stephen
664 Walton, Steven
665 Maxfield, Joseph
665 4 slaves
666 Allen, Joseph
667 Hosiear, Samll., senr.
667 Crowson, Richd.
668 Crawford, Andrew

668 Crawford, John
669 Sturgis, Daniell
670 Hill, Robt.
671 Chapman, Humphry
672 Holland, Nehemiah
672 Wattson, Jams.
673 Wattson, John
673 Waytt, Nathall.
674 Selbey, Parker
674 5 slaves
675 Davis, Charles
676 Benston, Joshua
677 Hill, Abraham
678 Hill, Jacob
679 Jackson, William
680 Wa[tt]son, Peter
680 Wa[ytt], Joseph
681 Duberley, Thos.
682 Jones, John
683 Vezey, Charles
683 Vezey, Wm.
684 Robins, Bodwine
684 4 slaves
685 Walton, Fisher
685 Hargis, Thos.
685 2 slaves
686 Dewey, Thomas O.
687 Hopkins, Matthew
687 Ayars, Richd.
687 Hares, Henry
688 Hopkins, William
689 Milburne, Thomas
690 Evens, John
691 Scarbrough, John
691 Daley, John
691 2 slaves
692 Hopkins, Nathall.
692 slave
693 Hopkins, Samll.
694 Holland, Benja.
694 2 slaves
695 Dreaden, John
696 Johnson, Peter
696 Johnson, Peter
697 Johnson, John
698 Hosiear, Samll., junr.
699 Johnson, William
699 Johnson, Ezekiah
700 Turner, William
701 Newton, Thomas
701 Newton, Thos.
701 Newton, Southy
702 Wise, Thomas
702 Mills, James
703 Newton, Jonathan
704 Taylor, Rodger
704 Answorth, Jobe
705 Tarr, Samll.
705 Newton, Jobe

705 Cornwill, John
706 Newton, Starling
707 Pope, John
707 Gurley, Gorge
707 4 slaves
708 Tarr, Michel
708 Tarr, Michel
709 Pope, Gorge
709 2 slaves
710 Pope, Samll.
710 slave
711 Booth, William
712 Ceary, Jeremiah
713 Wattson, Robt., senr.
713 Wattson, Charles
714 Slingo, Thomas
714 Slingo, Thos.
715 Nealson, William
715 Nealson, James
715 Nealson, Robt.
716 Selbey, Philip
716 Selby, Mattw.
716 Selbey, Danll.
716 Selbey, Phil.
716 Selbey, Wm.
716 7 slaves
717 Cord, William
717 Cord, Arthur
717 Cord, John
717 slave
718 Walker, John
718 2 slaves
719 Wagaman, Jacob
719 Wagaman, Ephram
719 Mcrall, John
719 Arnell, Larance
719 2 slaves
720 Rusill, Cuthbud
720 Wattson, Hurias
721 Willett, Ambrus
721 Wilett, Will.
721 Willett, Thos.
722 Hodge, Rolling
722 slave
723 Hodge, John, criple
723 Hodge, Rolling
724 Mallen, Christopher
725 Richardson, John
725 Richardson, Samll.
725 slave
726 Harman, Manewell
726 Colleck, Simon
727 Allen, John
728 Gill, John
729 Purnell, John
729 5 slaves
730 Scott, Robt.
730 Scott, Adam
730 Scott, Robt.

TAX LISTS OF SOMERSET COUNTY: 1730-1740

MATTAPANY/MONIE HUNDRED

731 Long, John
732 Ceary, Solomon
733 Wattson, Luke
734 Wimbroe, Paul
735 Moses, Joseph
736 Porter, Wm.
737 Due--, Wm.

   MONIE HUNDRED
738 Laws, Robert
738 Laws, Panter
738 Laws, Wm.
738 Wallace, Robert
738 Rose, Samll.
738 Wallace, George
738 slave Jack
738 slave Sampson
738 slave Bubo
739 Gale, George
739 M[au]ghon, Chrisr.
739 slave Joe
739 slave Sipeo
739 slave Dominick
739 slave Jamey
739 slave Limas
739 slave Jack
739 slave Nimrod
739 slave Ceasar
739 slave Jeany
739 slave Plinah
739 slave Beanda
739 slave Parthena
739 slave Nanne
739 slave Sarah
740 Bazwell, Thos.
741 Williams, Jno.
742 Jones, Lewis
742 Jones, Samll.
742 slave Jack
742 slave Ceasar
742 slave Moll
743 Laws, Jno.
743 slave Prince
743 slave Ceasar
744 Twifird, Wm.
745 Roe, Joseph
746 [Roe], Th[omas]
746 [Hop]kins,
  [George]
747 [Wi]ndsor,
  L[azarus]
747 W[inds]or, Jno.
747 [Wind]sor,
  illegible
747 [Wind]sor, J[ames]
748 [Dug]less, J[ohn]
749 [Roe], E[liz.]
749 [Roe, John]
750 [C]hain,
  [Alexander]

751 L[aws], Tho[s.]
751 slave Morreah
752 Macdorman, [Darby]
753 Miller, [Thomas]
754 Jones, Geo.
755 Windsor, Jno.
756 White, Francis
756 White, Thos.
756 White, Jno.
757 [Whi]te, Jno.
758 [Roberts], Jno.
758 Ro[berts], Tho.
759 Roberts, Rencher
760 Wallace, Mattw.
760 slave Tom
760 slave Sib
761 Wallace, Richd.
761 Wallace, Thos.
761 Wallace, James
761 slave Ceasar
761 slave Bess
762 Roberts, Edward
762 slave Jeffrey
762 slave Binah
763 Pollock, Joseph
763 Macdannell, Owen
764 Magrough, James
765 Waller, Majr.
766 Waller, Jno.
766 slave Jean
767 Irvin, George
767 Nickolson, Levin
767 slave Tobe
767 slave Cuffee
767 slave Jane
767 slave Jene
768 Martin, George
769 Stoughton, Wm.
769 slave Bussy
769 slave Simon
769 slave Jemmy
769 slave Sabinah
769 slave Sarah
770 Jones, Robert
770 Jones, Mitchel
770 Welch, Wm.
770 Macom, George
770 slave London
770 slave Amock
770 slave Dick
770 slave Jean
770 slave Rachel
771 Downs, Geoe.
771 Downs, Robt.
771 slave Bristo
771 slave Ned
772 Dorman, Jno.
773 Jones, Wm.
773 slave Will
773 slave Jame

773 slave Sue
773 slave Luse
774 Leatherbury, Jno.
774 Dorman, Ezekl.
774 slave Sambo
774 slave Pompe
774 slave Tony
774 slave Benn
774 slave Robbin
774 slave Bridgett
774 slave Bess
774 slave Rose
774 slave Nan
774 slave Nanne
775 Durham, Thos.
776 Covington, Thos.
777 Lawless, James
778 Jones, Daniel
778 Jones, Philimon
778 slave Doll
778 slave Whitehaven
779 Jones, Jno.
780 Jones, James
780 slave Busser
780 slave Dave
780 slave Sib
780 slave Moll
781 Hurst, Jno.
782 Dashiell, Thos.
782 Dashiell, Levin
782 slave Will
782 slave Jack
782 slave Harry
782 slave Joe
782 slave Whitehaven
782 slave Bess
782 slave Tamer
782 slave Hanah
782 slave Sarah
783 Wright, Thos.
783 Wright, Henry
783 Welch, Jno.
784 Spicer, Philip
785 Waller, Geoe.
785 Sasser, Wm.
786 Lu[ke], Williamson
787 Newman, Henry
787 Lake, Andrew
788 Dorman, Henry
789 Mongarr, Jno.
790 Puckem, Richard
791 Dorman, Marg[aret]
791 Smith, Jno.
792 Magraugh, Jno.
792 Hill, Wm.
793 Hobbs, Joy
794 Ho[bbs], Marsellass
795 Covington, Jno.
795 Wright, Zebelon
795 slave Sambo

1737 TAX LIST [Household number/Name/Remarks]

MONIE/NANTICOKE HUNDRED

795 slave Cuckow
795 slave Betty
795 slave Pegg
795 slave Dinah
796 Carey, Thos.
797 Carey, Rachel
797 Crouch, David
798 Shores, Jno.
798 Shores, Wm.
799 Costin, [M]athias
800 Hobbs, Thos.
800 Mongarr, Mattw.
801 Irvin, John
801 Nickolson, [Levin]

NANTICOKE HUNDRED

802 [Givans, Robert]
802 [Givans, George]
802 slave Seasar
802 slave Charles
802 slave Sampson
802 slave Hannah
802 slave Bess
803 Givins, James
803 slave Toby
803 slave Frank
804 Farington, William
805 Nicolas, Richard
806 Langston, Spear
807 Train, James
807 Train, James
807 Train, Roger
807 slave [Ro]bin
807 slave [Ro]ase
807 slave Benn
808 Hardey, James
808 slave Sambo
808 slave Jane
809 --nnit, George
810 W------, William
811 Kemp, Mathew
811 Kemp, John
811 Powel, James
812 Jones, John
813 Martin, John
814 Jacobs, Elizabeth
814 slave Sybb
815 Boadly, William
815 Mu----, James
816 [Nutter], Hewitt
816 slave Titus
816 slave Mingoe
817 Nutter, Matthew
818 Nutter, Christafer
818 slave Seaser
818 slave Tom
818 slave Sipueo
818 slave Jack
818 slave Barbarry
818 slave Roase
818 slave Harrey
819 Nutter, William
819 slave Phillip
819 slave Cato
819 slave Benn
819 slave Roase
819 slave Cattr.
820 Blewer, James
820 slave Nearrow
820 slave Judeth
821 Parsons, Francis
821 Sheridon, Ezekil
822 -----ine, illegible
823 ---erson, illegible
824 Done, illegible
824 Done, illegible
825 Hust, illegible
826 Macome, [Timoth]y
827 [Be]sick, illegible
828 Collier, [Robe]rt
828 Collier, [Geor]ge
828 Collier, [Robert]
828 slave --g
828 slave Sarah
829 ---lk-, illegible
830 W[a]lter, [Da]niel
831 Hickman, [Willi]am
831 Hickman, -------n
831 slave [M]urrear
831 slave [Jac]k
831 slave [Ro]se
831 slave Sambo
832 --allis, illegible
832 [---lis], illegible
833 illegible
834 illegible
835 ---nkins, illegible
835 illegible/slave
835 illegible/slave
836 --llis, illegible
837 ---als, illegible
837 illegible/slave
838 illegible
838 ----ards, illegible
839 Russell, James
839 Russell, Wm.
840 Russell, James
840 Syms, Archabl.
841 Dashiel, Joseph
841 Russell, Thos.
841 slave Randall
841 slave Sambo
842 Dashiel, Precila
842 slave Harry
843 Dashiel, Robert
843 slave Cago
843 slave Ta----
844 Bens[t]on, Mary
844 slave Will
844 slave Bess
845 Collier, Dowdy
846 Gale, John
846 [Coo]per, John
846 slave -----y
846 slave Jam[es]
846 slave Gallaway
846 slave Obed
846 slave Townside
846 slave Phebe
846 slave Judeth
846 slave Rose
846 slave Moll
847 Goselen, James
848 Ride[r], Wilson
849 [Rider], Hatel[y]
850 illegible, Char[les]
850 illegible, Hen[ry]
851 illegible, Benj[amin]
852 illegible, Josep[h]
853 illegible, Ma[ry]
853 illegible, Tho[mas]
853 slave illegible
854 Ac[worth, Thos.
854 slave illegible
855 [Parry], Ja[m]es
855 Parr[y], W[m.]
856 Chees[man], John
856 slave illegible
856 slave illegible
857 illegible, S------
857 slave illegible
858 illegible, Henry
859 Cottman, [Eb]enezer
859 Cottmon, Wm.
860 Fulton, William
861 Newbank, Molten
862 Callaway, Peter
862 Callaway, John
863 Henry, Robert
864 Collins, Ebenzr.
865 Collins, Thos.
866 Culver, John
867 Parramor, Thos.
868 P[arr]more, Betty
868 Parramore, John
869 Relph, Wm.
870 Allaphent, William
870 Ready, Cornelus
871 Olave[r], George
872 C---, [John]
873 Jones, [John]
874 Jones, [J]ames
875 McClure, Robert
876 Taylor, Abraham
876 slave Quashey
877 Beake, Isbel
877 Beake, [Isaac]
878 [Ho]fington, Jonathan

TAX LISTS OF SOMERSET COUNTY: 1730-1740

NANTICOKE HUNDRED

879 Hofing[ton], John	918 Wallac, Richd.	957 slave Amey
880 Killim, Edward	918 slave Hager	958 Polk, Charles
880 Killim, John	919 Anderson, John	958 Polk, Francis
880 slave Robin	920 Calwell, Thomas	958 Coapes, Wm.
880 slave Marrin	921 Calwell, Patrick	959 Polk, Ja[mes]
881 B[o]ice, John	922 illegible, Pet[er]	960 Haul, Jam[es]
882 Codrey, David	923 illegible, Jobe	961 Manlife, Emamuel
883 Kibble, John	924 illegible, Wm.	961 slave Quaco
884 Jarvis, Samull.	925 illegible, Dani[el]	962 Fisher, George
885 Thornes, Alexnd.	926 illegible, John	963 Polk, John
886 Melson, Samuell	927 illegible, M[oses]	963 slave Att---
886 Melson, Samuel	928 illegible, John	963 slave illegible
886 Churme, John	929 illegible, James	964 Owins, [Ro]bert
887 Coape, John	930 illegible, Jo[hn]	964 slave Cattey
887 Coape, Wm.	931 illegible, Jame[s]	965 Kimey, Walter
888 Right, Solomon	932 illegible, Ja[m]e[s]	966 Ingram, Isaac
889 Smith, Thomas	932 slave illegible	967 Ingram, Abraham
890 Poulson, Wm.	932 slave Sa---	967 Ingram, Abraham
891 Young, John	932 slave illegible	967 Ingram, David
892 Ellinsworth, Robert	933 illegible, Tho[mas]	967 Ingram, Jacob
893 Lynn, Aaron	933 illegible, R-----	967 slave Presilla
893 Robinis, Samuel	933 illegible, T[homas]	968 Fowler, illegible
893 slave Abrim	934 illegible, Henr[y]	969 [Co]llins, illegible
893 slave Bess	935 illegible, Sam[uel]	970 illegible
893 slave Jack	936 Bes----, Wm.	971 Brown, William
893 slave Jane	937 illegible	971 Comical, John
894 Gibins, John	938 illegible, James	971 Comical, Thos.
894 Gibins, Elixndr.	939 Ro----, T[ho]s.	972 Nowls, Edmond
895 Jenkins, Thos.	940 illegible, T[homas]	972 Nowls, Richd.
896 Wallter, Robert	941 illegible	972 Nowls, Edmond
897 Stilley, John	942 illegible, Henry	973 Langsten, William
897 Stilley, John	942 illegible, Jame[s]	973 Stevens, Isaac
898 Edge, Joshua	943 illegible, Pa----	974 Robertson, John
899 Edge, Robert	943 illegible, Jo---	975 Bradley, John
900 Paramore, James, jr.	943 illegible, Joh[n]	976 Deann, Charles
901 Boudger, James	943 illegible, Obedia[h]	976 Dean, Wm.
902 Sumon[s], Wm.	943 slave illegible	977 Boy[ce], Daniel
903 Callaway, Peter	944 Noal[s], Joh[n]	977 slave Bess
904 Kimey, Thos.	945 illegible, James	978 Dashiel, Mitchel
905 Thomson, George	945 slave illegible	978 Nicolds, George
906 Taylor, John	946 illegible, Isa[ac]	978 slave Venus
907 Kimey, Abraham	947 Jon---, Wm.	978 slave Bamoe
908 Downes, Robert	948 J-----, John	979 Morr[is], Thos.
909 King, Wm.	949 illegible, Wm.	980 Inglish, Wm.
910 Ki[ng], Phillip	949 slave illegible	981 Dunkin, James
911 Parramore, Mattw.	950 illegible, Thos.	982 Burne, James
911 Parramore, Ezekel	950 illegible, Alax[nder]	983 Roberson, Wm.
912 Write, Edward	951 illegible, Jona----	984 Hastten, Robt.
913 Parsons, John	952 illegible, Pet[er]	985 Hastten, Wm.
914 Thomson, Thos.	953 Will--, Charles	986 Willey, Jarrett
915 Calwe[ll], John	954 Brown, James	987 Mitchell, John
915 Calwell, Robert	955 Sharp, John	988 Benston, Henry, senr.
915 Garvil, Thos.	955 Sharp, Wm.	989 Buckworth, Charles
915 slave Sambo	955 Sharp, John	990 Greer, Lese
916 Walter, Nathn.	956 Willey, John	990 Greer, Wm.
916 Walter, John	956 slave Cossey	990 Macclanen, Joseph
916 Benston, George	957 Newbole, Francis	991 Rickords, John, jr.
917 Paramore, Joseph		

1737 TAX LIST [Household number/Name/Remarks]

WICOMICO HUNDRED

992 Gale, Levin, coll.
992 Leatherbury, Jno.
992 North, Jno.
992 Noble, Mark
992 Workman, Thomas
992 Leatherbury, Pearrey
992 slave Hope
992 slave Sambow
992 slave Honey
992 slave Jacob
992 slave Jack
992 slave Peter
992 slave Job
992 slave Ishmael
992 slave Plesent
992 slave Jehu
992 slave Robin
992 slave Parregit
992 slave Harrey
992 slave Jonathan
992 slave Will
992 slave Joyce, a woman
992 slave Zeporah, a woman
992 slave Bess, a woman
992 slave Moreah, a woman
993 Gilliss, Thos.
993 Peluit, Jno.
993 Cornwell, Robert
993 slave Stepney
993 slave Domnick
993 slave Namah
993 slave Peg
994 Harriss, William, snr.
994 Harriss, Jno.
994 Harriss, Charles
995 Harriss, Wm., jur.
996 Harriss, Richd.
996 Meclayn, Archeybald
997 Oston, Robert
997 Fowler, Jno.
997 slave Moll
998 Rencher, Thomas
998 slave Peter
998 slave Pompey
999 Rencher, Underwood
999 Leg, Benja.
999 slave Jack
1000 Ballard, Charles
1000 slave Ceasar
1000 slave Moreah
1001 Dashiell, Thomas, junr.
1001 slave Jack
1002 Cottman, Joseph
1002 Odaw, Owen
1002 slave Sarah
1003 Stevens, Richard
1003 slave Pumpow
1003 slave Alice
1004 Walker, Thomas
1004 slave Tom
1004 slave Jonathan
1004 slave Dinah
1004 slave Katherine
1005 Durham, James
1006 Harriss, George
1007 Hayman, James
1007 Hayman, Isaac
1008 Hayman, John
1009 Hayman, Charles
1010 To Elliss, Alice
1010 Chambers, Ewd., esqr.
1010 Horner, James
1010 slave Pubow
1010 slave Anna
1010 slave Moll
1011 Stuart, Patrick
1011 Folster, Jno.
1012 Gale, Mathias
1012 slave Ceasar
1012 slave Jack
1012 slave Ralph
1012 slave Stevan
1012 slave Dublin
1012 slave Rose
1012 slave Vilet
1012 slave Sarah
1013 Houlbrook, Thomas
1013 Shiles, John, junr.
1013 Alexander, Wm.
1014 Tate, Franciss
1015 Mode, Peter
1016 Roberson, William
1017 Lokey, Thomas
1018 Roberson, John
1019 Cottman, Benja.
1019 Numan, Jno.
1019 slave Sarah
1020 Cottman, William
1021 Howard, Thomass
1022 Noble, Isaack, jnr.
1023 Sulivant, William
1023 Noble, William
1024 Weatherbury, Jno.
1024 Tillman, Aron
1025 Mitchell, Richard
1025 Oday, John
1025 Hass, Gorg
1025 slave Patrick
1026 Mitchell, Benja.
1027 Shirman, Peter, snr.
1027 Shirman, Peter
1027 slave Tom
1027 slave Simon
1028 Alexander, Moses
1028 slave Tom
1029 Hayman, Charles, snr.
1030 Hales, John
1031 Attkins, Robert
1032 Alexander, Listen
1033 Pullet, Thos., snr.
1033 Pullet, Thos.
1033 Nox, William
1034 Polk, David
1034 slave Thamor
1035 Willson, George
1036 Bruerton, William, snr.
1036 Bruerton, William
1036 Bruerton, Jno.
1036 slave Patious
1037 Crouch, Jacob, snr.
1037 Crouch, Jacob
1037 Crouch, Thos.
1038 Tomson, John
1038 Mage, Samll.
1039 To Adams, Alexander, snr.
1039 Adams, Alexander
1039 slave Squash
1039 slave Isaac
1039 slave Rebecah
1039 slave Dinah
1040 Magee, George
1041 Dowdle, Christopher
1042 Baly, Benja.
1043 Baly, Geo.
1044 Ellis, Josep
1045 Christopher, Clemant
1046 Christopher, Ephraim
1047 Christopher, Jno., snr.
1047 Christopher, Joseph
1048 Meirs, John
1048 Meirs, Samll.
1049 Magee, Peter, snr.
1049 Magee, Peter
1050 Hobbs, Absolom
1050 slave Pollobus
1051 MaClanahan, Danll.
1052 Parsons, John
1052 Mitchell, Jno.
1053 Malone, Robert
1054 Hall, Phenix
1055 Shirman, John
1055 Osten, George
1055 slave Sye
1056 Kibble, William
1056 Magee, John

TAX LISTS OF SOMERSET COUNTY: 1730-1740

WICOMICO HUNDRED

1056 slave Peter
1056 slave Bess
1057 Foskey, Thomas
1058 Bounds, Jonathan
1058 slave Bess
1059 Phillips, Richard
1059 Phillips, Geo.
1060 Venables, William, snr.
1060 Venables, Joseph
1061 Mitchell, Isaac
1062 Gosley, Richard
1063 Davis, William
1064 Gosley, Mathew
1065 Morriss, Jeremiah
1066 Baley, Jonathan
1067 Beshaw, Jarrot
1067 Shirman, Isaac
1068 Gosley, Thos.
1069 Colier, Thos.
1069 slave Grace
1070 Cawdry, Jacob
1070 Beshaw, William
1071 Bluit, Thomas
1072 Jackson, Samll.
1072 slave Grace
1073 Redish, Jno.
1074 Crouch, Robert
1075 Morriss, Jacob
1075 Morriss, Josep
1075 Morriss, Jno.
1076 Howard, Jno.
1076 Taler, James
1077 Elliss, Francis
1078 Hill, Charles
1078 Elliss, Jno.
1078 Elliss, William
1079 Hillman, Edward
1080 Disheroon, Michal, snr.
1081 Gordy, Moses
1082 Crouch, John
1083 To Sharp, Geo.
1083 slave Moll
1083 slave Pompey
1083 slave Penney
1084 Carrey, Thos.
1084 Murfey, Danll.
1085 Porter, Joshua
1086 Salt, Balmforth
1087 To Todvine, Mary
1087 Todvine, Geo.
1088 Disheroon, John
1088 Caneday, Timothy
1088 slave Coffey
1088 slave Grace
1088 slave Fanney
1089 To Roach, Alice
1089 Roach, Isaac
1089 slave Tom
1089 slave Harrey
1089 slave Pegg
1089 slave Hannah
1090 Roach, Steven
1091 Shehon, John
1092 Jenkins, Jarvis, snr.
1092 Jenkins, Jno.
1092 Jenkins, Jarvis
1093 Disheroon, Michael, junr
1094 Disheroon, Jno., junr.
1095 Disheroon, William
1096 Todvine, Thomas
1097 Chadwick, James, snr.
1097 Chadwick, James
1098 Stanford, Joseph
1099 Adly, William, snr.
1099 Adly, Wm., junr.
1100 Griffin, John
1101 Ragly, Michael
1102 Christopher, John, snr.
1102 Talor, Jno.
1103 Cathell, James
1104 Daviss, Samll.
1105 Driskill, Moses
1105 Driskill, William
1106 Megraugh, William
1107 Driskill, Denniss
1108 Fooks, Benja.
1108 Fooks, William
1108 slave Pashon
1109 Revil, William
1109 slave Tom
1110 Cearrey, Levin
1111 Cearrey, Jonathan
1112 Toadvine, Henry
1112 Toadvine, Joshua
1112 slave Goliah
1112 slave Sarah
1112 slave Oxford
1112 slave Jane
1113 Toadvine, Isaac
1114 Vinson, Benja.
1115 Beshaw, Graves
1115 Beshaw, Giles
1116 Smith, James, junr.
1117 Hayman, William, snr.
1117 Hayman, Wm.
1118 Farlow, Jno.
1118 Rathbone, Andrew
1119 Davis, Danll.
1120 Davis, Thomas
1121 Lingo, Richd.
1122 Davis, Jno.
1122 Magee, Moses
1123 Shockley, Jno., junr.
1124 Shockley, Jonathan
1125 Shockley, Richd.
1126 Meglamery, George
1127 Dorman, Henry
1128 Dorman, Mager
1129 Lingo, Roberson
1130 Scady, Stevan
1131 Williss, Nethanel
1132 Ling, James
1132 Morris, Nethanel
1132 Ruock, James
1133 Kearsey, Patrick
1133 Kearsey, James
1134 Lingo, Jno.
1135 Perdue, Jno.
1135 Perdue, Geo.
1136 Meglamery, Edward
1136 Olivan, Mathey
1137 Hales, James
1138 Murfey, Joseph
1139 Smith, Moses
1140 Smith, James, snr.
1141 Persons, George
1141 Lokey, Alexander
1142 Smith, George
1143 Smith, David
1144 Smith, Archeybald
1145 Disheroon, Lewiss
1146 Disheroon, Jno., son Lewis
1147 Disheroon, Levin
1148 Meathwen, Thomas
1149 Turner, Samll.
1149 Turner, Joseph
1150 Mellson, Danll.
1151 Gordey, Peter
1152 Talor, Thomas
1153 Waill, John
1154 Cragin, Paul
1155 Springle, William
1156 Lenard, Joseph
1157 Cox, Hill
1158 Cox, Thos., snr.
1158 Cox, Thos.
1159 Tatum, Jno.
1160 Ready, Brion
1161 Coldwell, Jno., snr.
1161 Coldwell, Robert
1161 Goldsmith, Anthoney
1161 slave Will
1161 slave Coffey
1161 slave Doll
1161 slave Squash
1162 Handy, Isaack
1162 Coulbourn, Samll.

1737 TAX LIST [Household number/Name/Remarks]
WICOMICO HUNDRED

1162 slave Mumford
1162 slave Sharper
1162 slave Will
1162 slave Quameno
1162 slave Prue
1163 Vance, David
1163 Rigen, Teague
1164 To Crouch, Ann
1164 Crouch, Nicholas
1165 Stevans, William
1166 Crouch, Isaack
1167 Ruoc, John
1168 Scott, Geo.
1168 Maclane, John
1168 slave Sam
1168 slave Pompey
1168 slave Sanders
1168 slave Florak
1169 Scott, Day
1169 Carter, Phillip
1169 slave Hector
1169 slave Tom
1169 slave Sipeo
1169 slave Dido
1170 Dashiell, George, junr.
1170 slave Coffey
1170 slave Sipeo
1170 slave Dido
1171 Fowler, Thomas
1172 Lackey, Alexander
1172 Chambers, Samll.
1172 slave Toby
1172 slave Surthey
1172 slave Sam
1172 slave Robin
1172 slave Frank
1172 slave Sibb
1172 slave Amey
1173 Lewiss, Christopher
1174 Shiles, Jno., snr.
1174 slave Tom
1174 slave Hannabill
1175 Crockit, Richd.
1176 Crockit, Jno.
1177 Crockit, Robert
1177 slave Crap
1178 Willing, Thos.
1178 Willen, Robert
1178 slave Sarah
1179 Cawdry, Danll.
1179 slave Samson
1179 slave Sibb
1180 Dashiell, Matthias
1180 slave Sambow
1180 slave Ming
1180 slave Jane

1181 Evains, Jno., snr.
1181 Evains, Jno., jnr.
1181 slave Sambow
1182 Winder, Thomas
1182 slave Ming
1182 slave Rose
1183 Makemorie, James
1183 slave Bat
1183 slave Abner
1183 slave Pompey
1183 slave Rose
1184 To Waills, Heleney
1184 slave Leander
1184 slave Ordery
1185 Cawdry, Abraham
1185 Cawdry, Morgin
1186 Dashiell, Charles
1186 slave Jacob
1186 slave Peliner
1187 Willen, Edward
1188 Everton, Jno.
1188 Everton, William
1188 Stuart, Charles
1189 Nellson, William
1190 Jackson, Jno.
1191 Handy, Jno.
1191 slave Dick
1191 slave Tom
1191 slave Moll
1191 slave Jane
1191 slave Patience
1192 Dashiell, Geo., coll.
1192 White, Francis
1192 Evains, Jno.
1192 18 slaves
1193 Venables, Wm., junr.
1193 Toadvine, Jno.
1194 Gosley, Jno.
1195 Hardy, Robert
1195 Hardy, George
1195 Hardy, James, jnr.
1195 Bordman, Samll.
1195 Hardy, Benja.
1196 Bartly, Thomas
1196 Bartly, Paskey
1197 Twilley, George
1197 Larmore, John
1198 Fulerton, Alexander
1199 Nichols, Joseph
1200 Nichols, James
1201 Meirs, Robert
1202 Cawdry, Jno.
1203 Hitch, Elgit
1203 slave Cannundah
1203 slave Bonney
1203 slave Amey
1204 Hitch, Sam

1204 slave Jack
1205 Vinson, Thomas
1206 Lecat, John
1207 Low, Robert
1208 Hitch, Jno.
1208 Nichols, Richard
1208 slave Morah
1209 Bready, William
1210 Vinson, Thos., snr.
1211 Vinson, George
1211 Hitch, William
1212 Magee, Peter, jr.
1213 Evains, William
1214 Phillips, Thos.
1215 Collins, James
1216 Jarrit, William, free black
1216 [Jarrit], Comfort, wife
1217 Linch, Michaell
1218 Ricords, Jno.
1218 Ricords, James
1218 Ricords, Thos.
1219 Langcake, Francis
1219 Langcake, Stevan
1219 slave Jack
1219 slave Bess
1220 Langcake, George
1220 Tolbert, John
1220 Piper, Joseph
1221 Humphris, Thomas
1222 To Humphris, Mary
1222 Russell, Thomas
1223 Bird, Thomas, snr.
1223 Bird, William
1223 Bird, Benja.
1224 Bird, Thomas, jnr.
1225 Jonson, Samewell
1226 Price, John
1226 Price, Thomas
1226 Price, David
1226 Bredy, James
1227 Jones, Thomas
1228 Madox, Alexander
1228 slave Moreah
1229 Madox, William
1229 slave Abraham
1230 Covington, Thomas
1230 Covington, John
1230 slave Tom
1231 Gray, Allen
1232 Hall, Samewell
1232 Ready, Danll.
1233 Hern, William
1233 Hearn, Jno.
1233 slave Moll
1234 Lindol, Thomas
1235 Gordy, Peter
1236 Franey, Peter
1236 Franey, John

TAX LISTS OF SOMERSET COUNTY: 1730-1740

WICOMICO HUNDRED

1237 Hearn, Thos.
1237 slave Hanna
1238 Hearn, George
1239 Jonson, Purnall
1239 Todvine, William
1240 Hall, Thos.
1241 Venables, Benja.
1241 slave Pompey
1241 slave Bess
1241 slave Tom
1241 slave Will
1242 Willkins, James
1243 Lows, Henry
1243 Miles, John
1243 slave Jepthath
1243 slave Dover
1243 slave Jo
1243 slave Five Island
1243 slave Quamino
1243 slave Rose
1244 Piper, Christopher
1244 slave Sambow
1244 slave Toby
1244 slave Dick
1244 slave Greenidg
1244 slave Moll
1244 slave Sue
1245 Flehar, Thomas, mr.
1245 slave
1246 Willing, Thos., sr.
1246 Mackintier, Danll.
1246 Willin, Thos.
1246 Bruckshir, Wm.
1247 Shockley, John, senr.
1248 Dashiell, Arthur
1248 3 slaves
1249 Caldwell, Heugh
1250 Phillips, Jacob

1738 TAX LIST [Household number/Name/Remarks]

ANNEMESSEX HUNDRED

1 Davis, [Jo]hn
1 slave [Har]ry
1 slave [Cat]e
1 slave [Di]ck
1 slave [Jen]ny
2 Horsey, Stephen, [cap]t.
2 Horsey, [Joh]n
2 Killy, [James]
2 slave Sary
3 Roach, [Ch]arles
3 Megumery, [Thomas]
3 slave [Joe]
3 slave [Rose]
3 slave [Neom]ey
4 Roach, [John]
5 Cullen, [Hen]ry
6 Smith, [Jame]s
7 Starling, [Jo]hn, senr.
7 Starling, [He]nry
7 Starling, [Aa]ron
7 Claywell, Selby
8 Starling, Jno., jr.
9 Ward, Thos.
9 Ward, Jacob
9 Ward, Moses
9 slave Pompy
9 slave Fillis
10 Ward, James
11 Cullen, Jacob
11 Moore, Samuel
12 To Bird, Joseph
12 Blithe, Walter
12 Donnock, Wm.
13 Grimes, James
14 Wheler, Jno.
15 Bird, David
16 Moore, Wm.
17 Moore, Isaac
17 Parks, Jno., jur.
18 Juett, Wm.
18 slave Ned
18 slave Lonnon
19 Sumners, Jno.
19 Sumners, David
19 Sumners, Benjn.
20 Sumners, Thos.
20 Sumners, George
20 Sumners, Thos, jr.
20 Sumners, Samll.
21 Sumners, Jonathn.
22 Benson, Sollomon
23 Riggen, Jno., jr.
24 Readen, Jno.
25 Riggen, Jonathan
26 Ward, Cornelious
26 Riggen, Stephen
27 Ward, Stephen
28 Ward, Samuel
28 Ward, Jno.
28 Ward, Wm.
29 Riggen, John, senr.
29 Riggen, Wm.
29 Dukes, Robt.
30 Lord, Henry
31 Lord, Thos.
32 To Ward, Mary
32 Ward, Stephen, jr.
33 Lord, Frances
33 Lord, Randall
34 Doughety, John
34 Doughety, Nathn.
35 Davis, James
36 Miles, Henry
36 slave Phillis
36 slave Dinah
36 slave Robin
37 Frazer, Peter
38 Walton, Wm.
39 Caton, George
40 Coulbroun, Sollomon
40 Coulbroun, Soll.
40 slave Moreah
41 Coulbroun, Wm., jr.
41 mollatto Kate
42 Coulbroun, Wm., senr.
42 Coulbroun, Samll.
42 Coulbroun, Soll.
42 slave Quake
42 slave Lucy
43 Tayler, Wm.
44 Moore, Frances
44 Moore, Thos.
44 Moore, Jacob
45 Price, Edwd.
45 Price, Jno.
46 Gunby, Jno.
46 slave Jack
46 slave Kate
47 Bell, Thos.
47 slave Nan
48 Cottingham, Charles, jr.
49 Addams, David
49 Addams, Wm.
49 Addams, David
50 Addams, Thos.
51 Cohoone, Jno.
51 Cohoone, Henry
52 Lindsey, Thos.
53 Potter, Henry
54 Wheatly, Sampson
54 slave Jack
55 Connor, John, senr.
55 Connor, Jno., jr.
55 Connor, Levin
56 Johnson, John, junr.
56 Dize, Phill.
56 Mecanny, Patrick
57 Johnson, John, senr.
57 Flin, John
58 Kellam, John, jr.
59 Gunby, Kirk
59 Price, Johnson
60 White, John, senr.
60 Fordred, Wm.
60 Powell, Thos.
60 Powell, Benj.
61 Hearn, Edward
61 Lord, Alexdr.
62 Whittenton, Southy
62 slave Robin
62 slave Hannah
62 slave Sarah
62 slave Betty
63 Long, Randall
63 slave Sibb
64 Scott, Robt., senr.
64 Scott, Jno.
65 Readen, Peter
66 To Ore, Michael, senr.
66 Ore, Michael, jr.
67 Scandelin, Edward
68 Cottingham, Charles, sr.
68 Cottingham, Jno.
68 John[son], Joshua
69 Cottingham, Thos., jr.
70 Lankford, Joseph, jr.
71 Pewsey, Jno.
72 Long, Samll., merumsco
72 Long, Wm.
72 Long, David, jr.
73 Marshall, Samuell
73 Belmoset, Humphry
73 slave Gloster
74 Bywaters, Richd.
75 White, Jno., jr.
76 Long, Jeffery
76 Long, Saywell
76 slave Nish
77 Moore, Thos.
78 Porter, Joseph
79 Marshall, George
80 Addams, Dennis
81 Boston, Wm.
82 Brimegem, Walter
83 Beauchamp, Edmond
84 Beauchamp, Wm.
84 Trehearn, James, jr.
85 Bell, Anthony
85 Bell, Josephas
85 Riggen, Jonathan
86 Connor, Wm.
87 Maddux, Bell

TAX LISTS OF SOMERSET COUNTY: 1730-1740

ANNEMESSEX HUNDRED

88 Kellam, John, senr.
88 Outten, Purnell
89 White, Thos.
89 Wilson, Joseph
90 Prier, Thos.
90 Prier, Samll.
91 Wilson, George
92 Wilson, Jno., jr.
93 Long, David, senr.
94 Long, Daniel, jr.
95 Long, Daniel, senr.
95 slave Friendship
95 slave Jenny
96 Maddux, Thos.
97 To Maddux, Mary
97 slave Kate
98 Trehearn, James
98 Trehearn, Wm.
99 Tyler, Thos.
99 Crockett, Joseph
100 Tyler, Jno., senr.
100 Tyler, Jno., jr.
100 Tyler, Thos.
100 Tyler, David
101 To Parks, Arthur, sr.
101 Parks, Arthur, jr.
101 Parks, Jobe
102 Parks, John, ser.
102 Parks, Mark
102 Parks, Jno., jr.
103 Evins, Richd.
104 Mister, Wm.
104 Mister, Abraham
104 Mister, Benjn.
104 Topping, Samll.
105 Dixon, James
106 Evins, John
106 Evins, John, jr.
107 To Wheler, Samll.
107 Wheler, Jonahn.
108 Hoppkins, George
108 Hopkins, Jno.
108 Hopkins, Wm.
108 Hopkins, Chals.
108 Hopkins, George
109 Woolf, Henry
110 Horsman, Henry
111 Fogg, Daniell
112 Marshall, Thos.
113 Beauchamp, Robt.
114 Holland, Michaell, ser.
114 slave Sary
115 Holland, Michael, jr.
115 slave Moll
115 slave Tom
116 Horsey, Stephen, jr.
117 Horsey, Smith
118 To Horsey, Anne
118 slave Tamore
119 Horsey, Nathan.
119 Horsey, Outerbridge
119 Key, Wm.
119 slave Prince
119 slave Quamenor
119 slave Kook
119 slave Kate
119 slave Tarroh
119 slave Patience
120 Horsey, Isaac, coll.
120 Parks, Charles
120 slave Jonth.
120 slave Beck
121 Dixon, Wm.
121 Dixon, Ambros
121 slave Bess
121 slave Ben
121 slave Coffey
122 Dixon, Thos., senr.
122 Dixon, Thos., jr.
122 slave Harry
122 slave Dick
122 slave Toby
122 slave Gidden
122 slave Hannah
122 slave Dinah
123 Lankford, Benjamin
123 Lankford, Soll.
123 Ward, Richd.
123 slave Sesar
124 Lankford, Joseph, ser.
124 Lankford, Pewsey
125 Long, Jno.
125 Long, Coulbroun
125 slave Robin
125 slave Sary
126 Smith, Henry
126 Smith, Wm.
127 Williams, Thos., capt.
127 Owen, Thos.
127 slave Titus
127 slave Geo.
127 slave Addam
127 slave Tom
127 slave Addam
127 slave Jonas
127 slave Sary
127 slave Glasco
127 slave Gelico
128 Pewsey, Wm.
129 Williams, Thos., junr.
129 slave Dick
129 slave Quash
129 slave Sesar
129 slave Silly
130 free black Wat
131 Johnson, Wm.
132 To Owen, Elizth.
132 Owen, Wm.
133 Williams, Isaac
133 Doughety, James
133 Wood, David
133 slave Pleasant
134 Williams, [John]
134 Williams, Jacob
134 slave Sambo
134 slave Moll
135 Kings, Robt., coll. quarter
135 slave Mingo
135 slave Tamor
136 Sanders, Richd.
137 Beauchamp, Isaac
137 Porter, Wm.
137 slave Patience
138 Cattlin, Wm.
138 Learmouth, Alexdr.
138 slave Harry
139 Stockdell, Edwd.
139 slave Cato
140 To Lister, Jean
140 Lister, Thos.
140 slave Sesar
141 Whorton, Wm.
141 Cullen, Isaac
142 Tull, Sollomon
143 Long, Samll., annamessex
143 slave Samson
144 Trehearn, Jno.
145 Roach, Nathaniel
145 slave Sambo
146 Tull, Thos.
146 Lister, Wm.
147 Waters, Wm.
147 slave Goliah
147 slave Sambo
147 slave Bristah
147 slave Pompey
147 slave Dinah
148 Waters, John
148 slave Will
148 slave Sam
148 slave Dick
148 slave Berry
148 slave Jane
149 To Cotman, Mary
149 Cotman, Joseph
149 Cotman, Benjn.
149 slave Jean
150 Waters, Edwd.
151 To Waters, Elizth.
151 slave Ellick

1738 TAX LIST [Household number/Name/Remarks]

ANNEMESSEX/BALTIMORE HUNDREDS

151 slave Hannable
151 slave Sippeo
151 slave Hagar
151 slave Pegg
152 To Waters, Abgail
152 Waters, Richd.
152 slave David
152 slave York
153 Landen, Henry
154 Hall, Richd.
154 Hall, Charles, jr.
155 Hall, Charles, senr.
155 Davis, Richd.
156 Hall, William
157 Curtis, Charles
157 slave Dick
157 slave Toney
158 Sehoan, Thos.
158 Sanders, Thos.
158 slave Nan
158 slave Sary
159 Cottingham, Thos., sr.
159 Wilson, John
159 Owen, Philip
160 Scott, Robert, jr.

BALTIMORE HUNDRED
161 Fassitt, William
161 Mackcormack, Partrick
161 slave Will
161 slave Harry
161 slave Titus
161 slave Sambo
161 slave Rachell
161 slave Beck
162 Kinnett, Martain
162 Harberson, Samuel
163 Hudson, George
163 Willson, Isack
164 Fassitt, Mary, mrs.
164 slave Frank
164 slave Berry
164 slave Sew
164 slave Doll
165 Wyatt, William
165 Lathbery, Arthur
166 Hudson, David
166 Hudson, Wm.
166 Hudson, Absalam
167 Linch, Abraham
167 Whorton, Wm.
168 Holloway, John, sr.
168 Holloway, Aron
168 Holloway, Moses

169 Chase, Isaac
170 Burton, Jonathan
171 Hudson, John
172 Hudson, Richeard, jr.
173 Natman, John
174 Cobb, William
175 Boden, Able
176 Hickman, Richeard, ind. r.
177 Whorton, Thos.
178 Collings, William
178 Collings, Able
179 [Hudso]n, Andrew
180 Knock, Solomon
181 Derikson, Benjaman
181 Freeman, Wm.
182 Salomon, William
183 Aydlott, John, jur.
184 Derickson, Joseph
185 Robinson, Joshua
185 Derickson, Wm.
185 slave Bess
186 Howard, George, sr.
186 Howard, George, jr.
186 slave Kent
186 slave Bess
187 Howard, Nehemiah
188 Roberts, Thos., sr.
189 Roberts, Alexander
189 Roberts, Thos., jur.
190 Hopkins, Josiah
191 Blizard, Richeard
192 Walker, John
193 Hickman, Richard
194 Coe, Danil
195 Fassitt, Frankline
195 slave Bess
196 Aydlott, John, sr.
196 More, Wm.
197 Evans, John, ser.
198 Hudson, Richard, sr.
198 Hudson, John
198 Hudson, Henry
198 slave Coffee
198 slave Dick
198 slave Charles
198 slave Bik
199 Brumbely, Henrey
199 Brumbly, John
200 Aydlott, Thos.
200 Whorton, Charles
200 Melson, John
200 Munks, Wm.
201 Rickards, John
201 slave Simon
201 slave Boson
201 slave Moll

201 slave Brigg
202 Hattfield, William
203 Evens, Willm., sr.
203 Evens, Willm., jur.
203 Evens, Walter
204 Miller, Joseph, mr.
204 slave Tom
204 slave Charles
204 slave Jack
205 Evens, John, jnor.
206 Robins, Thos.
206 Rackliff, Rixam
206 slave Quash
206 slave Bess
207 Pridicks, Thos.
208 Walton, John
209 Smith, John, capt.
209 Smith, John
209 Smith, Thos.
209 Smith, Charles
209 slave Harry
209 slave Mirah
209 slave Bess
210 Kinnett, Willm.
210 slave Petter
211 Godard, Thos.
212 Gault, Wm.
213 Larrance, Henrey
214 Morris, Natthaniell
215 Whealey, Charles
215 Whealey, Natthell.
216 Fassitt, Lambard
216 slave Coe
217 Waters, Richeard
217 slave Jude
218 Gray, Joseph
218 slave Simon
218 slave Quacock
219 Bredell, James Stephen
219 Johnson, Jon.
219 slave Mendo
219 slave Adam
220 Tyer, Robard
221 Deal, John, jr.
222 Blizard, Thos.
223 Deall, John, sr.
224 Powell, Thos.
225 Gray, Thos.
226 Morrow, Robard
227 Mumford, Charles
228 Hardis, Hazzard
229 Russell, Andrew
230 Holloway, Joseph
231 Bessicks, Natthaell.
232 Bessicks, Absalam
233 Brittingham, Robard
233 Brittingham, Nathan
234 Wyatt, Joseph
234 Wyatt, Natthaill.

TAX LISTS OF SOMERSET COUNTY: 1730-1740

BALTIMORE HUNDRED

235 Nickelson, John
236 Low, Robard
237 Newbold, John
238 Whitehead, John
238 slave Catto
238 slave Silo
239 Hopkins, Samuel
239 slave Orson
240 Mumford, James
240 Wilson, John
241 Turvill, Prisgrave
241 Whalley, John
242 Deale, Archeabell
243 Perrey, James, sr.
243 Kent, John
244 Masey, John
245 Hall, Samuel
246 Roberson, Thos.
247 Johnson, John
248 Joseph, Ferdrick
249 Watson, John
249 Silvean, Timothay
249 Goodrick, Richeard
250 Gruphams, George
251 Gillstrap, Petter
252 Townsend, Boman
253 Beasey, Wm.
254 Johnson, Lenard
254 Harman, John
255 Dixson, Joyce, widow
255 Banks, Nibelett
255 Johnson, Leaven
256 West, Thos., jur.
257 West, George
258 West, Wm.
259 Hopkins, John
260 Whorton, Francis
260 Whorton, Rixam
261 Gibbins, Thos.
262 Smith, John, pineneck
262 Smith, Robard
262 Smith, Wm.
263 Cearey, Richeard
264 Barnett, James
265 Lewis, Josep
266 Lewis, William, sr.
267 Burton, Willm., mr.
267 Burton, John
267 slave Touse
267 slave Bomodo
267 slave Rachell
268 Wilson, John
269 Lewis, Wm., jr.
270 Walton, Teagle
271 Cambell, John
272 Roberson, Willm.

273 Lewis, Arthur
274 Collings, George
275 Hunnings, Phillip
276 Short, Edward, junr.
276 slave Sipe
277 Cade, Thos.
278 Cearey, Thos.
279 Johnson, Bathomew
280 Waples, Paul
280 slave Charles
280 slave Dublen
281 Anderson, Willm.
281 Anderson, Robt.
282 Hazzard, Willm.
282 slave Delfe
283 Massy, Katteran
283 Townsend, Willm.
284 Hazzard, David, sr.
284 Hazzard, Jon.
284 Gray, Jon.
284 slave Jacob
284 slave Dinah
285 Whorton, Henman
285 slave Ameroall
286 Rickards, John
287 Depray, John
288 Rickards, Jones
289 Whorton, Daniel, sr.
289 Whorton, Daniel
289 Whorton, George
290 Dasey, Thos., sr.
290 Dasey, Thos.
291 Morris, Wm.
292 Godwin, Ceasar, sr.
293 Godwin, Ceasar, jur.
294 Wise, Matthew
295 Smythers, Sergant, capt.
296 Godwin, Micheall, capt.
297 Purnell, John
297 Rackliff, Charles
297 slave Will
297 slave Toney
297 slave Toney
297 slave Darwell
297 slave James
297 slave Doll
297 slave Moll
297 slave Dinah
298 Jones, John
299 Whealey, Willm.
300 Hook, Willm.
301 Loggwood, Mary
301 Evens, Larrance
302 Smith, Abraham
303 Tingel, Mary

303 Tingle, Samuel
303 slave Harry
304 Hill, Johnson
304 Hill, Wm. Stevens
305 Hudson, Samuel
306 Eashom, John
307 Lyptrott, John
308 Harrison, Willm.
309 Rackliff, Elias
310 Folk, John
311 Lactham, Thos.
312 Smallwood, Samuel
313 Tayler, Samuel
314 Watson, Willm., sr.
314 slave Ceaser
314 slave George
314 slave Jude
314 slave Rose
315 Watson, Willm., jr.
316 Eevens, Ebenzear
317 Turvell, John
318 Jackson, Agness, widow
318 Jackson, John
319 Onorton, Isbell, widow
319 slave Jack
320 Fall, Abraham
321 Smith, William
321 Smith, John Onorton
322 Webb, Willm.
323 Tull, John, sr.
323 Tull, John, jr.
324 Purkins, Willm.
325 Conner, Daniel
326 Jefferson, Richeard
326 Jefferson, Richeard
327 Green, Ezekiell
328 Morris, Dennis
329 Morris, John
329 Hudson, Charles
329 slave Cate
330 Hopkins, Robard
330 slave Toben
331 Jones, Ebenezear
332 Simples, Paul
333 Radeney, Willm.
334 Priteyman, Thos.
335 Wails, Thos., snr.
336 Hogg, James
337 Morrow, James
338 Turvill, Willm.
338 Tayler, Josiah
339 Farrill, Thos.
340 Roberson, Micheall
340 Roberson, Wm.
340 Roberson, Michell
341 Masey, Wm.
342 Knock, Nehemiah
342 slave Nan

1738 TAX LIST [Household number/Name/Remarks]

BALTIMORE/BOGERTERNORTON HUNDREDS

343 Showell, Samuel
343 Larthbery, George
344 Looker, Wm.
345 Masey, Alexander
345 slave Jack
346 Purkins, Thos.
347 Boden, John
348 Clark, Joseph
349 Delaney, Jon. Partrick
350 Fisher, Bentnett
351 Patey, John
351 Patey, Powell
351 slave London
352 Harney, Thos., sr.
352 Harney, Thos., junr.
353 Miller, John
353 slave Primes
353 slave Pegg
354 Rackliff, Charles, capt.
354 Rackliff, Purnell
354 Rackliff, John
354 slave Robin
354 slave Kate
354 slave Matt
354 slave Will
355 Rickards, Willm.
356 Hampton, Mary, madam
356 slave Haneh
356 slave Petter
356 slave Hanable
356 slave Jack
356 slave Pegg
357 Collings, John
358 Collings, Thos.
359 Gault, Robard
359 Gault, John
360 Holland, Richeard
360 Holland, Samuel
360 slave Hanah
361 Alford, David
362 Crapper, Nathanell, junr
363 Bradford, Natthanell
364 Crapper, Natthanell, sr.
364 Crapper, Vimson
364 Crapper, John
364 slave Kiner
365 Wallis, Thomas
365 Nugen, Thos.
366 Camell, John
367 Morgen, Averey
367 Bowls, Zachrias
367 slave Hanah

368 Holloway, John, jur.
368 Quilling, John
369 Coffen, Thos., sr.
369 Coffen, John
369 Coffen, Thos.
369 Godwin, Daniell
370 Roberson, John
370 Roberson, George
370 Roberson, Joseph
371 Smith, Ann
371 Smith, Jonas
371 Wilegoos, Richeard
372 Gray, William
373 Hudson, William
373 Gray, Wm.
374 Fassitt, John
374 Caldwell, Augsteen
374 slave Mary
374 slave Lewsy
375 Fassitt, Rouse
375 slave James
375 slave Fillice
376 Crapper, Edmund, jr.
377 Bowen, Rodey, wdow
377 Bowen, Wm.
377 Bowen, John
377 slave Comny
378 Quilling, Joseph
378 Quilling, Beniamin
379 Whealler, John
379 Whealler, John
380 Coller, Petter
380 slave Pompey
380 slave Moll
380 slave Sarah
381 Crapper, Edmund, sr.
381 Camell, Solomon
381 slave Petter
381 slave Pompe
381 slave Mary
381 slave Febe
381 slave Dick
382 Johnson, David
383 Bradford, William
384 Linch, Alexander
385 Tingle, Littilson
385 Mankline, Richeard
386 Clark, Edward
387 Tingle, Hugh, sr.
387 Tingle, Hugh, jur.
387 Tingle, Joseph
388 Rogers, Solomon
388 slave Caine
389 Woodcraft, Richeard
390 Woodcraft, William
390 Praker, William
390 Typpens, Robard

391 Dolbey, William
392 Clark, Race
392 Clark, John
392 Clark, Benjaman
393 Stevenson, John
394 Mumford, Willm.
395 Hazard, David, junr.
395 unnamed/slave
396 Morris, Beavins

BOGERTERNORTON HUNDRED

397 Rownd, Edward
397 Davis, Thos.
397 Lawrie, William
397 slave
398 Thomson, James
399 Bowen, Litleton
399 slave
400 Bushop, John
401 Hammond, Jacob
402 Ratclife, Charles
403 Edwards, Benony
403 Edwards, James
404 Bowen, William
405 Jones, George
406 Jarmin, John
406 Jarmin, William
406 slave
407 Jarmin, John, junr.
408 Bowen, John
409 Truit, George, accomack
409 Truit, George, junr.
409 2 slaves
410 Morris, William
411 Burbridge, John
412 Marchment, Charles
413 Purnell, Mathew
413 Pointer, William
413 slave
414 Lewis, William
415 Hammond, John
415 Bassit, James
416 Bassit, John
417 Hammond, Isaac
417 Hammond, William
418 Smachie, William
419 Dunkin, Thos.
420 Webb, Samll.
421 Hammond, Edward
422 Timmons, John
422 Timmons, Samll.
422 Timmons, Aron
423 Swain, William
424 Jarmin, Robert
425 Smith, William
426 Timmons, Thomas
427 Timmons, Samll.
428 Timmons, Aron
429 Timmons, Joseph

TAX LISTS OF SOMERSET COUNTY: 1730-1740

BOGERTERNORTON HUNDRED

430 Truit, George, son of Job
431 Truit, Nehemiah
432 Hodge, Robert
432 slave
433 Bradford, John
434 Jarmin, George
435 Penniewell, Charles
436 Loe, George
437 Conner, Patrick
438 Greer, Ursula
438 Greer, John
439 Simpson, William
439 Simpson, Thomas
439 4 slaves
440 Templin, John
440 Templin, John, junr.
441 Midsley, Thomas
441 Penniewell, William
442 Guy, James
443 Richards, William
444 Crapper, Nehemiah
445 Davis, Edward
446 Davis, Samuell
447 Tull, Benjamin
447 Dukes, Thomas
448 Tadlock, Agnes
448 Tadlock, Edward
449 Crapper, Rixam
450 Smith, John
451 Rownd, James
451 5 slaves
452 Heather, Ephraim
452 slave
453 Heather, Ephraim, junr.
453 Templin, Richard
454 Porter, James
455 Blizard, Richard
456 Hadder, Warren
456 Davis, George
457 Williams, Thomas Nathll.
457 Williams, Samll.
458 Jones, Joseph
458 Jones, John
459 Timmons, William
460 Bravard, Adam
460 slave
461 Gray, John
462 Ingoe, James
463 Handcok, William
464 Powel, Thomas
464 Crisines, Ricahrd
464 Laycock, John
464 Brown, John
465 Williams, Argelus

466 Powell, Rachel
466 Smock, John
467 Purnell, Kathrine
467 2 slaves
468 Purnell, Walton
469 Steel, William
470 Smock, Henry
471 Griffen, Oliver
472 Selby, Parker, senr.
473 Pointer, Thomas
473 Pointer, Ratcliffe
473 Pointer, Turvill
473 2 slaves
474 Fletcher, Thomas
474 4 slaves
475 Turner, Henry
476 Mumford, James
476 Mumford, James, junr.
477 Truit, George, son Geo.
477 slave
478 Truit, John, junr.
479 Parker, Tabitha
479 4 slaves
480 Parker, Samll.
481 Parker, Charles
482 Parker, Phillip
483 Murray, David
483 Ayres, Harrison
484 Jarmin, William
485 Shohannas, William
486 Causey, John, tax free
486 Kinnady, Nehemiah Simmon
487 Parker, George
488 Adkins, Stenton
488 Adkins, Stephen
489 Jarmin, Job
490 Taylor, Phillip
490 Taylor, Elias
490 Taylor, Edmund
491 Penniewell, John
492 Burbridge, Edward
493 Dennis, William, junr.
494 Truit, George, son Jams.
495 Truit, James
496 Dennis, Donnock
497 Collins, Mary
497 Collins, Thomas
498 Collins, William
499 Collins, John
500 Penniwell, George
501 Porter, John
502 Davis, Thomas

503 Davis, William, senr.
503 Davis, Samll.
504 Davis, Robert, senr.
504 Davis, William
504 Davis, Ishmael
504 Davis, Benjamin
504 Davis, Robert
505 Powell, Samll.
506 Evans, Gammage
506 Cobb, Joseph
507 Hampton, Mary, maddam
507 4 slaves
508 Gornwell, John
509 Tayler, William
510 Townsend, Jeremiah
510 3 slaves
511 Townsend, Brickhouse
512 Murray, Dunkin
512 Duett, Nathll.
512 Huett, George
512 5 slaves
513 Ryley, Thomas
514 Whaley, William
515 Nock, John
516 Burton, John
517 Greer, Adam
518 Franklin, Edward
518 Andrews, Peel
518 Coffin, Joseph
519 Franklin, William
520 Alexander, Paul
521 Evans, Elias
522 Harmon, Edward
522 Harmon, Zachariah
523 Collins, Thomas
524 Truit, James, son James
524 Walton, William
525 Dazey, John
526 Evans, John
526 Evans, William
526 slave
527 Beddard, Richard
528 Lay, John
528 slave
529 Lay, Samll.
530 Banum, Bartholemew
531 Pointer, Elias
531 Kellum, Isaac
532 Scofield, Joseph
532 Scofield, John
532 2 slaves
533 Purnell, Thomas
533 6 slaves
534 Gilleland, John
534 2 slaves
535 Baker, John
536 Abbot, John

1738 TAX LIST [Household number/Name/Remarks]

BOGERTERNORTON HUNDRED

537 Waters, Patrick
538 Becket, Peter
539 Mumford, Thomas
540 Tull, Richard
541 Peel, Thoroughgood
542 Porter, Joseph
542 slave
543 Harmon, William
544 Crapper, Ebenezar
544 Crapper, Edmund
545 Crapper, Ebenezar, junr.
546 Collins, Solomon
547 Hudson, Dennis
547 2 slaves
548 Hudson, Major
549 Gillet, John
550 Dennis, William, senr.
551 Brittingham, William
551 Brittingham, Absolam
551 Brittingham, Nathll.
552 Brittingham, William, junr.
553 Brittingham, Solomon
554 Brittingham, Jeremiah
555 Ennis, Samuell
556 Ennis, Cornelius
557 Ennis, John
558 Ennis, William
558 Ennis, William, junr.
558 slave
559 Webb, Grace
559 Webb, Elisha
560 Brittingham, Isaac
560 Brittingham, Nathan
560 slave
561 Pepper, John
561 Pepper, William
562 Greer, Archibald
562 Greer, John
563 Shockley, John
564 Stevens, Samuell
565 Davis, William, seaside
565 slave
566 Houlston, William
566 Houlston, Charles
567 Macaly, John
568 Stephenson, James
568 Stephenson, Adam
568 Stephenson, Samuell
569 Bratton, James
570 Godfrey, Charles
571 Mason, Edmund
572 Dreyden, John
573 Sturgiss, John
573 Sturgiss, Littleton
574 Steel, James
574 Steel, Daniel
575 Truit, Phillip
575 Dreyden, Samll.
576 Truit, George, son Phi.
577 Mumford, George
578 Truit, William
579 Mcneil, Archibald
580 Dennis, Solomon
581 Dennis, Daniel
582 Scott, Mark
583 Devrox, John
583 Devrox, Cornelius
584 Johnson, Affradozi
584 slave
585 Johnson, John
586 Johnson, George
587 Johnson, Thomas
588 Bell, Adam
588 2 slaves
589 Hall, William
589 Hall, Phenix
589 2 slaves
590 Bratten, Samuell, senr.
590 Bratten, Hugh
591 Bratten, Samuel, junr.
591 Bratten, William
592 Bratten, James, junr.
593 Stevenson, Samuel
594 Richardson, Charles
594 slave
595 Richardson, Robert
596 Richardson, James
597 Victor, James
598 Selby, William
598 Selby, William, junr.
598 Houlston, Benja.
598 4 slaves
599 Selby, John
599 3 slaves
600 Clawell, Thomas
600 Patrick, Daniel
601 Purnell, Elisha
601 3 slaves
602 Bushop, William
603 Bushop, Benjamin
604 Bushop, Joseph
605 Porter, William
606 Patrick, Roger
607 Adkins, John
608 Houlston, John
609 Outten, John
610 Outten, Thomas
611 Driggus, John
612 Buncle, Alexander
613 Stuart, Peter
613 free black Will
614 Chaillie, Moses
614 2 slaves
615 Wildman, John
615 Murray, Samuel
615 Ainsworth, Job
615 Betsworth, Thomas
616 Atkinson, John
617 Murray, John
618 Vestry, Michael
619 Green, James
620 Robieson, William
621 Wells, Daniel
622 Jarmin, Henry
623 Lane, George
624 Spence, Adam
624 Scott, William
624 5 slaves
625 Ewart, James
625 slave
626 Austin, Elizabeth
626 slave
627 Henderson, Charles
628 Lamberson, John
629 Morris, Joseph
630 White, John
630 slave
631 Tobin, John
632 Marshal, Isaac
632 Marshal, Jacob
632 4 slaves
633 Handcock, Daniel
633 Handcock, William
634 Hall, Robert
634 Hall, Spence
634 slave
635 Teague, John
636 Teague, John, junr.
637 Ennis, Nathll.
638 Ake, John
639 Bowen, Edward
640 Pointer, John
641 Truit, Joseph
642 Stevenson, Hugh
643 Crapper, John
644 Stevens, William
645 Hall, Adam
646 Turner, Nickolas
647 Lues, Joseph
648 Richardson, William
649 Raine, Mathew
649 Rain, John
650 Bridgwaters, Emanuel

TAX LISTS OF SOMERSET COUNTY: 1730-1740

BOGERTERNORTON/MANOKIN HUNDREDS

650 Bridgewaters, Isaac
651 Davis, Robert, jr., Ind. Town
652 Davis, William, son Wm.
653 Warren, Nickolas
654 Warren, Robert
654 Gray, Nickolas
655 Rathbone, Robert
656 Bethard, William
657 Hamilton, Willm.
658 Jones, Thomas
659 Lyndall, Peter
660 Jenkins, John
661 Sturgis, Joshua
661 Laws, Ellijah
661 Laws, Belitha
662 Dennis, Wheatly
663 Timmons, James
664 Holland, William
665 Williams, Jonathan
666 Tingle, Daniel

MANOKIN HUNDRED
667 Pope, James
668 Heath, Abrah.
668 Heath, Jno.
668 Heath, Mat.
668 slave Sambo
669 Layfeild, Thom.
669 Layfeild, Willm.
669 Layfeild, David
670 Polk, Wm.
670 Gray, Allen
670 slave Otten
670 slave Abner
670 slave Hanah
670 slave Pleasnt
671 Gray, Wm.
671 Goldsmith, Tho.
671 slave Venus
672 Polk, James
672 slave Ogg
673 Heath, Dorman
674 Owens, Jno., sr.
674 Owens, Jno., jr.
675 Dorman, Mich.
676 Dorman, Mat.
676 Dorman, Nehmih.
676 slave Jack
676 slave Doll
677 Dorman, Wm.
678 Dobbin, Wm.
678 Brown, Geo.
679 Wilson, And.
680 Reynolds, Henry
680 Pingally, Tho.
680 slave Dino
681 Connelly, Pat.

682 Jones, Wm.
682 slave Guy
682 slave Anthony
682 slave Eve
683 Anderson, Jame.
683 McCane, Geo.
683 Haly, Tim.
683 Wright, Nehm.
683 slave Cudgo
683 slave Pegg
684 Anderson, Jno.
685 Allason, Pat.
685 slave Lott
685 slave Pallas
686 Lindow, Marg.
686 slave Josha
686 slave Bess
687 King, Char.
688 Train, James
688 slave Jack
688 slave Will
688 slave Beck
689 Swift, Rich.
690 Carnes, Jno.
691 King, Whit.
691 slave Tony
691 slave Tom
691 slave Pacy
692 Hall, Mary
692 Fisher, Henry
692 slave Nan
693 Dayly, Pat.
694 Floyd, Jno.
695 Chambers, Rich.
695 Collins, Saml.
695 Brewerton, Rich.
696 Smith, Rob.
696 Smith, Thos.
697 Hayman, Will.
697 Hayman, Benj.
698 Long, Sol.
698 Kendall, Wm.
698 slave Nan
699 Furnish, Jams.
700 Mathews, Pat.
700 Mathews, Wm.
701 McClammy, Wony
701 slave Frank
701 slave Medera
702 Bolar, Elenor
702 Bolar, Wm.
702 Bolar, James
703 Collins, Wm.
704 Tindall, Jams.
705 Morow, Alexr.
706 Strawbridge, James
706 slave David
706 slave Cuffy
706 slave Dick
706 slave Hagar

706 slave Jinny
707 Brown, Terrill
707 Gullett, Geo.
708 Gray, Jno.
708 slave Hannah
709 Layfeild, Rob.
710 Harris, Phil.
710 Sphere, Henry
711 Sheperd, Martin
712 Knott, Isaac
713 Culberson, Wm.
714 Thompson, And.
714 slave Cesar
715 Holland, Isaac
715 slave Oppo
716 Deer, Rose
716 Kane, Jams.
716 Tilman, Benj.
717 Tilman, Jos.
717 slave London
718 Givans, Tho.
719 Givans, Ann
719 slave Pleasant
720 Givans, Cath.
720 Tilman, Wm.
721 Tilman, Aron
721 slave Jack
722 Niblet, Burnet
722 slave Cuffy
723 Horsey, Jno.
723 Fiddy, Rand.
723 slave Nick
724 Outerbridge, Sar.
724 slave Bess
724 slave Dino
725 Mitchell, Anne
725 Mitchell, Rand.
725 slave Sarah
726 Mitchel, Tho.
727 Lebrooce, Benj.
728 Mathews, Will.
729 Banister, Tho.
729 Fiddy, Tho.
729 slave Oston
730 Revell, Rand.
730 Bayly, Tho.
730 slave Toby
730 slave Mathew
731 Roach, Wm.
731 slave Kitt
731 slave Patience
732 Walston, Boss
732 Walston, Joy
733 Revell, Chas.
733 Revell, Rand.
733 slave Venus
734 Bosman, Wm.
734 slave Dasoo
734 slave Bess
735 Tunstall, Jno.

1738 TAX LIST [Household number/Name/Remarks]

MANOKIN HUNDRED

735 Lord, Tho.
735 Grigg, Wm.
735 slave Lowhill
735 slave Thomboy
735 slave Sibby
735 slave Dick
735 slave Pompey
735 slave Sippy
735 slave Bess
735 slave Ratchell
735 slave Sibb
735 slave Norish
735 slave Somersett
735 slave Thom
735 slave Will
735 slave Truman
735 slave Dino
735 slave Isbell
735 slave Rose
736 Kellett, Rodger, c.
736 slave Whitehaven
736 slave Judah
736 slave Hannah
737 King, Rob., coll. sr.
737 King, Neh.
737 King, Rob., jr.
737 Andrews, Jno.
737 Hog, Step.
737 slave Fortune
737 slave Joshua
737 slave Long Cesar
737 slave Short Cesar
737 slave Joe
737 slave Obed
737 slave Ebo
737 slave Mannery
737 slave Will
737 slave Betty
737 slave Juday
737 slave Dida
737 slave Nann
737 slave Dido, jr.
738 Ares, Jac.
738 Walston, Obed.
738 Layfeild, Tho.
739 Harris, Jno.
739 slave Jack
740 Wilson, David, cap.
740 McGregore, Dirag
740 slave Harry
740 slave Cudgo
740 slave Kent
740 slave Pompey
740 slave Robbin
740 slave Bristo
740 slave Holyday
740 slave Nanny

740 slave Rose
740 slave Lancaster
741 Wilson, Sam., c.
741 slave Peter
741 slave Mumuda
741 slave Will
741 slave Sampson
741 slave Thom
741 slave Hannah
741 slave Nanny
741 slave Bess
741 slave Sarah
742 Holt, Jno.
742 Whitington, Jos.
743 King, Capel
743 Kenny, Jno.
743 slave Paragate
743 slave Titus
743 slave Jack
743 slave Kate
743 slave Rose
744 Turpen, Wm., secunds.
744 slave Cuffy
744 slave Mingo
744 slave Toby
745 McCalpen, Rob.
746 Bedford, James
747 Davis, Jno.
748 Fountain, Mary
748 Wright, Wm.
748 slave Nanny
748 slave Harclus
749 Fountain, Nich.
749 Brown, Alex.
749 slave London
749 slave Tom
749 slave Charles
749 slave Marrum
750 Turpen, Wm., jr.
750 Barratt, Henry
750 slave Will
750 slave George
750 slave Moll
751 Turpen, Will., sr.
751 Turpen, Jno.
751 Turpen, Whit.
751 Tull, Tho.
751 slave Jack
751 slave Tom
751 slave Toby
751 slave Phillis
752 Willis, Barnaby
752 Dorman, Wilson
753 Hammon, Charl.
754 Miles, Wm., sr.
754 Miles, Wm., jr.
755 Maddox, Daniel
755 slave Addam
755 slave Sarah

756 Abbott, Jno.
757 Maddox, Tho.
757 Maddox, Jno.
757 slave Will
757 slave Cesar
758 Tull, Saml.
759 Maddox, Laz.
759 slave Cuffy
759 slave Joe
760 Miles, Saml.
760 slave Ben
760 slave Dick
761 Butler, Nath.
761 slave Sarah
762 Tull, Jos.
762 Tull, Rich.
763 Tull, Esther
763 Tull, Step.
763 slave Moll
764 Sharp, Ben.
764 Bryan, Tho.
765 Walston, Thom.
765 Walston, Henr.
766 Walston, Willm.
767 Ford, Absolom
768 Mutt, Jno.
769 McDanil, David
770 Davis, Jno.
771 Davis, Arthur
772 Thompson, Jos.
773 McDaniel, Owen
774 Ballard, Henry, cap.
774 Wilks, Jno.
774 Cambell, Jno.
774 slave Cesar
774 slave Ventur
774 slave Jinny
774 slave Bendoo
774 slave Marylunn
775 Law, James
775 Brandon, Charl.
776 Metely, James
777 McGraw, Rob.
778 Obryan, Rich.
779 Denwood, Thom.
779 slave Cudgo
779 slave Will
779 slave Sorraw
779 slave Grace
779 slave Tamar
780 Denwood, Geo.
780 slave Ned
780 slave Moll
781 Brown, Tho.
781 Brown, Dav.
781 slave Cudgo
781 slave Jack
781 slave Bess
781 slave Will
782 Staples, James

TAX LISTS OF SOMERSET COUNTY: 1730-1740

MANOKIN/MATTAPANY HUNDREDS

782 slave Ben
783 Wolford, John
783 White, Jno.
783 slave Sampson
783 slave Rose
783 slave Moll
783 slave Truman
784 Fritzgeralld, Peter
784 slave Thom
785 Roberson, James
785 Roberson, Jno.
785 slave Toby
785 slave Jack
785 slave Nero
785 slave Cesar
785 slave Prue
785 slave Dino
785 slave Sciss
785 slave Phillis
786 Bosman, Geor., sr.
786 Bosman, Geo., jr.
786 slave Frank
787 Gilly, Jos.
787 Umphries, Ezek.
787 Ewell, Jedida
787 Bozman, Hitt
787 Mayly, Jno.
787 slave Boston
787 slave Truman
787 slave Rose
788 Bosman, Wm., jr.
788 Cowen, Alex.
789 Bosman, Mary
789 slave Sambo
790 Jones, Wm., goose crk.
790 Macomb, George
790 slave Pompey
791 McClammy, Wm.
791 Cambell, Neh.
791 slave Negro
791 slave Juda
792 Fosky, Benj.
793 Burgun, Daniel
793 Burgen, Wm.
794 Elsey, Jno.
794 Ballard, Arnal
794 slave Cesar
794 slave Sambo
794 slave Jishmael
794 slave Betty
794 slave Nanny
794 slave Sibb
795 Elesy, Sarah
795 Elesey, Arnal
795 slave Ned
795 slave Jack
795 slave Nann
795 slave Belindo

795 slave Fendar
796 Martin, Tho.
797 Ballard, Jarvis
797 Ballard, Wm.
797 Ballard, Jervis
797 Ballard, Char.
797 slave Rose
797 slave Amy
798 Young, Jno.
798 Young, Will.
799 Phebus, Geo., sr.
799 Phebus, Jno.
799 Bose, Sam.
799 slave Into
800 Phebus, Geo., jr.
801 Rigsby, Lewis
801 Cornelus, Cohil
801 slave Fendo
802 Horner, Geo.
802 Horner, Metildo
802 Horner, Jno.
802 Horner, Arnal
803 Crowder, Francis
804 Clark, Alex.
805 Cinnigum, Thom.
806 West, Will.
807 Kelly, John
808 Wilson, Geo.
808 slave Isbell
808 slave Betty
809 Whitingham, Heb.
809 Cundall, Jno.
810 Deniston, Rob.
811 Wheler, Eliz.
811 Jenkins, Sam.
812 Bosman, John, sr.
812 Bosman, John
813 McDorman, William
814 Benston, Geo.
814 Jones, Geo.
814 Benston, Mathw.

MATTAPANY HUNDRED

815 Pope, John
815 Taylor, Jobe
815 5 slaves
816 Hill, Johnson
817 Johnson, John
818 Johnson, Peter
818 Johnson, Peter
819 Scott, Robt.
819 Scott, Adam
819 Scott, Robt.
819 Wood, John
820 Milburne, Thomas
821 Mallen, Christopher
822 Allen, John
823 Benett, Mary, widow
823 Lenzey, Jams
823 Bennett, Edward

824 Guttry, Pattrick
824 Guttry, Jams
824 Guttry, Calab
825 Maxfeild, Joseph
825 4 slaves
826 Hogson, Rolling
826 slave
827 Hogson, John, an object
827 Hogson, Rolling
828 Allen, Joseph
828 Allen, Moses
829 Wattson, Luke
830 Hill, Jacob
831 Hill, Abraham
832 Pain, John
832 Pain, Moses
833 Duberley, Thomas
833 Duberley, Wm.
834 Wattson, Robt.
834 Wattson, Charles
834 slave
835 Wattson, John
836 Sturgis, Richard
837 Walton, Stephen
837 Walton, Stephen
837 Williams, Thomas
838 Jones, John
839 Karey, Solomon
840 Holland, Benja.
840 slave
841 Cord, William
841 Cord, Arthur
841 Cord, John
841 slave
842 Holland, Nehemiah
842 Andrus, Shepard
843 Odewey, Thomas
844 Davis, Charles
845 Selbey, Parker
845 5 slaves
846 Aydlott, William
846 2 slaves
847 Chapman, Humphry
847 Waytt, Nathall.
848 Wattson, Peter
849 Henderson, Biship
849 Wattson, Jams
850 Newton, Starling
851 Newton, Thomas
851 Newton, Southy
852 Gugsing, Benja.
853 Turner, William
854 Tarr, Samll.
854 Newton, Jobe
854 Cornwill, John
855 Selbey, Philip
855 Selby, Mattw.
855 Selby, Daniel
855 Selby, Philip

1738 TAX LIST [Household number/Name/Remarks]

MATTAPANY/MONIE HUNDREDS

855 7 slaves
856 Sturgis, Daniell
856 Answorth, Peter
857 Tarr, Michell
857 Tarr, Michel
858 Hill, Robt.
859 Wimbrough, Paul
860 Robins, Bowdwine
860 5 slaves
861 Nealson, William
861 Nealson, John
861 Bratton, John
862 Bratton, William
862 Willson, William
862 slave
863 Booth, William
863 Agnefeilds, Wm.
864 Jackson, Wm.
865 Clayuell, Peter, senr.
865 Clayuell, Shadrick
865 3 slaves
866 Clayuell, Peter, junr.
867 Richardson, John
867 Richardson, Samll.
867 slave
868 Evens, John
869 Hopkins, Samll.
870 Scarbrough, John
870 Wise, Ezekiell
870 Holdom, John
870 2 slaves
871 Dure, William
872 Samons, Benja.
872 Harman, Gorge
873 Vezey, Charles
873 Vezey, Wm.
874 Slocomb, Thomas
875 Johnson, William
876 Brownbill, Nathaniell
877 Answorth, William
877 Taylor, John
878 Nealson, Jams
878 Newton, Thomas
879 Hargis, Thomas
880 Harman, Emanewell
880 Collett, Simon
881 Rusell, Cuthbud
881 Wattson, Uriah
882 Hudson, Jonathan
883 Ceary, Jeremiah
883 Voan, William
884 Hill, Hutten
884 Richardson, John
885 Hosiear, Samll.
886 Porter, McClintuck
887 Pluder, Joseph
888 Pepper, William

889 Pepper, Tobias
890 Chambers, Jeremiah
890 2 slaves
891 Porter, William
892 Wagaman, Jacob
892 Wagaman, Ephram
892 Price, Elias
892 2 slaves
893 Calburd, William
894 Bichbord, William
895 Reed, Waltor
896 Taylor, Rodger
897 Fisher, Baley
898 Wattson, Robt., junr.
899 Newton, Jonathan
900 Purnell, John
900 6 slaves
901 Hopkins, Nathaniell
901 slave
902 Hopkins, Matthew
902 Ayars, Richard
903 Slingo, Thomas
903 Slingo, Thos.
903 Slingo, John
904 Pilshear, Moses
905 Venettson, Willums
905 Venettson, Nathan
906 Pope, Gorge
906 slave
907 Pope, Samll.
907 slave
908 Gill, John
909 Hill, Elisha
910 Walton, Elizth., widow
910 Walton, William
910 2 slaves
911 Willett, Ambrus
911 Willett, Wm.
911 Willett, Thomas
912 Pinegaley, Thomas
913 Jones, William
914 Wise, Thomas
914 Mills, James
915 Hall, John
915 Hall, Stephen
916 Dreadin, John

MONIE HUNDRED

917 Gale, George, capt.
917 Maughorn, Christopher
917 slave Joe
917 slave Scippeo
917 slave Siple
917 slave Dominick
917 slave Jeamey
917 slave Jack
917 slave Limas

917 slave Janey
917 slave Boandah
917 slave Parthenah
917 slave Palinah
917 slave Nimrod
917 slave Nanny
917 slave Sarah
918 Jones, Daniell
918 Jones, Phillimon
918 Willcox, William
918 slave Whitehaven
918 slave Doll
919 Carey, Thomas
919 Crouch, Thomas
920 To Carey, Rachel
920 Crouch, David
921 Covington, John
921 Briarhood, William
921 Wright, Zebulon
921 slave Sambo
921 slave Cuckkooe
921 slave Jean
921 slave Betty
921 slave Bess
921 slave Diner
922 Dashiell, Thomas
922 slave Will
922 slave Jack
922 slave Harrey
922 slave Bess
922 slave Tamer
922 slave Sarah
923 Waller, George
923 Sauser, William
924 Polke, Joseph
925 Leatherbury, John
925 Leatherbury, John, jr.
925 Jones, William
925 slave Pompey
925 slave Sambo
925 slave Benn
925 slave Toney
925 slave Adin
925 slave Bridgett
925 slave Nanny
925 slave Nann
925 slave Rose
925 slave Bess
926 Covington, Thoms.
926 Duhigg, Walter
927 Dorman, John
927 Dorman, Zedekiah
928 Dutham, Thomas
929 Lawless, Jams.
930 Jones, Wm.
930 slave Will
930 slave Janey
930 slave Sue
930 slave Lewsey

TAX LISTS OF SOMERSET COUNTY: 1730-1740

MONIE/NANTICOKE HUNDREDS

931 Downs, Robert
931 slave Ned
931 slave Bristoll
931 slave Frank
932 Jones, Robert
932 Jones, Mitchell
932 Jones, Benja.
932 Welch, William
932 slave London
932 slave Armock
932 slave Jeane
932 slave Rachell
933 Irving, George
933 Irving, John
933 slave Tobee
933 slave Cuffee
933 slave Janey
933 slave Jane
934 Spicer, Phillip
935 Lockwood, Wm.
936 Laws, Robert
936 Laws, Panther
936 Laws, Wm.
936 Walliss, Robert
936 Walliss, George
936 slave Bubo
936 slave Jack
936 slave Sampson
937 Husk, John
938 Waller, John
938 slave Jane
939 Stoughton, Wm., esqr.
939 Larey, Timothy
939 slave Bussah
939 slave Simon
939 slave Jeamey
939 slave Sabinah
939 slave Sarah
940 Wright, Thomas
940 Wright, Henry
941 Elzey, John, jur.
942 Shores, John
942 Shores, John
942 Shores, William
942 slave Palinah
943 Robbards, John
943 Robberts, Thoms.
944 Roberts, Edward
944 slave Jeoffrey
944 slave Binah
945 Waller, Major
946 Jones, Saml.
947 Walliss, Richard
947 Walliss, James
947 slave Ceesar
948 Walliss, Mathew
948 Waller, William
948 slave Tomm
948 slave Sibb

949 White, John, senr.
949 White, John
950 Winsor, John
951 White, Francis
951 White, Jno.
951 White, Thomas
952 Martin, George
953 Williams, Jno.
954 McDorman, Darbey
955 Cantwell, Thoms.
956 Bazzell, Thoms.
957 Jones, Lewis
957 Jones, Lewis
957 slave Jack
957 slave Ceesar
957 slave Moll
958 Jones, George
958 slave Adam
959 Laws, John
959 slave Prince
959 slave Ceesar
960 Miller, Thos.
961 Twyfoot, William
962 Laws, Thos.
962 slave Murreah
963 Roe, Joseph
963 Rollins, Charles
964 Douglass, John
965 Roe, Thomas
965 Jones, Charles
965 Chambers, Samuell
966 To Roe, Eliza.
966 Roe, John
967 Winsor, Lazarus
967 Winsor, Lazarus
967 Winsor, Phillip
967 Winsor, James
968 Chain, Alexander
969 Austin, Robert
969 Hopkins, George
970 Magraugh, James
970 Kindall, Pat.
971 Jones, James
971 Griggs, Henry
971 slave Bussah
971 slave Sibb
971 slave Mole
971 slave Davey
972 Mungar, Mathew
973 Puckham, Richard
974 Mungarr, John
975 Newman, Henry
976 Magraugh, John
976 Austin, George
976 Hill, William
977 Walliss, Thoms.
977 slave Jean
978 Hobbs, Thos.
979 Hobbs, Marcillass
980 Hobbs, Joy

981 To Dorman, Margarett
981 Smith, John
982 Dorman, Henry
983 Crouch, Jacob
984 Luke, Williamson

NANTICOKE HUNDRED

985 McClester, John, mr.
985 McClester, Samuell
985 slave Coffee
985 slave Sambo
985 slave Tomm
985 slave Adam
985 slave Siss
985 slave Abbee
985 slave Dagoe
985 slave Toney
985 slave Rose
986 Walliss, David
987 To Samuells, Amy
987 slace Cocoe
988 Hopkins, John, point
989 Barklett, John
989 Barklett, Abraham
989 Steward, Charles
990 illegible, John
991 Walter, John
991 Woodlaly, Joseph
992 Rotten, William
992 Rotten, Hezekiah
993 Martin, John
994 Dashiell, Joseph
994 Dashiell, Mitchell
994 slave Randall
995 Buckler, Nicholas
996 Quatermus, James
996 Judonee, Roger
997 Richardson, John
998 Hopkins, Stephen
998 Hopkins, David
999 Read, John
999 Read, Obadiah
999 Read, Hezekiah
999 slave Murreah
1000 Messicks, Nehemiah
1001 Messicks, Jacob
1001 Messicks, Joshua
1002 Stewart, Alexander
1002 slave Batt
1002 slave Frank
1003 Dashiell, William
1003 slave Bess
1003 slave Sibb
1004 Bounds, Joseph
1004 Russell, Thomas
1005 Game, Fortune
1005 Game, Anvill
1006 Dashiell, Levin
1006 slave Joe
1007 Sirman, Thomas

1738 TAX LIST [Household number/Name/Remarks]

NANTICOKE HUNDRED

1008 Dashiell, William
1009 Townsend, Benjn.
1009 slave illegible
1010 Williams, Richard
1010 Williams, John
1011 Henderson, Robert
1012 Dashiell, Bridgett
1012 Dashiell, Jessee
1012 slave Robin
1012 slave Will
1012 slave Jack
1012 slave James
1013 Hopkins, John
1013 Richardson, Wm.
1014 Hopkins, John
1014 Hopkins, Roger
1014 slave Sue
1015 Messick, Benjamin
1016 Moore, William
1017 Hickman, Arthur
1018 Walter, Robert
1019 Walter, Daniell
1020 Hickman, William
1020 Hickman, Jonathan
1020 slave Jack
1020 slave Sambo
1020 slave Murreah
1020 slave Rose
1020 slave Judah
1021 Winright, Cannon
1021 slave Quake
1022 Collier, Robert
1022 Collier, Robert
1022 Collier, George
1022 slave Sarah
1023 To Beard, Rebecca
1023 Beard, Lewis
1024 Beard, John
1025 L[arrimo]re, Thomas
1025 Larrimore, James
1026 To Ellingsorth, Eliz.
1026 Ellingsworth, Nehemiah
1026 Ellingsworth, William
1027 Husk, Joseph
1028 Anderson, John
1029 Macome, Timothy
1030 Ritchie, Archibald
1031 Dashiell, George, junr.
1031 slave Scippio
1031 slave Coffee
1032 Dunn, Richard
1032 Dunn, Nicholas
1032 Dunn, Thomas
1033 Walliss, John
1033 Walliss, Thomas
1034 Browne, Sidney
1035 Edwards, John
1036 Taylor, Anthony
1037 Game, Robert
1038 Gale, John, capt.
1038 slave Messenger
1038 slave Gamey
1038 slave Sambo
1038 slave Sambo
1038 slave Bashee
1038 slave Galloway
1038 slave Obed
1038 slave Townsee
1038 slave Judah
1038 slave Rose
1038 slave Sabbee
1038 slave Moll
1038 slave Sibb
1039 Dashiell, Robert
1039 slave Cudjoe
1039 slave Workington
1039 slave Tamer
1040 Dashiell, Priscilla
1040 slave Harrey
1041 McClester, Joseph
1041 McClester, Neal
1041 Gloster, Elijah
1041 slave Sampson
1042 Roberts, Rancher
1042 slave York
1043 Fluellin, Samuell
1043 slave Scillass
1044 Larramore, John
1044 slave Jammey
1044 slave Sambo
1045 Dashiell, Henry
1045 slave Gift
1045 slave Sam
1046 Collins, John
1047 Dean, John
1048 Sirman, William
1048 Sirman, Isaac
1048 Sirman, William
1049 Records, Alexr.
1050 Moore, William, junr.
1051 Moore, John, senr.
1051 Moore, James
1052 Wright, Solomon
1053 Rhodes, Timothy
1054 Green, Richard
1054 Green, Ezekiell
1055 Messick, Jacob
1056 Paul, George
1057 To Meginne, Betty
1057 Dobidee, James
1058 Giles, William
1058 Giles, William
1058 slave Florah
1059 Giles, Thomas
1060 Jackson, Thomas
1061 Rider, Bathley
1062 Jackson, Jonathan
1062 Jackson, Joshua
1062 Jackson, Ezekiell
1062 Parriss, John
1063 Richardson, Wm.
1063 Richardson, Benjn.
1064 Rider, Willson
1065 Russell, James, senr.
1065 Russell, William
1066 Ralph, Thomas
1066 slave Sambo
1067 To Benston, Mary
1067 slave Will
1067 slave Bess
1068 Collier, Dowdey
1069 Tulley, James
1070 English, Wm.
1071 Langsda[le], Wm.
1072 Twilley, Robert
1073 Weatherley, James
1073 slave Pegg
1074 Beake, Isabell
1074 Beak, Isaac
1075 Ellingsworth, Robert
1076 Nichollson, James
1077 Nichollson, Richard
1078 Robertson, John
1079 Steward, Catherine
1079 slave Tomm
1080 Caldwell, James
1080 Givans, William
1080 slave Bob
1080 slave Rose
1080 slave Sambo
1080 slave Hannah
1081 Russell, James
1081 Sims, Archibald
1082 Jones, Finch
1083 Ackworth, Thomas
1083 Tulley, Benjamin
1083 slave Moll
1083 slave Will
1084 Ackworth, Charles
1084 Church, John
1085 Darbey, Waller
1085 Marsey, Joseph
1086 Dean, Charles
1086 Dean, James
1087 Hoofington, Thomas
1088 Hoofington, Richard
1089 Taylor, William
1090 Scott, Windom
1091 Olliver, George

TAX LISTS OF SOMERSET COUNTY: 1730-1740

NANTICOKE HUNDRED

1091 Morrison, Thomas
1092 Sheredine, William
1092 Sheredine, Ezekiell
1093 Wright, Solomon
1094 Cope, John
1094 Cope, William
1094 Cope, William
1095 Kibble, John
1096 Lord, Moses
1097 Mellson, Samuell
1097 Mellson, Samuell
1098 Hoofington, Jonathan
1098 Gloster, Thomas
1099 Cordery, David
1100 Hoofington, John
1100 slave Iago
1100 slave Jane
1100 slave York
1100 slave Pleasant
1101 Hoofington, John
1102 Kellum, Edward
1102 Kellum, John
1102 slave Robin
1102 slave Bess
1103 Hicks, William
1103 Carmicole, John
1104 Jarviss, Samuell
1105 Cooper, Gabriell
1106 Cooper, Thomas
1106 Langsdale, Spear
1107 Twilley, George
1108 Gravenor, Thomas
1109 Willson, John
1110 Gilliss, John
1110 Gilliss, Thomas
1111 Jarrett, William
1111 Jarrett, Comfort
1112 Gaskenew, Mathew
1112 Allphew, Joseph
1113 Tulley, Joseph
1113 Riggen, [Ambrose]
1114 Smith, Thomas
1114 slave Doll
1115 Bennitt, George
1116 Taylor, Abraham
1116 slave Squash
1117 Hitch, Solomon
1117 Hitch, Adam
1117 Hitch, Levin
1117 slave Cook
1118 Acworth, Henry
1118 slave Judah
1119 Acworth, Samuell
1119 slave Sue
1120 Nutter, Christopher
1120 Dawson, John

1120 slave Sezar
1120 slave Tomm
1120 slave Sippeo
1120 slave Jack
1120 slave Harrey
1120 slave Barbarey
1120 slave Rose
1121 Kemp, Matthew
1121 Kemp, John
1122 Parramore, James
1122 Parramore, William
1123 Cheeseman, John
1123 Hardey, Benjamin
1123 slave Nanney
1124 Spolding, Alliott
1125 Polk, John
1125 slave Attee
1125 slave Sibb
1126 Townsend, Solomon
1127 Waller, Thomas
1127 Waller, Richard
1127 Oliver, Thomas
1128 Callaway, John, senr.
1129 Godard, John
1129 Goddard, Nathaniell
1129 Booth, George
1130 Sirman, THomas
1131 Carter, Thomas
1132 Dolbey, Peter
1132 Dollbey, John
1133 Lynn, Aaron
1133 slave Abraham
1133 slave Jack
1133 slave Bess
1133 slave Jane
1133 slave Pegg
1134 Parsons, Francis
1135 Messick, John
1135 Messick, Obadiah
1136 Owens, Robert
1136 Knox, John
1136 slave Kate
1137 Jones, Samuell
1138 Manlove, Emanuell
1138 slave Quacoe
1139 Jones, John
1140 Nutter, Betty
1140 slave Phillip
1140 slave Benn
1140 slave Cato
1140 slave Rose
1140 slave Catherine
1141 Traine, James
1141 slave Robin
1141 slave Rose
1141 slave Marian
1142 Kemmey, Walter
1142 Fleetwood, John

1143 Daughters, William
1143 Daughters, Thomas
1144 Andrews, John
1145 Isaacs, John
1146 Windsor, Henry
1146 Winsor, James
1147 Phillips, Richard
1147 Phillips, William
1148 Collins, John
1149 Bradley, John
1150 Phillips, Thomas
1151 Knowles, Edmund
1151 Knowles, Richard
1151 Knowles, Edmund
1152 Jones, James
1153 Brown, William
1153 Carmicle, Thomas
1153 slave Rose
1154 Langford, Thomas
1155 Moore, John
1156 Walter, Henry
1156 Walter, William
1157 McDowell, John
1158 Fulton, William
1159 Collins, Edmund
1160 Ralph, William
1161 Parramore, Elizabeth
1161 Parramore, John
1162 Olifant, William
1162 Beadey, Cornelius
1163 Callaway, Peter
1163 Callaway, John
1164 Backworth, Charles
1165 Mitchell, Alexander
1166 Brown, Thomas
1167 Vaughn, William
1167 Bacon, Dudson
1168 Parramore, Thomas
1169 McClanin, Joseph
1170 Culver, John
1171 Hardey, John
1172 Carter, Samuell
1173 Spear, Henry
1174 Spear, Robert
1175 Waller, Thomas
1176 Walliss, Richard
1176 slave Hagar
1177 McCluer, Robert
1178 Henrey, John
1178 Henrey, Hugh
1179 Lowe, Ralph
1179 Lowe, John
1180 Walliss, Richard
1180 Dawe, Henry
1181 Robertson, William
1182 Kinnig[am], Daniell
1183 Skilley, Daniell
1184 Floyd, Major
1185 Carter, Charles

1738 TAX LIST [Household number/Name/Remarks]

NANTICOKE HUNDRED

1186 Moore, William
1187 Greer, William
1188 Vance, Thomas
1189 Godard, Thomas
1189 Goddard, John
1189 Godard, Thomas
1190 Givans, John
1191 Ellingsworth, Richard
1192 Shiles, Edmund
1193 Beavins, Caleb
1194 Smith, David
1194 Beavins, John
1195 Tulley, Stephen
1195 Tulley, Joshua
1196 Tulley, Benjamin
1197 Moore, William
1197 Moore, Thomas
1198 Bennitt, Edward
1198 Bennitt, John
1199 Twyford, John
1200 Shiles, Thomas
1201 Johnson, David
1201 Murptey, James
1202 Phillips, John
1203 Smith, Thomas
1204 Cooper, Isaac
1205 Marsey, William
1206 Stilley, Mary
1206 Stilley, John
1207 Collins, Thomas
1207 Marsey, James
1208 Wiley, Jarred
1209 Moore, John, forrest
1210 James, John
1211 Rhodes, John
1212 Owten, John
1213 Callaway, Peter, jr.
1214 Thompson, George
1215 Callaway, John
1216 Bowlins, Thomas
1217 Callaway, John
1218 Callaway, Edward
1219 Parramore, Mathew
1219 Parramore, Ezekiell
1219 Parramore, Mathew
1220 Walter, Thomas
1221 Tindall, Charles
1222 Boyce, Daniell
1222 slave Tom
1222 slave Bess
1223 Boyce, John
1224 Godard, George
1225 Poke, John
1226 Wootten, Edward
1227 Cooper, James
1228 Benston, William
1229 Hosea, Mathew
1230 Stevens, John
1231 Waller, Nathaniell
1231 Waller, John
1232 Callaway, William
1232 Callaway, Benjamin
1233 To Fullton, Nicholas
1233 Fullton, John
1234 Records, John
1235 Phipps, John
1236 Johnson, Simon
1237 Owens, Peter
1238 Johnson, Thomas
1239 Houston, John
1240 Parsons, Charles
1241 Carter, William
1242 To Anderson, Mary
1242 Anderson, John
1243 Cottman, Ebenezer
1243 Cottman, William
1244 Dashiell, Mitchell
1244 Nicholson, George
1244 Marwell, Thomas
1244 slave Bamer
1244 slave Tobey
1244 slave Venus
1245 Langford, John
1245 Langford, Edward
1246 Langford, John
1247 Gastineau, George
1248 Nutter, Huett
1248 slave Mingo
1248 slave Tite
1249 Givans, Robert
1249 Givans, George
1249 slave Ceesar
1249 slave Charles
1249 slave Hannah
1250 Givans, James
1250 slave Frank
1251 Givans, John
1252 Rhodes, Daniell
1252 Acworth, Thomas
1253 West, James
1254 Cooper, Samuell
1255 To Weatherley, Charity
1255 Weatherley, William
1255 Weatherley, Joseph
1255 slave Levania
1256 Henry, Robert
1257 Williams, John
1258 Edge, Robert
1259 Edge, Joshua
1260 Puckam, Abraham
1261 Hardey, James
1261 Bradley, William
1261 slave Jane
1261 slave Sambo
1262 Farrington, William
1262 Austin, William
1263 Jones, William
1264 Hickman, Henry
1265 Killbey, John
1266 Oneall, John
1267 Samuells, Richard
1268 Hopkins, Daniell
1269 Robinett, Samuell
1270 Shortt, Edward
1270 Shortt, Abraham
1271 Mitchell, Richard
1272 Caldwell, Patrick
1273 Smith, John
1274 Bounds, Jacob
1275 Noble, John
1276 Baker, William
1277 Benston, Henry
1277 Benston, Mathew
1278 Sirman, Jobe
1279 Sirman, Peter
1280 Ing[rom], Robert
1281 Wa[lliss], Charles
1282 Sharp, John
1282 Sharp, William
1282 Sharp, John
1282 slave Nancey
1283 Phillips, John
1283 slave Mingo
1284 Short, John
1285 Mitchell, John
1286 King, Phillip
1287 Tatman, James
1288 Chipman, Parriss
1288 Bass, John
1288 slave Kate
1289 Willey, John
1289 slave Carsey
1290 Newbold, Francis
1290 slave Amey
1291 Parramore, Joseph
1292 Harvey, John
1293 Miles, Edward
1294 Downs, Robert
1295 Tomerline, Thomas
1296 King, William
1297 Parramore, James
1298 Houston, Robert
1299 Caldwell, John
1299 Caldwell, Robert
1299 slave Samuell
1299 slave George
1299 slave Henry
1299 slave Samboe
1300 Kenney, William
1301 Sumerlin, William
1302 Noble, Isaac
1303 Mellson, Joseph
1304 Mellson, Benjamin

TAX LISTS OF SOMERSET COUNTY: 1730-1740

NANTICOKE/POCOMOKE HUNDREDS

1305 Taylor, John
1306 Shockley, David
1306 Shockley, James
1307 Wright, Edward
1308 Wingate, Phillip
1308 Tatom, James
1308 slave Amey
1309 Potter, Josephus
1310 Hall, John
1311 Taylor, John
1311 Taylor, William
1312 Waller, Nellson
1313 Clifton, George
1313 Clifton, George
1313 Clifton, Thomas
1313 Clifton, Nehemiah
1313 Clifton, John
1314 Gray, William
1314 slave Coffee
1315 Lord, John
1316 Collins, Andrew
1316 slave Amey
1317 Newbank, Molton
1318 Langsdale, John
1318 Smith, James
1319 Felnellson, Elias
1320 Smith, Henry
1321 Ingrom, David
1322 Ingrom, Isaac
1323 Ingrom, Abraham
1323 Ingrom, Abraham
1323 Ingrom, James
1323 slave Priscilla
1323 slave George
1324 Polke, Charles
1325 Polke, Ephraim
1326 Hall, James
1327 Callaway, William, jr.
1328 Waller, Nathaniell, jr.
1329 Bowcher, James
1330 Winright, William
1331 Caldwell, Thomas
1332 Goslin, James
1333 Tulley, Stephen
1333 Tulley, Richard
1334 Collins, Thomas
1335 Jones, John
1336 Vincent, James
1337 C[ar]ter, John
1338 Oneall, James
1339 Messick, George
1340 Blewer, James
1340 slave Shero
1340 slave Judah
1341 Ainge, Francis
1342 Read, John, junr.
1342 Read, Zachariah
1342 slave Murreah

1343 Scott, George
1344 Mezick, Isaac
1345 Marvill, Thos.
1345 unnamed/slave
1346 Austin, Wm.
1347 Adams, Thos.
1348 Fisher, George
1349 Jones, Thos., point
1349 unnamed/slave
1350 Kennigan, Arthr.
1351 Powell, John
1352 Thorns, Alexr.

POCOMOKE HUNDRED
1353 Hayward, Thomas, mr.
1353 slave Sambo
1353 slave Sinnicho
1353 slave Jesper
1353 slave Tomm
1353 slave Cudjo
1353 slave Priss
1353 slave Rose
1353 slave Philliss
1353 slave Pleasant
1354 Denniss, John, mr. junr.
1354 slave Kingstone
1354 slave Jack
1354 slave Isaac
1354 slave George
1354 slave Patience
1354 slave Kate
1355 Probart, William, capt.
1356 Mitchell, Robert
1356 Mitchell, Joshua
1356 slave Townside
1356 slave Selbey
1357 Goddes, Robert
1357 slave Tom
1357 slave Pheebe
1358 Goore, Richard
1359 Handey, Elizabeth
1359 Handy, Thomas
1359 Handy, Stephen
1359 slave Harrey
1359 slave Judah
1359 slave Hagar
1360 Mills, William
1360 Mills, Samuell
1361 Mills, Jonathan
1362 Tull, George
1362 Tull, Jonathan
1362 slave Abner
1363 Tull, Noble
1364 Pilcher, John
1365 Pilcher, William
1366 Costin, Stephen

1366 Costin, Mathias
1366 slave Philliss
1367 Odeare, Stephen
1368 Costin, Isaac
1368 slave Coffee
1368 slave Andrew
1368 slave Pegg
1368 slave Jone
1368 slave Hannah
1368 slave Moll
1369 Stevens, William
1369 Clark, Thomas
1370 Dorman, Samuell, senr.
1370 Dorman, Samuell, junr.
1371 Stevens, Edward
1372 Cluff, Edward
1373 Paden, John
1373 Hall, John
1373 slave [Oxford]
1374 Dredon, David, junr.
1375 Broughton, Bruff
1375 Landen, John
1376 Broughton, John
1376 Broughton, Wm.
1377 Tillman, Giddion
1377 Maddux, Alexander
1377 Tillman, John
1377 slave Pompey
1378 Benston, George
1378 Benston, John, junr.
1379 Clogg, Samuell
1380 Perkins, John
1380 Perkins, Michaell
1381 Newbold, Thomas
1381 Brittingham, Elija
1381 Newbold, Purnall
1381 slave Patience
1382 Dredon, David, senr.
1382 Dredon, William
1382 Woods, David
1382 Thomson, John
1383 Hampton, Mary, madam
1383 Henry, Robert Jenckins
1383 Henry, John
1383 slave Tamill
1383 slave Chick
1383 slave Harry
1383 slave George Harrey
1383 slave Ceesar
1383 slave Adam
1383 slave Jeaney
1383 slave Lewsey
1383 slave Philliss

1738 TAX LIST [Household number/Name/Remarks]

POCOMOKE HUNDRED

1383 slave Patience
1384 Williams, John, mr.
1384 Venellson, Elisha
1384 slave illeg
1384 slave Harrey
1384 slave Robin
1384 slave Nimrod
1384 slave Pheenix
1384 slave Janey
1384 slave Sue
1384 slave Priss
1385 Tomlinson, Solomon
1385 slave London
1386 Peacock, Edward
1386 Peacock, John
1387 Schofield, Henry
1388 Fenton, Margarett
1388 Blair, Robert
1389 Benston, Thomas
1390 Powell, John
1390 Butler, Manewell
1390 slave Sarah
1391 Brooks, Richard
1391 slave Lett
1392 Powell, Levin
1393 Tomlinson, Saward
1393 slave Jonas Hodsson
1393 slave Pleasant
1394 Curvine, Thomas
1395 White, Archibald
1395 White, William
1396 White, John, poco.
1396 slave George
1396 slave Patience
1396 slave Nann
1397 Hall, John
1398 McCreddie, Alexander
1398 McCreddie, Solomon
1399 Nairne, Robert
1399 slave Toney
1399 slave Sarah
1399 slave Nanny
1399 slave Madge
1400 Nairn, James
1400 slave Harrey
1400 slave Will
1400 slave Moll
1401 Addams, Collings
1402 Dickerson, Isaac
1402 McCreddie, Alexander
1403 C[ollings], [Sam]uell
1404 illegible

1404 slave Tomm
1404 slave Darkis
1405 Millbourn, John
1406 Millbourn, Caleb
1406 slave Mingo
1406 slave Hannah
1407 Millbourn, Ralph
1408 Clifton, John
1409 Evans, Thomas
1409 Evans, William
1409 slave Janey
1410 Evans, John
1411 Benston, Benjamin
1412 Buyer, Robert
1412 Byer, Jonathan
1412 slave Harrey
1413 Merchant, Benjamin
1413 slave Adam
1414 Elliss, John
1415 Ruark, Edward
1416 Dickerson, Teague
1417 Caldwell, Joshua, capt.
1417 Hubbard, Richard
1417 Toadvine, John
1417 slave Addam
1417 slave Dinah
1417 slave Moll
1418 Cox, William
1418 slave Ceesar
1418 slave Doll
1419 Riggen, John, junr.
1419 slave Nann
1420 Dickerson, Charles
1420 Dickerson, John
1421 Riggen, Solomon
1422 Riggen, Charles
1422 Walltor, Cornelious
1422 slave Toney
1423 Riggen, John, senr.
1423 Riggen, John
1423 Riggen, Teague
1423 Riggen, Cornelius
1423 slave Janey
1424 Mathews, Teague
1425 Mathews, John
1426 Mathews, William
1427 Mathews, Samuell
1428 To Mathews, Mary
1428 Mathews, David
1428 slave Ceesar
1429 Adams, Samuell
1429 Adams, Jacob
1429 slave Janey
1430 Addams, Jacob
1430 Addams, Thomas
1430 Moore, Joseph

1430 slave Sampson
1430 slave Nann
1431 Kearsey, William
1431 Cottingham, John
1431 Cottingham, Willm.
1432 Kearsey, Samuell
1433 Boston, Isaac
1433 slave Tom
1433 slave Venus
1433 slave Jeoffrey
1434 Boston, Esau
1434 Boston, Esau, jr.
1435 Taylor, Robert
1435 Taylor, Robert, jr.
1436 Taylor, Elias
1437 Wood, William
1438 Addams, Isaac
1438 slave Dick
1438 slave Moll
1439 Owen, Moses
1439 slave Harrey
1440 Dikes, Edward
1440 Dikes, Daniell
1441 Adams, Hope
1442 [Adams], Phillip
1443 [Adams, George]
1443 Adams, George, jr.
1444 Adams, William, junr.
1445 Adams, William, senr.
1445 Adams, Phillip
1446 Daviss, Beachamp
1447 Beachamp, Marsey
1447 Beachamp, John
1448 Beachamp, Thomas
1449 Beachamp, Edward
1449 Beachamp, Levin
1449 slave Morey
1450 Porter, McKemmey
1450 Tull, James
1451 Gibbs, Abraham
1452 Allen, Francis, esqr.
1452 slave Frank
1452 slave Judah
1452 slave Margory
1452 slave Merear
1453 Atkinson, Angolo
1453 Ballance, Thomas
1454 Townsend, Charles
1454 Townsend, Solomon
1455 Scott, John, capt.
1455 slave Peter
1455 slave Mokey
1455 slave Rose
1455 slave Pheelace
1455 slave Hager
1455 slave Hogoe
1456 Porter, Francis

TAX LISTS OF SOMERSET COUNTY: 1730-1740

POCOMOKE HUNDRED

1456 slave Jack
1456 slave Sausiey
1456 slave Flora
1457 Townsend, Saul
1457 Warrington, Benjamin
1457 slave Will
1458 Beavins, Thomas
1459 Sheldon, John
1459 Obryan, Daniell
1459 slave Isaac
1460 Bennitt, William
1460 Kearsey, Robert
1460 Powell, Gabriell
1461 Townsend, James
1461 slave Guy
1461 slave Jack
1462 Taylor, Peter
1462 slave Cupid
1462 slave Jack
1462 slave Cork
1462 slave Fungee
1462 slave Pleasant
1462 slave Tomm
1463 Peall, Thomas
1463 Peall, Thomas, junr.
1463 slave Sampson
1464 Beavins, Roland
1464 Beavins, Wm.
1465 Beavins, Cornelius
1466 McAllen, Arthur
1467 Townsend, Wm. Bartley
1467 slave Abraham
1468 Andrews, John
1468 Andrews, Roberson
1469 Cottingham, Jonathan
1469 Cottingham, William
1469 Cottingham, Jno.
1470 Anderson, Mary
1470 Ottwell, Francis
1471 Donohoe, Sarah
1471 Donohoe, Daniell
1471 Donohoe, Teague
1471 Donohoe, John
1471 Donohoe, Dorman
1472 Dickerson, Cornelius
1472 slave Dinah
1472 slave Janey
1473 Townsend, Daniell
1473 Townsend, Dickerson
1473 Townsend, James
1473 slave Pegg
1474 Fogg, Moses
1475 Donohoe, Dorman
1475 --per, Samuel
1476 Dickerson, Edmond, jr.
1476 Townsend, Nathl.
1477 Dickerson, Edmond, senr.
1477 slave George
1478 Dickerson, Charles
1479 Mayo, Samuell
1480 Townsend, John
1480 Townsend, John, junr.
1480 Townsend, Marshall
1481 Lane, John
1482 Flemming, John
1482 slave Robin
1482 slave Pompey
1482 slave Joe
1482 slave Dinah
1482 slave Nann
1483 McCuddey, John
1483 Millbourne, Ralph
1484 Riggen, Darbey
1484 Riggen, John
1484 Riggen, Pearce
1484 Riggen, Teague
1485 Ottwell, Francis
1485 Ottwell, Solomon
1486 Ottwell, Charles
1487 Colebourn, John
1487 Colebourn, Wm.
1488 Townsend, Danford
1489 Wonnell, James
1489 Reading, Charles
1490 Harper, Francis
1491 Denston, John
1491 Denston, John, junr.
1491 Denston, Isaac
1492 Dukes, William
1492 Dukes, John
1493 Phillips, John
1493 Phillips, Ezekell
1494 Riggen, Joseph
1494 slave Ceesar
1495 Stutt, Archibald
1496 Gullett, Abraham
1497 Smulling, Randall
1497 Smulling, Nathaniell
1497 Smulling, Randall
1497 Smulling, William
1497 Magraine, John
1498 Ward, Joseph
1498 Ward, Cornelius
1498 Ward, Joseph, junr.
1498 slave Sarah
1499 Riggen, Ambrose, senr.
1499 Riggen, Teague
1500 Riggen, Teague
1500 Riggen, Teague, jr.
1500 slave Peter
1500 slave Nann
1501 Warwick, Arthur
1502 Flemming, Wm.
1503 Harriss, Robert
1503 slave Harrey
1503 slave Moll
1503 slave Toney
1503 slave Mingoe
1504 Harper, Edward
1504 Harper, John
1505 Harriss, Caleb
1505 Smith, John
1506 Taylor, Jacob
1507 Hadduck, Ignatius
1508 Harriss, Jeremiah
1509 Knight, Richard
1509 Knight, James
1509 slave Boatswain
1510 Harriss, John
1510 Harriss, Benton
1510 slave Tom
1511 Tull, John
1512 Atkinson, Samuell
1513 Atkinson, Joshua
1513 Evans, William
1513 Daviss, John
1513 slave T---
1513 slave Bess
1514 Atkinson, Isaac
1515 Buttler, Thomas
1516 Taylor, Samuell, senr.
1516 Taylor, George
1517 Taylor, Samuell, junr.
1518 Warrington, Thomas
1519 Jones, William
1520 Fountain, Nicholas
1521 Noble, James
1522 Wright, Randall
1523 Stevens, John
1524 Riggen, Ambrose, jr.
1525 Diar, John
1526 Ruark, John
1527 Crouch, Isaac
1528 Bell, John
1529 Kellum, John
1530 Townsend, Jeremiah
1531 Martin, James, capt.
1531 slave Pompey
1531 slave Mark
1531 slave Joe

1738 TAX LIST [Household number/Name/Remarks]

POCOMOKE HUNDRED

1531 slave Ceesar
1531 slave Nann
1532 To Whittington, Southy
1532 slave Ceasar
1533 Daviss, Nathaniell
1533 Daviss, Nathal., jr.
1533 Dukes, Robert
1534 Kitchen, William
1534 slave Bess
1535 Ball, Samuell
1536 White, Hannah
1536 White, John
1536 White, Wm.
1537 Selbey, Thomas
1537 Selbey, Thomas
1537 slave Sam
1538 Bennitt, John
1539 Johnson, Whittington
1539 Oldindman, John
1539 slave Betty
1539 slave Pleasant
1540 Nicholls, James
1540 slave Hannah
1541 Gurley, George
1542 Nicholls, Mathias
1543 Nicholls, Joseph
1543 Taylor, Mathias
1544 Beavins, John
1544 Beavins, Thomas
1544 Beavins, Rowland
1544 slave Sambo
1545 Beavins, Joshua
1546 Kellum, Joshua
1547 Breeman, James
1547 slave Tollomie
1548 Layfeild, George
1549 Blades, Benja.
1549 McFarline, Robert
1550 Whittington, William
1550 Whittington, Southy
1550 slave Southy's Robin
1550 slave Frank
1550 slave Abner
1550 slave Harrey
1550 slave Betty
1550 slave Bub
1550 slave Sarah
1550 slave Hannah
1551 Taylor, William
1551 Taylor, James
1552 Daviss, Joseph
1553 Laws, William
1554 McDaniell, James

1554 McDaniell, John
1554 Victor, Thomas
1555 Houston, Joseph, sr.
1555 Kellum, William
1555 slave Tom
1555 slave Bell
1556 Godfrey, Joseph
1557 Brumbley, Thomas
1558 Glass, Christopher, junr
1559 Glass, Christopher, sr.
1559 Glass, Elias
1559 slave Frank
1560 Sherrie, Job
1560 Murfey, John
1560 slave William
1560 slave Pompey
1560 slave Effey
1560 slave Janney
1561 Denniss, Valentine
1562 Denniss, John, senr.
1562 Denniss, Lazarus
1562 slave Joe
1563 Small, John
1563 Blades, Robert
1564 Henderson, John, jr.
1564 Henderson, John
1564 Henderson, Samuell
1565 Hough, Edmond
1565 slave Will
1565 slave Titus
1565 slave Scipio
1566 Sturgiss, Jonathan
1567 Prier, Webb
1568 Laws, John
1568 slave Tom
1569 Owten, Abraham
1569 Steene, James
1569 Odeare, John
1570 Morriss, Isaac
1570 slave Southey
1570 slave Benn
1570 slave Will Farmer
1570 slave Abner
1570 slave Sam
1570 slave Dinah
1571 Townsend, Littleton
1571 AllChurch, William
1572 Mellvin, Robert
1572 Mellvin, Robert
1573 Wheeler, Isaac
1573 Wheeler, Wm.
1573 slave Joe
1574 Mills, Moses
1574 slave Simon

1575 Maglaughlin, Charles
1576 Webb, John
1576 Webb, Solomon
1576 Webb, John, jr.
1576 Cook, Guy
1577 Paine, Joseph
1578 To Lindow, Margarett
1578 slave Moses
1579 Melvin, William
1580 Henderson, Jno., senr.
1580 slave Guy
1580 slave George
1580 slave Betts
1580 slave Jone
1580 slave Eve
1581 Henderson, Charles
1582 Lane, Wm., capt.
1582 slave Harrey
1582 slave Dick
1582 slave Quashabee
1582 slave Philliss
1583 Moses, Joseph
1584 Burnott, James
1585 Conner, William
1586 Mellton, John
1587 Brooks, Francis
1587 Brooks, Henry
1588 Jones, Edward
1588 Jones, Elisha
1589 Elliss, William
1590 Mills, Samuell
1590 Mills, Nathaniel
1590 Mills, Hugh
1590 Mills, John
1591 Mills, Smith
1592 Mills, Robert
1593 Mills, William, junr.
1593 Mills, Nathan
1593 Mills, Alexander
1594 Gillett, Samuell
1594 Weight, Joseph
1594 Gillett, William
1594 Gillett, Samuell, jr.
1594 slave Darkiss
1595 Gillett, John
1595 slave Harrey
1595 slave Nanny
1595 slave Rose
1596 Stephenson, Joseph
1596 Stephenson, William
1597 Piper, Isaac
1597 Whaley, John
1598 Stephenson, Robert
1599 Henderson, Jams.
1599 Henderson, John

TAX LISTS OF SOMERSET COUNTY: 1730-1740

POCOMOKE/WICOMICO HUNDREDS

1599 slave Adam
1600 Lambden, Thos.
1601 Henderson, Francis
1602 Henderson, Benjamin
1603 Lamberson, Abraham, [jun
1603 Lamberson, Samuell
1604 Ramsey, Charles
1604 Ramsey, John
1604 Ramsey, Barnett
1605 Merrill, John
1606 Hutton, John Booth
1607 Quinton, Phillip
1607 slave Jack
1607 slave Peter
1607 slave Tamer
1608 Quinton, Dixon
1609 Brittingham, Samuell
1610 Lindall, Robert
1611 Lamberson, Robert
1612 Dickerson, Eliza.
1612 Dickerson, Robert
1612 Dickerson, Francis
1612 Dickerson, Nehemiah
1613 Houston, James
1613 slave Kate
1614 Houston, Joseph, junr.
1614 slave Harrey
1614 slave Bess
1615 Dickerson, Peter
1615 slave Jack
1616 Brittingham, John, junr.
1617 Brittingham, William
1617 slave Rose
1618 Houston, John, senr.
1619 Brittingham, Thomas
1620 Brittingham, John, senr.
1620 slave Ceasar
1620 slave Nann
1621 Baker, James
1621 Hutcheson, James
1621 Wright, Comfort
1622 Young, Daniell
1623 Blades, John
1624 Newton, John
1625 Merrill, Joshua

WICOMICO HUNDRED
1626 Gale, Levin, coll.
1626 Noble, Mark
1626 Keeble, Thos.
1626 Fowler, Thos.
1626 Smith, Henry, capt.
1626 North, John
1626 slave Hope
1626 slave Jacob
1626 slave Jehue
1626 slave Robbin
1626 slave Jobe
1626 slave Will
1626 slave Jack
1626 slave Jamy
1626 slave Harry
1626 slave Franck
1626 slave Peter
1626 slave Ishmael
1626 slave Dick
1626 slave Harry
1626 slave Joyce
1626 slave Pullert
1626 slave Bess
1626 slave Ziporah
1626 slave Moreah
1626 slave Hannah
1627 Dashiell, George, col.
1627 White, Francis
1627 Emerson, Charles
1627 slave Pollie
1627 slave Nann
1627 slave Sam
1627 slave Franck
1627 slave Jane
1627 slave Dublin
1627 slave Sambo
1627 slave Robbin
1627 slave Young Sambo
1627 slave Harry
1627 slave Joe
1627 slave Benn
1627 slave Coffee
1627 slave Nell
1627 slave Cate
1627 slave Rose
1627 slave Saray
1627 slave Rose
1628 Mears, John
1628 Mears, Saml.
1629 Lackey, Alexr.
1629 Chambers, Saml.
1629 slave Tobey
1629 slave Sam
1629 slave Surrey
1629 slave Frank
1629 slave Robbin
1629 slave Sibb

1629 slave Amey
1629 slave Beck
1629 slave Grace
1630 Evans, John, senr.
1630 Evans, John, junr.
1630 slave Sambo
1631 Dashiell, Charles
1631 slave Jacob
1631 slave Pelinah
1632 Winwright, Stephen
1632 Winwright, John
1633 Willen, Edwd.
1633 slave Quoh
1634 Willen, Thos., senr.
1634 Willen, Robt.
1634 Willen, Thos., junr.
1634 slave Sarah
1634 slave Guimer
1635 Fowler, Thos.
1635 slave Moll
1636 Lowes, Henry
1636 slave Jepthah
1636 slave Dover
1636 slave Joe
1636 slave Five Islands
1636 slave Quomina
1636 slave Rose
1636 slave Bess
1637 Carey, Levin
1637 Talbott, John
1638 Hobbs, Absolom
1638 Stevens, Isaac
1638 slave Pollipus
1639 Malone, Robt.
1640 Parsons, John
1641 Macklanikin, Danl.
1641 Mitchell, John
1642 Hall, Phenix
1642 Taylor, James
1643 Standford, Joseph
1644 Vance, David
1644 Brown, Andrew
1645 Hayman, Charles, senr.
1646 Hayman, James
1646 Hayman, Isaac
1647 Hayman, John
1648 Hayman, Charles, junr.
1649 Raglin, Michl.
1650 Griffin, John
1651 Adley, William, senr.
1651 Adley, William, junr.
1652 Adkins, Robt.
1653 Hailes, John
1654 Shehorn, John

1738 TAX LIST [Household number/Name/Remarks]

WICOMICO HUNDRED

1655 Toadvine, Henry
1655 Toadvine, Joshua
1655 Savage, Wm.
1655 slave Goliah
1655 slave Oxford
1655 slave Sarah
1655 slave Jenney
1656 Fooks, Benjn.
1656 Fooks, William
1656 slave Patience
1657 Revill, Wm.
1657 slave Tom
1658 Furbish, Peter
1659 Neilson, William
1659 Neilson, John
1660 Everton, John
1660 Everton, Wm.
1661 Wilkins, James
1662 Shiles, John
1663 Cordrey, Danl.
1663 Collier, Nichs. Evans
1663 slave Sampson
1663 slave Sibb
1664 Scott, Day
1664 Carter, Philip
1664 slave Hector
1664 slave Tom
1664 slave Scipio
1664 slave Lucey
1665 Scott, George
1665 Maclane, John
1665 slave Sam
1665 slave Pompey
1665 slave Sandrus
1665 slave Florow
1666 Cordrey, Abram
1666 Cordrey, Morgan
1667 Wailes, Elinor
1667 slave Leander
1667 slave Audrey
1668 Driskell, Dennis
1668 Barry, James
1669 Davis, Saml.
1670 Christophers, John, junr
1671 Driskill, Moses
1671 Driskill, Wm.
1672 Cathell, James
1673 Carey, Thos.
1674 Shockley, Jonathn.
1675 Shockley, Jno., senr.
1675 Shockley, Jno., junr.
1675 Shockley, Wm.
1676 Shockley, Richd.
1677 Dormon, Henry
1678 Dormon, Majr.

1679 Lingo, Robinson
1680 Williss, Nathl.
1681 Scadey, Stephen
1682 Longoe, James
1682 Ruark, James
1682 Morris, Nathl.
1683 Kersey, Pat., senr.
1683 Kersey, Pat., junr.
1683 Kersey, James
1684 Lingo, John
1685 Perdue, John
1685 Perdue, George
1685 Scady, Jno.
1686 Parsons, George
1687 Maglamery, Edwd.
1687 Olliphent, Mathw.
1688 Lingo, Richd.
1689 Davis, John, junr.
1689 Magee, Mosses
1690 Davis, Danl.
1690 Davis, Thos.
1691 Smith, James, junr.
1692 Farlow, John
1693 Hill, James
1693 Cornwell, Robt.
1694 Murphey, Joseph
1695 Smith, Andrew
1695 Smith, Geo.
1696 Smith, Mosses
1697 Dashiell, Mathias
1697 slave Sambo
1697 slave Mingo
1698 Mackmorie, James
1698 slave Pompey
1698 slave Abner
1698 slave Rose
1699 Winder, Thos.
1699 slave Mingo
1699 slave Bess
1699 slave Harry
1700 Banks, Stephen
1701 Collier, Thos.
1701 slave Grace
1702 Hardie, Robt.
1702 Hardie, George
1703 Piper, Christopher
1703 slave Dick
1703 slave Sambo
1703 slave Tobey
1703 slave Moll
1703 slave Gwen
1703 slave Joe
1704 Vennables, Benjn.
1704 slave Tom
1704 slave Will
1704 slave Bess

1705 Smith, James, senr.
1705 Dougherty, James
1706 Smith, George
1707 Turner, Saml.
1707 Turner, Jos.
1708 Turner, Joshua
1709 Disharoon, Levin
1709 Smith, Archld.
1710 Melvin, Thos.
1711 Disharoon, John, forrest
1712 Smith, David
1713 Phillips, Jacob
1714 Disharoon, Lewis
1715 Vinson, Benjn.
1716 Cox, Hill
1717 Leonard, Jos.
1718 Pringle, Wm.
1719 Ready, Bryan
1720 Tatum, John
1721 Parsons, John, forrest
1722 Hairn, Thos.
1722 Hairn, Nehe.
1722 slave Hannah
1723 Hairn, George
1724 Hairn, William
1724 Hairn, Isaac
1724 Hairn, John
1724 slave Moll
1725 Gordie, Peter
1726 Morris, Jere.
1727 Mitchell, Alexr.
1728 Melson, Danl.
1729 Parsons, Robt.
1730 Ready, Thos.
1731 Creagin, Paul
1732 Taylor, Rebecca
1732 Taylor, John
1733 Lindell, Thos.
1734 Freeney, Peter
1734 Freeney, John
1735 King, Elizth.
1735 King, Hugh
1736 Larrimore, John, indian
1737 Price, John
1737 Price, Francis
1737 Price, David
1737 Price, Thos.
1738 Humphries, Thos.
1738 Morris, John
1739 Austin, William
1740 Ricketts, James
1741 Collins, James
1741 Langford, Thos.
1742 Collins, Richd.
1743 King, William
1744 Cordrey, John, senr.

TAX LISTS OF SOMERSET COUNTY: 1730-1740

WICOMICO HUNDRED

1744 Cordrey, John, jenr.
1745 Ricketts, John
1745 Ricketts, Thos.
1745 Moore, Isaac
1745 slave Tobey
1746 Humphries, Mary
1746 Russell, Thos. Alexr.
1747 Bird, Thos., senr.
1747 Bird, Wm.
1747 Bird, Benjn.
1748 Phillips, Richd.
1749 Hasty, Robt., senr.
1749 Hasty, Robt., junr.
1749 Hasty, Benjn.
1750 Hasty, Wm.
1751 Caldwell, Hugh
1752 Rathborne, Andrew
1753 Gray, Allen
1754 Hall, Saml.
1755 Covington, Thos.
1755 Covington, John
1755 slave Tom
1756 Lecatt, John
1756 slave Leah
1757 Mattux, Wm.
1757 slave Abram
1758 Mattux, Alexr.
1758 slave Mureah
1759 Vinson, George
1759 Hitch, Wm.
1759 Hitch, Jno., jr.
1760 Vinson, Thos., junr.
1760 Vinson, Thos., senr.
1761 Hitch, John, senr.
1761 Nichols, Richd.
1761 slave Mowear
1762 Hitch, Saml.
1762 slave Jack
1763 Flint, John
1763 Hailer, David
1764 Lynch, Michl.
1765 Johnson, Purnell
1766 Bready, Wm.
1767 Hall, Thos.
1768 Hitch, Elgate
1768 Piper, Joseph
1768 slave woman
1768 slave woman
1769 Lankake, George
1769 Ricketts, Joseph
1769 Green, Richd., junr.
1769 Evans, Wm.
1770 Lankake, Francis
1770 Lankake, Stepn.
1770 slave Jack
1770 slave Tobey
1770 slave Bess
1771 Burn, James
1772 Bird, Thos., junr.
1772 Bready, James
1773 Handy, John, capt.
1773 slave Dick
1773 slave Moll
1773 slave Jane
1773 slave Hagar
1773 slave Patience
1774 Caldwell, John
1774 Caldwell, Robt.
1774 slave Coffey
1774 slave Will
1774 slave Frank
1774 slave Doll
1774 slave Squash
1775 Stevens, Richd.
1775 slave Pompy
1775 slave Alice
1775 slave Scipio
1776 Hill, Charles
1776 Ellis, John
1776 Ellis, Wm.
1776 Ellis, Frans.
1777 Hillman, Edwd.
1778 Brereton, Wm., senr.
1778 Breereton, Wm., junr.
1778 Breereton, John
1778 slave Patience
1779 Christopher, John, senr.
1779 Christopher, Joseph
1780 Johnson, Saml.
1781 Mears, Robt.
1782 Nichols, James
1783 Nichols, Joseph
1784 Morris, Jacob
1784 Morris, Joseph
1785 Howard, John
1786 Disharoone, Ann
1786 Disharoon, Michl.
1787 Crouch, John
1787 Sharp,, widdow
1787 slave Pompy
1787 slave Mary
1787 slave Penny
1788 Porter, Joshua
1789 Bartlett, Thos.
1789 Bartlett, Paskey
1789 Bartlett, Thos., junr.
1790 Vennables, Wm.
1790 Bushaw, Joyles
1790 slave Amey
1791 Gosley, John
1792 Jackson, Saml.
1792 slave Grace
1793 Reddish, John
1794 Bailey, Jonathn.
1795 Gilliss, Thos.
1795 Gilliss, Levin
1795 Haith, Wm.
1795 slave Stepny
1795 slave Dominick
1795 slave Namor
1795 slave Pegg
1796 Chaddwicks, James
1796 Chaddwicks, James, junr.
1796 Chaddwicks, Jno.
1797 Waile, John
1798 T[oa]dvine, Isaac
1798 Toadvine, George
1799 Hayman, Wm.
1799 Hayman, Wm., junr.
1800 Maglamery, George
1801 Bushaw, Graves
1802 Disharroon, Jno., senr.
1802 Kennedy, Timothy
1802 slave Cuffey
1802 slave Grace
1802 slave Fanny
1803 Christopher, Clemt.
1804 Ellis, Joseph
1805 Adams, Alexr., revd.
1805 Adams, Alexr., junr.
1805 Adams, James
1805 slave Quash
1805 slave Glasgow
1805 slave Catoe
1805 slave Beck
1805 slave Dinah
1806 Magee, Peter, senr.
1806 Magee, Peter, junr.
1806 Magee, Thos.
1806 Magee, Saml.
1807 Magee, George
1807 Magee, John
1808 Weatherby, John
1809 Kibble, Wm.
1809 Logey, Ellick
1810 Bounds, Jonathn.
1810 slave Bess
1811 Dashiell, Arthr.
1811 Evans, John
1811 slave Benn
1811 slave Penny
1811 slave Betty

1738 TAX LIST [Household number/Name/Remarks]

WICOMICO HUNDRED

1812 Davis, Wm.
1813 Roach, Alice
1813 Roach, Isaac
1813 slave Tom
1813 slave Harry
1813 slave Pegg
1813 slave Hannah
1814 Roach, Stephen
1814 slave York
1815 Dowdle, Christopher
1816 Bailey, Benjn.
1817 Thompson, John
1818 Pullett, Thos., senr.
1818 Pullett, Thos., junr.
1818 Pullett, Wm.
1819 Polk, David
1819 slave Tamor
1820 Alexander, Agness
1820 Carey, Jonathn.
1821 Alexander, Moses
1821 slave Tom
1822 Sirmon, Peter, senr.
1822 Sirmon, John
1822 Sirmon, Peter
1822 slave Rose Dutton
1822 slave Tom
1822 slave Lemon
1823 Mitchell, Benjn.
1823 Johnson, Wm.
1823 Maggwiggen, Pat.
1824 Swillivan, Wm.
1824 Noble, Wm.
1825 Noble, Isaac
1826 Howard, Thos.
1827 Cottman, Wm.
1828 Cottman, Benjn.
1828 slave John Newman
1828 slave Sarah
1829 Robinson, John
1829 slave Sye
1830 Lockey, Thos.
1831 Roberson, Wm.
1832 Moode, Peter
1833 Walker, Thos.
1833 Makentire, Danll.
1833 Willin, Tho.
1833 slave Tom
1833 slave Jonathan
1833 slave Dinah
1833 slave Kate
1834 Foskey, Thos.
1835 Crouch, Robt.
1836 Fullerton, Alexr.
1837 Gosley, Mathw.
1838 Gosley, Richd.
1839 Mitchell, Isaac
1840 Vennables, Wm., senr.
1840 Vennables, Joseph
1840 Vennables, Pirkins
1841 Bushaw, Jarrott
1841 Hardy, James
1842 Gosley, Thos.
1843 Boarman, Saml.
1844 Cordrey, Jacob
1844 Bushaw, Wm.
1845 Christopher, Ephraim
1846 Cox, John
1846 slave Tom
1847 Hodgens, John
1848 Blewitt, John
1849 Cottman, Joseph
1849 Odaw, Owen
1849 slave Sarah
1850 Smith, Bridgett
1851 Jenkins, Jarvis, senr.
1851 Jenkins, John
1851 Jenkins, Jarvis, junr.
1852 Bayley, Geo.
1853 Stewart, Pat.
1853 Foster, Jno.
1854 Holbrook, Thos.
1854 Alexander, Wm.
1855 Gale, Mathias, capt.
1855 slave Stephen
1855 slave Ceasar
1855 slave Jack
1855 slave Ralph
1855 slave Dublin
1855 slave Rose
1855 slave Violett
1855 slave Sarah
1856 Ellis, Alice, mrs.
1856 Chambers, Edwd., esqr.
1856 Caldwell, Wm.
1856 slave Buboe
1856 slave Will
1856 slave Nanny
1856 slave Moll
1857 Harris, Wm., junr.
1858 Harris, Richd.
1859 Durham, James
1860 Harris, George
1861 Harris, Wm., senr.
1861 Harris, Charles
1861 Harris, Bloyce
1862 Dashiell, Thos., junr.
1862 slave Isaac
1863 Rencher, Thos.
1863 slave Peter
1863 slave Pompey
1864 Rencher, Underwood
1864 Logg, Benjn.
1864 slave Jack
1864 slave Murreah
1865 Ballard, Charles
1865 slave Murreah
1865 slave Caesar
1866 Jones, Jno.
1867 Dullany, Dennis
1868 Shiles, John
1868 slave Tom
1868 slave Anniball
1869 Crockett, John
1870 Crockett, Robt.
1870 slave Crap
1871 Toadvine, Thos.
1872 Disharoon, Michl.
1872 Knowles, Wm.
1873 Disharoon, John, junr.
1874 Disharoon, Wm.
1875 Right, Jere., junr.
1876 Cox, Thos., senr.
1876 Cox, Thos., junr.
1877 Parris, Geo.
1878 Sadler, Isaac
1879 Handy, Isaac
1879 Toadvine, Wm.
1879 slave Sharper
1879 slave Quomino
1879 slave Prew
1879 slave Mumford
1879 slave Will
1880 Fraizer, Hugh
1881 Hurt, Danl.
1882 Steevens, Wm.
1882 Rogers, Richd.
1883 Gordie, Moses
1884 Megee, Peter, jur.

1739 TAX LIST [Household number/Name/Remarks]

ANNAMESSEX HUNDRED

1 Hall, Richard
1 Hall, Charles
2 Hall, William
3 Waters, Abigil, mrs. for
3 Waters, Richard
3 slave David
3 slave York
4 Landin, Henry
5 Waters, Elizth., for
5 slave Armsbon
5 slave Scipio
5 slave Egg
6 Waters, Edward
6 slave Samson
7 Cottomon, Mary, for
7 Cottomon, Joseph
7 Cottomon, Benjan.
7 slave Jenney
8 Waters, Willm.
8 slave Jack
8 slave Sambo
8 slave Bristor
8 slave Pompey
8 slave Dinah
9 Roach, Nathaniel
9 slave Sambo
10 Trehern, John
11 Hall, Charles, senr.
11 Horn, Ezekiel
12 Tull, Thomas
12 Lyster, William
13 Tull, Solomon
14 Warton, William
15 Sehorn, Thomas
15 Sanders, Thomas
15 Mossis, Urisereebel
15 slave Nann
15 slave Mingo
16 Curtis, Charles
16 slave Dick
16 slave Toney
17 Long, Samuel
17 slave Samson
18 Cattlin, William
18 slave Harry
19 Stogdill, Edward
19 slave Coane
20 Lister, Jane, for
20 Lister, Thomas
20 slave Ceasor
21 Williams, John
21 Williams, Jacob
21 slave Sambo
21 slave Mol
22 Williams, Thomas, jur.
22 slave Dick
22 slave Ceasor
22 slave Quash
22 slave Lilley
23 Williams, Isaac
23 slave Plesent
24 Williams, Thomas, senr.
24 slave Titus
24 slave Adam
24 slave Tom
24 slave Jonas
24 slave Glaseo
24 slave Sarah
24 slave George
24 slave Adum
24 slave Geleco
25 Long, John
25 Long, Coulborn
25 slave Robbin
25 slave Sarah
26 Langford, Benja.
26 slave Cesar
27 Dixon, Thomas, senr.
27 Dixon, Thomas, junr.
27 slave Harry
27 slave Toby
27 slave Dick
27 slave Giddin
27 slave Hanna
27 slave Dina
28 Dixon, William
28 Dixon, Ambrose
28 slave Betty
28 slave Benn
28 slave Cuffy
29 Horsey, Isaac
29 Parks, Charles
29 slave Jonathan
29 slave Bek
30 Horsey, Nathl.
30 Horsey, Outerbridge
30 slave Catt
30 slave Patience
30 slave Prince
30 slave Quammino
30 slave Cook
30 slave Tarror
31 Horsey, Smith
31 Kelley, Jams.
31 slave Tamer
32 Horsey, Stephen
33 Holland, Michl., senr., for
33 slave Sarah
34 Holland, Michl., junr.
34 slave Moll
34 slave Tom
35 Smith, Henry
35 Smith, William
36 Cottingham, Thoms.
37 free black, Watt
38 Johnson, Willm.
39 Buttler, Emanuel
40 Pusey, William
41 Owen, Elizth., for
41 Owen, Phillip
41 Owen, William
42 Taylor, William
43 Coulborn, Saml.
44 Coulborn, Wm., senr.
44 Coulborn, Solomon
44 slave Quacor
45 Coulbourn, William, junr
45 slave Catt
46 Coulborn, Solomon, senr.
46 Coulborn, Solomon, junr.
46 slave Merrea
46 slave Nann
47 Walltom, William
48 Miles, Henry
48 slave Dina
48 slave Fellice
48 slave Robbin
49 Davis, James
50 Johnson, John, senr.
50 McKenney, Patrk.
50 Flin, John
50 Dyes, Silby
51 Johnson, John, junr.
52 Moore, Francis
52 Moore, Thomas
53 Lord, Henry
54 Dorothy, John
54 Dorothy, Nathl.
55 Lord, Thomas
56 Lord, Randale
56 Lord, Alexr.
57 Ward, Saml.
57 Ward, John
57 Ward, Wm.
58 Ward, Stephen
59 Ward, Cornelius
59 Riggon, Stephen
60 Riggon, Jno., senr.
60 Riggon, Wm.
60 Duks, Robt.
61 Riggon, Jno., jur.
62 Riggon, Jonan.
63 Benson, Solomon
64 Summers, Thomas, senr.
64 Summers, Geo.

1739 TAX LIST [Household number/Name/Remarks]

ANNAMESSEX HUNDRED

64 Summers, Thos., junr.
65 Summers, Jno.
65 Summers, David
65 Mungumirie, Thos.
65 Summers, Benj.
65 Summers, Richd.
66 Dewitt, Wm.
66 slave London
67 Bird, David
68 Moore, Wm.
69 Moore, Isaac
70 Wheeler, John
71 Ward, Thomas
71 Ward, Jacob
71 Ward, Moses
71 slave Pompey
71 slave Fellice
72 Ward, James
73 Grimes, James
74 Starling, Jno., senr.
74 Starling, Aaron
74 Starling, Jos.
74 Claywell, Selby
75 Starling, Jno., junr.
76 Starling, Henry
77 Smith, James
78 Bird, Joseph, for
78 Dunnock, Willm.
79 Cullin, Jacob
80 Roach, John
81 Cullin, Henry
82 Roach, Charles
82 Roach, Michael
82 slave Jo
82 slave Nenome
82 slave Rose
83 Claton, George
84 Davis, John
84 slave Harry
84 slave What
84 slave Dick
84 slave Su
84 slave Cate
84 slave Jenny
85 Horsey, Stephen
85 Horsey, John
85 slave Sarah
85 slave Robbin
86 Bloyd, Walter
87 Bell, Anthony
87 Bell, Josephas
87 Riggin, Jonathan
88 Bell, Thomas
88 slave Nann
89 Gunby, John
89 slave Jack
89 slave Cato
90 Killiam, John, junr.
91 Ward, Richard
92 Gunby, Kirk
93 Whittington, Surthy
93 slave Robin
93 slave Cesar
93 slave Hannah
93 slave Sarah
93 slave Betty
94 Harn, Edward
94 Ward, Stephen
95 White, John
95 Powell, Benjn.
95 Powell, Thoms.
96 Readin, John
97 Long, Randill
98 Scott, Robert, senior
98 Scott, John
99 Readin, Peter
100 Cottingham, Charles, sen
100 Cottingham, John
101 Cottingham, Charles, jun
102 Cottingham, Thomas
103 Linsey, Thomas
104 Adams, David
104 Adams, Wm.
104 Adams, David
105 Adams, Thomas
106 Pusey, John
107 Willson, John
108 Willson, George
109 Conoway, John, senr.
109 Conoway, Levin
109 Conoway, John, jur.
110 Conoway, Wm.
111 Whetly, Samson
111 slave Jack
112 Potter, Henry
112 slave Fellice
113 White, Thomas
113 Vison, Joseph
114 Trehern, James
114 Trehern, Wm.
115 Long, Daniel
115 slave Friendship
115 slave Jenny
116 Long, Saml.
116 Long, Wm.
116 Long, Davd.
117 Long, Jeffery
117 Long, Sowell
117 slave Nish
118 Hutcheson, Wm.
119 White, John
120 Marshell, Saml.
121 Moore, Thomas
122 Porter, Joseph
123 Bauchamp, Wm.
123 Bauchamp, Wm.
124 Bauchamp, Robt.
125 Bauchamp, Edmund
126 Bauchamp, John
127 Bauchamp, Isaac
127 slave Patience
128 Sanders, Richd.
128 Sanders, Wm.
129 King, Robert, coll. for
129 slave Mingo
129 slave Tamer
130 Summers, Jonan.
131 Fogg, Danl.
132 Horsman, Henry
133 Wooff, Henry
134 Hopkins, Geo.
134 Hopkins, Jno.
134 Hopkins, Wm.
134 Hopkins, Char.
134 Hopkins, Geo.
135 Mister, Wm.
135 Mister, Abra.
135 Mister, Benjn.
136 Evans, John, senr.
136 Evans, John, jun.
136 Loowill, John
137 Wheller, Jonathan
138 Tyler, Thomas, senr.
138 Crockett, Jos.
138 Topin, Saml.
139 Tyler, John
139 Tyler, David
139 Tyler, Thos.
140 Parks, Arthur, for
140 Parks, Arthur
140 Parks, John
140 Parks, Job
141 Evans, Richd.
142 Waters, John
142 Wood, David
142 slave Will
142 slave Sam
142 slave Dick
142 slave Berry
142 slave Jean
142 slave Mark
142 slave Sarah
143 Williams, Wm.
144 Scott, Robt., junior
144 Scott, George
145 Bywaters, Richard
146 Marshall, George
147 Boston, Wm.

TAX LISTS OF SOMERSET COUNTY: 1730-1740

ANNAMESSEX/BALTIMORE HUNDREDS

148 Brimagim, Water
149 Long, David, senior
150 Langford, Jos., senior
150 Langford, Solomon
150 Langford, Pusy
151 Langford, Jos., junior
152 Prior, Thomas
152 Prior, Saml.
153 Adams, Dennis
154 Fodred, William
155 Cohoone, John
155 Cohoone, Henry
156 Price, Edward
157 Keliam, John
157 Outen, Purnall
157 Keliam, William
158 Maddox, Bell
159 Maddox, Mary
159 slave Kate
160 Marshall, Thomas
161 Ore, Michl., senr.
161 Ore, Michl., junr.
162 Scandrel, Edwd.

BALTIMORE HUNDRED

163 Smith, John, capt.
163 Smith, John, jr.
163 Smith, Thos.
163 Smith, Charles
163 slave Harry
163 slave Bess
164 Miller, Joseph
164 slave Tom
164 slave Charles
164 slave Jack
165 Evens, John, sr.
166 Watson, John
166 Farlong, Nicholas
167 Hazzard, David, sr.
167 Hazzard, John
167 slave Jacob
167 slave Kate
168 Hazzard, William
168 Collings, Able
168 slave Dick
169 Johnson, John
170 Johnson, Lenord
171 Harmon, John
172 Morris, William
173 Tull, Richard
174 Hall, Samuel
175 Turvall, John
176 Fall, John
177 Smallwood, Samuel
178 Fall, Abraham
179 Crapper, Edmund, jr.
180 Shewell, Samuel
180 Larthbury, George
181 Turvell, William
181 Taylor, Josiah
181 Evans, Wm.
182 Harnays, Thos., sr.
182 Harnays, Thos., jr.
183 Banks, Neblitt
183 Johnson, Leavan Denard
184 Tull, John, jr.
185 Walker, John
186 Dasey, Thomas, sr.
186 Dasey, Thos., jr.
187 Whorton, Daniel, sr.
187 Whorton, Daniel, jr.
187 Whorton, George
187 Mooney, Charles
188 Kennett, William
188 slave Petter
189 Tapton, Samuel
190 Patey, John
190 Patey, Powell
190 slave Lonnon
191 Deal, Archabell
192 Smith, William
192 Smith, John Onorton
193 Rickards, William
194 Whorton, Henman
194 Burns, Joseph
194 slave Abner
195 Tingle, Mary, widow
195 slave Harry
196 Coe, Daniel
197 Linch, Alexander
198 Fassitt, Frankline
198 Besseks, Nathll.
198 slave Nann
199 Blizard, Richeard
200 Wood, Stephon
201 Hickman, Richeard
202 Nutman, John
203 Hudson, Samuel
204 Hudson, Richeard, jr.
205 Lathbury, Arthur
206 Wyatt, William
207 Aydlott, Thos.
207 Munks, Wm.
207 Hamelton, John
208 Rickards, John, jr.
209 Rickards, Joanes
210 Depray, John
211 Roberson, Thos.
212 Easom, John
213 Roberson, Joshua
213 Derickson, Wm.
213 slave Bess
214 Hudson, John
215 Rackliff, Charles, capt.
215 Rackliff, Purnell
215 slave Robin
215 slave Will
215 slave Cate
215 slave Topin
215 slave Matt
216 Crapper, Nathll., sr.
216 Crapper, Vinson
216 Crapper, John
216 slave Kiner
217 Turvell, Prisgrave
217 Jarman, Prisgrave
218 Mankline, Richeard
218 Kennett, John
219 Brumbly, Henry
219 Brumbly, John
219 Brumbly, Wm.
220 Mumford, John
221 Morgan, Avery
221 slave Hanah
222 Fassitt, Lambard
222 slave Coe
223 Crapper, Nathll., jr.
224 Bowen, Roday, widow
224 Bowen, William
224 Bowen, John
224 Bowen, Whittington
224 slave Comory
225 Pridix, Thomas
226 Woodcraft, William
226 Wilgoos, Thos.
226 Typpings, Robart
227 Tull, John, sr.
227 Clark, Joseph
227 Woods, John
228 Wise, Mathew
228 Wise, Ezeckell
229 Miller, John
229 slave Primas
229 slave Tom
229 slave Pegg
230 Hatfield, William
231 Perray, James
232 Collear, Petter
232 Hill, William Stevens
232 slave Pompey
232 slave Moll

1739 TAX LIST [Household number/Name/Remarks]

BALTIMORE HUNDRED

232 slave Sarah
233 Tingle, Littelton
233 Smith, John Jonas
234 Alford, David
235 Newbold, John
235 Whitehead, John
235 slave Cate
235 slave Cillo
236 Lockwood, Armorall
237 Lockwood, Mary, widow
237 Lockwood, John
238 Holloway, John, jr.
239 Kinnett, Martain
239 Harbrson, Samuel
240 Clark, Edward
241 West, George
241 Townsend, Wm.
242 Rickards, John, sr.
242 slave Boson
242 slave Prigg
242 slave Moll
243 Hudson, George
244 Evens, William, sr.
244 Evens, Wm.
244 Evens, Walter
245 Evens, John, sr.
246 West, Thos.
247 West, William
248 Howard, Nehemiah
249 Godwin, Ceaser, jr.
249 Godwin, Daniel
250 Robarson, Mickeall
250 Roberson, Wm.
250 Roberson, Mickeall
251 Woods, William
252 Hopkins, John
253 Haward, George, sr.
253 Haward, George, jr.
253 Woods, David
253 slave Kent
253 slave Bess
254 Godwin, Ceaser, sr.
255 Harris, George
256 Macomarack, Partrick
257 Hampton, Mary, madam
257 slave Jack
257 slave Hanable
257 slave Petter
257 slave Hanah
258 Bishop, Bowen
259 Brittingham, Robart
260 Fassitt, John
260 slave Meney
260 slave Lewsy
261 Crapper, Edmund, sr.
261 Camble, Solomon
261 slave Petter
261 slave Pompey
261 slave Dick
261 slave Sante
261 slave Phebe
262 Larrance, Henrey
262 Brewing, John
263 Walton, Mattha, widow
263 Davis, Robert
264 Pengolley, Thomas
265 Purnell, John
265 slave Will
265 slave Toney
265 slave Doll
265 slave Merah
265 slave Darnell
265 slave Dinah
265 slave James
266 Robins, Thomas
266 slave Prish
266 slave Bess
267 Roberson, John
267 Roberson, George
267 Roberson, Joseph
268 Godwin, Mickeall, capt.
268 Cooper, Charles
268 slave Bess
269 Holland, Benjamin
269 slave Joan
270 Latchamb, Thomas
271 Stevenson, John
272 Conner, Daniel
272 Rackliff, Nathll.
273 Wyatt, Joseph, sr.
273 Wyatt, Nathll.
273 Wyatt, Joseph, jr.
274 Coffen, Joseph
275 Adkins, John
276 Boden, John
277 Boden, Able
278 Delaney, John Partrick
279 Nickelson, John
280 Cobb, William
280 Tingle, Samuel
281 Bridell, James Stephn
281 Fisher, Bentall
281 slave Mendo
282 Gray, William
282 Baker, Wm.
283 Holloway, John, sr.
283 Holloway, Moses
283 Holloway, Aron
284 Linch, Abraham
285 Tyear, Robert
286 Gray, Thos.
286 Johnson, John
287 Deale, John, sr.
288 Moirey, James
289 Deale, John, jr.
290 Gray, Joseph
290 Conner, Partrick
290 slave Simon
290 slave Yoco
291 Blizard, Thomas
292 Whealey, Charles
293 Mumford, William
294 Mumford, Charles
295 Russell, Andrew
296 Moirey, Robart
297 Bessiks, Absalam
298 Holloway, Joseph
299 Harrison, William
300 Powell, Thomas
300 Ironbugh, John
301 Purkins, William
302 Purkins, Thomas
303 Webb, William
304 Onorton, Isbell, widow
304 Mills, Samuel
304 slave Jenney
305 Coffen, Thomas, sr.
305 Coffen, John
305 Coffen, Thos., jr.
306 Dolbey, William
307 Masey, Alexander
307 Rackliff, Charles
307 slave Jack
308 Carter, Joseph
308 Burnett, John
308 Goodrick, Wm.
309 Derickson, Benjaman
309 Freeman, Wm.
310 Derickson, Joseph
311 Roberts, Thos.
312 Roberts, Alexander
313 Hazzard, David, jr.
314 Aydlott, John, sr.
314 Moore, Wm.
315 Aydlott, John, jr.
315 Hapeney, William
316 Freeman, Sarah, widow
316 Jones, Edmund

TAX LISTS OF SOMERSET COUNTY: 1730-1740

BALTIMORE/BOGERTERNORTON HUNDREDS

317 Masey, John
317 Powell, Charles
317 Silivean, Timothy
318 Memford, James
319 Hudson, David
319 Hudson, William
319 Whorton, Rixam
320 Collings, John
321 Rackliff, Elias
322 Farrell, Thomas
323 Hogg, James
324 Collings, Thomas
325 Cade, Thomas
326 Joanes, John
327 Evens, Ebenezeah
328 Burton, William
328 Burton, Joshua
328 slave Adam
328 slave Touse
328 slave Conodo
328 slave James
328 slave Rachell
329 Powell, William
330 Burton, John
331 Lewis, William
332 MackDaniel, John
333 Barnett, James
334 Salman, William
335 Cambell, John
336 Joseph, Fedrick
337 Winser, Ann, widow
337 Winser, James
338 Wilson, John
339 Roberson, William
340 Collings, George
341 Hopkins, Robert
341 slave Toben
342 Johnson, Bertholomew
343 Short, Edward
343 slave Sepe
344 Hunnings, Phillip
345 Lowe, Robart
346 Liptrott, John
347 Brow, Micheall
348 Joanes, Ebenezah
348 Hudson, Charles
349 West, Thos.
350 West, Alexander
351 Kinney, Thomas
352 Hall, Joseph
353 Radeney, William
354 Priteyman, Thomas
355 Morris, Dennis
356 Morris, John
356 slave Cate
357 Jeaferson, Richeard, sr.
357 Jeaferson, Richd., jr.

357 Jeaferson, Absalam
358 Smith, Robart
359 Beasey, Elizbeath
359 Whorton, Charles
359 English, William
360 Cearey, Richeard
361 Oldson, Andrew
362 Green, Ezeckell
362 Green, David
363 Stevens, Samuel
364 Fassitt, Rouse
364 slave Fillis
364 slave James
365 Wallas, Thomas
366 Cambell, John, sr.
366 Cambell, John, jr.
367 Hopkins, Samuel, capt.
367 slave Orson
368 Johnson, David
369 Bradford, William
370 Woodcraft, Richeard
371 Bradford, Nathll.
372 Whorton, Francis
372 Whorton, Wm.
373 Lewis, Joseph
374 Walton, Teakell
375 Lewis, William
376 Grayhams, George
377 Smith, John, piney neck
377 Smith, William
378 Knock, Solomon
379 Morris, Bibbins
380 Whorton, Thomas
381 Townsend, Bowman
382 Collings, William
383 Hickman, Richeard
384 Fassitt, William, capt.
384 Brooks, Henry
384 slave Will
384 slave Titus
384 slave Sambo
384 slave Harrey
384 slave Rachell
384 slave Beck
384 slave Daniel
385 Fassitt, Mary, mrs. wido
385 slave Frank
385 slave Sue
385 slave Doll
385 slave Berey
386 Hudson, Richeard, sr.
386 Hudson, John
386 Hudson, Henry
386 slave Cuffe

386 slave Charles
386 slave Dick
386 slave Beck
386 slave Phillip
387 Morris, Nathall.
388 Masey, William
389 Rogers, Solomon
389 slave Cane
390 Tingle, Hugh, sr.
390 Tingle, Joseph
391 Tingle, Hugh, jr.
392 Smythers, Sargant, capt.
393 Waters, Richeard
394 Waples, Paul
394 Thorowgood, Paul
394 slave Charles
394 slave Dublen
394 slave Frank
395 Clark, Race
395 Clark, John
395 Clark, Benjm.
396 Godard, Thomas
397 Hargas, Thomas
398 Looker, William
399 Whealeys, Mary, widow
399 Whealey, Nathll.
400 Whealey, William
401 Lewis, Joseph, sr.
402 Quillings, Joseph
403 Smith, Abraham
403 Smith, Purnell Fleitcher
404 Gault, William
405 Gault, Robart
405 Gault, John
406 Walton, William, sr.
406 slave Ceaser
406 slave Jude
406 slave Rose
406 slave Comfort
406 slave George
407 Walton, William, jr.
408 Holland, Richeard
408 Holland, Samuel
408 slave Hanah
409 Hopkins, Josiah
410 Nock, Nehemiah
410 unnamed/slave
411 Taylor, Wm.

BOGERTERNORTON

412 Murray, Dunkin
412 Hewitt, George
412 5 slaves
413 Whaley, William
414 Ryly, Thomas

1739 TAX LIST [Household number/Name/Remarks]

BOGERTERNORTON HUNDRED

414 Evins, Larance
415 Greer, Adam
416 Burton, John
417 Qullin, Benjamin
418 Gornwell, John
419 Henry, John
419 3 slaves
420 Roach, James
421 Townsend, Brickus
422 Townsend, Jeremiah
422 Laton, George
422 3 slaves
423 Richards, William
424 Hodge, Robert
424 Hodge, Fleming
424 slave
425 Timmons, William
426 Timmons, Joseph
427 Timmons, Thomas
428 Timmons, James
429 Low, George
430 Mumford, Thomas
431 Bradford, John
432 Hadder, Warrin
433 Gray, John
433 Gray, William
434 Ingoe, James
435 Williams, Argulus
436 Powell, Samuel
437 Powell, Thomas
438 Williams, Thos. Nathaniel
438 Williams, Samuel
439 Davis, Benjamin
440 Smith, William
441 Lamberson, John
442 Jones, Joseph
442 Jones, John
443 Jarmon, Robert
444 Penewell, Charles
445 Trewitt, George
446 Trewitt, Nehemiah
447 Claywell, Thomas
448 Patrick, Roger
448 Patrick, Daniel
449 Selby, John
449 3 slaves
450 Bishop, William
451 Bishop, Joseph
452 Owten, John
453 Owten, Thomas
454 Victor, James
455 Holston, John
456 Richardson, Charles
456 slave
457 Richardson, Robert
458 Schofield, Joseph
458 Schofield, John
458 2 slaves

459 Selby, William, sr.
459 Selby, William, jur.
459 Holston, Benjamin
459 4 slaves
460 Purnell, Thomas
460 6 slaves
461 Ake, John
462 Bratton, Samuel, sr.
462 Bratton, Hugh
463 Bratton, James
463 Bratton, John
464 Bratton, William
465 Bratton, Samuel
466 Richardson, James
467 Stevenson, Samuel
468 McCally, John
469 Teague, John, sr.
469 Teague, John, jur.
469 Holston, Charles
470 Holston, William
471 Greer, Archibald
471 Greer, Solomon
472 Abbot, John
473 Pepper, John
474 Brittingham, Isaac
474 Brittingham, Nathan
474 slave
475 Ennis, William
475 Ennis, William
475 Ennis, John
475 slave
476 Ennis, Nathaniel
477 Ennis, Samuel
478 Ennis, Cornelius
479 Purnell, Elisha
479 2 slaves
480 Jones, Thomas
481 Porter, William
482 Driggus, John
483 Bat[so]n, Mordecai
484 Hall, William
484 Hall, [Pheni]x
484 2 slaves
485 Bell, Adam
485 slave
486 Johnson, Afradozie
487 Jonson, George
488 Johnson, Thomas
489 Deverix, John
489 Deverix, Cornelius
490 Scott, Mark
491 Godfrey, Charles
492 Mason, Edmond
493 Dredon, John
493 Dredon, Samuel
494 Sturgis, John

494 Sturgis, Litleton
495 Stevenson, James
495 Stevenson, Adam
495 Stevenson, Samuel
496 Steel, James
496 Steel, Daniel
497 Turner, Nicholas
498 Prier, Webb
499 Turner, Henry
500 Truitt, William
501 Truitt, Phillip
501 Taylor, Elias
502 Truitt, George
503 Mumford, George
504 Brittingham, William
504 Brittingham, Absalom
504 Brittingham, Nathl.
505 Brittingham, William
506 Brittingham, Solomon
507 Ennis, John
508 Davis, William
508 slave
509 Dennis, William
510 Handcock, Daniel
510 Handcock, Daniel
511 Hudson, William
512 Hudson, Majer
513 Hudson, Dennis
513 2 slaves
514 Gillaland,, widow
514 Magumery, Robert
514 2 slaves
515 Hall, Adam
516 Bowen, Edward
517 Webb, Grace
517 Webb, Elisha
518 Pointer, Thos.
518 Pointer, Rattliff
518 Pointer, Turvill
518 Church, Wm.
518 2 slaves
519 Pointer, Elias
520 Burbridge, John
521 Morris, William
522 Truitt, George
522 Truitt, George
522 2 slaves
523 Bowen, Littleton
523 slave
524 Bowen, George
525 Tomson, James
526 Bowen, John
527 Ratliff, Charles
528 Bowen, Wm.
529 Edwards, Benony

TAX LISTS OF SOMERSET COUNTY: 1730-1740

BOGERTERNORTON HUNDRED

530 Jarmon, John
530 Jarmon, Wm.
530 slave
531 Jarmon, John
532 Hook, William
533 Dunken, Thomas
534 Marchment, Charles
534 Hosier, Nathan
535 Mitchell, Thomas
535 2 slaves
536 Morris, Joseph
536 Vone, Wm.
537 Hammond, Jacob
538 Hammond, Edward
539 --------, William
540 Burbridge, Edward
541 Bassett, John
542 Hammond, John
543 Purnell, Mathew
543 slave
544 Holland, William
545 Lues, William
546 Timmons, John
546 Timmons, Aaron
547 Smoshie, William
548 Bassett, John
549 Evins, Gamage
550 Evins, Powell
551 Tingle, Daniel
552 Steel, William
553 Becketts, Peter
554 Fowler, Ursula
554 Neighenboroe, John
555 Baynom, Bartholomew
556 Lay, John
557 Franklyn, Edward
557 Harmon, Zachariah
558 Franklyn, Wm.
559 Alexander, Paul
559 Jaxon, John
560 Harmon, Edward
561 Truitt, John
562 Harmon, William
562 Harmon, Edward
563 Warrin, Nicholas
564 Collins, Thomas
565 Evens, Elias
566 Warren, Robert
566 Gray, Nicholas
567 Midsley, Thomas
567 Midsley, Wm.
568 White, John
568 slave
569 Rownd, Edward
569 Gibens, George
569 Davis, Thos.
569 slave
570 Lindell, Peter
571 McNeall, Archibald

572 Braford, Adam
573 Wells, Daniel
574 Robinson, Wm.
575 Spence, Adam
575 5 slaves
576 Buncle, Alexr.
576 3 slaves
577 Stewart,, [widow]
577 slave
578 Brumbly, Thos.
579 Wildman, John
579 Hubbard, Richd.
579 Bedsworth, Thos.
580 Adkinson, John
581 Shelly, Moses
581 2 slaves
582 Trewitt, George, i. town
583 Dennis, Wm., indn. town
584 Taylor, Philip
584 Taylor, Edmond
585 Jarmon, Joab
586 Williams, Littleton
587 Pennewell, Thos.
588 Collins, John
589 Collins, Mary
589 Collins, Thos.
590 Adkins, Stanton
590 Adkins, Stephen
591 Penewell, John
592 Dennis, Donnock
593 Murrain, Mathew
593 Murrain, John
594 Davis, William
594 Davis, Samuel
595 Murphey, John
596 Parker, George
597 Davis, Robert
597 Davis, Wm.
597 Davis, Ishmael
597 Davis, John
598 Davis, Robert
599 Davis, William
599 Davis, George
600 Bridgwaters, Isaac
601 Oshahannas, William
601 Davis, Samuel
602 Parker, Tabitha
602 3 slaves
603 Parker, Samuel
604 Parker, Charles
605 Parker, Philip
605 Canaday, Nehemiah Simons
606 Jarmon, William
607 Murray, David
607 Ayres, Harrison

608 Sturgis, Joshua
608 Laws, Elija
609 Fletcher, Thos., revd.
609 5 slaves
610 Webb, Samuel
611 Lowree, William
612 Smock, Henry
612 Smock, John
612 Smock, Saml.
613 Rownds, Catherine
613 4 slaves
614 Heather, Ephraim
614 2 slaves
615 Heather, Ephraim
616 Griffin, Oliver
617 Crapper, Ebenezer
617 Crapper, Edmond
618 Crapper, Ebenezer, jr.
619 Porter, Joseph
619 slave
620 Peall, Thorogood
621 Tull, Richard
622 Greer, Ursula
622 Greer, John
623 Handcock, [Wi]lliam
624 Watters, Patrick
625 Selby, Parker
626 Collins, Solomon
627 Stevens, William
628 Crapper, John
629 Porter, James
630 Tadlock, Agnes
630 Tadlock, Edward
631 Smith, John
632 Simpson, Thos.
632 4 slaves
633 Marshall, Isaac
633 Marshall, Jacob
633 2 slaves
634 Purnel, Walter
635 Purnel, Catherine
635 2 slaves
636 Da[z]ey, John
637 Crapper, Wrixham
638 Crapper, Nehemiah
639 Templin, John
639 Templin, Richard
640 Dennis, Solomon
641 Dennis, Daniel
642 Dennis, Wheatly
643 Murray, John
644 Truitt, Joseph
645 Porter, John
646 Timmons, Mary
646 Timmons, Saml.
647 Mumford, James
647 Mumford, James

1739 TAX LIST [Household number/Name/Remarks]

BOGERTERNORTON/MANOKIN HUNDREDS

648 Ev----, John
649 Clay[well], John
650 Daviss, Edwd.
651 Daviss, Samll.
652 Henderson, Charles
653 Timons, Aaron
654 Breveard, Adam
655 Timons, Joseph
656 Tull, Benja.
657 Jones, Geo.
658 Truit, James
659 Hammond, Isaac
660 Richardson, William
661 Beadard, William
662 Truit, Geo., senr.
662 slave

MANOKIN

663 Pope, James
664 Hath, Abraham
664 Hath, Matthew
664 slave Sambo
665 Layfield, Thos.
665 Layfield, Wm.
665 Layfield, David
666 Polk, Wm.
666 Gray, Allen
666 slave Oleon
666 slave Abner
666 slave Hannah
666 slave Pleasant
667 Gray, Wm.
667 slave Venus
668 Polk, James
668 slave Ogg
669 Wilson, George
669 slave Isbal
669 slave Betty
670 Wilson, Andrew
671 Dubbing, Wm.
672 Hath, Dorman
672 slave Goliath
673 [Holt, John]
673 Cl[ark], [T]hos.
673 Whittington, Joshua
674 Owens, John, sur.
674 Owens, John, junr.
675 Dorman, Michal
676 Dorman, Wm.
677 Dorman, Matthew
677 Dorman, Nehemiah
677 slave Jack
677 slave Doll
678 Layfield, Robert
679 Clark, Alexr.
680 Cuningham, Thos.
681 Horner, George, jur.
682 Horner, James
683 Crowder, Francis
684 Rigby, Lewis
684 Rigby, John
684 slave Fendow
685 Phebus, Geo., junr.
685 Horner, Wm.
686 Phebus, Geo., snr.
686 Phebus, John
686 slave Into
687 Martin, Thos.
688 Young, John
688 Young, Wm.
689 Horner, Geo., senr.
689 Horner, Mertiedo
689 Horner, John
689 Horner, Arnold
690 Elzey, Sarah
690 Elzey, Arnold
690 slave Ned
690 slave Jack
690 slave Naney
690 slave Belendo
690 slave Fendow
691 Elsey, John
691 Ballard, Arnold
691 slave Sambo
691 slave Cesar
691 slave Ishmael
691 slave Bess
691 slave Sibb
692 Fauscand, Benj.
693 McClemey, Wm.
693 Haley, Timothy
693 slave Nero
694 Gillies, Joseph
694 Ewwl, Jeddiah
694 Humphris, Ezekiel
694 Bozman, Huit
694 Malay, John
694 slave Bosen
694 slave Truman
694 slave Rose
695 Bozman, Geo., sr.
695 Bozman, Geo., jr.
695 slave Frank
696 Robinson, Jas., revrd.mr
696 Robinson, John
696 slave Jack
696 slave Cesar
696 slave Nero
696 slave Toby
696 slave Prue
696 slave Dinah
696 slave Philis
696 slave Siss
696 slave Pesek
697 Johns, Wm., goos creek
697 slave Pompey
698 Bozman, Mary
698 slave Whitehaven
698 slave Sambo
699 Bozman, Wm.
700 Burgan, Daniel
700 Burgan, Wm.
700 Burgan, Patrick
701 Staples, James
701 slave Ben
702 Wolford, John
702 slave Samson
702 slave Rose
702 slave Tamar
702 slave Moll
702 slave Tom
703 Bozman, John, sr.
703 Bozman, Jno., jr.
704 Brown, Thos.
704 slave Cudjo
705 Brown, David
705 slave Betty
705 slave Jack
705 slave Will
706 Anderson, Jno.
707 Dorman, Margret
707 Hill, Wm.
708 Megrah, Jean
708 Megrah, Robt.
709 Laws, James
709 Brandon, Charles
710 Obrian, Richard
711 Matlin, James
712 Denwood, Geo.
712 Smith, Thos.
712 slave Ned
713 Denwood, Thos.
713 slave Coga
713 slave Will
713 slave Sarner
713 slave Grace
713 slave Tamer
713 slave Toney
714 Lockwood, Wm.
715 Ballard, Henery
715 Wilks, Jno.
715 Campble, Jno.
715 Magrah, Richard
715 slave Cesar
715 slave Venter
715 slave Jeney
715 slave Mary
715 slave Bendow
716 Connely, Patrick
717 Alison, Patrick
717 slave Polles
718 Rondols, Henery
718 Rogers, John

TAX LISTS OF SOMERSET COUNTY: 1730-1740

MANOKIN HUNDRED

718 slave Didrah
719 Whittingham, Heber
719 Miller, James
720 Anderson, James
720 Right, Neh.
720 slave Cudjo
720 slave Pegg
721 Smith, Robt.
722 Smith, Magdalene
722 Smith, Wm.
723 Swift, Richard
724 Pringle, Wm.
725 Lendow, Margret
725 slave Joe
725 slave Bess
726 Johns, Wm.
726 Johns, Thos.
726 slave Antony
726 slave Eve
726 slave Gay
727 Hayman, Wm.
727 Hayman, Benj.
728 King, Whettinton
728 Kindall, Patrick
728 slave Tom
728 slave Pacey
729 Cox, Thos.
730 Hall, Mary
730 Fisher, Henery
730 slave Nan
731 Harriss, Phillip
731 Spear, Henery
732 Kearns, John
733 Shepherd, Martin
734 Chambers, [Richard]
734 Collens, Samll.
734 slave Pacey
735 Gullet, Abram
736 Gray, John
736 Gray, James
736 slave Hanah
736 slave Ned
737 Strabrige, James
737 slave Dane
737 slave Coffie
737 slave Dick
737 slave Hagar
737 slave Jeney
737 slave Sarah
738 Reavil, Charles
738 Right, Willm.
738 slave Hanah
739 Bozman, Wm.
739 slave Doso
739 slave Bess
739 slave Judah
740 Roch, Wm.
740 slave Kitt
740 slave Patrons

741 Ballard, Jarvis, sr.
741 Ballard, Wm.
741 Ballard, Jarvis, jur.
741 Ballard, Charles
741 slave Ann
741 slave Rose
742 Reavill, Randal
742 Baylies, Thos.
742 slave Toby
742 slave Matthew
743 Walston, Booz
743 Walston, Joy
744 West, Wm.
744 Cowen, Alexr.
745 Airs, Jacob
745 Walston, Obed
745 Turpin, Joshua, jur.
745 Layfield, Thos.
745 Dorothy, James
745 slave Jack
746 Outerbrige, Sarah
746 slave Priss
746 slave Dinah
746 slave Lonon
747 Culberson, Wm.
748 Thompson, Andrew
748 slave Cesar
749 Thompson, Joseph
750 McDonal, Owen
750 [Ar]globus, Cornelis
751 Hollen, Isaac
751 Furnace, James
751 slave Sippeo
752 ODear, Rose
752 Kain, James
752 Tilman, Benj.
753 Tilman, Joseph
753 slave Lonon
754 Tilman, Aaron
754 slave Jack
755 Givens, Cathrine
755 slave Sarah
756 Givens, Thos.
757 Givens, Ann
757 slave Pleasant
758 Niblet, Burnat
758 slave Coffe
759 Diniston, Robt.
760 Long, Solomon
760 Kindal, Wm.
760 slave Nan
761 Furnace, James
761 Coston, Matthias
761 Jenkins, Samll.
762 Mathews, Patrick
762 Matthews, Wm.

763 McClemey, Woney
763 slave Frank
764 Collins, Wm.
765 Boler, Elinor
765 Boler, Wm.
765 Boler, James
766 Tindal, James
767 Morrow, Alexr.
768 Brown, Tarral
768 Gullet, Geo.
769 Hayward, John
769 Burns, Patrick
770 Banaster, Thos.
770 slave Oston
771 Labrouss, Benj.
772 Matthews, Wm.
772 Fiddy, Thos.
773 Mitchal, Thos.
774 Mitchal, Ann
774 Michal, Rondal
774 slave Sarah
775 Killet, Rodger
775 slave Whitehaven
775 slave Judah
775 slave Hanah
776 Horsey, Sarah
776 Fiddy, [R]andal
776 slave Nick
777 Kinney, John
777 slave illegible
778 King, Robt.
778 King, Neh.
778 King, Robt., jur.
778 [Hog], Stephen
778 L[ane], Abraham
778 Turner, Wm.
778 Smith, Wm.
778 slave Fortin
778 slave Jesse
778 slave Long Cesar
778 slave Short Cesar
778 slave Manery
778 slave Obed
778 slave Eboe
778 slave Betty
778 slave Judith
778 slave Sue
778 slave Jude
778 slave Nanney
779 Horsey, John
779 Daley, Patrick
779 Killey, Hugh
780 King, Capell
780 King, Ephraim
780 slave Major
780 slave Pompy
780 slave Titus
780 slave Jack
780 slave Cate
780 slave Rose

1739 TAX LIST [Household number/Name/Remarks]

MANOKIN/MATTAPANY HUNDREDS

781 Tunstal, John	805 Tull, Jno.	813 slave Nell
781 Ladels, James	805 Turpin, Jno.	814 Davis, John
781 slave Sibey	805 Turpin, Whitty	815 Benson, Geo.
781 slave Pompy	805 slave Tom	815 Benson, Mathias
781 slave Lo Hill	805 slave Jack	
781 slave Tomboy	805 slave Toby	MATTAPANY HUNDRED
781 slave Dick	805 slave Cezar	816 Booth, William
781 slave Noris	805 slave Phillis	817 Cary, Jeremiah
781 slave Scipio	805 slave Medary	818 Walton, Robert, junr.
781 slave Bess	806 Turpin, Wm., junr.	819 Fisher, Baley
781 slave Rachal	806 slave Will	820 Willet, Ambrus
781 slave Sib	806 slave George	820 Willet, Wm.
781 slave Will	806 slave Moll	820 Willet, Thos.
781 slave Sanders	807 Maddox, Thos.	820 slave Jacob
781 slave Freeman	807 Maddox, Jno.	821 Duer, William
781 slave Tom	807 Cullin, Isaac	822 Selby, Parker
781 slace Cesar	807 slave Will	822 indian Jack
781 slave Dana	807 slave Sew	822 slave Gloster
781 slave Isbal	808 Fountain, Nicholis	822 slave Abraham
782 Killey, John	808 Copsey, Wm.	822 slave Isaac
783 King, Charles	808 slave Charles	822 slave Pegg
784 Knot, Isaac	808 slave Tom	822 slave Tamour
785 Davis, John	808 slave Lonon	823 Slingo, Thos., senr.
786 Davis, Arthur	808 slave Meream	823 Slingo, John
787 McDonnal, David	809 Fountain, Marey	824 Vannelson, William
788 Mott, John	809 Campable, Nehe.	824 Vannelson, Nathan
789 Ford, Abasolom	809 slave Mora	825 Sturgis, Richard
790 Walston, Wm.	809 slave Herculis	825 Sturgis, John
790 Walston, Henery	810 McCalpin, Robt.	826 Tarr, Mical, senr.
791 Sharp, Benj.	811 Wilson, David	826 Tarr, Mical, junr.
791 Bryan, Thos.	811 King, Jesse	826 Tarr, John
791 Mercht., Walter	811 Parkinson, Robt.	827 Bennit, Mary
791 Grumble, Benj.	811 slave Harrey	827 Linsey, James
792 McDorman, Wm.	811 slave Cudjo	827 Bennit, Edward
793 Tull, Esther	811 slave Robin	828 Pudrer, Joseph
793 Tull, Stephen	811 slave Kent	829 Porter, Mccluntuck
793 slave Moll	811 slave Pompy	830 Reed, Walter
794 Walston, Thos.	811 slave Bristo	831 Braton, William
795 Tull, Joshua	811 slave Moses	831 Braton, Thos.
796 Miles, Samll.	811 slave Lancaster	831 slave Gui
796 slave Dick	811 slave Nanney	832 Beachbord, William
796 slave Ben	811 slave Holiday	833 Long, John
797 Maddux, Lazarus	811 slave Rose	834 Pope, George
797 Tull, Richard	811 slave Venus	834 slave Bess
797 slave Coffe	812 Turpin, Wm., son to Jno.	835 Lane, Geo.
797 slave Joe	812 slave Coffe	836 Mallin, Christopher
798 Butler, Nathaniel	812 slave Toby	837 Taylor, Roger
798 slave Sarah	812 slave Mingo	837 Taylor, John
799 Abbit, John	813 Wilson, Samll.	838 Answorth, William
800 Miles, Wm., snr.	813 slave Petter	838 Answorth, Jobe
800 Miles, Wm., jur.	813 slave [Mummuda]	839 Peper, William
801 Maddox, Daniel	813 slave Will	840 Peper, Tobias
801 slave Addam	813 slave Tom	841 Brumbrill, Nathaniel
801 slave Sarah	813 slave Samson	842 Allen, John, senr.
802 Willis, Barnaby	813 slave Nanney	842 Allen, John
802 Dorman, Wilson	813 slave Hanna	843 Scott, Robt.,
803 Tull, Samll.	813 slave Joan	
804 Barrit, Henery	813 slave Bess	
805 Turpin, Wm., snr.	813 slave Sarah	
805 Tull, Thos.		

TAX LISTS OF SOMERSET COUNTY: 1730-1740

MATTAPANY HUNDRED

senr.
843 Scott, Dunken
843 Scott, Adam
843 Wilson, Wm.
844 Masfield, Joseph
844 slave York
844 slave Jack
844 slave Abigal
844 slave Pegg
844 slave Dennis
845 Waggaman, Ephraem
845 Harburd, William
845 slave George
845 slave Bess
845 slave Jubit
846 Cary, Sollomon
847 Boothouten, John
848 Pilsher, Moses
849 Hill, Abraham
850 Hill, Jacob
851 Watson, Petter
852 Watson, Luke
853 Hodson, Rowlon
853 slave Joe
854 Hodson, John
854 Hodson, Rowlon, junr.
855 Goodin, Benjamin
856 Allen, Joseph
856 Allen, Moses
857 Duberly, Thos.
858 Pane, John
858 Pane, Moses
859 Watson, John
860 Watson, Robt., ser.
860 Watson, Charles
860 slave Darkes
861 Watson, Jams.
861 Watson, Uriah
862 Chapman, Humphre
863 Vesey, Charles
863 Vesey, Wm.
864 Davis, Charles
865 Jones, John
866 Henderson, Bishop
867 Odue, Thos.
868 Aydelot, William
868 [Aydelot], Wm., junr.
868 slave Hector
868 slave Sesar
869 Jones, Wm.
870 Holland, Nehemiah
870 Cox, James
870 Andrues, Shipard
871 Britingham, Thos.
872 Wimbrough, Paul
873 Merill, Joseph
873 Harman, Geo.

874 Walker, John, fr.
874 slave Jack
874 slave Jobe
875 Jackson, William
876 Robins, Bowdin
876 slave Geo.
876 slave Jack
876 slave Roger
876 slave Frank
876 slave Sarah
877 Purnell, John
877 slave Tobe
877 slave Jacob
877 slave Nimrod
877 slave Geo.
877 slave Benn
877 slave Sarah
878 Cord, William
878 Cord, John
878 Cord, Arthur
878 slave Jane
879 Walton, William
879 slave Peter
879 slave Moll
880 Hill, Robt.
881 Waton, Stephen
881 [Waton], Stephen, junr.
881 Williams, Thos.
882 Scarborough, John
882 Ouldom, John
882 slave Dick
882 slave Nan
883 Eavans, John
884 Newton, Thos., senr.
884 Nuton, Thos., junr.
884 Newton, Southey
885 Sturgis, Daniell
886 Hill, Johnson
887 Hill, Hutten
888 Newton, Starling
889 Newton, Jobe
890 Nuten, Johnathan
891 Turner, William
892 Tarr, Samll.
892 Cornwell, John
892 Richardson, John
893 Hosier, Samll.
894 Milbourn, Thos.
895 Clarke, John
896 Pope, Samll.
896 slave Will
896 slave Hannah
897 Johnson, Peter
897 [Johnson], Peter, junr.
898 Johnson, John
899 Johnson, Leonard

900 Hudson, Johnathan
901 Johnson, William
902 Richardson, John
902 Richardson, Samll.
902 slave Rachel
903 Chericks, Jams.
904 Hopkins, Wm.
905 Hopkins, Samll.
906 Hall, John
907 Guttry, Patrick
907 Guttry, Calib
908 Slingo, Thos.
908 Hosiear, Edward
909 Porter, William
910 Vestry, Mical
911 Calburd, William
912 Sammons, Benja.
913 Pirce, Edward
913 slave Gui
914 Dreadin, John
915 Wise, Thos.
915 Drumd., Drake
915 Richardson, David
916 Hopkins, Mathew
916 Ayres, Richard
916 slave Sibman
917 Hopkins, Nathaniel
917 slave Abner
918 Claywell, Peter
918 Claywell, Shadrack
918 Mackrill, John
918 slave Geo.
918 slave Sambo
918 slave Jude
918 slave Hannah
919 Selby, Phillip
919 Selby, Mathew
919 Selby, Daniel
919 Selby, Phillip
919 Selby, Parker
919 slave Jack
919 slave Tom
919 slave Sambo
919 slave Pine
919 slave Sangra
919 slave Hannah
919 slave Meariah
920 Claywell, Peter, junr.
921 Handcock, Wm.
922 Slocum, Thomas
923 Nelson, William
923 Nelson, Jams.
923 Nelson, Robt.
923 Scott, Robt., junr.
924 Hardy, Hazzard

1739 TAX LIST [Household number/Name/Remarks]

MONIE HUNDRED

925 Wright, Thomas
925 Wright, Henry
925 Rose, Samll.
926 Shores, Jno.
926 Shores, Wm.
926 Shores, Jno., junr.
927 Elzey, Jno., junr.
928 Spicer, James
929 Waller, Major
930 Waller, Wm.
931 Sawser, Alice
931 Sawser, Wm.
931 Waller, Geor.
932 Pollock, Joseph
932 Bazwell, Charles
932 Neill, Jno.
933 Roberts, Edward
933 slave Jeffery
933 slave Cuffie
933 slave Binah
934 Roberts, Jno.
934 Roberts, Thomas
935 Williams, Jno.
936 Martin, George
937 McDarmond, Derby
938 Cantwell, Thos.
939 Windsor, Jno.
940 Wallace, Richard
940 Wallace, James
940 Stewart, Charles
940 slave Caesar
941 Wallace, Mathew
941 Haylor, David
941 slave Sib
941 slave Tom
942 White, Francis
942 White, Jno.
942 White, Thos.
943 White, Jno.
943 White, Jno., junr.
944 Spicer, Philip
945 Jones, Charles
946 Hurst, Jno.
947 Jones, Samll.
948 Jones, Lewis
948 Jones, Lewis, junr.
948 slave Jack
948 slave Moll
948 slave Caesar
949 Jones, George
949 slave Adam
950 Rawlins, Charles
950 Spicer, Jno.
951 Lawes, Thos.
951 Loyd, Thos.
951 slave Marrier
952 Roe, Joseph
953 Roe,, widdow
953 Sowards, Wm.
954 Chain, Alexander
955 Windsor, Lazarus
955 Windsor, Lazarus, junr.
955 Windsor, James
955 Windsor, Philip
956 Lawes, Jno.
956 slave Caeser
956 slave Prince
957 Miller, Thomas
958 Stoughton, Wm.
958 Lary, Timothy
958 slave Bussy
958 slave Simon
958 slave Jemme
958 slave Sarah
958 slave Sabina
959 Downs, Robert
959 slave Frans
959 slave Bristo
959 slave Ned
960 Jones, Robert, capt.
960 Jones, Mitchell
960 Jones, Benjamin
960 slave London
960 slave Amock
960 slave Jane
960 slave Rachell
961 Irvin, George
961 Irvin, John
961 slave Toby
961 slave Cuffee
961 slave Jane
961 slave Jane
962 Waller, John
962 slave Jean
963 Walsh, Wm.
964 Magraugh, James
965 Dashiell, Thomas
965 slave Will
965 slave Jack
965 slave Harry
965 slave Bess
965 slave Tamer
965 slave Sarah
966 Jones, Wm., capt.
966 slave James
966 slave Sue
966 slave Lucey
967 Gale, George, maj.
967 Maughan, Christr.
967 slave Joe
967 slave Dominick
967 slave Limas
967 slave Scipio
967 slave Jemy
967 slave Jack
967 slave Nimrod
967 slave Palinah
967 slave Sarah
967 slave Parthena
967 slave Nanny
967 slave Jenny
967 slave Beendah
967 slave Dinah
968 Cary, Thomas
968 Crouch, David
969 Cary, Rachell
969 Crouch, Thomas
970 Luke, Williamson
971 Howard, Thomas
971 Walter, John
972 Covington, Eleanor
972 Wright, Zebulon
972 slave Cucco
972 slave Sambo
972 slave Bess
972 slave Jean
972 slave Dinah
972 slave Pegg
973 Jones, Catherine
973 slave Bussey
973 slave Davey
973 slave Sibb
973 slave Moll
974 Squires, Edmund
975 Dorman, John
975 Dorman, Hezekiah
976 Leatherbury, Jno.
976 Leatherbury, Jno., junr.
976 Jones, Wm.
976 slave Toney
976 slave Pompy
976 slave Sambo
976 slave Robin
976 slave Ben
976 slave Bridgett
976 slave Rose
976 slave Nan
976 slave Bess
976 slave Candis
977 Jones, Daniel
977 Willcocks, Wm.
977 slave Doll
978 Covington, Thos.
978 Brookshaw, Manering
979 Durham, Thos.
980 Lawliss, James
981 Hobbs, Marcelious
982 Hobbs, Joy
983 Hobbs, Thomas
983 Hobbs, Stephen
983 Stevens, Isaac
984 Magraugh, Jno.
984 Smith, Jno.
985 Newman, Henry

TAX LISTS OF SOMERSET COUNTY: 1730-1740

MONIE/NANTICOKE HUNDREDS

986 Dorman, Henry, junr.
987 Puckam, Richard
987 Puckam, Jno.
988 Mungar, Jno.
989 Mungar, Mathew
990 Lawes, Robert
990 slave Boobo
990 slave Jack
990 slave Samson
991 Lawes, Panter
992 Lawes, Wm.
993 Wallace, Robert
993 Wallace, George
994 Wallice, Thomas
994 slave Bess

NANTICOKE HUNDRED
995 Maclester, John, captin
995 Maclester, Samuell
995 Maclester, George
995 Maclester, Neaill
995 slave Antoney
995 slave Cofee
995 slave Sambow
995 slave Tom
995 slave Andrew
995 slave Tony
995 slave Ben
995 slave Sis
995 slave Dino
995 slave Alex
995 slave Rose
996 Jones, Tho.
996 slave Messer
997 Hickman, Arthur
998 Bartlet, John
999 Walter, Danell
1000 Walter, Robart
1001 Bartlet, John
1001 Bartlet, Abraham
1002 Brown, Signe
1003 Wollis, John
1003 Wollis, Tho.
1004 Meseck, Isaac
1005 Macumb, Timothy
1006 Tailer, Abraham
1006 Taile, John
1006 slave Quash
1007 Govand, James
1007 slave Frank
1008 Gall, John, captt.
1008 Russell, Tho.
1008 slave Bartha
1008 slave Mese
1008 slave Jame
1008 slave Galaway
1008 slave Sambow
1008 slave Bob
1008 slave Sambow
1008 slave Orson
1008 slave Townsides
1008 slave Rose
1008 slave Judah
1008 slave Sib
1008 slave Pheby
1008 slave Moll
1008 slave Beck
1009 Train, James, snr.
1009 slave Roben
1009 slave Rose
1009 slave Meran
1010 Train, James
1010 slave Jack
1010 slave Bes
1010 slave Moll
1011 Caldwell, James
1011 Govand, Wm.
1011 slave Bob
1011 slave Rose
1011 slave Sambow
1011 slave Hanah
1012 Cotman, Eblineser
1012 Cotman, Nathanell
1012 Cotman, Wm.
1013 Parmore, Elizabeth
1013 Parmore, John
1013 Parmore, Beniamin
1014 Goddart, John
1014 Goddart, Nathanell
1014 Booth, George
1014 Wharton, Wm.
1015 Hix, Wiliam
1016 Nicholson, Ritchard
1016 slave Biner
1017 Chesman, John
1017 slave Nancy
1018 Acworth, Samull
1018 slave Sue
1019 Acworth, Henry
1019 Wertherly, Wiliam
1019 slave Sue
1020 Hickman, Wm.
1020 Hickman, Jonathan
1020 slave Jack
1020 slave Sambow
1020 slave Mareah
1020 slave Rose
1020 slave Juda
1021 Walter, John
1022 Dunn, Ritcard
1022 Dunn, Nicholis
1022 Dunn, Thos.
1023 Hust, Joseph
1024 Rotten, Wm.
1024 Rotten, Ezekeall
1025 Dashiell, George
1025 slave Cofey
1025 slave Sipeo
1026 Anderson, John
1027 Ritchey, Archable
1027 Macape, Wm.
1028 Larmore, Thos.
1028 Larmore, James
1029 Beard, John
1030 Bearde, Lewes
1031 Colier, Dowdy
1031 Colier, Robart
1032 Handerson, Robarte
1033 Colier, George
1034 Winright, Canan
1034 Winright, James
1034 slave Quaco
1035 Flueling, Samuell
1035 slave Siles
1036 Wertherly, James
1036 Wertherly, Joseph
1036 slave Toby
1036 slave Pegg
1037 Rhodes, Danell
1038 Govand, John
1038 slave Hager
1039 Acworth, Thos.
1040 Dashiell, Leven
1040 slave Joe
1041 Colier, Robarte, snr.
1041 slave Sarah
1041 slave Bess
1042 Dashiell, Henry
1042 slave Gift
1042 slave Sib
1043 Nutter, Christopher
1043 Dauson, John
1043 slave Seser
1043 slave Tom
1043 slave Sipeo
1043 slave Jack
1043 slave Hary
1043 slave Barbarry
1043 slave Rose
1044 Nutter, Hewit
1044 slave Tite
1044 slave Mingow
1044 slave Cogo
1045 Price, Robarte
1045 slave Nell
1046 Dunkin, James
1047 Oystin, William
1048 Benett, George
1049 Kemp, Mathew
1049 Kemp, John

1739 TAX LIST [Household number/Name/Remarks]

NANTICOKE HUNDRED

1050 Johnson, David
1051 Askely, Danell
1052 Maclester, Joseph
1052 slave Sambo
1053 Bluer, Margrett
1053 slave Narow
1053 slave Judah
1054 Kelamb, Edward
1054 Kelamb, John
1054 slave Maren
1054 slave Will
1055 Kebble, John
1056 Merriall, Tho.
1057 Larmore, Mary
1057 slave Cofey
1057 slave James
1058 Hopkins, John
1059 Hopkins, John, snr.
1059 Hopkins, Roger
1059 Eles, James
1059 slave Sarah
1060 Meseck, Beniamin
1061 More, Wm.
1062 Macants, Alexander
1063 Bounds, Joseph
1064 Game, Fortin
1064 Game, Annill
1065 Sturt, Alexander
1065 slave Batt
1065 slave Jeann
1065 slave Frank
1066 Dashiell, Wm.
1066 slave Bess
1066 slave Sibb
1066 slave Peter
1067 Dashiell, Wm.
1068 Deen, John
1069 Dashiell, Bridgett
1069 Dashiell, James
1069 Dashiell, Jesse
1069 slave Robin
1069 slave Will
1069 slave Jack
1070 Wiliams, Ritcard
1070 Wiliams, John
1071 Wollis, David
1072 Samuels, Ann
1072 slave Cocero
1073 Scott, George
1074 Scott, Windom
1075 Hofinton, Ritcard
1075 Hoofinton, Levi
1076 Gastinew, George
1077 Wollis, Ritcard
1078 Tailer, Wm.
1078 slave Nancy
1079 Darby, Walter
1079 Marcy, Joseph
1080 Tull, James
1080 Glaster, Thos.
1081 Oliver, George
1082 Jones, James
1082 Curmechell, John
1083 Jones, John
1084 Carter, John
1085 Andrews, John
1086 Relph, Wm.
1087 Vinson, James
1088 Roberson, Wm.
1089 Kenegin, Daniell
1090 Collings, John
1091 Edge, Robart
1092 Edge, Joshua
1093 Noulds, Edman
1093 Noulds, Edman
1094 Roberson, John
1094 Roberson, Wm.
1095 Walter, Henry
1095 Walter, John
1095 Walter, Wm.
1095 slave Beck
1096 Hardy, John
1097 Hopkins, Stephen
1097 Hopkins, David
1098 Hardy, James
1098 slave Jean
1099 Farinton, Wm.
1099 Austin, Wm.
1100 Govand, Robart
1100 slave Seser
1100 slave Charles
1100 slave Hanah
1100 slave Bess
1100 slave Sue
1101 Dashiell, Robart
1101 slave Caco
1101 slave Workinton
1101 slave Tamer
1102 Dashiell, Priscela
1102 slave Harry
1103 Benston, Mary
1103 Nicholson, Leven
1103 slave Will
1103 slave Bess
1103 slave Glasco
1104 Townsin, Benimin
1105 Woller, Nathanell
1106 Carter, Samuell
1107 Carter, Philip
1108 Elensworth, Elisab.
1108 Elensworth, Nehemiah
1109 Shockly, David
1109 Shockly, James
1109 Shockly, Saull
1109 slave Diner
1110 Collings, John
1111 Ritcherson, Wm.
1111 Ritch[erson], Beniamin
1112 Cooper, Isaac
1112 Price, Frances
1113 Coaper, Samuell
1113 Couper, Wm.
1114 Cooper, Tho.
1115 Couper, Gabrell
1116 Wilson, John
1117 Gravener, Tho.
1117 Carter, Wm.
1118 Smith, Thos.
1119 Young, Johew
1120 Brown, Wm.
1120 Camichell, Thos.
1120 slave Nancy
1121 Right, Soloman
1122 Rowell, Thos.
1123 Noulds, Ritchard
1124 Nuten, John
1125 Fulton, Wm.
1126 Culver, John
1127 Collings, Edman
1128 Hofinton, John
1129 Hofinton, Jonathan
1130 Hofinton, John, sr.
1130 slave Gogo
1130 slave Jean
1130 slave York
1130 slave Pleasant
1131 Melson, Samuell
1131 Melson, Samll.
1131 slave Randull
1132 Spear, Robert
1133 Wollis, Ritchard
1134 Quinton, Peter
1135 Quturmus, James
1136 Acworth, Thos.
1136 slave Will
1136 slave Moll
1137 Mitchell, Alexander
1138 Tatman, James
1139 Dodrall, James
1140 Rider, Hetely
1141 Rider, Wilson
1142 Russell, James, jur.
1142 Sims, Achable
1143 Russell, James
1144 Relph, Tho.
1144 slave Harry
1145 Goslee, James
1146 Reed, John
1146 Reed, Obediah

TAX LISTS OF SOMERSET COUNTY: 1730-1740

NANTICOKE HUNDRED

1146 slave Mareah
1147 Reed, John
1147 Reed, Ezakiah
1147 slave Pegg
1147 slave Hary
1148 Thornes, Alexandr
1149 Quturmus, James
1149 Quturmus, James
1150 Edwards, John
1151 Bucklee, Nicholis
1152 Martin, John
1153 Game, Robart
1154 Meseck, Nehemiah
1155 Meseck, Jacob
1156 Meseck, Elihew
1156 Meseck, Joshua
1157 Ritcharson, John
1158 Meseck, Jacob
1159 Reed, Zakariah
1160 Cope, John
1160 Cope, John
1161 Cordry, David
1161 Cordry, Morgin
1162 Hofinton, Thos.
1163 Deen, Charles
1163 Deen, James
1164 Bradly, John
1165 Floyd, Major
1166 Couper, Tho. Collings
1166 Marey, John
1167 Givands, John
1168 Collings, Thos.
1169 Stille, Mary
1169 Stille, John
1170 Mackdowell, John
1171 Carter, Charles
1172 Fulton, Nicholis
1172 Fulton, John
1173 Waller, Tho.
1174 Vahan, William
1175 Bacon, Dutson
1176 Calaway, John
1177 Stephens, John
1178 More, Wm.
1179 Greerer, Wm.
1180 Couper, James
1181 More, Wiliam, jur.
1182 Shiles, Edman
1183 Polk, John
1184 Waller, Thos., snr.
1184 Waller, Ritchd.
1184 Oliver, Thos.
1185 Rhodes, John
1186 Bolin, Tho.
1187 James, John
1188 Caldwell, John
1188 Caldwell, Robart
1188 slave Sambo
1189 Spoldin, Elizabeth
1189 Murphy, James
1190 Twiford, John
1191 Surman, Wm.
1191 Surman, Isaac
1191 Surman, Wm.
1192 Bennet, Edward
1192 Benett, John
1193 Benett, Elizabeth
1193 Bennet, Wm.
1194 Green, Ritchard
1194 Green, Ritchard
1194 Green, Ezekuell
1195 West, James, esqr.
1195 Fills, George
1196 More, Isaac
1197 Cox, John
1197 slave Tom
1198 Gills, Wm.
1198 Gills, Wm.
1198 slave Flora
1199 Giles, Thos.
1200 Jackson, Jonathan
1200 Jackson, Joshua
1200 Jackson, Ezekiell
1200 Jackson, Danell
1201 Jackson, Thos.
1202 Dashiell, Joseph
1202 Dashiell, Mitchell
1202 slave Randoll
1202 slave Bess
1203 Hitch, Soloman
1203 Hitch, Addam
1203 Hitch, Leven
1203 slave Frank
1203 slave Coak
1204 Surman, Jobe
1205 Calaway, Peter, snr.
1205 Calaway, John
1206 Calaway, Thos.
1207 Maclahen, Joseph
1208 Speare, Henry
1208 Speare, John
1209 Calaway, Petter
1210 Keny, Wiliam
1211 Caldwell, Thos.
1212 Caldwell, Patrick
1213 Philips, Ritchard
1214 Philips, Thos.
1215 Philips, Wm.
1216 Rickords, John, jur.
1216 Stogdill, George
1216 slave Rose
1217 Low, Relph
1217 Low, John
1218 Langford, John
1218 Langford, Edward
1218 Langford, Tho.
1219 Langford, John
1220 Anderson, Mary
1220 Anderson, John
1221 Langford, Thos.
1222 Vance, Thos.
1223 Right, Soloman
1224 Oystin, Wiliam
1225 More, John, snr.
1225 More, James
1226 Philips, John
1227 Tulle, Stephen
1227 Tulle, Joshua
1228 Tulle, Beniamin
1229 Jones, Finch
1230 King, Philip
1231 Calaway, John, snr.
1231 Calaway, Isaac
1232 Parmore, James
1232 Parmore, Wm.
1232 Parmore, Isaac
1233 Tulle, Stephen, jnr.
1233 Tulle, Ritchard
1233 Tulle, John
1233 Tulle, Danell
1234 Benston, Henry
1234 Benston, Henry
1234 Benston, Mathey
1234 Benston, George
1235 Calaway, Wm.
1235 Calaway, Beniamin
1236 Calaway, Wm., jur.
1237 Calaway, John
1238 Ange, Frannes
1238 Ange, Frannes
1239 Waller, Nathanell
1239 English, James
1240 Hozay, Mathew
1241 Godart, Tho.
1241 Godart, John
1241 Godart, Tho.
1242 More, John, forest
1243 Wootten, Edward
1244 Wootten, John
1245 Shurman, Thos.
1246 Calaway, Edward
1247 Gillis, John
1247 Gillis, Tho.
1248 Garritt, Wm.
1248 [Garritt],, wife
1249 Gastinew, Mathuren
1250 Acworth, Charles

1739 TAX LIST [Household number/Name/Remarks]

NANTICOKE HUNDRED

1250 Churn, John
1250 Olphy, Joseph
1251 Tulley, Joseph
1251 Riggin, Ambrus
1252 Tulle, Beniamin
1253 Smith, Thos.
1254 Paccumb, Abraham
1255 Powell, John
1256 Nicholson, James
1257 Elensworth, Robart
1258 Langsdell, Wm.
1259 Twille, Robart
1260 Dashiell, N.
1260 slave Tom
1260 slave Venus
1260 slave Bamaw
1261 Henry, John
1261 Henry, Hew
1261 Beek, Isaac
1262 Twille, George
1263 Macluer, Robart
1264 Dolby, Petter
1264 Dolby, John
1265 Smith, Henry
1266 Ingrom, Robart
1267 Kennigan, Arthur
1268 Miles, Edward
1269 Glas, John
1270 Noble, John
1271 Holston, Robart
1272 Holston, John
1273 Phips, John, esqr.
1274 More, John, deep creek
1275 Woller, Nelson
1276 Collings, Andrew
1276 slave Nancy
1277 Collings, Wm.
1278 Short, John
1279 Bivands, Calup
1280 Smith, David
1281 Langsdill, John
1281 Smith, James
1282 Bevands, John
1283 Bevands, Joshua
1284 Shorte, Abraham
1285 Hopkins, Danell
1286 Samuels, Ritchard
1287 Boyce, John
1288 Boyce, Danell
1288 slave Bes
1288 slave Will
1289 Wille, Jarett
1290 Waltter, Thos.
1291 Tailer, John
1292 Wingitt, Philip
1292 slave Amy
1293 Hall, Robart
1293 Morris, John
1293 Hall, Wm.
1293 slave Pris
1294 Clifton, George
1294 Clefton, Leven
1294 Clifton, Nehemiah
1295 Paull, George
1295 Nesom, Ben.
1296 Benston, Wm.
1296 Elensworth, William
1297 Oneall, James
1297 slave Biner
1298 Oneall, John
1299 Marcy, Wiliam
1300 Philips, John
1301 Hall, John
1302 Mezeck, George
1303 Mezeck, John
1303 Mezeck, Obedia
1304 Shiles, Thos.
1305 Carter, Thos.
1306 Tomson, George
1307 Venedson, Elias
1308 Owens, Petter
1309 Baker, Wm.
1309 Hall, Thos.
1310 Melson, Joseph
1311 Melson, Beniamin
1312 Hickman, Henry
1313 Ingrom, Jacob
1314 Potter, Josephus
1315 Hopkins, John
1316 Tindull, Charles
1317 Elensworth, Ritchard
1318 Smith, John
1319 Bounds, Jacob
1320 King, Wm.
1321 Parmore, Joseph
1322 Parmore, James
1323 Downes, Robart
1324 Persons, Charles
1325 Benston, Wm.
1326 Parmore, Ezekiell
1326 Parmore, Mathew
1327 Tomson, Charles
1328 Kemy, Abraham
1329 Ingrom, Abraham
1329 Ingrom, Abraham
1329 Ingrom, James
1329 slave George
1329 slave Pris
1330 Ingrom, David
1331 Ingrom, Isaac
1332 Hall, James
1333 Smith, David
1334 Hurny, John
1335 Wiliams, Charles
1336 Kemey, Walter
1337 Brown, Tho.
1338 Kemey, Thos.
1339 Dixon, Wm.
1340 Sanders, Andrew
1340 Sanders, Ritchard
1340 Sanders, Andrew
1341 Fortineare, Wm.
1342 Lewes, Arthur
1343 Lewis, Samuell
1343 Lewes, Leven
1344 Fisher, George
1345 Macady, John
1346 Owens, Robart
1346 slave Atte
1347 Polk, Charles
1348 Polk, Ephim
1349 Polk, John
1349 slave Atte
1349 slave Sip
1350 Polk, James
1351 Manlove, Amanull
1351 slave Quaco
1352 Jones, Samuell
1353 Sumerlin, Wm.
1353 Craycraft, George
1354 Lang[ston], Speare
1355 Newbold, Frances
1355 slave Ame
1356 Winright, Wm.
1357 Sharp, John
1357 Sharp, John
1357 slave Amee
1358 Buckworth, Charles
1359 Ubanks, Molten
1360 Bowger, James
1361 Rickords, Alexander
1362 Twiford, Wm.
1362 Twiford, Wm.
1363 Chipman, Parris
1363 Marvell, Robt.
1363 slave Cate
1364 Gray, Wm.
1364 Frigs, Robt.
1364 slave Cofie
1365 More, Wm., snr.
1365 More, Tho.
1365 Daughety, James
1365 slave Pegg
1366 Lynn, Arron
1366 Lyndas, Joseph
1366 slave Abraham
1366 slave Jack
1366 slave Jean
1366 slave Bess
1367 Persons, Frances
1367 Shorindon, Ezekiell

TAX LISTS OF SOMERSET COUNTY: 1730-1740

NANTICOKE/POCOMOKE HUNDREDS

1368 Waller, John
1368 Beach, Tho.
1369 Philips, Wm.
1370 Osborn, John
1371 Wille, John
1371 slave Danell
1371 slave Coffie
1372 Peterkin, James
1373 Tomson, Charles, jur.
1374 Jones, John, quantico
1375 Godard, George
1376 Stevens, John

POCOMOKE HUNDRED

1377 Hayward, Thos., mr.
1377 Larmouth, Alexr.
1377 slave Sambo
1377 slave Tom
1377 slave Jesper
1377 slave Cudjo
1377 slave Rose
1377 slave Priss
1377 slave Pleasant
1377 slave Philliss
1378 Denniss, John, jur.
1378 slave Kingstone
1378 slave Isaac
1378 slave George
1378 slave Patience
1378 slave Kate
1379 Probat, Willm., capt.
1380 Mitchell, Robert
1380 Mitchell, Joshua
1380 slave Selby
1381 Geddes, Robt.
1381 slave Tom
1381 slave Pheaby
1382 Handy, Elizth.
1382 slave Harry
1382 slave Hager
1382 slave Judea
1383 Handy, Thos.
1383 Handy, Stephen
1384 Mills, Wm.
1385 Mills, Jonathn.
1386 Tull, Noble
1387 Tull, George
1387 Tull, Jonathn.
1387 slave Abner
1388 Pilcher, William
1388 Mathews, John
1389 Pilcher, John
1390 Coston, Stephen
1390 slave Dinah
1391 Odear, Stephen

1392 Tull, John
1393 Costen, Isaac
1393 slave Coffee
1393 slave Andrew
1393 slave Ceesar
1393 slave Pegg
1393 slave Hannah
1393 slave Joan
1393 slave Moll
1394 Harriss, John
1394 Harriss, Benton
1394 slave Tom
1395 Harriss, Jeremiah
1396 Knight, Richd.
1396 slave Boatswain
1397 Knight, James
1398 Haddock, Ignatius
1399 Harper, Edwd.
1399 Harper, John
1400 Riggen, Teague, senr.
1400 Riggen, Teague
1400 Moore, Bradshaw
1400 slave Peter
1400 slave Dinah
1400 slave Nann
1401 Harriss, Robt.
1401 slave Harry
1401 slave Toney
1401 slave Mingo
1401 slave Moll
1402 Harriss, Caleb
1402 Smith, John
1403 Fleming, Wm.
1403 Benston, George
1404 Warwick, Arthr.
1404 Tillman, William
1405 Ward, Joseph
1405 Ward, Cornelius
1405 Ward, Joseph
1405 slave Sarah
1406 Riggen, Amrbose, senr.
1406 Riggen, Teague
1407 Long, Danl., junr.
1408 Smulling, Randl., senr.
1408 Smulling, Randl.
1408 Smulling, Nathl.
1408 Smulling, Wm.
1408 Magrain, John
1409 Riggen, Joseph
1409 slave Caesar
1410 Philips, John
1410 Philips, Ezekill
1411 Stutt, Archl.
1412 Denston, John, senr.
1412 Denston, John

1412 Denston, Isaac
1413 Brown, George
1414 Taylor, Jacob
1415 Dukes, Wm.
1416 Harper, Francis
1417 Wonnell, James
1417 Redding, Charles
1418 Dukes, Robt.
1419 Ottwell, Frans., senr.
1419 Outwell, Wm.
1420 Ottwell, Charles
1421 Riggen, Darby
1421 Riggen, John
1421 Riggen, Peirce
1421 Riggen, Teague
1422 Riggen, Ambrose, junr.
1423 Maccuddy, John
1423 Milbourn, Ralph
1423 Nichols, George
1424 Colebourn, John
1425 Townsend, Dantford
1426 Atkinson, Isaac
1427 Townsend, Elizth.
1427 slave Tawney
1428 Atkinson, Saml.
1428 Davis, John
1429 Atkinson, Joshua
1429 slave Abram
1429 slave Frank
1429 slave Bess
1430 Buttler, Thos.
1431 Johnson, Whittington
1431 slave Betty
1431 slave Pleasant
1432 Taylor, Saml., junr.
1433 Taylor, Saml., senr.
1433 Taylor, George
1434 Steevens, John
1435 Warrington, Thos.
1436 Ruark, John
1437 Crouch, Isaac
1438 Crouch, Nicholas
1439 Wright, Randl.
1440 Fountain, Nichs.
1441 Jones, Wm.
1442 Noble, James
1443 Hammond, Charles
1444 Dier, John
1445 Scott, Wm.
1445 Ross, David
1446 Laws, Wm.
1447 Taylor, James
1448 Beavans, John
1448 Beavans, Thos.

1739 TAX LIST [Household number/Name/Remarks]

POCOMOKE HUNDRED

1448 Beavans, Roland
1448 slave Sambo
1449 Kellum, Joshua
1449 Kellum, Isaac
1450 Glass, Christopher, junr
1451 Mackdaniel, James
1451 Victor, Thos.
1451 Mackdaniel, John
1451 Taylor, Mathias
1452 Broughton, James
1453 Whittington, William
1453 slave Frank
1453 slave Harry
1453 slave Abner
1453 slave Betty
1453 slave Sarah
1454 Houston, Joseph
1454 Kellum, Wm.
1454 slave Tom
1454 slave Bell
1454 slave Pegg
1455 Sturgace, Jonathn.
1456 Pope, John
1456 Pope, John
1456 Taylor, Jobe
1456 slave Cook
1456 slave Tom
1456 slave Harry
1456 slave Pegg
1456 slave Jenney
1457 Outton, Abram
1457 Andrews, Peale
1457 Dear, John
1457 slave Flowro
1458 Morris, Isaac, mr.
1458 slave Southy
1458 slave Will
1458 slave Abner
1458 slave Ben
1458 slave Sam
1458 slave Dinah
1459 Godfrey, Joseph
1460 Martin, James, capt.
1460 Neilson, John
1460 Brittingham, Nathl.
1460 slave Pompey
1460 slave Mass
1460 slave Joe
1460 slave Caesar
1460 slave Nann
1460 slave Dinah
1461 Dennis, John, senr. mr.

1461 Dennis, Lazs.
1461 slave Joe
1462 Denniss, Vallentine
1463 Glass, Christopher, senr
1463 Glass, Elias
1464 Purnell, Elisha
1464 slave Pipin
1465 Henry, Robt.
1466 Hough, Edmd.
1466 slave Will
1466 slave Scipio
1467 Townsend, Littleton
1467 Porter, John
1467 slave Abby
1467 slave Pompy
1467 slave Jenney
1468 Townsend, Jeremiah
1469 Kellum, John, jr. ind. town
1470 Taylor, Wm.
1471 Nichols, Joseph
1472 Davis, Joseph
1473 Nichols, Mathias
1474 Nichols, James
1474 slave Hannah
1475 Gurly, George
1476 Bennitt, John
1476 Reading, Michl.
1476 slave Cork
1477 Selby, Thos.
1477 Selby, Thos.
1477 slave Sam
1478 White, Hannah
1478 White, John
1478 White, Wm.
1479 Davis, Nathl., senr.
1479 Davis, Nathl.
1480 Kitchen, Wm.
1480 slave Betty
1481 Ball, Saml.
1482 Townsend, Wm. Bartho.
1483 Beavans, Cornelius
1484 Beavans, Rowland
1484 Beavans, Wm.
1485 Mackallin, Arthr.
1485 [Easom], John
1486 Peale, Thos., senr.
1486 Peale, Thos.
1486 slave Sampson
1487 Hambleton, Wm.
1488 Cottingham, Jonathn.
1488 Cottingham, Wm.
1488 Cottingham, John
1489 Beavans, Thos.
1490 Townsend, Charles
1490 Townsend, Solomon
1491 Scott, John, capt.
1491 Scott, Joseph
1491 Dougherty, Edmd.
1491 Goldsmith, Thos.
1491 slave Peter
1491 slave Hope
1491 slave Rose
1491 slave Phoeby
1492 Porter, Francis
1492 slave Jack
1492 slave Sawney
1493 Porter, McCemey
1493 Tull, James
1494 Allen, Francis, senr.
1494 Allen, Francis, junr.
1494 slave Sambo
1494 slave Frank
1494 slave Jeremi
1494 slave Judea
1494 slave Margery
1494 slave Murreah
1495 Gibbs, Robt.
1495 Gibbs, Abram
1496 Taylor, Peter
1496 slave Tom
1496 slave Cupitt
1496 slave Pleasant
1496 slave Fungeo
1496 slave Jack
1496 slave Fisher
1497 Atkinson, Angelo
1497 Dougherty, James
1497 Vallance, Thos.
1498 Ottwell, Frans., junr.
1498 Townsend, Marshall
1499 Bennett, Wm.
1499 Kersey, Robt.
1499 Powell, Gabriel
1499 Obryen, Danl.
1500 Sheldon, John
1500 Dukes, John
1500 slave Isaac
1501 Townsend, James
1501 slave Guy
1501 slave Jack
1502 Fogg, Moses
1503 Townsend, Danl.
1503 Townsend, Dickerson

TAX LISTS OF SOMERSET COUNTY: 1730-1740

POCOMOKE HUNDRED

1503 Townsend, James	1526 Jones, Edwd.	1557 Mulligen, Thos.
1503 slave Pegg	1526 Jones, Elisha	1557 Wright, Comfort, molatto
1504 Donohoe, Dormon	1527 Brooks, Francis	1558 Breemen, James
1504 Cooper, Saml.	1528 Mills, Saml.	1558 slave Tallomy
1505 Fleming, John	1528 Mills, Hugh	1559 Layfield, George
1505 Fleming, John, junr.	1528 Mills, John	1560 Jones, Richd.
1505 slave Robin	1529 Mills, Nathl.	1560 Mackfarlin, Robt.
1505 slave Pompy	1530 Elliss, Wm.	1561 Dickerson, Robt.
1505 slave Joe	1531 Gillett, Saml.	1561 Dickerson, Nehemiah
1505 slave Dinah	1531 Gillett, Wm.	1562 Dickerson, Francis
1505 slave Nancy	1531 Gillett, Saml.	1563 Blades, Benjn.
1506 Lane, John	1531 slave Dorcas	1563 Blades, Robt.
1507 Townsend, Saul	1532 Gillett, John	1564 Small, John
1507 Donoho, Dormon	1532 slave Harry	1565 Henderson, John, senr.
1507 slave Will	1532 slave Nanny	1565 slave Guy
1508 Townsend, John, senr.	1532 slave Rose	1565 slave George
1508 Townsend, John	1533 Steevenson, Joseph	1565 slave Bess
1508 Ottwell, Solomon	1533 Steevenson, Wm.	1565 slave Joan
1509 Dickerson, Charles	1534 Piper, Isaac	1565 slave Eve
1510 Dickerson, Cornelius	1534 Whaley, John	1566 Henderson, James
1510 slave Dinah	1535 Mills, Smith	1566 Henderson, John
1510 slave Jenney	1536 Mills, Wm., junr.	1566 slave Adam
1511 Dickerson, Edmd., junr.	1537 Mills, Nathn.	1567 Henderson, John, junr.
1511 Dickerson, Edmd., senr.	1537 Mills, Alexr.	1567 Henderson, Saml.
1511 slave George	1538 Mills, Robt.	1567 Henderson, John
1512 Donoho, Sarah	1539 Steevenson, Robt.	1568 Henderson, Charles
1512 Donoho, Teague	1540 Lamberson, Saml.	1569 Lambden, Thos.
1512 Donoho, Danl.	1541 Curreyos, Caleb	1569 Lambden, Richd.
1512 Donoho, John	1542 Lamberson, Abram	1570 Henderson, Francis
1513 Townsend, Comfort	1543 Ramsey, Charles	1571 Pitts, Robt.
1513 Townsend, Nathl.	1543 Ramsey, Jno.	1572 Blades, John
1514 Lindow, Margtt.	1543 Ramsey, Barnett	1572 slave Phillip
1514 slave Mosses	1543 Ramsey, Welbourn	1573 Henderson, Benjn.
1515 Brittingham, Elijah	1544 Merrill, John	1574 Young, Danl.
1515 slave Caesar	1545 Davis, Evans	1575 Conner, Wm.
1515 slave Nann	1546 Lane, Wm., capt.	1576 Benston, John, senr.
1516 Melvin, Robt.	1546 slave Harry	1576 Benston, John
1516 Melvin, Robt.	1546 slave Dick	1577 Cambroon, Evander
1517 Melvin, Wm.	1546 slave Phillis	1577 Hewdy, Hugh
1518 Mosses, Joseph	1547 Quinton, Philip	1578 Brittingham, Saml.
1519 Wheeler, Isaac	1547 slave Jack	1579 Brittingham, Micajh.
1519 Wheeler, Wm.	1547 slave Peter	1580 Steevens, Wm.
1519 slave Joe	1547 slave Tamor	1580 slave Mokey
1520 Mills, Mosses	1548 Quinton, Dixon	1581 Dormon, Saml., senr.
1520 slave Simon	1549 Lindall, Robt.	1581 Dormon, Saml.
1521 Burnett, James	1549 Cain, Thos.	1582 Paddin, John
1522 Bell, John	1550 Lamberson, Robert	1582 Hall, John
1523 Webb, John	1551 Houston, James	1582 slave Oxford
1523 Webb, Solomon	1551 slave Kate	1583 Cluff, Edwd.
1523 Webb, John	1552 Houston, John, senr.	
1523 Cook, Guy	1553 [Dickerson, Peter]	
1524 Pain, Joseph	1553 slave Jack	
1525 Melton, John	1554 Brittingham, John	
	1555 Brittingham, Wm.	
	1555 slave Rose	
	1556 Corvine, Thos.	
	1557 Baker, James	

1739 TAX LIST [Household number/Name/Remarks]

POCOMOKE HUNDRED

1583 Fetzhew, John
1584 Broughton, Bruff
1584 Lanyeard, Jno.
1585 Broughton, John
1585 Broughton, Willm.
1586 Tillghman, Giddeon
1586 Tillghman, John
1586 Maddox, Lazs.
1586 slave Pompey
1587 Steevens, Edwd.
1588 Clogg, Saml.
1589 Pirkins, John
1589 Pirkins, Michl.
1589 Whailey, Wm.
1590 Dreedon, David, junr.
1591 Newbold, Thos.
1591 Newbold, Purnell
1591 slave Patience
1592 Benston, Thos.
1593 Brookes, Richd.
1593 Brookes, Richd.
1593 slave Lett
1594 Powell, John
1594 slave Sarah
1595 Powell, Levin
1596 Dreedon, David, senr.
1596 Dreedon, Wm.
1596 Thompson, John
1597 Fenton, Margtt.
1597 Blair, Robt.
1598 Johnson, Joshua
1599 Hampton, Mary, madm.
1599 Henry, Robt. Jenckins, major
1599 Henry, John, capt.
1599 slave Tarrill
1599 slave Adam
1599 slave Harry
1599 slave Chick
1599 slave Lucey
1599 slave Philliss
1599 slave Jenny
1599 slave Patience
1599 slave Rose
1600 Williams, John, capt.
1600 Whittington, Southy
1600 Vernelson, Elias
1600 Porter, Wm.
1600 slave Jamey
1600 slave Harry
1600 slave Robbin
1600 slave Nimrod
1600 slave Phalix
1600 slave Robbin
1600 slave Titus
1600 slave Jenny
1600 slave Priss
1600 slave Sue
1601 Scholfield, Henry
1601 Sparkman, George
1602 Tomlinson, Seward
1602 Peacock, John
1602 slave Pleasent
1603 Tomlinson, Solomon
1603 Hogskin, Jonas
1603 slave London
1604 White, Archl.
1604 White, Wm.
1605 McCready, Alexr.
1606 White, John, pocomoke
1606 slave George
1606 slave Nan
1607 Hall, John
1608 Nearn, James
1608 slave Harry
1608 slave Cambridge
1608 slave Moll
1609 Nairn, Robt.
1609 slave Mag
1609 slave Nanny
1609 slave Sarah
1609 slave Jones
1610 Drummond, Francis
1611 Addams, Collins
1612 Dickerson, Isaac
1613 Collins, Saml.
1614 Milbourn, John
1615 Milbourn, Caleb
1615 slave Mingo
1615 slave Hannah
1616 Milbourn, Ralph
1617 Evans, Thos.
1617 Evans, Wm.
1617 slave Jenney
1618 Evans, John
1619 McCready, Solomon
1619 McCready, Alexr., junr.
1620 Baker, Henderson
1621 Holland, Wm., capt.
1621 slave Tom
1621 slave Dinah
1622 Benston, Benjn.
1623 Boyer, Robt.
1623 Boyer, Jona.
1623 Clifton, Geo.
1623 slave Harry
1623 slave Dorcass
1624 Clifton, John
1625 Elliss, John
1626 Rook, Edwd.
1626 Caton, Charles
1627 Cox, Wm.
1627 slave Ceaser
1627 slave Doll
1628 Riggen, John, junr.
1628 slave Nann
1629 Dickerson, Charles, junr
1630 Dickerson, Teague
1631 Riggen, Solomon
1631 Dickerson, John
1632 Riggen, Charles
1633 Caldwell, Joshua
1633 slave Jack
1633 slave Adam
1633 slave Dinah
1633 slave Moll
1634 Riggen, John, senr.
1634 Riggen, John
1634 Riggen, Teague
1634 Riggen, Cornelius
1634 slave Jenny
1635 Mathews, Teague
1635 Mathews, Philip
1636 Mathews, Wm.
1637 Mathews, John
1638 Mathews, Mary
1638 Mathews, David
1638 slave Jeofry
1639 Mathews, Saml.
1640 Adams, Saml.
1640 slave Jenny
1641 Adams, Jacob
1641 Adams, Thos.
1641 More, Joseph
1641 slave Sampson
1641 slave Nan
1642 Kersey, Wm.
1642 Cottingham, John
1642 Cottingham, Wm.
1643 Kersey, Saml.
1644 Boston, Isaac
1644 slave Jeffrey
1644 slave Venus
1644 slave Thomas
1644 slave Jenny
1645 Boston, Esaw, senr.
1645 Boston, Esaw
1646 Taylor, Robt., senr.
1646 Taylor, Robt.
1647 Taylor, Elias
1648 Woods, Wm.
1649 Adams, Isaac
1649 slave Dick
1649 slave Moll

TAX LISTS OF SOMERSET COUNTY: 1730-1740

POCOMOKE/WICOMICO HUNDREDS

1650 Owins, Mosses
1650 slave Harry
1651 Dikes, Edwd.
1651 Dikes, Danl.
1652 Adams, Hope
1652 slave Gloster
1653 Adams, Philip
1654 Adams, George
1654 Adams, George
1655 Adams, Wm., senr.
1655 Adams, Philip
1656 Adams, Wm., junr.
1657 Beauchamp, Edwd.
1657 Beauchamp, Levin
1657 slave Morie
1658 Beauchamp, Marsey
1659 Beauchamp, Thos.
1660 Davis, Beauchamp
1661 Mayo, Saml.
1662 Merrill, Joshua
1663 Henry, Robert Jenckins
1663 Whittney, Barrett
1664 Andrus, John
1664 Adrus, Robinson

WICOMICO HUNDRED

1665 Gale, Levin, coll.
1665 Roberson, Wm.
1665 slave Hope
1665 slave Jacob
1665 slave Jack
1665 slave Jemy
1665 slave Harry
1665 slave Robin
1665 slave Jehu
1665 slave Jobe
1665 slave Jonan.
1665 slave Will
1665 slave Old Henry
1665 slave Peter
1665 slave Joyce
1665 slave Plesent
1665 slave Bess
1665 slave Zipra
1665 slave Moreah
1665 slave Hanh.
1665 slave Franck
1665 slave Ishmael
1665 slave Dick
1666 Dashiell, Geor., coll.
1666 Morrison, Tho.
1666 Boadley, Wm.
1666 Crouch, Jno., jur.
1666 21 slaves
1667 Langcake, Fras.
1667 Langcake, Stepn.
1667 slave Jack
1667 slave Tobe
1667 slave Bess
1668 Heatch, John
1668 slave Mouah
1669 Heatch, Saml.
1669 slave Jack
1670 Flintt, John
1671 Heatch, Elgtt.
1671 Prise, Thos.
1671 Prise, Alex.
1671 Vinson, Geo.
1671 slave Bony
1671 slave Conuda
1672 Heatch, Wm.
1672 Heatch, Jno., jur.
1673 Collins, Jas.
1674 Cordrey, John
1674 Cordrey, Jno., jur.
1675 King, Wm.
1676 Vinson, Thos.
1676 Vinson, Thos., jur.
1677 Lecatt, John
1677 slave Leah
1678 Stevens, Wm.
1679 Maddux, Alexr.
1679 slave Geo.
1679 slave Moreah
1680 Maddux, Wm.
1680 slave Abram
1681 Gray, Allen
1682 Covington, Thos.
1682 Covington, Jno.
1682 slave Tom
1683 Hall, Saml.
1684 Ready, Bryan
1684 Ready, Cornelius
1685 Hearne, Thos.
1685 Hearne, Nehe.
1685 slave Hanh.
1686 Hearn, Geo.
1687 Cragin, Paul
1688 Caldwell, Hugh
1689 Haisten, Wm.
1690 Haistin, Robt.
1690 Haisten, Robt., jur.
1690 Haisten, Benj.
1691 Freny, Peter
1691 Freny, Jno.
1692 Lindow, Thos.
1693 Hearn, Wm.
1693 Hearn, Jno.
1693 Hearne, Isaac
1693 slave Moll
1694 King, Hugh
1695 Persons, Robt.
1696 Gordy, Peter
1697 Morris, Jeremh.
1698 Mellson, Danl.
1699 Phillips, Jacob
1700 Smith, David
1701 Roberts, Rencher
1702 Smith, Jams., jur.
1703 Smith, Archd.
1704 Disharoone, Lewis
1704 Dale, Jno.
1704 Canady, Timothy
1705 Cox, Thos.
1706 Cox, Hill
1707 Cox, Thos., jur.
1708 Disharoone, Jno., forrt.
1709 Disharoone, Levin
1710 Vinson, Benj.
1711 Right, Jeremh., jur.
1712 Tatom, Jno.
1713 Persons, Jno.
1714 Leonard, Jos.
1715 Tomson, Thos.
1716 Smith, Andw.
1716 Smith, Geo.
1716 Smith, Andw., jur.
1717 Turner, Saml.
1717 Turner, Jos.
1718 Turner, Joshua
1719 Smith, George
1720 Smith, Jas., sr.
1721 Smith, Moses
1722 Hill, James
1723 Murphey, Jos.
1724 Persons, Geo.
1724 Breuerton, Alexr.
1725 Kersey, Patrick
1725 Kersey, Jas.
1726 Lingo, Jno.
1727 Lingo, Jas.
1727 Ruock, Jas.
1727 Morris, Nathl.
1728 Sadler, Isaac
1729 Willis, Nathl.
1729 Savage, Wm.
1730 Lingo, Roberson
1731 Sceady, Stepn.
1732 Dorman, Majr.
1733 Dorman, Henry
1734 Lingo, Richd.
1735 Shockley, Richd.
1736 Perdue, Jno.
1736 Perdue, Geo.
1737 Niblett, Richd.
1737 Willis, Edmd.
1738 McGlamry, Edwd.
1738 Ollivin, Mathw.

1739 TAX LIST [Household number/Name/Remarks]

WICOMICO HUNDRED

1739 Davis, Danl.
1739 Davis, Thos.
1740 Megee, Peter, forrest
1741 Megee, Geo.
1741 Megee, Jno.
1742 Davis, Jno.
1742 Megee, Moses
1743 McGlamry, Geo.
1744 Waill, Jno.
1745 Collins, Richd.
1746 Toadvine, Isaac
1747 Toadvine, Jno.
1747 Toad[v]ine, Wm.
1748 Hay[man], Wm.
1748 Hay[man], Wm., jur.
1748 Hay[m]an, Nichs.
1749 Shockley, Jno.
1749 Shockley, Jno., jur.
1749 Shockley, Wm.
1750 Cary, Tho.
1751 Shockley, Jona.
1752 Driskill, Mosses
1753 Gordy, Mosses
1754 Davis, Saml.
1755 Adkins, Robt.
1756 Cathel, James
1757 Hailes, Jno.
1758 Tayler, John
1759 Chris[tof]er, Jno., jur.
1759 Chr[ist]ofer, Jacob
1760 [Drisk]ill, Dennis
1761 [Bush]aw, Graves
1761 To[advi]ne, Geo.
1762 Re[vill], Wm.
1762 slave Tom
1763 Foox, Benj.
1763 Fox, Benj., jur.
1763 slave Patience
1763 slave Jene
1764 Toadvine, Henry
1764 Toadvine, Josha.
1764 slave Goliah
1764 slave Sarah
1764 slave Flora
1764 slave Oxford
1764 slave Jeny
1765 Toadvine, Thos.
1766 Cary, Levin
1767 Roach, Alce
1767 Roach, Isaac
1767 slave Tom
1767 slave Pegg
1767 slave Hary
1767 slave Hanh.

1768 Roach, Stepn.
1768 Gol[d]smith, Ant.
1768 slave York
1769 Sheha[n]. Jno.
1770 Dish[aroon]e, Jno., sr.
1770 slave Coffey
1770 slave Grace
1770 slave Fanny
1771 Disharoone, Michl.
1772 Disharoone, Jno., jr.
1773 Disharoone, Wm.
1774 Ellis, Fra.
1774 Ellis, Wm.
1775 Stanford, Jos.
1775 Stanford, Jonan.
1776 Chadawicks, Jas.
1776 Chadawicks, Jno.
1777 Chadawicks, Jas., jur.
1778 Christofer, Epm.
1779 Tomson, Jno.
1780 Bayley, Benj.
1781 Raglin, Michl.
1782 Brown, Andw.
1783 Knox, Wm.
1783 Pollett, Wm.
1784 Adley, Wm.
1784 Adley, Wm., jur.
1784 Adley, Geo.
1784 Adley, Phillip
1785 Griffith, Jno.
1786 Hayman, Chas., son Wm.
1787 Hayman, Jno.
1788 Hayman, Ja.
1788 Hayman, Isaac
1789 Hayman, Cha.
1790 Pollett, Tho.
1790 Pollett, Thos., jur.
1790 slave Dinah
1791 Polk, David
1791 slave Tamer
1792 Laws, Jno.
1792 slave Tom
1793 Alexander, Mosses
1793 Polk, Jno.
1793 slave Tom
1794 Shurman, Peter
1794 Shurman, Peter
1794 slave Tom
1794 slave Lemon
1795 Shurman, Jno.
1796 Weatherbey, Jno.
1797 Mitchell, Benj.
1798 Mitchell, Jno.
1798 ADaugh, Owen

1799 Sillivin, Wm.
1799 Noble, Wm.
1800 Noble, Isaac
1801 Wilkins, James
1802 Cottman, Wm.
1803 Cottman, Jos.
1803 slave Sarah
1804 Roberson, Jno.
1804 slave Sy
1805 Lockey, Thos.
1806 Roberson, Wm.
1806 Macom, Geo.
1807 Moade, Peter
1808 Walker, Tho.
1808 slave Tom
1808 slave Jube
1808 slave Jonah
1808 slave Dinah
1808 slave Cate
1809 Mackintire, Danl.
1809 Crouckitt, Robt.
1809 Brucksher, Wm.
1809 Willing, Thos., jur.
1809 slave Crop
1810 Holbrook, Tho.
1811 Fouler, Tho.
1812 Ellis, Alce
1812 Chambers, Edwd., esqr.
1812 Caldwell, Wm.
1812 slave Will
1812 slave Bubo
1812 slave Harry
1812 slave Moll
1813 Gale, Matts.
1813 Noble, Marck
1813 slave Ceaser
1813 slave Jack
1813 slave Relph
1813 slave Dublin
1813 slave Stepn.
1813 slave Rose
1813 slave Violet
1813 slave Sarah
1814 Steuart, Patrick
1815 Harris, Wm.
1815 Harris, Cha.
1815 Harris, Bloyce
1816 Harris, Wm., jur.
1817 Harris, Richd.
1818 Durham, James
1819 Fouler, Jno.
1819 slave Mary
1820 Foskque, Tho.
1821 Dashiell, Thos., jur.
1821 slave Isaac
1822 Rensher, Tho.
1822 slave Peter

TAX LISTS OF SOMERSET COUNTY: 1730-1740

WICOMICO HUNDRED

1822 slave Pompy
1823 Rensher, Underwood
1823 Legg, Benj.
1823 slave Jack
1823 slave Moreah
1824 Ballard, Charles
1824 slave Seaser
1824 slave Moreah
1825 Jones, Jno.
1826 Dulany, Dennis
1827 Shiles, Jno.
1827 slave Tom
1827 slave Hanabel
1828 Crockitt, Jno.
1829 Leckie, Alex.
1829 Chambers, Sam.
1829 slave Toby
1829 slave Sam
1829 slave Surry
1829 slave Robin
1829 slave Franck
1829 slave Sibb
1829 slave Amey
1829 slave Grace
1829 slave Beck
1830 Evans, Jno.
1830 slave Sambo
1831 Dashiell, Charles
1831 slave Jacob
1831 slave Perlinah
1832 Fletchers, Thos.
1832 slave
1833 Willin, Edwd.
1834 Winright, Stepn.
1834 Winright, Jno.
1835 Shiles, John, jur.
1836 Nelson, Wm.
1836 Nelson, Jno.
1837 Everton, Jno.
1837 Everton, Wm.
1838 Forbus, Peter
1839 Willin, Tho.
1839 Willin, Robt.
1839 slave Guma
1839 slave Sarah
1840 Scott, Geo.
1840 McCaw, Jno.
1840 slave Sam
1840 slave Sanders
1840 slave Pomp
1840 slave Flolro
1841 Cordrey, Danl.
1841 Collier, N. Evens
1841 slave Samson
1841 slave Sib
1842 Cordrey, Abraham
1842 Dury, Danl.
1843 Scott, Day
1843 slave Hecter
1843 slave Tom
1843 slave Luecey
1843 slave Sue
1844 Austin, Edwd.
1844 James, Wm.
1845 Hardy, Robt.
1845 Hardy, Geo.
1845 Hardy, Ja.
1845 Hardy, Benj.
1846 Wailes, Helinah
1846 Richardson, Wm.
1846 slave Leander
1846 slave Peter
1846 slave Ordery
1846 slave Orris
1847 Dashiell, Matts.
1847 slave Sambo
1847 slave Mingo
1848 Mackmorie, Ann
1848 Foster, Jno.
1848 slave Pomp
1848 slave Rose
1848 slave Abner
1849 Banck, Stepn.
1849 slave Amey
1850 Winder, Thos.
1850 Rusell, Thos.
1850 slave Mingo
1850 slave Hary
1850 slave Bess
1851 Piper, Christ.
1851 slave Dick
1851 slave Sambo
1851 slave Moll
1851 slave Tobe
1851 slave Grenedg
1851 slave Sue
1852 Collier, Thos.
1852 slave Grace
1853 Venables, Benj.
1853 slave Tom
1853 slave Will
1853 slave Bess
1854 Goslen, Jno.
1855 Venables, Wm.
1855 slave Pompy
1856 Bartlett, Thos.
1856 Bartlett, Paskque
1856 Bartlett, Thos., jur.
1857 Prise, Jno.
1857 Christofer, Jos.
1857 Prise, David
1857 Piper, Jos.
1857 Bready, Ja.
1858 Byrd, Thos., se.
1858 Byrd, Benj.
1859 Byrd, Thos., jur.
1860 Nicholson, James
1861 Nicholson, Jos.
1862 Meares, Robt.
1862 Nicholson, Richd.
1863 Rickords, Jno.
1863 Rickords, Ja.
1863 Rickords, Thos.
1863 slave Tobe
1864 Humphris, Mary
1864 Humphris, Jos.
1865 Hall, Tho.
1866 Bready, Wm.
1866 Tolbert, Jno.
1867 Johnson, Purnall
1868 Johnson, Saml.
1869 Linch, Michl.
1870 Driskil, Wm.
1871 Hayler, David
1872 Handy, Isaac
1872 slave Quamino
1872 slave Sharper
1872 slave Prue
1872 slave Will
1872 slave Mumford
1873 Byrd, Wm.
1874 Parris, Geo.
1874 slave Nan
1875 Hobbs, Absolem
1875 slave Pulebus
1876 Handy, John
1876 slave Dick
1876 slave Ben
1876 slave Primus
1876 slave Jene
1876 slave Moll
1876 slave Hager
1876 slave Patience
1877 Jackson, Saml.
1877 slave Grace
1878 Morris, Jacob
1878 Morris, Jos.
1879 Howard, Jno.
1880 Ellis, Jno.
1881 Crouch, Jno.
1882 Sharp, Mary
1882 slave Moll
1882 slave Penny
1883 Porter, Joshua
1884 Henerickson, Peter
1885 Jenckins, Jarvis
1885 Jenckins, Jarvis, jur.
1885 Jenckins, Jno.
1886 Hillman, Edwd.
1887 Hill, Charles
1888 Ellis, Jos.
1889 Bayly, Geo.
1889 Bayly, Geo., jur.
1890 Baily, Jonathan
1891 Christofer, Jno.

1739 TAX LIST [Household number/Name/Remarks]

WICOMICO HUNDRED

1892 Christofer, Clemt.
1893 Doudle, Christ.
1894 N[o]les, Wm.
1895 [Gilli]s, Tho.
1895 [Gillis], Le[vin]
1895 H[ait]h, Wm.
1895 slave Stepny
1895 slave Tamor
1895 slave Domnick
1895 slave Pegg
1896 Adams, Alexr., revd.
1896 Adams, Alex., jur.
1896 Grig, Wm.
1896 slave Quosh
1896 slave Glasco
1896 slave Cato
1896 slave Beck
1896 slave Dinah
1897 Breuerton, Wm.
1897 Breuerton, Wm., jur.
1897 Breuerton, Jno.
1897 Breuerton, Saml.
1897 slave Patience
1898 Meares, John
1898 Meares, Saml.
1899 Megee, Peter
1899 [Me]gee, Peter, jur.
1899 [Meg]ee, Thos.
1900 [Co]ttman, Benj.
1900 slave Sarah
1901 E[va]ns, Jno., jur.
1901 slave Dinah
1902 McClain, Danl.
1903 Persons, Jno.
1904 Malone, Robt.
1905 Dashiell, Arthur
1905 Evans, Jno.
1905 slave Ben
1905 slave Penny
1905 slave Betty
1906 Shurman, Isaac
1907 Hall, Phenix
1907 Mitchell, Jno.
1908 Kibble, Wm.
1908 Megee, Saml.
1908 slave Peter
1908 slave Bess
1909 Stevens, Rachl.
1909 slave Pombo
1909 slave Sib
1909 slave Alce
1910 Lowes, Henry
1910 Willy, Artus
1910 Posel, Geo.
1910 Parratt, Thos.
1910 Waller, Saml.
1910 Willin, Jno.
1910 slave Jepter
1910 slave Joe
1910 slave Dover
1910 slave Rose
1910 slave Bess
1910 slave Five Islands
1910 slave Quomino
1911 Phillips, Richd.
1912 Bounds, Jonan.
1912 slave Bess
1913 Mitchell, Isaac
1914 Venables, Cathorin
1914 Venables, Jos.
1914 Venables, Perckins
1915 Cary, Jonan.
1916 Warrenton, Benja.
1916 Evans, Wm.
1916 Fookes, Young
1917 Davis, Wm.
1918 Goslen, Mathw.
1919 Goslen, Richd.
1920 Goslen, Thos.
1921 Bushaw, Jarrt.
1921 Bushaw, Giles
1922 Bluitt, Jno.
1923 Humphris, Thos.
1923 Morris, Jno.
1924 Evins, Wm.
1925 Crouch, Jacob
1926 Fulerton, Ja.
1927 Fulerton, Alexr.
1928 Reddish, Jno.
1929 Roggers, Richd.
1930 Crouch, Robt.
1931 Jackson, C. Domk.
1931 slave Judith
1931 slave Cate
1932 Cordrey, Jacob
1932 Bushaw, Wm.
1933 Caldwell, Jno.
1933 Caldwell, Robt.
1933 Benson, Geo., jur.
1933 slave Cuffie
1933 slave Will
1933 slave Doll
1933 slave Quosh
1934 Mellvin, Thos.
1935 Covington, Benj.
1936 Farlo, Jno.
1936 Farlo, Wm.
1937 Parris, Jno.
1938 Disharoone, Mich.

TAX LISTS OF SOMERSET COUNTY: 1730-1740

ANNAMESSEX HUNDRED

1 Hall, Richd.
1 Hall, Charles
2 Hall, Ezekil
3 Waters, Abigil, for
3 slave York
3 slave David
4 Waters, Elesibeth
4 slave Hannahbul
4 slave Sippo
4 slave Pegg
4 slave Alyo
5 Landin, Henry
6 Waters, Edward
6 slave Samson
6 slave Belindo
6 slave Flowre
7 Cotman, Mary
7 Cotman, Josept
7 Cotman, Bingaman
7 slave Gone
8 Waters, John
8 slave Will
8 slave Bery
8 slave Sam
8 slave Dick
8 slave Ned
8 slave Mark
8 slave Sarah
9 Waters, William
9 slave Gostiah
9 slave Hanover
9 slave Brister
9 slave Sambo
9 slave Pompey
9 slave Agethey
9 slave Dinah
10 Roach, Nathaniel
10 slave Sambo
11 Treharn, John
12 Sehorn, Thomas
12 Mositt, Umfris
12 slave Nan
12 slave Sarah
13 Tull, Sollomon
14 Warton, William
15 Long, Samll.
15 slave Samson
15 slave Quoreken
16 Curtis, Charles
16 slave Dick
16 slave Toney
17 Williams, John
17 slave Sambon
17 slave Mol
17 slave Ame
18 Williams, Jacob
18 slave Dick
18 slave Ginney
19 Beauchamp, Edmond
19 Dykes, Danl.

20 Catlin, William
20 slave Harry
21 Beauchamp, Isaac
21 slave Patience
22 Beauchamp, William
22 Beauchamp, Willm., jr.
23 Boston, William
24 Bremigim, Walter
25 Williams, Thomas, jr.
25 slave Dick
25 slave Seser
25 slave Quash
25 slave Billey
26 Williams, Isaac
26 Williams, Isaac, jr.
26 slave Plasant
27 Williams, Thomas, sr.
27 slave Titus
27 slave Addam
27 slave George
27 slave Tom
27 slave Addam
27 slave Jonas
27 slave Gelico
27 slave Glasco
27 slave Sarah
28 Long, John
28 Hogskin, Jonas
28 slave Robin
28 slave Sarah
29 Langford, Bengaman
29 slave Seasor
30 Dixon, Thomas
30 Dixo[n], Thomas, jr.
30 slave Gidin
30 slave Harry
30 slave Tobit
30 slave Dinah
30 slave Hannah
30 slave Peter
31 Dixon, Ambros
32 Dixon, William
32 Dixon, William, jr.
32 slave Ben
32 slave Cofey
32 slave Bettey
33 Horsey, Isaac, capt.
33 [Horsey], Jonathan
33 Parks, Charles
33 slave Beck
34 Horsey, Nathaniel
34 Horsey, Outterbridg
34 Johnson, Will.
34 slave Prenil
34 slave Quominy
34 slave Cate
34 slave Paticence

34 slave Cook
34 slave Tarrow
35 Horsey, Smith
35 Treharn, Jeams
35 slave Tamer
36 Horsey, Stephen, jr.
37 Holland, Michaeil, sr. for
37 slave Sarah
38 Taylor, William
39 Holland, Michaeil, jur.
39 slave Mol
39 slave Tom
40 Smith, Henry
41 Smith, William
42 Cottingham, Thomas
42 Oin, Phillip
43 Oin, Betty, for
43 Oin, William
44 Pusey, William
45 Colrn., William, sr.
45 Colborn, Sollomon
45 slave Quaco
46 Colrn., William, jur.
46 slave Cato
47 Coulborn, Sollomon
47 [Coulborn], Sollomon, son
47 slave Mereor
47 slave Nan
48 Davis, Jeams
49 Smith, Jeams
49 Regin, Jonathan
50 Miles, Henry
50 slave Robin
50 slave Dinah
50 slave Fillis
51 Johnson, John, sr.
51 Flin, John
52 Micaney, Patrick
53 Johson, John, jur.
54 More, Francis
55 More, Thomas
56 Cord, Thomas
57 Lord, Randil
58 Dorritey, John
58 Dorritey, Nathaniel
59 Cord, Henrey
60 Ward, Samll.
60 Ward, William
61 Ward, John
62 Ward, Steaphen
63 Ward, Cornellis
63 Rigin, Stephen
64 Rigin, John, jr.
65 Rigin, Jonathan
66 Rigin, John, sr.
66 Rigin, William
66 Ducks, Robert

1740 TAX LIST [Household number/Name/Remarks]

ANNAMESSEX HUNDRED

67 Benston, Saul	95 Bell, Anthoney	126 Madox, Bell
68 Summers, Thomas	95 Bell, Josephas	127 Madox, Thomas
68 Summers, George	95 Ward, Josshua	128 Madox, Mary, for
68 Summr., Samuel	96 Bell, Thomas	128 slave Cate
69 Lord, Ellicksander	96 slave Nan	129 White, Thomas
70 Sumers, Jonathan	97 Gunby, John	129 Willson, Josept
70 Sumers, Thomas	97 slave Cate	130 Treharn, Jeams
71 Whealler, Samuel, for	98 Gunby, Kirrk	130 Treharn, William
	99 Whittington, Suthar	131 Cohoon, John
71 [Whealler], Jonathan, son	99 slave Robin	131 Cohoon, Henry
	99 slave Seasor	132 Prier, Thomas
72 Readin, John	99 slave Hannah	132 Prier, Samuel
73 Sumers, John	99 slave Sarah	133 Long, Samuel
73 Sumers, David	99 slave Bettey	133 Long, William
73 Sumr., Bengaman	100 White, John	133 Long, Coulbourn
73 Sumr., Richard	100 Powel, Thomas	134 Long, Jeffrey
74 Banster, Charles	100 Powel, Bengaman	134 slave Ishmil
74 Phillips, Jeams	101 Moshel, Samll.	134 slave Sarah
75 Duit, William	102 Scott, Robert, ser.	135 Long, Daniel
75 slave Connon	102 Scot, George	135 slave Frindship
76 Ward, Thomas	103 Scott, John	135 slave Geney
76 Ward, Jacob	104 Scott, Robert, jr.	136 Long, David
76 Ward, Moses	105 Readin, Peter	137 Gullit, George
76 slave Pompey	106 Ore, Michaeil, for	138 White, John
77 Bird, David	106 [Ore], Michaeil, son	139 Bradley, William
78 More, Isaac		140 Bywaters, Richard
79 Williams, William	107 Scandons, Edward	141 Addams, Dennis
80 Sterlin, John, jr.	108 Langford, Joseph, sr.	142 Porter, Josept
81 Sterlin, Henry		143 Beauchamp, Mercey
82 Sterlin, John, sr.	108 Langford, Sollomon	144 Fordrid, William
82 Sterlin, Aron	108 Langford, Pusey	145 free black, What
82 Sterlin, Josept	109 Langford, Josept, junr.	146 Parks, Author, for
83 Grims, Jeams		146 Parks, John
84 Ward, Jeams	110 Cottingham, Thomas	146 Parks, Job
85 Cullin, Jacob	111 Cottingham, Charls	147 Tylor, Thomas
86 Bird, Arrabellow, for	111 Cottingham, John	147 Clayweel, Selvay
	112 Linzey, Thomas	147 Crockit, Josept
86 Dun--, William	113 Cottingham, Charl.	148 Tylor, John, sr.
87 Roach, John	114 Puzey, John	148 Tylor, Thomas
88 Roach, Charles	115 Addams, David	148 Tylor, David
88 Roach, Michaeil	115 Addams, William	149 Tylor, John, jur.
88 slave Jo	115 Addams, David	150 Evins, Richard
88 slave Rose	116 Harn, Edward	151 Evins, John
88 slave York	117 Addams, Thomas	151 Evins, John, jur.
88 slave Neomey	118 Willson, John	151 Evins, Thomas
89 Dize, Daniel	119 Willson, George	152 Mister, William
90 Cullin, Henry	120 Potter, Henry	152 Mister, Abraham
91 Claton, George	120 Olin, Thomas	152 Mister, Bengaman
92 Davis, John	120 slave Fillis	153 Hopkins, George
92 slave Harry	121 Wheatley, Samson	153 Hopkins, John
92 slave What	122 Wheatley, William	153 Hopkins, William
92 slave Dick	123 Connaway, William	153 Hopkins, George
92 slave Ginney	123 Conor, Phillip	153 Hopkins, Charles
92 slave Cate	124 Conaway, John	154 Wolf, Henry
93 Horsey, Stephen	124 Connaway, Levin	155 Horsman, Henry
93 Horsey, John	124 Conner, John, jur.	156 Fogg, Daniel
93 slave Daniel	125 Killiam, John	157 More, Thomas
93 slave Sarah	125 Killiam, William	158 Mashel, George
93 slave Robin	125 Outen, Purnal	159 Mashel, Thomas
94 Bloayd, Walter	125 Outten, Abraham	160 Killiam, John, jr.

TAX LISTS OF SOMERSET COUNTY: 1730-1740

ANNAMESSEX/BALTIMORE HUNDREDS

161 Lister, Jeane, for
161 Lister, Thomas
161 slave Sesor
162 Stodgdil, Cristen, for
162 slave Cate
163 King, Robert, coll. for
163 slave Tamer
163 slave Pompey
164 Hall, William
165 Johnson, John, sr., for
165 Dise, Philbey
166 Coulbourn, Samll.
167 Beachamp, Robert

BALTIMORE HUNDRED
168 Rackliff, Charles, capt.
168 Rackliff, Purnell
168 Rackliff, Charles
168 slave Robin
168 slave Will
168 slave Toppin
168 slave Cate
169 Fassitt, Lambard
169 slave Coffe
169 slave Capreall
170 Fassitt, John
170 free black Comfort
170 slave Lewe
170 slave Miney
171 Crapper, Natthanil, sr.
171 Crapper, Vincen
171 slave Kinny
172 Crapper, Edmond, sr.
172 Camble, Solomon
172 slave Petter
172 slave Dick
172 slave Sante
172 slave Pompy
172 slave Fills
173 Fassitt, Rouse
173 slave Sam
173 slave James
173 slave Fillis
174 Walton, Mattha, widow
174 Richeardson, John
175 Laurance, Henery
176 Walton, William, sr.
176 slave Ceaser
176 slave George
176 slave Jud
176 slave Rose
176 slave Comfort

177 Knock, Nehemiah
177 slave Nan
178 Crapper, Natthaniel, jr.
179 Wallis, Thomas
180 Coller, Petter
180 Coller, Kendell
180 slave Pompe
180 slave Moll
180 slave Sarah
181 Jones, John
182 Smallwood, Samuel
183 Fassitt, Mary, mrs. wido
183 slave Frank
183 slave Sue
183 slave Bery
183 slave Daull
184 Fassitt, William, capt.
184 Hamblon, Joseph
184 Brooks, Francis
184 slave Rachell
184 slave Sambo
184 slave Titus
184 slave Will
184 slave Hary
184 slave Beck
184 slave Daniel
185 Pattey, John
185 Pattey, Powell
185 slave London
186 Whealy, Mary, widow
186 Whealy, Natthaniel
186 Whealy, Elias
187 Morgan, Avery
187 slave Hanah
188 Gray, William
189 Pridix, Thomas
190 Crapper, Edmund, jr.
191 Purnell, John
191 slave Will
191 slave Darnel
191 slave Mary
191 slave Dinar
191 slave Fillis
191 slave Doll
191 slave James
191 slave Toney
191 slave Toney
192 Lay, Samuel
192 Rackliff, Rixam
193 Stevens, Samuel
194 Hudson, George
194 Aakey, Solomon
195 Walker, John, mulatto
196 Fisher, Bentual
197 Conner, Partrick

198 Tingle, Hugh
198 Tingle, Joseph
199 Clark, Edward
200 Aydlott, Thomas
200 Powell, Charles
201 Grace, Edward
202 West, George, sr.
202 West, George, jr.
203 Hopkins, Josiah
204 Woods, William
204 Woods, David
205 Woodcraft, William
205 Tippin, Robert
205 Mumford, John
206 Smith, Abraham
206 Smith, Purnell Fletcher
207 Newbold, John
207 slave Keato
207 slave Cillo
207 slave London
208 Lowrey, William
209 Stevenson, John
209 slave Harry
210 Webb, Wm.
211 Latchumb, Thomas
212 Clark, Joseph
213 Smith, William
213 Smith, John Onorton
214 Purkins, William
215 Conner, Daniel
216 Nickelson, John
217 Adkins, John
218 Linch, Abraham
219 Wyatt, Joseph, sr.
219 Wyatt, Natthaniel
220 Momford, James
221 Momford, William
222 Tull, John, jr.
223 Purkins, Thomas
224 Hudson, Samuel
225 Hudson, Richeard, jr.
226 Lathbury, Arthur
227 Wyatt, William
228 Linch, Alexander
229 Coe, Daniel
230 Derickson, Joseph
230 Freeman, Wm.
231 Wise, Matthew
231 Wise, Ezekiell
232 Daisey, Thomas, sr.
232 Daisey, Thos., jr.
233 Harney, Thomas, sr.
233 Harney, Thomas, jr.
234 Roberson, Joshua
234 Derickson, Wm.
234 Moore, Wm.
234 slave Bess
235 Evens, William, sr.

1740 TAX LIST [Household number/Name/Remarks]

BALTIMORE HUNDRED

235 Evens, Wm., jr.
235 Evens, Walter
235 Evens, Joshua
236 Waitt, John
237 Miller, Joseph
237 slave Tom
237 slave Jack
237 slave Charles
238 Gray, William
239 Evens, John, jr.
240 Whorton, Daniel, sr.
240 Whorton, Daniel, jr.
240 Whorton, George
240 Whorton, Baker
241 Rickards, John, sr.
241 Woods, John
241 slave Boson
241 slave Brigg
242 Whorton, Henman
242 slave Abrealer
243 Boden, John
244 Roberson, Thomas
244 Roberson, Joseph
245 Hazzard, William
245 slave Pheladelpha
246 Harges, Thomas
247 Godwin, Ceaser, sr.
248 Rickards, William
248 slave Moll
249 Rickards, John, jr.
249 Townsend, Wm.
250 Roberson, Michaell, sr.
250 Roberson, Michaell, jr.
250 Roberson, Wm.
251 Rogers, Solomon
251 slave Cane
252 Rathbone, Robart
253 Rickards, Jones
254 Depray, John
255 Masey, John
256 Aydlott, John, sr.
257 Morris, William
257 Godwin, Daniel
258 Dolby, William
259 Hodward, Nehemiah
260 Howard, George, sr.
260 Howard, George, jr.
260 slave Kent
260 slave Bess
261 Johnson, Lenard
261 Keth, John

262 Miller, John, mr.
262 slave Primas
262 slave Tom
262 slave Pegg
263 Dixson, Joyce, widow
263 Johnson, Leaven
264 Delany, John Partrick
265 Johnson, John
266 Boden, Able
267 Harmon, William
267 [Harmon], Betty, wife
268 Harmon, John
268 [Harmon], wife, molletto
269 Roberson, John
269 Roberson, George
269 Roberson, Joseph
269 Roberson, John
270 Banks, Neblitt
271 Godwin, Ceasar, jr.
272 Aydlott, John, jr.
273 Hopkins, John
274 Robarts, Alexander
274 Robarts, Thomas, jr.
275 Robarts, Thomas, sr.
276 Hall, Samuel
277 Evens, John, sr.
278 Tingle, Hugh, jr.
279 Perrey, James
280 Hatfield, William
281 Blizard, Thomas
282 Collings, John
283 Holland, Elezbath, sr., widow
283 Moore, David
283 Holland, Samuel
283 slave Hanah
284 Tingle, Samuel
285 Farrill, Thomas
286 Lockwood, Armesall
287 Lockwood, Mary, widow
287 Lockwood, John
288 Waters, Richeard
289 Looker, William
289 Quilling, John
290 Wood, Stephen
291 Brittingham, Robert
291 Brittingham, Nathan
292 Morrow, Robert
293 Morrow, James
294 Hogg, James
295 Deale, John, ser.
296 Gray, Thomas
297 Tyer, Robart

298 Powell, Thomas
299 Whealy, Charles
300 Cambell, John, sr.
300 Camble, John, jr.
300 slave Rick
301 Evens, Ebenezear
302 Godard, Thomas
303 Bessex, Natthaniel
304 Holloway, John, jr.
305 Turvell, Prisgrave
305 Garman, Prisgrave
306 Brewen, John
306 slave Matt
307 Russell, Andrew
308 Mumford, Charles
309 Hokins, Samuel, capt.
309 slave Orsen
310 Hudson, Richeard, sr.
310 Maccarthy, Charles
310 Hudson, Jon.
310 Hudson, Henry
310 slave Coffee
310 slave Dick
310 slave Beck
311 Turvell, William
311 Whealy, John
311 Taylor, Josiah
312 Walton, William, jr.
313 Harrison, William
314 Masey, Alexander
314 slave Jack
315 Hill, Johnson
316 Bowen, Rhodey, widow
316 Bowen, William
316 Bowing, John
316 Bowen, Whittington
316 slave Qaminy
316 slave Nead
317 Brumbly, Henry
317 Brumbly, John
317 Brumbly, Wm.
318 Holloway, John, sr.
318 Holloway, Moses
318 Holloway, Aaron
319 Showell, Samuel
320 Mackcormarick, Partrick
321 Hampton, Mary, madam
321 slave Jack
321 slave Petter
321 slave Hanah
322 Tingle, Lettleton
323 Deale, Archerbell, sr.
323 Deale, Archerbell, jr.
324 Broughton, William
325 Broughton, John

TAX LISTS OF SOMERSET COUNTY: 1730-1740

BALTIMORE HUNDRED

326 Deale, John, jr.
326 Truitt, Lettleton
327 Bridell, James Stephen
327 Backer, William
327 slave Mino
327 slave Jack
327 slave Huger
328 Gray, Joseph
328 slave Simon
328 slave Quaco
328 slave Coke
329 Morris, Natthaiel
329 [Morris], Eliz., wife
330 Gault, Robart
330 Gault, Obed
331 Gault, William
332 Gault, John
333 Kinnitt, Martain
333 Harbenson, Samuel
334 Mankline, Richeard
334 Kennitt, John
335 Bessex, Absalam
336 Alford, David
336 Bowls, Urias
337 Kennitt, William, sr.
337 Kennitt, Wm., jr.
337 slave Petter
338 Fall, John
339 Fall, Abraham
340 Rackliff, Elias
341 Taylor, Samuel
341 Hill, William Stevens
342 Stevens, William
343 Fassitt, Frankline
343 slave Nan
344 Wyatt, Joseph, jr.
345 Hickman, Richeard, jr.
346 Holloway, Joseph
347 Gillstrap, Petter
348 Coffen, Thomas, jr.
349 Coffen, Joseph
349 Coffen, John
350 West, William
351 Woodcraft, Richeard
352 Bradford, William
353 Easom, John
354 Whorton, William
354 Whorton, Rixam
355 Winser, Ann, widow
355 Winser, James
356 Joseph, Fedrick
356 Owens, Wm.
357 Hudson, John
357 Mackgumery, Robart
358 Tull, Richeard
359 Mills, Samuel
359 Burns, Joseph
359 slave Surrey
359 slave Jeney
360 Hazzard, David, sr.
360 Hazzard, John
360 slave Jacob
360 slave Dinar
360 slave Sis
361 Holland, Elezebath, jr., widow
361 Seveling, Timothas
361 slave Jud
362 Clark, Mary, widow
362 Clark, Roads
363 Collings, Thomas
363 Collings, Able
364 Pengalley, Thomas
365 Hudson, David, sr.
365 Hudson, David, jr.
365 Hudson, Wm.
366 Smith, John
366 Smith, Charles
366 Ardeley, John
366 slave Harrey
366 slave Bess
367 Robins, Thomas
367 Norton, John
367 FetchPartrick, Francis
367 slave Quash
367 slave Bess
368 Whealey, William
368 Rackliff, Natthaiel
369 Lewis, Joseph
370 Liptrott, John
371 Godwin, Michaell, capt.
371 slave Bess
371 slave Ceasar
372 West, Thomas, sr.
372 West, Thomas, jr.
373 Tingle, Mary, widow
373 slave Harrey
373 slave Lelley
374 Waples, Paul
374 slave Charles
374 slave Dublen
374 slave Frank
375 Smith, John, piney neck
375 Smith, William
376 Lewis, Joseph, sr.
377 Grayhams, George
378 Hapeney, Bingham
379 Walton, Teagele
380 Smith, Robart
381 Oldson, Androw
382 Mackdaniel, John
383 Mooney, Charles
384 Mumford, John
385 Barnett, James
386 Sammons, William
387 Lewis, William, sr.
388 Lewis, William, jr.
389 Burton, William
389 Burton, Joshua
389 slave Touse
389 slave Bomodo
389 slave James
389 slave Adam
389 slave Rachell
389 slave Hob
390 Camble, John
391 Wilson, John
392 Cade, Thomas
393 MacCooms, James
394 Jones, Ebenzear
394 Jones, Thomas
395 Lowe, Robart
396 Morris, Dennis
397 Radeney, William
398 West, Thomas, jr.
399 West, Alexander
400 Nier, Thomas
401 Cary, Richeard
402 Bishop, Bowen
403 Taylor, William
404 Short, Edward
404 slave Sepe
405 Hopkins, Robart
405 slave Tobe
406 Hunnings, Philip
407 Burton, John
408 Parsons, Robart
409 Johnson, Batholomew
409 Johnson, John
410 Morris, John
410 slave Kate
411 Gorselen, Richeard
412 Pride, John
413 Green, Ezekiell
413 Green, David
414 Hall, Joseph
415 Priteyman, Thomas
416 Jeaferson, Richeard, sr.
416 Jeaferson, Richeard, jr.
416 Jeaferson, Absalam
416 Jeaferson, John
416 Somerfield, Barnes
417 Blizard, Richeard
418 Whorton, Thomas
419 Derickson, Benjn.
420 Collings, William
421 Long, John
422 Dunk, John

1740 TAX LIST [Household number/Name/Remarks]

BALTIMORE/BOGERTERNORTON HUNDREDS

423 Morris, Bibbens
424 Knock, Solomon
425 Townsend, Boman
426 Whorton, Francis
427 Carter, Joseph
427 Goodrick, Wm.
427 Furlong, Nicklas
428 Hazzard, David, jr.
429 Hickman, Richeard
430 Coffen, Thomas, sr.
430 Coffen, William
431 Johnson, David
431 Evens, William
431 slave Fillis
431 slave Dinar
432 Hudson, Charles
433 Tull, John, sr.
433 Linch, John
433 Smith, Jonah
434 Clark, Race
434 Clark, John
434 Clark, Benjn.
435 Masey, William
436 Quilling, Joseph
437 Bunton, Jonathan
438 Wilegoos, Thomas

BOGERTERNORTON HUNDRED

439 Selby, William, sr.
439 Selby, William, jur.
439 3 slaves
440 Bishop, William
440 Outten, Abraham
441 Whittington, Southy, jr.
442 Outten, John
443 Porter, William, i.t.
444 Claywell, Thomas
444 slave
445 Patrick, Roger
446 Holston, John
447 Evans, John
448 Jones, Thomas
449 Bishop, Joseph
450 Ryly, Thomas
450 slave
451 Burton, John
451 Evans, Laurence
452 Quillin, Benjamin
453 Greer, Adam
454 Alexander, Paul
455 Daizey, John
456 Murray, Dunkin
456 Mchendrick, Walter

456 Rigs, John
456 5 slaves
457 Whailey, William
458 Tull, Thomas
458 Lidster, William
459 Lindell, Peter
459 Gray, Samuel
460 White, Rachell
460 White, William
460 slave
461 Lambertson, John
462 Greer, Ursula
462 Greer, John
463 Baynom, Bartholemew
464 Steell, William
465 Purnell, Thomas
465 6 slaves
466 Brittingham, Isaac
466 3 slaves
467 Davis, William, i.t.
467 slave
468 Braford, Adam
469 Ennis, Nathaniel
470 Ennis, William
470 Ennis, William
470 Ennis, John
470 Greer, Henry
470 slave
471 Ennis, John
472 Ennis, Cornelius
473 Pepper, John
474 Ennis, Samuel
475 Dennis, William
476 Handcock, Daniel
476 Handcock, William
477 Hudson, William
477 Gray, William
478 Hudson, Major
479 Brittingham, Nathl.
480 Greer, Archibald
480 Greer, George
480 Greer, Hampton
481 Brittingham, Solomon
481 Brittingham, Absalom
482 Rackliff, Charles
483 Brittingham, Jeremiah
484 Teague, John
484 Teague, John
485 Holston, William
486 McCauly, John
487 Truitt, Joseph
488 Timmons, Aaron
489 Roach, James
490 Guy, James
491 Townsend, Jeremiah
491 3 slaves

492 Henderson, Charles
493 Townsend, Brickus
494 Rownd, Catherin
494 5 slaves
495 Heather, Ephraim
495 slave
496 Heather, Ephraim
497 Selby, Parker
498 Crapper, John
499 Crapper, Ebenezer
499 Crapper, Edmond
500 Porter, Joseph
500 slave
501 Crapper, Ebenezer
502 Porter, James
503 Davis, Samuel
504 Crapper, Nehemiah
505 Long, David
506 Smith, John
507 Tadlock, Edward
508 Waters, Patrick
509 Tingle, Daniel
510 Evans, John
510 slave
511 Franklin, Edward
511 Powders, William
511 slave
512 Powel, Samuel
513 Hall, Spence
513 Hosier, Nathan
514 Brevard, Adam
514 Gray, Nicholas
514 slave
515 Powel, Thomas
516 Williams, Argulus
517 Lowe, George
518 Penewell, Charles
519 Jarman, George
520 Truitt, Nehemiah
521 Mumford, Thomas
521 Cobb, Joseph
522 Timmons, James
523 Timmons, Thomas
524 Smith, William
525 Jones, Joseph
525 Jones, John
526 Swain, William
527 Purnell, Mathew
527 slave
528 Lewis, William
529 Hook, William
530 Bassitt, John
531 Timmons, Samuel
532 Timmons, John
532 Timmons, Aaron
533 Hammond, Jacob
534 Edwards, Benoni
535 Hammond, Edward
536 Morris, Joseph
537 Midsley, Thomas

TAX LISTS OF SOMERSET COUNTY: 1730-1740

BOGERTERNORTON HUNDRED

537 Vaughn, William	574 Adkinson, John	614 Taylor, Philip
537 Midsley, William	575 McNeal, Archibald	615 Pennewell, John
538 Beckett, Peter	576 Spence, Adam	616 Pennewell, Thomas
538 Beckett, Deverix	576 5 slaves	617 Pennewell, John
538 illegible	577 Wells, Daniel	618 Collins, John
539 Mitchel, Thomas	577 free black Will	619 Collins, Mary
539 2 slaves	578 Robison, William	619 Collins, Thomas
540 Webb, Samuel	579 Stevenson, James	620 Williams, Littleton
541 Marchment, Charles	579 Stevenson, Adam	621 Parker, George
541 Hook, Henry	579 Stevenson, Saml.	621 Parker, Scofield
542 Richards, William	580 Godfrey, Charles	622 Davis, Ishmael
543 Hadder, Warrin	580 slave	623 Davis, William
543 Hadder, William	581 Hall, Margarett	624 Davis, Robert, sr.
544 Bradford, John	581 Hall, Fenix	624 Davis, Wm.
544 Bradford, John	581 Hall, John	624 Davis, Ishmael
545 Hodge, Robert	582 Bell, Adam	624 Davis, Robert
545 Hodge, Fleming	582 slave	624 Davis, John
545 slave	583 Deverix, John	624 Davis, Mathew
546 Truitt, George	583 Deverix, Cornelius	625 Murfey, John
547 Bedard, Richard	584 Johnson, Afradozey	626 Marshall, Isaac
548 Davis, Benjamin	584 slave	626 Marshall, Jacob
549 Evans, Gamage	585 Johnson, George	626 3 slaves
550 Evans, Powell	586 Johnson, Thos.	627 Neighnborough, Ursula
551 Warran, Nicholas	587 Dredon, John	627 Neighnborough, John
551 Warran, Wm.	588 Sturgis, John	628 Brittingham, William
552 Crapper, Wrixham	588 Sturgis, Littleton	628 Brittingham, Isaac
553 Evans, Elias	589 Steel, Daniel	629 Brittingham, William
554 Townsend, William	589 Steel, James	630 Brittingham, Nathan
555 Collins, Thomas	590 Turner, Nicholas	631 Scott, Mark
556 Taylor, William	591 Prier, Webb	632 Buncle, Alexander
557 Warrin, Robert	592 Turner, Henry	633 Purnell, Katherine
557 Harman, [Tom], mulato	593 Mumford, James	633 2 slaves
558 Harmon, Edward	593 Mumford, James	634 Purnell, Walter
558 Harmon, Edward	594 Truitt, George	634 slave
559 Smith, John Truitt	594 Truitt, George	635 Smock, Henry
560 Peele, Thorogood	595 Truitt, John	635 Smock, John
561 Tull, Benjamin	596 Murray, David	635 Smock, Henry
562 Simpson, Thomas	596 slave	636 Poynter, Thomas
562 Ayres, Harrison	597 Jarmon, William	636 Poynter, Ratliff
562 2 slaves	597 Bedord, Jarmon	636 Poynter, Turvil
563 Bratten, James	597 slave	636 2 slaves
563 Bratten, John	598 Parker, Tabitha	637 Webb, Grace
564 Bratten, Samuel	598 3 slaves	637 Webb, Elisha
565 Bratten, Samuel	599 Parker, Samuel	638 Bowen, Edward
566 Bratten, Hugh	599 Taylor, Edmond	639 Hall, Adam
566 Dreden, Saml.	600 Parker, Philip	639 Teague, Ralph
567 Scofield, Joseph	601 Parker, Charles	640 Rownd, Edward
567 Scofield, Benjamin	602 Shohanos, Wm.	640 Givan, George
567 slave	603 Davis, Robert	640 Renalds, William
568 Scofield, John	604 Davis, Thos.	640 2 slaves
569 Richason, Robert	605 Davis, George	641 Poynter, Elias
569 Mason, Edmond	606 Davis, William	642 Hudson, Dennis
569 Pepper, Wm.	606 Davis, Samuel	642 2 slaves
570 Richardson, Charles	607 Porter, John	643 Knock, John
570 slave	608 Dennis, Donock	644 Truitt, Joseph
571 Richardson, James	609 Atkins, Stanton	645 Hamond, Edward
572 Victor, James	610 Truitt, James	646 Bowen, William
573 Driggus, John	611 Adkins, Stephen	647 Swain, William
	612 Dennis, William	648 Franklyn, William
	613 Truitt, George	

1740 TAX LIST [Household number/Name/Remarks]

BOGERTERNORTON/MANOKIN HUNDREDS

649 Truitt, William
650 Truitt, George
651 Mumford, George
652 Kellam, William
653 Truitt, George, accok.
653 2 slaves
654 Truitt, George, jr.
655 Bowen, Littleton
655 Bowen, Geo.
655 slave
656 Bishop, John
657 Bowen, John
657 slave
658 Morris, William
659 Burbridge, Edwd.
660 Burbridge, John
661 Patrick, Roger
662 Jones, George
663 Bishop, Joseph
664 Collins, Solomon
665 Duncan, Thomas
666 Abbott, John
667 Truitt, George
668 Jarmon, John, sr.
668 Jarmon, William
668 slave
669 Jarmon, John, jur.
670 Fletcher, Thos., revd.
670 2 slaves
671 Ingoe, James
672 Sturgis, Joshua
672 Laws, Elijah
672 Laws, Bolitha
672 2 slaves
673 Hewitt, George
674 Murrain, Mathew
674 Murrain, John
675 Holston, Benjn.
676 Dennis, Solomon
677 Dennis, Daniel
678 Hammond, Isaac
679 Hammond, William
680 Greer, John
681 Hammond, John
682 Hampton, Mary, madm.
682 4 slaves
683 Dukes, Thos.
684 Dennis, Wheatly
685 Jarmin, Job
686 Holland, Wm.
687 Smachie, William
688 More, Wm.
689 Jarmin, Robert
690 Handcock, William
691 Blizard, Richard
692 Griffin, Oliver

693 Ake, John
694 Richardson, William
695 Williams, Thos. Nathll.
695 Williams, Samll.
696 Tayler, Samuell
697 Timmons, Joseph
698 Bradford, Nathaniel
699 Beadeard, William
700 Gray, John

MANOKIN HUNDRED

701 Sanders, Rich.
701 Sanders, Willm.
702 Miles, Willm., sr.
702 Miles, Willm.
702 Miles, Saml.
703 Turpen, Wm., sr.
703 Turpen, Whitt.
703 Tull, Thoms.
703 Tull, Jno.
703 slave Thom
703 slave Jack
703 slave Toby
703 slave Fillis
703 slave Medary
704 Turpen, Jno.
704 slave Cesar
704 slave Sary
705 Turpen, Willm., jr.
705 slave Will
705 slave George
705 slave Moll
706 Fountain, Nicholas
706 Fountain, Massy
706 Capsy, Willm.
706 slave Charles
706 slave London
706 slave Thom
706 slave Mirrin
707 Fountain, Mary
707 slave Rose
707 slave Hercles
708 Holland, Isaac
708 Furnish, Jams.
708 slave Appo
709 Dear, Rose
709 Cain, Jams.
709 Tilman, Benj.
710 Tilman, Joseph
710 slave London
711 Tilman, Aaron
711 slave Jack
712 Niblett, Burnett
712 slave Coffy
713 Gibbins, Cathar.
713 slave Sarah
714 Gibans, Anne
714 slave Pleasant
715 Gibbans, Thom.

716 Doniston, Robt.
717 Thompn., Andrew
717 slave Cesar
718 Thompn., Joseph
719 Hall, Jno.
719 Givan, Jno.
719 Clark, Thoms.
720 Outerbridge, Sarah
720 slave London
720 slave Priw
720 slave Dino
721 Horsey, Stephen
721 Megomery, Thoms.
721 slave Jenny
722 Walston, Bo[az]
722 Walston, Joy
723 Revell, Charles
723 Revell, Randl.
723 Revell, Curtis
723 Wright, Willm.
723 slave Hannah
724 Bosmon, Willm., sr.
724 slave Doso
724 slave Bess
724 slave Judy
725 Killy, Jno.
726 Roach, Willm.
726 slave Kitt
726 slave Patience
727 Bannister, Thos.
727 slave Dick
728 Labruce, Benj.
729 Mitchel, Thoms.
730 Mitchell, Ann
730 Mitchel, Rand.
730 Mitchel, Solom.
730 Mitchel, Stephen
730 slave Sarah
731 Ayres, Jacob
731 Walston, Obid.
731 Layfeild, Thom.
731 Turpen, Josh.
732 Horsey, Sarah
732 slave Nick
733 Horsey, Jno.
733 Kilby, Hugh
733 Baly, Tho.
734 Kerny, Jno.
734 slave Pliny
735 Shepard, Martin
735 Shepard, Peter
736 Long, Solomon
736 Kendall, Willm.
736 slave Nan
737 Furnich, Jams.
737 Jenkins, Saml.
738 Mathews, Pat.
738 Mathews, Willm.
739 Mitichell, Isaac
740 Culberson, Willm.

TAX LISTS OF SOMERSET COUNTY: 1730-1740

MANOKIN HUNDRED

741 Bowler, Willm.	768 Mathews, Wm.	779 slave Nanny
741 Bowler, Jams.	768 Fiddy, Rand.	779 slave Hannah
742 Collins, Willm.	768 slave Cudjo	779 slave Rose
743 Pringle, Wm.	768 slave Will	779 slave Sarah
744 Brown, Terrill	768 slave Sarah	779 slave Joney
745 Murrow, Alex.	768 slave Tamor	779 slave Nell
746 Tindal, Jams.	768 slave Grace	779 slave Tamar
747 Murrow, Saml.	768 slave Tony	780 King, Robt., col.
748 Howard, Jno.	769 Denwood, Geo.	780 King, Neh.
749 McClamy, Wony	769 slave Ned	780 King, Robt.
749 Mathews, Danl.	770 Megraw, Robt.	780 Leatherbury, Jno.
749 slave Frank	771 Brown, David	780 Lane, Ab.
750 Gullett, Abrah.	771 slave Jack	780 Smith, Will.
751 King, Whiting.	771 slave Will	780 Turner, Ab.
751 Condan, Alex.	771 slave Daniel	780 Hodge, Step.
751 slave Thom	771 slave Bess	780 slave Fortune
751 slave Nan	772 Brown, Mary	780 slave Jose
752 Dishal, Mary	772 slave Coco	780 slave Cesar
752 Fisher, Henry	773 Dorman, Marg.	780 slave Manary
752 slave Nan	773 Hill, Will.	780 slave Obadiah
753 Hayman, Will.	774 Lockwood, Will.	780 slave Ebo
753 Hayman, Benj.	775 Laws, James	780 slave Hope
754 Lindow, Marg.	776 Robinson, Jams.	780 slave Jenny
754 King, Charles	776 Robinson, Jno.	780 slave Betty
754 slave Jo	776 Welch, Will.	780 slave Judy
754 slave Bess	776 slave Jack	780 slave Dodo, sr.
755 Chambers, Rich.	776 slave Cesar	780 slave Will
755 Collins, Saml.	776 slave Naro	780 slave Didah, jr.
756 Smith, Magd.	776 slave Toby	780 slave Nan
756 Smith, Will.	776 slave Dino	780 slave Pacy
757 Smith, Rob.	776 slave Fillis	780 slave Long Cear
758 Swift, Richd.	776 slave Sise	781 Tunstal, Jno., capn.
759 Horner, Geo.	776 slave Perik	781 slave Lohill
760 Jones, Willm.	777 Willson, David	781 slave Siby
760 Jones, Thos.	777 King, Jesey	781 slave Tomboy
760 slave Guy	777 Parkason, Rob.	781 slave Dick
760 slave Anthony	777 Sanders, Tho.	781 slave Norrish
760 slave Eve	777 slave Harry	781 slave Sippio
761 Anderson, Jno.	777 slave Roben	781 slave Pompy
762 Anderson, Jams.	777 slave Bristo	781 slave Bess
762 Wright, Neh.	777 slave Cudjo	781 slave Sibb
762 slave Cudjo	777 slave Kent	781 slave Rachel
762 slave Pegg	777 slave Pompy	781 slave Somerst.
763 Reynod, Henry	777 slave Moses	781 slave Will
763 Rodgers, Jno.	777 slave Lancaster	781 slave Freeman
763 slave Dino	777 slave Holyday	781 slave Tom
764 Whitingn., Heb.	777 slave Nanny	781 slave Cesar
764 Miller, Jams.	777 slave Rose	781 slave Sarah
765 Connelly, Pat.	777 slave Venus	781 slave Isabell
766 Mately, Jams.	778 Turpen, Willm.	781 slave Bina
767 Ballard, Henry	778 slave Cuffy	781 slave Nanny
767 Wilks, Jno.	778 slave Toby	782 Harris, Philip
767 Megraw, Rich.	778 slave Mingo	782 Spear, Henry
767 C----, Thomas	779 Wilson, Saml.	783 Cox, Thos.
767 slave Cesar	779 Bod--, Jams.	784 Cullen, Isaac
767 slave Ventur	779 slave Peter	785 Layfeild, Thos.
767 slave Jenny	779 slave Mamedo	786 Pope, Jams.
767 slave Bindow	779 slave Will	787 Wilson, Geo.
767 slave Sarrah	779 slave Thom	787 slave Esabela
768 Denwood, Thos.	779 slave Sampson	787 slave Betty

1740 TAX LIST [Household number/Name/Remarks]

MANOKIN/MATTAPANY HUNDREDS

788 Layfeild, Robt.
789 Heath, Abrah.
789 slave Sambo
790 Wilson, Andw.
791 Dobbin, Wiln.
792 Gray, Wm.
792 Daly, Pat.
792 slave Venus
793 Polk, Jams.
793 slave Peter
793 slave Ogy
793 slave Pleasant
794 Gray, Jno.
794 Gray, Jam.
794 slave Hannah
794 slave Ned
795 Strawbidge, Jams.
795 slave David
795 slave Cuffy
795 slave Hago
795 slave Sarah
796 [Heath], Parthena
796 slave Quinney
797 Chase, Thos.
797 slave Dick
798 Owens, Jno.
798 Owens, Jno., jr.
799 Dorman, Mich.
800 Dorman, Wm.
801 Dorman, Frances, widw.
801 Dorman, Neh.
801 slave Jack
802 Cammel, Jno.
803 Mackdanll, David
804 Davis, Jno.
805 Davis, Arth.
806 Ford, Absolon
807 Wood, David
808 Mutt, Jno.
809 Sharp, Benj.
809 Cramell, Benj.
809 Marchan, Will.
810 Walston, Will.
810 Walston, Henry
811 Walston, Thos.
812 Tull, Easter
812 Tull, Steph.
812 slave Moll
813 Tull, Jos.
814 Tull, Saml.
815 Abbitt, Jno.
816 Barrit, Henry
817 Miles, Saml.
817 slave Dick
817 slave Ben
818 Butler, Nath.
818 slave Sarah
819 McDorman, Willm.
820 Maddox, Lazarus
820 slave Cuffy
820 slave Joe
821 Maddox, Danl.
821 slave Addam
821 slave Sarah
822 Maddox, Thoms.
822 Maddox, Jno.
822 slave Will
822 slave Sue
823 Willis, Barnaby
823 Dorman, Wilson
824 Cuningin, Thos.
825 Clark, Alex.
826 Ballard, Jarvis
826 Ballard, Will.
826 Ballard, Jarvis
826 Ballard, Arnold
826 Ballard, Charles
826 Ballard, Henry
826 slave Ame
826 slave Rose
827 Phebus, Geo.
827 Phebus, Jno.
827 slave Into
828 Horner, Geo.
828 Horner, Maltildo
828 Horner, Jno.
828 Horner, Arnold
828 Horner, Charles
829 Phebus, Geo., jr.
830 Martin, Tho.
831 Rigsby, Lewis
831 Rigsby, Jno.
831 slave Fendow
832 Crowder, Frans.
833 Elsey, Jno.
833 Elsey, Arnold
833 Read, Jos.
833 slave Sambo
833 slave Cesar
833 slave Hubo
833 slave Ismael
833 slave Isabell
833 slave Sib
833 slave Betty
833 slave Dino
833 slave Pacey
833 slave Moll
834 Lawless, Jams.
835 Elsey, Sarrah
835 Cordwell, Willm.
835 Elsey, Arnold
835 slave Ned
835 slave Jack
835 slave Charles
835 slave Belindo
835 slave Sarah
835 slave Nan
835 slave Fendo
836 Fosky, Benj.
837 Jones, Wm., gooce creek
838 McClammy, Willm.
838 McClammy, Whitty
838 Haley, Timothy
838 slave Tom
839 Bosmon, Mary
839 slave Sambo
839 slave Jean
839 slave Whitehaven
840 Horner, Jams.
841 Bosmon, Wm.
842 Gillis, Joseph
842 Mely, Jno.
842 Humpris, Ez.
842 Bullen, Jedediah
842 Compton, Isaac
842 Bosmon, Hewet
842 slave Truman
842 slave Bosson
842 slave George
842 slave Rose
843 Bosman, Geo.
843 Bosmon, Geo., jr.
843 slave Franck
844 Bosmon, Jno.
845 Walltim, Wm.
846 [Staples, James, dead]
846 slave Ben
847 Woolford, Jno.
847 Robens, Wm.
847 slave Sampson
847 slave Thom
847 slave Rose
847 slave Tamor
847 slave Moll
848 Brown, Thos.
848 slave Sampson
848 slave Kate
849 Allason, Pat.
849 slave Lott
849 slave Pallace
850 Parmor, Rich.
851 Young, Jno.
851 Young, Wm.
852 Burgin, Danl.
852 Burgen, Wm.
853 Revell, Randl.
853 slave Toby
853 slave Patience
854 Layfeild, Wm.
855 Benston, George
855 Binston, Matt.
855 Osten, George

MATTAPANY HUNDRED

856 Scarbrough, John
856 Holdom, John
856 slave Dick

TAX LISTS OF SOMERSET COUNTY: 1730-1740

MATTAPANY HUNDRED

856 slave Nan
857 Hopkins, Matthew
857 Ayars, Richd.
857 slave Ossen
858 Darlen, John
858 Holsten, Charles
859 Richardson, John
859 Richardson, Samll.
859 slave Rachall
860 Wise, Thomas
860 Richardson, David
861 Johnson, William
862 Johnson, John
863 Johnson, Lenard
864 Johnson, Peter, senr.
864 Johnson, Peter, junr.
865 Chadax, James
866 Newton, Starling
866 slave An
867 Newton, Jobe
868 Turner, William
869 Newton, Jonan.
870 Tarr, Samll.
871 Newton, Thomas
871 Newton, Thos., junr.
871 Newton, Southy
872 Milburne, Thomas
873 Pope, Samll.
873 slave Will
873 slave Hanah
874 Dreaden, John
875 Pope, Gorge
875 slave Bess
876 Lane, Gorge
876 Lane, William
877 Hill, Hutten
877 slave Plesent
878 Sturgis, Daniell
879 Selby, Philip
879 Selby, Mattw.
879 Selby, Daniell
879 Selby, Philip
879 Selby, Parker
879 slave Sangro
879 slave Jack
879 slave Sambo
879 slave Tom
879 slave Hanah
879 slave Morer
879 slave Dinah
880 Selby, Parker
880 slave Jack
880 slave Abraham
880 slave Gloster
880 slave Isaac
880 slave Tamer
880 slave Pege

881 Hill, Robt.
882 Hudson, Jonathan
883 Purnell, John
883 slave Tobey
883 slave Nemrod
883 slave Ben
883 slave Gorge
883 slave Jacob
883 slave Sarah
884 Walton, William
884 slave Moll
885 Walton, Stephen
885 Walton, Steven, junr.
885 Walton, Jobe
886 Cord, William
886 Cord, Arther
886 Cord, John
886 Cord, Joseph
886 slave Jean
887 Hudson, Jonathan
887 Cornwell, John
888 Samons, Benja.
888 Holland, Nehemiah
889 Coxx, Jams.
889 Harmon, Gorge
890 Wimbrough, Paul
891 Chapman, Humphry
892 Robins, Bowden
892 slave Gorge
892 slave Jack
892 slave Frank
892 slave Roger
892 slave Sarah
893 Calvart, William
894 Jones, William
895 Maxfeild, Joseph
895 slave York
895 slave Jack
895 slave Abegall
895 slave Peague
895 slave Denis
896 Wagaman, Ephram
896 Price, Benja.
896 slave Gorge
896 slave Tom
896 slave Bess
897 Walker, John, in Virgea.
897 slave Jack
897 slave Littelton
898 Jackson, William
899 Henderson, Bishop
900 Aydlott, William
900 Aydlott, Wm., junr.
900 slave Hector
900 slave Ceser
901 Vezey, Charles
901 Vezey, Ephram
902 Vezey, William

903 Watson, Robert
903 Watson, Charles
903 Paine, Paul
903 slave Darkey
903 slave Gorge
904 Watson, Uriah
905 Hodgson, Rolling
906 Merill, Joseph
907 Watson, John
908 Pain, John
908 Pain, Mosses
908 Pain, John
909 Duberley, Thomas
910 Hodgson, John, an object
910 Hodgson, Rolling, junr.
911 Allen, Joseph
911 Allen, Mosses
912 Hill, Jacob
913 Hill, Abraham
914 Wattson, Peter
915 Russell, Cuthbud
916 Watson, Luke
917 Pilcher, Mosses
918 Booth, John Outten
919 Hardes, Hazard
920 Ceary, Solomon
921 Ceary, Jeremiah
922 Wattson, Robt.
923 Fisher, Baley
924 Willett, Ambrus
924 Willett, Wm.
924 Willett, Thos.
924 slave Jacob
925 Slocumb, Thomas
925 Chapman, Eliga
926 Pepper, Tobias
927 Pepper, William
928 Brownbill, Nathanell
929 Allen, John, senr.
929 Allen, John, junr.
930 Brittingham, Thos.
931 Bechbord, William
932 Mallen, Christopher
933 Taylor, Rodger
933 slave Hanah
934 Reed, Waltor
935 Claywell, Peter, senr.
935 Claywell, Shadr.
935 slave Gorge
935 slave Sambo
935 slave Ben
935 slave Hanah
935 slave Jude
936 Puder, Joseph
936 Answorth, Peter
937 Lenzey, James
937 Benett, Edward

1740 TAX LIST [Household number/Name/Remarks]

MATTAPANY/MONIE HUNDREDS

937 Benett, William	968 White, John	1000 Hobbs, Joy
938 Answorth, William	969 Husk, John	1000 Stephens, Isaac
939 Porter, Clentuck	970 Roberts, John	1001 Hobbs, Mercilious
940 Tarr, Michell, senr.	970 Roberts, Thomas	1002 Howard, Thomas
940 Tarr, Michel, junr.	971 Martin, George	1003 Luke, Williamson
940 Tarr, John	972 Macdorman, Darby	1004 Durham, Thomas
941 Duer, William	973 Williams, John	1005 Wright, Zebulon
942 Sturgis, Richard	974 Windsor, John	1006 Weatherby, John
942 Sturgis, John	975 Miller, Thomas	1007 Jones, Mitchell
943 Venettson, Nathan	976 Chain, Alexander	1007 slave Bussy
944 Stevenson, Samll.	977 Douglass, John	1007 slave Davy
945 Westers, Michel	978 Windsor, Lazarus	1007 slave Jack
946 Bratton, William	978 Windsor, James	1008 Jones, Daniel
946 Bratton, Thos.	978 Windsor, Philip	1008 slave Doll
946 slave Guy	979 Roe, Sarah	1009 Covington, Thomas
947 Hall, John	979 Evins, John	1009 slave Moll
947 Hall, Stephen	979 Sewards, Wm.	1010 Covington, Eleanor
948 Hopkins, Samll.	980 Roe, Joseph	1010 slave Sambo
949 Hopkins, William	981 Lawes, Thomas	1010 slave Coco
950 Nelson, William	981 Loyd, Thomas	1010 slave Bess
950 Nelson, James	981 slave Murrier	1010 slave Jene
950 Patrick, Daniell	982 Jones, George	1010 slave Pegg
950 Nealson, Robt.	982 slave Adam	1010 slave Dinah
950 Nealson, Samll.	983 Lawes, John	1011 Chambers, Edward
951 Guttry, Pattrick	983 Lawes, John, jr.	1012 Cary, Thomas
951 Guttry, Calab	983 slave Prince	1012 slave Jone
952 Gittry, James	983 slave Ceasar	1013 Cary, Rachell
953 Porter, William	984 Jones, Lewis	1013 Crouch, David
954 Slingor, Thomas	984 Jones, Lewis, jr.	1014 Macomb, George
954 Slingor, John	984 slave Jack	1015 Gale, George
955 Slingor, Thomas, junr.	984 slave Moll	1015 Maughon, Christopher
955 Blizard, John	984 slave Ceasar	1015 slave Joe
956 Davis, Charles	985 Jones, Samll.	1015 slave Sipeo
956 Williams, Thos.	986 Waller, Major	1015 slave Dominick
957 Goodin, Benja.	987 White, Francis	1015 slave Jamey
958 Jones, John	987 White, Francis	1015 slave Limas
959 Whittington, William	987 White, Thomas	1015 slave Jack
959 slave Abner	988 Jones, Charles	1015 slave Nimrod
959 slave Sambow	989 White, John	1015 slave Mars
959 slave Sarah	989 White, John, jr.	1015 slave Isaac
959 slave Beaty	990 Wallace, Matthew	1015 slave Jack
960 Clawell, Peter, junr.	990 slave Tom	1015 slave Janey
	990 slave Sibb	1015 slave Palinah
MONIE HUNDRED	991 Wallace, Robert	1015 slave Beandah
961 Wright, Thomas	991 Wallace, George	1015 slave Parthenah
961 Wright, Henry	991 Wallace, Thomas	1015 slave Nany
961 Rose, Samll.	992 Wallace, Richard	1015 slave Sarah
961 slave Toby	992 Wallace, James	1015 slave Dinah
962 Elzey, John	992 slave Ceasar	1016 Lawes, Robert
963 Spicer, Philip	993 Roberts, Edward	1016 slave Bubo
964 Sasser, Wm.	993 slave Jeffry	1016 slave Jack
965 Spicer, James	993 slave Cuffee	1016 slave Samson
966 Neill, John	993 slave Binah	1017 Lawes, Panter
967 Pollock, Joseph	994 Mongar, Matthew	1018 Lawes, Wm.
967 Bazwell, Charles	995 Smith, John	1019 Irvin, George
	996 Dorman, Henry	1019 Irvin, John
	997 Newman, Henry	1019 slave Tobe
	998 Magraugh, John	1019 slave Cuffee
	999 Hobbs, Thomas	1019 slave Jane
	999 Hobbs, Stephen	

TAX LISTS OF SOMERSET COUNTY: 1730-1740

MONIE/NANTICOKE HUNDREDS

1019 slave Jeny
1020 Waller, John
1020 slave Jane
1020 slave Robin
1021 Waller, George
1022 Stoughton, Wm.
1022 slave Bussy
1022 slave Simon
1022 slave Jemy
1022 slave Sabina
1023 Jones, Robert
1023 Jones, Benjamin
1023 slave London
1023 slave Amock
1023 slave Jene
1023 slave Rachell
1024 Leatherbury, John
1024 Leatherbury, Charles
1024 Jones, Wm.
1024 Lunn, Mary
1024 slave Pompe
1024 slave Sambo
1024 slave Tone
1024 slave Ben
1024 slave Robin
1024 slave Will
1024 slave Jack
1024 slave Bridgett
1024 slave Rose
1024 slave Bess
1024 slave Hanne
1024 slave Candis
1025 Squires, Edwurd
1026 Downes, Margarett
1026 Downes, Robert
1026 slave Bristo
1026 slave Ned
1026 slave Frank
1027 Dashiell, Thomas
1027 slave Will
1027 slave Jack
1027 slave Harry
1027 slave Bess
1027 slave Tamor
1027 slave Sibb
1027 slave Sarah
1028 Jones, Wm.
1028 slave James
1028 slave Sue
1028 slave Lucey
1029 Dorman, John
1029 Dorman, Hezekiah
1029 slave Vilet
1030 Mongar, John
1031 Macgraw, James
1032 Shores, John
1032 Shores, William
1032 Shores, John

NANTICOKE HUNDRED
1033 McCloitser, John
1033 McCloister, Samuel
1033 McCloister, Geo.
1033 Taylor, Anthony
1033 slave Coffee
1033 slave Sambo
1033 slave Tom
1033 slave Adam
1033 slave Benn
1033 slave Ciss
1033 slave Abbo
1033 slave Dina
1033 slave Rose
1033 slave Tony
1034 McCloister, Nell
1035 Hopkins, Steven
1035 Hopkins, David
1036 Samuells, Ann
1036 slave Cokerow
1037 Wallace, David
1038 Dickeson, Teague
1039 McCants, Allexd.
1040 Brown, Signe
1041 Hickman, Wm.
1041 slave Jack
1041 slave Sambo
1041 slave Merreah
1041 slave Rose
1041 slave Jude
1042 Wallace, John
1043 Barklett, John, senr.
1043 Barklett, Abraham
1044 Barklett, John, jur.
1045 Hickman, Aurthur
1046 Dunn, Richard
1046 Dunn, Thos.
1047 Husk, Joseph
1048 Mackham, Timothy
1049 Walter, John
1050 Walter, Danel
1051 Dasheill, Geo., nantk.pt
1051 slave Coffee
1051 slave Sepio
1052 Beard, John
1053 Beard, Lewis
1054 Anderson, John, of tipgrum
1055 Rotten, Wm.
1055 Rotten, Hezeciah
1056 Larremore, Thos.
1056 Larremore, James
1057 Hinderson, Robrt
1057 Hinderson, Daniel
1058 Richass, Archable
1058 McCade, Wm.
1059 Collyar, Dowtte

1059 slave Mingo
1060 Collyar, Robrt, jur.
1061 Collyer, Geo.
1062 Collyer, Robert, senr.
1062 Griggs, Henry
1062 slave Sare
1062 slave Bess
1063 Winright, Cannon
1063 Winright, James
1063 slave Quokco
1064 Thorns, Allexd.
1065 Messick, Banjaman
1066 Hopkins, John, senr.
1066 Hopkins, Rodger
1066 slave Sue
1067 Hopkins, John, son John
1068 Dashiell, Henry
1068 slave Gift
1068 slave Sibb
1069 Dashiell, Bridgit
1069 Dashiell, James
1069 slave Robin
1069 slave Jack
1069 slave Will
1070 Game, Fortune
1070 Game, Anvill
1071 Fluallin, Samuel
1071 slave Sillas
1072 Larremore, Mary
1072 Larremore, Levin
1072 slave Coffee
1072 slave Jemmy
1073 Dashiell, Jessy
1074 Dashiell, Levin
1074 slave Joe
1074 slave Benn
1075 Deane, John
1076 Dashiell, Wm., senr.
1077 Bound, Joseph
1078 Dashiell, Wm., jur.
1078 slave Bess
1078 slave Sibb
1078 slave Peter
1079 Steward, Allexd.
1079 slave Benn
1079 slave Frank
1079 slave Jemmy
1080 Bucklar, Nicklos
1081 Richardson, John
1082 Messick, Jacob, senr.
1083 Messick, Jacob, jur.
1084 Messick, Nehemiah
1085 Reed, John, senr.

1740 TAX LIST [Household number/Name/Remarks]

NANTICOKE HUNDRED

1085 Reed, Ezekeil
1085 Reed, Jacob
1085 slave Harry
1085 slave Pegg
1086 Reed, John, jur.
1086 Reed, Obidiah
1086 slave Merreah
1087 Quotormus, James
1087 Quotormus, Partrick
1088 King, Capell
1088 King, Ephraim
1088 slave Margra
1088 slave Titus
1088 slave Jack
1088 slave Pompy
1088 slave Cate
1089 Townsand, Benjman
1090 Craycraft, Geo.
1091 Dashiell, Joseph
1091 Dashiell, N.
1091 slave Randal
1091 slave Bess
1091 slave Nearo
1092 Dashiell, Robrt
1092 slave Cage
1092 slave Tamor
1092 slave Workington
1093 Game, Robin
1094 Dashiell, Priscilla
1094 slave Harry
1095 Benson, Mary
1095 Nickelson, Levin
1095 Nickelson, John
1095 slave Will
1095 slave Dick
1095 slave Bess
1096 Russell, James, senr.
1096 Russell, Thos.
1096 Seems, Archable
1097 Russell, James
1098 Gale, John
1098 Beamore, Henry
1098 Knight, Richard
1098 Martin, John
1098 Shile, Thos.
1098 slave James
1098 slave Mesanger
1098 slave Bashow
1098 slave Glasgow
1098 slave Sambo
1098 slave Obidiah
1098 slave Sambo
1098 slave Jude
1098 slave Rose
1098 slave Phebe
1098 slave Moll
1098 slave Bett
1098 slave Dina
1098 slave Seba
1099 Ralph, Thos.
1099 slave Merreah
1100 Goslin, James
1101 Rider, Willson
1102 Hinderson, Wm.
1102 Hiderson, Benjman
1103 Jackson, Johnethan
1103 Jackson, Joshua
1103 Jackson, Danel
1104 Jackson, Thos.
1105 Gillis, Wm.
1105 Gills, Wm.
1105 slave Flora
1106 Gills, Thos.
1107 Burn, James
1108 Jones, John, quntico
1108 slave Plato
1109 Johnson, David
1110 Beanes, Geo.
1111 Oskelly, Danel
1112 Ostian, Wm.
1113 Spouldin, Eliz.
1113 Murfee, James
1114 Kemp, Mathew
1114 Dawson, John
1114 Green, Richard
1114 slave Sipio
1114 slave Alix
1115 Price, Robrt
1115 slave Nell
1116 Blure, Marget
1116 slave Jude
1117 Dunkin, James
1118 Cox, John
1118 slave Arculus
1118 slave Hagar
1119 Hardy, Geo., esqr.
1119 slave Ceasar
1119 slave Tom
1119 slave Sipio
1119 slave Jack
1119 slave Harry
1119 slave Barbery
1119 slave Rose
1119 slave Phillip
1119 slave Dina
1120 Nutter, Huitt
1120 slave Titt
1120 slave Mingo
1120 slave Bess
1121 Row, Elizb.
1121 Spencer, John
1122 Hardy, James
1122 slave Jean
1123 Train, James, senr.
1123 slave Rose
1123 slave Robin
1123 slave Benn
1123 slave Mingo
1124 Covington, Wm.
1124 Ostin, Henry
1124 slave Sibbo
1125 Givan, Robert
1125 Price, Thos.
1125 slave Ceasar
1125 slave Sevinah
1126 Givan, James
1127 Givan, John
1127 slave Hannah
1128 Taylor, Abraham
1128 Taylor, John
1128 slave South
1129 Caldwell, James
1129 Givans, Wm.
1129 slave Bob
1129 slave Sambo
1129 slave Rose
1129 slave Frank
1130 Dashiell, N., esqr.
1130 slave Tom
1130 slave Venus
1130 slave Barne
1131 Cottman, Ebenezer
1132 McKean, George
1132 McKean, Darbrook
1132 Friggs, Robrt
1132 slave Hager
1133 Henry, John
1133 Henry, Hugh
1134 Godart, Thos.
1134 Godart, John
1135 Langford, John, senr.
1135 Langford, Edward
1135 Langford, John, jur.
1136 Vance, Thos.
1137 Low, Ralph
1137 Low, John
1138 Phillips, Wm., rewostico
1139 Phillips, Richard, rewostico
1140 Anderson, John, quntico
1141 Phillips, Thos.
1142 West, James, esqr.
1142 slave Nann
1143 Langford, Thos.
1144 Green, Richard, esqr.
1144 Green, Ezekeil
1145 Ostian, Wm., jur.
1146 Phillips, John, quntico

TAX LISTS OF SOMERSET COUNTY: 1730-1740

NANTICOKE HUNDRED

1147 Tully, Stephen, senr.
1147 Tully, Benj.
1147 Tully, Joshua
1148 Tully, Stephen, jur.
1148 Tully, Richard
1148 Tully, Danel
1148 Tully, John
1149 More, John, quntico
1149 More, James
1150 More, Wm., quntico
1151 Mears, Robert
1152 Tyford, John
1153 Bennet, Edward
1154 Bennet, Elizb.
1154 Bennet, Wm.
1155 Shearman, Wm.
1156 Cheasman, Rachel
1156 Hardy, Benj.
1156 slave Nance
1157 Parremore, Elizabath
1157 Parremore, Isaac
1158 Train, James, jur.
1158 slave Jack
1158 slave Biack
1158 slave Will
1159 Acworth, Samuel
1159 slave Sue
1160 Acworth, Henry
1160 slave Dina
1161 Hitch, Solomon
1161 Hitch, Adam
1161 Hitch, Levin
1161 slave Cook
1162 Weathrley, Joseph
1163 Nickleson, Richard
1163 slave Sevina
1164 Weatherly, Wm.
1165 Weatherly, James
1165 slave Tobe
1165 slave Pegg
1166 Fullton, Wm.
1167 Nickleson, James
1167 slave Tom
1168 Einglish, Wm.
1169 Elensworth, Robrt
1170 Twilly, Robrt
1170 Olphie, Joseph
1171 Smith, Thos., nanticoke
1172 Rhods, Danel
1173 Tully, Joseph
1173 Riggin, Ambrose
1173 slave Charles
1174 Acworth, Charles
1174 Churn, John
1175 Tully, Benj.
1176 Acworth, Thos., senr.
1176 slave Will
1176 slave Moll
1177 Acworth, Thos., jur.
1178 Melson, Hytable
1178 Curmichall, John
1178 slave Randal
1179 Melson, Samuel
1180 Huffinton, Betty
1180 Piper, Joseph
1181 Codray, David
1181 Codray, Morghin
1182 Huffinton, John, senr.
1182 slave Jacob
1182 slave Pleasant
1182 slave Jenny
1182 slave York
1183 Huffinton, John, jnr.
1184 Simson, George
1185 Kellum, Edward
1185 Killum, John
1185 slave Robin
1185 slave Merrin
1186 Smith, Thos., barn creek
1187 Brown, Wm.
1187 slave Rose
1188 Gilliss, John
1189 Glaster, Thos.
1189 Gilliss, Thos.
1190 Cormichall, Thos.
1191 Andrew, John, handwright
1192 Vanables, Benj.
1192 Curtiss, Able
1192 slave Tom
1192 slave Will
1192 slave Bess
1193 Powall, John
1194 Hicks, William
1194 Mister, Charles
1195 Lanksdell, Wm.
1196 Willson, John
1197 Gravner, Thos.
1198 Carter, Wm.
1199 Taylor, Wm.
1199 slave Bess
1200 Darby, Walter
1201 Young, Jehu
1202 Jones, Finch
1203 Cooper, Isaac
1203 Price, Francis
1204 Hardy, John
1205 Coulvor, John
1206 Wright, Soloman, barn creek
1207 Kible, John
1208 Quinton, Peter
1209 Cooper, Thos.
1209 Price, David
1210 Cooper, Samuel
1210 Cooper, Wm.
1211 Coop, John
1211 Coop, Wm.
1212 Horsley, Richard
1213 Newton, John
1214 Armstrong, Hezeciah
1215 Wallace, Richard, carp.
1216 Huffinton, Richard
1216 Huffinton, Levin
1217 Marvel, Thos.
1218 Hufinton, Thos.
1219 Edge, Robrt
1220 Parremore, Thos.
1221 Dodreal, James
1222 Tyford, Wm.
1222 Tyford, Johnathan
1223 Noules, Edmund, senr.
1223 Noulls, Edmund
1224 Jackson, Samuel
1224 slave Grace
1225 Wallter, Henry
1225 Wallter, Wm.
1226 Oliphant, Wm.
1227 Jones, John
1228 Scott, Geo.
1228 Scott, Geo.
1229 Scoot, Windom
1229 Marvill, Robt.
1230 Deane, Charles
1230 Deane, James
1230 Deane, Charles
1231 Daw, Henry
1232 Noulls, Richard
1233 Magee, Peter
1233 Magee, Peter
1233 Magee, Thos.
1234 Rowell, Thos.
1235 Floyd, Magior
1236 Olipher, Geo.
1237 Robison, John
1237 Robison, Wm.
1238 More, Wm.
1238 More, Thos.
1238 slave Pegg
1239 Jones, James
1240 Kiniken, Danel
1241 Robison, Wms.
1242 Shills, John
1243 Collains, Thos.
1244 Mcdowell, John

1740 TAX LIST [Household number/Name/Remarks]

NANTICOKE HUNDRED

1245 Collains, Thos., cooper
1245 Jones, George
1245 Mercy, John
1246 Gibins, John
1246 Einglish, James
1247 Edge, Joshua
1247 Reed, Zechriah
1248 Carter, Phillip
1249 Carter, Charles
1250 Bally, Johnathan
1251 Carter, John
1252 Collains, Edmund
1253 Vinsin, James
1254 Maggunea, Elizibath
1254 Desten, James
1255 McClanan, Joseph
1256 Collains, John
1256 Turpin, Danel
1257 Wallor, Nethanel, senr.
1257 Wallor, John
1257 Wallor, Nethail
1258 Riukcords, John, junr.
1258 slave Deadford
1258 slave Bess
1259 Wallor, Thos., senr.
1259 Wallor, Richard
1260 Caldwell, Thos.
1261 Fullton, Nicklos
1261 Fullton, John
1262 Lynn, Aaron
1262 Jervice, Richard
1262 Battes, Edward
1262 Dreigs, Josephus
1262 slave Abram
1262 slave Jack
1262 slave Bess
1263 Jerad, Wm., free black
1263 Jerad, Comfort, free black
1264 Spear, Henry
1264 Spear, John
1265 McClure, Robrt
1266 Wallor, Nethaneil, jur.
1267 Wallor, Thos., jur.
1268 More, Wm., jur.
1269 Kenney, Wm.
1270 Caldwell, Partrick
1271 Tattman, James
1272 Polk, John, little creek
1273 Roads, John
1274 Williams, John
1275 Caldwell, John, jur.
1275 Caldwell, Robt.
1275 slave Sambo
1276 Ralph, Wm.
1276 Ralph, Thos.
1277 Bacon, Dutsand
1278 Wright, Solomon, quntico
1279 Wallace, Richard, ser.
1280 Godart, John
1280 Godart, Nethaneil
1280 Bouth, Geo.
1281 Callaway, John, senr.
1281 Callaway, Isaac
1282 Callaway, Wm., sen.
1282 Callaway, Benj.
1283 Callaway, Wm.
1284 Cooper, James
1285 Benson, Henry
1285 Benson, Mathew
1285 Benson, James
1286 Childs, Edmund
1287 Godart, George
1288 Callaway, John, jur.
1289 Callaway, John, son John
1290 Callaway, Edward
1291 Shearman, Thos.
1292 Bowelins, Thos.
1293 James, John
1294 Wootten, John
1295 Wootten, Edward
1296 Shearman, Job
1297 Hosea, Mathew
1298 Stevens, John
1299 More, Wm., jur. ind. fort
1300 Callaway, John, son of Peter
1301 Vaughan, Wm.
1302 Willy, Jerad
1302 Wartnaby, Wm.
1303 Cheapman, Paris
1303 Barnett, John
1303 Meashell, Joseph
1303 Bass, John
1303 slave Benn
1303 slave Philliss
1303 slave Katt
1304 Noble, John
1305 Parremore, James
1306 Downs, Robrt
1307 Kemmy, Abraham
1308 Benson, Wm., wimbascom
1309 King, Wm., w.s.
1310 Wright, Edward
1311 Paremore, Ezekeil
1312 Paremore, Joseph
1313 Thompson, Charles, ser.
1314 Littleton, Edmund
1315 Sanders, Andrew
1315 Sanders, Andrew
1316 Thompson, Charles, jur.
1317 Collains, Geo.
1318 Boudger, James
1319 Sumerlinn, Wm.
1320 Buckworth, Charles
1321 Parremore, Mathew
1322 Carter, Samuel
1323 Thompson, George
1323 Watson, John
1324 Dickson, Wm.
1325 Givans, George
1326 Houlston, John
1327 Oneal, John
1328 Baker, Wm.
1329 Shearman, Peter
1329 Mercys, Joseph
1330 Henry, Martian
1330 Hall, Thos.
1331 Rickords, Alexd.
1332 Oneal, James
1332 slave Dina
1332 slave Mingo
1333 Houlston, Robrt
1334 Rathborn, Andrew
1335 Phillips, Richard, nanticoke
1336 Hurt, Danel
1337 Clifton, Geo.
1338 Collains, John, ser.
1339 Oysborn, John
1340 Benson, Wm., deep creek
1341 Shiles, Thos.
1342 Persons, Frances
1343 More, John, deep creek
1344 Wallor, Nelson
1345 Phips, John, esqr.
1346 Collyer, Thos.
1346 slave Grace
1347 Crockett, Richard
1347 Fleetwood, John
1347 Esam, Benjman
1348 Hall, James
1349 Fisher, George

TAX LISTS OF SOMERSET COUNTY: 1730-1740

NANTICOKE/POCOMOKE HUNDREDS

1350 Newball, Frances
1350 slave Amie
1351 Willy, John
1351 slave Casaway
1351 slave Danell
1352 Callaway, Peter
1352 Dukes, John
1353 Wallor, Richard
1353 Oliver, Thos.
1354 Hickman, Henry
1355 Callaway, Thos.
1356 More, Isaac
1357 Spear, Robrt
1358 Owen, Peter
1359 Mitchell, Alex.
1360 Mercy, Wm.
1361 Owens, Robert
1361 slave Katt
1362 Jones, Samuel
1363 Polok, James
1364 Polok, Charles
1365 Polok, Ephreaim
1366 Polok, John
1366 slave Atte
1366 slave Sib
1367 Manlove, Manuel
1367 slave Quako
1368 Eingram, Abraham, senr.
1368 Ingram, James
1368 slave George
1368 slave Priscilla
1369 Collains, Wm.
1370 Smith, Henry
1371 Eingram, Abraham, jur.
1372 Eingram, Isaac
1373 Eingram, David
1374 Messick, Obidiah
1375 Collains, Andrew
1375 slave Lott
1375 slave Nann
1376 Tattman, Wm.
1377 Morgain, Joseph
1378 Samuels, Richard
1379 Samuels, Peter
1379 Lawson, Peter
1380 Hopkins, Danel
1381 Scoott, Wm.
1382 Harvay, John
1383 Keemy, Wallter
1384 Keemy, Thos.
1385 Brown, Thos.
1386 Williams, Charles
1387 Short, John
1388 Short, Abraham
1389 Puckam, Richard
1389 Puckam, John
1390 Bradley, John
1391 Carter, Thos.

1392 Cooper, Gabrill
1393 Dalby, Peter
1394 Grear, Wm.
1395 Henry, Robert
1396 Smith, David
1397 Bivins, Caleb
1398 Messick, John
1399 Sharp, John
1399 Sharp, Wm.
1399 Sharp, John
1399 slave Hannah
1400 Lord, John
1401 Bivans, John
1402 Johnson, Simon
1403 Hopkins, John
1404 Porter, Josephus
1405 Feenatson, Eliass
1406 Melson, Joseph
1407 Bound, Jacob
1408 Hickman, Jonathan
1409 Lanksdell, John
1409 Smith, James
1410 Coop, Wm.
1411 Elensworth, Nehemiah
1412 Wingitt, Phillip
1413 Eingram, Jacob
1414 Eingram, Robrt
1415 Messick, Robert
1416 Boyce, John
1417 Mcandtoush, Hugh
1418 Kiniken, Aurthur
1419 Elensworth, Richard
1420 Tindall, Charles
1421 Melson, Benjeman
1422 Hall, John
1423 Taylor, Wm., senr.
1424 Hall, Robrt
1424 Morriss, John
1424 slave Lilly
1425 Winright, William
1426 Phillips, Wm.
1427 Shockly, David
1427 slave Dina
1428 Shockly, James
1429 Shockly, Solomon
1430 Gray, Wm.
1430 slave Coffee
1431 Boyce, Danel
1431 slave Tom
1431 slave Bess
1432 Banks, Steven
1432 slave Quomono
1433 King, Phillip
1434 Persons, Charles
1435 Callaway, Sarah
1435 Callaway, Joseph
1436 Parremore, Elizbt.
1436 Parmore, Benj.
1436 Parremore, John

1437 Doughters, Wm.
1437 Doughters, Thos.
1438 Phillips, John
1439 McCloister, Josepj
1439 slave Samson
1440 Lewis, Aurther

POCOMOKE HUNDRED

1441 Hayward, Thomas, mr.
1441 slave Tom
1441 slave Jesper
1441 slave Cudgo
1441 slave Polk
1441 slave Rose
1441 slave Phelice
1441 slave Plesent
1442 Dennis, John, junr.
1442 Dennis, John
1442 Newton, John
1442 slave Kingston
1442 slave Isaac
1442 slave George
1442 slave Patience
1442 slave Cate
1443 Mitchell, Robert
1443 Mitchell, Joshua
1443 slave Selby
1444 Goddis, Robert
1444 slave Tom
1444 slave Phebe
1445 Goore, Jane, for
1445 Matthews, John
1446 Handy, Elizabeth
1446 slave Harry
1446 slave Hago
1446 slave Juda
1447 Handy, Thomas
1447 Handy, Stephen
1447 Mills, Robert
1448 Bell, John
1448 White, Nathaniel
1449 Mills, William, senr.
1450 Mills, Jonathan
1451 Tull, Noble
1452 Tull, George
1452 Tull, Jonathan
1452 slave Abner
1452 slave Dick
1453 Pilcher, William
1454 Pilcher, John
1455 Costin, Stephen
1456 Harris, John
1456 Harris, Benton
1456 slave Tom
1457 Costin, Isaac
1457 Costin, Oliver
1457 slave Cuffie
1457 slave Andrew
1457 slave Ceasar

1740 TAX LIST [Household number/Name/Remarks]

POCOMOKE HUNDRED

1457 slave Pegg
1457 slave Hanna
1457 slave Jean
1457 slave Moll
1457 slave Sawny
1458 Tull, John
1459 Knight, Richard
1459 slave Boson
1460 Long, Daniel, jur.
1461 Stutt, Archebd.
1462 Knight, James
1463 Harris, Jeremiah
1463 Harris, Spencer
1464 Odea, Stephen
1465 Harris, Caleb
1465 Harris, James
1466 Harper, Edward
1466 Harper, John
1467 Stephens, Edward
1468 Warrick, Arthur
1469 Riggin, Teague
1469 Riggin, Teague
1469 slave Peter
1469 slave Dina
1469 slave Nann
1470 Fleming, William
1471 Riggin, Ambroze, senr.
1471 Riggin, Teague
1472 Ward, Josph.
1472 Ward, Cornelius
1472 Ward, Josph.
1472 slave Sara
1473 Phillips, John
1473 Phillips, Ezekl.
1474 Harris, Robert
1474 slave Harry
1474 slave Tonny
1474 slave Mingo
1474 slave Moll
1475 Smulling, Randall
1475 Smulling, Nathanl.
1475 Smulling, William
1475 McGrain, John
1476 Riggin, Josph.
1476 slave Ceesar
1477 Denston, John
1478 Hadduck, Ignatius
1479 Brown, George
1480 Taylor, Jacob
1481 Dickerson, John
1482 Redding, Charles
1483 Dukes, William
1484 Harper, Francis
1485 Wonnell, James
1486 Dukes, Robert
1487 Smith, John

1487 Denston, Isaac
1488 Townsend, Elizabeth
1488 slave Tawny
1489 Townsend, Danford
1490 Coulborn, John
1491 McCuddy, John
1491 Mellbourn, Ralph
1491 Nicholas, George
1492 Riggin, Darby
1492 Riggin, John
1492 Riggin, Darby
1493 Otwell, Francis, senr.
1493 Otwell, William
1494 Otwell, Charles
1495 Fleming, John, senr.
1495 Fleming, John
1495 slave Robin
1495 slave Pompey
1495 slave Joe
1495 slave Dina
1495 slave Nanne
1496 Townsend, John, senr.
1496 Townsend, John
1496 Townsend, Marshell
1497 Cooper, Samuel
1498 Fogg, Mosses
1499 Donoho, Dorman
1500 Townsend, Daniel
1500 Townsend, Dickerson
1500 Townsend, James
1500 slave Pegg
1501 Mayo, Samuel
1502 Dickerson, Charles
1503 Dickerson, Edmund
1503 Marshell, William
1504 Dickerson, Cornelius
1504 Dickerson, Edmund, senr.
1504 slave Masey
1504 slave Jenny
1505 Donoho, Sarah
1505 Donoho, Daniel
1505 Donoho, Teague
1505 Donoho, Dormon
1505 Donoho, John
1505 slave George
1506 Townsend, James
1506 slave Guy
1506 slave Jack
1507 Bennett, William
1507 Kersey, Robert
1508 Otwell, Francis, jur.

1508 Daughtey, Edmond
1508 Otwell, Solomon
1509 Sheldon, John
1509 Hambleton, William
1509 slave Isaac
1510 Townsend, Solomon
1511 Townsend, Charles
1511 Townsend, Elias
1512 Townsend, Saul
1512 slave Will
1512 slave Adam
1513 Porter, Francis
1513 Taws, John
1513 slave Jack
1513 slave Sawny
1514 Porter, Mkkemey
1514 Tull, James
1515 Allen, Francis, senr.
1515 Allen, Willm.
1515 Tillman, Willm.
1515 slave Sambo
1515 slave Frank
1515 slave Jeremi
1515 slave Joe
1515 slave Majery
1515 slave Juda
1515 slave Merea
1516 Allen, Francis, jur.
1516 slave Jemmy
1517 Atkinson, Angelo
1517 Lorwill, John
1517 Vallence, Thomas
1517 slave Cubit
1518 Scott, John, capt.
1518 Scott, Joseph
1518 Goldsmith, Thomas
1518 slave Peter
1518 slave Hogo
1518 slave Will
1518 slave Jeane
1518 slave Phebe
1518 slave Rose
1519 Gibbs, Robt.
1520 Taylor, Peter
1520 slave Juda
1520 slave Fungo
1520 slave Plesent
1521 Peal, Thomas, senr.
1521 Peal, Thomas
1521 slave Samson
1522 Beavins, Thomas
1522 Beavins, Rowland
1522 Beavins, Rowland
1523 Beavins, William
1524 Beavins, Cornelius
1525 Andrus, John
1525 Andrus, Peal

TAX LISTS OF SOMERSET COUNTY: 1730-1740

POCOMOKE HUNDRED

1526 Cottingham, Willm.
1526 Cottingham, Jonathan
1526 Cottingham, John
1527 Bayly, Alexander
1528 Townsend, Willm. Bartlet
1528 slave Abraham
1529 Ball, Samuell
1529 Taylor, Job
1530 Kitchen, William
1530 slave Bess
1531 Townsend, Comfort, for
1531 Townsend, Nathl.
1532 White, Hannah
1532 White, John
1532 White, William
1533 Davis, Nathaniel
1533 Davis, Nathaniel
1533 Riggin, Pearce
1534 Selby, Thomas
1534 slave Sam
1535 Bennett, John
1535 slave Jack
1536 Atkinson, Samuel
1536 Holaday, Joseph
1536 slave James
1537 Atkinson, Joshua
1537 slave Frank
1537 slave Sam
1537 slave Bess
1538 Atkinson, Isaac
1539 Riggin, Ambroze, jur.
1539 Riggin, Teague
1540 Butler, Thomas
1541 Taylor, Samuel, jr.
1542 Taylor, Samuel, sr.
1542 Taylor, George
1542 slave Robbin
1543 Warington, Thomas
1544 [Rework], John
1545 Crouch, Isaac
1546 Crouch, Nicholas
1547 Right, Randall
1548 Fountain, Nicholas
1549 Jones, William
1550 Hammond, Charles
1551 Stevens, John
1552 Noble, James
1553 Laws, William
1554 Broughton, James
1555 Laws, John
1555 slave Joe

1556 Mkdanill, James
1556 Victor, Thoms.
1557 Taylor, James
1558 Beavins, John
1558 Beavins, Thoms.
1558 Beavins, Rowland
1558 slave Sambo
1559 Nicholas, Matthias
1560 Nicholas, James
1560 slave Hanna
1561 Nicholas, Joseph
1562 Brumble, Thomas
1563 Johnson, Whitington
1563 slave Bess
1563 slave Plessent
1564 Chelley, Mosses, capt.
1564 slave Simon
1564 slave Rose
1565 Davis, Jos.
1566 Selby, Thomas, junr.
1567 Houlston, Joseph
1567 slave Tom
1567 slave Bell
1567 slave Pegg
1567 slave Dina
1568 Kellem, Joshua
1568 Kellem, Isaac
1569 Glass, Christopher, jur.
1570 Jenkins, John
1570 Houston, Joseph
1570 Brittingham, Elisha
1571 Morris, Isaac
1571 Morris, Luke
1571 slave Benn
1571 slave Surthey
1571 slave Abner
1571 slave Will
1571 slave Dineh
1572 Godfrey, Joseph
1573 Glass, Christopher, senr
1574 Dennis, Valentine
1575 Dennis, John, senr.
1575 Dennis, Lazarus
1575 slave Joe
1575 slave Sue
1576 Sturgis, Jonathan
1576 slave Jack
1576 slave Dina
1577 Purnell, Elisha
1577 slave Pippin
1578 Martin, James, capt.

1578 Martin, John
1578 Nelson, John
1578 Olandman, John
1578 slave Pompey
1578 slave Mass
1578 slave Joe
1578 slave Nann
1578 slave Dinah
1579 Owten, Abraham
1579 Andrus, Roberson
1579 Dear, John
1579 slave Samson
1579 slave Phlora
1580 Davis, Thomas
1581 Hough, Edmund
1581 slave Cepio
1581 slave Frank
1582 Townsend, Littleton
1582 Glass, Elias
1582 slave Abbi
1582 slave Pompe
1582 slave Jenny
1583 Townsend, Jeremiah
1584 Kellem, John, indn. town
1585 Pope, John, senr.
1585 Pope, John
1585 slave Cook
1585 slave Tom
1585 slave Harry
1585 slave Pegg
1585 slave Jenny
1586 Taylor, Willm.
1587 MackAllen, Arthur
1588 Wildman, John
1588 slave Dina
1589 Lane, Willm., capt.
1589 Lane, Willm.
1589 slave Dick
1589 slave Harry
1589 slave Phelice
1590 Probart, William, capt.
1591 Lane, John
1592 Webb, John, senr.
1592 Webb, Solomon
1592 Webb, John
1592 Cook, Guy
1593 Pain, Joseph
1594 Mills, Mosses
1594 Mills, Alexandr.
1594 slave Simon
1595 Melvin, William
1596 Melvin, Robart, senr.
1596 Melvin, Robart
1597 Mosses, Joseph
1598 Wheeler, Isaac
1598 slave Joe

1740 TAX LIST [Household number/Name/Remarks]

POCOMOKE HUNDRED

1599 Burnett, James
1600 Mills, Samuel
1600 Mills, Hugh
1600 Mills, John
1600 slave Dina
1601 Mills, Nathal.
1602 Melton, John
1603 Brooks, Francis
1604 Gillit, John
1604 Benston, Danl.
1604 slave Harry
1604 slave Nann
1604 slave Roass
1605 Gillit, Samuel
1605 slave Darkiss
1606 Gillit, William
1606 Gillit, Samuel, jur.
1607 Jones, Edward
1607 Jones, Elisha
1608 Ellice, William
1609 Mills, Smith
1610 Stevenson, Joseph
1610 Stephenson, William
1611 Piper, Isaac
1611 Whaley, John
1612 Mills, William, junr.
1613 Mills, Nathen
1614 Mills, Robert
1614 Mills, Alexander
1615 Stevenson, Robert
1616 Lamberson, Samuel
1617 Lamberson, Abraham
1618 Lamberson, Sarah
1618 Lamberson, Henry
1619 Ramsey, Charles
1619 Taylor, James
1619 Ramsey, John
1619 Ramsey, Barnet
1620 Davis, Evin
1621 Merrill, John
1622 Merrill, William, jur.
1623 Quenton, Philip
1623 slave Jack
1623 slave Peter
1623 slave Tamer
1623 slave Phelice
1624 Quenton, Dixon
1625 Lindall, Robert
1625 Curyor, Caleb
1626 Baker, Henderson
1627 Henderson, Samuel
1627 slave Jack
1628 Brittingham, John
1629 Brittingham, William
1629 slave Rose
1630 Britingham, Samuel
1631 Curvin, Thomas
1632 Baker, James
1632 Mulagin, Thomas
1632 Wright, Comfort
1633 Conner, William
1633 Moore, Samuel
1633 Parks, Arthur
1634 Dickerson, Frans.
1634 Dickerson, Nehemiah
1635 Breeman, Cathern
1635 slave Talleme
1636 Layfield, George
1637 Dickerson, Robt.
1638 Houston, James
1638 slave Kate
1638 slave Dina
1639 Houston, John
1640 Blades, Benjamin
1640 Blades, James
1641 McCameren, Evender
1642 MkFarling, Robt.
1642 Henry, Hugh
1643 Britingham, Elijah
1643 Pecock, John
1643 Pecock, Willm.
1643 slave Nann
1644 Tomlinson, Soward
1644 slave Plesent
1644 slave Ceasar
1645 Benston, John, for
1645 Benston, George
1645 Benston, John
1646 Britingham, Micaijah
1647 Lamberson, Robert
1647 Steward, Francis
1648 Henderson, John, senr.
1648 slave Guy
1648 slave George
1648 slave Bess
1648 slave Joan
1648 slave Eve
1649 Henderson, James
1649 Henderson, John
1649 slave Adam
1650 Henderson, John, jur.
1650 Henderson, John
1651 Henderson, Charles
1651 Henderson, William
1652 Lambden, Thomas, mr.
1652 Lambdon, Richard
1653 Henderson, Francis
1654 Pitts, Robert
1654 Moriss, Bevins
1655 Blades, John
1655 slave Phelice
1656 Henderson, Benjn.
1657 Young, Danl.
1658 Jones, Richard
1659 Lindow, Margiret, for
1659 slave Mosses
1660 Stevens, William
1660 slave Harry
1661 Dorman, Samuel, sr.
1661 Dorman, Samuel
1661 Wheeler, William
1662 Padan, John
1662 slave Oxford
1663 Dreding, David, jr.
1664 Cluff, Edward
1664 Fittue, John
1665 Broughton, Bruff
1665 Cullingham, John
1665 Leonard, John
1666 Broughton, John
1666 Broughton, William
1667 Tillmen, Gidden
1667 Maddux, Alexandr.
1667 Telman, John
1667 slave Pompey
1668 Clogg, Saml.
1669 Purkins, John
1669 Purkins, Michl.
1669 Whaley, Willm.
1670 Newbold, Thomas
1670 Newbold, Purnall
1670 slave Patience
1671 Benston, Thomas
1672 Dreding, David, senr.
1672 Dreding, Willm.
1672 Thomson, John
1673 Powell, John
1673 Butler, Emanl.
1674 Powell, Levin
1675 Maddux, Alexr.
1675 slave Sarah
1676 Jackson, Nathanl.
1676 Tippin, Saml.
1677 Fenton, Margeret
1677 Blare, Robt.
1678 Bedoses, Hugh
1679 Scholfield, Henry
1679 Sparkman, George
1680 Williams, John, capt.
1680 Vernelson, Elisha
1680 Porter, William
1680 slave Jemmy

TAX LISTS OF SOMERSET COUNTY: 1730-1740

POCOMOKE/WICOMICO HUNDREDS

1680 slave Robbin
1680 slave Harry
1680 slave Nimrod
1680 slave Phenix
1680 slave Priss
1680 slave Sew
1680 slave Jenny
1681 Hampton, Mary, madm.
1681 Henry, Robt. Jenkins, major
1681 Henry, John, capt.
1681 Harbert, William
1681 Baker, John
1681 slave Chick
1681 slave Adam
1681 slave Tarrill
1681 slave Harry
1681 slave Jock
1681 slave Robbin
1681 slave Dirry
1681 slave Lewse
1681 slave Rose
1681 slave Phelice
1681 slave Jenny
1681 slave Patience
1682 Thomlinson, Abigal
1682 Thomlinson, Hampton
1682 slave London
1683 White, Archebauld
1683 White, William
1684 White, John
1684 slave George
1684 slave Nann
1685 Hall, John
1686 MkCready, Alexar.
1687 MkCready, Solomon
1688 Nearn, James
1688 slave Will
1688 slave Harry
1688 slave Moll
1688 slave Poll
1689 Dormon, Frans.
1690 Nearn, Robt.
1690 slave Tonny
1690 slave Sarah
1690 slave Magg
1690 slave Nanny
1691 Dickerson, Isaac
1692 Adams, Collings
1692 Moorain, Joseph
1693 Collings, Samuel
1693 slave Bett
1694 Melbourn, John
1694 slave Bess
1695 Melbourn, Caleb

1695 slave Mingo
1696 Melbourn, Ralph
1697 Evans, Thomas
1697 Evans, William
1697 slave Jenny
1698 Evans, John
1699 Harly, Peter
1700 Holland, William, capt.
1700 slave Tom
1700 slave Dina
1701 Benston, Benjn.
1702 Clifton, John
1703 Boyer, Robert
1703 Clifton, George
1703 slave Harry
1703 slave Darkis
1704 Ellis, John
1705 Cox, William
1705 slave Ceesar
1706 Riggin, John
1706 Cotingham, John
1706 slave Nann
1707 Dickerson, Charles
1707 slave Dina
1708 Riggin, Charles
1708 slave Dina
1709 Caldwell, Jos., capt.
1709 slave Jack
1709 slave Adam
1709 slave Moll
1709 slave Dina
1710 Riggin, Solomon
1711 Riggin, Mary
1711 Riggin, John
1711 Riggin, Teague
1711 Riggin, Cornelius
1711 slave Jenny
1712 Matthews, Teague
1712 Matthews, Philip
1713 Matthews, John
1714 Matthews, William
1715 Matthews, Samuel
1716 Matthews, Mary
1716 Matthews, David
1716 slave Jeffry
1717 Adams, Samuel
1717 Adams, Thomas
1717 slave Jenny
1718 Adams, Jacob
1718 slave Samson
1719 Kersey, William
1720 Kersey, Samuel
1721 Boston, Isaac
1721 slave Jeffery
1721 slave Venus
1721 slave Jenny
1722 Boston, Esau

1722 Boston, Esau
1722 Boston, Jacob
1723 Taylor, Elias
1724 Taylor, Robert
1724 Taylor, Robert
1724 Cotingham, William
1724 Melavery, Thoms.
1725 Woods, William
1726 Adams, Isaac
1726 slave Dick
1726 slave Will
1726 slave Moll
1727 Hutcheson, William
1728 Owen, Mosses
1728 slave Harry
1729 Dicks, Edward
1730 Adams, Hoap
1730 slave Gloster
1731 Adams, Philip, senr.
1732 Adams, William, senr.
1733 Adams, William, jur.
1734 Adams, Philip, jur.
1735 Adams, Geo., senr.
1735 Adams, Geo.
1736 Beachamp, Edward
1736 Beachamp, Willm.
1736 slave Moire
1737 Beachamp, John
1738 Beachamp, Thomas
1738 Beachamp, Levin
1739 Davis, Beachamp
1740 Dennes, Wheetley, for
1740 slave Diner
1741 Merrill, Joshua

WICOMICO HUNDRED
1742 Crouch, Jacob, senr.
1743 Crouch, Jacob, junr.
1744 Gosley, Thos.
1744 Bashaw, Giles
1745 Gosley, Matthew
1746 Mallone, Robert
1747 Christopher, Joseph
1747 Kersey, Patrick, junr.
1748 Crouch, Robert
1749 Parriss, John
1750 Jackson, Christ. Domk.
1750 Alexander, Wm.
1750 slave Ned
1750 slave Judith

1740 TAX LIST [Household number/Name/Remarks]

WICOMICO HUNDRED

1750 slave Kate	1774 Gray, Allen	1807 Smith, Archibald
1751 Handy, John	1775 Hall, Saml.	1808 Tate, Francis
1751 slave Dick	1776 Parsons, John, cyprus br	1808 Skeddy, John
1751 slave Ben	1777 Tatom, John	1809 Daviss, John
1751 slave Primus	1778 Leonard, Joseph	1810 Lindow, Thos.
1751 slave Jean	1779 Oliphant, Mathew	1811 Davis, Daniel
1751 slave Hagar	1780 Cox, Thos., junr.	1811 Davis, Thos.
1752 Daviss, Wm.	1781 Cox, Hill	1812 Maggee, Peter
1753 Bluett, John	1782 Cox, Thos., senr.	1812 Maggee, Moses
1754 Cordry, Jacob	1782 Cox, Daniel	1813 Caldwell, John, mr.
1754 Bashaw, Wm.	1783 Hill, Charles	1813 Caldwell, Robt.
1755 Humphries, Mary	1783 Elliss, Wm.	1813 slave Cuffe
1755 Humphries, Joseph	1783 Newberry, Wm.	1813 slave Scipio
1756 King, Wm.	1784 Dishroon, Levin	1813 slave Will
1757 Lank, Francis	1785 Dishroon, Lewis	1813 slave Doll
1757 Lank, Stephen	1785 Doyl, John	1813 slave Squash
1757 slave Jack	1786 Melvin, Thos.	1814 Shockley, John, senr.
1757 slave Toby	1787 Wright, Jerremiah, junr.	1814 Shockley, John, junr.
1757 slave Bess	1788 Smith, James, junr.	1814 Layfeild, David
1758 Hitch, Elgatt	1789 Roberts, Rencher	1815 Howard, John
1758 slave Bonny	1790 Vinson, Benjamin	1816 Morriss, Jacob
1758 slave Connundo	1791 Turner, Saml.	1817 Taylor, Samll.
1758 slave Amey	1791 Turner, Joseph	1817 slave Kingston
1759 Johnson, Purnall	1791 Turner, Rowland	1818 Bartlett, Pasque
1759 slave Rose	1792 Turner, Joshua	1818 Bartlett, Thos.
1760 Hall, Thos.	1793 Smith, Andrew, senr.	1819 Gosley, John
1761 Johnson, Samll.	1793 Smith, Andrew, junr.	1820 Piper, Christopher
1762 Breedy, Wm.	1793 Smith, George	1820 slave Dick
1763 Hall, David	1794 Smith, George	1820 slave Sambo
1764 Handy, Isaac	1794 Turpin, Matthew	1820 slave Toby
1764 slave Quameny	1795 Lingo, John	1820 slave Greenage
1764 slave Sharper	1796 Parsons, George	1820 slave Moll
1764 slave Prue	1796 Brereton, Alexander	1820 slave Sue
1764 slave Mumford	1797 Kersey, Patrick, senr.	1820 slave Whitehaven
1764 slave Will	1797 Kersey, James	1821 Winder, Thos.
1765 Dashiel, Arthur	1798 Perdew, John, senr.	1821 slave Mingo
1765 slave Ben	1798 Perdew, John, junr.	1821 slave Cudger
1765 slave Penny	1798 Perdew, George	1821 slave Benns
1765 slave Betty	1799 Maglammery, Edwd.	1821 slave Harry
1765 slave Cuffy	1799 slave Sambo	1821 slave Bess
1766 Hitch, Samll.	1799 slave Pheby	1822 Macmurray, Ann
1766 slave Jack	1800 Maggee, George	1822 Sirmon, Isaac
1767 Flint, John	1801 Lingo, Richd.	1822 slave Abner
1768 Hitch, John	1802 Deverix, John	1822 slave Rose
1768 slave Moyah	1802 Cannydy, Timothy	1823 Dashiel, Matthias
1769 Hitch, Wm.	1803 Smith, Moses	1823 slave Sambo
1770 Vinson, George	1804 Hill, James	1823 slave Rose
1770 Hitch, John, junr.	1805 Smith, James, senr.	1824 Wales, Eleanor
1770 Hitch, Nehemiah	1806 Murphy, Joseph	1824 Richardson, Wm.
1771 Vinson, Thos., senr.		1824 slave Leander
1771 Vinson, Thos., junr.		1824 slave Peter
1772 Lecatt, John		1824 slave Ordre
1772 slave Leah		1824 slave Orriss
1773 Covington, Thos.		1825 Cordry, Abraham
1773 Covington, John		1825 Day, Daniel
1773 slave Tom		1826 Scott, George, mr.
		1826 slave Sam

TAX LISTS OF SOMERSET COUNTY: 1730-1740

WICOMICO HUNDRED

1826 slave Sanders
1826 slave Pomp
1826 slave Flora
1827 Scott, Day
1827 slave Hector
1827 slave Tom
1827 slave Lucy
1828 Evans, John, senr.
1828 slave Sambo
1829 Evans, John, junr.
1829 slave Dinah
1830 Shiles, John, secundus
1831 Dashiel, Char
1831 slave Jacob
1831 slave Pliner
1832 Wainwright, Stephen
1833 Willin, Thos., senr.
1833 Willin, Thos., junr.
1833 Willin, Robt.
1833 slave Gunner
1833 slave Sarah
1834 Mackintire, Danl.
1834 Crockett, Robt.
1834 Brookshaw, Wm.
1834 slave Crop
1835 Nelson, Wm.
1835 Nelson, John
1836 Everton, John
1836 Everton, Wm.
1837 Furbush, Peter
1838 Williams, Richd.
1838 Williams, John
1839 Shiles, John, ferry
1839 slave Tom
1839 slave Hannibal
1840 Crockett, John
1841 Dulany, Dennis
1842 Fowler, John
1842 slave Mary
1843 Harriss, Wm., junr.
1844 Harriss, Richd.
1845 Willin, Edwd.
1846 Fletchers, Thos.
1846 slave
1847 Wilkins, James
1848 Foskey, Thos.
1849 Harriss, Wm., senr.
1849 Harriss, Charles
1849 Harriss, Bloys
1850 Dashiel, Thos.
1850 slave Isaac
1851 Renshaw, Thos.
1851 slave Peter
1851 slave Pompey
1852 Renshaw, Underwood
1852 slave Jack
1852 slave Maria
1853 Ballard, Charles
1853 slave Cesar
1854 Jones, John
1855 Gale, Matthias
1855 Noble, Mark
1855 slave Cesar
1855 slave Jack
1855 slave Ralph
1855 slave Stephen
1855 slave Dublin
1855 slave Rose
1855 slave Violat
1855 slave Sarah
1856 Stewart, Peter
1856 slave Nero
1857 Fowler, Thos.
1858 Holbrook, Thos., senr.
1858 Holbrook, Thos., junr.
1859 Walker, Thos.
1859 slave Tom
1859 slave Juba
1859 slave Jonathan
1859 slave Dinah
1859 slave Kate
1860 Murrah, Wm.
1860 slave Bella
1861 Cotman, Joseph
1861 slave Sarah
1862 Cotman, Wm.
1862 Chambers, Saml.
1863 Gale, Levin, coll.
1863 Robertson, Wm.
1863 Huttison, Robt.
1863 Raith, Jas.
1863 Smith, Jerremiah
1863 Henderson, James
1863 slave Hope
1863 slave Jack
1863 slave Jacob
1863 slave Robin
1863 slave Jonathan
1863 slave Will
1863 slave Harry
1863 slave Peter
1863 slave Parkitt
1863 slave Dick
1863 slave Frank
1863 slave Ishmael
1863 slave Carolus
1863 slave Pullert
1863 slave Bess
1863 slave Zipporah
1863 slave Maria
1863 slave Hannah
1863 slave Abigall
1864 Gilliss, Thos.
1864 Gilliss, Levin
1864 Heath, Wm.
1864 slave Stepney
1864 slave Dominick
1864 slave Nemoh
1864 slave Pegg
1865 Russell, George
1866 Cotman, Benj.
1866 Brown, Andrew
1866 slave Sarah
1867 Lackie, Alexandr.
1867 Collier, Evans
1867 slave Toby
1867 slave Robin
1867 slave Grace
1867 slave Beck
1867 slave Fortune
1868 Jones, Thos.
1868 slave Mercer
1868 slave Sam
1868 slave Surry
1868 slave Frank
1869 Records, John, senr.
1869 Records, Thos.
1869 slave Toby
1870 Christopher, John, senr.
1871 Christopher, Clement
1872 Knowles, Wm.
1873 Dowdle, Christopher
1874 Nicholson, Richard
1875 Adams, Alexander, senr.
1875 Adams, Alexandr., junr.
1875 Adams, John
1875 slave Quash
1875 slave Glascow
1875 slave Cato
1875 slave Beck
1875 slave Dinah
1876 Parriss, George
1876 Taylor, James
1876 slave Pompey
1877 Nicholson, James
1878 Nicholson, Joseph
1879 Bird, Thos., senr.
1879 Bird, Benj.
1880 Bird, Thos., junr.
1881 Bird, Wm.
1882 Price, John
1882 Maggee, John
1883 Collins, James
1884 Maddox, Wm.

1740 TAX LIST [Household number/Name/Remarks]

WICOMICO HUNDRED

1884 slave Abram
1885 Stephens, Wm.
1886 Humphries, Thos.
1886 Morriss, John
1887 Cordry, John, senr.
1887 Cordry, John, junr.
1888 Vennables, Wm.
1888 Russell, Wm.
1889 Hardy, Robert
1889 Hardy, James
1890 Dashiell, George
1890 Dashiell, Clemt.
1890 Russell, Thos.
1890 Piper, Benj.
1890 Crouch, John
1890 19 slaves
1891 Vennables, Catharine
1891 Vennables, Joseph
1891 Vennables, Perkins
1892 Howgene, Sarah
1892 Layton, Levin
1893 Rogers, Richd.
1894 Evans, Wm.
1895 Fullerton, Alexandr.
1896 Deshroon, John, son Lewis
1896 Dowhorty, James
1897 Maddox, Alexandr.
1897 slave George
1897 slave Maria
1898 Ready, Bryan
1898 Ready, Cornelius
1899 Craggan, Paul
1900 Caldwell, Hugh
1901 Hearn, Thos.
1901 slave Hannah
1902 Hearn, George
1903 Thomason, Thos.
1904 Hearn, Wm.
1904 Hearn, John
1904 Hearn, Isaac
1904 slave Moll
1905 Hearn, Nehemiah
1905 Maddox, Thos.
1906 Phillips, Jacob
1907 Smith, David
1908 Melson, Daniel
1909 Morriss, Jerremiah
1910 Gordey, Peter
1911 King, Hugh
1912 Freny, Peter
1912 Freny, John
1913 Hasten, Robt., senr.
1913 Hasten, Robt., junr.
1913 Hasten, Benj.
1914 Hasten, Wm.
1915 Longoe, James
1915 Ruark, James
1915 Morriss, Nathaniel
1916 Sadler, Isaac
1917 Williss, Nathaniel
1917 Williss, Edmund
1918 Lingoe, Robertson
1919 Skeddy, Stephen
1920 Dorman, Major
1921 Dorman, Henry
1922 Shockley, Richard
1923 Driskell, Moses
1924 Driskill, William
1925 Gordey, Moses
1926 Smullen, Randall
1927 Taylor, John
1928 Daviss, Samll.
1929 Cary, Thos.
1930 Cathwell, James
1930 Cathwell, Jonathan
1931 Christopher, John, junr.
1931 Christopher, Jacob
1932 Adkins, Robt.
1932 Warrington, Benj.
1933 Toadvine, Henry
1933 Toadvine, Joshua
1933 slave Goliah
1933 slave Oxford
1933 slave Sambo
1933 slave Sarah
1933 slave Jenny
1933 slave Flora
1934 Cary, Levin
1935 Shockly, Jonathan
1936 Hayman, Wm., senr.
1936 Hayman, Wm., junr.
1936 Hayman, Nick.
1937 Maglammery, George
1938 Toadvine, John
1939 Toadvine, Mary
1939 Toadvine, Wm.
1939 Toadvine, George
1940 Bashaw, Graves
1940 Talbott, John
1941 Robertson, Wm.
1942 Fooks, Benj., senr.
1942 Fooks, Benj., junr.
1942 Fooks, Wm.
1942 slave Patience
1942 slave Jean
1943 Deshroon, John, senr.
1943 slave Cuffey
1943 slave Grace
1943 slave Fanny
1944 Sehon, John
1945 Roach, Alice
1945 Roach, Isaac
1945 Goldsmith, Anthony
1945 slave Tom
1945 slave Harry
1945 slave Pegg
1945 slave Hannah
1946 Deshroon, John, junr.
1947 Deshroon, Wm.
1948 Revil, Wm.
1948 slave Tom
1949 Collins, Richd.
1950 Elliss, John
1951 Crouch, John
1952 Sharp, Mary
1952 slave Mary
1952 slave Penny
1953 Porter, Joshua
1954 Hillman, Edwd.
1955 Deshroon, Michael, junr.
1956 Jenkins, Jarvis, senr.
1956 Jenkins, Jarvis, junr.
1956 Jenkins, John
1957 Elliss, Franciss
1958 Deshroon, Michael, senr.
1959 Stanford, Joseph
1959 Stanford, Jonathan
1960 Toadvine, Thos.
1961 Christopher, Ephraim
1962 Elliss, Joseph
1963 Baily, George, senr.
1963 Baily, George, junr.
1964 Thomson, John
1965 Baily, Benj.
1966 Chadwicks, James, senr.
1967 Ragland, Michael
1968 Knox, Wm.
1969 Adley, Wm., senr.
1969 Adley, George
1969 Adley, Phillip
1970 Griffin, John
1971 Hayman, Charles, son Wm.
1972 Hayman, John
1973 Hayman, James
1973 Hayman, Isaac
1974 Hayman, Charles

TAX LISTS OF SOMERSET COUNTY: 1730-1740

WICOMICO HUNDRED

1975 Pullett, Thos., senr.
1975 Pullett, Wm.
1975 slave Dinah
1976 Pullett, Thos., junr.
1977 Polk, David
1977 slave Otern
1977 slave Abner
1977 slave Hannah
1977 slave Tahmer
1978 Alexander, Moses
1978 Alexander, John
1978 slave Tom
1979 Sirmon, Peter, senr.
1979 Sirmon, Peter, junr.
1979 Booth, Wm.
1979 slave Tom
1979 slave Lemon
1980 Sirmon, John
1981 Mitchell, Benj.
1982 Mitchell, John
1983 Swilvin, Wm.
1984 Austin, Edward
1984 James, Wm.
1985 Noble, Isaac
1985 Noble, Wm.
1986 Kibble, Wm.
1986 Maggee, Saml.
1986 slave Bess
1987 Morriss, Joseph
1987 slave Peter
1988 Sirmon, Jane
1988 Sirmon, Isaac
1989 Robinson, John
1989 slave Sy
1990 Lokey, Thos.
1991 Robinson, Wm.
1992 Mode, Peter
1993 Boadley, Wm.
1994 Macclanny, Danl.
1994 Mitchell, John
1995 Hobbs, Absalom
1995 slave Pollebus
1996 Mears, John
1996 Mears, Saml.
1997 Brereton, Wm., senr.
1997 Brereton, Wm., junr.
1997 Brereton, John
1997 Brereton, Saml.
1997 slave Patience
1998 Killett, Roger
1998 slave Whitehaven
1998 slave Hannah
1998 slave Judith
1999 Bounds, Jonathan
1999 slave Bess
2000 Linch, Michael
2001 Lowes, Henry, capt.
2001 Wiley, Erastus
2001 Pussell, George
2001 Parrett, Thos.
2001 Waller, Saml.
2001 Willin, John
2001 Morrison, Thos.
2001 Macknelly, John
2001 slave Jeptha
2001 slave Jo
2001 slave Dover
2001 slave Rose
2001 slave Five Islands
2002 Cordry, Danl.
2002 slave Samson
2003 Roach, Stephen
2003 slave York
2004 North, John
2005 Parsons, John
2006 Breedy, James

INDEX

-----, ANDREW [indian] 31-32, 33-35
-----, COMFORT [free black] 40-170
-----, DARKUS [mulatto] 30-1112
-----, HAGAR [indian] 36-629
-----, HARRY [molatto] 31-14
-----, JACK [indian] 33-695, 39-822
-----, JONATHAN [mollatto, mulatto/Johnathan] 33-43, 36-94
-----, KATE [molattoe Cate, mollatto Kate] 31-7, 35-98, 37-17, 37-88, 38- 41
-----, MARY [mulatto] 36-666
-----, NAN [molato] 35-665
-----, WATT [free black/What, W[at], Wat] 35-83, 36-107, 37-148, 38-130, 39- 37, 40-145
-----, WILL [free black] 38-613, 40-577
-----SON, ------E 36-1263
--PER, SAMUEL 38-1475

ABBOTT [Abbet(t), Ab(b)it(t), Abet, Abbot(t)]
   JOHN 30-634, 31-636, 33-598, 34-688, 35-621, 36-635, 38-536, 38-756, 39-472, 39-799, 40-666, 40-815
   WILLIAM 30-272, 31-141, 33-316, 34-573, 35-749, 36-649
ABDON, WILLIAM 30-1043, 31-973
ACWORTH [Ackworth]
   CHARLES 30-901, 31-872, 33-1021, 34-998, 35-1132, 36-930, 38-1084, 39-1250, 40-1174
   HENRY 30-868, 31-998, 33-894, 34-995, 35-113, 36-1040, 38-1118, 39-1019, 40-1160
   RICHARD 30-901, 31-872, 33-1021
   SAMUEL 30-900, 31-94, 31-940, 33-1002, 34-995, 34-1386, 35-1137, 38-1-18, 38-1119, 39-1018, 40-1159
   THOMAS 30-902, 31-889, 33-1022, 34-999, 35-1131, 36-929, 1083, 37-854, 38-1083, 38-1252, 39-1039, 39-1136, 40-1176, 40-1177
ADAMS [Addams]
   ABRAHAM 30-1108, 31-1264
   ALEXANDER [Alix., revd., junr., senr] 30-1442. 31-1423, 33-1564, 34-1546, 35-1523(2), 36-1581, 37-1039(2), 38-1805(2), 39-1896(2), 40-1875(2)
   CATHERINE [Cathorun, widw.] 33-1260
   COLLINS [Collens, Collins, Collings, Colons] 30-1114, 31-1271, 35-1451, 36-1307, 38-1401, 39-1611, 40-1692
   DAVID [D.] 30-86, 30-1095, 31-94, 31-1263, 33-104, 34-41, 34-1386, 35-101, 35-1423, 35-26, 37-9, 38-49(2) 39-104(2), 40-115, 40-115(2)

   DENNIS 30-1135, 31-1259, 33-1267, 34-1434, 35-1413, 36-121, 37-108, 38-80, 39-153, 40-141
   EDWARD 33-788
   GEORGE [jr., senr.] 30-1136, 31-1260, 33-1261, 34-1449, 35-1421, 36-1319, 38-1443(2), 39-1654(2), 40-1735(2)
   HOPE [Hoap] 30-1157, 31-1261, 33-1259, 34-1384, 35-1415, 36-1321, 38-1441, 39-1652, 40-1730
   ISAAC 31-1263, 33-1256, 34-1386, 35-1412, 36-1316, 38-1438, 39-1649, 40-1726
   JACOB 30-86, 30-1114, 30-1136, 31-94, 31-1271, 33-104, 33-1253, 34-41, 34-1390, 35-101, 35-1429, 36-26, 38-1429, 38-1430, 39-1641, 40-1718
   JAMES 38-1805
   JOHN 30-26, 31-1, 33- 35, 34-58, 35-71, 36-104, 40-1875
   PHILLIP [jur., senr.] 30-1157, 31-1258, 31-1271, 33-1253, 33-1262, 34-1390, 34-1433, 34-1434, 35-1413, 35-1416, 35-1429, 36-1293, 36-1320, 36-1322, 38-1442, 38-1445, 39-1653, 39-1655, 40-1731, 40-1734
   RACHEL [Rachell] 36-1318
   SAMUEL [Samuell] 30-1114, 31-1271, 33-1253, 34-1390, 35-1429, 36-1293, 38-1429, 39-1640, 40-1717
   THOMAS [junr., senr.] 30-86, 30-1095(2), 30-1114, 31-94, 31-1263, 33-104, 33-1256, 33-1257, 34-41, 34-1386, 34-1387, 35-101, 35-179, 36-27, 36-259, 37-10, 38-50, 38-1347, 38-1430, 39-105, 39-1641, 40-117, 40-1717
   WILLIAM [junr., senr, Willm.] 30-1135(2), 31-1259(2), 33-1267(2), 34-41, 34-1434, 35-101, 35-1413, 35-1414, 36-26, 36-1322, 36-1323, 37-9, 38-49, 38-1444, 38-1445, 39-104, 39-1655, 39-1656, 40-115, 40-1732, 40-1733
ADKINS [Attkins]
   ... [illegible] 30-719
   ELIZABETH 31-462, 34-367
   JACOB [At(t)kins, Akins] 30-1339
   JOHN 30-422, 31-1305, 33-344, 34-355, 35-375, 36-455, 37-617, 38-607, 39-275, 40-217
   JOSHUA 30-77
   ROBERT 30-1339, 31-1440, 33-1494, 34-1493, 35-1595, 36-1674, 37-1031, 38-1652, 39-1755, 40-1932
   SAMUEL 34-1203
   STANTON [Stenten, Stenton] 30-402, 31-472, 33-536, 34-491, 35-453, 36-420, 37-536, 38-488, 39-590, 40-609
   STEPHEN [Steven] 35-453, 36-420, 37-536, 38-488, 39-590, 40-611

INDEX

ADKINSON [Ackinson, A(d)keson, Adkitson, Atkinson, Ackinson]
  ANGELO [Aingelow, Angellow, Angolo] 30-1171, 31-1240, 33-1332, 34-1204, 35-1503, 36-1438, 38-1453, 39-1497, 40-1517
  ISAAC 30-1170, 31-1244, 33-1330, 34-1202, 35-1471, 36-1439, 38-1514, 39-1426, 40-1538
  JOHN 33-1331, 34-444, 36-539, 37-385, 38-616, 39-580, 40-574
  JOSHUA 31-89, 33-94, 34-25, 35-111, 36-43, 38-1513, 39-1429, 40-1537
  PATIENCE 30-1169, 31-1243
  SAMUEL 30-1169, 31-1243, 33-1329, 35-1470, 38-1512, 39-1428, 40-1536
  TIMOTHY 30-1281, 31-1375, 33-1592, 34-1695, 35-1741
ADLEY [Adly, Edly]
  GEORGE 39-1784, 40-1969
  PHILLIP 39-1784, 40-1969
  WILLIAM [junr., senr.] 30-1413, 31-1427, 33-1495, 34-1504, 35-1591, 36-1704(2), 37-1099(2), 38-1651(2), 39-1784(2), 40-1969
AKE [Aakey]
  JOHN 36-605, 37-479, 38-638, 39-461, 40-693
  SOLOMON 40-194
ALEXANDER [Alixander, Allexander, Elexander]
  AGNESS 38-1820
  JAMES 30-1373, 31-577, 31-1425, 33-1565, 34-1583
  JOHN 40-1978
  LISTAN [Lisan, Listen, Listian, Liston, Lestin] 31-1425, 33-1565, 34-1582, 35-1644, 36-1614, 37-1032
  MOSES 30-638, 30-1375, 31-662, 31-1429, 33-1081, 34-1584, 35-1590, 36-1700, 37-1028, 38-1821, 39-1793, 40-1978
  PAUL 30-351, 31-434, 37-403, 38-520, 39-559, 40-454
  SAMUEL 30-1374, 31-1428
  WILLIAM 30-1373, 31-1425, 33-1565, 34-1582, 35-1628, 36-1599, 37-1013, 38-1854, 40-1750
ALFORD [Aulford, Olford], DAVID 30-269, 31-138, 33-327, 34-293, 35-351, 36-279, 37-230, 38-361, 39-234, 40-336
ALL, JOHN 34-170
ALLCHURCH, WILLIAM 38-1571
ALLEN [Allin]
  FRANCIS [junr., senr.] 30-1165, 31-1200, 33-1274(2), 34-1307(2), 35-1466, 36-1435(2), 38-1452, 39-1494(2), 40-1515, 40-1516
  HENRY 31-45, 33-98, 34-45, 35-55, 36-74, 37-76

  JOHN [senr.] 30-659, 30-1165, 31-749, 31-1200, 33-744, 33-1274, 34-807, 35-840, 36-771, 37-727, 38-822, 39-842(2), 40-929(2)
  JOSEPH 30-54, 30-658, 31-38, 31-728, 33-77, 33-729, 34-67, 34-779, 35-33, 35-814, 36-74, 36-814, 37-76, 37-666, 38-828, 39-856, 40-911
  MOSES [Mosses] 38-828, 39-856, 40-911
  WILLIAM [Willm.] 40-1515
ALLISON [Alison, Allason, Elleson, Ellison]
  JOHN [Jon.] 30-231, 31-161, 33-249
  PATRICK 36-1455, 38-685, 39-717, 40-849
  RICHARD 35-369, 36-519
ALPHEY [Allphew, Olphie, Olphy], JOSEPH 38-1112, 39-1250, 40-1170
ANDERSON
  WIDOW 34-903
  ISAAC 33-1333
  JAMES [Jame.] 33-1058, 34-1110, 35-1019, 36-687, 38-683, 39-720, 40-762
  JOHN 30-810, 30-1029, 31-832, 31-904, 31-1048, 33-1079, 34-903, 35-943, 36-1206, 37-919, 38-684, 38-1028, 38-1242, 39-706, 39-1026, 39-1220, 40-761, 40-1054, 40-1140
  MARY 34-1200, 35-1464, 36-1432, 38-1242, 38-1470, 39-1220
  PEAL [Peale] 36-1507
  ROBERT 38-281
  ROGER 30-576
  SARAH 30-810, 31-832, 33-1079, 35-943
  THOMAS 30-1366
  WILLIAM [Willm.] 35-267, 38-281
ANDREWS [Adrus, Anders, Andraws, Andrew, Andru(e)s]
  JOHN 30-1179, 31-1180, 33-1087, 33-1339, 34-1042, 34-1228, 35-1508, 36-662, 36-1216, 36-1472, 38-737, 38-1144, 38-1468, 39-1085, 39-1664, 40-1191, 40-1525
  PEAL [Peale, Peall, Peel] 33-1339, 34-1228, 35-1508, 38-518, 39-1457, 40-1525
  ROBERTSON [Robinson, Roberson] 38-1468, 39-1664, 40-1579
  SHEPHARD [Sheperd, Shipard, Shepard] 35-1508, 36-1472, 38-842, 39-870
ANGE [Ainge]
  FRANCIS [Frances, Frannes] 34-1054, 36-997(2), 38-1341, 39-1238(2)
  JOHN 34-1120
ANGELO [Angeloe, Anglo], JAMES 33-541, 34-148

INDEX

ANSWORTH [Ainsworth]
  JOB [Jobe] 33-768, 35-790, 36-786, 37-704, 38-615, 39-838
  PETER 30-728, 34-725, 35-790, 38-856, 40-936
  SARAH [widow] 30-728, 31-680, 34-754, 35-789, 36-786
  WILLIAM 30-665, 31-681, 33-768, 34-744, 35-780, 36-769, 37-661, 38-877, 39-838, 40-938
ARABIA, JACOBUS [Arabin] 30-461, 31-427
ARDELEY, JOHN 40-366
ARGLOBUS, CORNELIS [[Ar]globus] 39-750
ARMSTRONG, HEZEKIAH [Hezeciah] 40-1214
  ARNOLD, [Arnald, Arnall, Arnell]
  [illegible] 30-708
  JAMES [Jams.] 34-799
  LAURENCE [Larance, Laurenc, Larraunce] 35-785, 36-821, 37-719
  WILLIAM 30-71, 31-79, 31-721, 33-767, 33-1251, 34-749, 34-1439, 35-49, 35-785, 36-821
ASCRIDGE [Ascridg, Eskridge], WILLIAM 30-577, 31-607, 33-663, 34-611, 35-604
ASHTON, THOMAS 33-3
ASKILLY [Askeley, Askely, Askiley, Keley, Kelley, Oskelly, Skilley], DANIEL 31-896, 33-887, 34-1104, 35-1243, 36-1011, 38-1183, 39-1051, 40-1111
AUSTIN [Astin, Astons, Austen, Osten, Ostian, O(y)stin, Osten, Oston]
  EDWARD 39-1844, 40-1984
  ELIZABETH 38-626
  GEORGE 31-1420, 35-1643, 36-1584, 37-1055, 38-976, 40-855
  HENRY 40-1124
  ROBERT 30-1392, 31-1420, 33-1602, 34-1610, 35-1624, 36-1600, 37-997, 38-969
  WILLIAM [jur.] 30-759, 30-875, 31-864, 33-1130, 33-1593, 34-968, 35-1161(2) 35-1624, 36-1104(2), 38-1262, 38-1346, 38-1739, 39-1047, 39-1099, 39-1224, 40-1112, 40-1145
AYDELOTT [Ayd(o)lott, Idlit, Idlot/Idlit, Idlot]
  BENJAMIN 30-145, 31-199, 33-213, 34-321, 35-245, 36-182
  JOHN [junr., senr.] 30-144(2), 31-201(2), 33-218, 33-219, 34-203, 34-326, 35-224, 35-309, 36-168, 36-185, 37-185, 37-375, 38-183, 38-196, 39-314, 39-315, 40-256, 40-272
  THOMAS 38-200, 39-207, 40-200
  WILLIAM [junr.] 30-724, 31-750, 34-755, 35-791, 36-764(2), 37-648, 38-846, 39-868(2), 40-900(2)
AYRES [Air(e)s, Ares, Ayars, Ayers, Eairs]
  HARRISON [Harson] 33-709, 34-805, 35-838, 36-842, 38-483, 39-607, 40-562
  HENRY 30-678, 33-707, 34-804, 35-837, 36-843
  JACOB [Jac.] 30-106, 31-2, 33-38, 38-738, 39-745, 40-731
  JOHN 30-681, 31-675
  RICHARD 33-709, 34-805, 35-838, 36-842, 37-687, 38-902, 39-916, 40-857

BACKWORTH [Backwor, Buckworth], CHARLES 30-1047, 33-995, 35-1171, 37-989, 38-1164, 39-1358, 40-1320
BACON [Baccon, Bacond], DUTSON [Dudson] 34-925, 35-968, 36-946, 38-1167, 39-1175, 40-1277
BAILY [Ba(i)ley, Balife, Baly(e), Bayl(e)y, Baylies]
  ALEXANDERS 40-1527
  BENJAMIN 31-1480, 33-1529, 34-1581, 35-1545, 36-1748, 37-1042, 38-1816, 39-1780, 40-1965
  GEORGE [junr., senr.] 30-1408, 31-1480, 33-1529, 34-1581, 35-1545, 36-1622, 37-1043, 38-1852, 39-1889(2), 40-1963(2)
  JONATHAN 30-1409, 31-1479, 33-1530, 34-1552, 35-1685, 36-1624, 37-1066, 38-1794, 39-1890, 40-1250
  SARAH 30-1410
  THOMAS 30-70, 31-78, 33-56, 34-109, 36-615, 38-730, 39-742, 40-733
BAKER [Bacer, Backer, Bacor]
  HENDERSON 31-1287, 33-1155, 34-1254, 35-1411, 36-1354, 39-1620, 40-1626
  JAMES 30-953, 31-1287, 33-1155, 34-1254, 35-1411, 36-1345, 38-1621, 39-1557, 40-1632
  JOHN 30-345, 31-491, 34-561, 35-589, 36-505, 38-535, 40-1681
  THOMAS 30-893, 31-953, 33-1606, 34-818, 34-1651, 35-1662
  WILLIAM 30-951, 31-1039, 33-863, 34-1181, 35-1246, 36-1142, 37-305, 38-1276, 39-1309, 39-282, 40-327, 40-1328
BALDREY, FRANCIS [Francies] 31-195, 33-212
BALL
  JOHN 31-881
  SAMUEL [Baull] 30-296, 34-1361, 38-1535, 39-1481, 40-1529
BALLANCE, THOMAS 38-1453
BALLARD [Ballerd]
  MRS. 31-1410, 33-1595, 34-1611

217

INDEX

ARNOLD [Arnal] 34-655, 35-669, 36-743, 38-794, 39-691, 40-826
   CHARLES 30-1445, 31-1402, 33-1596, 34-1613, 35-1622, 36-1607, 37-1000, 38-797, 38-1865, 39-741, 39-1824, 40-826, 40-1853
   ELEANOR [Eleanor, Elen., Elenar, Elener, Elinor, Elliner/mrs.] 30-629, 30-1446, 31-549, 33-556, 34-709, 35-657, 36-666, 36-1608
   ELIZABETH 35-1623
   HENRY [col., cap.] 30-628, 31-512, 33-555, 34-708, 35-656, 36-665, 38-774, 39-715, 40-767, 40-826
   JARVIS [Jarves/junr., senr.] 30-608, 31-629(2), 33-643(2), 34-655(2), 35-669(2), 36-743(2), 38-797(2), 39-741(2), 40-826(2)
   WILLIAM [Willam] 30-608, 31-629, 33-643, 34-655, 35-669, 36-743, 38-797, 39-741, 40-826
BANES [Beanes]
   GEORGE 30-1237, 40-1110
   JOHN 31-1476
BANISTER [Banaster, Banester, Banster]
   CHARLES 30-503, 31-509, 33-1211, 35-709, 36- 39, 37-106, 40-74
   THOMAS 30-505, 31-609, 33-665, 34-609, 35-709, 36-705, 38-729, 39-770, 40-727
BANKS [Banck]
   KIT 31-1127
   NIBLETT [Neblitt, Nibbling, Nibelett] 31-181, 33-200, 35-251, 36-266, 37-284, 38-255, 39-183, 40-270
   STEPHEN [Steven, Stepn.] 38-1700, 39-1849, 40-1432
BANUM [Bainum, Baynom], BARTHOLOMEW 33-461, 34-544, 35-574, 36-499, 37-499, 38-530, 39-555, 40-463
BARNETT, JOHN 40-1303
BARNS [Barnes], ROBERT 30-11, 31-577, 33-650, 34-3, 35-88
BARRETT [Barra(r)t, Barrit]
   HENRY 30-33, 30-1171, 31-43, 38-750, 39-804, 40-816
   SAMUEL 33-1580
BARRICK, WILLIAM 30-349
BARTHOLOMEW, SAMUEL [Betholemy] 34-1127, 35-1215
BARTLETT [Barklett, Barklett, Barkley, Bartl(e)y, Bartlit, Berklee]
   ABRAHAM 35-937, 36-969, 38-989, 39-1001, 40-1043
   JOHN [jur., senr] 30-796, 30-797, 31-823, 31-824, 33-1113, 33-1114, 34-894, 34-895, 35-936, 35-937, 36-968, 36-969, 38-989, 39-998, 39-1001, 40-1043, 40-1044

   PASQUE [Paskey, Paskque, Paskue, Pasky] 30-1471, 31-1363, 33-1416, 34-1655, 35-1670, 36-1549, 37-1196, 38-1789, 39-1856, 40-1818
   THOMAS [Barklett, Bartlit, Bartly/junr.] 30-1471, 31-1363, 33-1416, 34-1655, 35-1670, 36-1549, 37-1196, 38-1789(2), 39-1856(2), 40-1818
   WILLIAM 30-1471, 31-1365, 33-1416, 34-1656, 35-1669, 36-1550
BASHAW [Beshaw, Boushaw, Bushaw]
   ANN 30-1353
   GILES [Joiles, Joyles] 35-1702, 36-1635, 37-1115, 38-1790, 39-1921, 40-1744
   GRAVES 33-1542, 34-1573, 35-1567, 36-1659, 37-1115, 38-1801, 39-1761, 40-1940
   JARRETT [Jarrot, Garrott, Gerrard] 31-1514, 33-1562, 34-1690, 37-1067, 38-1841, 39-1921
   WILLIAM 36-1555, 37-1070, 38-1844, 39-1932, 40-1754
BASS, JOHN 34-1114, 35-1175, 36-1195, 38-1288, 40-1303
BASSITT [Bassett]
   ALICE [widd.] 30-437, 31-416
   JAMES 36-366, 37-587, 38-415
   JOHN 30-437, 31-416, 34-467, 35-531, 36-366, 37-588, 38-416, 39-541, 39-548, 40-530
BATSON, MORDECAI 39-483
BATTES, EDWARD 40-1262
BEACH, THOMAS 34-108, 35-93, 36-82, 37-121, 39-1368
BEACHBOARD [Beachbord, Bechbord, Bichbord], WILLIAM 30-666, 31-716, 33-754, 34-788, 35-822, 36-787, 38-894, 39-832, 40-931
BEADARD [Be(a)de(a)rd, Bed(d)ard, Beddart, Bedord, Bethard]
   JARMAN [Jarmon] 40-597
   RICHARD 30-400, 31-367, 33-488, 34-454, 35-518, 36-597, 37-419, 38-527, 40-547
   WILLIAM 30-446, 31-320, 33-377, 34-457, 36-464, 37-405, 38-656, 39-661, 40-699
BEAMORE, HENRY 40-1098
BEARD [Bearde]
   JOHN 30-816, 31-852, 33-1074, 34-908, 35-951, 36-1212, 38-1024, 39-1029, 40-1052
   LEWIS [Leuis, Lues, Lewes/junr., senr] 30-816(2), 31-852(2), 33-1074(2), 34-908(2), 35-951(2), 36-1210(2), 38-1023, 39-1030, 40-1053
   REBECCA 38-1023
BEAUCHAMP [Bauchamp, Be(a)cham(p), Beachamp, Beucham, Beachum]

INDEX

EDMUND [Edmond/junr.] 30-100(2),
31-23(2), 33-26, 33-109, 34-94,
35-122, 36-115, 37-131, 38-83,
39-125, 40-19
    EDWARD 30-1155, 31-1256, 33-1265,
34-1437, 35-1330, 36-1324, 38-1449,
39-1657, 40-1736
    ISAAC 30-25, 31- 32, 33-23, 34-97,
35-120, 36-112, 37-150, 38-137,
39-127, 40-21
    JOHN 30-100, 31-1109, 33-1263,
33-1265, 34-1382, 34-1437, 35-124,
35-1330, 36-1325, 38-1447, 39-126,
40-1737
    LEVIN 36-1324, 38-1449, 39-1657,
40-1738
    MARCY [Marcey, Marsey, Mercey] 30-1155, 35-1330, 36-1325, 38-1447,
39-1658, 40-143
    ROBERT 30-100, 31-23, 33-109,
34-92, 35-122, 36-749, 37-132,
38-113, 39-124, 40-167
    SARAH 34-92, 35-124
    SMITH 30-100
    THOMAS 30-1155, 31-1256, 33-1265,
34-1437, 35-1330, 36-1326, 38-1448,
39-1659, 40-1738
    WILLIAM [jr.] 30-21, 31-24, 33-25,
34-93, 35-123, 36-116, 37-132,
38-84, 39-123(2), 40-1736, 40-22(2)
BEAVANS [Beavens, Beavins, Bevens,
Bibbins, Bivan(d)s, Bivine]
    CALEB [Calib, Calup] 30-1193,
31-1147, 33-1360, 34-1356, 35-1372,
36-1489, 38-1193, 39-1279, 40-1397
    CORNELIUS 30-1182, 35-1482,
38-1465, 39-1483, 40-1524
    ELIAS 30-1182, 31-1181, 33-1338,
34-1226
    JOHN [junr.] 30-1193(2), 31-1147,
33-1354(2), 34-1283(2), 35-1357(2),
36-1445, 36-1492, 38-1194, 38-1544,
39-1282, 39-1448, 40-1401, 40-1558
    JOSHUA 30-1210, 31-1146, 34-1126,
35-1379, 38-1545, 39-1283
    ROLAND [Rowland,Rolond] 30-1182,
31-1181, 33-1338, 34-1226, 35-1481,
36-1473, 38-1464, 38-1544, 39-1448,
39-1484, 40-1522(2), 40-1558
    THOMAS [Thoms.] 30-1181, 31-1242,
33-1343, 33-1354, 34-1283, 34-1302,
35-1357, 35-1469, 36-1440, 36-1492,
38-1458, 38-1544, 39-1448, 39-1489,
40-1522, 40-1558
    WILLIAM 30-1182, 31-1181, 33-1338,
34-1226, 35-1481, 36-1473, 38-1464,
39-1484, 40-1523
BECKETT [Backitt, Becketts, Buket,
Peckett]
    DEVROX [Deverix] 40-538
    PETER 30-425, 31-321, 33-378,
34-411, 35-493, 36-374, 37-455,
38-538, 39-553, 40-538
    WILLIAM 37-455
BEDFORD, JAMES 38-746
BEDOSES, HUGH 40-1678
BEDSWORTH Betsford, Betsworth]
    JAMES [Jams.] 30-16, 31-13, 33-13,
34-690, 35-625, 36-628
    THOMAS 38-615, 39-579
BEEK [Beak(e), Beeck]
    ISAAC 36-1087, 37-877, 38-1074,
39-1261
    ISABEL [Isbel] 30-892, 36-1087,
37-877, 38-1074
BELL
    DOCTOR 31-457
    ADAM 30-379, 34-440, 35-434,
36-510, 37-502, 38-588, 39-485,
40-582
    ANTHONY [Antoney/junr., senr.]
30-71(2), 31-79, 31-81, 33-87(2),
34-32, 34-33, 35-49, 35-50, 36-44,
36-50, 38-85, 39-87, 40-95
    ISAAC 31-82, 33-126, 34-315,
35-306, 35-1454, 36-537, 37-381,
38-1528, 39-1522, 40 -1448
    JOSEPHAS [Josephus] 30-71, 34- 33,
35-49, 36-50, 37-44, 38-85, 39-87,
40-95
    THOMAS 30-71, 31-80, 33-88, 34-34,
35-116, 36-49, 37-63, 38-47, 39-88,
40-96
BELMOSET, HUMPHREY [Humphry] 38-73
BENNITT [Benett, Beniett, Bennit]
    EDWARD [senr.] 30-1039(2), 31-907,
33-886, 34-957, 35-999, 36-1132,
38-823, 38-1198, 39-827, 39-1192,
40-937, 40-1153
    ELIZABETH [Elesebeth/wido.]
31-907, 36-1133, 39-1193, 40-1154
    GEORGE [Gorge] 30-1039, 31-907,
33-1137, 34-957, 35-1158, 36-1101,
38-1115, 39-1048
    HENRY 33-84, 34-122, 35-6, 35-56
    JOHN 30-1039, 30-1083, 31-907, 33-1334, 33-1384, 34-1240, 34-1347,
35-999, 35-1478, 36-1133, 36-1434,
38-1198(2), 39-1192, 39-1476,
40-1535
    MARY [widow] 33-763, 34-787,
35-821, 36-791, 37-656, 38-823,
39-827
    WILLIAM 30-1255, 31-1227, 33-1277,
34-1306, 35-1461, 36-1133, 36-1400,
38-1460, 39-1193, 39-1499, 40-937,
40-1154, 40-1507
BENNS, JOHN 30-1429
BENSBOW, JOSHUA 31-730
BENSON
    GEORGE [jur.] 33-4, 548, 39-815,
39-1933
    HENRY 35-1070(2), 40-1285
    JAMES 40-1285

INDEX

JOHN 30-4, 31-22, 33-4, 35-1360
MARY 40-1095
MATHIAS 33-548, 39-815
MATTHEW 40-1285
SOLOMON 30-4, 31-22, 33-4, 37-75, 38-22, 39-63
THOMAS 35-986
WILLIAM 30-4, 31-22, 35-1072, 35-1073, 40-1308, 40-1340

BENSTON [Benstone, Binston]
ALEXANDER 30-1247, 31-1192, 33-1157
ANNE 35-1299
BENJAMIN 31-1287, 33-1155, 34-1254, 38-1411, 39-1622, 40-1701
DANIEL 40-1604
EDWARD 30-1232, 31-1301
GEORGE [Gorge] 30-539, 31-516, 31-1019, 33-949, 34-618, 34-1069, 34-1335, 35-648, 35-1360, 36-692, 36-1421, 37-916, 38-814, 38-1378, 39-1234, 39-1403, 40-855, 40-1645
HENRY [Henery/senr.] 30-998, 31-1019, 33-949(2), 34-1069(2), 36-1026(2), 37-988, 38-1277, 39-1234(2)
JOHN [junr, senr.] 34-1335, 36-1421, 38-1378, 39-1576(2), 40-1645(2)
JOSHUA 33-727, 35-856, 36-815, 37-676
MARY 37-844, 38-1067, 39-1103
MATHIAS [Mathais] 34-618, 35-648, 36-692, 40-855
MATTHEW [Mathey] 38-814, 38-1277, 39-1234
ROBERT [Robart] 30-549
SAUL 34-1335, 35-1360, 40-67
THOMAS 30-844, 30-1120, 31-944, 31-1114, 33-928, 33-1210, 34-945, 34-1415, 35-1263, 36-1259, 36-1265, 38-1389, 39-1592, 40-1671
WILLIAM [senr.] 30-999, 30-1138, 31-1015, 31-1251, 33-871, 33-1214, 33-950, 34-1095, 34-1174, 34-1414, 35-1408, 36-1165, 36-1168, 36-1266, 38-1228, 39-1296, 39-1325

BENTON [Bunton]
COMFORT 30-1054, 31-1208, 33-1285, 34-1336, 35-1494, 36-1407
JONATHAN 37-335, 40-437

BERRY [Barry. Berreu], JAMES 34-1665, 35-1661, 38-1668

BES----, WILLIAM 37-936

BESICKS, ... illegible 37-827

BESSIX [Besecks, Besek, Besseks, Bessen, Bessex, Bessicks, Bessiks, Bisick]
--- [Illgebile]
ABSOLOM [Absalam] 30-398, 31-320, 33-376, 34-256, 35-210, 36-204, 37-353, 38-232, 39-297, 40-335
NATHANIEL [Natthaell] 36-214, 37-357, 38-231, 39-198, 40-303
BENJAMIN 30-856, 31-952, 33-1081
JAMES 30-779, 35-1039, 36-1138
THOMAS 30-1141, 31-1101, 33-1234, 34-1422, 36-1300

BIRD [Byrd]
ANNABELLOW [Arrabellow] 40-86
BENJAMIN 37-1223, 38-1747, 39-1858, 40-1879
DAVID 30-59, 31-65, 33-70, 34-119, 35-11, 36-67, 37-67, 38-15, 39-67, 40-77
JOSEPH 30-64, 31-76, 33-78, 34-81, 35-8, 37-29, 38-12, 39-78
THOMAS [junr., senr] 30-1272(2), 31-1369(2), 33-1417(2), 34-1649(2), 35-1676(2), 36-1629(2), 37-1223, 37-1224, 38-1747, 38-1772, 39-1858, 39-1859, 40-1879, 40-1880
WILLIAM 33-1417, 34-1649, 35-1676, 36-1746, 37-1223, 38-1747, 39-1873, 40-1881

BISHOP, [Bushop]
BENJAMIN 30-347, 31-360, 33-346, 34-361, 35-382, 36-425, 37-610, 38-603
BOWIN [Bowen] 30-380, 31-307, 33-291, 39-258, 40-402
BRYAN [Brien] 34-283
CHARLES 30-358, 31-459
DAVID 30-347, 31-359, 33-345, 34-354
HENRY 31-1057, 33-854
JOHN [junr., senr] 30-347, 30-348, 31-341, 31-359, 33-345, 33-395, 34-354, 34-503, 35-374, 35-542, 36-563, 38-400, 40-656
JOSEPH 30-347, 31-359, 33-345, 34-354, 35-374, 36-412, 37-611, 38-604, 39-451, 40-449, 40-663
THOMAS 30-295
WILLIAM 30-489, 31-360, 33-346, 34-357, 35-378, 36-413, 37-607, 38-602, 39-450, 40-440

BLADES [Blaids]
BENJAMIN 31-1297, 33-1332, 34-1419, 35-1298, 36-1362, 38-1549, 39-1563, 40-1640
JAMES 40-1640
JOHN 31-1297, 33-1174, 34-1241, 35-1286, 36-1362, 38-1623, 39-1572, 40-1655
JOSEPH 33-1173, 34-1419
ROBERT 31-1285, 33-1173, 34-1419, 35-1298, 36-1372, 38-1563, 39-1563

BLAIR [Blaer, Blare, Blayer, Blear], ROBERT 30-1118, 31-1254, 33-1269, 34-1379, 35-1419, 36-1271, 38-1388, 39-1597, 40-1677

BLEWER, JAMES 37-820, 38-1340

INDEX

BLITHE [Bloayd, Bloyd], WALTER 38-12, 39-86, 40-94
BLIZARD [Blizsurd]
  BENJAMIN 30-292
  JOHN 40-955
  RICHARD [Richeard] 30-310, 31-421, 33-402, 34-373, 34-1141, 35-186, 35-479, 36-258, 36-371, 37-333, 37-480, 38-191, 38-455, 39-199, 40-417, 40-691
  THOMAS 35-179, 36-219, 37-332, 38-222, 39-291, 40-281
BLUER [Blure] MARGARET [Marget] 39-1053, 40-1116
BLUITT [Blewitt, Blueat, Bluett, Peluit]
  JOHN 35-1522, 36-1615, 37-993, 38-1848, 39-1922, 40-1753
  THOMAS 30-642, 31-592, 35-888, 36-896, 37-1071
BOADLEY [Boadley, Bodly]
  JOHN [35-1095
  WILLIAM 33-1130, 37-815, 39-1666, 40-1993
BOARDMAN [Bordman, Boar(e)man, Bormon]
  GRAVES 30-1356
  JOHN 30-30, 31-33, 33-400
  SAMUEL 33-1559, 34-1642, 35-1702, 36-1542, 37-1195, 38-1843
  SARAH [widow] 30-1356, 33-1559
BODEN [Bonton, Bouton, Bowden]
  ABLE [Abel] 31-170, 33-252, 34-214, 35-259, 36-261, 37-162, 38-175, 39-277, 40-266
  BENJAMIN 34-224
  JAMES 40-779
  JOHN 31-159, 33-250, 34-215, 35-166, 36-181, 37-161, 38-347, 39-276, 40-243
  SUSANNAH 36-242
  THOMAS 31-170, 33-251, 34-224
BODL, SAMUEL 35-1364
BONUM, WILLIAM 30-1066, 31-1236
BOOKS, FRANCIS 35-1291
BOOTH [Bouth]
  GEORGE 38-1129, 39-1014, 40-1280
  JAMES 31-76, 33-78, 34-80
  JOHN OUTTEN 39-847, 40-918
  ROGER 30-60, 31-69, 33-71, 34-47
  WILLIAM 30-719, 31-678, 33-778, 34-770, 35-858, 36-780, 37-711, 38-863, 39-816, 40-1979
BORDLEY [Boardly, Bodley], WILLIAM 30-856, 31-864, 34-967, 35-1162, 36-1103
BOSE, SAMUEL 38-799
BOSLEY, THOMAS [Baslee, Besle] 35-1011, 36-1124
BOSTON
  EBENEZER [Neser] 31-1267
  ESAU [Aesuc, Easah/jr., senr.] 30-1113, 33-1255, 34-1438, 35-1426, 36-1315, 38-1434, 38-1434, 39-1645, 39-1645, 40-1722, 40-1722
  ISAAC 30-1112, 31-1269, 33-1254, 34-1435, 35-1425, 36-1314, 38-1433, 39-1644, 40-1721
  JACOB 40-1722
  WILLIAM 30-23, 31-27, 33-27, 34-96, 35-125, 36-118, 37-155, 38-81, 39-147, 40-23
BOSWELL [Bassell, Baswell, Bazill, Bozsuell, Bazwell]
  CHARLES 39-932, 40-967
  JOHN 33-416
  THOMAS 30-753, 31-797, 33-803, 34-859, 35-922, 36-911, 37-740, 38-956
BOTTEN
  JOHN 30-190
  THOMAS 30-189
BOUGER [Boudger, Bowcher, Bowger]
  FRANCES [wido.] 31-987
  JAMES 31-987, 33-1092, 34-1137, 35-1175, 36-1196, 37-901, 38-1329, 39-1360, 40-1318
BOUNDS
  GEORGE 34-1366, 35-1468, 36-1469
  JACOB 30-973, 31-984, 34-1170, 35-1178, 36-1149, 38-1274, 39-1319, 40-1407
  JONATHAN 30-1421, 31-1431, 33-1552, 34-1559, 35-1686, 36-1564, 37-1058, 38-1810, 39-1912, 40-1999
  JOSEPH 30-834, 31-920, 33-1071, 34-929, 35-971, 36-1054, 38-1004, 39-1063, 40-1077
BOUTELL, BENJAMIN 31-1351
BOWIN [Boien, Boins, Bowen, Bowing]
  EDWARD 36-518, 38-639, 39-516, 40-638,
  GEORGE 30-396, 31-501, 34-367, 35-543, 36-565, 37-572, 39-524, 40-655
  JOHN 30-395, 31-145, 31-337, 33-148, 33-430, 34-234, 34-496, 35-348, 35-539, 36-295, 36-561, 37-370, 37-569, 38-377, 38-408, 39-224, 39-526, 40-316, 40-657
  LITTLETON 30-394, 31-503, 33-428, 34-498, 35-541, 36-562, 37-571, 38-399, 39-523, 40-655
  LUKE 30-396, 31-501
  RODAH [Rodey, Roday, Rodiah/widow] 30-278, 31-145, 33-148, 34-234, 35-348, 37-370, 38-377, 39-224, 40-316
  WHITTINGTON 39-224, 40-316
  WILLIAM 30-1344, 31-145, 31-462, 31-1447, 33-148, 33-393, 34-234, 34-367, 35-348, 35-468, 36-401, 37-370, 37-575, 38-377, 38-404, 39-224, 39-528, 40-316, 40-646

INDEX

BOWLER [Bolar, Bolend, Bolin, Booler]
    ELEANOR 35-643, 36-723, 38-702, 39-765
    JAMES 38-702, 39-765, 40-741
    WILLIAM [junr., senr.] 30-627, 31-543, 33-571, 34-625(2), 35-643, 36-723, 38-702, 39-765, 40-741

BOWLIN [Bolin, Bollen, Bowelins], THOMAS 33-1481, 34-1077, 35-1077, 36-1249, 38-1216, 39-1186, 40-1292

BOWLS
    URIAS 36-270, 40-336
    ZACHARIAH 37-311, 38-367

BOWMAN [Boweman], HENRY 33-218, 34-203, 35-224

BOYCE [Boice, Boyes, Bpuse]
    DANIEL [Danel] 30-969, 31-990, 33-1097, 34-1131, 35-1236, 36-1192, 37-977, 38-1222, 39-1288, 40-1431
    JOHN 31-906, 33-1029, 34-1010, 35-1118, 36-1085, 37-881, 38-1223, 39-1287, 40-1416
    WILLIAM 30-1106, 31-1210, 33-1143, 34-1251, 35-1503

BOYD, JOHN 34-671

BOYER [Boyen, Buyard, Buyer, Byer]
    JONATHAN 31-1120, 33-1230, 34-1402, 35-1443, 38-1412, 39-1623
    ROBERT 30-1101, 31-1120, 33-1230, 34-1402, 35-1443, 36-1295, 38-1412, 39-1623, 40-1703
    WILLIAM 34-1489

BOZMAN [Bausman, Bawsmon, Bazman, Bosman]
    GEORGE [jun., sener] 30-584, 30-605, 31-639, 31-643, 33-607, 33-636, 34-578, 34-661(2), 35-652, 35-725(2), 36-648, 36-658(2), 38-786(2), 39-695(2), 40-843(2)
    HUITT [Hewet, Hitt] 38-787, 39-694, 40-842
    JOHN [junr., senr.] 30-606, 31-646, 31-646, 33-606, 33-606, 34-678, 34-678, 35-752, 35-752, 36-656, 36-656, 38-812, 38-812, 39-703, 39-703, 40-844
    MARY 38-789, 39-698, 40-839
    WILLIAM [junr., senr., secundu] 30-510, 30-583(2), 31-637, 31-638(2), 33-588, 33-589(2), 34-663, 34-691(2), 35-653(2), 35-726, 36-729, 36-751, 38-734, 38-788, 39-699, 39-739, 40-724, 40-841

BRADFORD [Bradfoot, Braford, Brawfoot, Bredfoott]
    ADAM 30-265, 31-134, 33-338, 34-558, 35-586, 36-511, 39-572, 40-468
    JOHN 30-365, 31-483, 33-493, 34-556, 35-576, 36-569, 37-444, 38-433, 39-431, 40-544(2)
    NATHANIEL 30-444, 33-321, 34-171, 35-314, 36-233, 37-346, 38-363, 39-371, 40-698
    WILLIAM 30-365, 31-276, 33-494, 34-241, 35-345, 36-206, 37-297, 38-383, 39-369, 40-352

BRADLY [Bradley]
    JOHN 37-975, 38-1149, 39-1164, 40-1390
    WILLIAM 36-1116, 38-1261, 40-139

BRANDON, CHARLES 38-775, 39-709

BRAZIER [Braizer, Braser, Brasher, Brayser, Brozer]
    ANN [widw.] 33-1171, 34-1411
    JAMES 31-1190 33-1171, 34-1411, 35-548
    JAMES MUMFORD 36-567
    WILLIAM 30-1248, 31-1190

BREADY [Brady, Breedy]
    JAMES 37-1226, 38-1772, 39-1857, 40-2006
    JOHN 30-1269, 31-1368
    REBECCA [widow] 34-1669, 35-1675, 36-1632
    WILLIAM 34-1670, 35-1675, 36-1632, 37-1209, 38-1766, 39-1866, 40-1762

BREDELL [Bradwell, Bredall, Bredwell, Brid(w)ell]
    ISAIAH 30-217, 31-250, 33-273, 34-149, 35-195, 36-193, 37-323
    JAMES STEPHEN 31-250, 34-149, 36-193, 37-341, 38-219, 39-281, 40-327
    STEPHEN 30-217, 33-273, 35-195

BREEMAN
    CATHERINE [Cathern] 40-1635
    JAMES 33-1179, 34-671, 35-1289, 36-1346, 38-1547, 39-1558

BRERETON [Brearton, Breuerton, Brewerton(e), Brueton]
    ALEXANDER 36-1713, 39-1724, 40-1796
    JOHN 37-1036, 38-1778, 39-1897, 40-1997
    RICHARD 38-695
    SAMUEL 39-1897, 40-1997
    WILLIAM [junr., senr.] 30-1441, 31-1481(2), 33-1563, 34-1593, 35-1544(2), 36-1580(2), 37-1036(2), 38-1778(2), 39-1897(2), 40-1997(2)

BREVARD [Bravard, Breveard], ADAM 35-519, 36-570, 37-618, 38-460, 39-654, 40-514

BREWING [Brewen], JOHN 39-262, 40-306

BRIARHOOD, WILLIAM 38-921

BRIDGEWATERS, [son] 36-603

BRIDGEWATERS [Bridgints]
    EMMANUEL 30-468, 31-464, 33-520, 34-478, 35-442, 36-603, 37-560, 38-650
    ISAAC 35-442, 37-560, 38-650,

INDEX

39-600
BRIMAGIM [Bremigim. Brimegham, Brumegum], WALTER 30-102, 31-12, 33-29, 34-98, 35-126, 36-117, 37-133, 38-82, 39-148, 40-24
BRITT, JOHN 31-1102, 33-1235, 34-1450, 35-1452
BRITTINGHAM [Brettenham]
  ABSALOM 35-399, 36-394, 37-481, 38-551, 39-504, 40-481
  ELIJAH 38-1381, 39-1515, 40-1643
  ELISHA 40-1570
  ELIZABETH [Elesabth, Elezebeth] 33-274, 34-248, 35-196, 36-256, 37-332
  ISAAC 30-355, 31-343(2), 33-365, 34-387, 35-390, 36-475, 37-620, 38-560, 39-474, 40-466, 40-628
  JEREMIAH 30-485, 31-373, 33-363, 34-392, 35-398, 36-477, 37-624, 38-554, 40-483
  JOHN [junr., senr.] 30-1234, 31-1186, 33-1175, 34-1253, 35-1326, 36-1344, 38-1616, 38-1620, 39-1554, 40-1628
  JOSEPH [snr] 30-218, 31-258
  MICAJAH [Micaijah] 39-1579, 40-1646
  NATHAN 33-365, 35-390, 36-475, 37-620, 38-233, 38-560, 39-474, 40-291, 40-630
  NATHANIEL 36-394, 37-481, 38-551, 39-504, 39-1460, 40-479
  ROBERT [Robar(d)(t)] 31-258, 33-274, 34-248, 35-196, 36-256, 37-339, 38-233, 39-259, 40-291
  SAMUEL 38-1609, 39-1578, 40-1630
  SOLOMON 30-438, 31-372, 33-364, 34-393, 35-399, 36-394, 37-483, 38-553, 39-506, 40-481
  THOMAS 34-1260, 35-1287, 36-1353, 38-1619, 39-871, 40-930
  WILLIAM [junr., senr.] 30-355, 30-438(2), 31-372(2), 33-274, 33-364, 33-1154, 34-393(2), 34-1262, 35-399(2), 35-1279, 36-394, 36-395, 36-1352, 37-481, 37-482, 38-551, 38-552, 38-1617, 39-504, 39-505, 39-1555, 40-628, 40-629, 40-1629
BROADHEAD [Broahead], JOSEPH 35-896
BROOKS [Brookes]
  FRANCIS 33-1192, 34-1276, 36-1334, 38-1587, 39-1527, 40-184, 40-1603
  HENRY 33-1191, 34-1274, 35-1293, 35-1407, 36-1334, 38-1587, 39-384
  HUGH 36-1269
  PATRICK [Partrick] 31-567, 33-632, 34-699
  RICHARD 33-1209, 34-1418, 35-1407, 36-1269, 38-1391, 39-1593(2)
BROOKSHER [Brookshaw, Brucksher, Bruckshir, Brusher]
  ANN 30-1391
  MANARING [Manering, Manring] 33-841, 34-832, 35-878, 39-978
    WILLIAM 37-1246, 39-1809, 40-1834
BROUGHTON [Bratten, Bratton, Brauton, Brothon, Brotton]
  BRUFF [Brough] 30-1129, 31-1113, 33-1200, 34-1319, 35-1314, 36-1391, 38-1375, 39-1584, 40-1665
  HUGH 34-426, 35-422, 36-447, 37-469, 38-590, 39-462, 40-566
  JAMES [junr., senr] 30-379, 30-472, 31-457, 33-449, 34-404, 34-426, 35-421, 36-487, 36-515, 37-604, 37-605, 38-569, 38-592, 39-463, 39-1452, 40-563, 40-1554
  JOHN 30-716(2), 31-1123, 33-1202, 34-427, 34-1318, 35-423, 35-1315, 36-218, 36-1392, 37-351, 38-861, 38-1376, 39-463, 39-1585, 40-563, 40-325, 40-1666
  QUANTON 30-353
  SAMUEL [junr., senr] 30-472, 31-334(2), 31-335, 33-355, 33-357, 34-426, 34-427, 35-422, 35-423, 36-447, 36-448, 37-469, 37-470, 38-590, 38-591, 39-462, 39-465, 40-564, 40-565
  THOMAS 39-831, 40-946
  WILLIAM [junr.] 30-472, 30-716, 31-334, 31-713, 31-1123, 33-355, 33-714, 34-427, 34-795, 35-423, 35-826, 35-1315, 36-796, 36-1392, 37-603, 37-642, 38-591, 38-862, 38-1376, 39-464, 39-831, 39-1585, 40-324, 40-946, 40-1666
BROW, MICHAEL [Micheall] 39-347
BROWN [Browne]
  ALEXANDER 33-545, 34-604, 35-671, 36-625, 38-749
  ANDREW 38-1644, 39-1782, 40-1866
  DAVID [Browne/junr., senr.] 30-549, 30-609, 31-534, 31-535, 33-600, 33-642, 34-627, 34-628, 35-655, 36-748, 38-781, 39-705, 40-771
  GEORGE 36-679, 38-678, 39-1413, 40-1479
  JAMES 37-954
  JOHN 30-299, 30-1036, 30-1037, 31-332, 31-855, 31-955, 33-423, 33-1035, 34-494, 36-265, 38-464
  MARY 40-772
  REBECCA 35-754
  SIDNEY [Sidn(i)e 31-640, 33-681, 34-693, 35-697, 36-1003, 38-1034, 39-1002, 40-1040
  TARRILL [Terrell, Turvill] 30-507, 31-590, 33-687, 34-99, 38-707, 39-768, 40-744
  THOMAS 30-609, 30-1119, 31-534, 31-1115, 33-642, 34-627, 34-1416,

INDEX

35-655, 35-1262, 36-748, 36-1267,
38-781, 38-1166, 39-704, 39-1337,
40-848, 40-1385
    WILLIAM 30-904, 30-1213, 31-403,
31-1000, 33-504, 33-1023, 34-1002,
35-1128, 36-931, 37-971, 38-1153,
39-1120, 40-1187
BROWNBILL
    HENRY [Hendry] 30-732, 31-676, 33-769, 34-753, 35-788, 36-855
    JOHN 34-753, 35-788, 36-855
    NATHANIEL
BRUMBLEY [Brumbely, Bromly]
    HENRY 30-652, 31-747, 33-738,
34-784, 35-818, 36-774, 37-344,
37-660, 38-199, 38-876, 39-219,
39-841, 40-317, 40-928
    JOHN 37-343, 38-199, 39-219, 40-317,
    THOMAS 34-525, 38-1557, 39-578, 40-1562
    WILLIAM 39-219, 40-317
BRYAN [Brian, Bryon]
    JAMES 36-465
    RICHARD 30-523, 31-609, 34-609, 35-717
    THOMAS 33-594, 35-622, 38-764, 39-791
BUCKINGHAM [Beckingham], WILLIAM 34-942, 35-1039, 36-1138
BUCKLE/BUCKLER [Bucker, Bucklar, Buckle, Buckler, Buckley]
    CORNELIUS [Cornelious] 34-30, 35-112, 36-47, 37-45
    NICHOLAS [Nicklos, Nickliss] 31-1082, 33-1072, 34-932, 35-972, 36-944, 38-995, 39-1151, 40-1080
BULGER, RICHARD 30-510
BULL, PATRICK 34-1266
BUNCLE, ALEXANDER 34-568, 35-366, 36-513, 37-384, 38-612, 39-576, 40-632
BURBRIDGE [Burbadge, Burbage]
    EDWARD 30-392, 31-495, 33-542, 34-464, 35-528, 36-598, 37-562, 38-492, 39-540, 40-659
    JOHN 31-385, 33-436, 34-565, 35-553, 36-599, 37-565, 38-411, 39-520, 40-660
BURCAM [Burken, Burkim, Burkam]
    JAMES 30-885, 31-951
    ROGER 33-893, 34-987
BURCKETT, THOMAS 36-1397
BURGAN [Birgin, Burgen, Burgun]
    DANIEL [Danill] 30-618, 33-612, 34-683, 35-722, 36-716, 38-793, 39-700, 40-852
    PATRICK 39-700
    WILLIAM 39-700, 38-793, 40-852
BURK [Birk, Burke]
    JOHN 30-723, 31-1169, 33-1179
    PATRICK 31-533, 35-585

BURN [Burne], JAMES 30-861, 33-1410, 34-1694, 35-1168, 36-1100, 37-982, 38-1771, 40-1107
BURNETT [Barnet, Bearnett, Bernet, Burnitt, Burnott]
    JAMES 30-161, 30-1231, 31-221, 31-1167(2), 33-164, 33-1167, 34-334, 34-1443, 35-183, 35-1455, 36-321, 36-1336, 38-264, 38-1584, 39-333, 39-1521, 40-385, 40-1599
    JANE 35-1455
    JEAN [widw.] 33-1167, 34-1443
    JOHN 30-161, 31-218, 33-215, 34-203, 35-162, 36-267, 39-308
    MARY 30-161
BURNS
    JOSEPH 39-194, 40-359
    PATRICK 39-769
BURTON
    JOHN 30-164, 30-416, 31-226, 31-316, 33-170, 33-385, 34-262, 34-419, 35-159, 35-507, 36-357, 36-469, 37-241, 37-400, 38-267, 38-516, 39-330, 39-416, 40-407, 40-451
    JONATHAN 38-170
    JOSEPH 36-357
    JOSHUA [Joshuah] 31-226, 33-170, 34-262, 35-159, 37-241, 39-328, 40-389
    WILLIAM 30-164, 31-226, 33-170, 34-262, 35-159, 36-357, 37-241, 38-267, 39-328, 40-389
BUTLER
    EMMANUEL [Manewell, Manuell] 33-1207, 34-1312, 35-1259, 36-1274, 38-1390, 39-39, 40-1673
    NATHANIEL 30-512, 31-579, 33-651, 34-659, 35-620, 36-622, 38-761, 39-798, 40-818
    NICHOLAS 30-836
    THOMAS 30-1200, 31-1139, 33-1353, 34-1301, 35-1485, 36-1477, 38-1515, 39-1430, 40-1540
BUTT, JOHN 30-635, 31-514, 33-648, 34-571
BYWATERS [Beywatters, Buywaters], RICHARD [Richart] 30-1126, 31-1117, 33-1266, 34-1381, 35-117, 36-106, 37-147, 38-74, 39-145, 40-140

C---, JOHN? 37-872
CABB [Cobb]
    JOHN [junr., senr.] 30-191, 31-168(2)
    JOSEPH 35-168, 36-184
    NATHANIEL 30-198, 31-156, 33-255
    WILLIAM 30-200, 31-156, 33-254, 34-211, 35-167, 36-191, 37-167, 38-174, 39-280,
CABLE, WILLIAM 30-1420

INDEX

CADE
   CHARLES 30-711, 34-815, 36-1377
   THOMAS 36-247, 38-277, 39-325, 40-392,
CAIN [Ca(i)ne, Kain(e)]
   JAMES 30-638, 31-662, 33-1487, 34-595, 35-603, 36-675, 38-716, 39-752, 40-709
   THOMAS [Cane] 33-1183, 34-1256, 39-1549
   WILLIAM 30-639, 31-569, 35-605
CALDWELL [Cadwell, Calwell, Cardwell, Coldweld, Coldwell, Coldwill, Cordwell]
   AUGUSTUS [Agust(a)in, Augsteen, Augusten] 35-337, 36-197, 37-312, 38-374
   HUGH [Heugh, Hew] 30-1370, 31-1449, 33-1469, 34-1194, 34-1457, 35-1757, 36-1742, 37-1249, 38-1751, 39-1688, 40-1900
   JAMES 30-887, 31-1089, 33-1061, 34-986, 35-1112, 36-1081, 38-1080, 39-1011, 40-1129
   JOHN [junr., senr.] 30-294, 30-1008, 31-833, 31-1448, 33-952, 33-1474, 34-1045, 34-1451, 35-1062, 35-1516, 35-1649, 36-1240, 36-1754, 37-915, 37-1161, 38-1299, 38-1774, 39-1188, 39-1933, 40-1275, 40-1813
   JOSEPH [capt.] 33-1474, 35-1366, 40-1709
   JOSHUA [capt.] 30-1294, 31-1448, 34-1374, 36-1285, 39-1633, 38-1417
   PATRICK [Partrick] 30-1000, 31-836, 33-953, 34-1070, 35-1065, 36-1239, 37-921, 38-1272, 39-1212, 40-1270
   ROBERT 31-1448, 34-1451, 35-1062, 35-1649, 36-1240, 36-1754, 37-915, 37-1161, 38-1299, 38-1774, 39-1188, 39-1933, 40-1275, 40-1813
   THOMAS 33-957, 34-1112, 35-1055, 36-1238, 37-920, 38-1331, 39-1211, 40-1260,
   WILLIAM 30-630, 31-633, 33-551, 34-667, 35-905, 35-1112, 36-739, 38-1856, 39-1812, 40-835
CALHOON [Cahoone, Cohoon(e)]
   HENRY 38-51, 39-155, 40-131
   JOHN 30-82, 31-83, 33-106, 34-89, 35-132, 36- 36, 37-14, 38-51, 39-155, 40-131
CALLAWAY [Calleway]
   BENIAMIN [Beniamin] 38-1232, 39-1235 40-1282
   EDWARD 30-1006, 31-834, 33-943, 34-1062, 35-1060, 36-1060, 38-1218, 39-1246, 40-1290
   ISAAC 39-1231, 40-1281
   JOHN [junr., senr.] 30-1006(2), 30-1010, 31-834(2), 31-837, 33-933, 33-942, 33-944, 34-1061, 34-1063, 34-1094, 35-1045, 35-1058, 35-1059, 35-1061, 36-987, 36-996, 36-1030, 36-1031, 37-862, 38-1128, 38-1163, 38-1215, 38-1217, 39-1176, 39-1205, 39-1231, 39-1237, 40-1281, 40-1288, 40-1289, 40-1300
   JOSEPH 40-1435
   PETER [junr., snr.] 30-987, 30-1024, 31-1005, 31-1018, 33-958, 33-984, 34-1121, 35-1045, 35-1180, 36-987, 36-1164, 37-862, 37-903, 38-1163, 38-1213, 39-1205, 39-1209, 40-1352
   SARAH 40-1435
   THOMAS 33-984, 35-1045, 36-987, 39-1206, 40-1355
   WILLIAM [junr., snr.] 30-1010, 31-837(2), 33-933, 33-1469, 34-1052, 35-1056, 35-1057, 36-988, 36-989, 38-1232, 38-1327, 39-1235, 39-1236, 40-1282, 40-1283
CALVERT [Calburd, Colbord, Colburd, Colvart], WILLIAM 30-1117, 31-1253, 33-1270, 34-1378, 35-1266, 36-1270, 38-893, 39-911, 40-893
CAMBLE [Cambell, Cambill, Camble, Cammell, Cammile, Campable, Campbell]
   JOHN [jr., sr.] 30-156, 30-252, 30-517, 31-227, 31-282, 31-643, 33-171, 33-330, 33-555, 34-190, 34-277, 34-708, 35-275, 35-292, 35-656, 35-673, 36-269, 36-327, 36-665, 37-240, 37-309, 38-271, 38-366, 38-774, 39-335, 39-366(2), 39-715, 40-300(2), 40-390, 40-802
   NEHEMIAH [Neh.] 35-654, 36-649, 37-561, 38-791, 39-809
   SOLOMON 30-264, 31-133, 33-283, 34-188, 35-321, 36-313, 37-320, 38-381, 39-261, 40-172
CAMBRIDGE, WILLIAM 30-1147
CAMBROON [McCameren], EVANDER [Evender] 39-1577, 40-1641
CAMISS [Cames], JOHN 30-490, 31-508
CAMPBELL, JAMES 33-834
CANADAY [Canidor, Coniday, Kennady, Keneday, Kinnady]
   JOHN 31-1499, 34-1514, 35-1546, 36-1733
   NEHEMIAH 34-476, 36-439, 38-486, 39-605
   SIMMONS 31-463, 33-519
   TIMOTHY 37-1088, 38-1802, 39-1704, 40-1802
CANTWELL, THOMAS 30-1064, 31-1217, 33-670, 34-665, 35-612, 36-652, 38-955, 39-938
CAREYS [Kerrieys], THOMAS 30-174
CARMICHAL [Camichell, Carmical, Carmic(o)le, Comical, Curmechell,

INDEX

Cormichall, etc.]
   JOHN 35-1128, 36-931, 37-971, 38-1103, 39-1082, 40-1178
   THOMAS 37-971, 38-1153, 39-1120, 40-1190
CARNELL, THOMAS 34-1045
CARNEY, THOMAS [Kerney] 33-217
CARNIS, JOHN [Cairns, Carn(e)s, Kearns] 33-559, 34-638, 35-747, 36-719, 38-690, 39-732
CARNY [Carney]
   ANN 31-538
   ROBERT 30-559, 31-551, 34-624
CARR, JOHN 30-1293, 31-1344, 33-1442
CARSEY [Carzey, Cearsey, Corzey, Keirsey, Keirsie, Kersey, Kersie, Kezey, Kiersey]
   JAMES 37-1133, 38-1683, 39-1725, 40-1797
   JOHN 30-1320, 31-1459, 33-1458, 34-477, 35-441, 36-439
   PATRICK [junr., senr.] 30-1320, 31-1389, 33-1457(2), 34-1686(2), 35-1714(2), 36-439, 36-1725, 37-1133, 38-1683(2), 39-1725, 40-1747, 40-1797
   PETER 30-1153, 31-1266, 33-1252, 34-1388, 35-1428
   ROBERT 33-1252, 34-1388, 35-1428, 36-1289, 38-1460, 39-1499, 40-1507
   SAMUEL 30-1153, 31-1266, 33-1252, 34-1388, 35-1428, 36-1289, 38-1432, 39-1643, 40-1720
   WILLIAM 30-1153, 31-1389, 33-1260, 33-1457, 34-1389, 34-1686, 35-1402, 36-1289, 38-1431, 39-1642, 40-1719
CARTER [Cartor]
   CHARLES 30-1274, 31-1348, 33-991, 34-1050, 35-1073, 36-993, 38-1185, 39-1171, 40-1249
   JOHN [junr., senr.] 30-862, 30-863, 31-923, 31-1008, 33-990, 33-991, 34-1113, 34-1114, 35-1034, 35-1046, 36-994, 36-1044, 38-1337, 39-1084, 40-1251
   JOSEPH 33-220, 34-255, 39-308, 40-427,
   PHILLIP 30-864, 31-959, 33-986, 34-1044, 35-1143, 36-1112, 37-1169, 38-1664, 39-1107, 40-1248
   SAMUEL 30-862, 31-923, 33-991, 34-1113, 35-1046, 36-994, 38-1172, 39-1106, 40-1322,
   THOMAS 30-862, 31-923, 33-991, 34-1114, 35-1036, 36-994, 38-1131, 39-1305, 40-1391
   WILLIAM 38-1241, 33-991, 34-1113, 35-1143, 36-994, 39-1117, 40-1198
CARVEL [Garvil], THOMAS 35-1062, 37-915
CARWEEL, IGNATIOUS STEPHEN [Agnatius] 34-296

   THOMAS 34-337
CARY [Carey(s), Carrie(y), Cearr(e)y, Karrey, Kerey]
   WIDOW 34-1534
   FRANCIS [Fran.] 30-69, 31-1111, 33-125, 34-112, 35-131, 36-124
   JEREMIAH 30-1257, 33-1194, 34-1447, 35-852, 36-778, 37-712, 38-883, 39-817, 40-921
   JOHN 30-1244, 31-1189
   JONATHAN 30-1347, 31-1436, 33-1528, 34-1536, 35-1600, 36-1681, 37-1111, 38-1820, 39-1915
   LEVIN 30-1410, 31-1436, 33-1502, 34-1535, 35-1599, 37-1110, 38-1637, 39-1766, 40-1934
   NAOMI [Neomy, widw.] 33-1193, 34-1219
   RACHEL 34-883, 35-867, 36-880, 37-797, 38-920, 39-969, 40-1013
   RICHARD [Richeard] 30-158, 31-332, 33-169, 34-279, 35-161, 36-323, 38-263, 39-360, 40-401
   SOLOMON 30-719, 33-780, 34-771, 35-806, 36-776, 37-732, 38-839, 39-846, 40-920
   THOMAS 30-768, 31-236, 31-806, 31-1436, 33-183, 33-843, 33-1502, 34-268, 34-882, 34-153435-150, 35-866, 35-1601, 36-331, 36-879, 36-1660, 37-253, 37-796, 37-1084, 38-278, 38-919, 38-1673, 39-968, 39-1750, 40-1012, 40-1929,
   WILLIAM 30-1347, 31-237, 31-1436, 33-173, 33-1502, 34-272, 35-271
CASON, ALEXANDER 36-615
CATAN [Caton, Claton, Katon]
   CHARLES 39-1626
   GEORGE 34-4, 35-3, 36-19, 37-58, 38-39, 39-83, 40-91
CATHILL [Cathel, Cathill, Caththill, Cathwell, Chathell]
   JAMES 30-1326, 31-1468, 33-1489, 34-1497, 35-1575, 36-1671, 37-1103, 38-1672, 39-1756, 40-1930
   JONATHAN 40-1930
CATLIN [Catling]
   ROBERT 30-105, 33-21, 34-100, 35-125
   WILLIAM 30-105, 31-4, 33-21, 34-100, 35-75, 36-12, 37-110, 38-138, 39-18, 40-20
CAUSEY, JOHN 38-486
CAVENOUGH [Cavenock], JOHN 30-313, 31-386, 35-550
CHADWICKS [Chad(a)wicks, Chadwecks, Chadiwax]
   JAMES [junr., senr.] 30-1433, 30-1433, 31-1435, 31-1435, 33-1519, 33-1519, 34-1509, 34-1509, 35-1645, 35-1645, 36-1647, 36-1647, 37-1097, 37-1097, 38-1796, 38-1796, 39-1776,

INDEX

39-1777, 40-1966
  JOHN 38-1796, 39-1776
CHAILLIE [Chaillie, Challie, Chelley, Shellie, Shelly]
  MOSES [capt.] 31-1200, 34-442, 35-365, 36-534, 37-379, 38-614, 39-581, 40-1564
  PETER 34-442, 35-365
CHAIN [Chaine], ALEXANDER 31-534, 33-628, 34-626, 35-925, 36-916, 37-750, 38-968, 39-954, 40-976
CHAMBERLIN, WILLIAM 30-588
CHAMBERS [Chaimbers, Chamber, Chambres, Chambu(r)s]
  ALEXANDER 31-155, 33-255, 34-212
  EDWARD 30-630, 31-633, 33-551, 34-572, 35-1689, 36-1596, 37-1010, 38-1856, 39-1812, 40-1011
  JEREMIAH 30-1245, 31-1280, 33-1166, 35-1313, 36-1345, 38-890
  RICHARD 30-508, 31-520, 33-660, 33-1589, 34-641, 35-663, 36-663, 38-695, 39-734, 40-755
  ROBERT 30-1387, 31-1403
  SAMUEL 30-792, 31-1313, 33-826, 33-1414, 34-841, 35-898, 36-878, 37-1172, 38-965, 38-1629, 39-1829, 40-1862
CHANCLER [Chanchle, Chansler], George 30-220, 31-364, 33-395
CHAPELL, WILLIAM 30-508, 31-520
CHAPMAN [Chapmon, Chipman]
  EDWARD 30-726
  ELIJAH [Eliga] 40-925
  HUMPHREY [Humphre, Umphrey] 30-654, 31-736, 33-730, 34-768, 35-804, 36-805, 37-671, 38-847, 39-862, 40-891
  JOSHUA 33-1147
  MARGARET [Margrett] 31-753
  PARIS 35-1173, 36-1195, 38-1288, 39-1363
  RICHARD 33-1014
CHARLES, JOHN 30-476, 31-442, 34-567, 35-505, 37-397
CHASE [CHACE] ISAAC 37-334, 38-169, 40-797
CHEASEMAN [Cheesman], JOHN 30-899, 31-865, 33-1019, 34-997, 35-1135, 36-1041, 37-856, 38-1123, 39-1017
CHEASEMAN [Cheapman]
  PARIS 40-1303
  RACHELL 40-1156
CHERIX [Chadax, Chericks], JAMES 31-703, 39-903, 40-865
CHILD [Childs]
  EDMUND 40-1286
  JOHN 30-1449
  THOMAS 30-1263
CHRISTOPHER [Christofer]
  ARISTOBULUS [Arrostoblus, Aristobulus] 30-1173, 31-509, 33-1211, 34-1412
  CLEMENT [Clem, Clemon(t)] 30-1363, 31-1478, 33-1531, 34-1578, 35-1697, 36-1620, 37-1045, 38-1803, 39-1892, 40-1871,
  EPHRAIM [Ephram] 30-1411, 31-1531, 33-1521, 34-1517, 35-1698, 36-1619, 37-1046, 38-1845, 39-1778, 40-1961
  JACOB 39-1759, 40-1931
  JOHN [junr., senr.] 30-1305, 30-1363, 31-1462, 31-1478, 33-1491(2), 33-1531, 34-1498, 34-1578, 35-1571, 35-1571, 35-1697, 36-1621, 36-1672, 37-1047, 37-1102, 38-1670, 38-1779, 39-1759, 39-1891, 40-1870, 40-1931
  JOSEPH 33-1531, 34-1578, 35-1697, 36-1621, 37-1047, 38-1779, 39-1857, 40-1747,
  RICHARD 31-1477
  WRIXAM [Rickson, Rixon, Rixsom] 30-1434, 31-1517, 33-906, 35-1646
CHRISTY, JOHN [Christey, Cristee] 30-39, 31- 40
CHURCH
  SAMUEL 30-425, 31-322
  WILLIAM 36-575, 39-518
CHURN [Churine, Churme], JOHN 30-919, 31-926, 33-1033, 34-1008, 35-1029, 37-886, 38-1084, 39-1250, 40-1174
CLARK [Clarke, Clerk]
  ALEXANDER 30-490, 31-508, 34-648, 35-732, 36-651, 38-804, 39-679, 40-825
  BENJAMIN [Benjaman, Benjmen] 33-260, 34-222, 35-235, 36-350, 37-322, 38-392, 39-395, 40-434
  CHARLES 30-482, 31-431, 33-507, 34-570, 35-590
  DANIEL 30-314, 31-492, 33-418, 34-541, 35-536
  EDWARD 33-196, 34-154, 35-194, 36-307, 38-386, 39-240, 40-199
  JOHN 30-730, 31-275, 31-706, 33-260, 34-222, 35-235, 36-350, 37-322, 38-392, 39-395, 39-895, 40-434
  JOSEPH 35-235, 36-242, 37-337, 38-348, 39-227, 40-212,
  MARY [widow] 33-196, 34-154, 35-194, 36-307, 37-192, 40-362
  RACE [Rase/jr.] 30-206, 31-275, 33-260, 34-222, 35-235, 36-350(3), 37-322(2), 38-392, 39-395, 40-434
  ROADS 40-362
  THOMAS 38-1369, 39-673. 40-719
  WILLIAM 36-307, 37-192
CLAYWELL [Clauell, Clavell, Clawell, Clayweel, Clayuell]
  EZEKIEL [Ezecell] 30-643, 33-734, 34-791

INDEX

JOHN 39-649
PETER [junr., senr] 30-643, 30-649, 31-748, 31-757, 33-734, 33-735, 34-790, 34-791, 35-824, 35-825, 36-788, 36-792, 37-644, 37-651, 38-865, 38-866, 39-918, 39-920, 40-935, 40-960
SELBY [Selvay] 31-66, 33-69, 34-118, 35-19, 38-7, 39-74, 40-147
SHADRICK [Shadrack] 37-651, 38-865, 39-918, 40-935
THOMAS 30-383, 31-436, 33-342, 34-351, 35-370, 36-593, 37-613, 38-600, 39-447, 40-444
CLIFTON [Cleften, Clifen, Clifpton, Cliften]
DANIEL 31-1056
GEORGE [jnr., senr.] 30-1003(2), 31-997(2), 31-1120, 33-873(2), 33-1230, 34-1172(2), 34-1402, 35-1240(2), 35-1443, 36-1235(2), 36-1295, 38-1313(2), 39-1294, 39-1623, 40-1337, 40-1703
JOHN 30-1164, 31-1096, 33-1225, 34-1395, 35-1434, 36-1299, 38-1313, 38-1408, 39-1624, 40-1702
LEVIN 39-1294
NEHEMIAH 35-1240, 36-1235, 38-1313, 39-1294
PHILLIP 30-1004, 31-1013, 33-1477, 34-1677
THOMAS 34-1172, 35-1240, 36-1235, 38-1313
CLOCKER, DANIEL 37-231
CLOGG [Clegg], SAMUEL 30-1131, 31-1127, 33-1201, 34-1316, 35-1254, 36-1389, 38-1379, 39-1588, 40-1668
CLUFF, EDWARD 30-1130, 31-1126, 33-1199, 34-1320, 35-1252, 36-1387, 38-1372, 39-1583, 40-1664
COBB, JOSEPH 38-506, 40-521
COCANE, GEORGE 35-1406
COCKLING [Cocklin], FRANCIS 30-1173, 31-1183
COE [Cowe], DANIEL [Danil] 35-348, 36-286, 37-369, 38-194, 39-196, 40-229
COFFIN [Coffen, Coffine, Coffing, Cofien, Colfing]
JOHN [Jon.] 31-233, 33-242, 34-230, 36-386, 37-166, 38-369, 39-305, 40-349
JOSEPH 30-192, 31-233, 33-242, 34-230, 35-171, 36-165, 37-277, 38-518, 39-274, 40-349
THOMAS [jr., sr.] 30-192, 31-233, 33-242(2), 34-230(2), 35-176(2), 36-165(2), 37-276, 37-278, 38-369(2), 39-305(2), 40-348, 40-430
WILLIAM 35-501, 40-430
COGSBERRY [Cosere]
HENRY 30-35

HUGH 31-42
COLLETT [Colleck]
SIMON 37-726, 38-880
JAMES 33-1507, 34-1665, 35-1556, 36-1694
COLLIER [Colle(a)r, Collyar, Collyer, Coyllar]
BETTS 30-845
DOUBTY [Dowtee, Dot(e)y, Dowty, Dowd(e)y, Doughty] 30-818, 31-853, 33-1073, 34-910, 35-949, 36-1018, 37-845, 38-1068, 39-1031, 40-1059
GEORGE 33-1073, 38-1022, 39-1033, 40-1061
GEORGE BETTS 31-943, 33-929, 34-910, 35-953, 36-1017, 37-828
KENDALL 40-180
NICHOLAS EVANS 38-1663, 39-1841, 40-1867
PETER 30-259, 31-300, 33-311, 34-184, 35-335, 36-201, 37-362, 38-380, 39-232, 40-180
ROBERT [Robarte/jur., senr.] 30-818, 31-853(2), 33-1073(2), 34-910(2), 34-910, 35-953(2), 36-1017, 36-1018, 37-828(2), 38-1022(2), 39-1031, 39-1041, 40-1060, 40-1062
THOMAS 30-1354, 31-1506, 33-1558, 34-1545, 35-1536, 36-1563, 37-1069, 38-1701, 39-1852, 40-1346
COLLINS [Colens, Colins, Collains, Collings]
... illegible 37-969
ABLE 31-308, 36-244, 37-211, 38-178, 39-168, 40-363
ANDREW 30-456, 31-468, 33-878, 34-1163, 35-1210, 36-1148, 38-1316, 39-1276, 40-1375
CHARLES 30-424, 31-314
EBENEZER [Ebin] 33-985, 36-934, 37-864
EDMUND [Edmond, Edman] 30-1034, 31-1003, 34-1106, 35-1042, 38-1159, 39-1127, 40-1252,
GEORGE 31-856, 33-1003, 34-926, 35-268, 36-360, 37-244, 38-274, 39-340, 40-1317,
JAMES 30-1282, 31-845, 33-1085, 34-1075, 35-1764, 36-1745, 37-1215, 38-1741, 39-1673, 40-1883
JOHN [ser.] 30-240, 30-832, 30-1377, 31-308, 31-468, 31-862, 33-296, 33-529, 33-1070, 33-1088, 34-284, 34-517, 34-927, 34-1041, 35-198, 35-458, 35-969, 35-1090, 36-348, 36-434, 36-943, 36-1225, 37-225, 37-540, 38-357, 38-499, 38-1046, 38-1148, 39-320, 39-588, 39-1090, 39-1110, 40-282, 40-618, 40-1256, 40-1338,
MARY [widd.] 30-456, 31-468,

INDEX

33-529, 34-517, 35-458, 36-436,
37-541, 38-497, 39-589, 40-619
   PRICE 33-660, 34-641, 36-244,
   RICHARD 30-854, 30-1282, 31-1072,
35-1231, 38-1742, 39-1745, 40-1949
   SAMUEL 30-1102, 31-1100, 33-1239,
34-1425, 35-1410, 36-663, 36-1308,
37-496, 38-695, 38-1403, 39-734,
39-1613, 40-755, 40-1693
   SOLOMON 30-461, 31-427, 34-530,
35-595, 36-604, 38-546, 39-626,
40-664
   THOMAS [junr., senr.] 30-241,
30-366, 30-620, 31-294, 31-312,
33-295, 33-479, 34-295, 34-422,
34-1041, 35-298, 35-510, 35-1088,
36-207, 36-373, 36-436, 36-1223,
36-1226, 37-289, 37-440, 37-541,
37-865, 38-358, 38-497, 38-523,
38-1207, 38-1334, 39-324, 39-564,
39-589, 39-1166, 39-1168, 40-363,
40-555, 40-619, 40-1243, 40-1245
   WILLIAM 30-151, 30-457, 30-620,
31-216, 31-554, 33-228, 33-530,
33-572, 33-1366, 34-328, 34-518,
34-651, 35-277, 35-459, 35-642,
36-358, 36-435, 36-720, 37-211,
37-542, 38-178, 38-498, 38-703,
39-382, 39-764, 39-1277, 40-420,
40-742, 40-1369
COMPTON, ISAAC 40-842
CONDUM [Condun], EDWARD 30-1067
31-1219, 33-1297, 34-1209,
CONNELLY [Cunelo, Conerley, Conly]
   DARBY 30-553
   PATRICK 31-1185, 33-1275, 34-1227,
35-1284, 36-1331, 38-681, 39-716,
40-765
CONNOR [Conner]
   CORNELIUS 35-675
   DANIEL 30-288, 31-279, 33-324,
34-341, 38-325, 39-272, 40-215
   JOHN [junr., senr.] 30-88(2),
31-96, 33-111, 34-38(2), 35-98(2),
36-139(2), 37-23(2), 38-55(2),
40-124
   LEVIN 37-23, 38-55
   MICHAEL [Michall] 31-134, 33-338
   PATRICK 38-437, 39-290, 40-197
   PHILLIP 40-123
   RICHARD 31-727, 33-723, 34-817,
35-848
   WILLIAM 30-89, 30-1102, 31-97,
31-1097, 33-112, 33-1232, 34-37,
34-1252, 35-99, 35-1296, 36-140,
36-1366, 37-24, 38-86, 38-1585,
39-1575, 40-1633
CONNOWAY [Conaway]
   JOHN [jur., senr.] 39-109(2), 40-124
   LEVIN 39-110, 40-124
   WILLIAM 39-110, 40-123

COOK, GUY 38-1576, 39-1523, 40-1592
COOPER [Coaper, Coupper, Cupper]
   CHARLES 30-155, 33-163, 39-268
   GABRIEL [Gaby, Gabrill/junr.,
senr.] 30-911, 30-913, 31-927,
31-928, 33-987, 33-987, 34-1099,
34-1099, 35-1024, 35-1024, 36-924,
36-924, 38-1105, 39-1115, 40-1392
   ISAAC 30-915, 31-956, 33-989,
34-1098, 35-1026, 36-926, 38-1204,
39-1112, 40-1203
   JAMES 30-992, 31-1016, 33-939,
34-1060, 35-1071, 36-991, 38-1227,
39-1180, 40-1284
   JOHN 30-813, 31-858, 33-928,
34-945, 35-986, 36-1259, 37-846
   SAMUEL 30-914, 30-1085, 31-948,
31-1234, 33-988, 33-1320, 34-1102,
34-1235, 35-1025, 35-1480, 36-925,
36-1446, 38-1254, 39-1113, 39-1504,
40-1210, 40-1497
   THOMAS 30-911, 31-927, 33-987,
34-1099, 35-1024, 36-924, 38-1106,
39-1114, 40-1209
   WILLIAM 39-1113, 40-1210
COPE [Coape, Coop, Cope]
   JOHN 30-1401, 31-1490, 33-1594,
34-1570, 35-1525, 36-1570, 37-887,
38-1094, 39-1160(2), 40-1211
   THOMAS 40-767
   WILLIAM 30-1401, 31-1490, 33-1594,
34-1570, 35-1219, 35-1526, 36-1570,
37-887, 38-1094(2), 40-1211, 40-1410
COPSEY [Capsy, Coapes], WILLIAM 37-958, 39-808, 40-706
COR-, DANIEL 34-250
CORBETT [Corbitt], DANIEL 30-1357,
31-1503
CORD
   ARTHUR [Arter] 33-781, 34-748,
35-784, 36-763, 37-717, 38-841,
39-878, 40-886,
   HENRY 40-59
   JOHN 37-717, 38-841, 39-878,
40-886
   JOSEPH 40-886
   THOMAS 40-56
   WILLIAM [junr., senr.] 30-701,
31-673, 33-781, 33-781, 34-748,
35-784, 36-763, 37-717, 38-841,
39-878, 40-886
CORDRY [Cadry, Caudry, Caudrey,
Cawdroe, Cawdry, Codery, Codr(a)y,
Cordery]
   ABRAHAM [Abram] 30-1464, 31-1352,
33-1409, 34-1637, 35-1708, 36-1539,
37-1185, 38-1666, 39-1842, 40-1825
   DANIEL 30-1461, 31-1078, 31-1350,
33-1405, 34-1621, 35-1711, 36-1530,
37-1179, 38-1663, 39-1841, 40-2002
   DAVID 33-1030, 34-1012, 35-1114,
36-1086, 37-882, 38-1099, 39-1161,

INDEX

40-1181,
    EDWARD 30-921, 31-1078, 33-1030, 34-1011, 35-1115
    ISAAC [Isack] 30-877, 31-966, 33-1040, 34-1550, 35-1533
    JACOB 30-858, 31-1508, 33-1561, 34-1544, 35-1713, 36-1555, 37-1070, 38-1844, 39-1932, 40-1754
    JOHN [jur., snr] 30-1276, 31-1044, 31-1374, 33-1424, 34-1658, 35-1767, 36-1689, 37-1202, 38-1744(2), 39-1674(2), 40-1887(2)
    MORGAN [Morghin] 30-1464, 31-1352, 33-1424, 34-1544, 35-1713, 36-1689, 37-1185, 38-1666, 39-1161, 40-1181
CORNELIUS, COHIL 38-801
CORNON, CORNELIUS 30-1183
CORNWELL
    JOHN 36-834, 37-705, 38-854, 39-892, 40-887,
    ROBERT 33-1474, 34-1697, 35-1724, 36-1754, 37-993, 38-1693
    THOMAS 36-1240
COSTIN [Costen, Coston]
    ISAAC 30-1055, 31-1207, 33-1286, 34-1337, 35-1495, 36-1408, 38-1368, 39-1393, 40-1457
    MATHIAS [Mathies] 35-1494, 34-1215, 34-1336, 36-632, 38-1366, 37-799, 35-613, 36-1407, 39-761,
    OLIVER 40-1457
    STEPHEN 30-1057, 31-1209, 33-1284, 34-1258, 35-1497, 36-1406, 38-1366, 39-1390, 40-1455
COTTINGHAM [Cottengem, Cottinhame, Cottinhome]
    CHARLES [jr., sr.] 30-83, 30-83, 30-1180, 30-1344, 31-91, 31-91, 31-1135, 33-99, 33-99, 34-42, 34-43, 34-1329, 35-105, 35-106, 36-30, 36-31, 37-1, 37-2, 38-48, 38-68, 39-100, 39-101, 40-111, 40-113
    JOHN 30-83, 31-92, 33-99, 34-42, 34-1388, 35-105, 35-1428, 36-30, 36-103, 37-1, 37-5, 38-68, 38-1431, 38-1469, 39-100, 39-1488, 39-1642, 40-111, 40-1526, 40-1706
    JONATHAN 30-1180, 31-1135, 31-1135, 33-1344, 33-1344, 34-1329, 34-1329, 35-1493, 36-1442, 38-1469, 39-1488, 40-1526
    MARY 31-92
    THOMAS [jr., sr.] 30-10, 30-83, 31-91, 33-99, 33-106, 34-37, 34-42, 35-73, 35-105, 36-103, 36-153, 37-3, 37-5, 38-69, 38-159, 39-36, 39-102, 40-42, 40-110
    WILLIAM 30-1180, 31-1135, 33-1344, 34-1329, 35-1493, 36-1442, 38-1431, 38-1469, 39-1488, 39-1642, 40-1526, 40-1724
COTTMAN [Cotmon, Cottomon]

    BENJAMIN [Bingaman] 33-1543, 34-1595, 35-1635, 36-21, 36-1589, 37-118, 37-1019, 38-149, 38-1828, 39-7, 39-1900, 40-7, 40-1866
    EBENEZER [Eblineser, Ebin] 30-1030, 31-868, 33-1059, 34-1088, 35-1014, 36-957, 37-859, 38-1243, 39-1012, 40-1131
    JOSEPH [Josept] 30-7, 30-1382, 31-1407, 33-7, 33-1544, 34-1, 34-1596, 35-86, 35-1634, 36-21, 36-1590, 37-118, 37-1002, 38-149, 38-1849, 39-7, 39-1803, 40-7, 40-1861
    LAZARUS [Laz.] 30-7
    MARY 30-7, 31-16, 33-7, 34-1, 35-86, 36-21, 37-118, 38-149, 39-7, 40-7
    NATHANIEL 33-1059, 35-1014, 36-958, 39-1012
    WILLIAM 30-1383, 31-1408, 33-1574, 34-1594, 35-1636, 36-957, 36-1588, 37-859, 37-1020, 38-1243, 38-1827, 39-1012, 39-1802, 40-1862,
COULBOURN [Colborn, Colebourn, Colrn., Coulbourn(e), Coulbroun]
    ANN 30-40, 31-37, 33-51
    JOHN 30-1076, 31-1232, 33-1310, 34-1332, 35-1483, 36-1462, 38-1487, 39-1424, 40-1490
    MICHAEL 30-39, 33-50, 34-133, 35-1, 36-88
    SAMUEL 30-39, 31-51, 33-50, 34-133, 35-1, 36-88, 37-87, 37-1162, 38-42, 39-43, 40-166
    SOLOMON [junr., senr.] 30-39, 30-41, 30-41, 31-51, 31-52, 33-50, 33-52, 33-52, 34-84, 34-84, 34-133, 35-1, 35-2, 35-2, 36-87, 36-87, 36-88, 37-59, 37-59, 38-40, 38-40, 38-42, 39-44, 39-46, 39-46, 40-45, 40-47, 40-47
    WILLIAM [junr., senr.] 30- 39(2), 30-1076, 31-51(2), 33-50(2), 33-1310, 34-133(2), 34-665, 34-1332, 35-1(2), 35-1483, 36-88, 36-89, 36-1462, 37-87, 37-88, 38- 41, 38-42, 38-1487, 39- 44, 39- 45, 40- 45, 40- 46
COUSERLY, PATRICK 30-1258
COUSINS, THOMAS [Cussens] 34-587, 35-624, 36-638
COVINGTON [Coventoun, Covinton(e)]
    CAPTAIN 31-807
    ABRAHAM 30-783, 31-813
    BENJAMIN [Bingimin] 30-772, 31-333, 33-1510, 34-1466, 35-1773, 39-1935
    ELEANOR 39-972, 40-1010
    JOHN 30-779, 31-807, 33-844, 34-831, 35-876, 36-870, 37-795, 37-1230, 38-921, 38-1755, 39-1682,

INDEX

40-1773
  NEHEMIAH 31-764
  PHILLIP 30-779
  THOMAS 30-784, 30-1290, 31-814, 31-1394, 33-852, 33-1510, 34-823, 34-1466, 35-884, 35-1650, 36-872, 36-1685, 37-776, 37-1230, 38-926, 38-1755, 39-978, 39-1682, 40-1009, 40-1773
  WILLIAM 40-1124
COWARD, MARY 30-43
COWEN [Condan], ALEXANDER 38-788, 39-744, 40-751
COX [Cocks]
  DANIEL 40-1782
  HILL 31-1330, 33-1472, 34-1475, 35-1725, 36-1760, 37-1157, 38-1716, 39-1706, 40-1781
  JAMES 39-870, 40-889
  JOHN 38-1846, 39-1197, 40-1118
  THOMAS [junr., senr.] 30-1315, 31-1329, 33-1447, 34-1467, 35-1752(2), 36-1714(2), 37-1158(2), 38-1876(2), 39-729, 39-1705, 39-1707, 40-783, 40-1780, 40-1782
  WILLIAM 30-1097, 31-1094, 33-1228, 34-1428, 35-1440, 36-1281, 38-1418, 39-1627, 40-1705
CRAGIN [Cragen, Cragen, Craggan, Creagin, Grage, Grigin, Treagin]
  HUGH 34-1379
  PAUL 30-29, 31-35, 33-39, 34-36, 35-1727, 36-1762, 37-1154, 38-1731, 39-1687, 40-1899
  WILLIAM 36-662
CRAIGE [Creagh]
  CORNELIUS 34-1475
  WILLIAM 34-1475
CRAPPER
  EBENEZER [Ebenezar, Ebeynezar, Ebynezar/junr., senr.] 30-328(2), 31-340(2), 33-408, 33-409, 34-381, 34-382, 35-482, 35-483, 36-389, 36-390, 37-475, 37-476, 38-544, 38-545, 39-617, 39-618, 40-499, 40-501
  EDMUND [Edmand/jr., sr.] 30-264, 30-266, 31-133, 31-135, 33-160, 33-315, 34-174, 34-188, 35-197, 35-336, 36-285, 36-313, 37-228, 37-367, 38-376, 38-381, 38-544, 39-179, 39-261, 39-617, 40-172, 40-190, 40-499
  JOHN 30-458, 31-414, 34-384, 35-484, 36-391, 37-391, 38-364, 38-643, 39-216, 39-628, 40-498
  NATHANIEL [Netth./junr., senr.] 30-266(2), 31-135, 31-148, 33-143, 33-149, 34-166, 34-235, 35-300, 35-323, 36-282, 36-293, 37-229, 37-360, 38-362, 38-364, 39-216, 39-223, 40-171, 40-178

  NEHEMIAH [Nemiah] 30-450, 31-408, 33-464, 34-551, 35-579, 36-506, 37-447, 38-444, 39-638, 40-504, 31-408
  SOLOMON 30-266, 31-135, 33-143, 34-348, 35-328,
  VINCENT [Vencint, Vimson, Vincet] 31-148, 35-323, 36-293, 37-360, 38-364, 39-216, 40-171
  WRIXAM [Rixam, Wrixham] 30-451, 31-415, 33-410, 34-383, 35-485, 36-526, 37-448, 38-449, 39-637, 40-552
CRAWFORD [Crafford, Crauford, Crofford, Crowson]
  ANDREW 30-661, 31-754, 33-694, 34-739, 35-776, 36-826, 37-668
  JOHN 30-661, 30-1294, 31-1406, 33-694, 33-1557, 34-739, 34-1558, 35-776, 36-826, 37-668
  RICHARD 37-667
CRAY, WILLIAM 35-1729
CRAYCRAFT, GEORGE 39-1353, 40-1090
CRISINES, RICHARD 38-464
CROCKETT [Crocked, Crockitt, Croket, Crouckitt]
  JOHN 30-1451, 31-1317, 33-1394, 34-1619, 35-1605, 36-1527, 37-1176, 38-1869, 39-1828, 40-1840
  JOSEPH [Josept] 38-99, 39-138, 40-147
  RICHARD 33-1397, 35-1613, 31-1318, 36-1529, 40-1347, 30-1450, 37-1175, 34-1618
  ROBERT 30-1452, 31-1322, 33-1395, 34-1620, 35-1612, 36-1526, 37-1177, 38-1870, 39-1809, 40-1834
CROMWELL, THOMAS 35-983
CROUCH [Crouches, Croutch, Crouth, Crutch]
  ANN [Anne/widow] 31-1444, 34-1696, 35-1006, 37-1164
  DAVID 36-880, 37-797, 38-920, 39-968, 40-1013,
  ISAAC 30-1343, 31-1522, 33-1509, 34-1485, 35-1570, 36-1495, 37-1166, 38-1527, 39-1437, 40-1545
  JACOB [junr., senr.] 30-1262, 30-1402, 31-1366, 31-1521, 33-1507, 33-1508, 34-1696, 34-1663(2), 35-1568, 35-1758(2), 36-1553, 36-1582, 37-1037(2), 38-983, 39-1925, 40-1742, 40-1743
  JOHN [jur.] 30-1351, 31-1443, 33-1513, 34-1524, 35-1558, 36-1679, 37-1082, 38-1787, 39-1666, 39-1881, 40-1890, 40-1951
  NICHOLAS 31-1444, 33-1513, 34-1524, 35-1558, 36-1679, 37-1164, 39-1438, 40-1546
  ROBERT 30-1262, 31-1511, 31-1521, 33-1508, 34-1485, 35-1758, 35-1759,

INDEX

36-1553, 37-1074, 38-1835, 39-1930, 40-1748
   THOMAS 34-883, 35-867, 36-880, 37-1037, 38-919, 39-969,
CROWDER [Crouder], FRANCIS [Frans.] 30-617, 31-650, 33-617, 34-677, 35-748, 36-742, 38-803, 39-683, 40-832
CROWLEY [Crowly], TIMOTHY 34-711
CUDOGIN [Cordugon], DENNIS 33-1245, 34-1305
CULBERSON [Calverson, Colburson, Culverson], WILLIAM 30-766, 33-629, 34-624, 35-1336, 36-653, 38-713, 39-747, 40-740
CULENAN, JOHN 35-1314
CULLEN
  EDMUND 30-15, 31-10, 33-11, 34-61, 35-632
  HENRY 30-66, 31-73, 33-83, 34-121, 35-54, 36-54, 37-93, 38- 5, 39-81, 40-90
   ISAAC 34-61, 35-632, 37-113, 38-141, 39-807, 40-784
   JACOB 30-64, 31-76, 33-78, 34-81, 35- 8, 36-61, 37-29, 38-11, 39-79, 40-85
   NICHOLAS [Nichelos] 30-83, 31-91
CULLINGHAM, JOHN 40-1665
CULVER [Coluer, Coulvor], JOHN 30-838, 31-916, 33-1427, 34-1657, 35-1654, 36-933, 37-866, 38-1170, 39-1126, 40-1205
CUNNINGHAM [Cinegum, Cuningham, Cuningam, Cuningin, Cunungham, Kennigan, Kennigham, Kinigam, Kinigin, Kiniken, Kinnegen]
   ARTHUR 30-771, 31-541, 33-880, 34-1160, 35-361, 35-1205, 36-1013, 38-1350, 39-1267, 40-1418
   DANIEL 30-843, 31-974, 33-1039, 34-1116, 35-1092, 36-1221, 38-1182, 39-1089, 40-1240
   THOMAS 30-616, 31-630, 33-617, 34-689, 35-731, 36-654, 38-805, 39-680, 40-824
CURIOUS [Curreyos, Curyor], CALEB 39-1541, 40-1625
CURREY [Correy], PHILLIP 30-888, 31-1002, 33-1041
CURTIS [Curtice]
  ABLE 40-1192
  CHARLES 30-14, 31- 8, 33-17, 34-105, 35-76, 36-8, 37-153, 38-157, 39-16, 40-16
CURVINE [Carvine, Corbine], THOMAS 30-1248, 31-1190, 33-1171, 34-1411, 35-1300, 36-1368, 38-1394, 39-1556, 40-1631
CUSHADAY [Cashedie, Cusadey], OWEN 30-370, 33-370, 34-428
CUSHINEY [Cushney, Cusshene], JOHN 30-1440, 31-1495, 33-1586

CUSTIS, LEVIN 33-1589
CUTLASS [Cutless], JOHN 36-393

DAILY [Daley, Dayly], JOHN 30-1068, 31-1222, 33-1302, 34-1216, 36-1417, 37-691, 38-693, 39-779, 40-792,
DALE, JOHN 39-1704
DANIELSON, JANE [Jean/widow] 30-1031, 31-1074, 33-1057
DANTON [Denton, DONTON, Dunton]
  JONAS 33-1093, 34-1131, 35-1236, 36-1173
  WILLIAM 33-1097, 34-1135, 35-1236, 36-1173
DARBY [Darbey]
  DANIEL 30-970, 31-991, 33-1052, 34-1117
  JOHN 30-918, 31-905
  WALLER [Waller] 31-939, 30-1046, 33-1049, 34-1014, 35-1122, 36-974, 38-1085, 39-1079, 40-1200
DARLEN, JOHN 40-858
DASHIELL [Dalsheill, Dashiels, Dashiles, Deshiel(d)s, Dischall, Dishal, Dishield]
  DOCTOR 35-1520
  ARTHUR 36-1568, 37-1248, 38-1811, 39-1905, 40-1765
  BENJAMIN 30-841, 31-965
  BRIDGET [Bridgit] 36-1051, 38-1012, 39-1069, 40-1069
  CHARLES 34-1626, 35-1606, 36-1524, 37-1186, 38-1631, 39-1831, 40-1831
  CLEMENT 40-1890
  GEORGE [junr., senr/capt., major, coll.] 30-841, 30-1424, 30-1460, 31-965, 31-1415, 31-1507, 33-927, 33-1400, 33-1542, 34-1623, 35-1520, 35-1603, 36-1518, 36-1531, 37-1170, 37-1192, 38-1031, 38-1627, 39-1025, 39-1666, 40-1051, 40-1890
  HENRY 30-822, 31-859, 33-1042, 34-914, 35-958, 36-962, 38-1045, 39-1042, 40-1068
  JAMES [junr.] 30-556, 30-826, 31-857, 33-971, 33-1406, 34-920, 34-1640, 35-964, 35-964, 36-1051, 39-1069, 40-1069
  JESSE [Jessy] 39-1069, 38-1012, 40-1073
  JOSEPH 30-840, 31-945, 33-926, 34-943, 35-983, 36-1064, 37-841, 38-994, 39-1202, 40-1091
  LEVIN [Lewin] 30-778, 31-764, 33-826, 34-841, 35-896, 36-878, 37-782, 38-1006, 39-1040, 40-1074
  MAJOR [Magor] 34-1566
  MARY 40-752
  MATHIAS 31-1419, 33-1589, 35-1707, 37-1180, 38-1697, 39-1847, 40-1823
  MATTHEW 30-1259, 36-1536
  MITCHELL [Michell] 30-888,

INDEX

31-1002, 33-1041, 34-985, 35-1021, 37-978, 38-994, 38-1244, 39-1202
  N. [esqr.] 39-1260, 40-1091, 40-1130
  PRISCILLA [Precila, Priscela] 36-1258, 37-842, 39-1102, 38-1040, 40-1094
  ROBERT 30-841, 31-965, 33-927, 34-944, 35-984, 36-1257, 37-843, 38-1039, 39-1101, 40-1092
  THOMAS [junr., senr.] 30-778, 30-1396, 31-764, 31-1399, 33-826, 33-1599, 34-841, 34-1612, 35-896, 35-1620, 36-878, 36-1604, 37-782, 37-1001, 38-922, 38-1862, 39-965, 39-1821, 40-1027, 40-1850
  WILLIAM [jur., senr.] 30-833, 31-921, 33-931, 33-1401, 34-930, 34-1639, 35-970, 35-1755, 36-1052, 36-1538, 38-1003, 38-1008, 39-1066, 39-1067, 40-1076, 40-1078

DAUGHERTY [Daugh(e)t(e)y, Daughters, Dauhity, Dohety, Dohotey, Dorothy, Dorriety, Doughe(r)ty, Doughters, Doxtey]
  EDMUND [Edmond] 39-1491, 40-1508
  JAMES 30-814, 33-1127, 34-13, 34-966, 35-70, 35-1167, 36-108, 37-149, 38-133, 38-1705, 39-1497, 39-1365, 39-745, 40-1896
  JOHN 30-46, 31-39, 33-58, 34-125, 35-42, 36-81, 37-84, 38-34, 39-54, 40-58
  NATHANIEL 35-42, 36-81, 37-84, 38-34, 39-54, 40-58
    THOMAS 38-1143, 40-1437
    WILLIAM 33-866(2), 34-1178, 38-1143, 40-1437

DAVIDSON
  RACE [Rowes] 31-246
  WILLIAM 30-237, 31-246

DAVIS [Davies]
  MADAME [madom] 34-1365
  MAIDEN [maden] 33-1372
  ARTHUR [Auther/junr., senr.] 30-494, 31-570, 33-565, 33-590, 34-581, 34-585, 35-615, 36-631, 38-771, 39-786, 40-805
  BEAUCHAMP [Becham] 31-1257, 33-1263, 34-1380, 35-1417, 36-1327, 38-1446, 39-1660, 40-1739
  BENJAMIN [Benjamain] 33-523, 34-482, 35-445, 36-415, 37-557, 38-504, 39-439, 40-548
  CHARLES 30-693, 31-672, 33-726, 33-775, 34-756, 34-780, 35-792, 35-813, 36-770, 36-813, 37-675, 38-844, 39-864, 40-956
  DANIEL 30-1318, 31-1459, 33-1480, 34-1482, 35-1578, 36-1731, 37-1119, 38-1690, 39-1739, 40-1811
  EDWARD 30-331, 31-410, 33-465, 34-550, 35-580, 36-579, 37-446, 38-445, 39-650
  ELIZABETH 30-1134, 31-1173
  EVAN [Evin] 30-1173, 33-1182, 34-1263, 35-1301, 36-1367, 39-1545, 40-1620
  GEORGE 33-525, 34-483, 35-446, 36-419, 37-552, 38-456, 39-599, 40-605
  ISHMAEL [Eshmail] 30-307, 31-466, 33-523, 34-482, 35-445, 36-415, 37-557, 38-504, 39-597, 40-622, 40-624
  JAMES [Jeams] 30-44, 31-50, 33-56, 34-109, 35-47, 36-82, 37-55, 38-35, 39-49, 40-48
  JOHN [junr., senr.] 30-69, 30-593, 30-1157, 30-1319, 30-1323, 31-77, 31-615, 31-1175, 31-1258, 31-1388, 31-1457, 33-82, 33-543, 33-667, 33-1610, 34- 35, 34-579, 34-1481, 34-1483, 35-51, 35-626, 35-660, 35-1579, 35-1774, 36-52, 36-637, 36-757, 36-1732, 37-27, 37-1122, 38-1, 38-747, 38-770, 38-1513, 38-1689, 39-84, 39-597, 39-785, 39-814, 39-1428, 39-1742, 40-92, 40-624, 40-804, 40-1809
  JOSEPH 30-1201, 31-1172, 33-1375, 34-1355, 35-1367, 36-1509, 38-1552, 39-1472, 40-1565
  LAZARUS 31-318, 33-381, 34-756, 35-792, 36-770
  MATTHEW 40-624
  NATHANIEL [jr., senr.] 30-1207, 31-1175, 33-1347, 34-1362, 35-1362, 35-1362, 38-1533, 38-1533, 39-1479, 39-1479, 40-1533, 40-1533
  NEAL 33-1098, 34-1129
  PHILLIP 31-479, 33-525, 34-484, 35-446, 36-419, 37-552
  RICHARD 30- 2, 35-90, 36-5, 37-127, 38-155
  ROBERT [junr., senr.] 30-307, 30-466, 31-465, 31-466, 33-521, 33-523, 34-480, 34-482, 35-444, 35-445, 36-415(2), 36-437, 37-547, 37-557(2), 38-504(2), 38-651, 39-263, 39-597, 39-598, 40-603, 40-624(2)
  SAMUEL 30-1336, 31-479, 31-1469, 33-525, 33-1488, 34-483, 34-1491, 35-446, 35-1576, 36-418, 36-579, 36-1670, 37-446, 37-546, 37-1104, 38-446, 38-503, 38-1669, 39-594, 39-601, 39-651, 39-1754, 40-503, 40-606, 40-1928
  SARAH 33-82, 34- 35
  THEOPHILUS 31-352
  THOMAS 30-308, 30-1319, 31-466, 31-467, 31-1457, 33-522, 34-519, 35-460, 35-1578, 36-518, 36-582,

INDEX

36-1759, 37-551, 37-626, 37-1120,
38-397, 38-502, 38-1690, 39-569,
39-1739, 40-604, 40-1580, 40-1811
    TUDOR [Tudar] 30-1254, 31-1199,
33-1273, 37-464, 37-464
    WILLIAM [senr.] 30-307, 30-443,
30-1475, 31-346, 31-466, 31-479(2)
31-1509, 33-366, 33-443, 33-523,
33-525, 33-1555, 34-482, 34-483,
34-486, 34-526, 34-1553, 35-400,
35-411, 35-445, 35-446, 35-1535,
36-415, 36-418, 36-474, 36-1752,
37-490, 37-546, 37-557, 37-1063,
38-503, 38-504, 38-565, 38-652,
38-1812, 39-508, 39-594, 39-597,
39-599, 39-1917, 40-467, 40-606,
40-623, 40-624, 40-1752
DAWE [Daw], HENRY 38-1180, 40-1231
DAWSON [Dauson], JOHN 38-1120,
39-1043, 40-1114
DAY
    DANIEL 40-1825
    WILLIAM 33-188
DAZEY [Da(i)sey, Daizey, Das(i)ey,
Dasie]
    JOHN 30-344, 31-433, 33-486,
34-458, 35-522, 36-503, 37-418,
38-525, 39-636, 40-455
    THOMAS [jr, sr.] 30-132, 30-352,
31-198, 33-199, 34-157, 35-221,
36-301, 37-194, 38-290(2),
39-186(2), 40-232(2)
DEAL [Dal, Dalle]
    ARCHIBALD [Archable,
Archerbell/jr., sr.] 30-222, 31-260,
33-278, 34-317, 35-243, 36-219,
37-351, 38-242, 39-191, 40-323(2)
    JOHN [Dal, Dalle/junr., senr.,
sinor] 30-222, 30-225, 31-256,
31-257, 33-280, 33-281, 34-193,
34-196, 35-281, 35-282, 36-196,
36-218, 37-328, 37-329, 38-221,
38-223, 39-287, 39-289, 40-295,
40-326
    QUANTON 36-219, 37-351
DEAN [Daine, Deen]
    CHARLES 30-934, 31-912, 33-918,
34-1027, 35-1097, 36-1115, 37-976,
38-1086, 39-1163, 40-1230(2)
    JAMES 38-1086, 39-1163, 40-1230
    JOHN 30-831, 31-880, 33-968,
34-924, 35-956, 36-1053, 38-1047,
39-1068, 40-1075
    WILLIAM 37-976
DELAP [Defap, Delop], CHARLES
30-550, 31-616
DENNIS [Dones]
    DANIEL 30-1204, 31-452, 34-431,
35-1378, 36-417, 37-525, 38-581,
39-641, 40-677
    DONNOCK [Donick, Donuck/junr.]
30-454, 31-382, 33-451, 34-486,
35-448, 36-592, 37-526, 38-496,
39-592, 40-608
    JOHN [junr., senr, mr.] 30-1105,
30-1204, 31-1129, 31-1161, 33-1273,
33-1370, 34-1328, 34-1375, 35-1361,
35-1462, 36-1393, 36-1491, 38-1354,
38-1562, 39-1378, 39-1461,
40-1442(2), 40-1575
    LAZARUS 35-1361, 34-1328, 36-1491,
38-1562, 39-1461, 40-1575
    SOLOMON 30-1204, 31-452, 33-506,
34-430, 35-424, 36-416, 37-524,
38-580, 39-640, 40-676
    THEOPHILUS 30-1105
    VALENTINE [Volantine, Wollintine]
33-1370, 34-1328, 35-1361, 36-1491,
38-1561, 39-1462, 40-1574
    WHEATLY [Whetley] 31-1161,
33-1370, 34-1328, 35-425, 36-553,
37-628, 38-662, 39-642, 40-684,
40-1740
    WILLIAM [junr., senr] 30-319,
31-349, 33-399, 33-485, 34-371,
35-448, 35-473, 36-397, 36-421,
37-468, 37-630, 38-493, 38-550,
39-509, 39-583, 40-475, 40-612
DENNISON/DENSTON [Den(i)ston(e),
Diniston, Doniston]
    ROBERT 31-511, 33-613, 36-758, 38-
810, 39-759, 40-716
    ISAAC 38-1491, 39-1412, 40-1487
    JOHN [jnr., senr.] 30-1070,
31-1221, 33-1303, 34-1297(2),
35-1348(2), 36-1515(2), 38-1491(2),
39-1412(2), 40-1477
    ROBERT 34-692, 35-638
DENWOOD
    GEORGE 30-1372, 31-1516, 33-641,
34-613, 35-717, 36-689, 38-780,
39-712, 40-769
    THOMAS 31-541, 33-554, 34-711,
35-676, 36-738, 38-779, 39-713,
40-768
DEPRAY, JOHN 33-191, 34-152, 35-217,
36-190, 37-199, 38-287, 39-210,
40-254
DEPUTY, JAMES 31-909
DERICKSON [Derikson, Derrixon,
Direxson, Dirickson, Dirixson,
Dirkson]
    BENJAMIN [Benjamen] 30-148,
31-217, 33-232, 34-331, 35-278,
36-183, 37-286, 38-181, 39-309,
40-419
    JOSEPH 30-123, 31-206, 33-225,
34-327, 35-187, 37-187, 38-184,
39-310, 40-230
    WILLIAM 38-185, 39-213, 40-234
DEVERIX [Debvix, Devrox]
    CORNELIUS 34-434, 35-428, 36-452,
37-514, 38-583, 39-489, 40-583
    JOHN 31-417, 33-452, 33-1589,

INDEX

34-434, 34-1604, 35-428, 36-452, 36-1517, 37-514, 38-583, 39-489, 40-583, 40-1802
DIAL, JAMES 30-1340
DIAMOND [Daimond], RICHARD 33-646, 34-603
DICKERSON [Dickeson]
  CHARLES [junr., senr.] 30-1080, 30-1096, 31-1093, 31-1233, 33-1227, 33-1323, 34-1234, 34-1431, 35-1439, 35-1488, 36-1286, 36-1451, 38-1420, 38-1478, 39-1509, 39-1629, 40-1502, 40-1707
  CORNELIUS [Cornelis] 30-1081, 31-1132, 33-1322, 34-1238, 35-1492, 36-1448, 38-1472, 39-1510, 40-1504
  EDMUND [junr., senr.] 30-1078, 30-1079, 35-1489, 35-1491, 36-1449, 36-1450, 38-1476, 38-1477, 39-1511(2), 40-1503, 40-1504
  EDWARD [jur., senr.] 30-1096, 31-1233, 31-1093, 33-1318, 33-1341, 33-1317, 34-1233, 34-1232, 34-1431, 35-1261
  ELIZABETH 38-1612
  FRANCIS 33-1161, 34-1248, 35-1319, 36-1369, 38-1612, 39-1562, 40-1634
  ISAAC 30-1096, 31-1093, 33-1227, 34-1261, 35-1327, 36-1468, 38-1402, 39-1612, 40-1691
  JAMES 30-1230, 31-1306, 33-1161, 34-1248, 35-1319, 36-1369
  JOHN 30-1096, 31-1093, 33-1162, 34-1259, 35-1310, 36-1420, 38-1420, 39-1631, 40-1481
  NEHEMIAH 38-1612, 39-1561, 40-1634
  PETER [jur., senr.] 30-1096, 31-1293, 31-1093, 33-1227, 33-1162, 34-1259, 35-1310, 36-1376, 38-1615, 39-1553
  ROBERT 30-1230, 31-1306, 33-1161, 34-1248, 35-1319, 36-1369, 38-1612, 39-1561, 40-1637
  TEAGUE 33-1162, 34-1399, 35-1441, 36-1287, 38-1416, 39-1630
DICKINSON, JAMES 33-76
DIETON, [Diton], ISAAC 30-1194, 31-1158
DIKES [Dakes, Dicks, Dykes]
  DANIEL 36-837, 38-1440, 39-1651, 40-19
  EDWARD 30-73, 31-85, 33-91, 34-762, 35-122, 36-837, 38-1440, 39-1651, 40-1729
  JOHN 30-28, 30-80
DILCHER, JOHN PARSONS 31-1405
DISHAROON [Deshroon, Dish(a)roon(e), Disherone, Disherune, Dishrone]
  WIDOW 33-1518, 34-1526
  ANN 30-1435, 31-1445, 38-1786
  JOHN [junr., senr.] 30-1349(2), 30-1313, 31-1463(2), 31-1333, 33-1446, 33-1504, 33-1505, 34-1510, 34-1511, 34-1530, 35-1724, 35-1766, 35-1762, 36-1612, 36-1655, 36-1719, 37-1094, 37-1146, 37-1088, 38-1802, 38-1873, 38-1711, 39-1708, 39-1770, 39-1772, 40-1946, 40-1896, 40-1943
  LEVIN 30-1327, 31-1332, 33-1448, 34-1513, 35-1726, 36-1720, 37-1147, 38-1709, 39-1709, 40-1784
  LEWIS 30-1327, 31-1332, 33-1445, 34-1512, 35-1725, 36-1721, 37-1145, 38-1714, 39-1704, 40-1785
  MICHAEL [Mic(k)(a)ell/junr., senr.] 30-1350, 30-1435, 31-1445, 31-1499, 33-1506, 33-1518, 34-1514, 34-1526, 35-1546, 35-1550, 36-1611, 36-1654, 37-1080, 37-1093, 38-1786, 38-1872, 39-1771, 39-1938, 40-1955, 40-1958
  WILLIAM 30-1349, 31-1463, 33-1504, 34-1530, 35-1742, 36-1613, 37-1095, 38-1874, 39-1773, 40-1947
DIXON [Dickason, Dickeson, Dickson, Dikeson, Dikieson, Dixson]
  AMBROSE [Ambros, Ambross] 36-98, 37-141, 38-121, 39-28, 40-31
  CHARLES 31-220, 33-231
  HANNAH 30-150, 31-220, 33-231
  JAMES 34-74, 35-10, 36-147, 37-36, 38-105
  JOHN 31-196, 33-211
  JOYCE [widow] 38-255, 40-263
  STURGIS [Sturges, Stirges] 30-138, 31-194, 33-210, 34-310, 35-246, 36-266, 37-284
  TEAGUE 40-1038
  THOMAS [junr., Senr] 30-31, 31-40, 33-40, 34-16, 35-65(2), 36-99(2), 37-143(2), 38-122(2), 39-27(2), 40-30(2)
  WILLIAM [jr.] 30-35, 30-1436, 31-42, 33-42, 34-17, 34-1492, 35-63, 36-98, 37-141, 38-121, 39-28, 39-1339, 40-32(2), 40-1324
DOANESH, JARVIS [Juvns] 31-1028
DOBBIN [Dubbing], WILLIAM 35-363, 36-1498, 38-678, 39-671, 40-791
DOBBITY [Dobidee], JAMES 36-1518, 38-1057
DOCKEDAY, JAMES 30-106
DODRELL [Daudrell, Dodrall, Dodreal, Dodri(e)ll], JAMES 33-884, 34-1030, 35-1094, 36-1117, 39-1139, 40-1221
DOLBY [Dalby, Dollbey]
  JOHN 38-1132, 39-1264
  PETER 30-964, 31-1029, 33-912, 34-1142, 35-1198, 36-1179, 38-1132, 39-1264, 40-1393
  WILLIAM 36-346, 37-188, 38-391, 39-306, 40-258
DOLKIN, WILLIAM 34-132, 35-72, 36-15

INDEX

DONAS, ROBERT 31-1004
DONE, [illegible] 37-824(2)
DONELSON
  CAPTAIN 31-318
  CATHERINE 36-387
  JOHN [capt.] 30-349, 33-381, 34-416, 35-500
DONNOCK [Dunnock], WILLIAM 37-29, 38-12, 39-78, 40-86
DONOHO [Dennaho, Dineho, Donehow, Donohoe, Don(o)how, Dunehow]
  DANIEL 31-1230, 33-1319, 34-1444, 35-1490, 36-1443, 38-1471, 39-1512, 40-1505
  DORMAN [Dormond] 30-1085, 31-1234, 33-1320, 34-1235, 35-1480, 36-1446, 38-1471, 38-1475, 39-1504, 39-1507, 40-1499, 40-1505
  JOHN 38-1471, 39-1512, 40-1505
  NATHANIEL 30-1053, 33-853, 34-1191, 35-1213, 36-1244
  SARAH 38-1471, 39-1512, 40-1505
  TEAGUE 30-1072, 31-1230(2), 33-1319(2), 34-1444(2), 35-1490(2), 36-1443(2), 38-1471, 39-1512, 40-1505
  WILLIAM 30-157
DORMAN [Dormant, Dormon(d)]
  EZEKIEL 37-774
  FRANCES [widw.] 40-801
  FRANCIS 40-1689
  HENRY [junr.] 30-786, 31-560, 31-820, 33-837, 33-850, 34-835, 34-1681, 35-870, 35-1583, 35-1583, 36-864, 36-1708, 37-788, 37-1127, 38-982, 38-1677, 39-986, 39-1733, 40-996, 40-1921
  HEZEKIAH [Ezekiah, Zedekiah] 34-820, 35-885, 38-927, 39-975, 40-1029
  ISAIAH 36-876
  JOHN 30-787, 31-819, 33-851, 34-821, 35-886, 37-772, 38-927, 39-975, 40-1029
  MAJOR [Mager, Maior] 34-1681, 36-1708, 37-1128, 38-1678, 39-1732, 40-1920
  MARGARET [Margret] 35-753, 37-791, 38-981, 39-707, 40-773
  MATTHEW [junr., senr.] 30-542, 30-575, 31-532, 31-542, 33-583, 34-622, 35-664, 36-730, 38-676, 39-677
  MICHAEL [Michall] 30-543, 31-526, 33-584, 34-713, 35-700, 36-731, 38-675, 39-675, 40-799
  NEHEMIAH 35-664, 36-730, 38-676, 39-677, 40-801
  SAMUEL [junr., senr] 30-1107, 31-1128, 33-1196, 34-1322, 35-1251, 36-1388(2), 38-1370(2), 39-1581(2), 40-1661(2)
  WILLIAM 33-557, 33-583, 34-622, 35-610, 35-664, 36-730, 38-677, 39-676, 40-800
  WILSON 36-623, 38-752, 39-802, 40-823
DOUGLAS [Duglas, Dugless, Duglis]
  JOHN 33-792, 35-917, 36-903, 37-748, 38-964, 40-977
  VALENTINE [Volin tine] 31-510
DOWARD, ADAM 34-317
DOWDLE, [Doudell, Doudle, Dowdell], CHRISTOPHER 30-1364, 31-1497, 33-1523, 34-1521, 35-1647, 36-1616, 37-1041, 38-1815, 39-1893, 40-1873
DOWNES [Downs]
  GEORGE 30-772, 31-765, 33-825 34-843, 35-897, 36-882, 37-771
  MARGARET 40-1026
  ROBERT 30-772, 30-1015, 31-333, 33-982, 33-1384, 34-1105, 34-1347, 35-889, 35-1043, 36-883, 36-1160, 37-771, 37-908, 38-931, 38-1294, 39-959, 39-1323, 40-1026, 40-1306
DOYLE, JOHN [Doyl] 40-1785
DRAPER [Dreper]
  MR. 33-1094, 34-1134
  ALEXANDER 30-966, 31-1045
  WILLIAM 30-966, 31-1045, 33-1094, 35-1225, 36-1012
DREADEN [Drading, Dreadon, Dreden, Dreding, Dredon, Dreyden]
  DANIEL 34-1321
  DAVID [junr, senr.] 30-1094, 30-1152(2), 31-1252(2), 33-1198, 33-1271, 34-1313, 35-1258, 35-1418, 36-1279, 36-1280, 38-1374, 38-1382, 39-1590, 39-1596, 40-1663, 40-1672
  HANNAH [wid.] 30-452, 31-428
  JOHN [junr.] 30-452, 30-662, 31-428, 31-715, 33-446, 33-696, 34-400, 34-809, 35-414, 35-842, 36-483, 36-852, 37-523, 37-695, 38-572, 38-916, 39-493, 39-914, 40-587, 40-874
  ROBERT 30-453, 35-415, 36-484
  SAMUEL 38-575, 39-493, 40-566
  WILLIAM 30-1152, 31-1252, 33-1271, 34-1313, 35-1418, 36-1279, 38-1382, 39-1596, 40-1672
DREGGS [Dreigs], JOSEPHAS 40-1262
DRIFEN [Dufen], GEORGE 36-340, 37-237
DRIGUS [Driges, Drigguss, Drikens, Drogroes]
  DIBREX 30-234, 31-243, 33-307
  JOHN 34-441, 35-435, 36-512, 38-611, 39-482, 40-573
DRISKILL, WILLIAM , 36-1668, 37-1105, 38-1671, 39-1870, 40-1924
DRUMMOND [Drumd.]
  DRAKE 39-915
  FRANCIS 39-1610
DUBBERLY [Douberly]

INDEX

THOMAS 30-712, 31-733, 33-722, 34-775, 35-809, 36-808, 37-681, 38-833, 39-857, 40-909
   WILLIAM 38-833
DUCKS, THOMAS 35-400
DUER [Dicer, Ducar(e), Dur(e)],
WILLIAM 31-743, 33-764, 34-736, 35-773, 36-797, 37-737, 38-871, 39-821, 40-941
DUETT [Dueit, Judett, Juitt]
   NATHANIEL 30-278, 31-141, 33-148, 34-191, 35-324, 36-270, 37-400, 38-512
   WILLIAM 30-279, 31-146, 33-337, 34-197
DUFFEN [Desen], GEORGE 30-1186, 31-1157, 33-710, 34-812, 35-845
DUFFY [Dufey] JAMES 33-1274, 34-1307, 35-1466
DUGHING [Dughig, Duhig], WALTER 31-812, 33-841, 34-832, 35-878, 36-871, 38-926
DUKES [Dicks, Duck(e)s, Duks]
   JOHN 31-61, 33-93, 35-54, 36-1276, 38-1492, 39-1500, 40-1352
   ROBERT 30-53, 33-64, 33-1319, 34-129, 34-1444, 35-102, 35-1490, 36-1276, 36-1443, 37-81, 38-29, 38-1533, 39-60, 39-1418, 40-66, 40-1486
   THOMAS 31-357, 33-369, 34-529, 36-474, 37-484, 38-447, 40-683
   WILLIAM 30-1130, 31-1126, 33-1199, 34-1236, 35-1349, 36-1465, 38-1492, 39-1415, 40-1483
DULANEY [Dalany, Delaley, Delamati, Delanie, Deleney]
   DENNIS 38-1867, 39-1826, 40-1841
   JOHN PATRICK [Jon. Partrick] 31-299, 33-312, 35-319, 36-281, 37-226, 38-349, 39-278, 40-264
   PATRICK 34-186
   WILLIAM 30-1448, 31-1314, 33-1567, 34-1659, 36-1625
DUNCAN [Dunken, Dunkin]
   JAMES 30-871, 31-1081, 33-1135, 34-975, 35-1155, 37-981, 39-1046, 40-1117
   THOMAS 30-962, 33-419, 34-465, 35-529, 36-408, 37-566, 38-419, 39-533, 40-665
DUNK, JOHN 40-422
DUNN
   ELIZABETH 30-800
   NICHOLAS 36-1208, 38-1032, 39-1022
   RICHARD [Ritcard] 30-809, 31-831, 33-1099, 34-902, 35-942, 36-1208, 38-1032, 39-1022, 40-1046
   THOMAS 38-1032, 39-1022, 40-1046
DURGAN [Birgin], DANIEL 31-635
DURHAM [Dorham, Durram, Durrum, Dutham]

   JAMES [junr., senr.] 31-1422(2), 33-1601, 34-1608, 35-1616, 36-1602, 37-1005, 38-1859, 39-1818
   THOMAS 30-788, 31-817, 33-842, 34-824, 35-883, 36-875, 37-775, 38-928, 39-979, 40-1004
DURY, DANIEL 39-1842
DUSKEY [Driskell, Duskell, Duskie]
   DENNIS 30-1340, 31-1470, 33-1611, 34-1499, 35-1563, 36-1676, 37-1107, 38-1668, 39-1760
   MOSES 30-1334, 31-1438, 33-1487, 34-1490, 35-1564, 36-1668, 37-1105, 38-1671, 39-1752, 40-1923
   RICHARD 30-1338
DUSTON [Desten], JAMES 40-1254
DYER [Dear, Dius?, Diar, Dier(e), Diers]
   JOHN 33-1383, 34-1284, 36-1501, 38-1525, 39-1444
   ROBERT 33-568, 34-610
DYES [Dias, Dies, Dius, Dize]
   DANIEL 30-1098, 31-71, 33-73, 34-81, 35-8, 36-68, 40-89
   PHILBY [Filby, Silby] 30-48, 31-54, 33-55, 34-116, 37-77, 38-56, 39-50, 40-165
   ROBERT 30-84, 30-1098, 31-71, 33-73, 34-80, 35-710, 36-1399

EASOM [Esam, Eashom]
   BENJAMIN 40-1347
   JOHN 38-306, 39-212, 39-1485, 40-353
EDDES [Deeds, Eades, Edde, Edge, Eydes]
   JAMES 36-325
   LAURANCE [Larance, Larince, Laram] 30-256, 31-301, 33-162, 34-559, 35-588, 36-564
EDGE [Ege]
   JOSHUA 30-945, 31-977, 33-973, 34-1038, 35-1247, 36-1219, 37-898, 38-1259, 39-1092, 40-1247
   ROBERT 36-1218, 37-899, 38-1258, 39-1091, 40-1219
EDWARDS
   BENONY [Benjn., Bennoni] 30-373, 31-439, 33-348, 34-557, 35-392, 36-490, 37-586, 38-403, 39-529, 40-534
   JAMES 37-586, 38-403
   JOHN 31-643, 33-1388, 38-1035, 39-1150
ELGATE, WILLIAM 30-1288, 31-1386
ELLENSWORTH [Allensworth, Elling(s)worth, Elensworth]
   WIDOW [Elisab.] 34-1018, 35-1110, 39-1108, 38-1026
   NEHEMIAH 30-117, 33-1008, 34-1018, 35-1110, 38-1026, 39-1108, 40-1411
   RICHARD [Ritchard] 30-117, 30-117,

237

INDEX

31-125, 33-1008, 33-1008, 34-1018, 35-1110, 36-1122, 38-1191, 39-1317, 40-1419
  ROBERT 30-926, 33-1001, 34-1020, 35-1108, 36-1121, 37-892, 38-1075, 39-1257, 40-1169
  WILLIAM 38-1026, 39-1296
ELLIOTT, FRANCIS 34-1551, 35-1516
ELLIS [Elles, Ellice]
  MRS. 33-1591, 34-1603, 35-1627
  ALICE [Alce/Mrs.] 36-1596, 37-1010, 38-1856, 39-1812
  FRANCIS [Frank, Franses] 30-1431, 31-1500, 33-1556, 35-1553, 36-1651, 37-1077, 38-1776, 39-1774, 40-1957
  JAMES 39-1059
  JOHN 30-1099, 31-1095, 33-1229, 33-1515, 34-1405, 34-1580, 35-1442, 35-1562, 36-1296, 36-1650, 37-1078, 38-1414, 38-1776, 39-1625, 39-1880, 40-1704, 40-1950
  JOSEPH 31-1500, 34-1579, 35-1542, 36-1623, 37-1044, 38-1804, 39-1888, 40-1962
  MERRICK 30-1388, 31-1418
  THOMAS 30-1144
  WILLIAM 30-1219, 31-1305, 33-1149, 34-1293, 35-1282, 35-1547, 36-1335, 36-1650, 37-1078, 38-1589, 38-1776, 39-1530, 39-1774, 40-1608, 40-1783
ELZEY [El(e)s(e)y]
  CAPTAIN 34-667
  ARNOLD [Arnal] 30-630, 31-633, 31-633, 33-551, 34-572, 35-721, 36-740, 38-795, 39-690, 40-833, 40-835
  JOHN [juner, sener] 30-619, 30-619, 31-632, 31-632, 33-549, 33-549, 34-667, 35-672, 35-672, 36-739, 36-756, 38-794, 38-941, 39-691, 39-927, 40-833, 40-962
  SARAH [mrs.] 33-551, 34-572, 35-721, 36-740, 38-795, 39-690, 40-835
EMERSON, CHARLES 38-1627
ENGLISH [Einglish, Inglesh, Inglish]
  JAMES 39-1239, 40-1246
  ROBERT 31-960, 34-1067, 35-1037, 33-946
  THOMAS 30-300, 31-430, 33-448, 34-403, 35-420
  WILLIAM 30-926, 31-1061, 33-999, 34-1026, 35-1111, 37-980, 38-1070, 39-359, 40-1168
ENNIS [Inas, Ennes]
  CORNELIUS [Cornelious] 30-441, 31-458, 33-371, 34-531, 35-407, 37-486, 38-556, 39-478, 40-472
  JOHN 36-489, 37-621, 38-557, 39-475, 39-507, 40-470, 40-471
  MARY [widow] 30-441, 31-458, 33-371, 34-530, 35-406, 36-489, 37-489
  NATHANIEL 30-356, 31-345, 33-370, 34-528, 35-404, 36-407, 37-485, 38-637, 39-476, 40-469
  ROBERT [Robart] 30-762, 31-534
  SAMUEL 31-458, 33-371, 34-530, 35-406, 36-489, 37-489, 38-555, 39-477, 40-474
  WILLIAM [junr., senr.] 30-357, 31-344, 33-369, 34-529, 35-405, 36-405(2), 37-484(2), 38-558(2), 39-475(2), 40-470(2)
EV----, JOHN 39-648
EVANS [Eavans, Evains, E(i)(e)vens, Evines, Evin(s)]
  MRS. 34-1622
  ANN [widow] 33-1399
  CHARLES 35-503
  EBENEZER [Ebeynezar, Ebenezeah] 30-364, 31-310, 33-483, 34-425, 35-513, 36-212, 38-316, 39-327, 40-301
  EDWARD 30-364, 31-310
  ELIAS 30-202, 31-274, 33-388, 34-447, 36-386, 37-396, 38-521, 39-565, 40-553
  GAMMAGE [Gamadge] 1-366, 33-491, 34-452, 35-516, 36-548, 37-411, 38-506, 39-549, 40-549
  JOHN [jur., snr.] 30-114, 30-130, 30-131, 30-397, 30-1447, 30-1453, 30-114, 31-116, 31-176, 31-180, 31-309, 31-1313, 31-1325, 33-134, 33-155, 33-202, 33-483, 33-698, 33-1242, 33-1396(2), 34-144, 34-164, 34-297, 34-425, 34-752, 34-1625(2), 35-25, 35-236, 35-253, 35-512, 35-787, 35-1448, 35-1520, 35-1604(2), 36-148, 36-192, 36-310, 36-608, 36-845, 36-1303, 36-1518, 36-1525(2), 37-43, 37-233, 37-308, 37-409, 37-690, 37-1181(2), 37-1192, 38-106(2), 38-197, 38-205, 38-526, 38-868, 38-1410, 38-1630[2], 38-1811, 39-136(2), 39-165, 39-245, 39-883, 39-1618, 39-1830, 39-1901, 39-1905, 40-151(2), 40-239, 40-277, 40-447, 40-510, 40-979, 40-1698, 40-1828, 40-1829
  JOSHUA 34-1404, 40-235
  LAURENCE [Larance, Larraunce] 31-310, 33-483, 36-529, 37-231, 38-301, 39-414, 40-451
  LAZARUS 34-425
  MARY Mary 31-366
  POWELL 31-366, 33-477, 34-453, 35-517, 37-412, 39-550, 40-550
  RICHARD 38-103, 39-141, 40-150
  THOMAS 30-1100, 31-1098, 33-1231, 34-1403, 35-1447, 36-1304, 38-1409, 39-1617, 40-151, 40-1697
  WALTER 35-236, 36-192, 37-233,

INDEX

38-203, 39-244, 40-235
    WILLIAM [jr., sr] 30-130, 30-250, 30-1281, 31-180, 31-287, 31-1348, 31-1385, 33-155(2), 33-490, 33-951. 33-1463, 33-155, 34-291, 34-297(2), 34-1695, 35-236(2), 36-192(2), 36-275, 36-1747, 37-233(2), 37-409, 37-1213, 38-203(2), 38-526, 38-1409, 38-1513, 38-1769, 39-181, 39-244(2), 39-1617, 39-1916, 39-1924, 40-235(2), 40-431, 40-1697, 40-1894
EVE, GEORGE 33-1217
EVERTON
    JOHN 30-1454, 31-1324, 33-1387, 34-1632, 35-1611, 36-1520, 37-1188, 38-1660, 39-1837, 40-1836,
    WILLIAM 34-1632, 35-1611, 36-1520, 37-1188, 38-1660, 39-1837, 40-1836
EWART, JAMES 38-625
EWELL, JEDEDIAH [Bullen, Ewwl/Jedida] 38-787, 39-694, 40-842

FALL [Fault]
    ABRAHAM [Abram] 30-242, 31-298, 33-293, 34-282, 35-343, 36-278, 37-294, 38-320, 39-178, 40-339
    JOHN 31-295, 33-294, 34-283, 35-199, 36-277, 37-293, 39-176, 40-338
FARLOW [Farlo]
    JOHN 36-1754, 37-1118, 38-1692, 39-1936
    WILLIAM 39-1936
FARMER, WILLIAM 33-1372, 34-494
FARNALL, THOMAS 31-1423
FARRELL, WILLIAM 35-1682
FARRINGTON [Farentine, Farntine, Ferin(g)ton], WILLIAM 30-865, 31-955, 33-1035, 34-979, 35-1150, 36-1139, 37-804, 38-1262, 39-1099
FARWELL [Farrall, Fearwell, Fervell, Fervewl, Forwell], THOMAS 30-238, 31-296, 33-288, 35-333, 36-208, 37-290, 38-339, 39-322, 40-285
FASHE, CORNELIUS 36-741
FASSITT [Fassat]
    BENLES 34-175
    FRANKLIN [Franklyn, Frankline, Francling] 30-214, 31-268, 33-264, 34-300, 35-213, 36-344, 37-319, 38-195, 39-198, 40-343
    JOHN [Jon.] 30-270, 31-149, 33-161, 34-189, 35-317, 37-368, 38-374, 39-260, 40-170
    LAMBARD [Lambert, Lamburd] 33-141, 34-165, 35-316, 36-222, 37-311, 38-216, 39-222, 40-169
    MARY [mrs./wido] 36-295, 37-216, 38-164, 39-385, 40-183
    RACE [Rouce, Rous(e)] 31-131, 33-141, 34-165, 35-349, 36-225, 37-219, 38-375, 39-364, 40-173
    WILLIAM [capt./junr., sr./mr.] 30-213, 30-255, 30-256, 31-131, 31-301, 33-141, 33-162, 34-165, 34-175, 35-352, 36-235, 37-361, 38-161, 39-384, 40-184
FASTER [Folster] JOHN 35-1711, 37-1011, 38-1853, 39-1848
FEDDY [Feding, Ferding, Fidday, Fidd(e)y, Foedden]
    RANDALL [Randol 30-755, 31-802, 33-785, 35-923, 36-701, 38-723, 39-776, 40-768
    THOMAS 34-609, 35-709, 36-705, 38-729, 39-772
FENTON [Fanton]
    MARGARET [Margett/widow] 30-1118, 31-1254, 33-1269, 34-1379, 35-1419, 36-1271, 38-1388, 39-1597, 40-1677
    MARTIN [Marten] 30-104, 31-3, 33-22, 34-132, 35-72, 36-15
FERGUSON [Firguson, Forgerson], JOHN 30-619, 31-764
FILLS, GEORGE 39-1195
FINCH [Fintch], JOHN 31-531, 33-677, 34-698, 35-679, 36-664
FISHER
    BAILY [Baley] 30-656, 33-774, 34-1277, 38-897, 39-819, 40-923
    BARTHOLOMEW 33-638, 34-714
    BARTLETT [Bark(e)ly, Bartly, Bentnett] 30-560, 31-521, 35-701, 38-350
    BENTALL [Bentual, Bentill, Benton] 35-302, 36-284, 39-281, 40-196
    GEORGE 35-1221, 37-962, 38-1348, 39-1344, 40-1349
    HENRY 30-595, 31-596, 33-660, 34-641, 35-663, 36-663, 38-692, 39-730, 40-752
    SARAH 36-736
    THOMAS 34-347
FITZGERALD [Fargarrell, Fichgarll, Fisgarrard, Fitch Jarrill, Fittgarald, Fitzgarrell, Fitchjarril, Fritzgeralld]
    EDMUND 30-789, 31-815, 33-798, 34-846
    JOHN [Fittgarald] 31-1276
    PETER 30-558, 31-661, 33-683, 34-705, 35-718, 36-655, 38-784
FITZHUGH [Fetzhew, Fittue], JOHN 39-1583, 40-1664
FITZPATRICK [FetchPartrick], FRANCIS 40-367
FITZSIMMONS [Phidsimons], THOMAS 31-1340
FITZWATERS [Fishwater], HENRY 30-1209, 31-1179
FLEETWOOD [Fleatwood], JOHN 30-957, 31-1051, 33-1094, 34-1134, 35-1173, 36-1195, 38-1142, 40-1347
    THOMAS 30-175, 31-235, 33-183,

239

34-272, 35-1196, 36-1200
FLEMING [Flemen, Flemon]
  ISAAC 30-1084
  JOHN [junr., senr.] 30-1084,
31-1231, 33-1315, 34-1331,
35-1511, 36-1455, 38-1482,
39-1505(2), 40-1495(2)
  WILLIAM 30-525, 30-1084,
31-552, 31-1231, 33-1315,
34-1331, 35-1511, 36-1455,
38-1502, 39-1403, 40-1470
FLETCHER [Flehar], THOMAS
[revd./mr.] 30-421, 31-441,
33-438, 34-505, 35-554, 36-523,
37-590, 37-1245, 38-474, 39-1832,
39-609, 40-1846, 40-670
FLINT, JOHN 38-1763, 39-1670,
40-1767, 39-1670
FLOWITH, GEORGE 35-350
FLOYD [Flawed, Floid, Floyed]
  CATHERINE [Katron] 30-572
  JOHN 30-572, 31-596, 33-553,
34-715, 35-602, 36-672, 38-694
  MAJOR [Mager, Magi(o)r] 30-944,
31-976, 34-1080, 35-1247,
36-1220, 38-1184, 39-1165,
40-1235
FLUELLIN [Flualen, Fluallin,
Fluelling], SAMUEL 30-820,
31-873, 33-1139, 34-912, 35-954,
36-964, 38-1043, 39-1035, 40-1071
FLYNN [Flin], JOHN 37-86, 38-57,
39-50, 40-51
FOGG
  DANIEL 35- 30, 36-152, 37- 34,
38-111, 39-131, 40-156
  MOSES 34-1258, 35-1479,
36-1447, 38-1474, 39-1502,
40-1498
FOLK, JOHN 38-310
FOLLOWS, JOHN 33-835, 34-830,
36-727
FORBUSH [Furbish, Furbush], PETER
30-1396, 31-1399, 33-1612,
38-1658, 39-1838, 40-1837
FORD [Forge], ABSOLOM 30-514,
31-573, 33-593, 34-586, 35-616,
36-633, 38-767, 39-789, 40-806
FORDRED [Foddred] WILLIAM 31-589,
33-546, 34-576, 35-115, 38-60,
39-154, 40-144
FORSIGHT [Foresith, Forthsight]
  SARAH 37-215, 36-299
  THOMAS 30-217, 31-250, 33-147,
34-201, 35-304
FORTINEARE, WILLIAM 39-1341
FORTUNE [Fortin], JOHN 36-1435
FOSQUE [Faskey, Fasque, Fauscand,
Foskquy, Fosky]
  BENJAMIN 30-762, 33-824,
34-668, 35-746, 36-714, 38-792,
39-692, 40-836

  THOMAS 30-579, 31-624, 34-1562,
35-1692, 36-1566, 37-1057,
38-1834, 39-1820, 40-1848
FOSTER [Folster], JOHN 31-1312,
34-1623, 36-1597
FOUNTAIN [Fountin]
  MARCY [Massy/junr., sen.]
30-507, 30-631, 31-595, 34-606,
35-628, 36-626, 38-748, 39-809,
40-706, 40-707
  MICHAEL [junr.] 33-623
  NICHOLAS [ju., se.] 30-511,
31-590, 31-591, 33-545, 34-604,
34-650, 35-644, 35-671, 36-625,
36-1505, 38-749, 38-1520, 39-808,
39-1440, 40-706, 40-1548
  SAMUEL [Samewill] 30-631,
31-595
  THOMAS 30-631, 31-595, 33-558,
34-606, 35-628, 36-626
FOWLER [Farlor, Foler, Fouler]
  [illegible] 37-968
  ARTHUR 31-1035
  EDWARD 30-1392, 31-1420,
33-1603
  JOHN 30-527, 31-540, 31-1420,
35-703, 35-1649, 37-997, 39-1819,
40-1842
  THOMAS 30-1453, 31-1325,
33-1396, 34-1603, 35-1627,
36-1517, 37-1171, 38-1626,
38-1635, 39-1811, 40-1857
  URSULA 39-554
FRANKLIN, [Frankling, Franklyn]
  CHARLES 33-386
  EDWARD 30-359, 31-315, 33-386,
34-420, 35-508, 36-552, 37-401,
38-518, 39-557, 40-511
  WILLIAM 31-315, 33-1150,
34-420, 35-508, 37-402, 38-519,
39-558, 40-648
FRAZIER [Frasher, Frayzer,
Frazer]
  HUGH 33-1548, 38-1880
  PETER 30-42, 31-49, 33-53,
34-107, 35-44, 36-86, 37-57,
38-37
FREEMAN
  SARAH [widow] 39-316
  WILLIAM [jr., sr.] 30-153,
31-215, 31-215, 37-272, 37-272,
38-181, 39-309, 40-230
FREENY
  JOHN [Franey, Freaney, Freiny]
35-1731, 36-1744, 37-1236, 38-
1734, 39-1691, 40-1912
  PETER 30-1300, 33-1467,
34-1458, 35-1731, 36-1744,
37-1236, 38-1734, 39-1691,
40-1912
FRENCH, JOHN 37-381

INDEX

FRIGGS [Freaks]
   ROBERT 30-988, 31-982, 35-1224, 36-1146, 39-1364, 40-1132
   WILLIAM 35-1086
FUCHS [Fook(e)s, Foox, Fuckes]
   BENJAMIN [junr., senr./Bengimin] 30-1341, 31-1473, 33-1500(2), 35-1566, 36-1675, 37-1108, 38-1656, 39-1763(2), 40-1942(2)
   WILLIAM 36-1675, 37-1108, 38-1656, 40-1942
   YOUNG 39-1916
FULLERTON [Follerton, Fulertone]
   ALEXANDER [Alix.] 30-1474, 31-1501, 33-1577, 34-1541, 35-1745, 36-1552, 37-1198, 38-1836, 39-1927, 40-1895
   JAMES 30-1474, 31-1501, 33-1577, 34-1541, 35-1746, 36-1751, 39-1926
FULTON [Felton]
   JOHN 38-1233, 39-1172, 40-1261
   NICHOLAS 38-1233, 39-1172, 40-1261
   WILLIAM 30-970, 31-954, 33-1016, 34-982, 35-1044, 36-1073, 37-860, 38-1158, 39-1125, 40-1166
FURLONG [Farlong], NICHOLAS [Nicklas] 39-166, 40-427
FURNACE [Furnes, Furnis(h)]
   ANN 33-570, 35-637
   JAMES 30-626, 31-553, 33-573, 34-652, 35-645, 36-721, 38-699, 39-751, 39-761, 40-708, 40-737
   WILLIAM 30-498, 31-653

GABB, JOHN 30-249, 31-286
GABE, JOSEPH [Gabe, Gabey] 33-358, 34-1345
GADDES, ROBERT [Gaddass, Gaddis, Gades, Gaddes, Goddis] 30-1178, 31-1200, 33-1274, 34-1255, 35-1498, 36-1396, 38-1357, 39-1381, 40-1444
GALE [Gales]
   BETTY [madam, Mrs.] 31-761, 33-829, 34-838, 35-892
   GEORGE [capt., maj., Mr.] 30-775, 31-760, 33-830, 34-840, 35-893, 36-877, 37-739, 38-917, 39-967, 40-1015
   JOHN [capt.] 30-1045, 31-975, 33-930, 34-946, 35-997, 36-1261, 37-846, 38-1038, 39-1008, 40-1098
   LEVIN [hon. collonell.] 30-1398, 31-1405, 33-1589, 34-1604, 35-1519, 36-1517, 37-992, 38-1626, 39-1665, 40-1863
   MATHIAS [Mathias, Matts., capt.] 30-774, 33-847, 34-839, 35-894, 35-1770, 36-1598, 37-1012, 38-1855, 39-1813, 40-1855
GAME [Gam]
   ANVILL [Annill] 38-1005, 39-1064, 40-1070
   BETTY [Bety] 30-1049, 31-878, 33-1142, 36-1050
   ELENDER 33-1141
   FORTUNE [Forten, Fortin] 30-1049, 31-878, 33-1142, 34-919, 35-963, 36-1050, 38-1005, 39-1064, 40-1070
   ROBERT [Robart, Robin] 30-819, 31-854, 33-1141, 34-911, 35-957, 36-965, 38-1037, 39-1153, 40-1093
   ROSE 33-1142
   SAMBO [Sambow] 30-819, 31-854, 33-1068
GAMEWELL [Gamueall], GEORGE 35-923, 36-917
GARDNER, [Gardener] THOMAS [Thos.] 30-68
GARINS, SAMUEL [Samuell] 31-845
GARNILL, THOMAS 30-1442
GASTINEW [Gaskenew, Gastin(e)au, Gastinue]
   GEORGE 38-1247, 39-1076
   MATTHEW [Mathew, Mathuw, Mathuren, Mathewice] 30-1382, 35-1120, 36-1108, 38-1112, 39-1249
GAULT [Gatt, Gautt]
   JOHN 30-246, 31-278, 33-297, 34-252, 35-196, 36-318, 37-339, 38-359, 39-405, 40-332
   OBEDIAH [Obed] 40-330
   ROBERT [Robard, Robart] 30-246, 31-278, 33-297, 34-252, 35-358, 36-318, 37-339, 38-359, 39-405, 40-330
   WILLIAM [Willm.] 30-246, 31-278, 33-297, 34-252, 35-341, 36-227, 37-340, 38-212, 39-404, 40-331
GEORGE, WILLIAM 30-950, 35-1237
GIBBS [Gibb, Gibs]
   CAPTAIN 31-1131
   ABRAHAM [Abram] 30-1172, 31-1131, 33-1328, 34-1442, 36-1398, 38-1451, 39-1495
   ALEXANDER [Alxr.] 31-906
   ROBERT [capt.] 30-1172, 39-1495, 40-1519
GIBSON, GEORGE 30-1388, 31-1418
GILES [Chiles]
   EDMUND [Edmond] 35-1549, 36-1657
   JOHN 36-930
   THOMAS 30-855, 31-901, 33-1128, 34-955, 35-987, 36-1099, 38-1059,

INDEX

39-1199
    WILLIAM [jr/sr] 30-855(2), 31-901(2), 33-1126(2), 34-954(2), 35-988(2), 36-1098(2), 38-1058(2), 39-1198(2)
GILL, JOHN 33-771, 34-793, 36-841, 37-728, 38-908
GILLEGIN, BRYAN 30-559, 31-551
GILLEMORE, WILLIAM 34-31
GILLESPIE [Gilaspie, Gellasibey, Gillisphie]
   HENRY 30-835
   TERRANCE [Galaspie, Gellasibey/Tarrance] 33-835, 35-722
GILLETT
   GEORGE 34-1298
GILLETT [Gelitt, Gillit]
   JOHN [jur.] 30-325, 30-1224, 31-507, 31-1303, 33-390, 33-1145, 34-532, 34-1294, 35-462, 35-1285, 36-398, 36-1338, 37-460, 38-549, 38-1595, 39-1532, 40-1604
   SAMUEL [jr.] 30-1229, 31-1302, 33-1144, 34-1295, 35-1274, 36-1337, 36-1337, 38-1594, 38-1594, 39-1531, 39-1531, 40-1605, 40-1606
   WILLIAM 30-1224, 34-1295, 35-1274, 36-1337, 38-1594, 39-1531, 40-1606
GILLILAND [Gillaland, Gilland, Gilleland]
   WIDOW 39-514
   JOHN 30-277, 31-144, 33-322, 34-366, 35-467, 36-424, 37-459, 38-534
GILLININ, HUGH [Gillinin, Gillman] 30-297, 31-403
GILLIS [Gille, Gillies, Gillise, Gilly]
   JOHN 30-905, 33-1024, 34-1003, 35-1129, 38-1110, 39-1247, 40-1188   JOSEPH 30-633, 31-644, 33-640, 34-669, 35-728, 36-752, 38-787, 39-694, 40-842
   LEVIN 38-1795, 39-1895, 40-1864
   THOMAS [mr.] 30-1372, 31-1516, 33-1024, 33-1407, 34-1003, 34-1547, 35-1129, 35-1522, 36-935, 36-1615, 37-993, 38-1110, 38-1795, 39-1247, 39-1895, 40-1106, 40-1189, 40-1864
   WILLIAM 40-1105(2)
GILMORE [Gillmor], HUGH 36-538
GILSTRAP, PETER 31-199, 33-166, 34-287, 35-165, 36-163, 37-280, 38-251, 40-347
GIVANS [Gibans, Gibens, Gibins, Given(d)(s), Givbens, Given(s), Govan(d)(s), Goven]
   WIDOW [Gebins] 34-595

   ALEXANDER [Elixndr.] 33-945, 37-894
   ANN [Anne] 35-606, 36-712, 38-719, 39-757, 40-714
   CATHERINE [Katherine] 35-605, 38-720, 39-755, 40-713
   GEORGE 37-802, 38-1249, 39-569, 40-640, 40-1325
   JAMES 30-1468, 31-1087, 33-1060, 34-981, 35-1146, 36-1141, 37-803, 38-1250, 39-1007, 40-1126
   JOHN [junr., senr.] 30-622, 30-623, 31-656, 31-657, 31-978, 33-671, 33-672, 33-974, 33-1061, 34-594, 34-986, 34-1065, 34-1181, 35-1086, 35-1144, 36-1224, 37-627, 37-894, 38-1190, 38-1251, 39-1038, 39-1167, 40-719, 40-1127, 40-1246
   ROBERT [junr., senr.] 30-860, 30-989, 31-841, 31-938, 33-1011, 33-1012, 34-980, 34-1122, 35-1148, 35-1179, 36-1080, 37-802, 38-1249, 39-1100, 40-1125
   THOMAS 30-622, 31-657, 33-671, 34-594, 35-606, 36-322, 36-711, 37-248, 38-261, 38-718, 39-756, 40-715
   WILLIAM 38-1080, 39-1011, 40-1129
GLASS
   CHRISTOPHER [Christofer/junr., senr.] 30-1185, 31-1170(2), 33-1371(2), 34-1353(2), 35-1382(2), 36-1444, 36-1466, 38-1558, 38-1559, 39-1450, 39-1463, 40-1569, 40-1573
   ELIAS [Elis] 33-1371, 34-1353, 35-1382, 36-1444, 38-1559, 39-1463, 40-1582
   JOHN 30-1185, 31-1170, 34-1383, 35-1365, 39-1269
GLOSTER [Glaster]
   ELIJAH 38-1041
   SAUL [Saull] 36-1114
   SOLOMON 34-1008, 35-1120
   THOMAS 31-872, 33-1021, 34-998, 35-1119, 36-1084, 38-1098, 39-1080, 40-1189
GODDARD [Gathert, Godart(e), Godert]
   GEORGE 30-1379, 31-1412, 33-1582, 34-1047, 35-1075, 36-1025, 38-1224, 39-1375, 40-1287
   JOHN 30-1002, 31-1020, 33-951, 34-1048, 35-1068, 36-953, 36-1033, 38-1129, 38-1189, 39-1014, 39-1241, 40-1134,

INDEX

40-1280
   NATHANIEL [Nethaneil] 38-1129, 39-1014, 40-1280
   THOMAS 30-1367, 31-284, 31-1504, 33-151, 33-1581, 34-177, 34-1540, 35-340, 35-1007, 36-294, 36-953, 37-359, 38-211, 38-1189(2), 39-396, 39-1241(2), 40-302, 40-1134

GODFREY [Godfery, Gorfree]
   CHARLES 30-384, 31-432, 33-450, 34-432, 35-426, 36-411, 37-519, 38-570, 39-491, 40-580
   JOSEPH 30-1197, 31-1171, 33-1373, 34-1354, 35-1368, 36-1510, 38-1556, 39-1459, 40-1572

GODWIN [Godwen, Godweing, Godwen, Godwing, Godwing]
   CEASAR Ceaser/junr., senr.] 30-133(2), 31-190(2), 33-198(2), 34-156(2), 35-219(2), 36-309, 36-311, 37-195, 37-196, 38-292, 38-293, 39-249, 39-254, 40-247, 40-271
   DANIEL 33-198, 34-156, 35-219, 36-311, 37-195, 38-369, 39-249, 40-257
   MICHAEL [capt] 30-136, 31-191, 33-207, 34-306, 35-248, 37-285, 38-296, 39-268, 40-371

GOFF, JOSEPH 34-135

GOGEN/GOGIN [Gahagun, Gangun, Goging]
   DAVID 31-1281, 33-1191, 34-1274, 35-1293
   EDWARD 30-329, 31-418, 33-406

GOLDEN, JOHN 31-1501

GOLDSBOROUGH [Gouldberek], WILLIAM 34-942, 35-1039, 36-1138

GOLDSMITH [Gooldsmith]
   ANTHONY 30-1348, 31-1524, 34-1532, 35-1598, 37-1161, 39-1768, 40-1945
   CHARLES 36-668
   JOHN 30-534, 31-569, 33-580, 34-718, 36-668
   THOMAS [Tom] 30-1166, 31-1198, 33-1327, 34-1198, 35-1458, 36-682, 38-671, 39-1491, 40-1518

GOODING [Godwen, Gooden, Gooding], MOSES 30-197, 31-160, 33-248

GOODRICH [Goodrick, Goodrix, Gudrick]
   RICHARD [Richeard] 37-170, 38-249
   WILLIAM 30-162, 33-168, 34-289, 35-163, 36-163, 39-308, 40-427

GORDY [Gord(i)e]
   MOSES 30-1303, 31-1337, 33-1452, 34-1461, 35-1736, 36-1764, 37-1081, 38-1883, 39-1753, 40-1925
   PETER 30-1362, 31-1336, 33-1453, 34-1460, 35-1735, 36-1716, 37-1151, 37-1235, 38-1725, 39-1696, 40-1910

GORE [Goar, Goore]
   JAMES 30-463
   JANE 40-1445
   RICHARD 30-1104, 31-1237, 33-1278, 34-1371, 35-1322, 36-1395, 38-1358

GORNWELL, JOHN 33-458, 34-536, 35-562, 36-585, 37-407, 38-508, 39-418

GORSELEN, RICHARD 40-411

GOSLIN [Goselen, Goslae, Goslee, Gosley]
   EZEKIEL [Ezekill, Ezecell] 31-871, 33-1033
   JAMES 30-850, 31-877, 33-964, 34-949, 35-994, 36-1092, 37-847, 38-1332, 39-1145, 40-1100
   JOHN 30-1469, 31-1358, 33-1609, 34-1644, 35-1467, 35-1700, 36-1544, 37-1194, 38-1791, 39-1854, 40-1819
   MATTHEW 31-1404, 33-1573, 34-1549, 35-1534, 36-1557, 37-1064, 38-1837, 39-1918, 40-1745
   RICHARD 30-1469, 31-1358, 33-1560, 34-1554, 35-1537, 36-1558, 37-1062, 38-1838, 39-1919
   THOMAS 30-1358, 31-1510, 33-1560, 34-1548, 35-1531, 36-1556, 37-1068, 38-1842, 39-1920, 40-1744

GRACE, EDWARD 40-201

GRANT, JOHN 31-1402

GRAVENER, THOMAS 30-912, 33-1027, 34-1081, 35-1022, 36-928, 38-1108, 39-1117, 40-1197

GRAY [Grey, Grig]
   ALLEN 30-1194, 31-1159, 33-621, 33-1365, 34-634, 34-1448, 35-681, 35-1651, 36-678, 36-1686, 37-1231, 38-670, 38-1753, 39-666, 39-1681, 40-1774
   JAMES 39-736, 40-794
   JOHN [Jon./junr., senr.] 30-249, 30-522, 30-523, 31-192, 31-286, 31-518, 31-652, 33-218, 33-299, 33-676, 34-457, 34-637, 35-521, 35-688, 36-502, 36-681, 37-445, 38-284, 38-461, 38-708, 39-433, 39-736, 40-700, 40-794
   JOSEPH 30-219, 31-254, 33-275, 34-192, 35-180, 36-254, 37-350, 38-218, 39-290, 40-328
   MARY, widow 33-1333

243

INDEX

NICHOLAS [Nickolas] 30-343, 31-489, 33-484, 34-456, 35-522, 36-466, 37-418, 38-654, 39-566, 40-514
  SAMUEL 40-459
  THOMAS 30-219, 30-1168, 31-254, 31-1238, 33-279, 33-633, 33-676, 34-195, 34-607, 34-637, 35-283, 35-749, 36-200, 37-302, 38-225, 39-286, 40-296
  WILLIAM 30-223, 30-249, 30-547, 30-967, 31-255, 31-286, 31-517, 31-1032, 33-276, 33-298, 33-675, 33-1093, 34-194, 34-305, 34-623, 34-1135, 35-355, 35-635, 35-1234, 36-174, 36-317, 36-682, 36-1193, 37-204, 37-358, 38-372, 38-373, 38-671, 38-1314, 39-282, 39-433, 39-667, 39-1364, 39-1896, 40-188, 40-238, 40-477, 40-792, 40-1430

GRAYHAMS [Graham, Gruphams], GEORGE 35-182, 36-319, 38-250, 39-376, 40-377

GREEN
  DAVID 39-362, 40-413
  EZEKIEL [Ezecell, Ezekell, Zeckett] 30-925, 31-1062, 33-998, 34-1025, 35-1106, 36-337, 37-254, 38-327, 38-1054, 39-362, 39-1194, 40-413, 40-1144
  JAMES 30-1350, 34-928, 35-981, 38-619
  RICHARD [Dick, Ritchard/esqr., junr. 30-884, 31-891, 33-892, 34-963(2) 35-1010(2), 36-1125(2), 38-1054, 38-1769, 39-1194(2), 40-1114(2)
  THOMAS 35-73

GREER [Grear, Greerer, Greire, Grier]
  WIDOW 35-1053
  ADAM 30-471, 31-405, 34-418, 35-504, 36-385, 37-394, 38-517, 39-415, 40-453
  ARCHIBALD [Archabel] 31-1299, 33-1146, 34-1367, 35-396, 36-476, 37-497, 38-562, 39-471, 40-480
  ELIZABETH [Lese] 36-983, 37-990
  GEORGE 40-480
  HAMPTON 40-480
  HENRY 31-1299, 33-1146, 36-476, 40-470
  JAMES 33-1069
  JOHN 31-1299, 33-1146, 36-584, 37-430, 37-497, 38-438, 38-562, 39-622, 40-462, 40-680
  SOLOMON 39-471
  URSULA [Ursley] 33-460, 34-545, 37-430, 38-438, 39-622, 40-462
  WILLIAM 35-1053, 36-983, 37-990, 38-1187, 39-1179, 40-1394

GRIFFIN [Grifen]
  JOHN 30-1376, 31-1426, 33-1566, 34-1585, 35-1589, 36-1643, 37-1100, 38-1650, 40-1970
  OLIVER 30-1334, 31-1438, 33-403, 34-379, 35-498, 36-573, 37-474, 38-471, 39-616, 40-692

GRIFFITH, JOHN 39-1785

GRIGGS [Grigg]
  EDMUND 38-735
  HENRY 34-853, 36-963, 38-971, 40-1062

GRIMES [Grims]
  HENRY 34-251
  JAMES [Jeams] 33-72, 34-83, 35-12, 36-64, 37-65, 38-13, 39-73, 37-65, 40-83

GRINLESS [Grandless]
  JOHN 30-544, 31-569
  WILLIAM 31-517, 33-675, 34-623

GROOMS, WILLIAM 30-162

GRUMBLE, BENJAMIN [Cramell] 39-791, 40-809

GRUNDEY
  JOHN 30-744
  RENCHER [Rensher] 30-744

GUDGEON [Goodin(g), Gudgen, Gugsing], BENJAMIN 30-1094, 31-1191, 33-1158, 35-1295, 36-1342, 38-852, 39-855, 40-957

GUILD, JOHN 30-1474

GULLETT
  ABRAHAM 30-544, 31-599, 36-722, 38-1496, 39-735, 40-750
  GEORGE 33-1301, 36-722, 38-707, 39-768, 40-137

GULLIPS, JAMES 31-1184

GUNBY
  JOHN 30-72, 31-84, 33-89, 34-30, 35-112, 36-47, 37-45, 38-46, 39-89, 40-97
  KIRK [Kirrk] 30-80, 31-86, 33-92, 34-27, 35-113, 36-44, 37-46, 38-59, 39-92, 40-98

GURLEY [Garley, Gurling]
  GEORGE [Gorge] 30-685, 33-758, 34-732, 35-762, 36-1469, 37-707, 38-1541, 39-1475
  JOHN 30-825

GUTTRY [Gusttridge, Gutrey, Guttery, Guttridge]
  CALEB 38-824, 39-907, 40-951
  JAMES 33-751, 34-760, 35-797, 37-645, 38-824, 40-952
  PATRICK 30-663, 31-677, 33-751, 34-760, 35-797, 36-851, 37-645, 38-824, 39-907, 40-951

GUY [Gaiey], JAMES 33-162, 34-199, 35-303, 37-387, 38-442, 40-490

INDEX

HADDER [Haddock, Haddor, Hadduck]
    ANTHONY 30-449, 31-400, 33-379, 34-413, 35-495
    IGNATIOUS 34-1279, 35-1335, 36-1412, 38-1507, 39-1398, 40-1478
    WARREN [Warrin] 30-399, 31-486, 33-495, 34-569, 35-575, 36-364, 37-441, 38-456, 39-432, 40-543
    WILLIAM 40-543
HAILER [Hayler], DAVID 38-1763, 39-1871
HAISTEN [Hasitin, Hasteen, Hasten, Hastin(s), Hasty]
    BENJAMIN 35-1739, 36-1743, 38-1749, 39-1690, 40-1913
    ROBERT [junr., senr.] 30-1369, 31-1395, 33-1473, 34-1456, 35-1739, 36-1743, 37-984, 38-1749(2), 39-1690(2), 40-1913(2)
    WILLIAM 31-1395, 33-1473, 34-1456, 35-1739, 36-1743, 37-985, 38-1750, 39-1689, 40-1914
HALES [Hailes]
    JAMES 37-1137
    JEREMIAH 30-481, 31-444
    JOHN 30-557, 31-537, 33-1493, 34-1494, 35-1596, 36-1673, 37-1030, 38-1653, 39-1757
HALL
    ADAM 31-404, 33-453, 34-439, 35-433, 36-514, 37-471, 38-645, 39-515, 40-639
    ALEXANDER [junr., senr.] 30-555, 30-555, 31-602, 31-603, 33-547, 34-602, 35-665
    ANN 35-1693
    CHARLES [jr., senr.] 30-2, 31-20, 33-1, 34-6, 35-90, 36-5, 37-127, 38-154, 38-155, 39-1, 39-11, 40-1
    DAVID 40-1763
    EZEKIEL [Ezekil] 40-2
    GEORGE 33-725
    HENRY 34-797, 35-828, 36-844, 37-646
    JAMES 36-1016, 38-1326, 39-1332, 40-1348
    JOHN 30-3, 30-208, 31-178, 31-645, 31-719, 33-203, 33-667, 33-770, 34-7, 34-797, 34-1130, 35-828, 35-1190, 35-1399, 36-800, 36-1198, 36-1516, 37-646, 38-915, 38-1310, 38-1373, 38-1397, 39-906, 39-1301, 39-1582, 39-1607, 40-581, 40-719, 40-947, 40-1422, 40-1685
    JOSEPH [jr.] 30-209, 31-179, 33-333, 34-344, 35-311, 35-1106, 36-312, 36-337, 37-186, 37-254, 39-352, 40-414
    MARGARET 40-581
    MARY 36-760, 38-692, 39-730
    PHENIX [Fenex] 30-1316, 31-1495, 33-1547, 34-1565, 35-433, 36-514, 36-1569, 37-508, 37-1054, 38-589, 38-1642, 39-484, 39-1907, 40-581
    RICHARD 30-3, 31-21, 33-2, 34-5, 35-91, 36-4, 37-123, 38-154, 39-1, 40-1
    ROBERT 30-323, 31-460, 33-398, 34-533, 35-464, 36-396, 37-467, 38-634, 39-1293, 40-1424
    SAMUEL 31-204, 33-221, 33-1475, 34-319, 34-1468, 35-189, 35-1657, 36-194, 37-200, 37-1232, 38-245, 38-1754, 39-174, 39-1683, 40-276, 40-1775
    SPENCE 36-396, 38-634, 40-513
    STEPHEN 38-915, 40-947
    THOMAS 30-1287, 31-978, 31-1384, 33-1436, 34-1564, 35-1248, 35-1673, 36-337, 36-1630, 37-259, 37-1240, 38-1767, 39-1309, 39-1865, 40-1330, 40-1760
    WILLIAM 30-6, 30-322, 31-130, 31-404, 33-453, 33-545, 34-8, 34-439, 35-433, 35-750, 36-514, 36-617, 37-124, 37-508, 38-156, 38-589, 39-2, 39-484, 39-1293, 40-164
    WILLIAM STEPHEN 31-289
HALLER, WILLIAM DUBBIN 34-446
HALY [Hailey]
    NICHOLAS [Nicolis] 34-829, 5-890
    TIMOTHY 30-594, 31-509, 33-635, 34-613, 35-716, 36-687, 38-683, 39-693, 40-838
HAMFORD [Hamfort], JOHN 35-891
HAMILTON [Hambleton, Hambelton, Hamelton, Hamlton, Hamblon]
    JOHN 30-177, 39-207
    JOSEPH 40-184
    WILLIAM 30-266, 31-135, 33-381, 34-416, 35-1473, 36-409, 38-657, 39-1487, 40-1509
HAMLON
    FRANCIS [Francies] 30-258, 31-290, 33-303, 34-181
    JOHN 30-227, 31-261
HAMMOND [Hammon, Hanon, Haymond]
    CHARLES 30-386, 31-332, 31-1488, 34-680, 35-631, 36-618, 38-753, 39-1443, 40-1550
    DANIEL 30-553, 31-606
    EDWARD [junr., Senr] 30-389, 31-391, 31-1150, 33-415, 34-397, 34-463, 35-527, 35-534, 36-363, 36-555, 37-582, 38-421, 39-538, 40-535, 40-645

INDEX

ISAAC 30-388, 33-421, 34-469, 35-532, 36-566, 37-564, 38-417, 39-659, 40-678
JACOB 30-389, 31-496, 33-420, 34-455, 36-491, 38-401, 39-537, 40-533
JOHN [junr., senr.] 30-387, 30-390, 31-389, 31-390, 33-416, 34-467, 35-531, 36-366, 37-587, 38-415, 39-542, 40-681
NICHOLAS 31-1442
WILLIAM 31-1442(2), 35-530, 36-364, 37-564, 38-417, 40-679
HAMPTON, MARY [madam, mrs., widow] 30-236, 30-423, 30-1094, 31-248, 31-488, 31-1310, 33-286, 34-150, 34-1429, 35-204, 35-1506, 36-234, 36-587, 36-1262, 37-301, 38-356, 38-507, 38-1383, 39-257, 39-1599, 40-321, 40-682, 40-1681
HANDCOCK
DANIEL 30-412, 31-461, 33-394, 34-368, 35-469, 36-402, 37-466, 38-633, 39-510, 39-510, 40-476
WILLIAM [jr.] 30-409, 31-392, 33-407, 34-375, 36-402, 36-577, 37-466, 37-638, 38-463, 38-633, 39-623, 39-921, 40-476, 40-690
HANDY [Handay, Handey]
EBENEZER [Abennezer] 30-1306, 31-1334, 33-1444, 34-1601, 35-1727
ELIZABETH 34-1306, 35-1461, 36-1400, 38-1359, 39-1382, 40-1446
HAZZARD 39-924
ISAAC [mr.] 30-1283, 31-1366, 33-1438, 34-1673, 35-1671, 36-1701, 37-1162, 38-1879, 39-1872, 40-1764
JEAN [Jeane] 37-128
JOHN [capt., mr.] 30-1259, 31-1364, 33-1418, 34-1661, 35-1521, 36-1519, 37-1191, 38-1773, 39-1876, 40-1751
SAMUEL [junr.] 30-1103, 30-1259, 30-13, 31-1419, 31-1201, 31-7, 33-16, 33-1277, 33-16, 34-1306, 34-131(2), 35-884, 35-1461, 36-1400
STEPHEN 35-1461, 36-1400, 38-1359, 39-1383, 40-1447
THOMAS 30-13, 31-7, 33-15, 33-1277, 34-106, 34-1306, 35-77, 36-1, 38-1359, 39-1383, 40-1447
WILLIAM [mr.] 30-1103, 31-1201, 33-1277, 34-1306
HANGE, JOHN 33-959
HANLON, PATRICK [Handlin, Hanlen] 33-720, 34-758, 35-1249
HAPENEY
BINGHAM 40-378
WILLIAM 39-315
HARBERSON [Harbenson, Harbrson], SAMUEL 38-162, 39-239, 40-333
HARBURD [Harbert], WILLIAM 39-845, 40-1681
HARDING [Hardin, Hardy]
JOSEPH 30-561, 31-588, 33-587, 35-881
THOMAS 35-262
HARDIS, HAZZARD [Ardis, Hardes] 33-760, 35-783, 36-765, 37-327, 38-228, 40-919
HARDY [Hardey, Hardie]
BENJAMIN [Hardey] 33-1037, 37-1195, 38-1123, 39-1845, 40-1156
GEORGE [esqr.] 31-1355, 33-1412, 34-1642, 35-1702, 36-1542, 37-1195, 38-1702, 39-1845, 40-1119
JAMES [jnr.] 30-867, 31-1064, 33-1037, 34-977, 35-1151, 36-1045, 37-808, 37-1195, 38-1261, 38-1841, 39-1098, 39-1845, 40-1122, 40-1889
JOHN 30-1016, 31-913, 33-983, 34-1050, 35-1032, 36-932, 38-1171, 39-1096, 40-1204
JOSEPH 30-867, 31-1064, 33-1412, 34-716, 35-1151
ROBERT 30-1470, 31-1355, 33-1412, 34-1642, 35-1702, 36-1542, 37-1195, 38-1702, 39-1845, 40-1889
HARGIS [Hargas, Harkis], THOMAS 35-803, 36-822, 37-685, 38-879, 39-397, 40-246
HARLY, PETER 40-1699
HARMAN [Harmon]
BENJAMIN 36-856, 37-403
BETTY 40-267, 40-268
EDWARD 38-522, 39-560, 39-562, 40-558(2)
EMMANUEL [Emanewell, Immanuell, Manewell] 30-675, 31-710, 33-762, 34-816, 35-758, 36-860, 37-726, 38-880
GEORGE [Gorge] 37-663, 38-872, 39-873, 40-889
JOHN 35-831, 36-819, 37-401, 38-254, 39-171, 40-268
TOM 40-557
WILLIAM 33-460, 34-545, 35-573, 36-365, 37-417, 38-543, 39-562, 40-267
ZACHARIAH 33-459, 34-545, 35-492, 36-365, 37-401, 38-522, 39-557
HARNEY [-arrney, Harnays], THOMAS [jr., sr.] 36-157(2), 37-179, 38-352(2), 39-182(2), 40-233(2)

INDEX

HARPER
  ANN 34-1207
  EDWARD 30-1062, 31-1205,
33-1292, 34-1278, 35-1343,
36-1426, 38-1504, 39-1399,
40-1466
  FRANCIS 30-1089, 31-1248,
33-1283, 34-1208, 35-1350,
36-1464, 38-1490, 39-1416,
40-1484
  JAMES 30-1089
  JOHN 30-1091, 31-1311, 33-1282,
38-1504, 39-1399, 40-1466
  MOSES 30-1089
  RICHARD 30-1056
  WILLIAM 30-932, 31-912
HARPWHEEL [Herpweel], ROBERT 30-273
HARRIS [Hares(h)]
  ANN 30-1139
  BENTON 31-1203, 33-1288,
34-1217, 35-1338, 36-1410,
38-1510, 39-1394, 40-1456
  BLOYCE [Bloys] 38-1861,
39-1815, 40-1849
  CALEB [Calep] 30-1063, 31-1214,
36-1294, 38-1505, 39-1402,
40-1465
  CHARLES 34-1606, 35-1619,
36-1610, 37-994, 38-1861,
39-1815, 40-1849
  GEORGE 30-1394, 31-1422,
33-1601, 34-1609, 35-1615,
36-1592, 37-1006, 38-1860, 39-255
  HENRY 37-687
  JAMES 40-1465
  JEAN 30-1394
  JEREMIAH 30-741, 31-785,
33-800, 34-1280, 35-1339,
36-1411, 38-1508, 39-1395,
40-1463
  JOHN 31-1203, 31-1398, 33-1288,
33-1404, 33-1600, 34-1217,
34-1606, 35-1338, 35-1619,
36-1410, 36-1610, 37-994, 38-739,
38-1510, 39-1394, 40-1456
  PHILLIP 30-835, 31-919, 33-972,
34-931, 35-696, 36-698, 38-710,
39-731, 40-782
  RICHARD 30-1395, 31-1398,
33-1600, 34-1606, 35-1619,
36-1603, 37-996, 38-1858,
39-1817, 40-1844
  ROBERT 30-1065, 31-1218,
33-1296, 34-1334, 35-1341,
35-1775, 36-1424, 36-1684,
38-1503, 39-1401, 40-1474
  SPENCER 40-1463
  WILLIAM [junr., senr] 30-1393,
30-1395, 31-1398, 31-1421,
33-1600, 33-1605, 34-1606,
34-1607, 35-1618, 35-1619,
36-1601, 36-1610, 37-994, 37-995,
38-1857, 38-1861, 39-1815,
39-1816, 40-1843, 40-1849
HARRISON [Hareshson]
  JOHN 30-778, 31-975, 33-826
  WILLIAM 30-220, 31-253, 33-154,
34-338, 35-285, 36-354, 37-299,
38-308, 39-299, 40-313
HARRY [Harrey, Herry], GEORGE 30-12, 35-1268
HARVEY [Harvay, Harve, Hurvey]
  JOHN 30-974, 31-1052, 33-895,
34-1157, 35-1202, 36-1145,
38-1292, 40-1382
  THOMAS [Harney, Harniey]
30-295, 31-203, 34-314
  WILLIAM 30-1012, 31-838, 33-959
HARWOOD, RICHARD [Harewood]
30-1442, 31-1423, 33-1319,
34-1373
HASS, GEORGE 37-1025
HATCH, RICHARD 30-1478
HATFIELD, WILLIAM 35-1314,
36-1392, 38-202, 39-230, 40-280
HATH [Haith, Heath]
  ABRAHAM [junr., sener]
30-576(2), 31-508, 31-530(2),
33-543, 33-679(2), 34-617,
34-631, 34-695, 35-677, 35-678,
36-735, 36-754, 38-668, 39-664,
40-789
  ANN 36-679
  DORMAN [Dormand] 30-641,
31-530, 33-678, 34-614, 35-699,
36-732, 38-673, 39-672
  JACOB 30-573, 31-608, 33-637
  JOHN [junr., senr.] 34-617,
34-1694, 35-678, 36-754, 36-754,
38-668
  MATTHEW 38-668, 39-664
  PARTHENA 40-796
  WILLIAM 30-537, 31-556, 33-620,
34-636, 38-1795, 39-1895, 40-1864
HAUL, JAMES 37-960
HAYFIELDS [Agnefeilds,
Haynefield], WILLIAM 36-780, 38-863
HAYLOR, DAVID 39-941
HAYMAN [Haman, Hamon, Haymon,
Heman]
  WIDOW 33-1498
  ARTHUR [Arther] 30-596, 31- 523
  BEMJAMIN 30-596, 31-522, 33-579,
34-697, 35-694, 36-713, 38-697,
39-727, 40-753
  CHARLES [junr., senr.] 30-1332,
30-1438, 31-1437, 33-611,
33-1498, 33-1564, 34-1538,
34-1546, 35-1556, 35-1587,
36-1641, 36-1644, 37-1009,

INDEX

37-1029, 38-1645, 38-1648,
39-1786, 39-1789, 40-1971,
40-1974
   EDWARD [Hillman] 34-1527
   ISAAC 30-1438, 31-1437,
33-1498, 34-1538, 35-1587,
36-1641, 37-1007, 38-1646,
39-1788, 40-1973
   JAMES 30-1438, 31-1437,
33-1498, 34-1538, 35-1587,
36-1641, 37-1007, 38-1646,
39-1788, 40-1973
   JOHN 30-1438, 31-1437, 33-1498,
34-1539, 35-1588, 36-1642,
37-1008, 38-1647, 39-1787,
40-1972
   NICHOLAS [Nick.] 39-1748,
40-1936
   SARAH 31-1437
   WILLIAM [junr., snr.] 30-596,
30-1332, 31-522, 33-579,
33-1486(2), 34-697, 34-1503(2),
35-694, 35-1577(2), 36-713,
36-1665(2), 37-1117(2), 38-697,
38-1799(2), 39-727, 39-1748(2),
40-753, 40-1936(2)
HAYNES, FRANCIS 30-1007
HAYS, JAMES 34-831
HAYWARD
   JOHN 39-769
   THOMAS [mr.] 30-1254, 31-1199,
33-1272, 34-1196, 35-1249,
36-1399, 38-1353, 39-1377,
40-1441
   WILLIAM 30-988
HAZZARD
   [------y] 36-250
   ARTHUR [Arter] 34-161, 35-191
   BENJAMIN 35-249
   BENONY 34-308
   CONARD 30-127
   DAVID [junr., senr] 30-126(2),
31-183, 33-195(2), 34-161(2),
35-191, 35-220, 36-158, 36-159,
37-189, 37-190, 38-284, 38-395,
39-167, 39-313, 40-360, 40-428
   HENRY 36-924
   JOHN [Jon.] 38-284, 39-167,
40-360
   WILLIAM 30-135, 31-183, 33-195,
35-191, 36-158, 37-189, 38-282,
39-168, 40-245
HEARN [Ha(i)rn, Hearne, Hearon,
Heren, Hern(e), Heron]
   EDWARD 30-75, 31-88, 33-93,
34-26, 35-110, 36-42, 37-49,
38-61, 39-94, 40-116
   GEORGE [34-1452, 35-1648,
36-1737, 37-1238, 38-1723,
39-1686, 40-1902
   ISAAC 38-1724, 39-1693, 40-1904
   JOHN 30-1451, 35-1730, 36-1738,
37-1233, 38-1724, 39-1693,
40-1904
   NEHEMIAH [Nehe.] 31-1396,
33-1471, 34-1452, 35-1648,
36-1737, 38-1722, 39-1685,
40-1905
   THOMAS 30-1297, 31-1396,
31-1397, 33-1470, 33-1471,
34-1452, 34-1463, 35-1648,
36-1737, 37-1237, 38-1722,
39-1685, 40-1901
   WILLIAM 30-1298, 31-1397,
31-1508, 33-1470, 33-1561,
34-1463, 35-1532, 35-1730,
36-1738, 37-1233, 38-1724,
39-1693, 40-1904
HEATHER, EPHRAIM [Epheraim,
Ephiraim/jr., snr.] 30-309(2),
31-419(2), 33-405(2), 34-376(2),
35-480(2), 36-470(2), 37-472,
37-473, 38-452, 38-453, 39-614,
39-615, 40-495, 40-496
HENDERSON [Handerson,
Hi(n)derson]
   BENJAMIN 30-1220, 31-1165,
33-1164, 34-1242, 35-1281,
36-1361, 38-1602, 39-1573,
40-1102, 40-1656
   BISHOP [Biship, Bishup] 30-655,
31-758, 33-731, 34-769, 35-805,
36-818, 37-662, 38-849, 39-866,
40-899
   CHARLES 30-318, 30-1240,
31-380, 31-1286, 33-1180, 34-547,
34-1244, 35-596, 35-1308, 36-580,
36-1359, 37-639, 38-627, 38-1581,
39-652, 39-1568, 40-492, 40-1651
   DANIEL 40-1057
   FRANCIS 31-1168, 33-1181,
34-1249, 35-1283, 36-1360,
38-1601, 39-1570, 40-1653
   JAMES 30-1221, 31-1277,
33-1169, 34-1243, 35-1307,
36-1370, 38-1599, 39-1566,
40-1649, 40-1863
   JOHN [junr., senr.] 30-1218,
30-1225, 31-1197, 31-1278,
33-1168, 33-1169, 33-1172,
34-1243, 34-1245, 34-1250,
35-1306, 35-1307, 35-1318,
36-1358, 36-1370, 36-1371,
38-1564(2), 38-1580, 38-1599,
39-1565, 39-1566, 39-1567(2),
40-1648, 40-1649, 40-1650(2)
   ROBERT [Robarte] 30-817,
31-851, 33-1077, 34-909, 35-952,
36-1209, 38-1011, 39-1032,
40-1057
   SAMUEL 35-1306, 36-1371,
38-1564, 39-1567, 40-1627
   WILLIAM 33-611, 34-573, 35-542,
36-563, 40-1102, 40-1651

INDEX

HENRICKSON [Henerickson] PETER 39-1884

HENRY [Henerey, Henrey, Hewdy]
  HUGH [Hew] 35-1020, 36-1065, 38-1178, 39-1261, 39-1577, 40-1133, 40-1642
  JOHN [capt.] 30-289, 30-1027, 31-1001, 31-1310, 33-1054, 33-1217, 34-1096, 34-1429, 35-1020, 35-1506, 36-1065, 36-1262, 38-1178, 38-1383, 39-419, 39-1261, 39-1599, 40-1133, 40-1681
  MARTIN [Martain, Martian] 33-1458, 34-1475, 40-1330
  ROBERT [capt.] 31-1001, 33-1054, 33-1217, 34-1096, 35-1020, 35-1506, 36-1071, 36-1262, 37-863, 38-1256, 39-1465, 40-1395
  ROBERT JENKINS [Jenckins] 34-1429, 38-1383, 39-1599, 39-1663, 40-1681

HICK, SOLOMON 31-952

HICKMAN [Hickmen, Hickmon, Hikman]
  [-------n] 37-831
  [illegible] 36-1005
  ARTHUR [Arther] 33-1105, 34-900, 38-1017, 39-997, 40-1045
  HENRY 33-1104, 34-893, 35-944, 36-1004, 38-1264, 39-1312, 40-1354
  JAMES 33-867, 34-1177, 35-1238, 36-1007
  JONATHAN 36-1202, 38-1020, 39-1020, 40-1408
  JOSHUA 30-798, 31-874, 33-1106, 34-893, 35-935
  RICHARD [Richeard/junr., senr.] 30-147, 30-152, 31-214, 31-269, 33-226, 33-263, 34-254, 34-329, 35-230, 35-276, 36-338, 37-269, 37-331, 38-176, 38-193, 39-201, 39-383, 40-345, 40-429
  WILLIAM [junr., senr.] 30-805, 30-806, 31-931, 31-932, 33-1103, 33-1104, 34-896, 34-897, 35-945, 35-946, 36-1202, 37-831, 38-1020(2), 40-1041

HICKS [Hix]
  LEVIN 35-1039, 36-1138
  WILLIAM 31-539, 33-1033, 33-658, 34-1007, 38-1103, 39-1015, 40-1194

HICKSON, JOSEPH 30-1002, 31-1020, 33-846, 34-906, 35-38

HIGGINS, NATHANIEL 36-541

HIGGMAN, BENJAMIN 30-1455

HIGHWAY [Haighway, Hi(e)way, Hyway]
  ABRAHAM 30-176, 30-957, 34-1451

  ISAAC 30-1341, 31-1473, 34-1533, 36-806

HILL
  WIDOW 33-1456, 34-1480, 36-250
  ABRAHAM 30-657, 31-732, 33-721, 34-778, 35-812, 36-810, 37-677, 38-831, 39-849, 40-913
  ANN 31-208, 33-206, 34-308, 35-249
  BENJAMIN 33-206
  BENONY [Benone] 31-208
  CHARLES 30-1431, 31-1500, 33-1515, 34-1580, 35-1547, 36-1650, 37-1078, 38-1776, 39-1887, 40-1783
  COMFORT 33-302
  ELISHA [Lishea] 30-687, 33-758, 34-732, 35-769, 36-828, 37-640, 38-909
  HUTTON [Hutten] 30-688, 33-759, 34-733, 35-770, 36-829, 37-641, 38-884, 39-887, 40-877
  JACOB 37-678, 38-830, 39-850, 40-912
  JAMES 33-1456, 34-1480, 35-1718, 36-1727, 38-1693, 39-1722, 40-1804
  JOHN 30-564, 31-613, 33-565, 34-607, 34-1546, 35-658, 35-1523
  JOHNSON [junr.] 30-248, 30-687, 31-289, 31-698, 33-382, 33-758, 34-417, 34-732, 35-502, 35-769, 36-244, 36-828, 37-584, 37-640, 38-304, 38-816, 39-886, 40-315
  NICHOLAS 34-548
  RICHARD 33-462, 34-407, 35-490, 36-290
  ROBERT 30-248, 30-689, 31-289, 31-685, 33-784, 34-740, 35-777, 36-858, 37-584, 37-670, 38-858, 39-880, 40-881
  THOMAS 30-1329
  WILLIAM 34-834, 35-502, 35-872, 36-866, 37-792, 38-976, 39-707, 40-773
  WILLIAM STEPHENS 36-244, 38-304, 39-232, 40-341

HILLMAN [Hillmon], EDWARD 30-1432, 31-1529, 33-1517, 35-1548, 36-1652, 37-1079, 38-1777, 39-1886, 40-1954

HINDMAN, JACOB [Hinman] 30-1165, 31-1200

HITCH [Heatch, Hitches, Hith]
  WIDOW 34-1001, 35-1130
  ADAM 30-1277, 36-1046, 38-1117, 39-1203, 40-1161
  ELGATE [Elgit] 30-1277, 31-1382, 33-1430, 34-1671, 35-1661, 36-1746, 37-1203, 38-1768, 39-1671, 40-1758

INDEX

JOHN [junr., senr] 30-1280, 31-1379, 33-1429, 34-1675, 35-1660, 36-1635, 37-1208, 38-1759, 38-1761, 39-1668, 39-1672, 40-1768, 40-1770
LEVIN [Leven] 38-1117, 39-1203, 40-1161
MARY [widow] 33-1431, 36-935
NEHEMIAH 40-1770
SAMUEL 30-1271, 31-1380, 33-1428, 34-1674, 35-1748, 36-1637, 37-1204, 38-1762, 39-1669, 40-1766
SOLOMON 30-897, 33-1014, 34-992, 35-1139, 36-1046, 38-1117, 39-1203, 40-1161
WILLIAM 34-1676, 35-1655, 36-1634, 37-1211, 38-1759, 39-1672, 40-1769

HOBBS
ABSOLOM 40-1995, 39-1875, 30-1403, 35-1524, 36-1575, 37-1050, 38-1638, 33-1537, 31-1487, 34-1572
JOY [junr.] 30-780, 30-1403, 31-1487, 31-809, 33-832, 33-1537, 34-827, 34-1572, 35-1524, 35-874, 36-868, 36-1575, 37-793, 38-980, 39-982, 40-1000
MERCILIOUS [Marsellass, Marcelious, Marsallas, Marthelus, Marthillias, Mathelli] 30-777, 31-808, 33-831, 34-828, 35-875, 36-869, 37-794, 38-979, 39-981, 40-1001
NOBLE 30-747, 31-793
STEPHEN 39-983, 40-999
THOMAS 30-781, 31-810, 33-833, 34-826, 35-873, 36-867, 37-800, 38-978, 39-983, 40-999

HODGE [Hodg, Hog]
FLEMING 39-424, 40-545
JOHN 30-1430, 31-1509, 34-1583, 36-1700, 37-723
RICHARD 30-1397, 31-1532
ROBERT 30-426, 31-485, 33-455, 33-724, 34-540, 35-567, 36-367, 37-434, 38-432, 39-424, 40-545
ROLAND [Rolling] 37-722, 37-723
STEPHEN 38-737, 39-778, 40- 780

HODGSON [Hodson, Hogson]
JOHN [Hodson] 38-827, 39-854, 40- 910
ROBERT 34-818
ROLAND [Rolan, Roling, Rowlon/junr.] 31-726, 33-724, 34-813, 35-846, 36-812, 38-826, 38-827, 39-853, 39-854, 40-905, 40-910

HOGG, JAMES 36-299, 37-215, 38-336, 39-323, 40-294

HOGSKIN [Hoggskin]
JAMES 36-1313
JONAS 39-1603, 40-28
SUSAN [Sue] 36-1313

HOLBROOK [Holdbrook, Holdbroke Holebrook, Houlbrook, Houlbrouk], THOMAS [junr., senr.], 30-1389, 31-1315, 33-1604, 34-1602, 35-1628, 36-1599, 37-1013, 38-1854, 39-1810, 40-1858(2)

HOLDER [Houlder], SAMUEL 34-946, 35-1161

HOLDOM, JOHN 38-870, 39-882, 40-856

HOLIDAY [Holaday], JOSEPH 40-1536

HOLLAND [Hallond, Hollond]
BENJAMIN 30-725, 31-752, 33-773, 34-758, 35-794, 36-802, 37-694, 38-840, 39-269
ELIZABETH [Elezbath/jr., sr.] 40-283, 40-361
ISAAC 33-20, 34-104, 35-636, 36-710, 38-715, 39-751, 40-708
JOHN 30-202, 31-153, 33-257, 34-209
MICHAEL [jnr., sr.] 30-36, 30-37, 31-47, 31-48, 33-47, 33-48, 34-124, 35-5, 36-91(2), 37-92, 38-114, 38-115, 39-33, 39-34, 40-37, 40-39
NEHEMIAH 30-723, 31-756, 33-760, 34-759, 35-796, 36-801, 37-672, 38-842, 39-870, 40-888
RICHARD 30-267, 31-137, 33-319, 34-296, 35-337, 36-197, 37-312, 38-360, 39-408
SAMUEL 38-360, 39-408, 40-283
WILLIAM [capt.] 30-380, 30-1140, 31-1099, 33-47, 33-1233, 34-564, 34-1401, 35-403, 35-1445, 36-492, 36-1301, 37-487, 38-664, 39-544, 39-1621, 40-686, 40-1700

HOLLOWAY [Halaway, Hallaway, Hallay]
AARON 40-318, 37-303, 38-168, 39-283, 40-318
JOHN [junr., senr.] 30-216, 30-293, 31-251, 31-252, 31-405, 33-269, 33-270, 34-183, 34-182, 35-203, 35-206, 36-248, 36-347, 37-303, 37-325, 38-168, 38-368, 39-238, 39-283, 40-304, 40-318
JOSEPH [Halla(y)way, Hallay] 30-216, 33-271, 34-179, 35-205, 36-249, 37-355, 38-230, 39-298, 40-346
MOSES 37-303, 38-168, 39-283, 40-318

HOLSTON [Hol(e)stone, Holsten, Houlston]
BENJAMIN 30-1195, 33-710, 36-510, 37-595, 38-598, 39-459,

INDEX

40-675
  CHARLES 33-361, 34-364, 36-510, 37-495, 38-566, 39-469, 40-858
  JAMES 30-1226
  JOHN [junr., senr.] 30-372, 30-1227, 30-1228, 31-438, 33-360, 34-353, 34-1342, 35-373, 36-454, 36-1194, 37-614, 38-608, 39-455, 39-1272, 40-446, 40-1326
  JOSEPH 40-1567
  ROBERT 39-1271, 40-1333
  WILLIAM 30-382, 31-355, 33-361, 34-388, 35-394, 36-473, 37-495, 38-566, 39-470, 40-485

HOLT, JOHN 36-554, 37-377, 39-673

HOLTON, JOHN [Holtone] 30-1295

HOOK
  HENRY 40-541
  WILLIAM 30-376, 31-447, 33-499, 35-331, 36-229, 38-300, 39-532, 40-529

HOOPCRAFT [Hapcraft, Happeraft, Hopcraft], THOMAS 30-1116, 31-1125, 33-1295, 34-1210

HOPKINS [Hopkens]
  BENJAMIN 30-507, 31-12, 33-669, 34-604, 35-671
  CHARLES 35-27, 36-150, 37-32, 38-108, 39-134, 40-153
  DANIEL 38-1268, 39-1285, 40-1380
  DAVID 36-999, 38-998, 39-1097, 40-1035
  GEORGE 30-116(2), 31-124, 33-129, 33-789, 34-139, 34-853, 35-27, 35-923, 36-150, 36-917, 37-32, 37-746, 38-108(2), 38-969, 39-134(2), 40-153(2)
  HAMPTON [Hamton] 30-677
  JEAN [wido.] 33-1043
  JOHN [junr., senr.] 30-116, 30-682, 30-802, 30-825, 30-825, 31-124, 31-883(2), 31-885, 33-129, 33-157, 33-1069, 33-1108, 34-139, 34-323, 34-892, 34-918(2), 35-27, 35-263, 35-934, 35-962(2). 36-150, 36-161, 36-1002, 36-1049(2), 37-32, 38-108, 38-259, 38-988, 38-1013, 38-1014, 39-134, 39-252, 39-1058, 39-1059, 39-1315, 40-153, 40-273, 40-1066, 40-1067, 40-1403
  JOSIAH 30-682, 33-156, 34-325, 35-222, 36-170, 38-190, 39-409, 40-203
  MATTHEW 30-697, 31-694, 33-709, 34-805, 35-838, 36-842, 37-687, 38-902, 39-916, 40-857
  NATHANIEL [junr.] 30-677, 30-678, 31-674, 33-707, 34-804, 35-837, 36-843, 37-692, 38-901, 39-917
  ROBERT [senr.] 30-824, 30-824, 31-822, 31-886, 33-1043, 34-916, 35-960, 36-1020, 38-330, 39-341, 40-405
  ROGER [Rodger] 36-1049, 38-1014, 39-1059, 40-1066
  SAMUEL [capt./junr, senr.] 30-265, 30-682(2), 31-134, 31-679, 33-338, 33-702(2), 34-345, 34-796(2), 35-357, 35-827, 36-275, 36-849, 37-317, 37-693, 38-239, 38-869, 39-367, 39-905, 40-309, 40-948
  STEPHEN 30-792, 31-822, 33-1111, 34-888, 35-929, 36-999, 38-998, 39-1097, 40-1035
  WILLIAM 30-691, 33-129, 33-703, 34-139, 34-773, 35-27, 35-829, 36-150, 36-850, 37-688, 38-108, 39-134, 39-904, 40-153, 40-949
  WILLIAMS 37-32

HORN, EZEKIEL 39-11

HORNER [Horney]
  ARNOLD [Arnal] 38-802, 39-689, 40-828
  CHARLES 40-828
  GEORGE [junr., senr.] 30-613(2), 31-623, 31-633, 33-609, 33-618, 34-670, 34-870, 35-705, 35-706, 36-747, 38-802, 39-681, 39-689, 40-759, 40-828
  JAMES 30-613, 31-623, 33-618, 34-670, 35-706, 36-1596, 37-1010, 39-682, 40-840
  JOHN 34-670, 35-706, 36-747, 38-802, 39-689, 40-828
  MATILDA [Maltildo, Martilda, Mertiedo. Metildo, Till, Tull] 30-613, 31-623, 33-618, 35-706, 36-747, 38-802, 39-689, 40-828
  WILLIAM 30-615, 31-631, 34-677, 35-729, 39-685

HORSEY [Horsee, Horsy]
  ANNE 38-118
  HANNAH 34-681
  ISAAC [capt., coll.] 30-34, 31-41, 33-43, 34-18, 35-61, 36-94, 37-140, 38-120, 39-29, 40-33
  JOHN 30-564, 31-613, 33-668, 34-672, 35-735, 37-62, 38-2, 38-723, 39-85, 39-779, 40-93, 40-733
  JONATHAN 40-33
  NATHANIEL 30-33, 31-43, 33-44, 34-19, 35-62, 36-97, 37-139, 38-119, 39-30, 40-34
  OUTERBRIDGE [Outterbridg] 36-97, 37-139, 38-119, 39-30, 40-34
  REVILL [Revell] 30-553, 31-606, 33-661

INDEX

SAMUEL 30-32, 31-44, 33-45, 34-20, 35-60
SARAH 34-612, 35-745, 36-701, 39-776, 40-732
SMITH 30-32, 31-45, 33-45, 34-20, 35-60, 36-93, 37-137, 38-117, 39-31, 40-35
STEPHEN [capt./junr., senr] 30-32, 30-70, 31-46, 31-78, 33-46, 33-86, 34-21, 34-123, 35-59, 35-115, 35-736, 36-51, 36-92, 37-62, 37-138, 38-2, 38-116, 39-32, 39-85, 40-36, 40-93, 40-721
WILLIAM 30-554, 31-606, 33-662
HORSLEY, RICHARD 40-1212
HORSMAN, HENRY 30-118, 31-114, 33-130, 34-140, 37-33, 38-110, 39-132, 40-155
HOSIEAR [Hosay, Hosea, Hosey, Hosiear(e), Hosier, Hozay, Hozeir] EDWARD 39-908
MATTHEW 30-991, 31-994, 33-937, 34-1118, 35-1080, 36-1023, 38-1229, 39-1240, 40-1297
NATHAN 39-534, 40-513
SAMUEL [junr., senr] 30-660, 30-660, 31-751, 33-701, 34-726, 34-757, 35-763, 35-793, 36-825, 36-831, 37-667, 37-698, 38-885, 39-893
HOUGH [Huff], EDMUND [Edw.] 30-1211, 31-1155, 33-1366, 34-1346, 35-1358, 36-1486, 38-1565, 39-1466, 40-1581
HOUGIN [Hodgen(s), Hodgin, Houghgens, Hougine, Howgene]
JOHN 33-1547, 35-1644, 38-1847
SARAH [widow] 30-1474, 31-1501, 33-1577, 40-1892
WILLIAM 30-1353
HOUSTON [Houstone]
BENJAMIN 31-1177, 33-1346, 34-803
GEORGE 30-1259
JAMES 31-1288, 33-1152, 34-1369, 35-1278, 36-1356, 38-1613, 39-1551, 40-1638
JOHN [junr., senr] 31-1276, 31-1289, 33-1151, 33-1363, 34-1368, 35-1317, 35-1374, 36-1357, 38-1239, 38-1618, 39-1552, 40-1639
JOSEPH [junr., senr.] 30-1192, 31-1153, 31-1290, 33-1153, 33-1364, 34-1344, 34-1370, 35-1316, 35-1499, 36-1355, 38-1555, 38-1614, 39-1454, 40-1570
ROBERT [jur.] 30-1205, 31-1292, 33-1362, 34-1343, 35-1375, 38-1298
HOVINGTON [Hofin(g)ton, Hoofinton, Huffin(g)ton]
ELIZABETH [Betty] 40-1180
JOHN [junr., senr.] 30-919, 30-920, 31-924, 31-926, 33-1032, 33-1034, 34-1008, 34-1009, 35-1120, 35-1121, 36-1078, 36-1114, 37-879, 38-1100, 38-1101, 39-1128, 39-1130, 40-1182, 40-1183
JONATHAN 30-920, 31-925, 33-1031, 34-1006, 35-1119, 36-1084, 37-878, 38-1098, 39-1129
LEVI 39-1075
LEVIN 40-1216
RICHARD [Ritcard] 30-929, 31-1076, 33-916, 34-1029, 35-1100, 36-1062, 38-1088, 39-1075, 40-1216
THOMAS 30-930, 31-1073, 33-919, 34-1028, 35-1099, 36-972, 38-1087, 39-1162, 40-1218
HOWARD [Haward, Hodward]
GEORGE [junr., senr.] 30-159, 31-213(2), 33-220(2), 34-255(2), 35-225(2), 36-221(2), 37-183(2), 38-186(2), 39-253(2), 40-260(2)
JOHN 30-1400, 31-1528, 33-1516, 34-1528, 35-1555, 36-1649, 37-1076, 38-1785, 39-1879, 40-748, 40-1815
NEHEMIAH [Nemiah] 30-159, 31-213, 33-220, 34-255, 35-227, 36-179, 37-181, 38-187, 39-248, 40-259
THOMAS 30-1390, 31-1533, 33-1414, 34-1633, 35-1633, 36-1587, 37-1021, 38-1826, 39-971, 40-1002
HOWELL, JOHN 31-780, 35-1079
HUBBARD [Hubbord], RICHARD 4-1308, 35-1406, 38-1417, 39-579
HUDSON [Hodson, Hutson]
ABSALOM 33-246, 34-204, 35-175, 38-166
ANDREW 38-179
CHARLES 35-274, 38-329, 39-348, 40-432
DAVID [jr., sr.] 31-173, 33-246, 34-204, 35-175, 36-257, 37-296, 38-166, 39-319, 40-365(2)
DENNIS [Donis] 30-483, 31-425, 33-391, 34-534, 35-465, 36-404, 37-458, 38-547, 39-513, 40-642
GEORGE 30-195, 33-246, 34-385, 37-172, 38-163, 39-243, 40-194
HENRY 38-198, 39-386, 40-310
JOHN [Jon.] 30-710, 30-210, 31-272, 33-163, 34-245, 35-233, 35-334, 36-210, 36-399, 37-345, 37-358, 38-171, 38-198, 39-214,

INDEX

39-386, 40-310, 40-357
   JONATHAN [Johnathan, Jonathun] 30-668, 33-716, 35-795, 36-835, 38-882, 39-900, 40-887, 40-882
   MAJOR 37-461, 35-463, 36-400, 38-548, 39-512, 40-478
   MARGARET [widow] 30-380, 31-353
   RICHARD [junr., senr.] 30-249, 30-207, 31-273, 31-286, 33-299, 33-144, 34-292, 34-243, 35-231, 35-334, 36-341, 36-210, 37-321, 37-358, 38-198, 38-172, 39-204, 39-386, 40-225, 40-310
   ROLAND [Rowland] 30-710
   SAMUEL 30-211, 31-274, 33-145, 34-244, 35-178, 36-342, 37-314, 38-305, 39-203, 40-224
   WILLIAM 30-378, 31-288, 31-1195, 33-298, 34-305, 35-175, 35-355, 36-257, 36-317, 37-296, 37-300, 38-166, 38-373, 39-319, 39-511, 40-365, 40-477

HUGG, JOANNA [Hugge/Johanah, wido.] 30-997, 31-1017

HUGGINS [Huggans, Hugin]
   CHARLES 30-940, 31-1060
   ROGER 30-1091, 31-1311

HUGHES, WILLIAM [Hues, Hughs] 33-641, 34-610, 35-585

HUITT [Heugitt, Hewitt, Huett]
   GEORGE 36-292, 38-512, 39-412, 40-673
   THOMAS [Thommis] 30-628

HULL
   BEAUCHAMP [Beacham] 30-1154
   DANIEL 30-20, 31-25, 33-30, 34-99
   EDWARD 30-1154, 31-1257, 33-1263, 34-1381
   JOHN 30-925

HUMPHRIES [Humfris, Humphris, Umphri(e)s]
   CAPTAIN 34-1648
   EZEKIEL 38-787, 39-694, 40-842
   JOSEPH 39-1864, 40-1755
   MARY 35-1677, 37-1222, 38-1746, 39-1864, 40-1755
   THOMAS [junr., sr.] 30-1260, 31-1371(2), 33-1408(2), 34-1648, 35-1677, 36-1696, 37-1221, 38-1738, 39-1923, 40-1886

HUNNINGS, PHILLIP [Hunins] 34-274, 38-275, 39-344, 40-406

HUNT, JOHN 30-1365, 31-568

HUNTER, JOHN 35-1173

HURNY, JOHN 39-1334

HURST
   JOHN 35-25, 36-142, 36-899, 37-31, 37-781, 39-946
   JOSEPH 30-804
   WILLIAM 30-794

HURT, DANIEL 31-1433, 38-1881, 40-1336

HUSK
   JOHN 30-114, 30-636, 31-774, 33-804, 34-862, 35-913, 38-937, 40-969
   JOSEPH 38-1027, 40-1047

HUST
   [illegible] 37-825
   JOHN 38-742
   JOSEPH 31-933, 33-1107, 34-898, 35-939, 36-1058, 36-1203, 39-1023
   LAZARUS [Lazrs,] 33-1071, 34-929, 35-951
   WILLIAM 31-825, 33-1044, 34-937

HUTCHESON
   JAMES 38-1621
   ROBERT [Huttison] 40-1863
   WILLIAM 39-118, 40-1727

HUTTON
   ABRAHAM [Abram] 30-1202
   JOHN BOOTH 36-1511, 38-1606

HYMINONS, THOMAS 30-980

INGOE, JAMES [Ingo] 36-556, 37-307, 38-462, 39-434, 40-671

INGRAM [Eingram, Ingrim, Ingrom, Ingrum]
   ABRAHAM [jur., senr.] 30-957, 31-1051, 33-875, 34-1166(2), 35-1211(2), 36-1214(2), 37-967(2), 38-1323(2), 39-1329(2), 40-1368, 40-1371
   DAVID 33-875, 35-1211, 36-1214, 37-967, 38-1321, 39-1330, 40-1373
   ISAAC 30-957, 30-959, 31-1025, 33-875, 34-1166, 35-1212, 35-1241, 36-1008, 37-966, 38-1322, 39-1331, 40-1372
   JACOB 30-291, 30-960, 31-232, 31-1051, 33-182, 34-270, 35-269, 36-336, 36-1009, 37-967, 39-1313, 40-1413
   JAMES 38-1323, 39-1329, 40-1368
   ROBERT 30-983, 31-1026, 33-881, 34-1159, 35-1195, 36-1183, 38-1280, 39-1266, 40-1414

INLOES [Inloes, Indlos]
   ABRAHAM 30-167
   THOMAS [Thom.] 30-171, 31-238

IRONBUGH, JOHN 39-300

IRONSHIRE
   ISAAC 30-429, 31-368, 33-487
   MARY 34-455

IRVING [Arvin, Erving, Ewing, Irvin, Irwing]
   GEORGE 30-766, 31-771, 33-818, 34-873, 35-901, 36-886, 37-767, 38-933, 39-961, 40-1019
   JOHN 33-640, 34-669, 35-728, 36-752, 37-801, 38-933, 39-961, 40-1019

ISAACS, JOHN [Isaac, Isaacks] 33-912, 34-1128, 35-1234, 36-1192,

INDEX

38-1145

J-----, JOHN 37- 948

JACKSON [Jaxon, Jeckson]
  AGNES [widow] 36-463, 37-438, 38-318
  CHRISTOPHER DOMINIC 39-1931, 40-1750
  DANIEL 39-1200, 40-1103
  EZEKIEL 34-953, 35-989, 36-1096, 38-1062, 39-1200
  HENRY 35-599, 36-457
  JOHN 33-1409, 36-463, 36-1533, 37-1190, 37-438, 38-318, 39-559
  JONATHAN [Johnethan, Johanathen] 30-851, 31-934, 33-1125, 34-203, 34-953, 35-989, 36-1096, 38-1062, 39-1200, 40-1103
  JOSHUA 33-1125, 34-953, 35-989, 36-1096, 38-1062, 39-1200, 40-1103
  NATHANIEL 40-1676
  SAMUEL 30-909, 31-844, 33-1084, 34-1109, 35-1744, 36-1551, 37-1072, 38-1792, 39-1877, 40-1224
  THOMAS 30-851, 36-1097, 38-1060, 39-1201, 40-1104
  WILLIAM 35-851, 36-817, 37-679, 38-864, 39-875, 40-898

JACOBS
  WIDOW 34-971
  EDWARD [moluto] 30-630
  ELIZABETH 35-1157, 36-1106, 37-814
  WALTER 30-859, 31-1065, 33-1132
  WILLIAM [Will] 30-629

JAMES
  DUNCAN [Dunkin] 36-1107
  JOHN 30-1268, 31-1357, 33-936, 34-1058, 35-1076, 36-1037, 38-1210, 39-1187, 40-1293
  WILLIAM 39-1844, 40-1984

JARMAN [Garman, German, Jannan, Jarmin, Jarmon]
  GEORGE 30-488, 31-494, 33-417, 34-466, 35-530, 36-571, 37-579, 38-434, 40-519
  HENRY 30-448, 31-446, 33-541, 34-523, 35-591, 36-458, 37-382, 38-622
  JOB [Joab] 30-403, 31-473, 33-537, 34-490, 35-452, 36-431, 37-537, 38-489, 39-585, 40-685
  JOHN [junr., senr.] 30-311, 31-497, 33-422(2), 34-493(2), 35-537(2), 36-525(2), 37-576, 37-577, 38-406, 38-407, 39-530, 39-531, 40-668, 40-669
  PARRIS 31-509, 33-647
  PRISGRAVE 39-217, 40-305
  ROBERT 30-439, 31-484, 33-411, 34-460, 35-524, 36-568, 37-433, 38-424, 39-443, 40-689
  WILLIAM 30-440, 31-493, 33-414, 34-472, 35-438, 36-525, 36-549, 37-555, 37-576, 38-406, 38-484, 39-530, 39-606, 40-597, 40-668

JARRETT [Garot, Gerett, Jarritt, Jerad]
  JARRETT 33-1423, 34-1108, 36-1691, 37-1216, 38-1111, 39-1248, 40-1263
  WILLIAM 31-1483, 33-1423, 34-1108, 36-1691, 37-1216, 38-1111, 39-1248, 40-1263

JARVIS [Jarves, Jarvice, Jarvise, Jarwile, Jervice]
  RICHARD 40-1262
  SAMUEL 34-1633, 35-1633, 36-993, 37-884, 38-1104
  WILLIAM 30-33, 30-607, 31-647, 33-588, 34-691, 35-741

JEFFERSON [Jeaferson, Jeoferson]
  ABSOLOM [Jeaferson] 39-357, 40-416
  JOHN [Jeaferson] 40-416
  RICHARD [Richeard/jr., sr.] 33-336, 34-265, 35-360, 36-333, 37-372(2), 38-326(2), 39-357(2), 40-416(2)

JENKINS [Garviss, Genkins, Ginkens, Ginkins, Gynkins, Jankins, Jenckins, Jinkins]
  BENJAMIN 33-150
  CHRISTOPHER 30-1127, 31-1119
  JARVIS [Garviss, Jervice/junr., senr.] 30-1428, 31-1530, 33-1527, 34-1518, 35-1541, 36-1648, 37-1092(2), 38-1851(2), 39-1885(2), 40-1956(2)
  JOHN 30-493, 30-669, 31-575, 33-594, 34-349, 34-602, 34-1518, 35-538, 35-1541, 36-254, 36-532, 36-1648, 37-188, 37-623, 37-1092, 38-660, 38-1851, 39-1885, 40-1570, 40-1956
  SAMUEL 36-753, 38-811, 39-761, 40-737
  THOMAS 30-948, 33-901, 34-1133, 35-1083, 36-1147, 37-895

JOHNSON [Jnoson, Johnston, Johson, Jonson]
  ABRAHAM 33-1274, 34-1307, 35-1466
  AFRADOZI [Afradozey, Afradozia, Afreya Doze, Afriadoze] 30-447, 31-342, 33-454, 34-435, 35-431, 36-459, 37-510, 38-584, 39-486, 40-584
  BARTHOLOMEW [Batholomwma, Bathomew, Bertholomew] 35-272, 36-352, 37-247, 38-279, 39-342,

INDEX

40-409
  BENJAMIN 30-254
  DAVID 30-235, 30-858, 31-244,
31-947, 33-283, 33-1129, 34-239,
34-969, 35-287, 36-202, 37-371,
38-382, 38-1201, 39-368, 39-1050,
40-431, 40-1109
  ELIZABETH [widw.] 30-1191,
31-1151, 33-1355, 34-1364
GEORGE 30-447, 31-342, 33-454,
34-436, 35-429, 36-461, 37-512,
38-586, 39-487, 40-585
  HEZEKIAH [Ezekiah, Hixakiah]
30-729, 33-704, 34-724, 36-838,
37-699
  JOHN [Jon./junr., senr.] 30-48,
30-48, 30-138, 30-447, 30-674,
31-54, 31-54, 31-194, 31-342,
31-704, 33-55, 33-55, 33-210,
33-454, 33-706, 34-72, 34-116,
34-342, 34-435, 34-762, 35-45,
35-46, 35-307, 35-431, 35-799,
36-84, 36-84, 36-351, 36-460,
36-837, 36-1476, 37-80, 37-86,
37-302, 37-373, 37-511, 37-697,
38-56, 38-57, 38-219, 38-247,
38-585, 38-817, 39-50, 39-51,
39-169, 39-286, 39-898, 40-51,
40-53, 40-165, 40-265, 40-409,
40-862
  JOSHUA 30-1120, 31-1286,
33-1210, 34-1246, 35-1260,
36-1435, 38-68, 39-1598
  LEONARD [Lenard, Linard,
Linoard] 30-137, 31-193, 33-208,
34-309, 35-247, 36-172, 37-282,
38-254, 39-170, 39-899, 40-261,
40-863
    LEVIN [Leaven] 35-246, 36-351,
37-284, 38-255, 40-263
    LEVIN DENARD [Leaven] 39-183
  MARY 35-1373
  NATHANEIEL 33-1096
  PETER [junr., senr.] 30-673,
31-708, 33-705, 34-727, 35-764,
36-836(2), 37-696(2), 38-818(2),
39-897(2), 40-864(2)
  PURNELL [Purnall] 31-1383,
33-1437, 34-1672, 35-1672,
36-1631, 37-1239, 38-1765,
39-1867, 40-1759
  SAMUEL [Samewell] 30-447,
31-342, 33-454, 33-1437, 35-1674,
37-1225, 38-1780, 39-1868,
40-1761
  SIMON 35-1206, 36-1190,
38-1236, 40-1402
  THOMAS 30-447, 30-955, 31-342,
31-441, 31-988, 33-438, 33-454,
33-902, 34-437, 34-505, 34-1150,
35-430, 35-1229, 36-462, 36-1200,
37-513, 38-587, 38-1238, 39-488,

40-586
  WHITTINGTON 36-1490, 38-1539,
39-1431, 40-1563
  WILLIAM 30-14, 30-729, 31-8,
31-686, 33-90, 33-704, 34-56,
34-724, 35-73, 35-761, 36-95,
36-838, 37-104, 37-699, 38-131,
38-875, 38-1823, 39-38, 39-901,
40-34, 40-861
JON---, WILLIAM 37-947
JONES [Gones, Joanes, John(e)s,
Jons]
  ABRAHAM 30-1171, 31-1240,
33-1332, 34-1230, 35-1272
  ANN [widw.] 33-1279, 34-1372,
35-1321
  BENJAMIN 38-932, 39-960,
40-1023
  CATHERINE 39-973
  CHARLES 30-751, 31-801, 33-789,
34-853, 36-705, 38-965, 39-945,
40-988
  DANIEL 30-783, 30-1035, 31-813,
31-842, 33-845, 34-833, 35-879,
36-873, 37-778, 38-918, 39-977,
40-1008
  EBENEZER [Ebenezah] 30-175,
31-235, 33-186, 34-267, 35-155,
36-334, 37-256, 38-331, 39-348,
40-394
  EDMUND 39-316
  EDWARD 30-1235, 31-1282,
33-1148, 34-1273, 35-1294,
36-1343, 38-1588, 39-1526,
40-1607
  ELISHA 34-1273, 35-1294,
36-1343, 38-1588, 39-1526,
40-1607
  ELIZABETH 31-766
  FINCH 30-1273, 31-1370,
33-1586, 34-1692, 35-1117,
36-1079, 38-1082, 39-1229,
40-1202
  GEORGE 30-386, 30-771, 31-498,
31-767, 33-424, 33-548, 33-823,
34-470, 34-618, 34-845, 35-535,
35-648, 35-899, 36-581, 36-692,
36-885, 37-568, 37-754, 38-405,
38-814, 38-958, 39-657, 39-949,
40-662, 40-982, 40-1245
  JAMES [junr, senr.] 30-776,
30-1020, 30-1035, 31-812, 31-842,
31-1010, 33-841, 33-979, 33-1121,
34-832, 34-1078, 34-1084, 35-878,
35-1036, 36-871, 36-1043, 37-780,
37-874, 38-971, 38-1152, 39-1082,
40-1239
  JOHN [Jon./capt.] 30-255,
30-721, 30-771, 30-776, 30-873,
30-1017, 31-131, 31-723, 31-812,
31-846, 31-1012, 33-306, 33-481,
33-748, 33-841, 33-992, 33-1065,

INDEX

33-1131, 34-302, 34-554, 34-806,
34-832, 34-970, 34-1086, 35-290,
35-839, 35-1035, 35-1160,
35-1620, 36-768, 36-975, 36-1105,
36-1609, 37-361, 37-682, 37-779,
37-812, 37-873, 38-298, 38-458,
38-838, 38-1139, 38-1335,
38-1866, 39-326, 39-442, 39-865,
39-1083, 39-1374, 39-1825,
40-181, 40-525, 40-958, 40-1108,
40-1227, 40-1854
  JOSEPH 30-414, 31-331, 33-412,
34-462, 35-526, 36-382, 37-436,
38-458, 39-442, 40-525,
    LEWIS [Luas/junr.] 30-746,
31-792, 33-796, 34-858, 35-864,
36-861, 37-742, 38-957, 38-957,
39-948, 39-948, 40-984, 40-984
    MATHIAS 30-784, 31-814, 34-832
    MATTHEW 30-493, 31-575, 34-33,
35-49, 36-50, 37-44
    MITCHELL 33-640, 34-669,
35-728, 36-752, 37-770, 38-932,
39-960, 40-1007
    PHILEMON [Philimon] 37-778,
38-918
    RICHARD [Ritchard] 30-754,
31-800, 33-786, 34-700, 34-854,
35-924, 36-915, 39-1560, 40-1658
    ROBERT [capt.] 30-771, 31-767,
33-823, 34-845, 35-898, 36-884,
37-770, 38-932, 39-960, 40-1023
    SAMUEL 30-746, 31-786, 33-796,
34-858, 35-864, 36-861, 37-742,
38-946, 38-1137, 39-947, 39-1352,
40-985, 40-1362
    THOMAS 30-772, 31-333, 31-1296,
33-823, 33-1189, 34-845, 34-1269,
35-898, 35-1305, 36-210, 36-889,
36-1380, 37-1227, 38-658,
38-1349, 39-480, 39-726, 39-996,
40-394, 40-448, 40-760, 40-1868
    WILLIAM [Williams/capt., junr.,
senr.] 30-521, 30-582, 30-640,
30-773, 30-1008, 31-567, 31-641,
31-763, 31-833, 31-1142, 33-608,
33-639, 33-827, 33-956, 33-1279,
33-1378, 34-660, 34-696, 34-878,
34-1348, 34-1372, 35-650, 35-674,
35-895, 35-1063, 35-1321,
35-1391, 36-647, 36-695, 36-890,
36-1336, 36-1500, 37-773, 38-682,
38-790, 38-913, 38-925, 38-930,
38-1263, 38-1519, 39-697, 39-726,
39-869, 39-966, 39-976, 39-1441,
40-760, 40-837, 40-894, 40-1024,
40-1028, 40-1549
JORDINE [Jorden, Jourdine], AARON
30-1058, 31-1212, 33-1290,
34-1220, 35-1342, 36-1414

JOSEPH
  FREDERICK [Fedrick] 30-166,
31-228, 33-334, 35-264, 37-238,
38-248, 39-336, 40-356
  JEREMIAH 35-1194
JUDONEE, ROGER 38-996
JUETT, WILLIAM [Dewitt, Duit]
35-15, 36-71, 37-73, 38-18,
39-66, 40-75

KELLAM [Calem, Cellam, Celum,
Cillim, Kelamb, Keliam, Kellem,
Kellum, Killi(a)m]
  EDWARD 30-918, 31-871, 33-1033,
34-1007, 35-1125, 36-1113,
37-880, 38-1102, 39-1054, 40-1185
  ISAAC 33-91
  ISAAC [Kellem, Kellum] 34-28,
35-114, 36-45, 37-19, 38-531,
39-1449, 40-1568
  JOHN [junr., senr.] 30-73(2),
31-85(2), 31-1153, 33-91(2),
33-1033, 33-1364, 34-28, 34-29,
34-1007, 34-1357, 35-114(2),
35-1371, 36-45, 36-46, 36-1113,
36-1488, 37-19, 37-20, 37-880,
38-58, 38-88, 38-1102, 38-1529,
39-90, 39-157, 39-1054, 39-1469,
40-125, 40-160, 40-1185, 40-1584
  JOSHUA 30-73, 31-85, 34-89,
35-1436, 38-1546, 39-1449,
40-1568
  WILLIAM 33-1364, 34-1344,
35-1499, 36-1497, 38-1555,
39-157, 39-1454, 40-125, 40-652
KELLASON, WILLIAM 31-771
KELLETT [Killett], ROGER [Rodger]
38-736, 39-775, 40-1998
KELLEY [Kill(e)y(e)]
  GEORGE 34-1037, 35-1084, 36-326
  HUGH 39-779
  JAMES 30-70, 33-86, 34-123,
35-115, 36-51, 37-62, 38-2, 39-31
  JOHN 30-34, 30-564, 31-41,
31-613, 31-1051, 33-316, 33-668,
33-874, 34-336, 34-681, 34-1169,
35-749, 35-1222, 36-729, 38-807,
39-782, 40-725
  NICHOLAS [Nicklas, Nickoles]
30-349, 31-318, 33-381, 35-180,
36-246
KELNICK, THOMAS 33-1316
KEMEY [Ke(e)my, Keme, Kemeny,
Kemmy, Kimey]
  ABRAHAM 36-1155, 37-907,
39-1328, 40-1307
  JOHN 36-1156
  THOMAS 37-904, 39-1338, 40-1384
  WALTER 35-1199, 36-1169,
37-965, 38-1142, 39-1336, 40-1383
KEMP [Camp, Kempe]
  JOHN 30-1447, 31-944, 33-1542,

INDEX

34-946, 35-997, 36-1261, 37-811, 38-1121, 39-1049
    MATTHEW 37-811, 38-1121, 39-1049, 40-1114
KENDALL [Cundall, Kindall, Kindell]
    JOHN [Cundall] 38-809
    PATRICK 33-648, 34-571, 35-690, 38-970, 39-728
    WILLIAM 33-93, 34-28, 35-113, 36-42, 37-144, 38-698, 39-760, 40-736
KENNEY [Kemey]
    HENRY 34-1167
    JOSEPH 30-169, 31-240, 33-174,
    LAZARUS [Laseres, Lazares] 31-239, 33-175
    STEPHEN 30-170, 31-239, 33-175
    WILLIAM 30-170, 34-1043, 35-1064, 36-1034, 38-1300, 40-1269
KENNITT [Kennett, Kinnett]
    JOHN 39-218, 40-334
    MARTIN [Kennet/Martain(e) 30-244, 31-307, 33-291, 34-242, 35-286, 36-298, 37-338, 38-162, 39-239, 40-333,
    WILLIAM [Kinette/jr, sr.] 30-247, 31-285, 33-301, 34-280, 35-339, 36-211, 37-295, 38-210, 39-188, 40-337(2)
KENNY [Kerny, Kinn(e)y]
    JOHN 33-829, 34-838, 35-892, 36-738, 38-743, 39-777, 40-734
    WILLIAM 39-1210
KENT, JOHN 38-243
KERSEY, WILLIAM 31-128
KETH, JOHN 40-261
KEY, WILLIAM 37-85, 38-119
KIBBLE [Keeble, Kebble, Kibbell]
    WIDOW 34-1561
    JOHN 33-1550, 34-1576, 35-1539, 37-883, 38-1095, 39-1055, 40-1207
    THOMAS 38-1626
    WILLIAM [junr., senr.] 31-1515(2), 33-1550, 33-1550, 34-1561, 35-1687, 36-1567, 37-1056, 38-1809, 39-1908, 40-1986
KILLBY [Killbey]
    HUGH 40-733
    JOHN 38-1265
    WILLIAM 33-128, 34-65
KING [Kings]
    COLONEL 34-571
    BENJAMIN 30-540, 31-593
    CAPELL [Capbell, Capill, Capwell, Kepwell/capt.] 30-637, 30-1465, 31-1351, 31-649, 33-680, 34-695, 35-689, 36-737, 38-743, 39-780, 40-1088
    CHARLES 38-687, 39-783, 40-754

    DUNCAN 30-750, 31-779, 33-586
    ELEANOR [Eliner] 30-570, 31-60
    ELIZABETH 31-601, 38-1735
    EPHRAIM 39-780, 40-1088
    HUGH 38-1735, 39-1694, 40-1911
    JAMES 30-24, 30-1301, 31-26, 31-1339, 33-28, 34-95, 35-121, 36-755
    JESSE [Jesey] 39-811, 40-777
    JOHN 31-599, 33-659, 34-666, 35-600, 36-669
    NEHEMIAH 30-635, 31-514, 33-648, 34-571, 35-690, 36-662, 38-737, 39-778, 40-780
    PHILLIP 30-1021, 31-1007, 33-909, 34-1144, 35-1185, 36-1162, 37-910, 38-1286, 39-1230, 40-1433
    PLANNER 34-664, 35-626, 36-609
    ROBERT [col./junr., senr./majr., col] 30-101, 30-635, 31-31, 31-514, 33-34, 33-648, 34-90, 34-571, 35-119, 35-690(2), 36-110, 36-662(2), 37-152, 38-135, 38-737(2), 39-129, 39-778(2), 40-163, 40-780(2)
    WHITTINGTON [Whettinton, Whit., Whitenton, Whiting.] 30-595, 31-599, 33-659, 34-666, 35-600, 36-670, 38-691, 39-728, 40-751
    WILLIAM 30-1014, 31-1009, 33-910, 34-1143, 35-1187, 36-1161, 36-1697, 37-909, 38-1296, 38-1743, 39-1320, 39-1675, 40-1309, 40-1756
KINNEY [Kinne]
    THOMAS 39-351
    WILLIAM 30-1005, 31-1022, 33-947
KINSEY [Kinnisey], JOHN 30-261
KIRKMAN, ROGER [Rodger] 34-1123, 35-1183, 36-1153
KITCHIN [Kidchin], WILLIAM 31-1353, 34-575, 35-724, 36-1475, 38-1534, 39-1480, 40-1530
KNIGHT [Knite]
    JAMES 30-1060, 31-1247, 33-1289, 34-1281, 35-1337, 36-1413, 38-1509, 39-1397, 40-1462
    JOSHUA 30-1060, 31-1247
    RICHARD [Richart] 30-1060, 31-1247, 33-1289, 34-1281, 35-1337, 36-1413, 38-1509, 39-1396, 40-1098, 40-1459
KNOT [Not], ISAAC [Issack] 30-566, 31-563, 33-645, 34-597, 36-671, 38-712, 39-784
KNOWLES [Noals, Noles, Nould(s), Noules, Noulls, Nowils, Nowlews, Nowls]

INDEX

    EDMUND [Edman/senr.] 30-936, 31-1077, 33-914, 34-1035, 35-1093, 36-1120, 37-972(2), 38-1151(2), 39-1093(2), 40-1223(2)
      JOHN 37-944
      RICHARD 31-1077, 33-914, 34-1035, 35-1093, 36-1120, 37-972, 38-1151, 39-1123, 40-1232
      SAMUEL 30-416
      WILLIAM 38-1872, 39-1894, 40-1872
KNOX [Nocks, Nox]
    JOHN 34-1188, 38-1136
    ROBERT 30-1437, 31-1472, 33-1497, 34-1506, 35-1593, 36-1703
    WILLIAM 30-520, 33-1497, 34-1506, 35-1593, 36-1703, 37-1033, 39-1783, 40-1968

LA---, JOHN 30-699
LABRUCE [Bruce, Debruce, Labrouss, Lebrooce, Leebruse, Libruse], BENJAMIN [Beniamon] 30-597, 31-611, 33-562, 34-642, 35-740, 36-706, 38-727, 39-771, 40-728
LACKEY [Lackie, Leckie]
    ALEXANDER 30-1459, 31-1349, 33-1402, 34-1624, 35-1614, 36-1757, 37-1172, 38-1629, 39-1829, 40-1867
    PATRICK 30-25
LAHY [Lahee, Lake, Layhe, Layhill] ANDREW 34-836, 35-871, 36-865, 37-787
LAHYDILL, SPEAR [Speir] 35-1663
LAKE, BENJAMIN 36-1606
LAMARD, JOSEPH 31-1448
LAMBDEN [Lambdon, Lamdon]
    RICHARD 39-1569, 40-1652
    THOMAS [mr.] 31-1169, 33-1179, 34-1420, 35-1457, 36-1373, 38-1600, 39-1569, 40-1652
LAMBERSON [Lambertson]
    ABRAHAM [jr.] 30-1222, 31-1193, 33-1187(2), 34-1267(2), 35-1328(2), 36-1379(2), 38-1603, 39-1542, 40-1617
      HENRY 40-1618
      JOHANNAS [Johannus] 31-1194, 33-1186
    JOHN 30-1250, 31-1188, 33-1170, 34-1309, 35-1311, 36-1349, 38-628, 39-441, 40-461
    ROBERT 31-1188, 33-1170, 34-1309, 35-1311, 36-1350, 38-1611, 39-1550, 40-1647
    SAMUEL 33-1187, 34-1267, 35-1328, 36-1379, 38-1603, 39-1540, 40-1616
    SARAH 40-1618
LANCAKE [Langcake, Lank(c)ake]
    FRANCIS [Fras.] 30-1264, 31-1372, 33-1432, 34-1666, 36-1698, 37-1219, 38-1770, 39-1667
    GEORGE 30-1274, 31-1348, 33-1433, 34-1667, 37-1220, 38-1769
    STEPHEN 34-1666, 36-1698, 37-1219, 38-1770, 39-1667
LANDEN [Landin, Landon, Londin], HENRY 30-6, 31-18, 33-6, 34-580, 35-92, 36-6, 37-126, 38-153, 39-4, 40-5
LANDMAN [Landen, Lanman] JOHN 30-1210, 33-1345, 34-1197, 36-1476, 38-1375
LANE [Layn]
    ABRAHAM [Ab.] 39-778, 40-780
    GEORGE 30-1217, 31-451, 31-709, 34-722, 35-759, 36-451, 37-612, 38-623, 39-835, 40-876
    JOHN 31-1226, 33-1307, 34-1299, 35-1351, 36-1461, 38-1481, 39-1506, 40-1591
    WILLIAM [capt., mr.] 30-1241, 31-1307, 34-1251, 35-1459, 36-1340, 38-1582, 39-1546, 40-876, 40-1589(2)
LANG, JOHN 31-369, 36-848
LANGSDELL/LANGSTON [Langsdale, Langsdill, Langston, Lank(s)dell, Lankson]
    JOHN 30-1048, 31-1036, 33-879, 34-1161, 35-1204, 36-1184, 38-1318, 39-1281, 40-1409
    SPEAR 30-893, 31-1036, 33-1026, 36-981, 37-806, 38-1106, 39-1354
    WILLIAM 30-892, 31-954, 33-1018, 34-1097, 35-1027, 36-1066, 37-973, 38-1071, 39-1258, 40-119
LANK
    FRANCIS 35-1680, 40-1757
    GEORGE 35-1681, 36-1699
    STEPHEN 40-1757
LANKFORD [Lan(g)ford, Langfort]
    BENJAMIN 30-107, 31-34, 33-39, 34-14, 35-66, 36-100, 37-144, 38-123, 39-26, 40-29
    EDWARD 34-1079, 35-1016, 36-955, 38-1245, 39-1218, 40-1135
    JOHN [jur., senr.] 30-1033, 31-1072, 33-1120(2), 34-1079(2), 35-1016(2), 36-955, 36-956, 38-1245, 38-1246, 39-1218, 39-1219, 40-1135(2)
    JOSEPH [junior, senior] 30-107(2), 31-103(2), 33-39, 33-101, 34-86(2), 35-57, 35-58,

INDEX

36-32, 36-34, 37-7, 37-8, 38-70, 38-124, 39-150, 39-151, 40-108, 40-109

   PEWSEY [Pus(e)y] 38-124, 39-150, 40-108

   SOLOMON 33-101, 34-86, 35-57, 36-32, 37-7, 38-123, 39-150, 40-108

   THOMAS 30-886, 31-957, 33-1119, 34-1090, 35-1012, 36-955, 36-1111, 38-1154, 38-1741, 39-1218, 39-1221, 40-1143

LANSDELL   See Langsdell/Langston.

LARAMORE [Larimore, Larmore, Larremore, Larrimore, Leremor]

   JAMES 35-948, 36-1211, 38-1025, 39-1028, 40-1056

   JOHN [senr.] 30-821(2), 31-888(2), 33-1140, 33-1397, 34-913, 34-1618, 35-955, 35-1613, 36-963, 36-1527, 37-1197, 38-1044, 38-1736

    LEVIN 40-1072

    MARY 39-1057, 40-1072

    THOMAS [junr., senr.] 30-814(2), 30-821, 31-849(2), 31-888, 33-1075, 33-1140, 34-913, 34-907, 35-948, 36-1211, 38-1025, 39-1028, 40-1056

LAREY [Lairy, Lare, Lary], TIMOTHY 30-617, 31-650, 34-677, 35-748, 36-742, 38-939, 39-958

LARREN, TEAGUE 33-617

LATCHAM, [Lactham, Latchamb, Latchim, Latchumb], THOMAS 30-273, 31-300, 33-253, 34-303, 35-291, 36-209, 37-291, 38-311, 39-270, 40-211

LATHBURY [Larthbery, Lathberey, Lethbery, Lithbery

   ABIGAIL [Abgile, Abgail] 30-212, 31-271

   ARTHUR [Arter] 30-212, 31-271, 33-144, 34-212, 35-231, 36-341, 37-313, 38-165, 39-205, 40-226

    GEORGE 35-170, 37-320, 38-343, 39-180

LAUGHINGHOUSE [La(r)thinghouse, Laugh House, Loughinghours], WILLIAM 33-146, 34-198, 35-289, 36-264, 37-212

LAURENCE, [Larrance] HENRY 35-326, 36-289, 37-227, 38-213, 39-262, 40-175

LAWLESS [Ladels, Lales, Lawliss]

   JAMES 34-844, 35-905, 36-877, 37-777, 38-929, 39-781, 39-980, 40-834

   JOHN 31-625

LAWS [Law, Lawes, Lows]

   BOLITHA [Belitha] 37-622, 38-661, 40-672

   ELIJAH [Elija] 38-661, 39-608, 40-672

   JAMES 30-531, 31-529, 33-599, 34-615, 35-667, 36-685, 38-775, 39-709, 40-775

   JOHN [jr.] 30-748, 31-795(2), 33-1376, 34-849, 34-1282, 35-862, 35-1353, 36-919, 36-1497, 37-622, 37-743, 38-959, 38-1568, 39-956, 39-1792, 40-983(2), 40-1555

   LAZARUS 36-1497

   PANTER [Panther, Panthur, Painter] 30-767, 31-768, 33-822, 34-842, 35-900, 36-862, 37-738, 38-936, 39-991, 40-1017

   ROBERT 30-767, 31-768, 33-822, 34-842, 35-900, 36-862, 37-738, 38-936, 39-990, 40-1016

   THOMAS 30-750, 31-796, 33-791, 34-851, 35-860, 36-912, 37-751, 38-962, 39-951, 40-981

   WILLIAM 30-767, 30-1184, 31-768, 33-822, 33-1376, 34-842, 34-1282, 35-900, 35-1354, 36-862, 37-738, 38-936, 38-1553, 39-992, 39-1446, 40-1018, 40-1553

LAWSON, PETER 40-1379

LAY [Leay]

   JOHN 30-296, 31-413, 33-387, 34-421, 35-509, 36-467, 37-398, 38-528, 39-556

   SAMUEL 38-529, 40-192

   WILLIAM 37-399

LAYCOCK, JOHN 38-464

LAYFIELD [Lafild, Layfeild, Layfild

   CATHERINE [widw] 33-1156, 34-1252

   DAVID 35-1596, 38-669, 39-665, 40-1814

   GEORGE 30-1252, 31-1284, 33-1156, 34-1252, 35-1288, 36-1364, 38-1548, 39-1559, 40-1636

   ROBERT 30-528, 31-537, 33-574, 38-709, 39-678, 40-788

   THOMAS 30-538, 30-1252, 31-538, 31-1284, 36-677, 38-669, 38-738, 39-665, 39-745, 40-731, 40-785

   WILLIAM 30-557, 31-537, 33-574, 36-677, 38-669, 39-665, 40-854

LAYTON [Laton]

   GEORGE 39-422

   LEVIN 40-1892

LEARMOUTH [Larmouth], ALEXANDER 38-138, 39-1377

LEATHER, STEPHEN 34-594

LEATHERBURY [Leatherberry, Lesherbury, Letherbur(e)y]

   CHARLES 40-1024

   JOHN [junr., mr.] 30-782, 33-848, 34-820, 34-946, 35-885,

INDEX

35-1519, 36-876, 36-1517, 37-774, 37-992, 38-925(2), 39-976(2), 40-780, 40-1024
   PERRY [Parr(e)y 34-820, 35-885, 36-872, 37-992
   THOMAS 30-633, 31-644, 33-1536, 35-1520
LECATT [Lecate]
   BARTHOLOMEW 30-1286
   JOHN 30-1286, 31-1327, 33-1607, 34-1473, 35-1761, 36-1692, 37-1206, 38-1756, 39-1677, 40-1772
LEE, JOHN [jnr., snr.] 33-476(2)
LEGG [Leggs, Ligg, Logg],
BENJAMIN 30-19, 31-5, 34-1616, 35-1621, 37-999, 38-1864, 39-1823
LEONARD [LanyeardM Leanord, Lenard], JOHN 39-1584, 40-1665
   JOSEPH 30-1294, 34-1698, 35-1750, 36-1730, 37-1156, 38-1717, 39-1714, 40-1778
LESULL
   DAVID 34-639
   ROBERT 34-639, 35-687
   THOMAS 34-639, 35-687
   WILLIAM 34-639, 35-687
LEWIS [Lewes, Lues, Luwes]
   ARTHUR [Aurther] 36-328, 37-243, 38-273, 39-1342, 40-1440
   CHRISTOPHER 35-1710, 36-1532, 37-1173
   JOSEPH [sr.] 33-178, 36-320, 37-262, 38-265, 38-647, 39-373, 39-401, 40-369, 40-376
   LEVIN 39-1343
   SAMUEL 39-1343
   WILLIAM [jr., sr.] 30-349, 31-318, 31-572, 33-458, 33-648, 34-249, 34-1218, 35-552, 35-1340, 36-320, 36-530, 37-239, 37-262, 38-266, 38-269, 38-414, 39-331, 39-375, 39-545, 40-387, 40-388, 40-528
LINCH [Lynch]
   ABRAHAM 30-201, 31-155, 33-245, 34-206, 35-257, 36-175, 37-168, 38-167, 39-284, 40-218
   ALEXANDER 30-198, 31-158, 33-285, 34-240, 35-202, 36-198, 37-298, 38-384, 39-197, 40-228
   CORNELIUS [Curnelus] 30-1279, 31-1378
   JOHN [junr., senr] 30-179, 30-201, 31-155, 31-205, 33-159, 33-255, 34-212, 34-320, 35-188, 40-433
   MICHAEL [Mikell] 33-1425, 34-1693, 35-1740, 36-1633, 37-1217, 38-1764, 39-1869, 40-2000
LINDALL [Glindell, Lendell, Lindell, Lindow, Lyndall]. See also Lindow.
   PETER 30-442, 31-505, 33-384, 34-563, 36-594, 37-585, 38-659, 39-570, 40-459
   ROBERT 30-470, 31-354, 33-354, 34-1311, 35-1312, 36-1350, 38-1610, 39-1549, 40-1625
   THOMAS 38-1733
LINDONE, JOHN 35-147
LINDOW [Lendow, Lindan, Lindo, Lindol]
   JAMES 30-594, 30-1236, 31-533, 33-604, 34-620, 35-702, 35-1515
   MARGARET 36-667, 38-686, 38-1578, 39-725, 39-1514, 40-754, 40-1659
   THOMAS 30-1296, 31-1342, 33-1468, 34-1454, 35-1737, 36-1740, 37-1234, 39-1692, 40-1810
LINGO [Ling, Lingoe, Lingow]
   DANIEL 30-1310, 31-1519, 33-935, 34-1057
   JACOB 30-1321, 33-1460, 34-1680, 35-1582
   JAMES 36-1710, 37-1132, 39-1727
   JOHN 30-1317, 31-1392, 33-1459, 34-1687, 35-1756, 36-1726, 37-1134, 38-1684, 39-1726, 40-1795
   RICHARD 33-1116, 34-1682, 35-1580, 36-1758, 37-1121, 38-1688, 39-1734, 40-1801
   ROBERT 33-1461
   ROBERTSON [Roberson, Robinson, Robison, Robeson] 30-1335, 31-1518, 34-1679, 35-1585, 36-1707, 37-1129, 38-1679, 39-1730, 40-1918
LINSEY [Lenzey, Lindsey, Linz(e)y]
   JAMES 33-763, 35-821, 36-791, 37-656, 38-823, 39-827, 40-937
   THOMAS 31-1113, 35-104, 36-35, 37-51, 38-52, 39-103, 40-112
LIPTROTT, JOHN [Liptroatt, Lyptrott] 30-275, 31-1152, 33-325, 34-207, 35-237, 36-240, 37-343, 38-307, 39-346, 40-370
LISTER [Lidster, Lyster]
   JANE [Jean(e)] 33-20, 34-104, 35-95, 36-114, 37-130, 38-140, 39-20, 40-161
   THOMAS 30-19, 35-95, 36-114, 37-130, 38-140, 39-20, 40-161
   WILLIAM 30-19, 30-19, 31-5, 35-95, 36-114, 37-130, 38-146, 39-12, 40-458
LITTLETON, EDMUND 40-1314
LLOYD [Lawed]
   THOMAS 39-951, 40-981

INDEX

TUCKER 30-586
WILLIAM 34-108, 35-93
LOCKEY [Locee, Locke, Logey, Lokey, Lokie]
  ALEXANDER [Ellick] 37-1141, 38-1809
  JOHN 30-1382, 31-1407
  THOMAS 30-1379, 31-1413, 33-1538, 34-1599, 35-1630, 36-1593, 37-1017, 38-1830, 39-1805, 40-1990
LOCKWOOD [Logwood]
  ARMORALL [Armale, Armesall] 30-250, 39-236, 40-286
  JOHN 39-237, 40-287
  MARY [widow] 38-301, 39-237, 40-287
  RICHARD 30-250, 31-287, 33-300, 34-291, 35-297, 36-203, 37-316
  WILLIAM 30-530, 31-539, 33-685, 34-629, 35-707, 36-686, 38-935, 39-714, 40-774
LOGEY, ALEXANDER [Loge, Logen, Login] 0-1065, 31-1218, 33-1296, 34-1334
LOLEY, JAMES 33-1543
LONG
  COULBOURN 30-95, 33-121, 34-127, 35-1269, 36-1273, 37-653, 38-125, 39-25, 40-133
  DANIEL [junr., senr.] 30-119(2), 31-107(2), 33-120, 33-123, 34-113, 34-114, 35-134, 35-138, 36-126, 36-129, 37-97, 37-100, 38-94, 38-95, 39-115, 39-1407, 40-135, 40-1460
  DAVID [jr., senr.] 30-96, 30-119, 31-106, 31-107, 33-120, 33-121, 34-115, 34-127, 35-136, 35-138, 36-128, 36-130, 37-99, 38-72, 38-93, 39-116, 39-149, 40-136, 40-505
  JEFFREY [Jeoffrey] 30-17(2), 31-9(2), 33-122, 34-128, 35-135, 36-127, 37-98, 38-76, 39-117, 40-134
  JOHN 30-1110, 31-1265, 33-1384, 34-52, 34-389, 35-67, 35-853, 36-101, 37-142, 37-731, 38-125, 39-25, 39-833, 40-28, 40-421
  RANDALL 30-68, 30-78, 31-113, 33-96, 34-23, 35-108, 36-40, 37-48, 38-63, 39-97
  SAMUEL [junr., senr.] 30-17, 30-96, 31-9, 31-106, 33-18, 33-121, 34-60, 34-127, 35-78, 35-136, 36-14, 36-128, 37-99, 37-111, 38-72, 38-143, 39-17, 39-116, 40-15, 40-133
  SOLOMON 30-624, 31-550, 33-624, 34-649, 35-647, 36-724, 38-698, 39-760, 40-736
  SOWELL [Sawell, Saywell] 30-17, 34-1412, 36-127, 37-129, 38-76, 39-117
  WILLIAM [mr.] 30-96, 31-106, 33-121, 33-1143, 34-127, 35-136, 36-128, 37-99, 38-72, 39-116, 40-133
LONGO [Longer, Longoe, Longow], JAMES 30-1307, 31-1455, 33-1462, 34-1684, 35-1716, 38-1682, 40-1915
LOOKER, WILLIAM [Lucker] 35-199, 36-353, 37-218, 38-344, 39-398, 40-289
LOOWILL, JOHN 39-136
LORD [Laud]
  ALEXANDER [Ellicksander] 30-49, 33-59, 34-69, 35-40, 36-57, 37-22, 38-61, 39-56, 40-69
  FRANCIS 30-49, 31-56, 33-59, 34-69, 35-40, 36-57, 37-21, 38-33
  HENRY 30-56, 31-56, 33-59, 34-44, 35-103, 36-58, 37-22, 38-30, 39-53
  JOHN 30-92, 31-56, 33-87, 34-33, 35-40, 38-1315, 40-1400
  MOSES 38-1096
  RANDALL 31-88, 33-59, 34-69, 35-40, 36-57, 38-33, 39-56, 40-57
  THOMAS 30-49, 31-56, 33-59, 34-69, 34-707, 35-40, 35-719, 36-57, 36-704, 37-21, 38-31, 38-735, 39-55
LORWILL, JOHN 40-1517
LOWE [Loe, Low, Lowant, Lows]
  CAPTAIN 34-1543
  CHARLES 31-774, 33-815, 34-169, 35-356, 36-292, 37-349
  GEORGE 30-385, 30-474, 31-354, 33-352, 34-360, 35-381, 36-432, 37-432, 38-436, 39-429, 40-517
  JOHN 34-1087, 35-1015, 36-959, 38-1179, 39-1217, 40-1137
  RALPH [Rase, Reafe, Relph] 30-1032, 31-1046, 33-1056, 34-1087, 35-1015, 36-959, 38-1179, 39-1217, 40-1137
  ROBERT [Robin] 33-1056, 34-1087, 35-1015, 36-959, 37-1207, 38-236, 39-345, 40-395
  WILLIAM 31-1136
LOWRY [Lawrie, Lowree], WILLIAM 37-458, 38-397, 39-611, 40-208
LOWS [Lewes, Lewis, Lowes]
  MRS. 33-1579
  ARTHUR [Art(h)er 31-230, 33-179, 34-275, 35-266
  HENRY [capt.] 30-1417, 31-1505, 35-1747, 36-1554, 37-1243, 38-1636, 39-1910, 40-2001
  JOSEPH 30-165, 31-229, 34-276, 35-265

INDEX

WILLIAM [Lewes, Lewis] 31-231, 35-265
LUKE [Luak]
  WILLIAM 30-1236
  WILLIAMSON [Luak] 33-836, 34-880, 35-868, 36-881, 37-786, 38-984, 39-970, 40-1003
LYNDAS, JOSEPH 39-1366
LYNN [Lin]
  AARON 30-948, 31-1048, 33-1087, 34-1042, 35-1083, 36-1144, 37-893, 38-1133, 39-1366, 40-1262
  JOHN 36-1144

MACABE [Macabe, Makab], HENRY 30-815, 31-850
MACADY, JOHN 39-1345
MACALLEN [Mackallen, Mackallin], ARTHUR MackAllen, Arthur 39-1485, 40-1587
MACAM, GEORGE 34-660
MACAPE, WILLIAM 39-1027
MACAY, JOHN 36-1102
MACCOOMS, JAMES 40-393
MACDANIEL [MackDaniel, Mac(k)dannel, Mackdanll, McDonill, McDonnall, Makdanil, Mkdanill, McDannish]
  ALLEN 30-1149, 31-1121, 33-1246, 34-1408, 35-1401
  DAVID 30-592, 31-571, 33-591, 34-583, 35-614, 36-630, 38-769, 39-787, 40-803
  JAMES 30-1231, 31-595, 33-1380, 34-1289, 35-1355, 36-1496, 38-1554, 39-1451, 40-1556
  JOHN 34-869, 38-1554, 39-332, 39-1451, 40-382
  MOSES 30-1149, 31-1121, 33-1246, 34-1408, 35-1401
  OWEN 33-812, 35-910, 36-895, 37-763, 38-773, 39-750
  RANDALL 31-630, 33-614, 34-676
MACDORMAN [McDarmond, McDormon, McDurmock]
  DARBY 35-863, 36-910, 37-752, 38-954, 39-937, 40-972
  WILLIAM 30-513, 31-574, 34-658, 36-644, 38-813, 39-792, 40-819
MACDOWELL [Mackdowll, McDowell], JOHN 30-883, 31-892, 33-891, 34-1019, 35-1087, 36-1229, 38-1157, 39-1170, 40-1244
MACINTIRE [Mackinteer, Mackintyre], DANIEL 33-680, 34-695
MACINTOSH [Makentosh, Mcandtoush], HUGH 34-292, 40-1417
MACKEN, HUGH 33-220
MACKEY [Mcckeey, Makeey], MICHAEL [Mikeall] 30-860, 31-938

MACMANUS [Mackmanus], JAMES 30-459
MACMURRAY [Mackmorey, Mackmorie, Mak(e)morie, McMorry, McMorie]
  ANN 39-1848, 40-1822
  JAMES 30-1466, 31-1354, 33-1411, 34-1641, 35-1705, 36-1540, 37-1183, 38-1698
MACNEAL [McNeale, McNeil], ARCHIBALD 34-443, 35-364, 37-521, 38-579, 39-571, 40-575
MACORPINT, ROBERT 33-1465
MACOWEN [Mackowen], THOMAS 33-84
MACOY [Macoye], JOHN 31-939, 33-1393, 34-1627, 35-1608
MADDEN, TIMOTHY [Tim] 36-1625
MADDOX [Maddux, Madix, Mattax, Mattex, Mattix, Mattox, Muttex]
  ALEXANDER 30-91, 30-1291, 31-100, 31-1377, 33-1584, 34-1465, 35-1653, 36-1688, 37-1228, 38-1377, 38-1758, 39-1679, 40-1667, 40-1675, 40-1897
  BELL 30-91, 31-100, 33-117, 34-40, 35-97, 36-138, 37-18, 38-87, 39-158, 40-126
  DANIEL 30-568, 31-583, 33-653, 34-601, 35-634, 36-643, 38-755, 39-801, 40-821
  JOHN 36-634, 38-757, 39-807, 40-822
  LAZARUS 30-497, 30-1127, 31-580, 31-1119, 33-595, 33-1203, 34-598, 34-1330, 35-742, 35-1253, 36-645, 38-759, 39-797, 39-1586, 40-820
  MARGARET 36-1276
  MARY 36-137, 37-17, 38-97, 39-159, 40-128
  THOMAS [junr., senr.] 30-91, 30-567, 31-100, 31-581, 33-117, 33-596, 34-40, 34-577, 35-97, 35-723(2), 36-634, 37-105, 38-96, 38-757, 39-807, 40-127, 40-822, 40-1905
  WILLIAM 30-1292, 31-1376, 33-1585, 34-1464, 35-1652, 36-1687, 37-1229, 38-1757, 39-1680, 40-1884
MAGAN, JOHN 30-1174, 31-1204
MAGEE [Magey, Magge, McGee, Megee] GEORGE 30-1324, 31-1458, 33-1522, 34-1520, 35-1540, 36-1617, 37-1040, 38-1807, 39-1741, 40-1800
  JOHN 30-1325, 31-1484, 33-1615, 34-1483, 35-1579, 36-1567, 37-1056, 38-1807, 39-1741, 40-1882
  MOSES 37-1122, 38-1689, 39-

INDEX

1742, 40-1812
    PETER [junr., senr.] 30-1323, 30-1407, 31-1484, 31-1485, 33-1484, 33-1533, 34-1568, 34-1575, 35-1527, 35-1529, 36-1578, 36-1749(2), 37-1049(2), 37-1212, 38-1806(2), 38-1884, 39-1740, 39-1899(2), 40-1233(2), 40-1812
    SAMUEL 33-1610, 35-1540, 36-1617, 37-1038, 38-1806, 39-1908, 40-1986
    THOMAS 38-1806, 39-1899, 40-1233
MAGGWIGGEN, PATRICK 38-1823
MAGLIN, JOHN 33-1086
MAGOO, THOMAS 31-87
MAGRAUGH [Ma(c)graw, Macgrah, Magrach, McGra, Magrah, Magrough, McGra, Megra(ug)h, Mograw]
    DAVID 30-628, 31-512
    JAMES 30-517, 31-509, 33-626, 34-877, 35- 902 , 36-887, 37-764, 38-970, 39-964, 40-1031
    JEAN 30-538, 31-548, 34-616, 35-714, 36-688, 39-708
    JOHN 30-526, 31-547, 33-834, 34-834, 35-872, 36-866, 37-792, 38-976, 39-984, 40-998
    RICHARD 39-715, 40-767
    ROBERT 31-548, 33-684, 34-616, 35-714, 36-688, 38-777, 39-708, 40-770
    WILLIAM 30-529, 31-545, 33-686, 34-630, 35-1565, 36-1669, 37-1106
MALCOLM [Macom(b), Macumb, Makin, Makum, Malco(l)m, Malkem, Mocum]
    GEORGE 31-769, 33-619, 35-650, 36-656, 37-770, 38-790, 39-1806, 40-1014
    ROBERT 30-770, 31-769, 33-619, 34-822, 35-887
    TIMOTHY 30-807, 31-829, 33-1101, 34-901, 35-940, 36-1205, 37-826, 38-1029, 39-1005, 40-1048
MALINGO, JACOB 31-816
MALLALY [Mallaly, Mallile, Maybillie], PATRICK 30-1337, 31-1439, 33-1490
MALLIN [Mallen, Mullin], CHRISTOPHER 30-486, 33-755, 34-794, 35-849, 36-784, 37-724, 38-821, 39-836, 40-932
MALONE [Mallone, Malloon, Maylone, Mellone, Molone], ROBERT 30-1406, 31-1485, 33-1534, 35-1528, 36-1750, 37-1053, 38-1639, 39-1904, 40-1746
MALONEY [Molonie], PATRICK 30-458
MAN, THOMAS 34-1691
MANARING [Mannering, Manwering], ABRAHAM 33-554, 34-505, 35-477, 36-574, 37-462
MANKLYN [Manklin(e), Menklyn] RICHARD 30-239, 31-297, 33-287, 34-301, 35-344, 36-273, 37-292, 38-385, 39-218, 40-334
MANLOVE [Maniste, Manlef, Manlife, Manliff, Manlose], EMMANUEL [Amanll., Manuel] 30-976, 31-1034, 33-855, 34-1190, 35-1214, 36-1185, 37-961, 38-1138, 39-1351, 40-1367
MARCHMENT
    CHARLES 30-1246, 33-695, 34-1410, 35-547, 36-493, 37-578, 38-412, 39-534, 40-541
    WILLIAM 30-1246
MARCY [Marey, Marsey, Masey, Mercey, Mercys, Mers(i)ey]
    ADKINS [Atkins, Attkens, Edkins] 30-129, 31-182, 33-201, 34-163, 35-252, 36-361, 37-306
    ALEXANDER 30-257, 31-303, 33-310, 34-185, 35-318, 36-230, 37-363, 38-345, 39-307, 40-314
    ELIZABETH 30-949
    HENRY 33-1027, 35-1022
    JAMES 38-1207
    JOHN 30-128, 31-181, 33-200, 33-1049, 34-162, 34-1014, 34-1149, 35-251, 35-1127, 37-304, 38-244, 39-317, 40-255, 40-1245
    JOSEPH 38-1085, 39-1079, 40-1329
    THOMAS 30-291, 30-967, 33-904
    WILLIAM 30-254, 30-260, 30-949, 31-292, 31-1040, 33-308, 33-904, 34-237, 34-1147, 35-1230, 36-1143, 37-365, 38-341, 38-1205, 39-388, 39-1299, 40-435, 40-1360
MAREY, JOHN 39-1166
MARINER [Mairner, Morner], HENRY 31-211, 33-229, 34-258
MARSHALL [Marchel, Marshell, Mashel, Meashell, Moshel]
    GEORGE 30-22, 31-28, 33-31, 34-101, 35-127, 36-119, 37-134, 38-79, 39-146, 40-158
    ISAAC 30-271, 31-136, 33-317, 34-191, 35-313, 36-231, 37-457, 38-632, 39-633, 40-626
    JACOB 30-271, 34-1338, 36-231, 37-457, 38-632, 39-633, 40-626
    JOSEPH 40-1303
    SAMUEL 30-1109, 31-1262, 33-1258, 34-1385, 35-1422, 36-120, 37-135, 38-73, 39-120, 40-101
    THOMAS 30-1109, 31-24, 33-31, 34-101, 36-676, 37-136, 38-112, 39-160, 40-159
    WILLIAM 40-1503
MARTIN [Martain]

INDEX

GEORGE 30-745, 31-784, 33-797, 34-860, 35-920, 36-906, 37-768, 38-952, 39-936, 40-971
  JAMES [capt.] 30-464, 31-333, 33-1384, 34-1347, 35-1352, 36-1481, 38-1531, 39-1460, 40-1578
  JOHN 30-795, 31-1084, 35-1159, 36-1260, 37-813, 38-993, 39-1152, 40-1098, 40-1578
  THOMAS 30-958, 31-767, 33-820, 34-879, 35-744, 36-715, 38-796, 39-687, 40-830
MARVILL [Marvel, Marwell, Mervell] RICHARD 35-1105
  ROBERT 36-942, 39-1363, 40-1229
  THOMAS 30-927, 31-1063, 33-920, 34-1021, 35-1105, 36-942, 38-1244, 38-1345, 40-1217
MASEY, WILLIAM 36-315
MASON [Masen, Meason]
  ABRAHAM 30-700, 31-669, 33-772, 34-750, 35-786
  EDMUND 34-383, 35-597, 36-482, 37-534, 38-571, 39-492, 40-569
MASSEY [Massy]
  CATHERINE [Katteran] 38-283
  THOMAS 31-1025
MATHIS [Mathas, Matthes]
  KENDALL [Kindal, Kindell] 31-1293, 34-1259
  MARY 36-1514
  PATRICK [Partrick] 30-625, 31-610, 35-737
  ROBERT 30-74
  THOMAS 34-1375
  WILLIAM 30-74, 35-712, 36-1514
MATLASON, JOHN 34-233
MATLIN [Macklin, Mately, Matle(n), Metely, Metlain], JAMES 30-533, 31-528, 33-838, 34-825, 35-704, 36-697, 38-776, 39-711, 40-766
MATTHEWS [Mathas, Mathews, Matthues]
  DANIEL 40-749
  DAVID 38-1428, 39-1638, 40-1716
  JOHN 30-1159, 31-1274, 33-1224, 34-1392, 35-1433, 38-1425, 39-1388, 39-1637, 40-1445, 40-1713
  MARY 38-1428, 39-1638, 40-1716
  PATRICK 33-625, 36-726, 38-700, 39-762, 40-738
  PHILLIP 39-1635, 40-1712
  ROBERT 31-1271, 33-1253, 34-609
  SAMUEL 30-1158, 31-1275, 33-1223, 34-1394, 35-1430, 38-1427, 39-1639, 40-1715
  TEAGUE 30-1156, 31-1272, 33-1219, 34-1391, 35-1432, 38-1424, 39-1635, 40-1712

  THOMAS 33-624, 35-1462
  WILLIAM 31-89, 31-291, 31-1273, 33-108, 33-304, 33-1222, 34-186, 34-609, 34-1393, 35-1431, 36-707, 38-700, 38-728, 38-1426, 39-762, 39-772, 39-1636, 40-738, 40-768, 40-1714
  WILLIAM KENDALL 33-1162
MAUGHON [Maughone, Maughonr], CHRISTOPHER 31-760, 33-830, 35-893, 36-877, 37-739, 38-917, 39-967, 40-1015
MAXFIELD [Masfield, Maxfeild, Mcfeilds, Mexfild], JOSEPH 31-720, 33-782, 34-801, 35-834, 36-820, 37-665, 38-825, 39-844, 40-895
MAYLY [Malay, Mely], JOHN 38-787, 39-694, 40-842
MAYO [Mahow,], SAMUEL 30-1077, 31-1134, 33-1316, 34-1230, 35-1487, 36-1452, 38-1479, 39-1661, 40-1501
MCALLEN, ARTHUR 38-1466
MCCADE, WILLIAM 40-1058
MCCALANAN [Macklanikin], DANIEL 38-1641
MCCALLAN [Macolin, McCalagan, McCallian, McCollegin, Mccallagan], HUGH 30-1061, 31-664, 33-648, 34-571, 35-690, 36-662
MCCALPIN [Maelpin, McCalpen], ROBERT 35-1728, 36-7, 38-745, 39-810
MCCANALLS [Mackinally, Maconeley, Makanells], JOHN 30-1353, 31-1508, 33-1579
MCCANE [MacCane], GEORGE 36-998, 38-683
MCCANNY [McCane, McCennie, McKenney, Mecanny, Micaney], PATRICK 30-41, 31-52, 33-51, 34-133, 35-2, 36-1581, 37-59, 38-56, 39-50, 40-52
MCCANTS [Macance], ALEXANDER 30-827, 31-884, 33-1434, 39-1062, 40-1039
MCCARTHY [Maccarthy], CHARLES 40-310
MCCARTNICK, PATRICK 31-405
MCCAULEY [MacCales, Macal(e)y, McCally, Mcaley], JOHN 30-470, 31-356, 33-362, 34-389, 35-395, 36-486, 37-494, 38-567, 39-468, 40-486
MCCAW, JOHN 39-1840
MCCAY [Mekie], JOHN 30-277
MCCLAIN [Maclaine, Maclan(e), McClanan, McCone, McGlenne, McLane, McLean, Meclane, Meclayn]
  ARCHIBALD 35-994, 36-1261, 37-

INDEX

996
   DANIEL 30-1399, 31-1491, 33-1540, 34-1569, 39-1902
    JOHN 36-1534, 37-1168, 38-1665
  ROBERT 34-1574
MCCLANNY, DANIEL 35-1530, 40-1994
MCCLATT, JONATHAN 31-41
MCCLEMMY [McClammy, McClemm(e)y, Mclamey]
   WHITTY 40-838
   WILLIAM 30-634, 31-636, 33-611, 34-573, 35-654, 36-649, 38-791, 39-693, 40-838
    WONEY 33-633, 34-573, 35-651, 36-661, 38-701, 39-763, 40-749
MCCLESTER [Maclester, McClister, McCloister]
   GEORGE [capt., mr.] 33-1138, 39-995, 34-887, 35-928, 36-923, 40-1033
    JOHN 30-791, 31-821, 33-1138, 34-887, 35-928, 36-923, 38-985, 39-995, 40-1033
    JOSEPH 30-846, 31-866, 33-1010, 34-942, 35-1039, 36-1138, 38-1041, 39-1052, 40-1439
    NEAL [Neaill, Nell] 30-846, 31-866, 33-1010, 34-942, 35-1039, 36-1138, 38-1041, 39-995, 40-1034
    RANDALL 35-1226, 36-1215
    SAMUEL 30-791, 31-821, 33-1138, 34-887, 35-928, 36-923, 38-985, 39-995, 40-1033
   WILLIAM, 30-791, 31-821
MCCLURE [Macclure, Macluer, Meclure]
   ROBERT 30-1019, 31-961, 33-977, 34-1082, 35-1033, 36-1032, 37-875, 38-1177, 39-1263, 40-1265
MCCNALLY [Macknelly]
   JOHN 40-2001
MCCORMICK [Mackcormack, Mackcormarick, Mackcunick, Macomarack, McConnock, McCormuck]
   PATRICK 33-316, 34-173, 35-338, 36-409, 38-161, 39-256, 40-320
MCCOY [Mackcioy, Mecoy, Mackcioy]
   JAMES 36-313, 37-348
   JOHN 37-348
MCCREADY [McCreddie, McCred(e), McCredey, McRedde, MkCready/junr.]
   ALEXANDER 30-1150, 31-1110, 33-1248(2), 34-1409(2), 35-1400(2), 38-1398, 38-1402, 39-1605, 39-1619, 40-1686
    SOLOMON 35-1400, 38-1398, 39-1619, 40-1687
MCCUDDY [Maccudd(e)y] 33-1311, 34-1222, 35-1501, 36-1456, 38-1483, 39-1423, 40-1491

MCFARLIN [Mackfarlin, McFarline, McFarling]
   ROBERT McFarline Robert 38-1549, 39-1560, 40-1642
MCGINNES [Maginey, Megenes, Maggunea, Mcginey, Meginne]
   WIDOW 34-966, 35-1167
   ELIZABETH [Betty] 38-1057, 40-1254
    JEAN [Jenn/wido.] 31-909, 33-1127
MCGLAMMERY [Maglam(e)r(e)y, Maglimmery]
   EDWARD 30-1312, 31-1391, 33-1464, 34-1685, 35-1717, 36-1712, 37-1136, 38-1687, 39-1738, 40-1799
   GEORGE 30-1311, 31-1446, 33-1483, 34-1488, 35-1573, 36-1661, 37-1126, 38-1800, 39-1743, 40-1937
   WILLIAM 33-1435, 34-1669, 35-1574
MCGRAINE
   JOHN [Magrain] 36-1431, 38-1497, John 39-1408, 40-1475
MCGREGORY
   DIRAG [McGregore] 38-740
MCHENDRY [McHendery, McHenry, McHendrick]
   CHARLES 30-1233, 31-1196, 33-766
   WALTER 33-766, 40-456
MCINTIRE [Mackintier, Mackintire, Mackintoie, Makentire]
   DANIEL 31-1312, 36-1757, 37-1246, 38-1833, 39-1809, 40-1834
MCKEAN
   DARBROOK 40-1132
   GEORGE 40-1132
MCKINSEY
   PATRICK 30-471
MCLAUGHLIN [Maglachlan, McGlalchlin]
   CHARLES 38-1575
   DOMINICK 30-1260, 31-1516
   ROBERT 34-1471
MCLALIN [Macclanen, Maclahen, Maclalin, Maglolin, Mcglaclen, Meglohlin]
   JOHN 30-947, 31-980, 34-1040, 35-1085
   JOSEPH 30-989, 36-1038, 37-990, 39-1207
MCLANNON [MaClanahan, Maclanin, Maclenen, McClanan]
   DANIEL 36-1573, 37-1051
   JOSEPH 33-1058, 34-1110, 35-1019, 38-1169, 40-1255
MCPHERSON [Mcherson]
   PETER 30-483
MCRAIL [Mackiell, Mackrill,

INDEX

Mcrall]
   JOHN 30-692, 33-747, 37-719, 39-918

MEARS [Meares, Meirs, Moors]
   JOHN 30-1425, 31-1482, 33-1532, 34-1577, 35-1696, 36-1579, 37-1048, 38-1628, 39-1898, 40-1996
   ROBERT 30-1425, 31-1482, 33-1532, 34-1577, 35-1696, 36-1574, 37-1201, 38-1781, 39-1862, 40-1151

MEARS, SAMUEL 37-1048, 38-1628, 39-1898, 40-1996

MEATHWEN, THOMAS 37-1148

MELAVERY, THOMAS 40-1724

MELLS, JAMES 35-760

MELSON
   BENJAMIN 31-863, 33-996, 34-1024, 35-1189, 36-1077, 38-1304, 39-1311, 40-1421
   DANIEL 35-1733, 36-1718, 37-1150, 38-1728, 39-1698, 40-1908
   HYTABLE 40-1178
   JOB 34-1192
   JOHN 38-200, 36-1076
   JOSEPH 30-923, 31-863, 33-908, 35-1189, 36-1197, 38-1303, 39-1310, 40-1406,
   SAMUEL [junr., senr.] 30-923(2), 31-863(2), 33-996(2), 34-1024(2), 35-1116(2), 36-1076(2), 37-886(2), 38-1097(2), 39-1131(2), 40-1179
   JOHN 31-1282, 33-1163, 34-1275, 35-1290, 36-1333, 38-1586, 39-1525, 40-1602

MELVIN
   ROBERT [junr., senr.] 30-1223, 31-1164, 33-1178, 34-1292, 35-1276(2), 36-1332(2), 38-1572(2), 39-1516(2), 40-1596(2)
   THOMAS 35-1638, 36-1724, 38-1710, 39-1934, 40-1786
   WILLIAM 30-1223, 31-1164, 33-1178, 34-1292, 35-1276, 36-1332, 38-1579, 39-1517, 40-1595

MERCHANT [Marchan(t)]
   BENJAMIN 35-1502, 36-1297, 38-1413
   WALTER 39-791
   WILLIAM 40- 809

MERCY, HENRY 34-1081

MEREDAY, JOHN 33-1134, 34-976

MERRILL [Merrell, Merriall]
   JOHN 30-1245, 31-1280, 33-1166, 34-1264, 35-1304, 36-1374, 38-1605, 39-1544, 40-1621
   JOSEPH 31-1187, 33-1184, 34-1310, 35-1313, 36-1351, 39-873, 40-906
   JOSHUA 30-1245, 31-1280, 34-1375, 35-1517, 36-1512, 38-1625, 39-1662, 40-1741
   THOMAS 39-1056
   WILLIAM [jur.] 40-1622

MERRITT, LUKE 37-231

METHERD, JONATHAN 31-200

MEZICK [Meseck, Mesek, Messex, Messick, Messicks, Messix, Meseck/jur., senr.]
   BENIAMIN 30-807, 31-829, 33-1101, 34-917, 35-961, 36-1048, 38-1015, 39-1060, 40-1065
   ELIHU [Elihew] 33-1038, 34-935, 39-1156
   GEORGE 30-952, 31-1050, 33-900, 34-1185, 35-1242, 36-1010, 38-1339, 39-1302
   ISAAC 30-808, 31-830, 33-1100, 34-904, 35-941, 36-1201, 38-1344, 39-1004
   JACOB 30-1041, 30-1050, 31-970, 31-972, 33-1038, 33-1066, 33-1102, 34-935, 35-975, 35-976, 36-1253, 36-1255, 38-1001, 38-1055, 39-1155, 39-1158, 40-1082, 40-1083
   JAMES 35-1241, 36-1009
   JOHN 30-952, 31-1050, 33-900, 34-1185, 35-1241, 36-1009, 38-1135, 39-1303, 40-1398
   JOSHUA 38-1001, 39-1156
   JULIAN [Juell] 34-901, 35-953
   NATHANIEL 31-970
   NEHEMIAH 30-1050, 33-1066, 34-936, 35-977, 36-1254, 38-1000, 39-1154, 40-1084
   OBEDIAH 31-1050, 33-900, 34-1185, 35-1241, 36-1009, 38-1135, 39-1303, 40-1374
   ROBERT 40-1415

MIDDLETON, DANIEL [senr.] 30-954(2)

MIDSLEY [Midgley]
   THOMAS 30-367, 31-399, 33-461, 34-544, 35-571, 36-575, 37-408, 38-441, 39-567, 40-537

MIDSLEY, WILLIAM 39-567, 40-537

MIFLIN, THOMAS 34-1592

MILBOURN [Melbourn, Milborn(e), Milbroune]
   WIDOW 31-1104
   CALEB 30-1142, 31-1104, 33-1237, 34-1423, 35-1449, 36-1305, 38-1406, 39-1615, 40-1695
   JOHN 30-1143, 31-1105, 33-1238, 34-1424, 35-1450, 36-1306, 38-1405, 39-1614, 40-1694
   MARY 35-1449

INDEX

    RALPH 31-1103, 33-1236, 34-1400, 35-1446, 36-1302, 38-1407, 38-1483, 39-1423, 39-1616, 40-1491, 40-1696
    THOMAS 30-685, 31-682, 33-711, 34-810, 35-843, 36-853, 37-689, 38-820, 39-894, 40-872

MILES
    EDWARD 35-882, 36-751, 38-1293, 39-1268
    HENRY 30-45, 31-53, 33-54, 34-108, 35-48, 36-85, 37-56, 38-36, 39-48, 40-50
    JOHN 31-763, 33-827, 34-878, 35-895, 36-890, 37-1243,
    SAMUEL 30-496, 31-578, 33-652, 34-654, 35-619, 36-646, 38-760, 39-796, 40-702, 40-817
    WILLIAM [junr., senr] 30-515, 31-585, 33-655, 34-582, 35-633, 36-619(2), 38-754(2), 39-800(2), 40-702(2)

MILHARD, RICHARD 31-1413

MILLER [Millar]
    JAMES 33-793, 34-856, 39-719, 40-764
    JOHN [Jon./mr.] 30-197, 30-749, 30-1094, 31-160, 31-794, 33-248, 33-793, 34-223, 34-856, 35-258, 36-178, 37-275, 38-353, 39-229, 40-262
    JOSEPH [mr.] 31-249, 33-204, 34-231, 35-308, 36-236, 37-201, 38-204, 39-164, 40-237
    PETER 30-1430, 31-1494, 33-1520, 34-1515, 35-1543
    THOMAS 30-749, 31-794, 33-794, 34-850, 35-927, 36-907, 37-753, 38-960, 39-957, 40-975
    WILLIAM GRAY 36-176

MILLS
    WIDOW 31-1295
    ALEXANDER 30-1242, 31-1298, 33-1150, 34-1266, 35-1324, 36-1382, 38-1593, 39-1537, 40-1594, 40-1614
    HUGH 33-1176, 34-1270, 35-1303, 36-1339, 38-1590, 39-1528, 40-1600
    JAMES 34-723, 36-839, 37-702, 38-914
    JOHN 30-1242, 31-1298, 33-1150, 36-1339, 38-1590, 39-1528, 40-1600
    JONATHAN 30-1093, 33-1280, 34-1206, 35-1271, 36-1401, 38-1361, 39-1385, 40-1450
    MARY [widw.] 30-1253, 33-1177, 34-1271, 35-1277
    MOSES 31-1295, 33-1177, 34-1272, 35-1277, 36-1329, 38-1574, 39-1520, 40-1594
    NATHAN 33-1150, 34-1266, 35-1324, 36-1382, 38-1593, 40-1613
    NATHANIEL 30-1242, 30-1243, 31-1298, 31-1304, 33-1176, 34-1270, 35-1303, 36-1339, 38-1590, 39-1529, 39-1537, 40-1601
    ROBERT 30-1242, 31-1298, 38-1592, 39-1538, 40-1447, 40-1614
    SAMUEL [junr.] 30-1093, 30-1243, 31-1245, 31-1304, 33-1176, 33-1280, 34-1206, 34-1270, 35-1271, 35-1303, 36-1339, 36-1402, 38-1360, 38-1590, 39-304, 39-1528, 40-359, 40-1600
    SMITH 33-1177, 34-1271, 35-1277, 36-1381, 38-1591, 39-1535, 40-1609
    WILLIAM [junr., senr.] 30-1093, 30-1242, 31-1245, 31-1298, 33-1150, 33-1280, 34-1206, 34-1265, 35-1271, 35-1325, 36-1382, 36-1401, 38-1360, 38-1593, 39-1384, 39-1536, 40-1449, 40-1612

MISTER
    ABRAHAM 35-26, 36-149, 37-37, 38-104, 39-135, 40-152
    BENJAMIN 35-26, 36-149, 37-37, 38-104, 39-135, 40-152
    CHARLES 40-1194
    WILLIAM 30-113, 30-113, 31-118, 33-133, 34-146, 35-26, 36-149, 37-37, 38-104, 39-135, 40-152

MITCHELL [Michall, Mitchal]
    ALEXANDER 33-1582, 34-1588, 35-1075, 36-1025, 38-1165, 38-1727, 39-1137, 40-1359
    ANN 33-561, 35-692, 36-703, 38-725, 39-774, 40-730
    BENJAMIN 30-1379, 31-1412, 33-1570, 34-1588, 35-1639, 36-1576, 37-1026, 38-1823, 39-1797, 40-1981
    ISAAC 30-587, 31-566, 33-561, 34-1556, 35-1538, 36-1561, 37-1061, 38-1839, 39-1913, 40-739
    JAMES 31-401
    JOHN 30-1379, 31-1412, 33-1571, 34-1589, 35-1069, 35-1530, 36-1163, 36-1573, 37-987, 37-1052, 38-1285, 38-1641, 39-1798, 39-1907, 40-1982, 40-1994
    JOSHUA 35-1460, 36-1394, 38-1356, 39-1380, 40-1443
    RANDALL [Rondal] 30-92, 38-725, 39-774, 40-730

INDEX

RICHARD 30-1380, 33-1569, 34-1587, 35-1640, 36-1577, 37-1025, 38-1271
  ROBERT 30-1106, 31-1210, 33-1276, 34-1326, 35-1460, 36-1394, 38-1356, 39-1380, 40-1443
    SOLOMON 40-730
    STEPHEN 40-730
    THOMAS 30-587, 31-388, 31-566, 33-437, 33-561, 34-502, 34-694, 35-549, 35-693, 35-1075, 36-702, 37-570, 38-726, 39-535, 39-773, 40-539, 40-729
MODE [Moad(e), PETER 30-1386, 31-811, 33-840, 35-1632, 36-1594, 37-1015, 38-1832, 39-1807, 40-1992
MOLLESTON, JOHN 31- 5
MOLLISON, JOHN 35-461, 36-527
MONKS [Munks], WILLIAM 33-208, 34-344, 35-308, 36-258, 37-273, 38-200, 39-207
MONTERY, DANIEL 30-556
MONTGARR [Mangare, Mongarr, Montgair, Mungar(e)]
  JOHN 30-780, 31-808, 33-839, 34-837, 35-869, 36-863, 37-789, 38-974, 39-988, 40-1030
    MARY [widow] 30-1404, 33-1535
    MATTHEW 30-1404, 31-809, 33-1535, 34-828, 35-874, 36-867, 37-800, 38-972, 39-989, 40-994
MONTGOMERY [Mackgumery, Magumery, McGumery, MeGomrame, Megumrey, Megummerah, Mungumirie]
  JOHN 37-459
  ROBERT 31-144, 36-424, 39-514, 40-357
    THOMAS 30-76, 34-51, 35-51, 36-52, 38-3, 39-65, 40-721
MOO [Moe], JOHN 30-610, 31-49, 31-648, 33-605
MOONEY, CHARLES 39-187, 40-383
MOORAIN, JOSEPH 40-1692
MOORE
  WIDOW 33-994, 35-1054
  BRADSHAW 39-1400
  CATHERINE [Catron/wido.] 30-1026, 31-963
  DAVID 40-283
  FRANCES/FRANCES 30-47, 31-55, 33-57, 34-75, 35-43, 35-148, 36-83, 37-85, 38-44, 39-52, 40-54
    ISAAC 31-55, 33-57, 34-75, 34-141, 34-964, 35-32, 35-148, 35-1004, 36-66, 36-83, 36-951, 37-68, 38-17, 38-1745, 39-69, 39-1196, 40-78, 40-1356
    JACOB 30-47, 34-75, 35-43, 36-83, 37-85, 38-44
    JAMES 36-951, 38-1051, 39-1225, 40-1149,
    JOHN [junr., senr.] 30-42, 30-47, 30-876, 30-878, 30-1005, 31-55, 31-890, 31-1021, 31-1059, 33-57, 33-955, 33-1059, 33-1123, 34-76, 34-107, 34-687, 34-964, 34-1051, 34-1089, 35-148, 35-1004, 35-1009, 35-1066, 36-83, 36-951, 36-954, 36-1028, 38-1051, 38-1155, 38-1209, 39-1225, 39-1242, 39-1274, 40-1149, 40-1343
    JOSEPH 38-1430, 39-1641
    SAMUEL 30-63, 34-27, 35-149, 36-44, 38-11, 40-1633
    THOMAS 30-47, 30-98, 31-30, 31-55, 33-33, 33-61, 34-75, 34-110, 35-43, 35-129, 36-83, 36-125, 36-1131, 37-95, 38-44, 38-77, 38-1197, 39-52, 39-121, 39-1365, 40-55, 40-157, 40-1238
    WILLIAM [junr., senr.] 30-63, 30-812, 30-876, 30-879, 30-1026, 31-74, 31-849, 31-875, 31-890, 31-963, 33-81, 33-994, 33-1075, 33-1122, 33-1137, 34-922, 34-960, 34-1000, 34-1072, 35-13, 35-149, 35-1003, 35-1054, 35-1166, 36-224, 36-950, 36-978, 36-999, 36-1131, 37-375, 38-16, 38-196, 38-1016, 38-1050, 38-1186, 38-1197, 39-68, 39-314, 39-1061, 39-1178, 39-1181, 39-1365, 40-234, 40-688, 40-1150, 40-1238, 40-1268, 40-1299
MORGAN [Morgain, Morgen, Morgine, Morgyine]
  AVERY [Evirey] 30-287, 33-160, 34-250, 35-301, 36-286, 37-369, 38-367, 39-221, 40-187
  JOSEPH 40-1377
  WALTER 30-743, 31-781, 33-616, 34-675, 35-734
MORNIE [Morn], JOHN 30-532, 31-527
MORRIS [Morres, Moires]
  WIDOW 33-1578
  ALEXANDER 37-197
  BEAVANS [Bibbens] 30-154, 31-225, 33-235, 34-330, 35-185, 36-324, 37-251, 38-396, 39-379, 40-423, 40-1654
  DENNIS 30-141, 31-241, 33-181, 34-261, 35-152, 36-252, 37-279, 38-328, 39-355, 40-396
  ELIZABETH 40-329
  ISAAC 30-1201, 31-1160, 33-1374, 34-1333, 35-1377, 36-1482, 38-1570, 39-1458, 40-1571
  JACOB 30-1473, 31-1527, 33-1578, 34-1662, 35-1554, 36-1680, 37-1075, 38-1784,

INDEX

39-1878, 40-1816
  JEREMIAH 30-1399, 31-1491,
33-1540, 34-1571, 35-1694, 36-1559,
37-1065, 38-1726, 39-1697, 40-1909
  JOHN 30-168, 31-241, 33-185,
33-317, 34-191, 34-263, 35-151,
35-503, 36-330, 36-409, 36-1680,
37-264, 37-1075, 38-329, 38-1738,
39-356, 39-1293, 39-1923, 40-410,
40-1424, 40-1886
  JOSEPH 30-479, 30-1473, 31-338,
31-1527, 33-435, 34-501, 35-546,
35-1554, 36-522, 37-592, 37-1075,
38-629, 38-1784, 39-536, 39-1878,
40-536, 40-1987
  JUDITH [Juda, Judy] 30-1473,
31-1527
  LUKE 30-1201, 31-1160, 33-1374,
34-1333, 35-1377, 40-1571
  MICHAEL 33-905, 34-1145, 35-1083,
36-1145
  NATHANIEL 37-1132, 38-214,
38-1682, 39-387, 39-1727, 40-329,
40-1915
  SARAH 30-141, 31-189, 33-197
  THOMAS 37-79
  WILLIAM 30-141, 30-479, 31-189,
31-338, 33-197, 33-433, 34-155,
34-500, 35-359, 35-545, 36-308,
36-543, 37-197, 37-591, 38-291,
38-410, 39-172, 39-521, 40-257,
40-658
MORRISON, THOMAS 38-1091, 39-1666,
40-2001
MORROW
  JAMES 36-224, 38-337, 40-293
  ROBERT 36-223, 38-226, 40-292
MOSES [Mossis]
  EDWARD 33-44
  JOSEPH 37-735, 38-1583, 39-1518,
40-1597
  URISEREEBEL 39-15
MOSITT, HUMPHRIES [Umfris] 40-12
MOTT JOHN 36-53, 37-61, 39-788
MU----, JAMES 37- 815
MUIDMAN, THOMAS [Marderman] 33-644,
34-703
MUIR, ROWLAND [More/Rolland] 30-742,
31-782
MULESTO, JOHN 34-343
MULLIGAN, THOMAS [Mulligen] 39-1557,
40-1632
MULROW
  ALEXANDER [Elexander] 30-545,
31-544
  DANIEL [Mellrow/Danill] 30-545,
31-544
MUMFORD
  [illegible] 37- 529
  CHARLES 31-293, 33-272, 34-247,
35-207, 36-213, 37-326, 38-227,
39-294, 40-308

  GEORGE 31-375, 33-445, 34-394,
35-408, 36-508, 38-577, 39-503,
40-651
  JAMES [Memford, Momford/junr.,
senr.] 30-229, 30-317, 31-264,
31-374, 33-282, 33-441, 34-298,
34-398, 35-201, 35-412(2), 36-247,
36-524(2), 37-531(2), 38-240,
38-476(2), 39-318, 39-647(2),
40-220, 40-593(2)
  JOHN 39-220, 40-205, 40-384
  THOMAS 30- 229, 33-272, 34-451,
35-208, 38-539, 39-430, 40-521
  WILLIAM [Momford] 30-215, 31-267,
33-265, 34-246, 35-211, 36-274,
37-336, 38-394, 39-293, 40-221
MUNROW, ALEXANDER [Munro] 33-627
MURIDON, JOHN 33-1133
MURPHEY
  DANIEL [Murfey] 36-1694, 37-1084
  JAMES [Mufey, Murfee, Murfey,
Murptey] 30-856, 31-896, 34-968,
35-1157, 36-1103, 38-1201, 39-1189,
40-1113
  JOHN [Murfey] 34-630, 34-1678,
38-1560, 39-595, 40-625
  JOSEPH [Murfee, Murfey, Murphie]
30-1377, 31-1390, 33-1479, 35-1719,
36-1735, 37-1138, 38-1694, 39-1723,
40-1806
MURRAY
  DANIEL 33-1232
  DAVID 31-482, 33-515, 34-471,
35-437, 36-557, 37-556, 38-483,
39-607, 40-596
  DUNCAN [Donkin, Dunken, Dunkin]
30-471, 31-405, 33-380, 34-415,
35-499, 36-409, 37-393, 38-512,
39-412, 40-456
  JAMES [Moirey, Morrah] 30-221,
31-259, 33-268, 34-200, 35-158,
35-279, 37-356, 39-288
  JOHN [Marraugh, Murah] 30-297,
30-790, 31-403, 33-504, 33-849,
33-902, 34-445, 34-803, 35-362,
35-836, 36-536, 37-383, 38-617,
39-643
  RICHARD [Morrah, Murrah] 33-675,
36-682
  ROBERT [Moirey, Murrey] 30-232,
31-259, 33-275, 34-257, 35-280,
39-296
  SAMUEL 38- 615
  WILLIAM [Murrah] 40-1860
MURROW, ALEXANDER [Murroh] 34-599,
35-640, 36-725, 38-705, 39-767,
40-745
  DAVID 30-677
  RICHARD 34-623, 35-635
  SAMUEL Murrow, Saml. 40-747
MUTT, JOHN 38-768, 40-808

INDEX

NAIRN [Nairne, Naron, Nearn, Nearon]
    JAMES 30-1147, 31-1108, 33-1240, 34-1427, 35-1397, 36-1310, 38-1400, 39-1608, 40-1688
    ROBERT [senr, junr.] 30-1145, 30-1146, 31-1106, 31-1107, 33-1241, 34-1406, 35-1398, 36-1309, 38-1399, 39-1609, 40-1690

NAPMAN [Natman, Nottman, Nutman],
JOHN 31-224, 35-232, 36-343, 38-173, 39-202

NEASOM, JOHN 30-835

NEIGHENBOROUGH [Neighenboroe, Neighnborough]
    JOHN 39-554, 40-627
    URSULA 40-627

NELSON [Nealson, Neilson, Nellson, Nilson]
    HUGH 30-1194, 31-1158, 33-1369, 34-1352
    JAMES 33-713, 34-766, 35-1359, 36-798, 37-715, 38-878, 39-923, 40-950
    JOHN 30-1457, 31-1321, 33-1391, 34-1629, 35-1411, 38-861, 38-1659, 39-1460, 39-1836, 40-1578, 40-1835
    ROBERT 37-715, 39-923, 40-950
    SAMUEL 40-950
    WILLIAM 30-720, 30-1456, 31-712, 31-1323, 33-713, 33-1389, 34-766, 34-1630, 35-857, 35-1610, 36-798, 36-1521, 37-715, 37-1189, 38-861, 38-1659, 39-923, 39-1836, 40-950, 40-1835

NESOM, BENJAMIN [Ben.] 39-1295

NEWBERRY, WILLIAM 40-1783

NEWBOLD [Neubeld, Newbald, Newball, Newbole, Neweble, Nubold]
    FRANCIS [Frances] 30-981, 31-941, 33-860, 34-1184, 35-1220, 36-1243, 37-957, 38-1290, 39-1355, 40-1350
    JOHN 30-251, 31-280, 33-328, 34-168, 35-295, 36-228, 37-307, 38-237, 39-235, 40-207
    PURNELL [Purnall] 35-1329, 36-1275, 38-1381, 39-1591, 40-1670
    THOMAS 31-1118, 33-1207, 34-1312, 35-1329, 36-1275, 38-1381, 39-1591, 40-1670

NEWMAN [Neuman, Nueman, Numan]
    HENRY 30-528, 31-546, 33-836, 34-836, 35-871, 36-865, 37-787, 38-975, 39-985, 40-997
    JOHN 35-1361, 35-1635, 36-1589, 37-1019

NIBLETT [Nirblit]
    BURNETT [Burnall, Burnell, Burnit] 30-1190, 33-567, 34-590, 35-609, 36-674, 38-722, 39-758, 40-712
    RICHARD 39-1737

NICHOLS [Nicholas, Nicholds, Nickals, Nickles, Nickols, Nickorles, Nicolds, Nicols]
    ELIZABETH 31-1150
    GEORGE 37-978, 39-1423, 40-1491
    JAMES 31-1148, 33-1356, 34-1339, 35-1385, 36-1483, 37-1200, 38-1540, 38-1782, 39-1474, 40-1560
    JOHN 31-1149, 33-1357, 34-1340, 35-1384, 36-239
    JOSEPH 31-1149, 33-1358, 34-1341, 35-1388, 36-1484, 37-1199, 38-1543, 38-1783, 39-1471, 40-1561
    MATHIAS [Marthias] 30-697, 33-709, 34-805, 35-1386, 36-1485, 38-1542, 39-1473, 40-1559
    RICHARD 37-805, 37-1208, 38-1761
    WILLIAM 31-43, 33-50

NICHOLSON [Nicholdson, Nicholsons, Nickellson, Nicoldson]
    WIDOW 34-934
    ELIZABETH [Betty] 33-1004, 36-1228
    GEORGE 36-1057, 38-1244
    JAMES 30-1215, 30-1267, 30-895, 31-935, 31-1356, 33-1015, 33-1420, 34-994, 34-1653, 35-1169, 35-1667, 36-1067, 36-1627, 38-1076, 39-1256, 39-1860, 40-1167, 40-1877
    JOHN 30-1052, 30-1216, 31-914, 37-163, 38-235, 39-279, 40-216, 40-1095
    JOSEPH [Jos.] 30-1216, 30-1266, 31-1347, 33-1421, 34-1652, 35-1666, 36-1626, 39-1861, 40-1878
    LEVIN 37-767, 37-801, 39-1103, 40-1095
    RICHARD [Ritchard] 30-896, 30-1266, 31-893, 31-1347, 33-1000, 33-1419, 34-993, 34-1654, 35-1109, 35-1668, 36-1213, 38-1077, 39-1016, 39-1862, 40-1163, 40-1874
    ROGER 30-839, 31-915

NIER, THOMAS 40-400

NISBETT, WILLIAM 30-635, 31-514

NOBLE [Nobell, Nobles]
    ISAAC [Isack/junr., senr] 30-985, 30-986, 30-1381, 31-985, 31-986, 31-1411, 33-924, 33-1572, 34-1136, 34-1590, 35-1172, 36-1186, 36-1586, 37-1022, 38-1302, 38-1825, 39-1800, 40-1985
    JAMES [senr.] 30-1122, 30-1187, 31-1145, 33-1176, 33-1381, 34-1270, 34-1287, 35-1393, 36-1503, 38-1521, 39-1442, 40-1552
    JOHN 33-1095, 34-1139, 35-1174, 35-1641, 36-1517, 38-1275, 39-1270, 40-1304
    MARK [Marck, Marke] 30-1398, 31-1405, 33-1589, 35-1519, 36-1517, 37-992, 38-1626, 39-1813, 40-1855
    WIDOW 33-1095, 34-1139, 35-1174
    WILLIAM 36-1585, 37-1023, 38-1824, 39-1799, 40-1985

INDEX

NOCK [Knock]
  JOHN 30-416, 31-316, 33-385, 34-419, 35-506, 36-527, 37-500, 38-515, 40-643
  NEHEMIAH 33-385, 34-419, 36-316, 37-364, 38-342, 39-410, 40-177
  SOLOMON 37-252, 38-180, 39-378, 40- 424
  WILLIAM 34-176

NORTH
  WIDOW 33-1553
  EDWARD 30-1418, 31-1432
  JOHN 33-1553, 34-1566, 35-1520, 37-992, 38-1626, 40-2004
  WILLIAM 30-1418, 31-1432

NORTON, JOHN 40-367

NOTTINGHAM [Notingame], BENJAMIN 33-1096, 34-1132, 35-1235

NUGEN, THOMAS 38-365

NUTON [Newton, Notton, Nuten]
  CHRISTOPHER [Chripther] 30- 932, 31-1023, 33- 921
  JOB [Jobe] 34-731, 35-768, 36-832, 37-705, 38-854, 39-889, 40-867
  JOHN 30-939, 33-922, 34-1036, 35-1091, 36-1118, 38-1624, 39-1124, 40-1213, 40-1442
  JONATHAN 30-687, 33-719, 34-737, 34-759, 35-774, 36-833, 37-703, 38-899, 39-890, 40-869
  PATIENCE 30- 939
  SOUTHY 36-832, 37-701, 38-851, 39-884, 40-871
  STARLING 30-670, 35-768, 36-1467, 37-706, 38-850, 39-888, 40-866
  THOMAS [junr, senr] 30-670, 31-702, 33-718(2), 34-731(2), 35-768(2), 36-832(2), 37-701(2), 38-851, 38-878, 39-884(2), 40-871(2)

NUTTER
  CHRISTOPHER [Ch., Christafer] 30-873, 31-846, 33-1064, 34-974, 35-1152, 36-1136, 37-818, 38-1120, 39-1043
  ELIZABETH [Betty] 38-1140
  HUITT [Hewit, Huet] 30-870, 33-1136, 34-972, 35-1156, 36-1137, 37-816, 38-1248, 39-1044, 40-1120
  JOHN HUITT 31-1085
  MARGARET [Margrett] 30-872, 31-946
  MATTHEW 30-870, 31-1079, 33-1013, 34-988, 35-1154, 36-1109, 37-817
  WILLIAM 30-874, 31-936, 33-1082, 34-973, 35-1153, 36-1135, 37-819

NUTWELL [Nettwell], BRUNT [Briantt] 30-803, 31- 981, 33-1089

OBEAR [Obeer, Obeir] ISAAC [Isack] 30-65, 31-67, 33-74, 34-97, 35-905, 36-864

OBRYAN [Obrian, Obrien, Obrion, Obryen,]
  CHRISTOPHER [Chris.] 33-1274, 34-1324, 35-1323
  CLARK 35-5
  DANIEL 38-1459, 39-1499
  RICHARD 33-665, 36-655, 38-778, 39- 710
  THOMAS 34-600, 36-640

ODAY [Adaugh, Adaw, Aday, Daye, Odaw]
  HENRY 31-1486, 35-1018
  JOHN 31-1486, 33-1569, 34-1589, 35-1640, 36-1577, 37-102511
  OWEN 30-1405, 31-1486(2), 34-1596, 35-1634, 36-1590, 37-1002, 38-1849, 39-1798

ODEAR [Dear, Deer, Odea, Odeare]
  WIDOW 34-646
  FURNACE [Farness] 30-621, 31-658, 33- 634, 34-645
  JAMES 35-651
  JOHN 30-1188, 31-665, 33-1379, 34-1350, 38-1569, 39-1457, 40-1579
  ROSE 36-675, 38-716, 39-752, 40-709
  STEPHEN [Steven/junr., senr.] 30-621(2), 31-658, 31-659, 33-569, 33-634, 34-644, 35-1346, 36-1415, 38-1367, 39-1391, 40-1464

ODUE [Dewey, Odewey, Odewey, Odiewey, Odwe] THOMAS 31-668, 33-783, 34-745, 35-781, 36-823, 37-686, 38-843, 39-867

OGILSBUS [Oglisbus] JOHN 31- 514

OLDINDMAN [Olandman] JOHN 38-1539, 40-1578

OLDSON, ANDREW 39-361, 40-381

OLIN, THOMAS 40-120

OLIPHANT [Allaphent, Olefentt, Oleyfent, Olifant, Olivan, Ollifen, Ollifan]
  GEORGE [Gorge] 31-962
  JOHN 30-1312, 31-1455
  MATTHEW 33-1464, 34-1685, 35-1717, 36-1712, 37-1136, 38-1687, 39-1738, 40-1779
  WILLIAM 31-922, 34-1111, 35-1038, 37-870, 38-1162, 40-1226

OLIVER [Olave[r], Olefen, Olefer, Olifer, Olifir, Olipher]
  GEORGE 30-1018, 33-978, 34-1083, 35-1031, 36-992, 37-871, 38-1091, 39-1081, 40-1236
  THOMAS 35-1037, 38-1127, 39-1184, 40-1353
  WILLIAM [Olefen, Olifir] 30-869, 33-980, 36- 977

OLPHEY, JOHN 30- 903

ONEAL [Onail, Oneall, Neal, Neial, Neil]
  HENRY [Hennery] 30-77, 31-89, 34-25

INDEX

JAMES 30-966, 31-1045, 33-903, 34-1148, 35-1227, 36-1178, 38-1338, 39-1297, 40-1332
    JOHN 30-757, 30-956, 31-861, 31-989, 33-812, 33-861, 34-869, 34-1183, 35-910, 35-1228, 36-1177, 38-1266, 39-932, 39-1298, 40-966, 40-1327
    THOMAS 36-704
ONORTON [Onarton]
    ISABEL [Isbell/widow] 38-319, 39-304
    JOHN 30-122, 31-186, 33-192, 34-160, 35-218, 36-265
ORE, MICHAEL [Michaeil, Michl./jur., senr.] 37-60(2), 38-66(2), 39-161(2), 40-106(2)
OSARVAND, WILLIAM 33-952
OSBURN [O[z]burn, Osborn, Oysborn], JOHN 33-870, 39-1370, 40-1339
OSHOHANAS [Oshahannas, Oshohanies, Oshohannas, Oshonus, Sheehanus, Shohanis, Shohannas, Shohanos], WILLIAM 30-469, 31-463, 33-519, 34-476, 35-440, 36-440, 37-548, 38-485, 39-601, 40-602
OUTERBRIDGE
    JOHN [capt.] 31-129, 35-751, 36-708
    SARAH 38-724, 39-746, 40-720
    THOMAS 37-139
OUTTEN [Houten, Ottwell, Oughton, Oulden, Outton, Outwell, Owten]
ABRAHAM 31-1162, 33-1367, 34-1338, 35-1370, 36-1507, 38-1569, 39-1457, 40-440, 40-125, 40-1579
    EDWARD 30-993
    JOHN [junr., senr.] 30-90(2), 30-990, 31-98, 31-360, 33-118(2), 33-346, 34-39(2), 34-357, 35-96(2), 35-378, 36-413, 37-608, 38-609, 38-1212, 39-452, 40-442
    PURNELL [Purnal] 38-88, 39-157, 40-125
    THOMAS 33-346, 34-357, 35-378, 37-609, 38-610, 39-453
WILLIAM 36-413
OUTWELL [Autwill, Oatwell, Oldwell, Ottell, Ottwell]
    CHARLES 30-1082, 31-1133, 33-1314, 34-1304, 35-1509, 36-1428, 38-1486, 39-1420, 40-1494
    FRANCIS [Frans./junr., senr.] 30-1073, 30-1088, 31-1129, 31-1228, 33-1313, 33-1324, 34-1235, 34-1300, 35-1505, 35-1509, 36-1429, 36-1450, 38-1470, 38-1485, 39-1419, 39-1498, 40-1493, 40-1508
    SOLOMON [Solm.] 30-1073, 31-1228, 33-1115, 36-1429, 38-1485, 39-1508, 40-1508
    WILLIAM 39-1419, 40-1493

OWARS [Ores, Ouws], EPHRAIM [Ephram] 31-886, 33-1066, 36-1254
OWINS [Oin, Owen(s)]
    EDWARD 33-1017, 34-1660 35-1663
    ELIZABETH [Betty, Elisa.] 31-110, 33-127, 34-64, 35-69, 36-109, 37-154, 38-132, 39-41, 40-43
    EPHRAIM [Epharim, Ephrem] 34-936, 35-977
    JOHN [junr., sur.] 30-541, 31-525, 33-585, 34-657, 35-666, 36-728, 38-674, 38-674, 39-674, 39-674, 40-798, 40-798
    MOSES [Mosses, Mosis] 30-8, 31-589, 33-1550, 35-57, 37-154, 38-1439, 39-1650, 40-1728
    PETER [31-1528, 33-862, 34-1182, 35-1239, 36-1167, 38-1237, 39-1308, 40-1358
    PHILLIP [Philip] 31-110, 33-127, 34-64, 35-69, 36-109, 37-154, 38-159, 39-41, 40-42
    ROBERT [Robart] 30-978, 31-1054, 33-857, 34-1188, 35-1217, 36-1245, 37-964, 38-1136, 39-1346, 40-1361
    THOMAS 36-104, 37-103, 38-127
    WILLIAM 37-154, 38-132, 39-41, 40-43, 40-356

PADED [Pading], JOHN 34-1270
PADEN [Padan, Paddin] JOHN 31-1304, 33-1176, 35-1257, 36-1386, 38-1373, 39-1582, 40-1662
PAIN [Paine, Pane]
    JOHN 30-714, 33-1386, 34-772, 35-807, 36-809, 37-647, 38-832, 39-858, 40-908(2)
    JOSEPH 30-714, 33-722, 34-772, 35-1387, 36-1330, 38-1577, 39-1524, 40-1593
    MOSES [Mosses] 37-647, 38-832, 39-858, 40-908
    PAUL 40-903
PALLIS, JOHN 30-633
PARAMORE [Parimore, Parmor(e), Parramor, Parremore]
    WIDOW 35-1041
    BENJAMIN [Beniamin] 39-1013, 40-1436
    ELIZABETH [Betty, Elizbt.] 37-868, 38-1161, 39-1013, 40-1157, 40-1436
    EZEKIEL 35-1182, 36-1036, 37-911, 38-1219, 39-1326, 40-1311
    ISAAC 39-1232, 40-1157
    JAMES [junr] 30-898, 31-958, 33-1020, 34-996, 35-1136, 35-1188, 36-1042, 36-1171, 37-900, 38-1122, 38-1297, 39-1232, 39-1322, 40-1305
    JOHN 37-868, 38-1161, 39-1013, 40-1436
    JOSEPH 30-995, 34-1046, 35-1186,

INDEX

37-917, 38-1291, 39-1321, 40-1312
   MATTHEW [Mattw.] 30-1001, 31-835, 33-954, 34-1049, 35-1182, 36-1036, 37-911, 38-1219(2), 39-1326, 40-1321
   RICHARD 30-1304, 31-1467, 33-1492, 34-1496, 35-1745, 40-850
   THOMAS 30-667, 30-1013, 31-699, 31-1006, 33-948(2), 34-1068(2), 35-1041, 36-985, 37-867, 38-1168, 40-1220
   WILLIAM 38-1122, 39-1232
PARIS
   GEORGE 38-1877, 39-1874, 40-1876
   JOHN 31-17, 33-1593, 38-1062, 39-1937, 40-1749
PARKER
   CHARLES 30-401, 31-370, 33-517, 34-475, 35-592, 36-441, 37-553, 38-481, 39-604, 40-601
   GEORGE 30-401, 31-480, 33-524, 34-479, 35-443, 37-544, 38-487, 39-596, 40-621
   ISAAC 31-121, 33-131, 34-145, 35-31
   JOHN 30-401(2), 34-1055
   PHILLIP 30-401, 30-1129, 33-353, 33-518, 36-442, 39-605, 40-600, 31-481, 31-1113, 34-474, 34-1319, 35-593, 37-554, 38-482
   SAMUEL 30-401, 31-370, 33-38, 33-516, 34-473, 35-439, 36-438, 37-559, 38-480, 39-603, 40-599
   SCHOLFIELD [Scofield] 40-621
   TABITHA 31-370, 36-438, 37-559, 38-479, 39-602, 40-598
PARKERSON [Parkason]
   JOHN 30-818, 31-930, 33-1045
   PARKERSON, ROBERT [Parkason] 40-777
PARKINSON, ROBERT 39-811
PARKS [Park]
   ARTHUR [Author/jr, sr.] 30-108, 30-112, 31-122(2), 33-136(2), 34-136(2), 35-22(2), 36-60, 36-142, 37-39, 37-74, 38-101(2), 39-140(2), 40-146, 40-1633
   CHARLES 36-94, 37-140, 38-120, 39-29, 40-33   ISAAC 30-110, 37-41
   JOB [Jobe] 35-22, 36-142, 37-39, 38-101, 39-140, 40-146
   JOHN [jr., senr] 30-108, 30-112, 31-122, 31-123, 33-135, 33-136, 34-136, 34-138, 35-22, 35-24, 36-142, 36-143, 37-40, 37-68, 38-17, 38-102(2), 39-140, 40-146
   MARK [Marke] 31-123, 33-135, 34-138, 35-24, 36-143, 37-40, 38-102
PARRATT [Parrett], THOMAS 39-1910, 40-2001
PARRY WILLIAM 37-855
PARSONS [Parson, Persons]

   CHARLES 33-905, 34-1146, 35-1188, 36-1172, 38-1240, 39-1324, 40-1434
   FRANCES 39-1367, 40-1342
   FRANCIS 30-842, 31-967, 33-1009, 34-941, 35-982, 36-1252, 37-821, 38-1134
   GEORGE 30-1427, 31-1493, 33-1484, 34-1484, 35-1572, 36-1713, 37-1141, 38-1686, 39-1724, 40-1796
   JOHN 30-1426, 31-1492, 33-1541, 34-1567, 35-1765, 36-1199, 36-1571, 37-913, 37-1052, 38-1640, 38-1721, 39-1713, 39-1903, 40-1776, 40-2005
   ROBERT [Robart] 31-887, 35-1463, 36-1458, 38-1729, 39-1695, 40-408
PATRICK
   DANIEL 35-372, 36-412, 37-616, 38-600, 39-448, 40-950
   MATTHEW 30-371
   ROGER [Rodger] 33-343, 34-352, 35-372, 36-425, 37-610, 38-606, 39-448, 40-445, 40-661
PATTEY [Patty, Paty]
   JOHN 30-254, 31-291, 33-304, 34-180, 35-329, 36-199, 37-220, 38-351, 39-190, 40-185
   POWELL 31-291, 36-199, 37-220, 38-351, 39-190, 40-185
PAUL [Pall, Pawl]
   GEORGE [30-1051, 33-1044, 34-937, 35-978, 36-1047, 38-1056, 39-1295
   JACOB 30-1050
   WILLIAM [Willm.] 33-1564
PEACOCK [Pecock]
   EDWARD 30-1121, 31-1255, 33-1268, 34-1376, 35-1420, 36-1272, 38-1386
   JOHN 38-1386, 39-1602, 40-1643
   WILLIAM [Willm.] 40-1643
PEAL [Paul, Peale, Peal, Peall, Peel, Peele]
   THOMAS [junr., senr.] 30-1178, 31-1182, 33-1337, 34-1225, 35-1507, 36-1471, 38-1463(2), 39-1486(2), 40-1521(2)
   THOROUGHGOOD [Thorowgood, Thorogood] 30-1178, 31-136, 33-326, 34-294, 35-353, 36-384, 37-222, 37-274, 38-541, 39-620, 40-560
PENEWELL [Peniewell, Penniwell]
   ANN [Anne/wid.] 30-467, 31-470
   CHARLES 30-302, 31-469, 33-532, 34-515, 35-455, 36-495, 37-456, 38-435, 39-444, 40-518
   GEORGE 33-531, 34-516, 35-457, 36-423, 37-545, 38-500
   JOHN 30-306, 31-420, 33-404, 34-377, 35-457, 36-422, 37-543, 38-491, 39-591, 40-615, 40-617
   RICHARD 30-467, 31-341, 33-534
   THOMAS 30-391, 31-506, 33-533, 34-516, 35-456, 36-427, 37-632, 39-587, 40-616

INDEX

WILLIAM 30-467, 31-470, 33-531, 34-381, 35-584, 37-635, 38-441

PEPPER
  JOHN 30-374, 31-440, 33-349, 35-376, 36-517, 37-596, 38-561, 39-473, 40-473
  TOBIAS 30-650, 35-820, 37-658, 39-840, 31-741, 33-739, 34-786, 36-772, 38-889, 40-926
  WILLIAM 30-651, 31-226, 31-744, 33-170, 33-737, 34-262, 34-785, 35-159, 35-819, 36-517, 36-773, 37-596, 37-659, 38-561, 38-888, 39-839, 40-569, 40-927

PERDUE [Perdew]
  GEORGE 37-1135, 38-1685, 39-1736, 40-1798
  JOHN [junr., senr.] 30-1322, 31-1456, 33-1463, 34-1688, 35-1715, 36-1711, 37-1135, 38-1685, 39-1736, 40-1798(2)

PERKINS [Pirkins, Purkins]
  HUGH 34-445, 35-394
  JOHN 30-1124, 31-1250, 33-1205, 34-1314, 35-1255, 36-1277, 38-1380, 39-1589, 40-1669
  MICHAEL [Michall] 30-1125, 31-1249, 33-1204, 34-1315, 38-1380, 39-1589, 40-1669
  MITCHELL [Michell, Mitchell] 35-1256, 36-1278
  SARAH [widdow] 30-1125, 31-1249, 33-1204, 34-1315, 35-1256, 36-1278
  THOMAS 30-283, 31-154, 33-256, 34-213, 35-171, 36-349, 37-164, 38-346, 39-302, 40-223
  WILLIAM 30-1125, 31-1249, 33-1204, 34-1315, 35-1256, 36-243, 37-288, 38-324, 39-301, 40-214

PERRY [Parrey], JAMES [junr., sr.] 30-182, 31-207, 33-205, 33-1507, 34-304, 34-1486, 35-261, 35-1569, 36-291, 36-1658, 36-1694, 37-182(2), 37-855, 38-243, 39-231, 40-279

PETERKIN [Betriken, Pittrikine]
  DAVID 33-180, 34-217, 35-310, 36-215
  JAMES 39-1372

PEWSEY [Peusey, Puissey, Puesey, Puisey, Pusey]
  ALICE [Ayles] 30-81, 31-104
  JOHN 30-81, 31-104, 33-100, 34-15, 35-144, 36-29, 37-4, 38-71, 39-106
  WILLIAM 30-27, 31-33, 33-103, 34-57, 35-68, 36-105, 38-128, 39-40, 40-44

PHEBUS [Febus/juner, sener]
  GEORGE 30-614, 30-615, 31-622, 31-631, 33-550, 33-552, 34-685, 34-686, 35-668, 35-729, 36-744, 36-745, 38-799, 38-800, 39-685, 39-686, 40-827, 40-829
  JOHN 34-685, 35-668, 36-744, 38-799, 40-827, 34-685, 39-686
  SAMUEL [Febus] 30-614, 31-622, 33-550, 34-685, 35-668
  WILLIAM 31- 622

PHILLIPS
  EZEKIEL [Ezekill, Ezekel] 38-1493, 39-1410, 40-1473
  GEORGE 31-1506, 33-1433, 34-1667, 35-1681, 36-1699, 37-1059
  JACOB 30-1308, 31-1338, 33-1472, 34-1455, 35-1738, 36-1741, 37-1250, 38-1713, 39-1699, 40-1906
  JAMES [Jeams] 30-503, 40-74
  JOHN 30-499, 30-1359, 31-843, 33-1083, 33-1301, 34-965, 34-1298, 35-1163, 35-1345, 36-329, 36-1126, 36-1418, 38-1202, 38-1283, 38-1493, 39-1226, 39-1300, 39-1410, 40-1146, 40-1438, 40-1473
  RICHARD [Ritchard/junr., senr.] 30-1359, 30-1361, 31-843, 31-1319, 33-1083, 33-1554, 34-1073, 34-1557, 35-1030, 35-1771, 36-1231, 36-1562, 37-1059, 38-1147, 38-1748, 39-1213, 39-1911, 40-1139, 40-1335
  THOMAS 30-1359, 31-1513, 34-1074, 35-1017, 36-1230, 37-1214, 38-1150, 39-1214, 40-1141
  WILLIAM 33-1083, 34-273, 34-1074, 35-274, 35-1006, 36-359, 36-1126, 38-1147, 39-1215, 39-1369, 40-1138, 40-1426

PHIPPS, JOHN 30-801, 31-828, 33-868, 34-1176, 35-932, 36-1233, 38-1235, 39-1273, 40-1345

PILCHER [Pilchard, Pilcherd, Pilshear, Pilsher, Pilshiar]
  EDWARD 31-1248
  JAMES 33-1195, 36- 775
  JOHN 30-1059, 31-1209, 33-1284, 34-1218, 35-1273, 36-1405, 38-1364, 39-1389, 40-1454
  MOSES 33-1193, 34-1219, 35-1350, 36-1330, 37-647, 38-904, 39-848, 40-917
  WILLIAM 30-1139, 34-1207, 35-1272, 36-1404, 38-1365, 39-1388, 40-1453

PINGALLEY [Dingally, Pengalley, Pengolley, Pilgalley, Pinegaley], THOMAS 30-1252, 31-1284, 34-1308, 35-1259, 36-1274, 38-680, 38-912, 39-264, 40-364

PIPER
  BENJAMIN 36-1078, 40-1890
  CHRISTOPHER 30-1261, 31-1359, 33-1413, 34-1643, 35-1701, 36-1543, 37-1244, 38-1703, 39-1851, 40-1820
  ISAAC 31-1300, 33-1190, 34-1325, 35-1292, 36-1341, 38-1597, 39-1534, 40-1611
  JOSEPH 36-1113, 37-1220, 38-1768,

INDEX

39-1857, 40-1180
  WILLIAM 30-868, 31-998, 33-894
PIPERBANES, ISAAC 34- 796
PITTS
  JOHN 30-1251
  ROBERT 39-1571, 40-1654
PLANNER, WILLIAM [capt., majr.] 30-26, 31-1, 33-37, 34-12
PLUDER [Pudderrer, Puddihny, Puddrah, Puder, Pudrer], JOSEPH 33-690, 34-734, 35-855, 36-790, 37-655, 38-887, 39-828, 40-936
PLUNKETT, HONOR [Oner] 30- 639
POINTER [Pinter, Poynter]
  CHARLES 36- 576
  EDWARD 30-361, 31-350
  ELIAS 30-410, 31-505, 33-513, 34-504, 35-476, 37-634, 38-531, 39-519, 40-641
  JOHN 31-424, 33-502, 34-504, 35-494, 37-478, 38-640
  NATHANIEL [Natl.] 30-484, 31-424, 33-512, 34-374, 35-478
  NEHEMIAH 35- 470
  RATCLIFF [Ratcklife, Ratliff] 31-348, 33-400, 34-513, 35-474, 36-507, 37-477, 38-473, 39-518, 40-636
  THOMAS 30-419, 31-348, 33-400, 34-513, 35-474, 36-507, 37-477, 38-473, 39-518, 40-636
  TURVILLE [Turvil 35-474, 36-507 37-477, 38-473, 39-518, 40-636
  WILLIAM [Willm./senr.] 30-410, 30-484, 30-1424, 31-495, 31-1409, 33-397, 33-400, 33-1542, 34-369, 34-535, 35-470, 35-528, 36-403, 36-507, 38-413
POLK [Poak, Polke, Polok]
  CHARLES [Ch.] 30-977, 31-1055, 33-858, 34-1187, 35-1218, 36-1014, 37-958, 38-1324, 39-1347, 40-1364
  DAVID 30-516, 31-660, 33-621, 34-1700, 35-1754, 37-1034, 38-1819, 39-1791, 40-1977
  EPHRAIM [Epharim, Ephim, Ephreaim] 35-1218, 36-1014, 38-1325, 39-1348, 40-1365
  FRANCIS 37-958
  GEORGE [Gorge] 31- 971
  JAMES 30-535, 31-562, 33-622, 34-719, 35-680, 35-1216, 36-680, 36-1015, 37-959, 38-672, 39-668, 39-1350, 40-793, 40-1363
  JOHN 30-979, 30-997, 31-1017, 31-1033, 33-856, 33-940, 34-1060, 34-1189, 35-1071, 35-1216, 36-990, 36-1015, 37-963, 38-1125, 38-1225, 39-1183, 39-1793, 39-1349, 40-1366, 40-1366
  WILLIAM 30-516, 31-660, 33-621, 34-634, 36-678, 35-681, 38-670, 39-666

POLLETT
  THOMAS [junr.] 31-1424(2), 34-1507, 39-1790(2)
  WILLIAM 39-1783
POLLOCK
  WIDOW 31-778
  DAVID 30-758, 36-1682
  JOSEPH 30-757, 31-780, 33-812, 34-869, 35- 910, 36-895, 37-763, 38-924, 39- 932, 40- 967
POLSON [Poulson], WILLIAM 31-924, 33-1032, 34-1005, 35-1124, 36-1063, 37-890
PONTON, ROBERT 30-381
POPE
  GEORGE [Gorge] 30-684, 31-696, 33-777, 34-763, 35-800, 36-785, 37-709, 38-906, 39-834, 40-875
  JAMES 30-536, 31-557, 33-575, 34-619, 35-685, 36-683, 38-667, 39-663, 40-786
  JOHN [senr.] 30-644, 31-695, 33-690, 34-734, 35-771, 36-782, 36-1445, 37-707, 38-815, 39-1456(2), 40-1585(2)
  RICHARD 30-1366, 31-1482, 33-1592, 34-1581
  SAMUEL 30-683, 31-697, 33-697, 34-808, 35-841, 36-859, 37-710, 38-907, 39-896, 40-873
PORTER
  FRANCIS 30-1175, 31-1239, 33-1326, 34-1201, 35-1484, 36-1431, 38-1456, 39-1492, 40-1513
  HUGH 30-1104, 31-1237
  JAMES 33-527, 34-552, 35-583, 37-388, 38-454, 39-629, 40-502
  JOHN 30-408, 31-478, 33-526, 34-485, 35-447, 35-583, 36-369, 36-433, 37-539, 38-501, 39-645, 39-1467, 40-607
  JONATHAN 30-1104,, 31-1237, 33-1311, 34-1222, 35-1484, 36-531, 30-1104
  JOSEPH [Josept] 30-99, 31-29, 33-32, 30-413, 31-412, 33-372, 34-102, 34-406, 35-128, 35-487, 36-122, 36-369, 37-94, 37-389, 38-78, 38-542, 39-122, 39-619, 40-142, 40-500
  JOSEPHAS 40-1404
  JOSHUA 30-1472, 31-1526, 33-1580, 34-1664, 35-1551, 36-1653, 37-1085, 38-1788, 39-1883, 40-1953
  MCCEMMY [Mackemey, McCimey, Mkkemey] 30-1175, 31-1239, 33-1326, 34-1201, 35-1484, 36-1431, 38-1450, 39-1493, 40-1514
  MCCLINTUCK [Clentuck, Mccluntuck 30-664, 31-745, 33-742, 34-789, 35-823, 36-789, 37-654, 38-886, 39-829, 40-939

INDEX

WILLIAM 30-330, 30-459, 30-1069, 31-437, 31-1223, 33-343, 33-1304, 34-102, 34-352, 34-1296, 35-128, 35-372, 35-854, 36-122, 36-444, 36-846, 37-94, 37-615, 37-736, 38-137, 38-605, 38-891, 39-481, 39-909, 39-1600, 40-443, 40-953, 40-1680

POSEL, GEORGE 39-1910

POTTER
  ANNE 30-85, 31-93, 34-44
  HENRY 30-85, 31-93, 33-108, 34-44, 35-102, 36-28, 37-11, 38-53, 39-112, 40-120
  JOSEPHAS [Josefas] 30-85, 31-93, 33-897, 34-1155, 35-1192, 36-1189, 38-1309, 39-1314

POW, JOHN 31-1326, 33-1396

POWDERS, WILLIAM 40-511

POWELL
  BENJAMIN [Bengaman] 38-60, 39-95, 40-100
  CHARLES 30-284, 31-270, 33-262, 39-317, 40-200
  GABRIEL 34-24, 35-108, 36-1438, 39-1499, 38-1460
  JAMES 37-811
  JOHN [Powall] 30-1137, 31-1116, 33-1208, 34-1417, 35-1264, 36-1268, 38-1351, 38-1390, 39-1255, 39-1594, 40-1193, 40-1673
  JOSEPH 35-1200, 36-1043
  LEVIN [Leving] 31-1288, 35-1264, 36-1356, 38-1392, 39-1595, 40-1674
  RACHEL [widdow] 30-435, 31-363, 34-451, 38-466
  SAMUEL 30-433, 31-364, 33-489, 34-449, 35-515, 36-589, 37-414, 38-505, 39-436, 40-512
  SUSANNAH 30-284, 31-270, 33-262
  THOMAS [junr., senr.] 30-224, 30-435, 31-262, 31-277, 31-363, 34-23, 34-178, 34-450, 35-109, 35-284, 35-598, 36-43, 36-356, 36-547, 37-50, 37-224, 37-413, 38-60, 38-224, 38-464, 39-95, 39-300, 39-437, 40-100, 40-298, 40-515
  WILLIAM 39-329

PRAKER, WILLIAM 38-390

PRICE [Prise]
  ALEXANDER [Elix.] 31-1367, 31-1370, 34-1671, 35-1681, 39-1671
  BENJAMIN 40-896
  DAVID 30-715, 35-1683, 36-1628, 37-1226, 38-1737, 39-1857, 40-1209
  EDWARD 33-79, 34-126, 35-53, 36-55, 37-90, 38-45, 39-156, 39-913
  ELIAS 38-892
  EVE 30-1270
  FRANCIS [Frances, Frank] 31-950, 33-79, 33-1050, 34-126, 34-1674, 35-53, 35-1029, 36-55, 36-938, 38-1737, 39-1112, 40-1203
  JOHN 30-1278, 31-1381, 33-1426, 34-1668, 35-53, 35-1664, 36-55, 36-1628, 37-1226, 38-45, 38-1737, 39-1857, 40-1882
  JOHNSON 35-53, 36-55, 38-59
  ROBERT [Robart] 39-1045, 40-1115
  THOMAS 33-79, 34-126, 35-1664, 36-1628, 37-1226, 38-1737, 39-1671, 40-1125

PRIDE, JOHN 40-412

PRIDOX [Predox, Pridicks, Pridix, Produx] THOMAS 30-276, 31-143, 33-320, 34-346, 35-315, 36-287, 37-217, 38-207, 39-225, 40-189

PRINGLE, WILLIAM 38-1718, 39-724, 40-743

PRIOR [Prier, Pryer]
  JOHN WEBB 37-528
  SAMUEL 37-15, 38-90, 39-152, 40-132
  THOMAS 30-93, 31-102, 33-116, 34-49, 35-141, 36-133, 37-15, 38-90, 39-152, 40-132
  WEBB [Weeb] 31-417, 33-452, 34-434, 35-428, 36-452, 38-1567, 39-498, 40-591

PRITCHETT, WILLIAM 30-113, 35-1610

PRITEYMAN [Briteyman, Prietyman], THOMAS 34-266, 35-157, 36-332, 37-260, 38-334, 39-354, 40-415

PROBART [Probat/capt.], WILLIAM 38-1355, 39-1379, 40-1590

PUCKHAM [Paccumb, Pookum, Puckem, Pukum]
  ABRAHAM 30-611, 38-1260, 39-1254
  JOHN 39-987, 40-1389
  RICHARD 30-1442, 31-1523, 33-1525, 34-1516, 36-734, 37-790, 38-973, 39-987, 40-1389

PULLETT
  ABRAHAM 35-642
  THOMAS [junr., senr.] 30-1439, 33-1526, 35-1753, 36-1683(2), 37-1033(2), 38-1818(2), 40-1975, 40-1976
  WILLIAM 38-1818, 40-1975

PURNELL [Purnall]
  BENJAMIN [Benjamain 33-351, 34-359, 35-393, 36-485
  CATHARINE [Katharine/Mrs.] 30-445, 31-319, 33-375, 34-409, 35-488, 36-410, 37-454, 38-467, 39-635, 40-633
  ELISHA 30-442, 31-455, 33-359, 34-386, 34-1345, 35-389, 35-1383, 36-586, 36-1480, 37-498, 38-601, 39-479, 39-1464, 40-1577
  JOHN [Mr.] 30-272, 30-731, 31-141, 31-666, 33-316, 33-750, 34-169, 34-742, 35-356, 35-756, 36-292, 36-824, 37-349, 37-729, 38-297,

INDEX

38-900, 39-265, 39-877, 40-191, 40-883
   MATTHEW 30-304, 31-496, 33-420, 34-524, 35-533, 36-520, 37-561, 38-413, 39-543, 40-527
   THOMAS 30-418, 31-454, 33-351, 34-359, 35-379, 36-478, 37-597, 38-533, 39-460, 40-465
   WALTER [Walton] 33-375, 34-409, 35-488, 36-410, 37-454, 38-468, 39-634, 40-634
PUSSELL, GEORGE 40-2001
PUZEY, JOHN 40-114

QUARTERMUS [Quotormus, Quturmus]
   ISAIAH 31-978, 33-974
   JAMES 30-1044, 31-969, 33-1007, 34-940, 35-980(2), 36-1251, 38-996, 39-1135, 39-1149(2), 40-1087
   PATRICK 40-1087
QUILLING [Quellin(g), Quillin]
   BENJAMIN Benjmen] 31-147, 33-152, 34-339, 35-354, 36-233, 37-318, 38-378, 39-417, 40-452
   JOHN 31-147(2), 33-152, 34-339, 35-354, 36-353, 37-346, 38-368, 40-289
   JOSEPH 30-280, 33-152, 34-189, 35-354, 36-271, 37-318, 38-378, 40-436
   MARY 31-147, 33-152, 34-339
QUILLINS, JOSEPH 39-402
QUINTON [Quenton]
   DIXON [Dickson] 31-1279, 33-1159, 34-1257, 35-1280, 36-1347, 38-1608, 39-1548, 40-1624
   PETER 39-1134, 40-1208
   PHILLIP 30-1238, 31-1279, 33-1159, 34-1257, 35-1280, 36-1348, 38-160739-1547, 40-1623

RACKLIFE [Rackliff(e), Ratcliff, Ratlide, Ratlife, Ratliff(e)]
   CHARLES [capt., senr.] 30-268, 30-272(2), 31-139, 31-140, 31-141, 33-316, 33-326, 33-425, 34-169, 34-249, 34-495, 35-350, 35-356, 35-391, 36-288, 36-292, 37-218, 38-297, 38-354, 38-402, 39-215, 39-307, 39-527, 40-168(2), 40-482
   EDWARD 30-268
   ELIAS 30-240, 31-308, 33-296, 34-284, 35-346, 36-348, 37-292, 38-309, 39-321, 40-340
   JOHN 31-285, 33-301, 34-280, 35-339, 37-583, 38-354
   NATHANIEL 36-226, 39-272, 40-368
   PURNELL [Purnal) 31-140, 35-350, 36-288, 37-218, 38-354, 39-215, 40-168
   WRIXAM [Rixam] 31-141, 33-316, 34-169, 35-356, 38-206, 40-192

RADISH [Reddish], JOHN 30-1352, 31-1502, 33-1576, 34-1542, 35-1759, 36-1553, 37-1073, 38-1793, 39-1928
RAGLIN [Ragland, Ragley], MICHAEL [Mikell] 30-1476, 31-1471, 33-1496, 34-1505, 35-1594, 36-1664, 37-1101, 38-1649, 39-1781, 40-1967
RAINE [Murrain, Rain, Ryan]
   JOHN 34-487, 35-449, 36-428, 37-558, 38-649, 39-593, 40-674
   MATTHEW 30-406, 31-476, 33-539, 34-487, 35-449, 36-428, 37-558, 38-649, 39-593, 40-674
RAITH, JAMES 40-1863
RALPHFIELD, SPENCER 36-827
RAMSEY
   BARNETT 38-1604, 39-1543, 40-1619
   BARRETT 31-1291
   CHARLES 31-1291, 33-1185, 34-1268, 35-1302, 36-1378, 38-1604, 39-1543, 40-1619
   JOHN 33-1185, 35-1302, 36-1378, 38-1604, 39-1543, 40-1619
   WELBOURN 39-1543
RANDALLS, WILLIAM 34-572
RATHBONE [Rathbon]
   ANDREW 30-1294, 34-1112, 35-1649, 36-1754, 37-1118, 38-1752, 40-1334
   RICHARD 30-297
   ROBERT 33-508, 34-525, 37-563, 38-655, 40-252
RAY, JAMES 30-1166, 31-1198, 33-1327
READ [Reed, Reid]
   EZEKIEL [Hezekiah, Ezekeil, Ezakiah] 38-999, 39-1147, 40-1085
   JACOB 40-1085
   JAMES 36-827
   JOHN [junr., senr.] 30-1042(2), 31-968(2), 33-692, 33-1005(2), 34-939(2), 35-767, 35-979(2), 36-827, 36-1059, 36-1055, 38-999, 38-1342, 39-1146, 39-1147, 40-1085, 40-1086
   JOSEPH 40-833
   OBEDIAH 35-979, 36-1250, 38-999, 39-1146, 40-1086
   THOMAS 36-1250
   WALTER 33-695, 36-787, 37-652, 38-895, 39-830, 40-934
   WILLIAM 36-1056
   ZACHARIAH [Zacharies, Zechriah] 31-968, 33-1005, 34-939, 35-979, 38-1342, 39-1159, 40-1247
READEN [Reading, Redden, Redding, Riddin]
   CHARLES 30-80, 31-86, 31-1240, 33-92, 34-1373, 35-1491, 36-1463, 38-1489, 39-1417, 40-1482
   JOHN 33-66, 34-48, 35-34, 36-73, 37-77, 38-24, 39-96, 40-72
   MICHAEL 31-1232, 36-14331, 39-1476
   PETER 30-87, 31-55, 33-62, 33-140,

INDEX

34-48, 36-136, 37-52, 38-65, 39-99, 40-105

RECORDS [Ricords]
   ALEXANDER 30-1275, 31-1373, 33-1422, 35-1002, 38-1049
   BENJAMIN [Ben. son] 30-1275, 31-1014, 34-1647
   JAMES 33-1422, 34-1647, 37-1218
   JOHN [sr., jur.] 30-1023, 30-1275, 31-960, 31-1373, 33-1422, 34-1647, 35-254, 36-1695, 37-1218, 38-1234, 40-1869
   JOSEPH 30-1275, 31-1373, 33-1422
   THOMAS 34-1647, 36-1695, 37-1218, 40-1869

REDDY [Ready]
   BRYAN [Brian, Bryant] 33-1466, 34-1468, 35-1729, 36-1728, 37-1160, 38-1719, 39-1684, 40-1898
   CORNELIUS 35-1038, 36-977, 37-870, 38-1162, 39-1684, 40-1898
   DANIEL 35-1729, 37-1232
   JAMES 33-1466
   JOHN 30-1299, 31-1343, 33-1476
   NICHOLAS 30-1299, 31-1343
   THOMAS 30-1299, 31-1343, 34-1689, 35-1113, 36-1739, 38-1730

REIGHAN, JAMES 34-844

RELPH
   ANN 30-1047
   THOMAS [Ralph(e)] 30-849, 31-860, 33-962, 34-950, 35-995, 36-1088, 38-1066, 39-1144, 40-1099, 40-1276
   WILLIAM [Ralph, Relpte] 30-1022, 31-1011, 33-981, 34-1085, 35-1040, 36-986, 37-869, 38-1160, 39-1086, 40-1276

RENCHER [R(e)ancher, Renshaw, Rensher]
   THOMAS 30-1443, 31-1400, 33-1598, 34-1615, 35-1621, 36-1605, 37-998, 38-1863, 39-1822, 40-1851
   UNDERWOOD [Honorwood, Wood] 30-1444, 31-1401, 33-1597, 34-1614, 35-1763, 36-1606, 37-999, 38-1864, 39-1823, 40-1852

REVILL [Re(a)vell, Reavill]
   CHARLES 30-593, 31-615, 33-667, 34-579, 35-659, 36-611, 38-733, 39-738, 40-723
   CURTIS 40-723
   RANDALL [Randul] 30-589, 31-618, 33-563, 34-671, 35-661, 36-613, 38-730, 38-733, 39-742, 40-723, 40-853
   WILLIAM 34-671, 35-662, 36-1639, 37-1109, 38-1657, 39-1762, 40-1948

REYDEN, ROBERT 31-383

REYNOLDS [Renalds, Renalls, Reno(l)ds, Ronalds, Rondols, Runels]
   HENRY 33-1245, 34-1308, 35-1406, 38-680, 39-718, 40-763
   JOHN 30-103, 30-1389, 31-1143, 31-1315, 33-1377, 33-1604
   RICHARD 30-173, 31-242, 33-172, 34-264, 35-154
   WILLIAM 40-640

RHODE, JOHN [Rode] 30-690

RHODES [R(h)oad(e)s, Rodes]
   DANIEL 30-891, 31-1070, 33-1063, 34-983, 35-1144, 36-1083, 38-1252, 39-1037, 40-1172
   JOHN 30-1260, 31-1371, 33-991, 35-1050, 36-1029, 38-1211, 39-1185, 40-1273
   TIMOTHY [junr., senr.] 30-882, 30-891, 31-869(2), 33-890, 33-1063, 34-959, 34-983, 35-1164(2), 36-1130, 38-1053

RICKARDS [Richards, Rickards, Rickcords, Ricords,]
   JOHN [junr., sr.] 30-134, 30-178, 31-175, 31-188, 33-190, 33-223, 34-153, 34-260, 35-215, 36-156, 36-189, 37-202, 37-235, 38-201, 38-286, 39-208, 39-242, 40-241, 40-249
   JONES [Jonnas, Joanes] 31-187, 33-189, 34-151, 35-216, 36-188, 37-198, 38-288, 39-209, 40-253
   WILLIAM 30-428, 31-394, 33-456, 34-260, 34-514, 35-254, 35-568, 36-156, 36-497, 37-202, 37-435, 38-355, 38-443, 39-193, 39-423, 40-248, 40-542

RICHARDSON [Richason, Richeson, Richison, Richeardson, Richerson, Ritcharson]
   BENJAMIN 38-1063, 39-1111
   CHARLES 30-346, 31-347, 33-353, 34-363, 35-384, 36-446, 37-600, 38-594, 39-456, 40-570
   DAVID 39-915, 40-860
   JAMES 30-455, 31-347, 33-356, 34-365, 35-386, 37-599, 38-596, 39-466, 40-571
   JOHN 30-679, 30-837, 31-711, 31-917, 33-700, 33-758, 33-1006, 34-721, 34-732, 34-933, 35-757, 35-769, 35-973, 36-828, 36-840, 36-1256, 37-640, 37-725, 38-867, 38-884, 38-997, 39-892, 39-902, 39-1157, 40-174, 40-859, 40-1081
   JONES 30-124, 36-449
   ROBERT 30-462, 31-369, 33-354, 34-364, 35-385, 36-445, 37-601, 38-595, 39-457, 40-569
   SAMUEL 35-760, 36-840, 37-725, 38-867, 39-902, 40-859
   THOMAS 30-286
   WILLIAM 30-462, 30-852, 31-333, 31-876, 33-966, 33-1006, 34-440, 34-933, 34-952, 35-387, 35-973, 35-990, 36-516, 36-1095, 37-602,

INDEX

38-648, 38-1013, 38-1063, 39-660,
39-1111, 39-1846, 40-694, 40-1824
RICHEY [Richass, Richee, Richtie,
Rickee, Rickey, Ritchey, Ritchie]
  ARCHIBALD [Archable, Archbuld]
31-970, 33-1078, 34-921, 35-950,
36-1207, 38-1030, 39-1027, 40-1058
RICKETTS, JAMES 38-1740
RICORDS [Rickards, Ricketts,
Rickordsm Riukords]
  ALEXANDER 34-1101, 36-949,
39-1361, 40-1331
    BENJAMIN 35-1679
    JAMES 35-1678, 39-1863
    JOHN [junr.] 33-960, 34-1100,
35-1170, 35-1678, 36-1236, 37-991,
38-1745, 39-1216, 39-1863, 40-1258
    JOSEPH 38-1769
    THOMAS 35-1678, 38-1745, 39-1863
RIDER [Ryden, Ryder]
  HATHLY [Hathley, Hetely, Hatly]
30-853, 31-902, 33-961, 34-1115,
35-991, 36-1094, 37-849, 38-1061,
39-1140
  JAMES [jur.] 31-942(2), 33-1557,
34-1558, 35-1649
   RICHARD 30-853, 31-902, 33- 965
   WILSON 30-853, 31-902, 33-965,
34-951, 35-992, 36-1093, 37-848,
38-1064, 39-1141, 40-1101
RIGGIN [Regin, Riggen, Rigging,
Riggon]
  AMBROSE [Ambr(o)(u)s,
Ambroze/junr., senr.] 30-671,
30-1066, 30-1271, 31-1202, 33-1300,
33-1309, 33-1431, 34-1001, 34-1211,
34-1231, 35-1130, 35-1332, 35-1465,
36-1420, 36-1460, 36-1695, 38-1113,
38-1499, 38-1524, 39-1251, 39-1406,
39-1422, 40-1173, 40-1471, 40-1539
  CHARLES 30-1163, 31-1092, 33-1226,
34-1398, 35-1438, 36-1284, 38-1422,
39-1632, 40-1708
  CORNELIUS 38-1423, 39-1634, 40-1711
  DARBY 30-1074, 31-1229, 33-1312,
34-1445, 35-1510, 36-1427, 38-1484,
39-1421, 40-1492(2)
  ELIZABETH 30-1163, 34-1397,
35-1437, 36-1283
  JOHN [junr., senr., secundes]
30-53(2), 30-1160(2), 30-1162,
31-59, 31-109, 31-1090(2), 31-1092,
31-1311, 33-64(2), 33-1221(2),
33-1226, 33-1309, 34-129(2),
34-1396, 34-1436(2), 35-36(2),
35-1403, 35-1435(2), 35-1510, 36-23,
36-77, 36-1282, 36-1288(2), 36-1427,
37-72, 37-78, 38-23, 38-29, 38-1419,
38-1423(2), 38-1484, 39-60, 39-61,
39-1421, 39-1628, 39-1634(2), 40-64,
40-66, 40-1492, 40-1706, 40-1711
  JONATHAN 30-53, 31-59, 33-64,
34-130, 35-35, 35-110, 36-78, 37-25,
37-79, 38-25, 38-85, 39-62, 39-87,
40-49, 40-65
  JOSEPH 30-1067, 31-1219, 33-1297,
34-1209, 35-1334, 36-1425, 38-1494,
39-1409, 40-1476
  MARY 40-1711
  PIERCE [Pearce, Pease, Pierce]
31-1229, 33-1312, 34-1296, 35-1510,
36-1460, 38-1484, 39-1421, 40-1533
  SAMUEL 30-1161, 31-1091, 33-1220,
34-55, 35-133
  SOLOMON 33-1226, 34-1397, 35-1437,
36-1283, 38-1421, 39-1631
  SOLOMON 40-1710
  STEPHEN [Steven] 30-53, 30-1160,
31-1090, 33-64, 33-1221, 34-129,
34-1436, 35-37, 35-1435, 36-78,
36-1288, 37-81, 38-26, 39-59, 40-63
  TEAGUE [jr., senr] 30-1064,
30-1066, 31-1202, 31-1217, 33-1221,
33-1294, 33-1300, 33-1312, 34-1211,
34-1212, 34-1436, 34-1445, 35-1332,
35-1347, 35-1435, 35-1510, 36-1288,
36-1420, 36-1423(2), 36-1427,
37-1163, 38-1423, 38-1484, 38-1499,
38-1500(2), 39-1400(2), 39-1406,
39-1421, 39-1634, 40-1469(2),
40-1471, 40-1539, 40-1711
  WILLIAM 30-505, 33-1243, 34-390,
35-36, 36-77, 37-78, 38-29, 39-60,
40-66
RIGGS, JOHN 40-456
RIGSBY [Rigbey, Rigby, Rigsbe(e)]
  JOHN 39-684, 40-831
  LEWIS 30-616, 31-630, 33-614,
34-676, 35-675, 36-741, 38-801,
39-684, 40-831
RILEY, GEORGE 33-1117
RINGROSE [Ring Rose, Ringrow,
Rinsrose], DANIEL 31- 531, 33-605,
34-1604
RO-----, THOMAS 37-939
ROACH [Roa(t)ch(es), Roch, Rotch,
Rouch]
  ALICE [Ealse, Else/mrs./widow]
30-1348, 31-1524, 33-1503, 34-1529,
35-1598, 36-1638, 37-1089, 38-1813,
39-1767, 40-1945
  CHARLES 30-590, 31-1524, 33-80,
34-53, 35-7, 36-59, 37-106, 38-3,
39-82, 40-88
  DANIEL 30-12, 34-59, 35-647
  ISAAC [Isack] 30-590, 31-617,
33-1503, 34-1529, 35-52, 36-1638,
37-1089, 38-1813, 39-1767, 40-1945
  JAMES 39-420, 40- 489
  JOHN 30-65, 31-67, 33-81, 33-1125,
34-54, 34-1563, 35-52, 36-60, 37-28,
38-4, 39-80, 40-87
  MICHAEL [Michaeil] 39-82, 40-88
  NATHANIEL 30-12, 33-14, 34-59,

INDEX

35-143, 36-10, 37-116, 38-145, 39-9, 40-10
   SAMUEL 31-68, 33-107, 34-63, 35-145
   SARAH Roaches] 30-87, 31- 95
   STEPHEN [Steven] 30-1348, 31-1524, 33-1503, 34-1529, 35-1598, 36-1638, 37-1090, 38-1814, 39-1768, 40-2003
   WILLIAM 30-590, 31-617, 33-564, 34-674, 35-733, 36-616, 38-731, 39-740, 40-726
ROBBINS [Robens]
   BOWDIN [Bodwine, Bowdwine] 34-800, 37-684, 38-860, 39-876, 40-892
   ELIZABETH [widow] 31-722, 33-749, 34-800, 35-832, 36-857
   THOMAS 30-718, 36-857, 38-206, 39-266, 40-367
   WILLIAM 40-847
ROBERTS [Robards, Robarts]
   WIDOW 31-783
   ALEXANDER 30-139, 31-214, 33-209, 34-153, 35-190, 36-216, 38-189, 39-312, 40-274
   EDWARD 30-740, 31-791, 33-810, 34-868, 35-911, 36-892, 37-762, 38-944, 39-933, 40-993
   JOHN 31-783, 33-762, 33-811, 34-665, 34-733, 34-861, 35-770, 35-919, 36-838, 36-909, 37-758, 38-943, 39-934, 40-970
   JOSEPH 30-594, 31-533, 33-560, 35-739
   RENCHER [Rancher, Renshaw] 31-783, 33-811, 34-833, 37-759, 38-1042, 39-1701, 40-1789
   ROBERT 30-67, 31-75
   SAMUEL 31-212, 33-224, 34-318, 35-188
   THOMAS [jr., sr.] 30-140, 30-140, 31-212, 31-212, 33-224, 33-226, 34-318, 34-327, 34-861, 35-190, 35-919, 36-216, 36-909, 37-221, 37-304, 37-324, 37-758, 38-188, 38-189, 38-943, 39-311, 39-934, 40-274, 40-275, 40-970
ROBERTSON [Robarson, Roberson]
   MR. 35-673
   ANDREW 30-242, 31-298, 33-292, 34-281, 36-276, 37-295
   DAVID 30-946, 31-979, 33-975, 34-1039
   GEORGE 36-162, 38-370, 39-267, 40-269
   JAMES [revd.] 30-632, 31-645, 33-610, 34-608, 36-657, 38-785
   JOHN 30-632, 30-931, 30-1382, 31-645, 31-910, 33-610, 33-917, 34-608, 34-1033, 35-673, 35-1098, 36-162, 36-657, 36-973, 37-374, 37-974, 37-1018, 38-370, 38-785, 38-1078, 39-267, 39-1094, 39-1804, 40-269(2)
   JOSEPH 37-374, 38-370, 39-267, 40-244, 40-269
   JOSHUA 36-300, 37-283, 37-374, 39-213, 40-234
   MICHAEL [Mickeall/jr., sr.] 36-166, 37-210, 38-340(2), 39-250(2), 40-250(2)
   THOMAS 36-160, 37-281, 38-246, 39-211, 40-244
   WILLIAM 30-941, 30-1385, 31-964, 33-976, 33-1575, 34-438, 34-938, 35-974, 36-166, 36-1222, 36-1756, 37-210, 37-983, 37-1016, 38-272, 38-340, 38-1181, 38-1831, 39-250, 39-339, 39-1088, 39-1094, 39-1665, 39-1806, 40-250, 40-1863, 40-1941
ROBINETT [Robinnut/sr.], SAMUEL 35-1173(2), 36-1247, 36-1248, 37-893, 38-1269
ROBINSON [Robi(e)son, Robyson]
   [illegible] 37- 505
   ANDREW 35-342
   GEORGE 30-188, 31-163, 33-236, 34-228, 35-260
   HANNAH 33-503
   JAMES [revrd. mr.] 39-696, 40-776
   JOHN 30-188, 31-163, 31-1404, 33-236, 34-228, 34-1598, 35-260, 35-1631, 36-1591, 38-1829, 39-696, 40-776, 40-1237, 40-1989
   JOSHUA 31-209, 33-158, 34-324, 35-226, 38-185
   JOSIAH 30-181
   MARY 30-181, 31-209
   MICHAEL [Michel] 30-180, 31-210, 33-230, 34-259, 35-255
   THOMAS 30-135, 31-192, 33-209, 34-307, 35-250
   WILLIAM 30-369(2), 31-358(2), 31-1406, 33-503, 34-1597, 35-255, 35-432, 35-1629, 36-542, 38-620, 39-574, 40-578, 40-1237, 40-1241, 40-1991
ROCHESTER, RALPH 34-707
RODGERS [Rogers]
   JOHN 39-718, 40-763
   RICHARD 38-1882, 39-1929, 40-1893
   SAMUEL 36-807
   SOLOMON 33-241, 34-208, 35-238, 37-171, 38-388, 39-389, 40-251
RODNEY [Rad(e)ney] WILLIAM 35-156, 37-257, 38-333, 39-353, 40-397
ROE [Poe, Row(e)]
   WIDOW 31-803, 39-953
   ELIZABETH 34-885, 36-914, 37-749, 38-966, 40-1121
   ISAAC 35-698
   JOHN 34-1634, 36- 914, 38- 966, 37- 749
   JOSEPH 30-752, 31-799, 33-790, 34-852, 35-859, 36-918, 37-745,

INDEX

38-963, 39-952, 40-980
  SARAH 40-979
  THOMAS 30-751, 31-801, 33-789, 34-853, 35-923, 36-917, 37-746, 38-965
ROLAND, ELIZABETH 31-1124
ROLLINS [Rawlins], CHARLES 38-963, 39-950
ROSE, SAMUEL 31-807, 33-795, 34-865, 35-915, 36-902, 37-738, 39-925, 40-961
ROSS, DAVID 39-1445
ROTTEN
  EZEKIEL [Ezekeall] 39-1024
  HEZEKIAH 38-992, 40-1055
  JOSIAH [Josias] 30-928, 31-1075, 33-923, 34-1023, 35-1101, 36-1061
  JOSIAS 34-1023
  WILLIAM 38-992, 39-1024, 40-1055
ROUND [Rownd(s), Rowin]
  CATHERINE [Catherin] 39-613, 40-494
  EDWARD [capt.] 30-476, 31-442, 33-514, 34-558, 35-585, 36-518, 37-626, 37-636, 38-397, 39-569, 40-640
  JAMES 30-475, 31-401, 33-510, 34-380, 35-481, 36-393, 37-386, 38-451
ROWELL, THOMAS 30-937, 33-883, 35-1102, 36-939, 39-1122, 40-1234
RUARK [Rewark, Roark]
  BRYAN 30-464, 31-333
  EDWARD [Rook] 38, 1415, 39-1626
  JAMES [Roark, Ruock, Ruoke] 34-1481, 36-1710, 37-1132, 38-1682, 39-1727, 40-1915
  JOHN [Rewark, Roark, Ro(u)ock, Ruoc, Rework] 30-769, 31-762, 33-828, 34-1495, 36-1494, 37-1167, 38-1526, 39-1436, 40-1544
  WILLIAM [Ruke] 30-594, 31-1424
RUSSELL [Russie, Rusill]
  ANDREW [Androw] 30-228, 31-266, 33-266, 34-299, 35-209, 36-205, 37-354, 38-229, 39-295, 40-307
  CUTHBURD [Cuthbud, Cuthburt] 31-759, 33-746, 34-802, 35-835, 36-767, 37-720, 38-881, 40-915
  GEORGE 40-1865
  JAMES [junr., senr] 30-847, 30-848, 31-1066, 31-1067, 33-961, 33-963, 34-947, 34-948, 35-993, 35-996, 36-1090, 36-1091, 37-839, 37-840, 38-1065, 38-1081, 39-1142, 39-1143, 40-1096, 40-1097
  RICHARD 30-578, 31-626
  THOMAS [Thos. Alexr.] 31-1066, 33-961, 34-947, 35-996, 36-1090, 36-1536, 37-841, 37-1222, 38-1004, 38-1746, 39-1008, 39-1850, 40-1096, 40-1890

  WILLIAM 30-933, 31-609, 31-911, 34-947, 35-996, 36-1090, 37-839, 38-1065, 40-1888
RYCRAFT, RICHARD 36-1397
RYLEY [Railey, Realy, Reily, R(e)yley], THOMAS 30-363, 31-317, 33-382, 34-417, 35-501, 36-529, 37-395, 38-513, 39-414, 40-450

SADLER, ISAAC 38-1878, 39-1728, 40-1916
SAILOR, JOHN 30-1, 34-605
SALISBURY [Solsberry], WILLIAM 33-137, 34-135, 35-22
SALT, BALMFORTH 34-1665, 35-1556, 36-1705, 37-1086
SAMMONS
  BENJAMIN [Benoney] 31-755, 33-776, 34-792, 35-833, 36-856, 37-663, 38-872, 39-912, 40-888
  WILLIAM [Salmon, Salomon] 30-146, 31-218, 33-233, 34-332, 36-263, 37-287, 38-182, 39-334, 40-386
SAMUELS
  WIDOW 34-889
  ABEL 30-1266, 31-1347
  ANN [Amy/widow] 33-1110, 35-931, 36-1001, 38-987, 39-1072, 40-1036
  PETER [junr, senr.] 30-794, 30-963, 31-825, 31-1058, 33-876, 34-1165, 35-1208, 40-1379
  RICHARD [Richard/senr.] 30-793, 30-963, 31-827, 31-1031, 33-877, 34-1164, 35-1209, 38-1267, 39-1286, 40-1378
SANDERS [Sandus]
  ANDREW 39-1340(2), 40-1315(2)
  RICHARD [Ritchard] 30-500, 31-565, 33-24, 33-674, 34-91, 35-118, 36-111, 37-151, 38-136, 39-128, 39-1340, 40-701
  THOMAS 33-24, 34-91, 35-118, 36-111, 37-151, 38-158, 39-15, 40-777
  WILLIAM 39-128, 40-701
SANDWITH, WILLIAM 34-1351, 36-521, 37-589
SASSER [Saucer, Sawser]
  ALICE 39-931
  WILLIAM 35-909, 36-888, 37-785, 38-923, 39-931, 40-964
SAULS, JOHN 33-240
SAVAGE [Savige]
  GEORGE 36-1475
  WILLIAM 31-1405, 33-1589, 38-1655, 39-1729
SCADY [Scadey, Sheydy, Skeddy]
  ELIZABETH 35-1581
  JOHN 35-1581, 36-1709, 38-1685, 40-1808
  STEPHEN 35-1581, 36-1709, 37-1130, 38-1681, 39-1731, 40-1919

INDEX

SCANDLIN [Scandalon, Scandons, Scandrel], EDWARD 31-53, 33-102, 34-46, 35-56, 36-33, 37-53, 38-67, 39-162, 40-107
SCARBOROUGH [Scarbrough]
  MADAM 35-1363
  JOHN 31-683, 33-710, 34-803, 35-836, 36-844, 37-691, 38-870, 39-882, 40-856
SCHOLFIELD [Schofield, Sco(e)field, Scolfield, Scoolfield]
  BENJAMIN 40-567
  HENRY 1130-1134, 31-1124, 33-1215, 34-1413, 35-1267, 36-1264, 38-1387, 39-1601, 40-1679
  JOHN 33-358, 34-385, 35-388, 36-414, 37-606, 38-532, 39-458, 40-568
  JOSEPH 30-1239, 31-361, 33-358, 34-385, 35-388, 36-414, 37-606, 38-532, 39-458, 40-567
SCOTT [Scott] CAPTAIN 31-1198
  ADAM 37-730, 38-819, 39-843
  ANDREW 33-1587
  DAY [mr.] 30-1462, 31-1466, 33-1404, 34-1635, 35-1710, 36-1532, 37-1169, 38-1664, 39-1843, 40-1827
  DUNCAN [Dunken] 39-843
  GEORGE [mr.] 30-906, 30-1462, 31-895, 31-1465, 33-1025, 33-1403, 34-1032, 34-1636, 35-1103, 35-1709, 36-941, 36-1534, 37-1168, 38-1343, 38-1665, 39-144, 39-1073, 39-1840, 40-102, 40-1228(2), 40-1826
  JOHN [capt., junr.] 30-79, 30-1166, 31-90, 33-97, 33-1327, 34-22, 34-1198(2), 35-107, 35-1458, 35-1458, 36-37, 36-1430(2), 37-54, 38-64, 38-1455, 39-98, 39-1491, 40-103, 40-1518
  JOSEPH 39-1491, 40-1518
  MARK 30-321, 31-384, 33-509, 34-433, 35-427, 36-453, 37-515, 38-582, 39-490, 40-631
  ROBERT [junr., senr.] 30-79, 30-79, 30-706(2), 31-90, 31-717, 33-97, 33-715, 33-715, 34-22, 34-22, 34-782, 34-782, 35-107, 35-146, 35-816, 35-816, 36-37, 36-38, 36-799, 37-54, 37-107, 37-730, 37-730, 38-64, 38-160, 38-819, 38-819, 39-98, 39-144, 39-843, 39-923, 40-102, 40-104
  THOMAS 30-1071, 31-1225, 33-1305
  WILLIAM 33-715, 34-733, 35-816, 37-504, 38-624, 39-1445, 40-1381
  WINDOM [esqr.] 30-907, 31-1080, 33-997, 34-1022, 35-1104, 36-940, 38-1090, 39-1074, 40-1229
SEAHORN [Seahan, Seahawne, Sehoan, Seho(r)n, Shenane, Shehorn]
  JOHN 30-1416, 31-1460, 33-1499, 34-1522, 35-1597, 36-1656, 37-1091, 38-1654, 39-1769, 40-1944
  THOMAS 30-1259, 31-1419, 33-1589, 34-946, 35-1519, 38-158, 39-15, 40-12
SELBY [Sebry, Selbie]
  DANIEL 30-698, 33-693, 34-738, 35-775, 36-761, 37-716, 38-855, 39-919, 40-879
  JOHN 31-402, 33-347, 34-356, 35-377, 36-450, 37-594, 38-599, 39-449
  MATTHEW 30- 698 , 33- 693 , 34- 738 , 35- 775 , 36- 761 , 37- 716 , 38- 855 , 39- 919 , 40- 879
  PARKER [senr.] 30-411, 30-699, 31-422, 31-692, 33-403, 33-695, 34-378, 34-741, 35-497, 35-778, 36-471, 36-762, 37-488, 37-674, 38-472, 38-845, 39-625, 39-822, 39-919, 40-497, 40-879, 40-880
  PHILLIP [junr.] 30-698(2), 31-691, 33-693(2), 34-738(2), 35-775(2), 36-761(2), 37-716(2), 38-855(2), 39-919(2), 40-879(2)
  THOMAS [junr.] 30-1208, 31-1174, 33-1348, 34-1363, 35-1518, 35-1518, 38-1537(2), 39-1477(2), 40-1534, 40-1566
  WILLIAM [junr., senr.] 30-460, 30-698, 31-426, 33-340, 33-693, 34-358, 34-738, 35-380, 35-775, 36-443(2), 36-761, 37-595(2), 37-716, 38-598(2), 39-459(2), 40-439(2)
SEWARD [Sewards, Sowards], WILLIAM 39-953, 40-979
SEYMOUR [Seamour, Semour], DIGBY 30-631, 31-52
SHANKLING [Shanklin], WILLIAM 34-1266, 35-1324, 36-1383
SHANKS, BENJAMIN 31-805, 33-615, 34-720, 35-738, 36-660
SHARLY, JAMES 30-370
SHARP [Sharpe]
  CAPTAIN 34-1531
  WIDOW 38-1787
  BENJAMIN [Ben.] 30-493, 31-575, 33-594, 34-600, 35-622, 36-640, 38-764, 39-791, 40-809
  GEORGE 30-1371, 31-1525, 33-1512, 35-1557, 36-1678, 37-1083
  JOHN 30-982, 31-1053, 33-874, 34-1171, 35-1223, 36-1241, 37-955(2), 38-1282(2), 39-1357(2), 40-1399(2)
  MARY 39-1882, 40-1952
  WILLIAM 37-955, 38-1282, 40-1399
SHAW, JONATHAN 30-562, 31-597, 33-603, 34-653
SHEHAN [Shehe, Shihea],
  PETER [Potter] 30-898, 31-718, 33-

INDEX

699, 34-751
SHELDON [Shilden], JOHN 30-1167, 31-1236, 33-1341, 34-1440, 35-1477, 36-1433, 38-1459, 39-1500, 40-1509
SHEPHARD [Shepard, Sheperd, Ship(h)ard]
  MARTIN 33-657, 34-643, 35-646, 36-700, 38-711, 39-733, 40-735
    MATTHEW 30-563, 31-598
    PETER 40-735
SHERIDAN [Sheradan, Shiradon, Shireden, Sheredine, Sheridine, Sheridon, Shiradon, Shorindon, Shuraden, etc.]
  DAVID 31-945, 33-926, 34-943, 35-983
    EZEKIEL 37-821, 38-1092, 39-1367
    JOHN 30-844, 31-1315
    WILLIAM [ ] 35-1028, 36-1123, 38-1092
SHERRY [Sherrie, Surrey], JOB 30-622, 31-657, 33-671, 34-589, 38-1560
SHILES [Shales, Shiels, Shills]
  EDMUND [Edman] 38-1192, 39-1182
  JOHN [junr., snr., secundus] 31-1316, 33-1393, 33-1613, 34-1617, 35-1617, 35-1769, 36-1528, 36-1541, 37-1013, 37-1174, 38-1662, 38-1868, 39-1827, 39-1835, 40-1242, 40-1830, 40-1839
    PATRICK 30-859, 31-937
    THOMAS 31-1320, 33-1393, 34-1627, 35-1608, 36-1102, 38-1200, 39-1304, 40-1098, 40-1341
SHIRLEY [Sherley], JAMES 31-352, 33-396
SHOCKLEY [Shokley]
  DAVID 30-968, 31-1049, 33-1115, 34-1128, 35-1232, 36-1246, 38-1306, 39-1109, 40-1427
  JAMES 31-1049, 33-1115, 34-1128, 35-1232, 36-1246, 38-1306, 39-1109, 40-1428
  JOHN [junr, senr.] 30-1333, 31-1341, 31-1441(2), 33-368, 33-1485(2), 34-1487(2), 35-402, 35-1560(2), 36-583, 36-1666(2), 37-493, 37-1123, 37-1247, 38-563, 38-1675(2), 39-1749(2), 40-1814(2)
  JONATHAN [Jont.] 30-1333, 31-1441, 33-1485, 34-1487, 35-1561, 36-1667, 37-1124, 38-1674, 39-1751, 40-1935
  RICHARD 31-1441, 33-1485, 34-1487, 35-1560, 36-1666, 37-1125, 38-1676, 39-1735, 40-1922
    SAMUEL 33-1115
    SAUL 39-1109
    SOLOMON 34-1128, 35-1232, 40-1429
    WILLIAM 30-324, 31-453, 31-1441, 36-1666, 38-1675, 39-1749
SHORES [Showrs]
  EDWARD 33-805, 34-848, 35-908
  JOHN [junr. 30-760, 31-776, 33-814, 34-872, 35-907, 36-894, 37-798, 38-942(2), 39-926(2), 40-1032(2)
  WILLIAM 30-760, 31-776, 33-814, 34-872, 35-907, 36-894, 37-798, 38-942, 39-926, 40-1032
SHORT [Short(e)]
  ABRAHAM 35-1196, 36-1176, 38-1270, 39-1284, 40-1388
  EDWARD [junr., senr.] 30-958(2), 31-234, 31-1037, 31-1038, 33-177, 33-898, 34-271, 34-1154, 35-270, 35-1196, 36-335, 36-1176, 37-246, 38-276, 38-1270, 39-343, 40-404
  JOHN 30-958, 31-1423, 33-898, 34-1153, 35-1201, 38-1284, 39-1278, 40-1387, 36-1175
SHOWELL [Shewell]M SAMUEL 30-294, 31-265, 33-267, 34-253, 35-212, 36-346, 37-320, 38-343, 39-180, 40-319
SHOWER [Shawr], ABRAHAM 31-707
SIMMONS [Sumons], WILLIAM 37-902
SIMPLES, PAUL 37-258, 38-332
SIMPSON [Simson]
  ARCHIBALD 31-1418, 33-1274
  GEORGE 40-1184
  RICHARD 30-281, 31-281, 33-331, 34-148, 35-294, 36-353, 37-263
  THOMAS 33-462, 34-548, 35-578, 36-528, 37-450, 38-439, 39-632, 40-562
  WILLIAM 30-431, 31-395, 33-462, 34-548, 35-578, 36-528, 37-450, 38-439
SINGLETON, JOHN 36-1301
SIRMAN [Serman, She(a)rman, Shirman, Shurman, Sirmon, Sormon, Surman]
  EDWARD [junr, ser.] 30-1402, 31-1489, 35-1694, 36-1574, 33-1539, 30-1477, 34-1571
  ISAAC 35-998, 36-1134, 37-1067, 38-1048, 39-1191, 39-1906, 40-1822, 40-1988
  JANE 40-1988
  JEAN [Jeane 31-1488, 36-1578
  JOB [Joab] 30-1477, 31-1489, 34-1168, 35-1245, 36-1152, 38-1278, 39-1204, 40-1296
  JOHN 30-633, 31-644, 33-1568, 34-1586, 35-1643, 36-1584, 37-1055, 38-1822, 39-1795, 40-1980
  PETER 30-942, 30-1378(2), 31-1043, 31-1414(2), 33-906, 33-962, 33-1568(2), 34-950, 34-1586(2), 35-1244, 35-1642(2), 36-1151, 36-1583(2), 37-1027(2), 38-1279, 38-1822(2), 39-1794(2), 40-1329, 40-1979(2)
  THOMAS [junr., senr.] 30-829,

INDEX

30-832, 30-996, 31-862, 31-879,
31-996, 33-969, 33-1070, 34-923,
34-927, 34-1076, 35-966(2), 35-1074,
36-961, 36-1035, 38-1007, 38-1130,
39-1245, 40-1291
   WILLIAM 30-1040, 31-908, 33-885,
34-956, 35-998, 36-1134(2),
38-1048(2), 39-1191(2), 40-1155
SKENE [Skean, Skeen, Skein], ROBERT
30-762, 31-768, 33-822, 34-871,
35-906
SLINGO [Slinger, Slingoe, Slingor]
   JOHN 38-903, 39-823, 40-954
   THOMAS [jnr., snr.] 30-298,
30-727, 31-450, 33-505(2),
33-712(2), 34-761(2), 35-798(2),
36-847(2), 37-714(2), 38-903(2),
39-823, 39-908, 40-954, 40-955
SLOAN, JAMES 34-1453
SLOCUMB [Slocom]
   BENTON 34-1421
   RILEY 35-89
   THOMAS 34-1426, 35-1269, 38-874,
39-922, 37-653, 33-1247, 36-1273,
40-925
SMACHIE [Smoshie], WILLIAM 35-471,
36-372, 37-567, 38-418, 39-547,
40-687
SMALL, JOHN 31-1283, 33-1160,
34-1247, 35-1297, 36-1365, 38-1563,
39-1564
SMALLWOOD, SAMUEL 35-200, 36-355,
37-376, 38-312, 39-177, 40-182
SMITH
   WIDOW 33-669
   ABRAHAM 30-477, 31-424, 33-502,
34-412, 35-494, 36-498, 37-465,
38-302, 39-403, 40-206
   ANDREW [junr., senr.] 30-487,
31-396, 34-543, 35-570, 36-368,
37-431, 38-1695, 39-1716(2),
40-1793(2)
   ANN 36-195, 37-166, 38-371
   ARCHIBALD [Archable, Archeybald]
33-41, 33-1450, 34-134, 34-1476,
35-64, 35-1661, 36-102, 36-1722,
37-1144, 38-1709, 39-1703, 40-1807
   BRIDGET 38-1850
   CHARLES 37-273, 38-209, 39-163,
40-366
   DAVID 30-1048, 30-1309, 31-1452,
33-882, 33-1454, 34-1158, 34-1478,
35-1203, 35-1721, 36-1174, 36-1734,
37-1143, 38-1194, 38-1712, 39-1280,
39-1333, 39-1700, 40-1396, 40-1907
   EDWARD 30-546, 31-536
   GEORGE 30-1330, 31-1454, 33-1450,
34-1477, 35-1722, 36-368, 36-1723,
37-431, 37-1142, 38-1695, 38-1706,
39-1716, 39-1719, 40-1793, 40-1794
   HENRY [capt.] 30-29, 31-35, 33-41,
34-134, 35-64, 36-102, 37-6, 38-126,
38-1320, 38-1626, 39-35, 39-1265,
40-40, 40-1370
   JAMES [Jeams/junr., senr.] 30-48,
30-1309(2), 31-54, 31-1367, 31-1453,
33-55, 33-1455, 33-1608, 34-116,
34-1161, 34-1479, 34-1650, 35-45,
35-1204, 35-1665, 35-1695, 36-84,
36-1572, 36-1733, 37-86, 37-1116,
37-1140, 38-6, 38-1318, 38-1691,
38-1705, 39-77, 39-1281, 39-1702,
39-1720, 40-49, 40-1409, 40-1788,
40-1805
   JEREMIAH 40-1863
   JOHN [Jon./capt./junr., senr.]
30-160(2), 30-177(2), 30-430,
30-477, 30-506, 30-972, 31-174(2),
31-221(2), 31-398, 31-591, 33-165,
33-222(2), 33-392, 33-600, 33-913,
33-1293, 34-147(2), 34-286, 34-535,
34-628, 34-1140, 35-181, 35-312(2),
35-466, 35-753, 35-1193, 35-1395,
35-1722, 36-154(2), 36-217, 36-600,
36-694, 36-1150, 36-1294, 37-268,
37-273(2), 37-449, 37-791,
38-209(2), 38-262, 38-450, 38-981,
38-1273, 38-1505, 39-163(2), 39-377,
39-631, 39-984, 39-1318, 39-1402,
40-366, 40-375, 40-506, 40-995,
40-1487
   JOHN JONAS 39-233
   JOHN ONORTON 38-321, 39-192,
40-213
   JOHN TRUITT 33-477, 34-423, 40-559
   JONAH 40-433
   JONAS [Jones] 30-193, 31-171, 33-244, 34-202, 38-371
   MAGDALENE [Magdillon] 33-581,
35-695, 36-684, 39-722, 40-756
   MOSES 30-1309, 31-1453, 33-1455,
34-1479, 35-1720, 36-1736, 37-1139,
38-1696, 39-1721, 40-1803
   PURNELL FLETCHER [Fleitcher]
39-403, 40-206
   ROBERT [Robard] 30-160, 30-524,
31-221, 31-519, 33-67, 33-165,
33-582, 34-286, 34-632, 35-181,
35-691, 36-217, 36-694, 37-268,
38-262, 38-696, 39-358, 39-721,
40-380, 40-757
   STEPHEN [Steven] 33-869, 34-1175,
35-1224
   THOMAS 30-177, 30-546, 31-174,
31-519, 31-536, 33-222, 33-555,
33-582, 33-601, 33-1047, 34-147,
34-631, 34-632, 34-708, 34-1013,
35-312, 35-691, 35-1147, 36-154,
36-694, 36-1074, 36-1140, 37-273,
37-889, 38-209, 38-696, 38-1114,
38-1203, 39-163, 39-712, 39-1118,
39-1253, 40-1171, 40-1186
   WILLIAM [Doctor] 30-204, 30-415,
30-598, 30-1256, 31-151, 31-397,

INDEX

31-619, 33-259, 33-459, 34-134,
34-216, 34-546, 35-64, 35-173,
35-572, 36-102, 36-167, 36-362,
36-1184, 37-6, 37-158, 37-429,
37-633, 38-126, 38-262, 38-321,
38-425, 39-35, 39-192, 39-377,
39-440, 39-722, 39-778, 40-41,
40-213, 40-375, 40-524, 40-756,
40-780
   WILLIAM PORTER 31-411
SMOCK
   HENRY 30-360, 31-423, 33-401,
34-372, 35-475, 36-596, 37-637,
38-470, 39-612, 40-635(2)
   JOHN 33-401, 34-372, 35-475,
36-596, 37-637, 38-466, 39-612,
40-635
   SAMUEL 39-612
SMULLING [Smullen]
   NATHANIEL 34-1213, 35-1333,
36-1416, 38-1497, 39-1408, 40-1475
   RANDALL [Randuplh, Randl./jr.,
senr.] 30-1086, 31-1220, 33-1298(2),
34-1213(2), 35-1333(2), 36-1416(2),
38-1497(2), 39-1408(2), 40-1475,
40-1926
   WILLIAM 36-1416, 38-1497, 39-1408,
40-1475
SMYTHERS, SARGANT [capt.] 36-345,
37-265, 38-295, 39-392
SNEAD [Sneed], BRYAN 33-1476
SOCKWELL, GEORGE 30-421, 33-1543,
34-1591
SOMERFIELD, BARNES 40-416
SPARKMAN [Spartman], GEORGE 33-22,
39-1601, 40-1679
SPEAR [Spear(e), Sphere]
   HENRY 30-1025, 30-835, 31-840,
31-919, 33-972, 33-993, 34-931,
34-1071, 35-696, 35-1047, 36-698,
36-995, 38-710, 38-1173, 39-731,
39-1208, 40-782, 40-1264
   JOHN 39-1208, 40-1264
   ROBERT 33-993, 34-1071, 35-1047,
38-1174, 39-1132, 40-1357
SPECKS, ROBERT 34-1604
SPEEDEN
   JAMES 30-1243
   ROBERT 30-1243
SPENCE [Spens]
   ADAM [junr., senr.] 30-465,
30-473, 31-448, 31-449, 33-341,
33-497, 34-520(2), 35-436, 36-540,
37-504, 38-624, 39-575, 40-576
   JOHN 31-803, 33-615, 34-886
SPENCER, JOHN 40-1121
SPIBY [Spibe(y), Spyb(i)e], JONATHAN
30-72, 31-84, 33-89, 34-30, 35-29
SPICER [Spicier, Spiser]
   JAMES 30-1450, 39-928, 40-965
   JOHN 39-950
   PHILLIP [Phillup] 30-551, 31-627,

33-688, 34-710, 35-730, 36-898,
37-784, 38-934, 39-944, 40-963
SPOLDING [Spolding, Spouldin]
   ELIZABETH 39-1189, 40-1113
   ELLIOTT [Alliott] 38-1124
SPRINGLE
   CHARLES 34-481
   WILLIAM 37-1155
SPROGLE [Sprogal], GODFREY 33-1589,
34-665
SPRUANCE [Spruens], JOHN 30-8,
31-15, 33-624, 34-649
SQUIRES, EDMUND [Edward] 39-974,
40-1025
STANFORD [Standford, Stangford]
   JONATHAN 39-1775, 40-1959
   JOSEPH 30-1434, 31-1517, 33-1614,
34-1508, 35-1646, 36-1646, 37-1098,
38-1643, 39-1775, 40-1959
STANTON [Stanthin]
   EDWARD 30-45
   JONATHAN 30-790
   WILLIAM 33-510
STAPLES, JAMES 30-612, 31-642,
33-642, 34-704, 35-708, 36-691,
38-782, 39-701, 40-846
STARLING [Sterlin]
   AARON [Aron] 30-63, 31-74, 33-74,
34-85, 35-9, 36-62, 37-30, 38-7,
39-74, 40-82
   HENRY 30-63, 31-74, 33-74, 34-85,
35-9, 36-62, 37-30, 38-7, 39-76,
40-81
   JOHN [junr., senr] 30-63(2),
31-74(2)
33-74(2), 34-85(2), 35-9(2), 36-62,
36-63, 37-30, 37-64, 38-7, 38-8,
39-74, 39-75, 40-80, 40-82
   JOSEPH [Josept] 39-74, 40-82
STEARNS, WILLIAM 36-504
STEEL [Steale, Steall, Steele]
   AUGUSTUS [Augustes] 33-315
   DANIEL 30-320, 31-381, 34-401,
35-416, 36-588, 37-517, 38-574,
39-496, 40-589
   JAMES 30-320, 31-381, 34-401, 34-
1353, 35-416, 36-588, 37-517,
38-574, 39-496, 40-589
   WILLIAM 31-381, 34-412, 35-474,
36-588, 37-517, 38-469, 39-552,
40-464
STEEN [Stain, Steain, Steene], JAMES
31-746, 33-708, 35-551, 36-392,
38-1569
STEPHENS [Steevens, Stepeans,
Stephins, Stevens]
   ANN 30-1423
   EDWARD 30-1084, 31-1128, 33-1315,
34-1323, 35-1320, 36-1385, 38-1371,
39-1587, 40-1467
   ELEANOR 36-1385
   ISAAC 31-1430, 33-1582, 34-828,

INDEX

35-875, 36-869, 37-973, 38-1638, 39-983, 40-1000
  JOHN 30-994, 30-1187, 30-1422, 31-995, 31-1145, 31-1496, 33-941, 33-1382, 33-1549, 34-1119, 34-1288, 34-1563, 35-1081, 35-1394, 35-1691, 36-1024, 36-1504, 38-1230, 38-1523, 39-1177, 39-1376, 39-1434, 40-1298, 40-1551
  RACHEL 39-1909
  RICHARD 30-1419, 31-1434, 33-1551, 34-1560, 35-1690, 36-1565, 37-1003, 38-1775
  SAMUEL 30-352, 31-357, 33-367, 34-527, 35-401, 36-472, 37-491, 38-564, 39-363, 40-193
  THOMAS 30-1418, 33-1617, 34-1701, 35-1082
  WILLIAM 30-1107, 30-1349, 31-456, 33-478, 33-1197, 33-1511, 34-560, 34-1323, 34-1702, 35-1320, 35-1743, 36-1384, 36-1702, 37-392, 37-1165, 38-644, 38-1369, 38-1882, 39-627, 39-1580, 39-1678, 40-342, 40-1660, 40-1885

STEPHENSON [Stevenson, Stephinsin]
  [Illegible] 37-527
  ADAM 36-488, 37-520, 38-568, 39-495, 40-579
  HUGH [mr., revd.] 30-486, 33-440, 34-553, 35-587, 36-551, 38-642
  JAMES 30-301, 31-429, 33-447, 34-402, 35-419, 36-488, 37-520, 38-568, 39-495, 40-579
  JOHN 30-203, 31-152, 33-258, 34-218, 35-172, 36-220, 38-393, 39-271, 40-209
  JOSEPH 30-203, 31-1303, 33-1145, 36-1513, 38-1596, 39-1533, 40-1610
  LUCY [Lesey/wid.] 30-455
  ROBERT 31-1304, 38-1598, 39-1539, 40-1615
  SAMUEL 36-551, 37-520, 38-568, 38-593, 39-467, 39-495, 40-579, 40-944
  WILLIAM 31-152, 33-258, 34-218, 36-1513, 38-1596, 39-1533, 40-1610

STEWART [Steward, Stuard, Stu(a)rt]
  DOCTOR 30-1388
  WIDOW 34-635, 35-686, 39-577
  ALEXANDER 30-556, 31-1312, 33-1401, 34-1639, 35-1706, 36-1537, 38-1002, 39-1065, 40-1079
  CATHERINE 36-998, 38-1079
  CHARLES 33-1109, 34-914, 35-958, 36-1521, 37-1188, 38-989, 39-940
  FRANCIS 40-1647
  JOHN 30-1173, 30-1398, 31-1183, 31-1405, 33-1593, 34-1605
  PATRICK 31-1418, 33-1593, 34-1605, 35-1626, 36-1597, 37-1011, 38-1853, 39-1814

  PETER 35-367, 36-535, 37-380, 38-613, 40-1856
  SARAH [mrs., widow.] 33-1336, 34-1199, 35-1504
  WILLIAM [revd.] 30-518, 31-513, 33-578

STILLEY [Stiley(s), Stille]
  JOHN 36-1227, 37-897(2), 38-1206, 39-1169
  MARY [wido.] 30-944, 31-976, 34-1080, 36-1227, 38-1206, 39-1169

STOCKDELL [Stocdill, Stogdell, Stogdill]
  EDWARD 30-18, 31-6, 33-19, 34-103, 35-94, 36-13, 37-112, 38-139, 39-19
  GEORGE 39-1216
  KRISTIN [Cristen] 40-162

STOCKWELL
  GEORGE 31-441, 35-554
  THOMAS 30-120, 31-72

STONE, JAMES 36-406

STORY [Storrie]
  WIDOW 31-813
  SUSANNAH 35-880, 36-874

STOUGHTON [Staughton/mr, esqr.], WILLIAM 30-762, 31-774, 33-815, 34-844, 35-905, 36-922, 37-769, 38-939, 39-958, 40-1022

STRAWBRIDGE [Strabrige, Strabritt, Strobridg]
  JAMES 30-517, 31-559, 33-576, 34-640, 35-649, 36-629, 38-706, 39-737, 40-795
  THOMAS 37-261

STREET, MENSFEET 30-249

STRINGER, GEORGE 30-761, 31-777

STURGIS [Sturgace, Sturges, Sturgis]
  DANIEL 30-690, 33-692, 34-730, 35-767, 36-827, 37-669, 38-856, 39-885, 40-878
  JOHN [junr., senr.] 30-672, 30-690, 31-693, 31-700, 33-691, 34-729, 35-417, 36-468, 37-516, 38-573, 39-494, 39-825, 40-588, 40-942
  JONATHAN 30-1203, 31-1163, 33-1368, 34-1351, 35-1500, 36-1508, 38-1566, 38-1566, 39-1455, 40-1576
  JOSEPH 34-1282
  JOSHUA 30-1184, 31-1136, 33-1376, 35-1353, 36-1497, 37-622, 38-661, 39-608, 40-672
  LITTLETON 34-729, 36-468, 37-516, 38-573, 39-494, 40-588
  RICHARD 30-645, 31-714, 33-752, 34-819, 35-766, 36-794, 37-643, 38-836, 39-825, 40-942

STUTT [Stitt], ARCHIBALD Archebild, Arsbill] 30-519, 31-558, 33-577, 34-596, 35-755, 36-693, 38-1495, 39-1411, 40-1461

SUCH [Shuch, Sucth], OLIVER [Olifer]

INDEX

30-1368, 31-1461, 33-1514, 34-1525, 35-1552
SULLIVAN [Seveling, Shelerneng, Sillivan, Silivain, Silivean, Sulivant, Sulevan, Swillaven, Swillifant, Swilivin, Syllavan]
   MICHAEL [Michell] 30-811, 31-1083, 33-1014
   TIMOTHY [Timothas] 30-1442, 31-1423, 33-141, 36-305, 37-170, 38-249, 39-317, 40-361
   WILLIAM 30-1381, 31-1411, 33-1572, 34-1590, 35-1637, 36-1585, 37-1023, 38-1824, 39-1799, 40-1983
SUMERLIN, WILLIAM 38-1301, 39-1353, 40-1319
SUMMERS [Sumners, Sumnres, Sumr.]
   BENJAMIN [Bengaman] 36-75, 37-74, 38-19, 39-65, 40-73
   DAVID 30-57, 31-62, 33-65, 34-73, 35-18, 36-75, 37-74, 38-19, 39-65, 40-73
   GEORGE 30-55, 31-61, 33-66, 34-68, 35-16, 36-76, 37-75, 38-20, 39-64, 40-68
   JOHN 30-57, 31-62, 33-65, 34-73, 35-18, 36-75, 37-74, 38-19, 39-65, 40-73
   JONATHAN 30-55, 31-61, 33-66, 34-71, 35-17, 36-72, 37-71, 38-21, 39-130, 40-70
   RICHARD 39-65, 40-73
   SAMUEL 38-20, 40-68
   THOMAS [junr., senr.] 30-55(2), 31-61, 33-66, 34-68(2), 35-16(2), 36-76(2), 37-75(2), 38-20(2), 39-64(2), 40-68, 40-70
SWAINE [Swain]
   JOHN 30-74
   WILLIAM 30-414, 31-331, 33-413, 34-461, 35-525, 36-494, 37-437, 38-423, 40-526, 40-647
SWIFT, RICHARD 30-491, 31-515, 33-544, 34-591, 35-670, 36-696, 38-689, 39-723, 40-758
SYMS [Seems, Sims], ARCHIBALD [Archable] 37-840, 38-1081, 39-1142, 40-1096

TADLOCK [Tatlock]
   AGNES 34-405, 35-486, 36-388, 37-453, 38-448, 39-630
   EDWARD 34-405, 35-281, 35-486, 36-388, 37-453, 38-448, 39-630, 40-507
TALBOT [Talbort, Talburt, Tolbat, Tolbert], John 34-1499, 35-214, 35-1563, 36-1658, 37-1220, 38-1637, 39-1866, 40-1940
TALL, JOHN 30-243
TALLMAN, JAMES 36-844
TANNER, JOHN [Tanna] 33-636, 34-661, 35-725, 36-658

TAPTON, SAMUEL 39-189
TARR
   JOHN 30-647, 39-826, 40-940
   MICHAEL [Mikell, Michall/junr., senr.] 30-646, 31-688, 33-743, 34-735, 35-772, 36-793, 37-708(2), 38-857(2), 39-826(2), 40-940(2)
   SAMUEL 30-668, 31-705, 33-716, 34-725, 35-762, 36-834, 37-705, 38-854, 39-892, 40-870
TATE
   FRANCIS 33-549, 34-667, 35-715, 36-699, 37-1014, 40-1808
   THOMAS 33-639, 34-696, 35-715
TATMAN
   JAMES 33-925, 34-1092, 35-1078, 38-1287, 39-1138, 40-1271
   WILLIAM 30-993, 40-1376
TATUM [Tatom, Tetum]
   JAMES 38-1308
   JOHN 30-1314, 31-1331, 33-1443, 34-1470, 35-1749, 36-1729, 37-1159, 38-1720, 39-1712, 40-1777
   THOMAS 34-1470
TAWS, JOHN 40-1513
TAYLOR [Tailer, Tailor, Taler, Talor, Talyr, Tayler(s), Taylour]
   ABRAHAM 30-890, 31-903, 33-1062, 34-984, 35-1145, 36-1082, 37-876, 38-1116, 39-1006, 40-1128
   ANTHONY 34-366, 35-985, 36-1110, 38-1036, 40-1033
   EDMUND [Edmond] 38-490, 39-584, 40-599
   ELIAS [Elies] 30-93, 31-113, 33-116, 33-760, 34-49, 34-743, 35-141, 35-779, 36-854, 36-1291, 37550, 38-490, 38-1436, 39-501, 39-1647, 40-1723
   GEORGE 33-1352, 34-1285, 35-1380, 36-1478, 38-1516, 39-1433, 40-1542
   HOPE 30-1249, 31-1270, 33-1249
   JACOB 34-1211, 35-1332
36-1425, 38-1506, 39-1414, 40-1480
   JAMES 30-1213, 35-1305, 35-1693, 36-1492, 36-1568, 37-1076, 38-1551, 38-1642, 39-1447, 40-1557, 40-1619, 40-1876
   JOB [Jobe] 38-815, 39-1456, 40-1529
   JOHN 30-350, 30-728, 33-19, 33-753, 34-734, 34-811, 34-1498, 35-771, 35-789, 35-1200, 36-782, 36-783, 36-1191, 36-1393, 36-1672, 37-661, 37-906, 37-1102, 38-877, 38-1305, 38-1311, 38-1732, 39-837, 39-1006, 39-1291, 39-1758, 40-1128, 40-1927
   JOHN JONES 36-288
   JOHN LEE 30-326
   JOSEPH 30-350, 30-1284, 31-443, 31-1387, 33-480, 34-459
   JOSIAH 30-645, 36-465, 37-352,

INDEX

38-338, 39-181, 40-311
   MATHIAS 38-1543, 39-1451
   PETER 36-1470, 38-1462, 39-1496, 40-1520
   PHILLIP 30-686, 31-689, 33-756, 34-743, 35-779, 36-854, 37-550, 38-490, 39-584, 40-614
   REBECCA 38-1732
   ROBERT [jr., senr.] 30-1111, 31-1268, 33-1250, 34-1432, 35-1427, 36-1290(2), 38-1435(2), 39-1646(2), 40-1724(2)
   ROGER [Rodger] 33-753, 33-1177, 34-811, 34-1271, 35-844, 35-1277, 36-783, 36-1381, 37-704, 38-896, 39-837, 40-933
   SAMUEL [junr., senr.] 30-1196(2), 31-1140(2), 33-1352, 34-1285, 34-1285, 35-331, 35-1380, 35-1381, 36-229, 36-1478, 36-1479, 37-342, 38-313, 38-1516, 38-1517, 39-1432, 39-1433, 40-341, 40-696, 40-1541, 40-1542, 40-1817
   THOMAS 30-1302, 31-1335, 33-704, 33-1451, 34-727, 34-1462, 35-771, 35-1734, 36-792, 36-1715, 37-1152
   WALTER 30-282, 33-332, 35-296
   WILLIAM [senr.] 30-38, 30-916, 31-36, 31-443, 31-894, 33-49, 33-480, 33-1051, 33-1360, 34-66, 34-447, 34-1017, 34-1356, 35-4, 35-523, 35-1123, 35-1200, 35-1372, 36-90, 36-479, 36-937, 36-1191, 36-1489, 37-89, 37-619, 38-43, 38-509, 38-1089, 38-1311, 38-1551, 39-42, 39-411, 39-1078, 39-1470, 40-38, 40-403, 40-556, 40-1199, 40-1423, 40-1586
   WILLIAM RIGGIN 33-540
TEAGUE [Tegue]
   JOHN [junr., senr.] 30-492(2), 31-362(2), 34-391(2), 35-397(2), 36-591(2), 37-492(2), 38-635, 38-636, 39-469(2), 40-484(2)
   RALPH 40-639
   WILLIAM 31-362, 34-522, 35-584
TEMPLIN [Templing]
   JOHN [junr.] 33-467, 34-555, 35-581, 36-370, 37-451, 38-440, 38-440, 39-639
   RICHARD 36-370, 37-473, 38-453, 39-639
TENEY
   JOHN 33-1370
   JOHN GEORGE 30-1422
THOMPSON [Thom(a)son, Thomson, Tom(e)son, Tompson]
   ANDREW [/junr.] 30-503, 31-564, 33-674, 33-731, 34-700, 34-700, 34-756, 35-683, 35-683, 35-831, 36-709, 38-714, 39-748, 40-717
   CHARLES [jur., senr] 36-1158, 36-1159, 39-1327, 39-1373, 40-1313, 40-1316
   GEORGE 30-1275, 31-1014, 33-934, 34-1056, 35-1181, 36-1157, 37-905, 38-1214, 39-1306, 40-1323
   JAMES 30-305, 31-387, 33-429, 34-497, 35-540, 36-560, 37-573, 38-398, 39-525
   JOHN 33- 674 30-503, 30-1415, 31-564, 31-1498, 33-1524, 34-700, 34-1519, 35-683, 35-1699, 36-1618, 37-1038, 38-1382, 38-1817, 39-1596, 39-1779, 40-1672, 40-1964
   JOSEPH 31-515, 33-544, 34-665, 38-772, 39-749, 40-718
   SARAH 36-755
   THOMAS [ ] 33-1443, 36-1753, 37-914, 39-1715, 40-1903
   WILLIAM [junr.] 30-503, 31-564, 33-674, 34-701, 35-684
THORNES [Thorns]
   ALEXANDER [Elxdr.] 31-1042, 33-864, 34-1180, 35-967, 36-1204, 37-885, 38-1352, 39-1148, 40-1064
   EDWARD 30-943, 31-1041, 33-865, 34-1179
THOROUGHGOOD [Thorowgood, Throgood], PAUL 34-288, 35-164, 36-180, 39- 394
TIER [Tyear, Tyer, Tyre, Tyrie]
   ROBERT 30-214, 31-268, 33-264, 35-305, 36-255, 37-330, 38-220, 39-285, 40-297
TILLMAN [Telman, Tillghman, Tillman, Tilmon, Tullmon]
   AARON 30-599, 31-655, 33-673, 34-593, 35-607, 36-673, 37-1024, 38-721, 39-754, 40-711
   BENJAMIN 34-591, 35-636, 36-724, 38-716, 39-752, 40-709
   GIDEON [Gidding, Giddion] 30-1189, 31-1144, 33-1206, 34-1317, 35-1250, 36-1390, 38-1377, 39-1586, 40-1667
   JOHN 30-601, 31-654, 38-1377, 39-1586, 40-1667
   JOSEPH 30-600, 31-651, 33-566, 34-589, 35-608, 36-749, 38-717, 39-753, 40-710
   MOSES 34-592, 35-603
   ROUSE 34-591
   ROSE 35-636
   SOLOMON 35-589
   WILLIAM 36-505, 38-720, 39-1404, 40-1515
TIMMONS [Timions]
   AARON 30-335, 31-328, 33-473, 34-512, 35-558, 36-377, 36-381, 37-423, 37-428, 38-422, 38-428, 39-546, 39-653, 40-488, 40-532,
   FRANCIS 30-334, 31-325, 33-334, 33-468, 34-506
   JAMES 30-338, 31-330, 33-475, 34-509, 35-559, 36-379, 37-427,

INDEX

38-663, 39-428, 40-522
   JOHN 30-341, 31-324, 31-826,
33-469, 34-511, 35-555, 36-380,
37-428, 38-422, 39-546, 40-532
   JOSEPH 30-337, 31-329, 33-474,
34-510, 35-556, 36-378, 37-424,
38-429, 39-426, 39-655, 40-697
  MARY 39-646
  SAMUEL 30-339, 31-327, 33-472,
34-508, 35-555, 35-561, 36-381,
36-572, 37-426, 37-428, 38-422,
38-427, 39-646, 40-531
   THOMAS 30-336, 30-1289, 31-326,
33-470, 34-507, 35-557, 36-376,
37-425, 38-426, 39-427, 40-523
   WILLIAM 30-226, 30-340, 31-323,
33-471, 34-510, 35-560, 37-422,
38-459, 39-425
TINDALL [Tindell, Tindoll, Tindull]
   CHARLES 30-971, 33-899, 34-1151,
35-1194, 36-1187, 38-1221, 39-1316,
40-1420
   JAMES 30-625, 31-1213, 33-1291,
34-633, 35-641, 36-718, 38-704,
39-766, 40-746
TINGLE [Tindle, Tingel]
   DANIEL 31-365, 33-490, 34-448,
35-514, 36-546, 37-410, 38-666,
39-551, 40-509
   HUGH [Hough/junr., senr.] 30-183,
30-185, 31-162, 31-166, 33-237(2),
34-227(2), 35-177(2), 36-186(2),
37-234(2), 38-387(2), 39-390,
39-391, 40-198, 40-278
   JOHN 30-184, 31-167, 33-239,
34-226, 35-239, 36-187, 37-205
   JOSEPH 38-387, 39-390, 40-198
   LITTLETON [Lettleton, Littilson,
Littleting] 31-156, 33-158, 34-223,
35-258, 36-195, 37-169, 38-385,
39-233, 40-322
   MARY [widow] 38-303, 39-195,
40-373
   SAMUEL 30-155, 30-434, 35-167,
36-191, 37-288, 38-303, 39-280,
40-284
TINNIS, WILLIAM 34-523
TIPPENS [Tippin, Typpens, Typpings],
ROBERT 38-390, 39-226, 40-205
TIPPETT [Tippit], THOMAS 34-1626,
35-1607, 36-253, 37-249
TOBIN, JOHN 38-631
TOCKLES [Tockell], WILLIAM 30-574,
31-587
TODVINE [Toadvine, Todevine]
   GEORGE 36-1662, 37-1087, 38-1798,
39-1761, 40-1939
   HENRY 30-1345, 31-1464, 33-1501,
34-1533, 35-1559, 36-1640, 37-1112,
38-1655, 39-1764, 40-1933
   ISAAC 30-1342, 33-1583, 34-504,
36-1663, 37-1113, 38-1798, 39-1746

   JOHN 31-1520, 33-1507, 34-1665,
35-1566, 36-1694, 37-1193, 38-1417,
39-1747, 40-1938
   JOSHUA 37-1112, 38-1655, 39-1764,
40-1933
   MARY [widow] 30-1342, 31-1520,
33-1583, 34-1502, 35-1772, 36-1662,
37-1087, 40-1939
   NICHOLAS 30-1346, 31-1345
   THOMAS 30-1345, 31-1464, 33-1501,
34-1533, 35-1562, 37-1096, 38-1871,
39-1765, 40-1960
   WILLIAM 34-1502, 36-1663, 37-1239,
38-1879, 39-1747, 40-1939
TOLINSON, JOHN 33-830
TOLLMAN, JAMES 35-778
TOMLIN [Tomerlin(e)]
  NABOTH 31-1122
  SAMUEL 31-1122, 33-1216
  SEWARD [Sayward] 31-1122, 33-1212
  SOLOMON 31-1122, 33-1216
  THOMAS 38-1295
TOMLINSON [Thomlinson, Timilinson,
Tomblinson, Tomerlinson, Tomlins,
Tomslon]
  DOCTOR 36-724
  ABIGAIL 34-1410, 35-1405, 40-1682
  EDWARD 30-1123
  HAMPTON 40-1682
  HENRY [Harry] 31-15, 33-19,
34-54, 35-676
  SAMUEL 30-1123
  SEWARD [Sayward, Soward] 34-1377,
35-1404, 38-1393, 39-1602, 40-1644
  SOLOMON 30-1123, 34-1410, 35-1405,
38-1385, 39-1603
TOPPING [Tippin, Topin], SAMUEL 38-
104, 39-138, 40-1676
TOW, JONAS 30-722, 31-670
TOWNSEND [Tousend, Toundson,
Tow(n)sand, Tow(e)nsand, Towsin,
Townson]
   BENJAMIN [mr.] 34-1537, 35-1602,
36-947, 38-1009, 39-1104, 40-1089
   BOWMAN 30-194, 31-169, 33-243, 34-
205, 35-174, 36-245, 37-305, 38-252,
39-381, 40-425
   BRICKHOUSE [Brickus] 30-417,
31-339, 33-457, 34-538, 35-564,
36-545, 37-421, 38-511, 39-421,
40-493
   CHARLES [junr., senr.] 30-1176,
30-1176, 31-1141, 31-1239, 33-1342,
34-1223, 35-1472, 36-1437, 38-1454,
39-1490, 40-1511
   COMFORT 34-1303, 35-1474, 39-1513,
40-1531
   DANFORD 31-1224, 33-1308, 34-1441,
36-1459, 38-1488, 39-1425, 40-1489
   DANIEL 30-1132, 31-1211, 33-1321,
34-1237, 35-1514, 36-1441, 38-1473,
39-1503, 40-1500

INDEX

DICKERSON 34-1237, 35-1514, 36-1441, 38-1473, 39-1503, 40-1500
 ELIAS 30-1176, 31-1141, 33-1342, 34-1223, 35-1472, 40-1511
 ELIZABETH 30-1075, 31-1224, 33-1308, 34-1441, 36-1457, 39-1427, 40-1488
 JAMES 30-1133, 31-1235, 33-1335, 34-1239, 35-1476, 36-1436, 36-1441, 38-1461, 38-1473, 39-1501, 39-1503, 40-1500
40-1506
 JEREMIAH 30-356, 30-417, 31-339, 33-457, 33-466, 34-537, 34-1361, 35-563, 36-544, 36-1506, 37-420, 38-510, 38-1530, 39-422, 39-1468, 40-491, 40-1583
 JOHN 30-1082(2), 30-1177, 30-1181, 31-1133(2), 31-1177, 31-1241, 33-1264, 33-1324(2), 33-1325, 34-1224, 34-1229(2), 35-1473, 35-1486(2), 36-1453(2), 38-1480(2), 39-1508(2), 40-1496(2)
 LITTLETON 30-1257, 31-1130, 33-90, 33-1264, 34-1327, 35-1356, 36-1487, 38-1571, 39-1467, 40-1582
 MARSHALL 38-1480, 39-1498, 40-1496
 NATHANIEL 38-1476, 39-1513, 40-1531
 PAUL 33-1325
 SAUL 30-1177, 31-1241, 34-1224, 35-1473, 36-1454, 38-1457, 39-1507, 40-1512
 SOLOMON 30-1176, 30-1212, 31-1141, 31-1154, 33-1342, 33-1359, 34-1223, 34-1358, 35-1472, 35-1475, 36-1437, 36-1499, 38-1126, 38-1454, 39-1490, 40-1510
 WILLIAM 30-342, 31-393, 33-373, 34-415, 34-1223, 34-1303, 35-565, 35-1472, 36-164, 36-383, 36-1437, 37-235, 37-631, 38-283, 39-241, 40-249, 40-554
TOWNSEND, WILLIAM BARKLEY [Wm. Bartho., Wm. Bartley, Willm. Bartlet] 35-1474, 36-1487, 38-1467, 39-1482, 40-1528
TRADOR, WILLIAM 34-774
TRAIN [Tra(i)n(e)]
 JAMES [junr., senr/] 30-866(2), 31-937(2), 33-1036(2), 34-978(2), 35-1149(2), 36-1089(2), 37-807(2), 38-688, 38-1141, 39-1009, 39-1010, 40-1123, 40-1158
 ROGER 30-866, 31-937, 33-1036, 34-978, 35-1149, 36-1089, 37-807
TRAVIS [Traverse], RICHARD 33-440, 34-553, 35-587, 36-551
TREHEARN [Trahern, Treharn, Treherne]
 JAMES [Jeams/jr.] 30-12, 30-95, 31-14, 31-105, 33-14, 33-119, 34-7, 34-52, 35-139, 35-1399, 36-115, 36-131, 38-84, 38-98, 39-114, 40-35, 40-130]
 JOHN 30-12, 31-14, 33-14, 34-59, 35-81, 36-9, 37-115, 38-144, 39-10, 40-11
 WILLIAM 38-98, 39-114, 40-130
TRUITT [Trewitt, Truit, Truett]
 BENJAMIN 30-303, 31-499
 ELEANOR [Ellenir/widow] 30-315, 31-378
 GEORGE [junr., senr] 30-233, 30-316, 30-354, 30-377, 30-420, 31-277, 31-371, 31-377, 31-445, 33-431, 33-431, 33-434, 33-439, 33-444, 33-496, 34-395, 34-397, 34-489, 34-499(2), 34-539, 35-409, 35-411, 35-451, 35-544(2), 35-566, 36-430, 36-558, 36-559, 36-595(2), 36-606, 37-442, 37-530, 37-533, 37-580(2), 37-581, 38-409(2), 38-430, 38-477, 38-494, 38-576, 39-445, 39-502, 39-522(2), 39-582, 39-662, 40-546, 40-594(2), 40-613, 40-650, 40-653, 40-654, 40-667
 HENRY 31-502, 33-432
 JAMES 30-404, 31-475, 33-538, 34-488, 35-450, 36-429, 37-538, 38-495, 38-524, 39-658, 40-610
 JOHN [junr.] 30-393, 31-313, 31-445, 33-439, 34-397, 35-411, 35-511, 36-375, 36-558, 37-439, 37-530, 38-478, 39-561, 40-595
 JOSEPH 30-375, 31-500, 33-500, 34-521, 35-594, 36-543, 37-593, 38-641, 39-644, 40-487, 40-644
 LITTLETON 40-326
 MARY [widow] 30-420
 MICHAEL 34-499
 NEHEMIAH 30-420, 31-371, 33-496, 34-539, 35-566, 36-607, 37-443, 38-431, 39-446, 40-520
 PHILLIP 33-443, 38-575, 39-501
 SAMUEL 30-407, 31-477, 33-528, 34-370, 35-472
 THOMAS 30-405, 31-474, 37-549
 WILLIAM 30-312, 31-376, 33-442, 34-396, 35-410, 36-509, 37-532, 38-578, 39-500, 40-649
TULL [Till]
 BENJAMIN 30-332, 31-409, 33-466, 34-549, 35-582, 36-496, 37-390, 38-447, 39-656, 40-561
 ESTHER 30-495, 34-588, 35-611, 36-642, 38-763, 39-793, 40-812
 GEORGE [mr.] 30-1092, 31-1246, 33-1281, 34-1205, 35-1270, 36-1403, 38-1362, 39-1387, 40-1452
 JAMES 38-1450, 39-1080, 39-1493, 40-1514
 JOHN 30-205, 30-502, 30-1059, 31-150(2), 31-636, 31-1206,

INDEX

33-142(2), 33-558, 33-1287,
34-221(2), 34-606, 34-1221,
35-234(2), 35-628, 35-1496,
36-171(2), 36-626, 36-1409, 36-1491,
37-156(2), 38-323(2), 38-1511,
39-184, 39-227, 39-805, 39-1392,
40-222, 40-433, 40-703, 40-1458
  JONATHAN 35-1270, 36-1403,
38-1362, 39-1387, 40-1452
  JOSEPH 38-762, 40-813
  JOSHUA [Joshew] 30-495, 31-576,
33-649, 34-587, 35-624, 36-638,
39-795
  NOBLE 30-1092, 31-1246, 33-1281,
34-1205, 35-1270, 36-1403, 38-1363,
39-1386, 40-1451
  RICHARD 30-333, 31-406, 31-584,
33-374, 33-649, 34-408, 34-588,
35-491, 35-611, 36-590, 36-642,
37-452, 38-540, 38-762, 39-173,
39-621, 39-797, 40-358
  SAMUEL [Samewill] 30-585, 31-582,
33-592, 34-706, 35-623, 36-636,
38-758, 39-803, 40-814
  SOLOMON 31-584, 33-654, 34-584,
35-79, 36-11, 37-114, 38-142, 39-13,
40-13
  STEPHEN 34-588, 35-611, 36-642,
38-763, 39-793, 40-812
  THOMAS 30-10, 30-511, 31-11,
33-10, 33-654, 34-11, 34-584, 35-80,
35-634, 36-2, 36-620, 38-146,
38-751, 39-12, 39-805, 40-458,
40-703
  WILLIAM 30-10, 30-1090, 33-10
TULLEY [Tulle]
  BENJAMIN 30-881, 30-938, 31-898,
31-956, 33-889, 33-1050, 34-958,
34-1107, 35-1029, 35-1165, 36-936,
36-1129, 38-1083, 38-1196, 39-1228,
39-1252, 40-1147, 40-1175
  DANIEL 39-1233, 40-1148
  JAMES 30-938, 31-950, 33-1050,
34-1107, 35-1029, 36-938, 38-1069
  JOHN 39-1233, 40-1148
  JOSEPH 30-920, 31-906, 33-1050,
34-1015, 35-1133, 36-970, 38-1113,
39-1251, 40-1173
  JOSHUA 38-1195, 39-1227, 40-1147
  RICHARD 35-1001, 36-1127, 38-1333,
39-1233, 40-1148
  STEPHEN [junr., senr] 30-880,
30-1038, 31-897, 31-899, 33-888,
33-889, 34-958, 34-961, 35-1001,
35-1165, 36-1127, 36-1128, 38-1195,
38-1333, 39-1227, 39-1233, 40-1147,
40-1148
TUNSTALL, JOHN [Jon./capt.] 30-565,
31-509, 33-647, 34-707, 35-719,
36-704, 38-735, 39-781, 40-781
TURK, MAGNUS [Magne, Magnes] 30-18,
31-1346, 33-1483, 34-1547, 35-1170

TURNER
  ABRAHAM 40-780
  EDWARD 35-1723, 34-1476, 36-1722
  HENRY 30-318, 31-379, 34-399,
35-413, 36-481, 37-522, 38-475,
39-499, 40-592
  JOHN 30-1199, 31-1138, 33-1350,
34-1360, 35-1389
  JOSEPH 37-1149, 38-1707, 39-1717,
40-1791
  JOSHUA 36-1722, 38-1708, 39-1718,
40-1792
  NICHOLAS 30-1331, 31-1451, 34-429,
35-418, 36-480, 37-518, 38-646,
39-497, 40-590
  ROLAND [Rowland] 40-1791
  SAMUEL [junr.] 30-1198, 30-1331,
31-1137, 31-1451, 33-1349, 33-1449,
34-1359, 34-1476, 35-1723, 36-1722,
37-1149, 38-1707, 39-1717, 40-1791
  WILLIAM 30-671, 31-701, 33-717,
34-728, 35-765, 36-830, 37-700,
38-853, 39-778, 39-891, 40-868
TURPIN [Turpen]
  DANIEL 40-1256
  HANNAH 36-750
  JOHN [senr.] 30-569, 31-594,
33-546, 34-574, 34-647, 35-630,
35-720, 36-624, 38-751, 39-805,
40-704
  JOSHUA [jur.] 39-745, 40-731
  MATTHEW 40-1794
  WHITTINGTON [whit., Whitt(e)y] 36-
624, 38-751, 39-805, 40- 703
  WILLIAM [jr., sr./capt.] 30-502,
30-509, 30-569, 31-524, 31-589,
31-594, 33-38, 33-546, 33-553,
33-598, 34-574, 34-621, 34-647,
35-601, 35-630, 35-720, 36-621,
36-624, 36-746, 38-744, 38-750,
38-751, 39-805, 39-806, 39-812,
40-703, 40-705, 40-778
TURVILE [Turvell]
  JOHN 31-307, 33-291, 34-238,
35-341, 36-297, 37-223, 38-317,
39-175
  PRISGRAVE 31-313, 33-289, 34-238,
35-346, 36-244, 37-352, 38-241,
39-217, 40-305
  WILLIAM 30-245(2), 31-306(2),
33-289, 33-290, 34-238, 34-285,
35-346, 35-347, 36-280, 37-231,
38-338, 39-181, 40-311
TUSTER [Justian, Tuftin]
  BENTALL 37-629
  WILLIAM 30-349, 31-318, 33-381,
34-558, 35-500
TWILLY [Tweley,Twille]
  ELIZABETH [Elzebett/wido.] 30-895,
31-999
  GEORGE 30-895, 31-999, 33-1000,
34-993, 35-1141, 36-1547, 37-1197,

INDEX

38-1107, 39-1262
   ROBERT 30-895, 31-900, 33-1053, 34-1016, 35-1141, 36-1068, 38-1072, 39-1259, 40-1170
TWOMAN, JOHN 34-1328
TWYFORD [Twifird, Twiford, Twyfoot, Tyford]
   JOHN 30-1037, 31-896, 33-887, 34-962, 35-1000, 36-948, 38-1199, 39-1190, 40-1152
    JONATHAN 40-1222
    WILLIAM 37-744, 38-961, 39-1362(2), 40-1222
TYLER [Tailer, Tiler, Tylor]
   DAVID 38-100, 39-139, 40-148
   HAES 37-42
   JOHN [junr., senr.] 30-110, 30-111, 31-119, 31-121, 33-138, 34-137, 35-21(2), 36-146(2), 37-42(2), 38-100(2), 39-139, 40-148, 40-149
    JOSIAH 34-170
    SAMUEL 31-289
    THOMAS 30-109, 31-120, 33-137, 34-135, 35-20, 36-145, 36-146, 37-31, 38-99, 38-100, 39-138, 39-139, 40-147, 40-148
TYLER, WALTER 31-279, 34-290

UBANKS, MOLTON [Newbank/Molten] 34-1152, 35-1207, 36-1242, 37-861, 38-1317, 39-1359
UPTON, THOMAS 33-1588, 34-1634, 35-1712
USEARS, JOHN 30-813, 31-848

VALLANCE, THOMAS [Vallence] 39-1497, 40-1517
VANCE [Vaunce]
   ALEXANDER [junr., sr.] 30-1345, 30-1414, 31-1464, 31-1475, 33-1501, 34-1501, 35-1592
   DAVID 30-1412, 31-1474, 33-1616, 34-1523, 35-1586, 36-1645, 37-1163, 38-1644
   THOMAS 30-1372, 31-1516, 33-1407, 35-676, 36-690, 38-1188, 39-1222, 40-1136
VAUGHAN [Vahan, Vaun, Voan, Vohan, Vone, Voyhn] WILLIAM 30-830, 30-1173, 31-881, 33-778, 33-967, 34-770, 34-925, 35-968, 36-837, 36-945, 37-641, 38-883, 38-1167, 39-536, 39-1174, 40-537, 40-1301
VEAZEY [Beasey, Besiey, Bessey, Bewsiey, Vesey, Veze(y)]
   CHARLES 30-653, 31-737, 33-765, 34-814, 35-847, 36-804, 37-683, 38-873, 39-863, 40-901
    ELIZABETH [Elizbeath] 39-359
    EPHRAIM [Ephram] 40-901
    WILLIAM 30-163, 31-223, 33-168, 34-289, 35-163, 36-283, 36-804, 37-250, 37-683, 38-253, 38-873, 39-863, 40-902
VENABLES [Vanables, Venibles, Vennab(a)ls, Vinibles]
   BENJAMIN 30-1467, 31-1360, 33-1415, 34-1645, 35-1127, 35-1684, 36-1545, 37-1241, 38-1704, 39-1853, 40-1192
   CATHERINE [Cathorin] 39-1914, 40-1891
   JOHN 30-1355, 31-1511, 33-1546
   JOSEPH [senr] 30-1468, 31-1360, 35-1688, 36-1560, 37-1060, 38-1840, 39-1914, 40-1891
   PERKINS [Perckins, Pirkins] 38-1840, 39-1914, 40-1891
   WILLIAM [junr., senr.] 30-1360, 30-1468, 31-1360, 31-1512, 33-1415, 33-1545, 34-1555, 34-1646, 35-1683, 35-1688, 36-1546, 36-1560, 37-1060, 37-1193, 38-1790, 38-1840, 39-1855, 40-1888
VENATSON [Feenatson, Felnellson, Funnelson, Phunelson, Vannelson, Vanatson, Vatnatson, Venedson, Fenelson, Venadson, Venellson, Vene(a)tson, Vernelson]
   ELIAS 30-812, 31-847, 33-1076, 34-905, 35-947, 36-1188, 38-1319, 39-1307, 39-1600, 40-1405
   ELISHA [Elige] 33-1076, 34-905, 35-1751, 36-1263, 38-1384, 40-1680
   NATHAN 34-781, 35-815, 36-795, 37-657, 38-905, 39-824, 40-943
   WILLIAM 30-717, 34-781, 35-815, 36-795, 39-824
   WILLIAMS [Willums] 31-684, 33-779, 37-657, 38-905
VESSELLS [Wassells, Wepells]
   EPHRAIM 30-121(2), 33-67, 34-117
   JAMES 30-58, 31-63, 33-67, 34-117
VESTRY [Vestrey, Westers, Westrons, Westry]
   MICHAEL [Mickel] 30-716, 33-714, 34-795, 37-503, 38-618, 39-910, 40-945
VICTOR
   JAMES 33-350, 34-362, 35-383, 36-456, 37-598, 38-597, 39-454, 40-572
   MAGDALENE [Magladen] 33-350, 34-362
   THOMAS 36-456, 37-598, 38-1554, 39-1451, 40-1556
VINCENT [Vinson, Venson, Vincon, Vinsin, Vinsent, Vinson]
   BENJAMIN 31-1393, 33-1440, 34-1469, 35-1656, 37-1114, 38-1715, 39-1710, 40-1790
   GEORGE 30-1285, 31-1393, 33-1425, 34-1676, 35-1655, 36-1634, 37-1211,

INDEX

38-1759, 39-1671, 40-1770
  JAMES [junr.] 30-1265, 31-1328, 33-1441, 35-1089, 36-1237, 38-1336, 39-1087, 40-1253
  THOMAS [junr., senr.] 30-1265, 30-1285, 31-1328, 31-1393, 33-1439, 33-1440, 34-1469, 34-1472, 35-1656, 35-1659, 36-1636, 36-1761, 37-1205, 37-1210, 38-1760(2), 39-1676(2), 40-1771(2)

VISON, JOSEPH 39-113

W------, WILLIAM W------, William 37- 810

WAFERS [Wafer], IGNATIOUS 31-1362, 35-1134, 36- 971

WAGGAMAN
  EPHRAIM 33-733, 34-799, 35-831, 36-819, 37-719, 38-892, 39-845, 40-896
  HENRY 30-702
  JACOB 30-702, 31-724, 33-733, 34-799, 35-831, 36-819, 37-719, 38-892
  WILLIAM 30-702

WAILES [Wails, Wales/snr.]
  ELEANOR [Helinah, Heleney] 37-1184, 38-1667, 39-1846, 40-1824
  JOHN 30-901, 33-1028
  JOSEPH 31-1353, 33-1410, 34-1638, 35-1704, 36-1535
  THOMAS 38- 335

WAKER
  JOHN 35-330
  WILLIAM 35-153

WALE [Waile, Waill, Wale]
  JOHN 31-871, 34-174, 35-1658, 36-1693, 37-1153, 38-1797, 39-1744
  WILLIAM 37-404

WALKER [Wolker]
  JAMES 30-737, 31-634
  JOHN 30-677, 30-703, 31-725, 33-707, 33-732, 34-325, 34-798, 35-830, 36-238, 36-1217, 37-207, 37-718, 38-192, 39-185, 39-874, 40-195, 40-897
  THOMAS 30-1387, 31-1403, 33-1590, 34-1600, 35-1625, 36-1595, 37-1004, 38-1833, 39-1808, 40-1859

WALLACE [Waless, Walles, Wallis, Wollace, Wollis]
  CHARLES 38-1281
  DAVID 30-739, 31-790, 33-809, 34-891, 35-933, 36-1000, 38-986, 39-1071, 40-1037
  GEORGE 37-738, 38-936, 39-993, 40-991
  JAMES 30-739, 31-790, 33-809, 34-867, 35-912, 36-901, 37-761, 38-947, 39-940, 40-992
  JOHN 30-750, 31-796, 35-861, 36-920, 38-1033, 39-1003, 40-1042
  JOSEPH 30-1463
  MATTHEW 30-738, 31-789, 33-808, 34-866, 35-915, 36-900, 37-760, 38-948, 39-941, 40-990
  RICHARD [senr.] 30-739, 30-1028, 30-1384, 31-790, 31-870, 31-1430, 33-809, 33-1055, 33-1478, 34-867, 34-1031, 34-1195, 35-912, 35-1018, 35-1048, 36-901, 36-1072, 36-1232, 37-761, 37-918, 38-947, 38-1176, 38-1180, 39-940, 39-1077, 39-1133, 40-992, 40-1215
  ROBERT 33-1384, 34-1347, 35-889, 36-883, 37-738, 38-936, 39-993, 40-991
  THOMAS 30-253, 30-739, 31-283, 31-790, 33-329, 33-809, 34-167, 34-867, 35-293, 35-903, 35-912, 36-270, 36-901, 36-920, 37-310, 37-761, 38-365, 38-977, 38-1033, 39-365, 39-994, 39-1003, 40-179, 40-991
  WILLIAM 30-748, 31-795

WALLER [Wallear, Wallor, Walear, Woller/junr., senr.]
  GEORGE 30-785, 31-779, 33-802, 34-847, 35-909, 36-888, 37-785, 38-923, 39-931, 40-1021
  JOHN 30-763, 30-1440, 31-772, 33-817, 33-945, 34-875, 34-1064, 35-903, 35-1052, 36-891, 36-979, 37-766, 38-938, 38-1231, 39-962, 39-1368, 40-1020, 40-1257
  MAJOR 30-764, 31-773, 33-821, 34-874, 35-904, 36-897, 37-765, 38-945, 39-929, 40-986
  NATHANIEL [junr., senr.] 30-1009, 30-1011, 31-839, 31-1088, 33-945, 33-946, 34-1064, 34-1065, 35-1051, 35-1052, 36-979, 36-980, 38-1231, 38-1328, 39-1105, 39-1239, 40-1257(20, 40-1266
  NELSON 30-763, 31-772, 33-821, 34-876, 35-1008, 36-1690, 38-1312, 39-1275, 40-1344
  RICHARD [ser.] 34-1066, 35-1050, 36-984, 38-1127, 39-1184, 40-1259, 40-1279, 40-1353
  ROBERT 33-946
  SAMUEL 39-1910, 40-2001
  THOMAS 30-1011(2), 31-839(2), 33-946(2), 34-1053, 34-1066, 35-1049, 35-1050, 36-982, 36-984, 38-1127, 38-1175, 39-1173, 39-1184, 40-1259, 40-1267
  WILLIAM 30-765, 31-786, 33-821, 34-881, 35-877, 36-921, 38-948, 39-930

WALSTON [Walstone, Wolston]
  BOAZ [Boos, Booz, Bows] 33-565, 30-603, 31-614, 34-581, 35-658, 36-612, 38-732, 39-743, 40-722

INDEX

HENRY 33-594, 34-600, 35-622, 36-639, 38-765, 39-790, 40-810
JOSEPH 33-602, 34-712, 35-618, 36-623
JOY 30-3, 31-21, 33-2, 34-5, 35-91, 36-4, 37-123, 38-732, 39-743, 40-722
OBEDIAH 36-612, 38-738, 39-745, 40-731
THOMAS 30-493, 31-575, 33-689, 34-656, 35-617, 36-639, 38-765, 39-794, 40-811
WILLIAM 30-493, 31-575, 33-602, 34-712, 35-618, 36-641, 38-766, 39-790, 40-810

WALTER [Walltor]
CORNELIUS 38-1422
DANIEL 30-800, 31-827, 31-1024, 33-915, 33-1109, 34-890, 34-1034, 35-930, 35-1096, 36-966, 36-1119, 37-830, 38-1019, 39-999, 40-1050
HENRY 30-935, 31-1024, 33-915, 34-1034, 35-1096, 36-1119, 38-1156, 39-1095, 40-1225
JOHN 30-799, 31-1086, 33-915, 33-1112, 34-899, 34-1034, 35-944, 35-1096, 36-967, 36-1119, 37-916, 38-991, 39-971, 39-1021, 39-1095, 40-1049
NATHANIEL 37-916
ROBERT 33-1112, 34-899, 35-944, 36-1228, 37-896, 38-1018, 39-1000
THOMAS 30-747, 30-965, 33-1096, 34-1132, 35-1235, 36-1181, 38-1220, 39-1290
WILLIAM 34-1034, 35-1096, 36-1119, 38-1156, 39-1095, 40-1225

WALTON [Walltom]
BENJAMIN 31-132, 33-309, 34-232
COMFORT 35-320
ELIZABETH [widow] 38-910
FISHER 30-692, 31-671, 33-747, 34-746, 35-782, 36-822, 37-685
JOB 40-885
JOHN [jr.] 30-368, 31-305, 33-314, 34-340, 35-327, 36-232, 38-208
MARTHA Walton, Mattha widow 39-263
MARTHA [Mattha/widow] 40-174
RICHARD 30-368, 31-311, 33-482, 34-424
ROBERT [junr.] 39-818
STEPHEN [junr., senr.] 30-693(2), 31-667, 33-761(2), 34-747(2), 35-783(2), 36-765(2), 37-664(2), 38-837(2), 39-881(2), 40-885(2)
TEAGUE [Teagele, Teagle, Teakell] 38-270, 39-374, 40-379
WILLIAM [junr., senr.] 30-262(2), 31-132(2), 31-153, 33-154, 33-313(2), 34-187(2), 34-756, 35-325(2), 35-783, 36-296, 36-314(2), 37-315(2), 38-38, 38-524, 38-910, 39-47, 39-406, 39-407, 39-879, 40-176, 40-312, 40-845, 40-884

WARD
CORNELIUS 30-52, 30-1087, 31-109, 31-1215, 33-63, 33-1299, 34-70, 34-1214, 35-37, 35-1344, 36-24, 36-1419, 36-1474, 37-81, 38-26, 38-1498, 39-59, 39-1405, 40-63, 40-1472
JACOB 30-62, 31-64, 33-68, 34-82, 35-14, 36-69, 37-70, 38-9, 39-71, 40-76
JAMES [Jeams] 30-62, 31-64, 33-68, 34-82, 34-1559, 35-14, 36-70, 37-69, 38-10, 39-72, 40-84
JOHN 30-56, 33-61, 34-79, 35-39, 36-79, 37-83, 38-28, 39-57, 40-61
JOSEPH [junr.] 30-1087, 31-1215, 33-1299, 34-1214, 35-1344, 36-1419, 36-1419, 36-1474, 36-1474, 38-1498, 38-1498, 39-1405, 39-1405, 40-1472, 40-1472
JOSHUA 40-95
MARY 30-30, 37-25, 38-32
MOSES 36-69, 37-70, 38-9, 39-71, 40-76
RICHARD 33-84, 34-122, 35-6, 36-56, 37-93, 38-123, 39-91
SAMUEL 30-56, 31-58, 33-61, 34-79, 35-39, 36-79, 37-83, 38-28, 39-57, 40-60
STEPHEN [junr., senr.] 30-50, 30-51, 31-57, 31-60, 33-60, 33-62, 34-77, 34-78, 35-38, 35-41, 36-25, 36-80, 37-49, 37-82, 38-27, 38-32, 39-58, 39-94, 40-62
THOMAS 30-62, 31-64, 33-68, 34-82, 35-14, 36-69, 37-70, 38-9, 39-71, 40-76
WILLIAM 36-79, 37-83, 38-28, 39-57, 40-60

WARE, ROBERT 30-74
WARNER, ISAAC 31-1032, 33-176
WARREN [Warran, Warrin, Warrent]
NICHOLAS 30-343, 31-489, 33-484, 34-456, 35-520, 36-500, 37-415, 38-653, 39-563, 40-551
ROBERT 30-279, 30-342, 31-490, 33-485, 34-457, 35-521, 36-501, 37-416, 38-654, 39-566, 40-557
WILLIAM 40-551

WARRINGTON [Warranton, Warrenton, Worington]
BENJAMIN 33-1332, 34-1204, 35-1503, 36-1497, 38-1457, 39-1916, 40-1932
THOMAS 30-1195, 31-1308, 33-184, 33-1351, 34-1286, 35-1390, 36-1493, 38-1518, 39-1435, 40-1543

WARTNABY, WILLIAM 40-1302

INDEX

WARWICK [Warrick, Worwick], ARTHUR 30-1088, 31-1216, 33-1295, 34-1210, 35-1331, 36-1422, 38-1501, 39-1404, 40-1468

WATERS [Warters]
  ABIGAIL [mrs.] 33-3, 34-8, 35-87, 36-20, 37-122, 38-152, 39-3, 40-3
  EDWARD 31-111, 35-85, 36-22, 37-120, 38-150, 39-6, 40-6
  ELIZABETH [mrs.] 30-6, 31-18, 33-5, 34-2, 35-93, 36-18, 37-121, 38-151, 39-5, 40-4
  JOHN 30-8, 31-15, 33-8, 34-9, 35-84, 36-16, 37-117, 38-148, 39-142, 40-8
  LITTLETON 30-6, 31-18
  PATRICK 30-1173, 31-282, 33-511, 34-414, 35-496, 36-578, 38-537, 39-624, 40-508
  RICHARD 33-5, 33-316, 34-2, 35-93, 36-465, 37-232, 38-152, 38-217, 39-3, 39-393, 40-288
  WILLIAM [junr., senr.] 30-5, 30-9, 31-17, 31-19, 33-9, 34-10, 35-83, 36-17, 37-119, 38-147, 39-8, 40-9

WATKINS [Wotikins], WILLIAM 35-1299

WATSON [Wattson]
  WIDOW 30-734
  CHARLES 30-656, 33-745, 34-767, 35-803, 36-806, 37-713, 38-834, 39-860, 40-903
  JAMES 30-490, 30-734, 33-746, 34-802, 35-796, 36-801, 37-672, 38-849, 39-861
  JOHN 30-704, 31-734, 33-774, 34-774, 35-808, 36-305, 36-807, 36-816, 37-170, 37-673, 38-249, 38-835, 39-166, 39-859, 40-907, 40-1323
  LUKE 30-713, 31-729, 33-728, 34-777, 35-811, 36-811, 37-733, 38-829, 39-852, 40-916
  MOSES 31-739, 33-740, 34-764, 35-801, 36-779, 37-650
  PETER 30-722, 31-731, 33-720, 34-776, 35-810, 36-766, 37-680, 38-848, 39-851, 40-914
  ROBERT 30-656, 30-705, 31-735, 31-738, 33-741, 33-745, 34-767, 34-783, 35-803, 35-817, 36-777, 36-806, 37-649, 37-713, 38-834, 38-898, 39-860, 40-903, 40-922
  URIAH 33-746, 34-802, 35-810, 38-881, 39-861, 40-904
  URIAS [Hurias] 36-767, 37-720
  WILLIAM [jr., sr.] 38-315, 38-314

WAPLES, PAUL [Wayaples, Wayiaples] 30-158, 31-222, 33-167, 34-288, 35-164, 36-180, 37-274, 38-280, 39-394, 40-374

WEATHERBY [We(a)therbey, Weatherbury]
  JOHN 33-583, 34-698, 35-627, 36-627, 37-1024, 38-1808, 39-1796, 40-1006

WEATHERLY [Wertherly, Wetheley, Weatherlee, Witherley]
  WIDOW 35-1140
  CHARITY 36-1070, 38-1255
  ELIZABETH [wid] 31-1047
  JAMES 30-857, 31-1047, 33-1081, 34-990, 35-1142, 36-1069, 38-1073, 39-1036, 40-1165
  JOSEPH 38-1255, 39-1036, 40-1162
  RICHARD 36-1070
  WILLIAM [jur.] 30-894, 31-929, 33-1080, 33-1080, 34-991, 34-991, 35-1668, 38-1255, 39-1019, 40-1164

WEBB [Weeb]
  [illegible] 37-457
  ELISHA 30-480, 31-504, 33-426, 34-523, 35-591, 36-458, 38-559, 39-517, 40-637
  GRACE [widd.] 30-480, 31-504, 34-468, 38-559, 39-517, 40-637
  JOHN [junr., senr.] 30-349, 31-1294(2), 33-1195(2), 34-468, 34-1290(2), 35-1275(2), 36-1328(2), 38-1576(2), 39-1523(2), 40-1592(2)
  MARK 31-150, 33-142, 34-221
  SAMUEL 30-303, 31-446, 33-427, 34-542, 35-569, 36-550, 37-463, 38-420, 39-610, 40-540
  SOLOMON 31-1294, 33-1385, 34-1290, 35-1275, 36-1328, 38-1576, 39-1523, 40-1592
  WILLIAM 30-205, 31-306, 33-187, 34-220, 35-256, 37-157, 38-322, 39-303, 40-210

WELCH [Welcks, Walsh, Welsh]
  JAMES 33-1589, 34-1604, 35-717
  JOHN 34-871, 35-906, 36-893, 37-783
  WILLIAM 34-678, 35-728, 36-884, 37-770, 38-932, 39-963, 40-776

WELL, WILLIAM 36-241

WELLS, DANIEL 34-494, 35-432, 36-542, 38-621, 39-573, 40-577

WEST
  ALEXANDER 30-172, 34-1162, 39-350, 40-399
  ANTHONY 30-501, 31-604, 33-670, 34-702, 35-639, 36-709
  GEORGE [jr., sr.] 30-139, 31-200, 33-215, 34-312, 35-244, 36-302, 38-257, 39-241, 40-202(2)
  JAMES [esqr.] 30-885, 31-951, 33-893, 34-987, 35-1011, 36-1124, 38-1253, 39-1195, 40-1142
  RANDALL 30-602
  THOMAS [jr., sr.] 30-143, 30-1151, 31-202, 31-242, 33-216, 33-335, 34-269, 34-313, 35-228, 35-273, 36-303, 37-176, 37-255, 38-256,

INDEX

39-246, 39-349, 40-372, 40-372, 40-398
  WILLIAM 30-142, 30-504, 31-197, 31-605, 33-214, 33-682, 34-311, 34-682, 35-229, 35-713, 36-304, 36-614, 38-258, 38-806, 39-247, 39-744, 40-350

WHALEY [Wale, Whalie, Whealey, Whaliey, Wale]
  CHARLES 31-142, 33-153, 34-172, 35-299, 37-347, 38-215, 39-292, 40-299
  EDWARD 30-274, 31-142
  ELIAS 40-186
  JOHN 31-306, 33-289, 34-238, 35-346, 36-280, 38-241, 38-1597, 39-1534, 40-311, 40-1611
  MARY [widow] 31-142, 33-153, 37-347, 39-399, 40-186
  NATHANIEL 37-347, 38-215, 39-399, 40-186
  WILLIAM [junr., senr.] 30-125, 30-274, 31-139, 31-177, 31-911, 33-318, 33-383, 33-668, 34-173, 34-316, 35-332, 35-338, 36-226, 37-348, 38-299, 38-514, 39-400, 39-413, 39-1589, 40-368, 40-457, 40-1669

WHARTON [Warton, Whorton]
  BAKER 40-240
  CHARLES 38-200, 39-359
  DANIEL [jr., sr.] 30-123, 31-184, 33-194, 34-159, 35-192, 36-306(2), 37-236(2), 38-289(2), 39-187(2), 40-240(2)
  FRANCIS 30-196, 31-219, 33-234, 34-333, 35-184, 36-262, 37-267, 38-260, 39-372, 40-426
  GEORGE 37-236, 38-289, 39-187, 40-240
  HEMMON [Henman] 30-123, 31-185, 33-193, 34-158, 35-193, 36-155, 37-191, 38-285, 39-194, 40-242
  THOMAS 36-175, 37-266, 38-177, 39-380, 40-418
  WILLIAM 30-1398, 31-590, 33-12, 34-62, 34-333, 35-89, 35-184, 36-3, 36-262, 37-113, 37-267, 38-141, 38-167, 39-14, 39-372, 39-1014, 40-14, 40-354
  WRIXAM [Ricksam] 36-245, 37-305, 38-260, 39-319, 40-354

WHEATLY [Whetly]
  JOHN 37-231
  SAMPSON 30-87, 31-95, 33-115, 34-36, 35-100, 36-135, 37-26, 38-54, 39-111, 40-121
  WILLIAM 30-87, 30-934, 40-122

WHEELER [Whealler]
  EDWARD 33-1188, 34-1291
  ELIZABETH 36-753, 38-811
  ISAAC 31-1166, 33-1188, 34-1291, 35-1456, 36-1375, 38-1573, 39-1519, 40-1598
  JOHN [junr., senr.] 30-61, 30-263(2), 31-70, 31-304(2), 33-305(2), 34-120, 34-236(2), 35-322(2), 36-65, 36-229, 36-272, 37-66, 37-271(2), 38-14, 38-379(2), 39-70
  JONATHAN 38-107, 39-137, 40-71
  SAMUEL 30-115, 31-117, 33-139, 38-107, 40-71
  WILLIAM 36-1375, 38-1573, 39-1519, 40-1661

WHITE [Whight]
  ARCHIBALD 30-1151, 31-1112, 33-1218, 34-1407, 35-1453, 36-1312, 38-1395, 39-1604, 40-1683
  ESTHER [mrs.] 35-1265
  FRANCIS 30-735, 31-787, 33-806, 34-863, 35-918, 36-905, 36-1548, 37-756, 37-1192, 38-951, 38-1627, 39-942, 40-987(2)
  HANNAH 31-1176, 35-1369, 38-1536, 39-1478, 40-1532
  HENRY 31-1176, 33-1361, 34-1459, 35-1732, 36-1717
  ISAAC 31-127
  JOHN [junr., senr.] 30-76, 30-97(2), 30-736, 30-948, 30-1102, 30-1148, 30-1206, 31-87, 31-108, 31-787, 31-788, 31-1097, 31-1109, 33-95, 33-124, 33-389, 33-799, 33-806, 33-1232, 33-1244, 34-24, 34-111(2), 34-863, 34-865, 34-1421, 34-1430, 35-109, 35-130(2), 35-914, 35-918, 35-1369, 35-1396, 35-1444, 36-41, 36-123, 36-902, 36-905, 36-1298, 36-1311, 37-50, 37-96, 37-406, 37-756, 37-757, 38-60, 38-75, 38-630, 38-783, 38-949(2), 38-951, 38-1396, 38-1536, 39-95, 39-119, 39-568, 39-942, 39-943(2), 39-1478, 39-1606, 40-100, 40-138, 40-968, 40-989(2), 40-1532, 40-1684
  MAJOR 30-1206
  NATHANIEL 40-1448
  RACHEL 40-460
  THOMAS 31-99, 33-114, 33-806, 34-50, 34-863, 35-142, 35-918, 36-134, 36-905, 37-16, 37-756, 38-89, 38-951, 39-113, 39-942, 40-129, 40-987
  WILLIAM 30-1115, 31-126, 31-1309, 33-1211, 33-1218, 34-1407, 34-1412, 35-1453, 36-1312, 38-1395, 38-1536, 39-1478, 39-1604, 40-460, 40-1532, 40-1683

WHITEHEAD, JOHN 34-458, 36-228, 38-238, 39-235

WHITTINGHAM
  mr. 31-1125
  HEBER 30-1116, 33-1213, 36-699,

INDEX

38-809, 39-719, 40-764
   SURY 31-302
   WILLIAM 35-711
WHITTINGTON
   JOSEPH 38-742
   JOSHUA 39-673
   SOUTHY 33-1345 [jr.] 30-1210, 31-1146, 33-339, 34-1197, 35-1512, 35-1751, 36-48, 36-1263, 36-1476, 37-47, 38-62, 38-1532, 38-1550, 39-93, 39-1600, 40-99, 40-441
   WILLIAM [junr., senr.] 30-432, 30-1214, 31-435, 31-1156, 33-339(2), 34-350(2), 35-371, 35-1376, 35-1512, 38-1550, 39-1453, 40-959
WHITTNEY, BARRETT 39-1663
WIANT, JOHN 30-676
WILCOX [Wilcocks, Woolcocks]
   GEORGE 30-327, 31-336, 33-501
   JOHN 30-552, 31-555, 33-631, 34-717
   WILLIAM 35-655, 36-748, 38-918, 39-977
WILDGOOSE [Wil(e)goos(e)]
   RICHARD 33-247, 35-241, 36-184, 37-203, 38-371
   THOMAS 34-229, 35-241, 36-184, 37-203, 39-226, 40-438
WILDMAN, JOHN 35-368, 36-533, 37-378, 38-615, 39-579, 40-1588
WILEY, ERASTUS [Artus] 39-1910, 40-2001
WILKINS [Wilkinson], JAMES 30-1391, 31-1418, 33-1591, 37-1242, 38-1661, 39-1801, 40-1847
WILKS, JOHN 30-628, 33-605, 34-708, 35-656, 36-665, 38-774, 39-715, 40-767
WILL--, CHARLES 37-953
WILLEY [Welley, Wille]
   JARRETT [Jared] 37-986, 38-1208, 39-1289, 40-1302
JOHN 33-859, 34-1186, 35-1219, 36-1199, 37-956, 38-1289, 39-1371, 40-1351
WILLIAMS [Wilems, Wiliams]
   [illegible] 37-535(2), 37-560
   ARGULUS 30-232, 31-263, 33-463, 34-566, 36-601, 38-465, 39-435, 40-516
   CHARLES 30-975, 31-1030, 33-896, 34-1156, 35-1197, 36-1180, 39-1335, 40-1386
   HENRY 30-38, 31-112
   ISAAC [jr.] 30-106, 31-2, 33-36, 34-13, 35-70, 36-108, 37-149, 38-133, 39-23, 40-26(2)
   JACOB 35-74, 36-113, 37-109, 38-134, 39-21, 40-18
   JEREMIAH 31-798, 33-801
   JOAB 30-436
   JOHN [capt., mr.] 30-104, 30-157, 30-398, 30-478, 30-749, 30-1024, 30-1259, 31-3, 31-407, 31-471, 31-795, 31-1088, 31-1419, 33-8, 33-22, 33-373, 33-535, 33-938, 34-132, 34-407, 34-492, 34-857, 34-1059, 34-1254, 35-74, 35-454, 35-489, 35-921, 35-965, 35-1067, 35-1751, 36-113, 36-520, 36-904, 36-960, 36-1027, 37-109, 37-741, 38-134, 38-953, 38-1010, 38-1257, 38-1384, 39-21, 39-935, 39-1070, 39-1600, 40-17, 40-973, 40-1274, 40-1680, 40-1838
   JONATHAN 30-478, 31-471, 33-535, 34-492, 35-454, 36-426, 38-665
   LITTLETON [Lettilton] 31-471, 33-535, 34-492, 35-454, 36-426, 39-586, 40-620
   NATHANIEL 37-501
   PRISGRAVE 30-362, 31-351, 33-376, 34-410, 35-492, 36-602, 37-625
   RICHARD [Ritcard] 30-828, 31-882, 33-970, 34-922, 35-965, 36-960, 38-1010, 39-1070, 40-1838
   SAMUEL 30-427, 31-487, 33-492, 34-562, 35-577, 36-466, 37-501, 38-457, 39-438, 40-695
   THOMAS [junr., senr., capt., mr.] 30-25(2), 31-32(2), 33-35(2), 33-773, 34-58(2), 34-747, 35-71, 35-73, 35-792, 36-96, 36-104, 36-770, 37-103, 37-145, 37-648, 38-127, 38-129, 38-837, 39-22, 39-24, 39-881, 40-25, 40-27, 40-956
   THOMAS NATHANIEL 30-427, 31-487, 33-492, 34-562, 35-577, 36-466, 38-457, 39-438, 40-695
   WILLIAM 31-115, 34-142, 35-23, 36-144, 37-38, 39-143, 40-79
WILLIN [Willen, Willing]
   [--rey/mr.] 30-285
   EDWARD 31-1417, 33-1392, 34-1628, 35-1768, 36-1523, 37-1187, 38-1633, 39-1833, 40-1845
   JOHN 39-1910, 40-2001
   ROBERT 33-1390, 34-1631, 35-1609, 36-1522, 37-1178, 38-1634, 39-1839, 40-1833
   THOMAS [junr., senr.] 31-1416, 33-1390, 34-1631, 35-1609, 36-1522(2), 37-1178, 37-1246(2), 38-1634(2), 38-1833, 39-1809, 39-1839, 40-1833(2)
WILLISS
   BARNABY 30-580, 31-586, 33-597, 34-679, 35-629, 36-623, 38-752, 39-802, 40-823
   EDMUND 39-1737, 40-1917
   NATHANIEL 34-1683, 35-1584, 36-1706, 37-1131, 38-1680, 39-1729, 40-1917

INDEX

WILLITT
  AMBROSE 30-648, 31-740, 33-736, 34-765, 35-802, 36-781, 37-721, 38-911, 39-820(2), 40-924
  THOMAS [Tom] 30-648, 36-781, 37-721, 38-911, 40-924
  WILLIAM 33-736, 34-765, 35-802, 36-781, 37-721, 38-911, 39-820, 40-924
WILSON [Willson]
  ANDREW 38-679, 39-670, 40-790
  DAVID [capt.] 30-491, 31-515, 33-543, 34-664, 35-626, 36-609, 38-740, 39-811, 40-777
  EPHRAIM 30-490, 31-508
  FRANCIS 30-1091
  GEORGE 30-94, 31-101, 33-113, 34-51, 35-140, 36-132, 36-759, 37-12, 37-1035, 38-91, 38-808, 39-108, 39-669, 40-119, 40-787
  ISAAC 34-239, 35-288, 38-163
  ISRAEL 30-290, 31-245, 33-284, 36-177, 37-165
  JAMES 30-602, 33-664, 34- 684
  JOHN 30-64, 30-94, 30-290, 30-511, 30-910, 31-76, 31-101, 31-110, 31-245(2), 31-770, 31-949, 33-85, 33-105, 33-110, 33-283, 33-819, 33-1026, 34-87, 34-88, 34-239, 34-278, 34-1103, 35-137, 35-160, 35-213, 35-1023, 35-1409, 36-141, 36-298, 36-339, 36-927, 36-1292, 37-13, 37-119, 37-242, 37-319, 38-92, 38-159, 38-240, 38-268, 38-1109, 39-107, 39-338, 39-1116, 40-118, 40-391, 40-1196
  JOSEPH 30-94, 33-114, 34-50, 35-142, 36-134, 37-16, 38-89, 40-129
  MARY 33-284
  ROBERT 30-548, 31-561, 33-630, 34-638, 35-682
  SAMUEL [capt.] 33-544, 34-665, 35-612, 36-610, 38-741, 39-813, 40-779
  SARAH 36-733
  WILLIAM 30-94, 31-101, 35-1620, 37-642, 38-862, 39-843
WIMBROUGH [Wimbroe, Wimbror], PAUL 33-726, 35-850, 36-803, 37-734, 38-859, 39-872, 40-890
WINDER, THOMAS 30-1468, 31-1361, 33-1398, 34-1699, 35-1703, 36-1541, 37-1182, 38-1699, 39-1850, 40-1821
WINDSOR [Win(d)ser, Winsor, Winzer]
  [illegible] 37-747
  ANN 39-337, 40-355
  HENRY 30-984, 31-982, 33-1090, 34-1138, 35-1177, 36-1006, 38-1146
  JAMES 36-913, 36-1006, 37-747, 38-967, 38-1146, 39-337, 39-955, 40-355, 40-978
  JOHN 30-756, 30-988, 31-804, 31-983, 33-787, 33-807, 33-1091, 34-855, 34-864, 34-1125, 35-916, 35-926, 35-1176, 36-917, 36-1182, 37-747, 37-755, 38-950, 39-939, 40-974
  LAZARUS [junr.] 30-756, 31-804, 33-787, 34-855, 34-855, 35-926, 35-926, 36-913, 36-913, 37-747, 38-967, 38-967, 39-955, 39-955, 40-978
  MARY [widow] 34-864, 35-916
  PHILLIP 38-967, 39-955, 40-978
WINGATE [Wingett, Wingitt], PHILLIP 30-961, 31-1027, 33-907, 34-1193, 35-1191, 36-1166, 38-1308, 39-1292, 40-1412
WINRIGHT [Wainwright, Whinwrite, Windright, Winrite]
  CANNON 30-823, 31-887, 33-1067, 34-915, 35-959, 36-1019, 38-1021, 39-1034, 40-1063
  JAMES 39-1034, 40-1063
  JOHN 30-823, 31-886, 33-872, 34-1174, 35-959, 36-1234, 38-1632, 39-1834
  STEPHEN 30-823, 31-887, 34-1375, 35-1468, 36-1469, 38-1632, 39-1834, 40-1832
  WILLIAM 31-918, 33-872, 34-1173, 35-1233, 36-1170, 38-1330, 39-1356
WISE
  EZEKIEL 30-644, 33-710, 34-803, 35-836, 36-844, 37-180, 38-870, 39-228, 40-231
  MATTHEW 30-680, 31-690, 33-227, 34-322, 35-223, 36-169, 37-180, 38-294, 39-228, 40-231
  THOMAS 30-676, 31-687, 33-757, 34-723, 35-760, 36-839, 37-702, 38-914, 39-915, 40-860
WONELL, JAMES 30-1255, 31-1227, 33-1306, 34-1373, 35-1513, 36-1463, 38-1489, 39-1417, 40-1485
WOODCRAFT
  JOHN 30-186, 31-164
  MARY 30-230, 31-172, 33-247, 34-229, 35-241
  RICHARD 30-187, 31-165, 33-238, 34-335, 35-240, 36-260, 37-206, 38-389, 39-370, 40-351
  THOMAS 30-230, 31-172, 33-247, 34-229
  WILLIAM 30-230, 31-172, 33-247, 34-225, 35-242, 36-184, 37-203, 38-390, 39-226, 40-205
WOODLAL, JOSEPH 38-991
WOODS [Wood]
  ADAM 30-236, 31-247
  DAVID 36-108, 37-149, 38-133, 38-1382, 39-142, 39-253, 40-204, 40-807
  JOHN 30-917, 31-1068, 33-497,

INDEX

34-520, 37-184, 38-819, 39-227, 40-241
   ROBERT 33-323, 37-184
   STEPHEN 39-200, 40-290
   THOMAS 30-917, 31-1068
   WILLIAM 30-1110, 31-362, 31-1265, 33-498, 33-1251, 34-1439, 35-1424, 36-1317, 38-1437, 39-251, 39-1648, 40-204, 40-1725

WOOLF, HENRY 33-132, 34-143, 35-28, 36-151, 37-35, 38-109, 39-133, 40-154

WOOLFORD
   JOHN 31-621, 33-644, 34-703, 35-743, 36-717, 38-783, 39-702, 40-847
   MARTHA 30-597, 31-648
   ROGER 30-581
   THOMAS 35-743

WOOTEN [Wooten, Wouten]
   EDWARD 31-993, 33-925, 34-1092, 35-1078, 36-1021, 38-1226, 39-1243, 40-1295
   JOHN 31-992, 33-932, 34-1093, 35-1079, 36-1022, 39-1244, 40-1294
   THOMAS 30-1458

WORD [Worder], SUSANNAH [Sesannah/widw.] 30-1183, 31-1178, 33-1340

WORKMAN, THOMAS 37-992

WOTS, JAMES 31-508

WRIGHT [Right, Rite, Winright(1), Write]
   ABEL 30-591, 31-612, 33-666, 34-673
   COMFORT 31-1285, 34-1254, 35-1308, 36-1360, 38-1621, 40-1632
   EDWARD 30-924, 31-912, 33-911, 34-1124, 35-1184, 36-1154, 37-912, 38-1307, 40-1310
   EZEKIEL [Ezecll.] 34-1091
   HENRY 30-759, 31-775, 33-813, 34-871, 35-906, 36-893, 37-783, 38-940, 39-925, 40-961
   JEREMIAH [junr., senr.] 30-1328(2), 31-1450(2), 33-1482, 35-1760(2), 36-1763, 38-1875, 39-1711, 40-1787
   JOHN 33-666, 34-673, 36-1269
   JUDITH [widow] 35-1013
   NEHEMIAH 38-683, 39-720, 40-762
   RANDALL 30-603, 31-614, 33-667, 34-1349, 35-1392, 36-1502, 38-1522, 39-1439, 40-1547,
   SAUL [Saulle] 36-976
   SOLOMON 30-924, 30-1036, 31-867, 31-1071, 33-1048, 33-1124, 34-989, 35-1005, 35-1107, 36-952, 37-888, 38-1052, 38-1093, 39-1121, 39-1223, 40-1206, 40-1278
   THOMAS 30-759, 31-775, 33-813, 34-871, 35-906, 36-893, 37-783, 38-940, 39-925, 40-961
   WILLIAM [ser.] 30-889, 30-1394, 31-855, 31-855, 33-1118, 33-1118, 34-1091, 34-1091, 35-1013, 38-748, 39-738, 40-723, 40-1425
   ZEBULON 35-1141, 37-795, 38-921, 39-972, 40-1005

WYATT [Waitt, Waytt, Wate, Weight]
   JOHN 40-236
   JOSEPH [junr., senr.] 30-199(2), 31-157(2), 33-253(2), 34-210(2), 35-168, 36-237, 36-766, 37-160, 37-680, 38-234, 38-1594, 39-273(2), 40-219, 40-344
   NATHANIEL 30-733, 31-157, 31-742, 36-237, 37-160, 37-673, 38-234, 38-847, 39-273, 40-219
   WILLIAM 30-199, 31-157, 33-261, 34-219, 35-169, 36-173, 37-313, 38-165, 39-206, 40-227

WYE [Wey]
   MARY 31-620
   WILLIAM [revrend, junr] 30-571, 31-663, 34-884, 34-884, 35-865, 36-659, 33-816

YANKSWAW, JOHN 33-75m

YOUNG
   WIDOW 34-1010, 35-1118
   CHARLES 30-922, 31-906, 33-1029
   DANIEL 31-1283, 33-1165, 34-1446, 35-1309, 36-1363, 38-1622, 39-1574, 40-1657
   GEORGE 33-750, 34-742
   JEHU [Jehew, Johew] 33-1046, 36-1075, 39-1119, 40-1201
   JOHN 30-604, 31-628, 33-656, 34-662, 34-1004, 35-727, 35-1126, 36-650, 37-891, 38-798, 39-688, 40-851
   PAUL 30-1240
   RACHEL 36-1075
   WILLIAM 30-908, 31-1069, 33-1046, 34-1004, 35-1126, 38-798, 39-688, 40-851

www.ingramcontent.com/pod-product-compliance
Lightning Source LLC
Chambersburg PA
CBHW082035230426
43670CB00016B/2667